JOHN HOSKYNS, SERJEANT-AT-LAW

by

Baird W. Whitlock
Chairman, Humanities,
Language, and Literature
Midwestern State University

i

Library of Congress Catalog Card Number: **81-40426**

To Joan

iv

Acknowledgments

While I was working on the biography of John Donne for my thesis at the University of Edinburgh in the early 50s, I kept running across the figure of John Hoskyns, who more and more appeared to be the innovator and leading wit of the group of young poets that Donne met at Oxford and continued to as- sociate with throughout his life. Yet none of my friends and fellow scholars seemed to know anything about Hoskyns. It was at that time that I decided to do a full-length study of the man, although I knew little of him. The list of those who should be thanked for their help goes back, therefore, to include the staff of the library of the University of Edinburgh, who extended themselves in every pos- sible way to be helpful. The same is true of the staff of the British Museum, especially of the Man- uscript Room, whose sense of humor helped lighten many a weary day; Noel Blakiston and the staff of the Public Record Office; and the staff of the Na- tional Library of Wales. Grants from Case Insti- tute of Technology (now Case-Western Reserve) and San Francisco State University made travel to Eng- land and necessary research materials possible; Midwestern State University assisted with the typ- ing.

It was not until I was well into my early re- search that I discovered Louise Osborn's doctoral work on Hoskyns. It was, of course, invaluable as a guide to manuscript sources. It led me to four close personal friendships: Sir Benedict and Lady Ann Hoskyns at Harewood, Great Oakley, Essex, and Henry and Mary Hornyold-Strickland (and later their son Thomas) at Sizergh Castle, Kendal, Umbria. The muniment rooms and strongboxes of these families contain most of the extant papers of the Serjeant. Searches in the library at Winchester College led to another long-standing friendship, with the then- archivist John H. Harvey. All of these people have extended their friendship to include dealing kindly with groups of students I have brought to England through the years. The Serjeant could not have

v

wished for more understanding descendants and care-
takers of his writings. Another valued friendship
that had to remain epistolary but that yielded a
very valuable manuscript of Hoskyns' poems was
with Sir Geoffrey Keynes, the great Donne biblio-
grapher.
The list of those in England (besides those
already mentioned) who helped me search out material is a long one, but it is a pleasure to be able
to acknowledge their help: in Hereford, Violet
Buchanan and J.F.W. Sherwood at the Hereford City
Library, and Mr. Bray at the Town Clerk's Office;
F. C. Morgan at the Cathedral Library and Meryl
Jancey at the Hereford County Library; in Winchester, Jack Blakiston at the College Library; in
Shrewsbury, Mary C. Hill at the County Record Office; in Great Rissington, the Rev. W. H. Bates;
in Ilchester, the Rev. C. Large; in London, H.A.C.
Sturgess at the Middle Temple Library.

Official acknowledgment for permission to use
materials is gratefully given to The Wardens and
Fellows of Winchester College; The Dean and Chapter of Hereford Cathedral; the Henry E. Huntington
Library; and His Grace the Duke of Buccleuch.

TABLE OF CONTENTS

I.   An Ingeniose Man   1

II.   School Days   23

III.   College Years   45

IV.   Inner Barrister of the Middle Temple   87

V.   Directions of Speeche & Stile   137

VI.   Marriage and Hereford City   167

VII.   The 1604 Parliament: Round One   191

VIII.   Interlude   215

IX.   Rounds Two and Three   221

X.   The M. P. as Poet   283

XI.   Rounds Four and Five   331

XII.   The Company of Wits   381

XIII.   The Addled Parliament   427

XIV.   Life in the Tower   469

XV.   Restoration   495

XVI.   Serjeant-at-Law   575

XVII.   A New Life   635

XVIII.   The Allotted Span   687

PREFACE

In the following book. John Hoskyns' life and
writings speak for themselves. All of the available information (except for the actual Latin
texts) is present so that the reader can draw his
or her own conclusions about the man. There is no
psychological analysis because it would be idiotic
to do such analysis when there is so little information on Hoskyns' childhood or his relations with
his parents to work with. The emphasis is on the
daily life of a man who was well known and admired
by most of the leading figures of a fascinating
period of literary and governmental history. I
have tried to give a sense of what it meant to
grow up within a close group of literary friends,
to slog through the daily work of House of Commons
meetings, to make a sometimes shaky living as a
lawyer and circuit judge, to live as a prisoner in
the Tower of London, and even to act as a careful
landowner on the borders of Wales. Except for the
limits of space, I have tried to include everything Hoskyns said or wrote. For complete latin
texts, the reader will have to refer to Louise
Osborn's doctoral work on Hoskyns published by
Yale; and for the complete Directions either to
Osborn or Hoyt Hudson's edition. All new material
not printed in earlier sources has been included.

Portrait of John Hoskyns by John Hoskyns and Self Portrait with Family
(See p. 534)

The "Trusty Servant" at Winchester
(See p. 33)

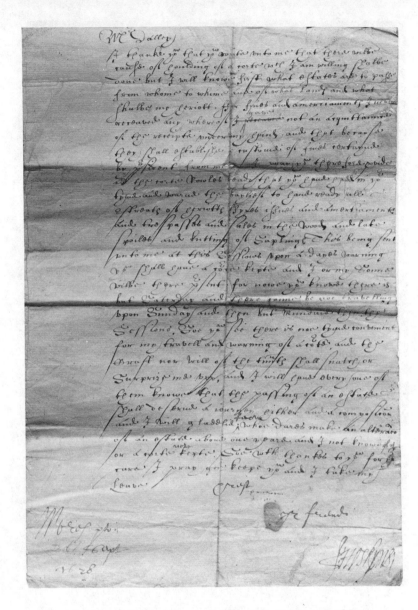

Letter of Instruction to James Dalley
(See p. 652)

xiii

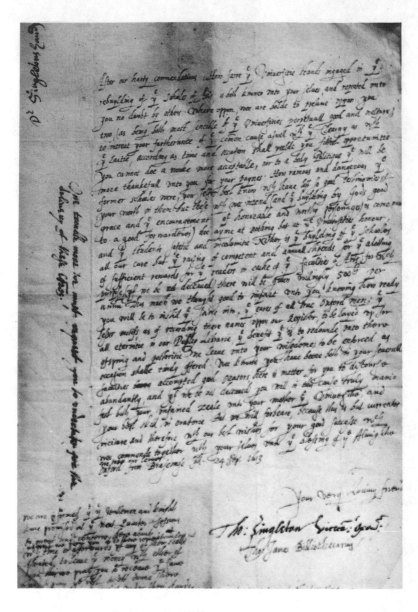

Fund-raising Letter from Oxford
(See p. 415)

(See p. 415)

CHAPTER I

An Ingeniose Man

> His conversation was exceedingly pleasant,
> and [he] would make verses on the Roade,
> where he was the best Company in the
> world. He was a great master of the Latin
> and Greke languages; a great Divine; made
> the best Latin Epitaphs of his time. He
> understood the Lawe well, but [was] worst
> at that.[1]

So runs a short summary of the life of one of the
leading wits of the late sixteenth and early seventeenth century. The biographer, John Aubrey,
probably knew as much about his subject as he did
any of the many men whose lives he chronicled at
the end of the 1600s, for he was a close friend
of John Hoskyns' son Sir Benedict Hoskyns, and often quoted the son about his father and other members of the family.[2] The irony of the passage is
that the person described as "worst at" law was
one of the great counselors of the realm, ranking
with the leading lawyers of the age and sitting on
the bench of His Majesty's Assizes in Wales from
1621 until his death in 1638. We shall have reason to see both the accuracy of Aubrey's description of Hoskyns' personality and the error of his
judgment of Hoskyns' legal ability.

Any study of the years from Elizabeth's reign
through the early stages of Parliamentary control
in England should, by all rights, contain a considerable amount of information about John Hoskyns,
but such is not the case. Except for an edition
of his Directions for Speech and Style by Hoyt
Hudson in 1935, a collection of his writings and a
brief biography by Louise Osborn in 1937, and occasional references to him in collections of Elizabethan lyrics, Parliamentary studies of the Addled Parliament of 1614, and books on the development of rhetorical theory, this friend of poets

1

and statesmen goes almost unnoticed.[3] It is safe
to say that even among modern sixteenth and seventeenth century scholars Hoskyns is the least known
figure who was considered important to his own
contemporaries. Yet in his own age he was recognized as one of the great wits, if not indeed the
leading wit of the circle of literary and political friends that met in the Mermaid Tavern.[4] A
list of his friends and associates reads like a
catalogue of the great men of the period, and his
activities cover the full range of Jacobean and
Caroline life. He missed being a complete Elizabethan only because his travels and adventures
were limited to England and Wales; he never seems
to have shared his friends' desire to wander on
the continent or to join in any military ventures.

    To be considered a "Son of Ben" was one of
the highest attainments of the poets of this time,
and young Benedict Hoskyns once tried for the title by asking Ben Jonson himself. Ben replied,
"No, I dare not; 'tis honour enough for me to be
your Brother: I was your Father's sonne, and 'twas
he that polished me, I do acknowledge it."[5] This
was not idle compliment, a practice that Jonson
did not indulge in anyway. He used extended passages from John Hoskyns' rhetoric in his own critical writings, without, it must be noted, bothering to identify them as by Hoskyns. But he was
not the only writer of the time to be "polished"
by Hoskyns. Sir Walter Ralegh gave John his History of the World to revise while they were fellow
prisoners in the Tower of London. Indeed, Aubrey
describes Hoskyns as Ralegh's Aristarchus, imply-
ing that his work was of the same level as that of
the great head of the Alexandrian Library who edited the works of such men as Homer, Anacreon, and
Pindar. Anthony à Wood, writing at the same time
as Aubrey, said of Hoskyns,

        He was the most ingenious and admired Poet
        of his time, and therefore much courted by
        the ingenious Men then living. There were
        few or none that published Books of Poetry,
        but did celebrate his Memory in them, es-

pecially his Contemporary in New Coll. named
Joh. Owen the Epigrammatist, and fewer but
did lay them at his Feet for approbation before they went to Press.

Wood also listed him among the "noted scholars of his time... Will. Cambden, Sir Jo. Harrington the Poet, Ben. Johnson, Jo. Selden, Facete
Hoskyns, R. Corbet of Ch. Ch. Christ's Church."6
John Donne was a close friend, and their lives
touched from the time they were together at Oxford
until the Dean of St. Paul's died in 1631. At
least one poem that long was attributed to Donne
seems now to have been written by Hoskyns. Their
mutual friend, Sir Henry Wotton, close associate
of the Earl of Essex, English Ambassador to Venice,
and Provost of Eton College, actually was closer
to Hoskyns than to Donne in many events in their
lives, and he and John together made the kind of
horseback poetry that Aubrey mentioned in his
sketch. William Camden, the great teacher of Westminster School and leading historian of his age,
was a teacher of Hoskyns for a year and by 1605
had collected the epigrams of his former charge.
Nicholas Hill, "one of the most learned men of his
time: a great mathematician and philosopher and
traveller and a poet,"7 was another of his friends
and was partially responsible for Hoskyns' interest in the scientific developments of his day.
Whether one could say that Sir Francis Bacon was a
friend is questionable, as they tangled in debates
more than once on the floor of the House of Commons
but they were certainly well acquainted. The list
of John's friends and close associates would have
to extend to all of the major parliamentary figures of the early seventeenth century, as he worked closely with them on committees, record searches
in the Tower of London, and in debates in Commons.
He was one of the permanent members of the Mermaid
Tavern group and was a close friend of Lionel Cranfield, who rose to the position of Lord Treasurer
of the realm. It is likely that his work in the
Marches of Wales drew him into intimate contact
with all of the groups of courtiers and artists
surrounding the Earl of Bridgewater, Lord Presi-

3

dent of the Council of the Marches of Wales, and
we know from other sources that he was on friendly
terms with such central figures of the government
as Lord Egerton, Lord Chancellor of England, father of the Earl of Bridgewater and one-time employer of John Donne. Oxford University thought
enough of their former student to involve him in
alumni fund-raising drives, and the Bishop and
Chapter of Hereford Cathedral entrusted many of
their legal affairs to his guidance.

But if his friendships covered all walks of
life, so did his various activities and interests.
He was one of the major landowners of Herefordshire, at least an amateur scientist, a painter,
composer, and, of course, poet. As we have already noted, he was a leading lawyer, judge, and
member of Parliament. Through his brother, he was
involved in the business life of London; because
of the requirements of his various careers, he was
an athlete of no mean ability, at least on horseback. And above all, he was a wit. His conversation, his letters, his prose and poetry were all
admired by those who valued this quality in themselves and others. The Oxford English Dictionary
definition of "wit" for 1579 reads, "Quickness of
intellect or liveliness of fancy, with capacity of
apt expression; talent for saying brilliant or
sparkling things, especially in an amusing way."
Hoskyns' wit included the serious play of associa-
ting thoughts and expression in a way "calculated
to surprise and delight by its unexpectedness" as
well as the humorous play of ideas at any level--
and Hoskyns played at every level, from high seriousness to low earthiness. This play of wit char-
acterizes all of his activities from the classroom
and dormitory of his schools through his more serious fooling at Oxford--too serious for the autho-
rities there--through the dramatic performances of
members of the Middle Temple, to his personal letters, his debates in Parliament, his imprisonment
in the Tower of London, indeed, to his death bed.

Luckily we have a mass of material to work
with in studying this man's life, material which

4

sheds light on his friends and on his age. His letters have been preserved in family collections and various archives; his law cases in the Public Record Office; his speeches in parliamentary records and diaries; his poems and prose in the manuscript collections of the British Museum and elsewhere--and cut into the marble of tombs of friends and associates. Unfortunately, most of his poetry is lost. Aubrey writes: "He had a booke of Poemes, neatly written by one of his Clerkes, bigger then Dr. Donne's Poemes, which his sonn Benet lent to he knowes not who, about 1653, and could never heare of it since." Any honest critic of his work would have to admit, however, that it is unlikely that we would gain a great deal by finding the volume. We have multiple copies of those poems which his contemporaries found important, and they reveal a talent that was more impressive to those contemporaries than it is to us. In the twentieth century Hoskyns must remain of interest largely because of the light he casts on others and on his age rather than for the strength of his own poetic genius. This is not to undervalue his genuine gifts and abilities, but it is important to keep judgments about him reasonable rather than to try to make a major poet of him.

****

At some time between 1 March 1566 and 20 August 1566[8] John Hoskyns was born on a farm called "Mouncton" or Monkton on a hill southwest of the small village of Llanwarne, in Herefordshire.[9] The property had been in the family's hands since at least 1510, when the Prior of Llanthony Abbey granted a John Hoskins of Monkton a lease of certain premises for forty years.[10] The geographical attribute given this Hoskyns indicates that he was already established on at least part of the Monkton property, which, incidentally, is still divided into two farms, Upper and Lower Monkton. Upper Monkton has a three storey house with stone rubble walls and timber framing with brick nogging and a roof covered with stone slates. The main block has a projecting porch built in the early seventeenth century. Lower Monkton is a two storey

building with cellars and attics, with wings built
at the same time as the porch on Upper Monkton.[11]
In 1522, the Prior demised these lands, and those
held by a Thomas Hoskyns, to another John Hoskyns
(the first's son) and his mother Margaret Jones.
In so doing he noted that the John Hoskyns mentioned in the 1510 lease had held these lands in
Monkton for sixty years.[12] The family relationship
with the Abbey undoubtedly went back several centuries on this or nearby property. Monkton was a
chapelry and grange and probably a cell to Llanthony Abbey.[13] Aubrey states, "Mounckton belonged
to the priory of Llantony juxta Glocester, where
his ancestors had the office of cupbearer (or
'pocillator') to the prior. I have heard there
was a windowe given by one Hoskyns there, as by
the inscription did appeare."[14] Llanthony Abbey
was originally founded by Hugh de Lacy[15] some ten
miles due west of Llanwarne on one of the most un-
inviting pieces of land in the generally forbidding
range known as the Black Mountains. The monks, unhappy about their location, requested transfer to
a more amiable climate, and one segment of the community established a new center near Gloucester.
As early as 26 June 1336, however, a John Hoche-
kynes is listed among the witnesses at a Hereford
Inquisition,[16] and it is likely that the family
was already established at Monkton in some service
capacity to the Abbey.[17]

The records of the 1522 lease also indicate
that the Hoskyns and Jones families were already
quite close. The Jones owned the manor and court
in Llanwarne itself,[18] and they and the Hoskyns
were extremely close, intermarrying at least twice,
serving Hereford in Parliament, and engaging in
various land suits against each other or together
against smaller landowners in the area. Margery
Jones, John's mother, was born in 1534, as her son
refers to her, in a poem written in prison in 1614,
as being then four score years old. (John's father
was born earlier.) Margery was the sister of the
Thomas Jones who represented Hereford in the last
two parliaments of Queen Elizabeth.[19] Unlike his
nephew, Jones spoke very little in Parliament, and

when he did, he played it very safe. Indeed, in a
speech he gave on 3 December 1601, he sounded far
more like Polonius than the relative of a famous
wit:

> It is now my chance to Speak something,
> and that without Humming or Hawing. I
> think this Law is a good Law; Even Reck-
> oning makes long Friends; As far goes the
> Penny, as the Penny's Master. Vigilantibus
> non dormientibus jura subveniunt. Pay the
> Reckoning over Night, and you shall not be
> troubled in the Morning. If ready Money
> be Mensura Publica, let every Man cut his
> Coat according to his Cloth. When his old
> Suit is in the Wain, let him stay till that
> his Money bring a new Suit in the Increase.
> Therefore, I think the Law to be good, and
> I wish it a good Passage.[20]

It took a friend of young Hoskyns, William Hackwell,[21] to get Commons back into some kind of discussion uncluttered by such a collection of old
saws. One wonders how the elder Jones got along
with his witty and sometimes bawdy young nephew.

John Hoskyns was the grandson of John Hoskyns
as well as the son of John Hoskyns; the brother of
John Hoskyns as well as the nephew of John Hoskyns.
The habit of naming more than one person in each
generation by the same name is the despair of any
biographer working with materials open to him at
this period of history. Discovering the family
background of the poet John Donne, for example, is
made particularly difficult by the fact that almost every Donne family at the time, in London or
Wales, had at least two Johns in each generation.
In the Hoskyns family a differentiation was made
in one generation, that immediately preceding the
subject of this biography, by referring to the
first-born as "John the Elder" or "John Hoskyns of
Byton." He took his branch of the family northwest to an area some fifteen miles north and west
of Hereford and developed a large holding of farmland there. The only complication that he brings

into the family records is that there were two
Thomas Hoskyns in that family, and it is not at
all clear whether they were brothers, uncle and
nephew, or cousins. The fact that there two wives
in that branch of the family named Sibyl doesn't
help a great deal either.

The husband of Margery Jones was "John Hoskyns
the Younger" or "John Hoskyns of Monkton." Two of
his children were Johns: our man is known in the
records as John Hoskyns or, later on, Serjeant
Hoskyns. His geographical attributes are listed
as "of Monkton," "of Hereford," or "of Morehampton"
depending on the period of his life and his chief
residence. His younger brother is usually identified as "Doctor Hoskyns" because of the LL D degree he gained at Oxford and his continued use of
that title as a minister. His one geographical
attribute is "of Ledbury," the parish in which he
spent much of his life, located ten miles east of
Hereford. Obviously both of them grew sick and
tired of the complexity of similar names, for neither of them named any of his sons "John," although
Serjeant John did, in his first marriage, gain a
stepson of the same name. For the purposes of this
book, we shall stick with calling the principal
subject simply "John" and his brother by his usual
title, "Dr. John."

In 1558, both of John's paternal grandparents
died, the husband on 17 July and Elizabeth his
wife on 27 August. Their wills in the National
Library of Wales give a good idea of the family
situation at the time. John Hoskyns of Mounton,
parish of Llanwarne, asked to be buried in the
churchyard of Llanwarne, a spot now completely
overgrown but still surrounding the remains of the
ruined church which nestles next to a bend in the
river Gamber. After the usual small gifts to the
local church and to "the Mother churche" of Hereford, he says that if his wife, Elizabeth, marries
again, she must give forty pounds "to Thomas Gethyn and Richard Baker to the vse of William Margaret Johane Alice and Anne my children equally
betwyxte them to be devided And to the lengest ly-

8

```
                                              John Hoskyns
                                              of Llanwarne      =
                                              d.1558


John the Elder=Alice                          John the Younger=Margery Jones
of Byton                                      d.1607           b.c.1534
will 1587                                                      still living 1617


                                              Oswald=Elizabeth Wooley
                                              d.1618  d.a.1632


William=ElizBourne  Mary        Magdalen Elizabeth Elinor=Mr.Taylor  Margery=E.Bagshaw  Katherine=A.Roe
b.a.1609            b.a.1609     b.a.1611 b.a.1611                    b.a.1614           b.a.1618
d.1655             d.1631        one of these mar-                                       (m.a.1639)
                                 ried a Mr. Masters


John=Elizabeth Scudamore   Charles   dau.=Jones   Oswald   Benedicta=Wm. Gwillim
of Bernithen


                                              John the Elder=Alice
                                              of Byton


Thomas  =Margery   Johanna=Roger Hill   Katherine   John            (Richard?)=Anne
of Byton, =2nd wife,                                 =Sibyl
Uphampton  sibyl                                     of Langarren,
or Shobdon                                           godson of
d.1637                                               Thomas of
                                                     St. Weonards
                                                     d.1614


Katherin Walter Sibyl   Henry  Johanna  Anne =John Gwillim  Margaret=R.Beddoe  Elizabeth Margery
                        D.1615          b.1595 (m.1624)      b.1598 (m.1626)    b.1601    b.1605
                                                                                d.1630    d.1632
```

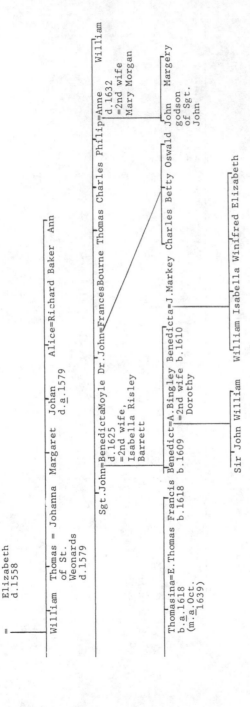

Elizabeth
d.1558

=

William   Thomas = Johanna   Margaret   Johan   Alice=Richard Baker   Ann
           of St.   d.a.1579
           Weonards
           d.1579

Sgt.John=BenedictaMoyle   Dr.John=FrancesBourne   Thomas Charles Philip=Anne   William
d.1625   d.1632
=2nd wife,   =2nd wife
Isabella Risley   Mary Morgan
Barrett

                                                                    John   Margery
                                                                    godson
                                                                    of Sgt.
                                                                    John

Benedict=A.Bingley   Benedicta=J.Markey   Charles Betty Oswald
b.1609 =2nd wife   b.1610
         Dorothy

Thomasina=E.Thomas Francis
b.a.1618
(m.a.Oct.
  1639)

Sir John William

                    William Isabella Winifred Elizabeth

Benedicta Moyle=Francis Bourne

Walter   Frances=Dr.John   Elizabeth=Wm.Hoskyns   John=Margaret Bourne
d.1610   d.1601   b.1601
                                                         d.1627

ver or lyvers of them." If she does not remarry,
she is to "marye my presand children" and give
them dowries according to her power. He also gives
a special gift of fifty shillings to John the
younger over and above the six pounds, thirteen
shillings and four pence that his son owes him but
can now keep. All the rest is to go to Elizabeth,
who is also his executor. Both John the younger
and John the elder, who received nothing from the
will, signed as witnesses.

The sickness which killed the husband took
the wife just a little over a month later. Elizabeth Hoskyns wrote her will as a "wedow sycke in
body." Besides restating the main legacies of her
husband's will, she gave an extra forty shillings
and two pieces of pewter to William, Margaret,
Joan, Alice, and Anne. To the four girls she gave
the beds and bedding, towels, sheets, etc., in e-
qual parts. Five of her grandchildren received
two sheep each, and two of them, the sons of Alice
and Richard Baker, larger sums of money. All the
residue, after debts and burial expenses, went to
John the younger, Thomas, and William "in theyre
dysposycion and dyscrescon." John the younger,
who is here identified as her second son, and Margaret were named the executors. As in her husband's will, no mention is made of any bequest to
her eldest son, John Hoskyns of Byton. This is
probably due to the fact that he was already well
established as a land-owner in a different part of
the shire and had cut some of the close ties with
the rest of the family.

At any rate, following these and other wills
of the family[22] we know that when the poet was
born, he had a very large number of relatives living nearby. On his father's side alone, there were
three uncles, five aunts, and nine cousins, not
counting in-laws.[23]

The young child born in 1566 seems to have
given almost immediate signs of brilliance. Aubrey
has the family ages wrong, but his story has the
ring of truth about it, considering John's later

11

accomplishments:

> He had a brother, John, D.D., a learned man,
> Rector of Ledbury and canon of Hereford, who,
> I thinke, was eldest, who was designed to be
> a Scholar, but this John (the Serjeant) would
> not be quiet, but he must be a Scholar too.
> In those dayes boyes were seldome taught to
> read that were not to be of some learned pro-
> fession. So, upon his instant importunity,
> being then ten years of age, he learned to
> reade, and, at the yeare's end, entred into
> his Greeke grammar. This I have heard his
> sonne, Sir Benet Hoskyns, knight and baronett,
> several times say.[24]

What Aubrey says of him as a grown-up probably
held true of him as a child as well: "He was a very
strong man, and valiant, and an early riser in the
morning (scil., at four in the morning). He was
black-eyed and had black hayre." Life on a large
farm w-uld account for the early rising and the
physical strength.

One of his brothers, Oswald, was older, but
he early left the family home and established a
thriving business in London. There is some question as to whether another brother, Thomas, was
also older than John, but the records of the Middle Temple refer to John as the "second son." When
Thomas was born we do not know, but he always played a subordinate role in the family and never did
much except to work on the family farm in Didley,
four miles over the hill to the northwest, and act
as a general overseer for his more successful brother. Four other brothers, Dr. John, Charles,
Phillip, and William, were to be born in later
years. Of the last, William, we know nothing but
the name; that probably indicates that he died
while still a child. It is evident from many accounts that the family put a high priority on good
education and training, and it may be that a tradition mentioned in the Dictionary of National
Biography is the reason--that they were descendants of William of Wykeham, founder of Winchester

College. There is, however, no available evidence
to show such a relationship. What is more likely
is that the first son was given the more usual
treatment of being set up in a trade in London and
that the importunity of the second, described by
Aubrey, led the family to educate the remaining
children in a more advanced way. Certainly the
Hoskyns were well-to-do and could afford the kind
of early tutoring required for bright children.

It would also appear that John's father was
socially ambitious. According to several sources,
the family was granted a Coat of Arms about the
year 1572.[25] This action was usually the result of
a family trying to establish its social position,
as it was in the case of the Shakespeares. Aubrey
placed John Hoskyns' crest at a much later date:
"I have heard that when he came out of the Tower,
his Crest was graunted him (I believe) for his
bold Spirit, and (I suppose) contrived by himselfe,
viz. a Lyon's head couped or, breathing fire. The
Serjeant would say jocosely that it was the only
Lyon's head in England that tooke Tobacco." His
friendship with Sir Walter Ralegh, the man who popularized smoking in England, makes that remark particularly interesting. Both stories could, of
course, be true, as a crest and a family coat of
arms are not the same thing. The Hoskyns' family
arms are elsewhere described as "Party per azure &
gules a Chevron between 3 lioncells rampand or
lang [elongated] & armmd counterchanged of the
pale."[26]

At about the same time his father was trying
to increase the family holdings as well, in what
seems to have been a questionable enough way to
lead to several lawsuits. Two suits in Chancery
addressed to Sir Nicholas Bacon, Francis Bacon's
father, undated but obviously before 1575, bring
charges against John Hoskyns the Younger of Monkton. They both concern property lying in the valley to the east of Monkton and just south of Llanwarne, across the main Hereford-Monmouth road. A
David Waythan of Trevase Farm claimed he legally
owned one messuage (a dwelling house with its out-

13

buildings) in Trevase, a four acre meadow called
Tresynet, and one hundred acres belonging to this
messuage and others in Penecoid and Trevase, which
he bought from Hoskyns and William Jones of Much
Birch on 8 September 1567 for "threescore and ten
poundes." It was a complicated situation, however.
Apparently he sold it back to them on the condition
that if he paid them the seventy pounds before 1
October 1569, he could reenter his possessions. He
said he had fulfilled the bargain, but they still
held the bond he signed for two hundred marks and
had begun a Common Law suit on the basis of the
bond. He asked the Court to restrain them. Jones
and Hoskyns gave a joint answer that seems a trifle
less than forthright. First of all they claimed
that "the bill of complaint is insufficient in the
Law to be answered vnto" and is the result of malice. They granted all that Waythan said, but added that there were other things to be done according to the bond of a very material nature which he
had not done. For example, they were to have free
use of the property, but Waythan kept them from it.
Then they had him jailed in London, but he got out
on bail. They had brought suit in the Exchequer,
and Waythan was now trying every means to keep that
suit from coming about because it was well grounded
in the law. As is usual in such cases, they asked
to be dismissed with costs.[27] Whatever the relative
merits of the case, it is interesting to note one
of the common occurrences of Elizabethan legal battles: a defendant in one branch of the legal system, such as Chancery, would bring his own suit a-
gainst his prosecutors in another branch, such as
the Exchequer. Later on John Hoskyns would use
the same device in his battles--and have it used
against him as well.

At about the same time Thomas Browne brought a
second complaint about lands in exactly the same
area.[28] Browne was probably the grandson of the
man who sold the Monkton property to the Hoskyns
family at the time of the dissolution of the monasteries. The family remained important in the area
all through the period under discussion and later
in the seventeenth century regained possession of

14

Monkton. Browne now claimed that he was lawful owner of sixty acres of land and buildings in "Pencoyde Trevare [Trevase] ¢ Mighelchurche" and that by some chance his deeds, leases, etc., had come into John Hoskyns the Younger's hands, and that the latter had entered the lands and conveyed them to himself and "dyuerse of his frendes to yor Orator vnknowen." Since he didn't know where the documents were, he could not give specific information about them and wanted a court order to obtain them as well as a subpoena for Hoskyns to appear in the matter.

The subpoena obviously worked, as at a later date John Hoskyns the Younger went to London and gave his testimony before Justice Richardson in Westminster. It would be unlikely that his young son John would have accompanied him on such a long trip, but anyone who reads the intimate records of the time is astonished by the apparent ease and frequency with which the long and difficult horseback ride was made between London and the outlying districts of England. John Hoskyns was later to remark that "all those that came to London were either Carrion or Crowes." In this case his father seems to have been one of the Carrion. In his answer to Browne's charges, he pled innocent, claimed that "he doeth not intermeddle with the said landes," nor does he have any documents concerning the lands, nor has he "wrongefullie entred into the premysses" nor conveyed any of the lands secretly to friends, nor anything else in the charge. He asked to be "dysmyssed with his costes and chardges boren and susteined for his wrongefull vexacon in this behalf."

It is impossible to tell which of these cases came first or to discover how they ended, but they would seem to indicate that John's father and one of the Jones family tried to move into the lands that lay between them and ran up against more trouble than they bargained for. The lack of any further indentures, leases, bequests or remarks in letters about this property would seem to indicate that they lost in their move and gave up any fur-

15

ther attempt. John's father did, however, own
lands in the general area of Tretire and Michaelchurch, just south of Trevase and Pencoyd, up to
the day of his death.

The little we know of Hoskyns' life during his
first twelve years sets the tone for the rest of
it. He grew up in an atmosphere of land dealings
with farm property in the neighborhood which was
to occupy most of his life; his close relatives
were already involved in the activities of Parliament, where he was to gain fame; his precocious wit
and intellect were already recognized and abetted
by his family, and he had shown a liking for and
ability in the classics which was to give him a
nearly unrivalled reputation later on; on the
slopes of the family farm in Monkton, he learned
how to ride and oversee the growth and harvesting
of crops, when to plant both those crops and fruit
trees, how to plant the hedgerows that offered protection from the winter winds sweeping off the
Welsh mountains, all of those small items of practical knowledge that he shows in his letters from
London to his wife or children later on. He must
have learned his lesson well, for from his twelfth
year until his twenty-sixth he was at school or
college and only infrequently visited his home. A-
nother thing he learned from his father and his
early experience: to choose farm lands that had a
gentle slope for proper drainage to accomodate the
wet weather of the border areas and to buy acreage
that faced south to take full benefit of the sun
throughout the year in a land at the same longitude
as Labrador. All of the property which he bought,
leased, or handled shared these characteristics.
Thus both his practical bent and intellectual development came early. From whom he gained his
sense of humor is less clear. Certainly his father
showed little sign of it. Perhaps it was a gift of
his mother, who lived with him to a ripe old age,
and the Jones branch of the family. But whatever
the source, it was to show up in his own temperament as soon as he left the family home and journeyed to London to begin his formal education.

Footnotes for Chapter I

1. Aubrey's Brief Lives, Oliver L. Dick. ed. (1949). All quotes from Aubrey will be from this edition unless noted otherwise. The life of John Hoskyns covers pp. 168-71.
2. Andrew Clark, in his justly famous edition of Brief Lives (1898), says, "The lives of Isaac Barrow, and of (Serjeant-at-Law) John Hoskyns, may serve as specimens of a fair copy" as he comments on Aubrey's manuscript. (I, 3, n. f.) Dick notes (p. xii) that Aubrey "rarely made a fair copy of anything that he had written because, as he confessed, he wanted patience to go thorough Knotty Studies." The impetus for Aubrey's biography of Hoskyns seems to have been a letter from Anthony a Wood dated 11 Nov. 1667:
   You may remember when you were at Oxon, that you promised upon my enquirie &c., to obtained some intelligence concerning Dr. Joh: Hoskyns sometimes of New Coll: of his birth death and buriall, his bookes that he wrote and that might be worthie memorie of him. If you please to informe me as soone as you can, I shall take it for a verie great favour from your hands. 'Tis probable you might upon recollection informe me also of others that were Oxford men. (pp. lviii-ix.)
3. In footnote 2 to her introductory chapter of The Life, Letters and Writings of John Hoskyns, pp. 216-17, Dr. Louise Osborn gives a good list of references to Hoskyns up to that time (1937). She does not, however, list entries in such local publications as the Woolhope Club Transactions (Hereford). Since 1937 the number of references has, of course, increased but at a very small rate. Only Rosamund Tuve's notice of Hoskyns' place in the development of rhetorical study in her volume on Elizabethan imagery has treated Hoskyns in any really serious way.
4. Although we will have reason to study this group at length in Chap. 12, it seems worthwhile to note here that the Mermaid Tavern group is not what it often is claimed to be. It does

17

not, for example, include Shakespeare, Beaumont and Fletcher. Prof. I. A Shapiro has analyzed the full make-up of the group in "The 'Mermaid Club'", Modern Language Review, Vol. XLV, 1950.

5. The final clause and some additional wording appear in the version of the story in Aubrey's life of Ben Jonson.

6. Anthony Wood, Athenae Oxoniensis (2nd ed., 1721), cols. 614-615. The O.E.D. defines "facete" as witty, pleasant or humorous. The list of scholars appears in the biographical note on John Davies, co. 506.

7. John Aubrey, Letters written by eminent persons ...and Lives of eminent men (1813), II, 393.

8. In Clark's edition of Aubrey, there is a note that Anthony Wood added to the Aubrey manuscript the birth date of "St. Mark's day" (April 25). The Winchester College records quoted in Chapter 2 indicate, however, that he was thirteen on or before 1 March 1579 (Registrum Primum Wint Coll., p. 93) and that he took the oath usually administered on the completion of a student's fifteenth year on 20 August 1581 (Liber prothocollorum de iuramentis tam Sociorum quam Scholarium... from 1576).

9. Osborn, following an inaccurate footnote in Clark's edition of the Brief Lives, equates Mouncton with Monnington-upon-Wye. Aside from the fact that this is about twelve miles off target as the crow flies, it would make absolute nonsense of all of Hoskyns' activities as a land-holder and pater familias of the various branches of the family, a role which he played with great seriousness and sincerity. Monnington is northwest of Hereford; Monkton and Llanwarne due south.

10. Charles Robinson, The Mansions of Herefordshire (1872), p. 185.

11. Royal Commission on Historical Monuments, Herefordshire, Vol. I (1931), p. 178. Plate 20 is a photograph of Upper Monkton.

12. In 1528 the same property was demised to John Hoskins, Elizabeth his wife, and John and Johan,

their children.
13. Thomas Blount's Collection, Vol. II, f. 53
(Hereford City Library MSS). Also John H. Matthews, Collections towards the History and Antiquities of the County of Hereford... Hundred
of Wormelow (Hereford, 1912), p. 20; and Harley
6726, f. 125v.
14. Aubrey, Clark ed., p. 416. The Monkton property probably was the same type of holding as the
parish of Weobly: Hugh de Lacy "presented the
tithes of the parish of Weobly to the Abbey of
Lantony as part of its endowment, in virtue of
which present the Chapter of that Abbey became
patrons of the Vicarage, which was held by
them down to the time of the dissolution of the
monasteries, A.D. 1535." Canon H. W. Phillpott,
Woolhope Club Transactions (Hereford, 1888),
p. 250.
15. This famous conqueror and governor of Ireland
died in 1186.
16. Matthews, Collections, p. 20.
17. One family tradition is that the Hoskyns came
originally from Kent "where they were of considerable antiquity." MSS Add. 23,929, f. 286.
John Matthews, a descendant of the family, notes
that Monkton was sold to one Thomas Browne at
the time of the suppression of the monasteries,
that he became the sole proprietor, and that his
sons Edmund and George had the manor by gavel-
kind inheritance (the custom of dividing a deceased man's property equally among his sons,
O.E.D.), Collections, p. 102. As an indication
of the value of the property, the annual value
of the cure (office of Curate) of Orcop, which
was part of this holding, was £5 11s 10d in
1535. (from Valor Ecclesiasticus, 1535) quoted
in Collections, p. 110. On 8 October 1541,
John Hoskyns was a witness about lands in Orcop.
#44, Papers from The Mynde in the National Li-
brary of Wales. In 1553, King Edward VI granted the property which "did heretofore appertain
to the Abby of Lantony in Com. Glocester, together wth the Advowson of the Rectory or Church
by the name of the Mannor of Moncton-Lanwarne,
wth all messuages, mills, landes, Tenem^ts and

19

herdetamtes in Monkton ϵ Lanwarne" to Thomas Browne, William Breton, and their heirs. Pat. 7 Ed. 6 pars. 7., quoted in Blount's Collections. A lease in the possession of Sir Benedict Hoskyns at Harewood, Gt. Oakley, Essex, supports this sale to Browne and Breton.

18. Robinson, Mansions,p. 185.
19. John Duncomb, Collections towards the History... of... Hereford (Hereford, 1804), p. 353.
20. Heywood Townshend, Historical Collections... Four last Parliaments of Q. Elizabeth(1680),p.283
21. One of the names where a choice of spelling must be made arbitrarily. Parliamentary records vary from Hakewill to Hakewell to Hackwill to Hackwell. As his closest friends chose to use the last, I have elected to do the same.
22. John Hoskyns the elder of Byton, January 1587 Will. National Library of Wales, Early Hereford Wills; Thomas Hoskyns, of the parish of St. Weonards, 5 Oct. 1579 Will. NLW, Early Hereford Wills.
23. See genealogical table, p.9 for the relationships as far as I have been able to discover them from leases, wills, family letters, etc. Although I do not claim it to be complete, it is certainly more accurate than any previous study.
24. The final sentence is in the Clark edition, p. 416. Lansdowne 702, f. 54v, contains material excerpted from Anthony Wood's papers and includes an account of Hoskyns with the following version: "while he was a Child he was very importunate wth his ffather to be a scholar--at 10 years of age he began A B. C ϵ by ye years end he was got in his greek Grammer for he was a person of a prodigious memory ϵ gt strength of Body."
25. H. Hoskyns of Harewood, in an 1832 letter, says that Serjeant John Hoskyns' father was given a new crest. MSS Add. 23,929, f. 286. Also W. R. Williams, The History of the Great Sessions in Wales 1542-1830 (Brecknock, 1899), p. 173.
26. Thomas Dingley, History from Marble, Vol. I, p. 40(Camden Society ed. 1867). Clark describes the coat of arms and crest in a note on p. 424 of his edition of Aubrey.

27. Public Record Office, C.2, W 7/46.
28. P.R.O. C. 2, B 24/11.

CHAPTER II

School Days

Some time during 1578 the twelve year old farm lad and reader of Greek and Latin rode off to London and school, if Aubrey's brief note is accurate. He says that Hoskyns "was a yeare at Westminster." There are several reasons for believing Aubrey. First, there is his general accuracy on the facts of Hoskyns' life, gleaned in large measure from the poet's son and grandson. Second, it would explain why William Camden should have made the group of epitaphs by Hoskyns the core of his whole collection of contemporary witty epitaphs of England when he published his Remains Concerning Britain in 1605. Camden was the famous teacher of Westminster School, instructor of young Ben Jonson, and general historian of England and the Elizabethan period. He would probably have kept up an interest in his more brilliant pupils, even though they remained under his tutelage for a short time. It would certainly be no indication of failure for Hoskyns to move on to Winchester College after a year, for Winchester ranked then, as it does now, as one of the finest schools in Britain. It is true that Aubrey notes of Hoskyns' career at Westminster, "and not speeding there," but the possible meaning of that phrase is ambiguous at best.

There is another reason for believing he went to Westminster, and that is his close friendship with Ben Jonson. Herford and Simpson, in their great edition of Ben Jonson's works, analyze the relationship between these two in various places in their first volume. They take more for granted than I think possible, but their conclusions are worth noting. Jonson himself described his youth to William Drummond of Hawthornden as follows: "he   Jonson   himself was Posthumous born a moneth after his fathers decease, brought up poorly, putt to school by a friend (his master Cambden) after taken from it, and put to ane other Craft (I thinke was to be a Wright or Bricklayer)." The parenthetical

23

explanations are those of Drummond. Herford and
Simpson, however, footnote "a friend" as "Probably
Sir John Hoskins."[1] One obvious problem with the
note is that Hoskyns was never knighted. In another place[2] the editors explain, "Apart from Camden,
the only person whose claim to the honour appears
to be at all plausible is the distinguished lawyer
John Hoskyns, of whom Aubrey reports a pleasant
tradition." They then quote Aubrey's report of
Benedict Hoskyns' conversation with Jonson about
becoming his "son." It is a little difficult, however, to see how twelve-year-old John Hoskyns could
have put six-year-old Ben Jonson to school. It is
true that the Hoskyns family could afford it, and
it may even be possible (but unlikely) that John's
older brother Oswald was already successfully established in the clothing business in London by
this time. Thus young John might have influenced
someone else in the family to befriend a bright,
young, fatherless child that John met in the
streets of Westminster. It seems to me, however,
more likely that Drummond was right and that as
conscientious a teacher as Camden would have
brought into the school the obviously precocious
Jonson child. He would have been more likely to
know of such a neighborhood child than would Hoskyns. Under any circumstances, however, it is
pleasant to think of the friendship of John and
Ben beginning at such an early age, with the six-
year-older boy from Herefordshire taking the young,
fatherless Londoner under his wing.

We know very little about Westminster School,
"a publique Schoole for Grammer, Rhetoricke, Poe-
trie, and for the Latine and Greeke Languages,"[3]
at this time because the records have been lost.
But we do know some things that can help to show
the influences on young Hoskyns. For example, we
know the method that Camden used to teach his young
charges how to write poetry. Jonson said of his
own approach to poetry (again to Drummond): "That
he wrote all his first in prose, for so his master,
Camden, had learned him."[4] Much of Hoskyns' verse,
especially his earlier poetry, shows signs of this
method of composition. We also know that Camden

24

emphasized the study of the classics, and Hoskyns'
large body of poetry in Latin, poetry whose skill
and precision is lost on modern audiences because
of its language, would indicate this early training which would have been reinforced by his work
at Winchester College. Hoskyns would probably
have agreed with Jonson's praise of his teacher:

Camden, most reverend head, to whom I owe
All that I am in arts, all that I know.
(How nothing's that?) to whom my countrey owes
The great renowne, and name wherewith shee goes.
Then thee the age sees not that thing more grave,
More high, more holy, that shee more would
crave.
What name, what skill, what faith hast thou in
things!
What sight in searching the most antique
springs!
What weight, and what authoritie in thy speech!
Man scarse can make that doubt, but thou canst
teach.[5]

But Aubrey's note on Hoskyns' lack of success
at Westminster as well as our knowledge of Hoskyns'
character and physical prowess indicate that the
boy did not spend all of his time within the con-
fines of the school located through the long tun-
nel at the end of the greater cloister of Westminster Abbey. On his daily visits for worship to
the Abbey itself, his reaction may well have been
similar to that of Washington Irving two centuries
later:

I entered from the inner court of Westminster
School, through a long, low, vaulted passage,
that had an almost subterranean look, being
dimly lighted in one part by circular perfor-
ations in the massive walls. Through this
dark avenue I had a distant view of the cloisters, with the figure of an old verger, in his
black gown, moving along their shadowy vaults,
and seeming like a spectre from one of the
neighboring tombs. The approach to the abbey
through these gloomy monastic remains prepares

25

the mind for its solemn contemplation. The
cloisters still retain something of the quiet
and seclusion of former days.6

Although it is true that throughout his life Hoskyns
showed a genuine concern for his own spiritual life
and for the condition of the church in general, it
is likely that visions of Rome and Athens were more
in his thoughts than those of medieval grandeur at
this stage of his life. His "strong constitution"
as a youth also makes it plausible that he took e-
very opportunity possible for getting away from the
school and playing in the general area of Westminster, perhaps running past Westminster Hall and the
Gothic church where Parliament met and where he was
later to become so well-known, to play on Westminster steps, watching the boats and barges that carried members of the court to and from the City of
London, the great metropolis located around the
bend of the great river but still visible above the
flat river banks of Southwark and the low houses
and theaters on the Bankside.

As we do not know the date of his arrival in
London, we cannot tell which events of 1578 he either saw or heard about during his first year at
school. There would undoubtedly have been much
talk among the schoolboys about the sorcerer Simon
Pembroke, accused of "divelling in Southwark, being a figure flinger; and vehemently suspected to
be a Coniurer," who fell dead in the church of St.
Saviour, Southwark, just before his trial began,
"ratling a littlc in the throat, and neuer spake
word after." The Judge undoubtedly proclaimed the
common verdict, that "it was the iust iudgement of
God towards those that vsed Sorcery, and a great
example to admonish other to feare the iustice of
God." No doubt the boys at Westminster were duly
admonished. There were the usual events at Tyburn
gallows to draw a schoolboy with sufficient time
and energy to run across the fields and see a man
like John Nelson, who, because he denied the Queen's
supremacy, "was drawne from Newgate to Tiborne, and
there hanged, bowelled and quartered." The boys
would, of course, have brought rolls or fruit to

26

keep off hunger during the proceedings. At the end
of August 1578 Martin Frobisher returned from the
"Islands of Ice" with his disappointing load of
fool's gold, and in late January 1579 Hoskyns and
his friends would have been aware of the arrival
of the Count Palatine of the Rhine and the following festivities, including "a valiant Iusting and
running at the Tilt at Westminster" on February 1st.
As it was a Sunday, the schoolboys would have made
every effort to be present.

February brought with it a schoolboy's delight,
"such aboundance of snow, that on the fift in the
morning, the same was found in London to lye two
foote deepe iu [sic] the shallowest, and otherwise
being driuen by the winde, very boysterous in the
Northeast, on bankes, an ell or yard and halfe
deepe." The joys of snowball fights in February
would have turned to the extreme discomfort of insufficient heating by April, even for a healthy lad.

Sir Nicholas Bacon, Lord Keeper of the Great
Seal, died in February also, and perhaps young Hoskyns already knew of his own family's dealings with
that important man in earlier lawsuits. He had not
yet come into controversy with Bacon's son, Francis,
although within twenty years the two would be
crossing literary swords and soon after Parliamentary ones in the buildings on the other side of the
Abbey.

Certainly he would have seen the Queen either
on horseback around Westminster or boating on the
river, the latter a common occurrence that this
summer proved dangerous. On July 17th a young man
named Thomas Appeltree was firing a gun at random
while rowing on the Thames in a boat with two or
three children of Her Majesty's Chapel and hit one
of the bargemen of Her Majesty's private barge.
Her Majesty, with her usual aplomb, "neuer bashed
thereat," but helped care for the man. Later she
pardoned young Appeltree, but not until the rope
had been placed around his neck on the gibbet.[7] It
is hard to know whether Elizabeth was indulging in
her flare for the dramatic or practicing her usual

27

indecision.

We have some idea of student life at Westminster at the time, and the traditions help to supply Aubrey's loss of memory: "There were many pretty stories of him when a schooleboy, which I have forgott." Sir Nicholas L'Estrange, in his collection of "Jests and Stories," most of which are funny and rude, recounts two stories of Westminster School that may have involved Hoskyns, although there is no reason to presume that they do. They may well be considered typical, however. One tells of two boys that slept in one bed. All the boys had to rise at 6 a.m. (perhaps hard on many, but not on Hoskyns, who is described constantly as an early riser) to go to prayers. One night the other boys in the dorm took ropes, threw them over a beam above the bed, and lifted the bed with its sleeping occupants up to the ceiling. The next morning the bell rang as usual, the two boys lept from the bed, and very nearly killed themselves.[8]

On another occasion one of the boys had a pot of butter sent to him from his family, and the other boys discovered it. They tried to pick the cover from the pot, which was locked, but failed. Being resourceful, they put the pot next to the fire, "For, because They could not come at it, They made It come out to Them."[9] It is no wonder, with such carrying on, that Hoskyns did not speed well at Westminster. The life at his next school was to be a good deal more rigorous.

In the **Registrum Primum Wint Coll** of Winchester College, third on the list of entries beginning on August 30, 1579, is "Jo: Hoskyns de Mownton 13 annorum primo Martij post admiss 15º Dec. Hereford."[10] As indicated earlier, this does not necessarily mean that Hoskyns was born on the 1st of March 1566, but only that he was born by that date. It does not mean, either, that he arrived in Winchester on December 15th. He might well have been there earlier as a Commoner and was simply made a Scholar as an opening occurred. In spite of the biography in the **Dictionary of National Biography**, all the evidence indicates that he was not a Founder's Kin.

28

There were none that year. Certainly nowhere does
Hoskyns himself claim any kinship with the estimable founder of Winchester College, William of
Wykeham, who also founded New College at Oxford.
That he honored Wykeham is clear enough, but he
studiously avoided any mention of a family connection when, twenty years later, he praised the man:

> to giue that Bishopp his right that built
> two absolute Colledges at his owne charges
> and endowed them wth lands; looke downewards,
> how rare a thinge in theise dayes for a P^{r}lat
> not to graunt long leases, Diminish the re-
> venues of his fee, how lawdable it is but to
> repaire the ruines of his owne decayed pal-
> laces and churches, how magnificent an act
> it is thought fo^r a Nobleman to build an
> hospitall, how royall fo^r two o^r three princes
> to erect one Colledge and can there bee such
> vnthankfullnesse as to beare but one ordinary
> remembrance of him that enriched his Byshop-
> pricke, built two the most famous nurseries
> of lerning in the land was liberall to all
> wants in his life and left worthy bequests
> to all Degrees at his Death.[11]

With his entry at Winchester College, our
knowledge of John Hoskyns' activities becomes quite
firm for the rest of his life. We begin to see
the poetry that he wrote and the activities in
which he was involved. We also meet the friends
with whom he was to maintain contact throughout
his life. For any understanding of the poetry of
the late Elizabethan and early Jacobean age, the
reader must keep in mind the circle of friends that
formed early and changed very little throughout
their lifetime. Most of them did not publish their
poems during their lifetime because it was considered beneath the dignity of a gentleman to rush into print. The poetry takes for granted a clique
of equally informed friends, friends who would immediately understand and enjoy the display of wit,
the immense learning, and the playing of the game
which are all part and parcel of this poetry. It
was not meant to astound or obscure, for the writer

29

could count on a reader or group of readers who would immediately understand and appreciate. John Donne's admonition to the reader in his unpublished work of 1601, The Progresse of the Soule, makes the situation clear: "I will have no such Readers as I can teach." They had all been through the same education, studied the same classical writers, read the same medieval theology and science. And they delighted in the recognition of their peers. It was enough to circulate their works in manuscript, for such manuscript copies would eventually reach all the audience that they were concerned with. Perhaps more important for any critic who wishes to mix his biography and poetic criticism in an unthinking way, they all knew that when they used Ovid or Lucretius as the basis for their love lyrics or elegies, their readers would not be tempted to read such works as autobiography. They could distinguish between an allusion and a confession. The first was what they were after; gossip could take care of the other.

At least seven of Hoskyns' close friends were at Winchester during the five years that he stayed there, receiving training mainly in the classics. On 8 November 1577, John Gifford, aged 12, entered the school.[12] He was to become one of the most famous physicians of the age and the personal doctor of Hoskyns during the latter's infrequent bouts of sickness. He also seems to have collected some of Hoskyns' verse and poems about Hoskyns' imprisonment in 1614. On 6 March 1578, Henry Martin, aged 14, entered from Basinghall, London. He and Hoskyns were to share many debates and committee assignments during their years in Parliament. John Owen arrived from the west country on August 12th, at the age of 12. We shall have reason to examine his poems in praise of Hoskyns later on. Like Hoskyns, he was best known for his short works; indeed he was one of the leading epigrammatists of the age and celebrated all of the leading figures of the court and city of London. He seems never to have lost his affection and admiration for his classmate from Hereford who was the same age. Nearly a year after Hoskyns' entry, on 25 August 1580, Peter

Woodgate of Hawkhurst, aged 12, entered the College. He was to die young, while still at University, and Hoskyns would write one of his earliest epitaphs for his friend; it is still carved on the wall of the cloisters of New College. On 22 August 1581, John Davies, the youngest of the group, arrived at the age of 11. Not only were he and Hoskyns to be fellow students at the Middle Temple, but Davies was to become one of the best known, although not always the most admired poets of the group. Just two years before Hoskyns went on to Oxford, Thomas Bastard was to enter at the age of 13, on 27 March 1582. His collection of poetry and his friendship with John Donne were to insure his continuing memory in following centuries. He seems never, however, to have fully entered into the community of respect that the rest held for each other. His poetic life is charged with an obvious attempt to be accepted as an equal in ability with the group whose personal friendship he enjoyed. Unfortunately, he does not always seem to have been able to distinguish between verses that he and one of the others actually wrote. The ending of his life was a mean one. Anthony Wood describes his last days in which he apparently went insane, fell into debt, and died in prison in 1618.

The seventh fellow student is the least easy to register. Izaak Walton says of Henry Wotton:

> when time and diligent instruction had made him fit for a removal to an higher Form (which was very early) he was sent to Winchester-School: a place of strict Discipline and Order: that so, he might in his youth be moulded into a Method of living by Rule, which his wise Father knew to be the most necessary way, to make the future part of his life, both happy to himself, and useful for the discharge of all business, whether publick or private.[13]

Unfortunately, Wotton must have been a Commoner at the College as his name does not appear in the list of Scholars or in any other record of the College.

31

It seems absolutely certain that he did attend at
this period, however. It is easy to chart the
friendship of Wotton and Hoskyns and their many
activities together. But Wotton's career was to
outshine all of his contemporaries at Winchester,
and he seems to have kept a kind of personal distance in almost all of his relationships, perhaps
with a conscious eye to his own uncluttered advancement, perhaps because of a sense of his own family's superiority in the social scale.[14] This same
distance and yet friendship colors his relationships with such University associates as John Donne.
It would appear, incidentally, that Wotton was the
main connection between Donne and Hoskyns at the
time of the arrival of the three of them in Oxford.
We have already noted that Hoskyns and Wotton wrote
at least one poem together, and there is evidence
that they wrote different versions of another poem
later on.

Aubrey gives us a good picture of Hoskyns'
life and reputation at Winchester:

He was a yeare at Westminster; and not speeding there, he was sent to Winton Schole,
where he was the Flower of his time. He was
of a strong constitution, and had a prodigious
memorie. Besides his excellent naturall memorie, he acquired the artificiall way of memorie.[15] I remember I have heard that one time
he had not made his exercise (verse) and
spake to one of his Forme to shew him his,
which he sawe. The schoolmaster presently
calles for the Exercises, and Hoskyns told
him that he had writ it out but lost it, but
he could repeate it, and repeated the other
boye's exercise (I think 12 or 16 verses)
only at once reading over. When the boy who
really had made them shewed the Master the
same, and could not repeate them, he was
whipped for stealing Hoskyn's Exercise...

The Latin verses in the quadrangle at
Winton-colledge, at the Cocks where the Boyes
wash their hands, where there is the picture

32

of a good Servant, with asses eares and Hind's
feet, a padlock on his Lippes, etc. very
good hieroglyphick, with a hexastique in Latin underneath (which I doe not remember).
It was done by the Serjeant when he went to
school there; but now finely painted.

Although Aubrey forgot the Latin verse, Winchester
College did not, and it remains one of the treasures of the college, kept in good repair to this
day, although the board on which it is painted now
hangs in a dark hallway rather than in the quadrangle. Aubrey was right in saying that it was
repainted "finely." Luckily we have a copy of its
earlier form as it was originally painted by Hoskyns at the same time as he wrote the verse:

Effigiem Servi si vis spectare Probati,
Quisquis es, haec oculos pascat Imago Tuos.
Porcinum Os quocunque cibo jejunia sedat.
Haec Sera, consilium nefluat, arcta premit.
Dat patientem Asinus Dominis jurgantibus Aurem:
Cervus habet celeres ire, redire, Pedes.
Laeva docet multum tot Rebus onusta laborem:
Vestis munditiem: Dextera aperta Fidem,
Accinctus Gladis; Clypeo munitus: & inde
Vel se, Vel Dominum, quo tueatur, Habet.

The English translation below it may also be by
Hoskyns. Luckily for the modern reader, he often
did an English version at the same time he wrote
his Latin verse, at least in the case of his
shorter poems.

A Trusty Servant's Portrait would you see,
This Emblematic Figure well Survey:
The Porker's Snout, not Nice in diet shews:
The Padlock Shut, no Secrets He'll disclose.
Patient, the Ass, his Masters wrath will hear.
Swiftness in Errand, the Staggs Feet declare;
Loaded his Left Hand, apt to Labour saith;
The Vest, his Neatness: Open Hand his Faith.
Girt with his Sword; his Shield upon his Arm:
Himself & Master He'll protect from Harm.[16]

We have another poem of a more ambitious kind
dating from Hoskyns' Winchester days. It is not
possible to date the year, but we do know that it
was written for Pentecost Sunday. Our only dat-
able manuscript copy is from 1598, when it is recorded that the verses were sent to Mr. Percival
at Sir Robert Cecil's house. It is clear from
this address that Hoskyns was already known as a
poet by the end of the century among the highest
officials at the Elizabethan Court. The poem itself is interesting because it shows the reading
that Hoskyns was doing at Winchester which was to
be of importance in his own development of rhetorical style and theory. One section of his 1599
<u>Directions</u> <u>of</u> <u>Speeche</u> <u>and</u> <u>Stile</u>, that on letter-
writing, shows an obvious debt to Lipsius; it is
this section that Ben Jonson was to life in its
entirety and without acknowledgement when he put
together his own rhetorical and critical commonplace book, <u>Discoveries</u>. Justus Lipsius (Joest
Lips) was a <u>Flemish</u> philologist who lived from 1547
to 1606. He was known for his examination and collection of inscriptions and manuscripts as well as
for such works as the <u>Epistolica</u> <u>Institutio</u>, which
influenced the section of <u>Directions</u> mentioned a-
bove. He studied at Cologne, Rome, and Louvain
and ultimately returned to Louvain as professor of
Latin. Hoskyns used this estimable scholar as his
foil for a witty if somewhat youthful investigation
of the kind of minor problem one runs up against in
school lessons. He wonders why the syllable "Cos"
appears on the calendar in Winchester College:

> In Syllabam <u>Cos</u>, in Pentecost Dom. in
>   schola Wintoniensi.

Dic mihi Semesas Lipsi scrutate figuras
  Qui de Romano marmore mira sapis
Cos positum nostris an sit pro Consule fastis
  Vt<u>que</u> sit hoc cuius Consulis acta notet....[17]

Why Hoskyns should have been concerned with
such a minor linguistic detail on Pentecost Sunday
instead of with the religious meaning of the birthday of the church is oneone's guess. The poem, as

I have said, is a witty one, based on the double
meaning of the Latin word "Cos," which can either
mean "whetstone" or can be used as an abbreviation
for "Consul." Roman dating was marked by the con-
sulate of the year rather than by a year number, as
we mark our calendars. He asks Lipsius, who has
"studied half-eaten letters, who knows wonderful
things about Roman marble," whether Cos is "placed
on our calendars instead of consul," and if so,
"the acts of what Consul does it denote?" He
praises Lipsius for restoring the lost remains of
mutilated words and says that through his skill the
letter which is lost in a previous shipwreck is restored to its manuscript, and "sense returns." He
claims that Lipsius' restorations are better than
that accomplished by Phoebus on the mangled limbs
of the son of Theseus and better than the restoration of Pelops' arm, for in the latter case "Life
was not restored." He asks Lipsius, who "can do
all things with Words," to tell him what the single
word Cos means. Lipsius replies, but too late,
"For Justus does not act so well at Louvain," (that
certainly must have won the best Latin-English pun
award for the year!)

This is right, this less so, that more correct
But I never change anything from the old manu-
                    script.
If I remember well the words of the Capitoline
                    manuscripts,
Hear, Boy, what the Cos at Winchester means.
Aemilius Lepidus and Laetus Pomponius mark
The favorable times of the year by their
                    auguries.
Is it not so? Or perhaps Domitius in this
                    same year
Ordered soldiers who were on maneuvers to
                    return home.
Or is it thus? The righteous whetstone sharpen-
                    ed the Roman axes
When public indignation sought vengeance on a
                    forbidden crime.
But even this I doubt, and if my best opinion
                    is demanded,
I do not know what this word Cos means.

35

Both meanings, Hoskyns says, are attractive, and
as for Lipsius, "You can keep the precision of
the worn whetstone for yourself." Hoskyns will
listen to any other meanings, even though given by
Chalcas, as if they were given by Cassandra--in o-
ther words, he won't believe them.

If the subject matter is slight, this early
poem already shows Hoskyns' ability at writing Latin verse of a very high technical level. His metrical sense is always good, and his Latin is usually very pure. Kenneth Fleissner, to whom I am
much indebted for a careful scrutiny of the Latin
poetry and for excellent suggestions on transla-
tions of the poems, has pointed out that there are
only about ten medieval words in all of Hoskyns'
Latin verse. He relies heavily, as did most of
his friends in both their Latin and English verse,
on Ovid. More than most, he sticks to Augustan
language and metrics; it is, in other words, strictly classical and quite difficult. His references
reveal a tremendously learned person, and he shows
a quite remarkable knowledge of ancient history.
It is often necessary to work with the most ab-
struse sources for his mythological references,
and some are still not identifiable.

Obviously, however, Hoskyns did not spend all
of his time at Winchester writing Latin verse, although a major part of his studies would have been
in reading the classics and doing daily exercises
in Latin. On 20 August 1581, John Hoskyns took
his oath to abide by everything in Wykeham's Statutes. His name appears last on the list for that
day.[18] As the oath was to be administered on the
completion of a student's fifteenth year, although
this was not a hard and fast rule, we have reason
to accept a 1566 birth date as the correct one.
The Scholars were administered the oath in the
chapel of the college, and they agreed to follow
the forty-six clauses of the Statutes. These
clauses give us a thorough knowledge of the make-
up of the college and the daily routine of the students. Under the first clause we find that the
College was to consist of a Warden, seventy Scho-

lars, ten fellows, three Chaplains, and three lay
Clerks. There also were a schoolmaster and an
usher. There were exact rules for the choice of
Scholars: Clause two lists Founder's Kin first,
then natives of parishes in which one of the two
Colleges (Winchester and New College) had property,
then certain counties. It would appear that Hoskyns qualified under the second category, as the
College had extensive holdings in Herefordshire.
Under the original Statutes, "Candidates must be
pauperes et indigentes, towardly and well-mannered
('manners makyth man'); quick to study, well behaved and grounded in Latin grammar, reading, and
plain song. No candidate as a general rule is to
be under eight or over twelve years of age."

It is obvious that on both scores of age and
indigency, Hoskyns had entered the school in opposition to the rule. As to the first, his year at
Westminster probably was in his favor; as to the
second, already the private schools of England had
shifted from institutions favoring the poor to
those catering in large measure to the children of
the well-to-do. On all other points Hoskyns was
an admirable candidate, except perhaps for the
well-behaved part. The entry on the requirement of
the knowledge of plainsong is an interesting one.
It may be that Hoskyns already had the love of music that was to continue throughout his life, or it
may be that he gained that affection while at Winchester. Aubrey notes that in his later life, "He
made an antheme (gett it) in English to be sung at
Hereford Minster at the assizes; but Sir Robert
Harley (a great Puritan) was much offended at it."
Unfortunately, Aubrey apparently did not "gett it."
John's interest and abilities in singing in a lighter vein are also noted by Aubrey in the life of Dr.
Ralph Kettel, head of Trinity College, Oxford. Kettel "sang a thin shrill high Treble, but there was
one J. Hoskins who had a higher, and was wont to
playe the wag with the Doctor to make him straine
his voyce up to his."[19] John's voice would have
been changing at Winchester, but he apparently kept
a strong falsetto, a characteristic not at all unusual in men who have had good training as boy so-

37

pranos.

One ordeal that Hoskyns had to go through was
that of tonsure, unless he had already had that
extreme form of haircut while at Westminster, as
it was a strict rule for entering Scholars at Winchester. As he was probably not a Founder's Kin,
he would not have had the advantage of help by "one
of the discreeter and more advanced scholars to su-
perintend his studies." Later on he may well have
been one of the tutors appointed in this way. Nor,
as a regular Scholar, would his linen and woollen
clothing, bedding, shoes, and other necessaries
have been provided. Every Scholar, except a Founder's Kin, had to leave on completing his 18th year
unless he was already on the roll of New College,
in which case he could stay until he went to New
College or completed his 19th year.

The student's life at the College was quite
limited and had a monastic air about it:

> Every member of the Society is to dine and
> sup in Hall daily... not to have more than
> five dishes... During dinner and supper a
> scholar chosen by the schoolmaster is to read
> aloud passages from the 'Lives of the Saints',
> the 'Dicta Doctorum', or Holy Writ, the o-
> thers keeping silence... everyone shall leave
> hall after dinner or supper is over, so soon
> as the loving cup shall have passed round once
> among the Fellows... on festivals when the
> drinking is done, they need not retire till
> curfew: and on festivals in winter, when a
> fire is on the hearth [The fire in the Hall
> was on an open hearth. The smoke made its
> way out through louvers in the ceiling until
> 1819.] , the company present may, for re-
> creation's sake, spend a moderate time in
> singing or other honest amusements, such as
> reciting lays, reading chronicles, or talking
> of the wonders of the universe, and other sub-
> jects befitting the gravity of churchmen.

We can be certain that Hoskyns took a leading part in such entertainment, perhaps even straining to the limit subjects befitting the gravity of churchmen. If he didn't, it was the only period of his life when that was true.

The regulations in clause 17 would have been the hardest for a young boy brought up on a farm in the hills and fields of Herefordshire: "No scholar may go into the town or Soke [the district under the jurisdiction of the town] without leave. No Fellow, scholar, or servant may keep dogs, hawks, or ferrets, or have nets, or perform military exercises, or play any game, or shoot or throw anything within or near the buildings." Of course, there were the extensive playing fields to wander in, or the banks of the Itchen where Walton was later to spend so much time fishing. Nor were the students allowed to "grow long hair or a beard, or wear shoes with peaks or hoods with frogs, or wear a sword or dagger, or frequent taverns, shows, or other improper places." To guard against infractions of such rules, the gates were to be closed at sunset and remain closed until daybreak, and the walls of Winchester College even to this day appear almost impregnable. A side note is that no female servants were to be employed at the college except for a laundress.

Infractions against the monastic rule were treated harshly: "A scholar may be removed if convicted of any crime or immorality, or if he enter any religious order, or marry, or absent himself from College more than a month in any year." Overseeing Hoskyns and his associates at this time was Thomas Stempe as Warden. Soon after, John Harmer, "a subtle Aristotleian," was to take over, and during his term in office he was to be one of the translators of the King James Bible, being assigned, with seven other men, the four gospels, the Book of Acts, and Revelation. Hoskyns was to deal with Harmer when he leased lands in Herefordshire from his former school.

And so for five years Hoskyns was to live, ex-

39

cept for periods of less than a month each year, at Winchester College, studying the classics and rudiments of law and theology, gaining a reputation at an early age for his ability as a Latin poet and a boy with a prodigious memory. He must have spent long hours in the noble Romanesque Cathedral with the longest nave in England, passing by the tomb of William Rufus, whose burial reputedly caused the original tower to crash down as a sign of divine displeasure at the act, looking at the burial boxes of the kings of Anglo-Saxon England resting on their elevated rack around the choir. Like Keats he may have loved to wander along the Itchen River south of town until he reached St. Cross Hospital with its great Romanesque Chapel, and asked and received the traveller's dole of beer and bread that still is offered at the front gate. The city of Winchester itself had all of the shops a young boy could ask for, and the remains of William the Conqueror's palace as well as the round table of King Arthur in the palace on the hill--for was this not Camelot?--would have called up the romance of the past.

Hoskyns never lost his attachment to his childhood school, and he made sure that two of his brothers also attended, bringing the influence of his friends at court to pave the way. He became one of the large leaseholders of the College for property in Herefordshire as well. It must have been with considerable regret as well as anticipation that he made the necessary move to the other of Wykeham's foundations, New College, Oxford.

Footnotes for Chapter II

1. C.H.Herford and Percy Simpson, Ben Jonson (Oxford, 1925), I, 139, 164.
2. Ibid., p. 3.
3. From a description of the Colleges and Schools within the city of London by G.B.Knight added to Stow's Annales (1631), p. 1066.
4. Witherspoon and Warnke, edd., Seventeenth-Century Prose and Poetry (2nd ed.,1963), p. 130.
5. Helen White, et al., edd., Seventeenth-Century Verse and Prose (1961), I, 125-26.
6. Washington Irving, "Westminster Abbey," in Oxford Anthology of American Literature, W. R. Benet and N. H. Pearson, edd, (1947), I, 245.
7. The events recorded here for 1578 and 1579 are from John Stow, Annales, pp. 684-86.
8. Harley 6395, #107.
9. Ibid., #108.
10. p. 93.
11. From Directions of Speeche & Stile, MSS Add. 15,230, f. 15; See Chap. 5.
12. The entries for all of the friends mentioned in this section (except for Henry Wotton) are in the Registrum Primum, pp. 92-94.
13. Izaak Walton, The Lives of John Donne, Sir Henry Wotton.... (Oxford World Classics, 1950), p..99.
14. Wotton was no more saintly than the rest of his friends, however. Ben Jonson once told of an incident which occurred at Leith when Wotton visited the court of James VI of Scotland:
    Sir Henry Wotton, befor his Majesties going to England, being disguised at Leith on Sunday, when all the rest were at church, being interrupted of his occupation by ane other wenche who came in at the door cryed out "Pox on thee, for thou hast hindered the procreation of a chyld", and betrayed himself.
    (Logan Pearsall Smith, The Life and Letters of Sir Henry Wotton (Oxford, 1907), I, 42, n. 2.
15. This sentence is found in Clark's edition of Aubrey, p. 421.
16. Both Latin and English versions are painted on

41

boards at Winchester College, but there is some reason to doubt that the English version is by Hoskyns (see Osborn, p. 280). I think we have reason to believe, however, that Hoskyns wrote an English version which has remained traditional at the College. The spelling and punctuation are more ancient than the 19th century version quoted by Osborn. Certainly the English lacks the directness and vigor of the Latin original, in which, for example, the stag "has swift feet to go, to return," and the viewer, "whoever you are," is urged to "feast your eyes on this Image." And the wonderful motion of line six with its running trochees and dactyls, broken by the first comma and turned into an iamb for "redire," is lost in the English. The background of the painting and verse, with their models in France, is summed up by Herbert Chitty in two articles, in Notes and Queries, October 1915, and The Wykehamist, No. 652, 4 Nov. 1924. In the latter article Chitty quotes from the Bursar's Accounts for 1611-12, in which the figure is already a "veterem effigiem." He also provides a reproduction of the original drawing and the Latin verse. There seems no reason to question Aubrey's version of Hoskyns' activity.

17. MSS Add. 15,227, ff. 48v-49. The poem is 40 lines in length and is signed "Hosequinus." It should be noted that Osborn's text is faulty in several places, perhaps because of typographical errors in publishing. She quotes, in her footnotes to the poem (p. 280), a prologue and ending from the other copy of the poem, MS. Hatfield 204.43, which establishes a dream "frame" for the poem.

Hoskyns would have appreciated Laurence Sterne's more famous reference to Lipsius in Tristram Shandy: "But you forget the great Lipsius, quoth Yorick, who composed a work the day he was born; -- They should have wiped it up, said my uncle Toby, and said no more about it." (Riverside Edition, 1965), p. 313.

18. Liber prothocollorum de iuramentis tam Sociorum from 1576. The Statutes are printed in Chap. 5 of T.F.Kirby's Annals of Winchester College

(London, 1892).
19. Aubrey, Dick ed., p. 185.

CHAPTER III
College Years

On 5 March 1585 Hoskyns went up to New College, Oxford, as a probationary fellow, although the term did not begin until April 21st.[1] He probably spent some weeks or even months in Hereford between Winchester and Oxford. There he would have seen once again the younger brother who was now three and a half years old. Dr. John Hoskyns was born on or before 29 September 1581, perhaps as early as 29 February.[2] These two brothers were to follow similar tracks through their college and university days, and for most of his life the younger brother had a room in John's house, which he apparently thought of as his own home.

From the time of his entry into Oxford, Hoskyns would have been able to get home with more ease than he had while at Winchester. There would be much longer vacations and no regulations on the amount of time one could spend at home during those vacations. Hereford and the borders of Wales were well represented at Oxford as well, and there would be all kinds of company to share the ride back across Gloucestershire. Oxford was also a good deal nearer than either London or Winchester had been.

But it also seems obvious that Hoskyns at this point preferred the college company of his fellows to the country atmosphere of Monkton farm. Hoskyns entered Oxford with one of the most illustrious groups of students ever to enter in such a short period of time, and he unquestionably ranked as one of the intellectual leaders of the group, if not the unquestioned leader. As the most brilliant student from Winchester, he would have been heard from before he even set foot on campus. As one of the older students in the group, he would have assumed leadership in many ways. By the time he left, he would have increased his fame as a writer of Latin epitaphs and elegies and added to it his even greater fame as a writer of humorous epitaphs.

45

The group of friends from Winchester either
were at New College or would soon arrive. Henry
Martin had entered on 19 August 1582 and remained
until 1595, after he had earned his D.C.L. The famous preacher Lancelot Andrewes advised Martin to
study civil and canon law, which he did, becoming
King's Advocate in 1609 and a Judge in the Admiralty Court in 1617. He and John worked closely together as late as 1628 in helping to frame the Petition of Right. John Owen arrived on 2 October
1584 and left in 1591 with a Bachelor of Laws degree. John Gifford entered on 30 August 1586 and
remained the longest of all, not leaving until 1598,
then a full-fledged M.D. Thomas Bastard did not arrive until 27 August 1588 and only stayed thee
years from that date, graduating in 1591.[3]

Henry Wotton matriculated nearly a full year
before Hoskyns, on 5 June 1584, but it is always
possible that they came up together if Clark and
Wood are right in saying that Hoskyns had entered
as a Probationary Fellow that same June. Wotton
had soon moved from New College to Hart Hall and
taken up rooms with Richard Baker, who was later
to memorialize both Wotton and Donne in his mammoth
Chronicle of the Kings of England.[4] Baker, a six-
teen-year-old boy from Kent, had entered Hart Hall
on the same day that John Donne and his brother
Henry, aged 12 and 11 respectively, had done, 23
October 1584. Donne came from a strong Catholic
background, descended from the family of Sir Thomas
More. He had had training in Latin and French and
was to spend much of his time at Oxford becoming
deeply immersed in Spanish literature and thought.
Because of his unwillingness to take the Oath of
Supremacy, Donne would leave about 1588 without
taking his degree.[5] As the grandson of the most famous English epigrammatist, John Heywood, Donne undoubtedly joined in the game of writing short, witty epigrams, perhaps under the guidance of Hoskyns,
for it is quite clear that this whole group of writers and courtiers became close friends while at
Oxford.

46

Another John Davies came up from Hereford on 2 July 1585 and entered Magdalen College. His exact situation at the University is not clear. His poems seem to indicate that he was not, at least for very long, a student, although Wood describes him as being educated at Oxford. It is certain that he was a writing master there, and he wrote several poems in praise of Magdalen College. Later on, while living at London, he was to have Prince Henry as a pupil, and Fuller was to call him the most skillfull penman of his age. Some of Hoskyns' works were to be copied out by him, and the two were apparently friends until Davies died in 1618. Like Hoskyns, Davies was a great epigrammatist and in 1610 published The Scourge of Folly, a collection of about 300 epigrams on all of the well-known people of the time, including Shakespeare, Jonson, Daniel Joseph Hall, Marston, and Fletcher. Two of them, as we shall see, were addressed to his friend Hoskyns. Davies also contributed commendatory verses for several of the same books as Hoskyns, and he prefaced his 1603 poem Microcosmos with "A Request to the City of Hereford," which would have been duly noted by the then Deputy Steward of the City and its representative in Parliament, Hoskyns.

The other John Davies, later to be Attorney General for Ireland, also came up from Winchester in 1585 to enter Queen's College, but he left soon after and entered the Middle Temple on 3 February 1588. This did not keep him from getting his degree from Oxford in 1590. For a time he was ostracized from the group of friends because of his actions, but he managed to return to their good graces, though Donne and Hoskyns both were critical of his sonnets.

One of the key figures in the group arrived in December 1585: Richard Martin, one of Hoskyns' closest friends and probably the most congenial of the entire crew, who was made Recorder of London in 1618 and apparently died of financial embarrassment when he found the amount of graft he was supposed to pay for obtaining the position was more than he could afford, arrived at Broadgates Hall (Pembroke College)

47

on 10 December. Hoskyns wrote his epitaph. which
still stands in the Middle Temple church, one of
the few items that remained undestroyed in the
bombing of this famous Romanesque building during
World War II.

Finally, two other friends should be noted,
one who arrived at Oxford before Hoskyns left Winchester and the other who arrived after Hoskyns
had completed his B.A. Hugh Holland, a Welshman
from Denbigh, entered Balliol College on 1 March
1583. He had gone to Westminster School and had
had William Camden as his teacher. It is very possible that he and Hoskyns had been fellow students
there. In 1589 he was to leave Oxford and move to
Trinity College, Cambridge, perhaps because of his
conversion to Roman Catholicism. Walton said that
John Donne made a similar move in 1588 for religious reasons, although there is no evidence to
support his claim. Whether John Davies of Hereford
or John Donne was in any way responsible for Holland's conversion it is not possible to discover.
It is important, however, to see how very little
difference the struggle between Protestantism and
Roman Catholicism made in the forming of collegiate and artistic friendships at the time. On leaving Cambridge, Holland travelled on the continent
and even reached Jerusalem. His religion obviously
kept him from the preferment he sought on returning
to England, and he "grumbled out the rest of his
life in visible discontentment."[6] Later on, however,
he was patronized by Buckingham and was buried in
Westminster Abbey in 1633. Like the others he contributed verses to various books and was a member
of the Mermaid Tavern group.

On 15 January 1588, Benjamin Rudyard matriculated from St. John's College after being educated
at Winchester, where he arrived after Hoskyns had
left. Apparently he did not graduate from Oxford
but went on to New Inn in 1589 and the Middle Temple in April 1590. He was called to the bar on 24
October 1600. He was to be associated with the government side in Parliament from 1620 to 1640, although he gradually became a middle-of-the-roader.

His relations with Hoskyns seem to have been basically friendly, and Aubrey notes him among those
close friends of John that include Ralegh, Donne,
John Owen, Richard Martin, and Henry Wotton. However, the Rudyard entry is unique, to say the least:
"Sir Benjamin Ruddyer, with whom it was once his
[Hoskyns] fortune to have a quarrel and fought a
Duell with him and hurt him in the Knee, but they
were afterwards friends again." When the duel took
place is not easily ascertained; it could have been
during the short years during which they were both
at Oxford, or it could have been during the longer
years during which they were both law students in
London. The latter seems the more likely. During
the Christmas season of 1597-98, however, they were
close friends and fellow performers and writers in
the **Prince** d'Amour, given in the Middle Temple.
Rudyard is often given credit for writing the play,
although it is probable that he wrote only a part.

Hoskyns' main statement on friendship in the
Directions **of** **Speeche** **and** **Stile** clearly refers to
his relationship with Rudyard:

> Yo^r freind hath esteemed better of his owne
> stomacke, then of the eternall loue vowed
> betwixt you and p^rferreth the tryall of his
> vallo^r before the regard of both your cre-
> ditts, wch must die howsoever either of you
> or both surviue the Combate; would you not
> iudge him vnworthy to bee yor freind that
> began not his fidelitie wth an inviolable
> covenant never to bee yor enemye[7]

On the basis of our knowledge of the two friends
and of this passage, I think we may safely say
that Rudyard demanded the duel. It is also likely
that the duel occurred not long before this passage was written at the Middle Temple in 1599.

It would be difficult if not impossible to
describe the exact nature of the studies that occupied Hoskyns during his years at New College.
From his later interests and writings, we would be
safe in supposing that he continued his interest

in and study of the classics and history. A mere listing of references to classical authors and events in the Directions gives an indication of his background: Aristotle, Hermogenes, Quintillian, Demosthenes, Cicero, Themistocles, Coriolanus, Eriphile, Tarpeia, Isocrates, Plutarch. Verres, Alexander, Urbinus, Draco, Milo, Titerinus, Polybius, Tacitus, Aesop, Scipio Africanus, St. Augustine, and on and on. And Hoskyns' references are not those of slight acquaintance; they reveal close familiarity with the sources.

From Aubrey's remarks, we are also safe in saying that he continued his study of theology, which was an important part of the education of all students at both of William of Wykeham's foundations. His knowledge of science was undoubtedly furthered at University, and he already began to associate with those members of the aristocracy whose interest in the New Philosophy or science was a matter of comment at the Elizabethan court. Like his friends Wotton and Donne, he undoubtedly became involved in the study of languages, and although he may not have been as deeply involved in Spanish as Donne, his interest ranged sufficiently wide to enable him nearly forty years later to write Latin, Greek, and Hebrew inscriptions and poetry on the walls of his estate at Morehampton. He also began those studies of the law which would prepare him for his calling to the Bar at the Middle Temple. Put another way, his study was a continuation of the medieval trivium (grammar, logic, and rhetoric) and quadrivium (arithmetic, geometry, astronomy, and music) which was still the heart of the liberal arts education of European universities.

For us the most important part of his growth, however, was outside the classroom in the association of his friends, all of whom were involved in the writing of poetry. Most of his longer poems we can date with assurance. His shorter works give more trouble. Aubrey, as we have seen, said that he made the best Latin epitaphs of his time, and William Camden thought enough of his English epitaphs to collect them. Most of the short Eng-

lish epitaphs were probably written while he was at
Oxford, one of them definitely so:

> Mr Hoskines, his owne Epitaphe when he was
> sicke, beinge fellow in New Colledge
> in Oxforde.
> Reader, I wo'ld not haue the mistake
> deade or alive I deserve not thy knowledge;
> onlie but this that my bones may make
> parte of the dust of soe worthie a Colledge.
> That I spente I had; y^t I gaue I haue; y^t I
> lefte I loste.[8]

The epitaph is a nice gesture to the college he felt
such a close affection for all his life; the L'envoi
is a good example of the wit that made Hoskyns so
popular with his own generation. The metrical form
of alternate nine and eleven syllable lines is handled easily and with remarkable variety for a single
quatrain. It is no wonder that other epigrammatists
recognized his skill from the start.

William Camden introduced his collection of
Hoskyns' epitaphs in this way:

> But I fear now I have overcharged the Reader's
> mind, with doleful, dumpish and uncomfortable
> Lines; I will therefore for his recomfort end
> this part with a few conceited, merry, and
> laughing Epitaphs, the most of them composed
> by Master John Hoskins, when he was young,
> and will begin with the Bellows maker of Oxford.
> Here lieth John Cruker, a maker of Bellows,
> His crafts-master and King of good fellows,
> Yet when he came to the hour of his death.
> He that made Bellows, could not make breath.[9]

By the number of times it appears in manuscript
collections, it is clear that this obvious play of
wit caught the fancy of the time. It reveals the
love of verbal play and puns that is so much a part
of Shakespeare's attraction to the audiences of the
period, even though Samuel Johnson in a more "re-
fined" age would find it offensive and we in ours
find it often childish, or at least childlike.

It is difficult to know just how many of the
epitaphs that follow in Camden's collection of 1605
are actually by Hoskyns.[10] It is probably safe to
include the Latin epitaph on the ballad maker Elderton who, as Camden explained, "did arm himself
with Ale (as old Father Ennis did with Wine) when
he ballated."

Hic situs est sitiens atque ebrius Eldertonus
Quid dico hic situs est? hic potius sitis est.

The oral pun on situs, this place where Elderton
lies, and sitis, the thirst he feels even though
he is drunk, would have been especially appreciated
by John's undergraduate friends. He probably also
wrote the English epitaph that Camden includes next:

Here is Elderton lyeing in dust,
Or lyeing Elderton, chose which you lust.
Here he lyes dead, I doe him no wrong,
For who knew him standing, all his life long.

The next four are even more likely by John.

Here lyeth Thom Nicks bodie
Who liued a fool and dyed a nodye:
As for his soule aske them that can tell,
Whether fooles soules go to heauen or to hell.

The second is on an old Priest,

Hic est Durandus positus sub marmore duro,
An sit saluandus ego nescio, nec ego curo.

The flip, "Whether he is well [saved] I do not know,
nor do I care" is not in John's usual manner. The
only real wit in the poem is in the positioning of
the parallel forms "Durandus" and "saluandus" and
"duro" and "curo" which implies a double meaning
in the last of both to cure and to care.

Camden identifies the third subject as "our
Countreyman, old Sparges,

        Here lyeth father Sparges
        That died to saue charges.

The fourth could have been an attempt by John to
make the form carry part of the meaning of the poem
in what was going to be a more common practice of
the Baroque:

        Here lyeth he
        Which with himself could neuer agree.

The disagreement of line lengths fits the message
of the poem.

        Two other epigrams seem certainly to be by
Hoskyns because of their close physical association
in the text with other epigrams by him which we
will consider later on:[11]

        Here lyeth Richard a Preene,
        One thousand, fiue hundred, eighty nine,
        Of March the 22. day,
        And he that will die after him may.

                * * * * * * * *

        Here lyes the man that madly slaine,
        In earnest madnesse did complaine,
        On nature, that she did not giue,
        One life to loose, another to liue.

        There are several other epitaphs by Hoskyns in
the Farmer Chetham MS which, although they have no
time identification, probably date from the Oxford
days, although there is no way to prove it. One is
on Sir Thomas Gresham, the famous Elizabethan financier and friend of Cecil, who built the Royal Exchange and founded Gresham College, but whose greatest popular fame is owing to his dictum that bad
money drives out good. Gresham died in 1579, and
the poem could date from any time after that.

                Of Sr Tho. Gressam.
        Here lyes Gressam vnder ground
        as wise as fifty thousand pound;
        he never refused the drinck of his freind,
        drinke was his life and drunck was his ende.[12]

53

The judgment seems a trifle less than fair. The
Rev. Mr. Grosart had some basis for his note, "It
grates on one to read the above Verses on the 'magnificent' Gresham."[13] It also seems to us now a very
impolitic poem for a young man who was soon to become a friend of the family of Sir William Cecil.

John's other epitaphs in the Chetham MS are
typical of the many circulating at the time, although they are free from the usual bawdiness of
those written by his friends during this period.[14]

Here lyeth the bodie of Hugh Poache
headed like a herringe, bellied like a Roache:
god of his mercy send him his grace,
for he never had heare, growe on his face.[15]

* * * * * * * * * * * *

Of Swifte.

Here lyes Swifte that swiftlie fledd
all company alive, and lived as deade;
when death ran for Swifte he was verie glad
That so might he shifte of those few freindes
                              he hadd:
Away he wo'ld in hast, noe man could intreate
                              him,
yet nowe here he lyes, yf the wormes have not
                              eate him.[16]

* * * * * * * * * * * *

An Ep: one a man for doyinge nothinge.

Here lyes the man was borne and cryed
tould three score yeares, fell sicke and dyed.[17]

It would be hard to tell how many gravestones of
England and New England bore versions of this epitaph, but it must be in the hundreds.

Here lyes the man w[th]owte repentaunce,
whose death hath lost him much acquaintaunce.[18]

The Chetham MS. has two other short poems by
Hoskyns that may well come from this early period,
although both the language and control argue for a

later day, say the years at the Middle Temple. They
are worth including at this point, however, to see
the growth in Hoskyns' control over the same elements of wit, puns, and verbal twists from the expected or familiar.

Of ye losse of time. Par J. Hoskins.

If life be time y^t here is spent
and time on earth be cast away
Who so his time hath here mispent
hath hastned his owne dying day.
So it doth proue a killing crime
to massacre our living time.

If doing nought be like to death,
of him y^t doth Camelion wise
take only paines to draw his breath
the passers by may pasquilize
not here he liues: but here he dyes.[19]

What seems at first glance a rather superficial
poem of wit takes on much more weight when it is
read with care. The double meaning of "living" in
the last line of the first stanza brings with it a
touch of pathos which supports the religious argument of the first two lines. The image of the Cha-
melion, which is easily passed over because of the
flow of the verse, is a metaphor of telling power
in relation to the person who sits motionless, un-
blinking, in the sun, "doing naught." Obviously
the implications reach far beyond the person who is
merely stationary. The use of the anti-genre, in
this case of an epitaph on a living person, adds to
the power of the short piece. Short as it is, it
matches the wit and poetic ability of the young
Donne of the earliest Songs and Sonets, although it
willingly stays within the older traditions of Elizabethan poetry rather than moving into the rebellion of the "strong lines" of poets like Donne and
Chapman.

The other poem, an epigram rather than an epitaph, is aimed at one of the playwrights of the day,
probably one of the University wits who were straining after their model, Seneca. It too could come

55

from the London period rather than the days at Oxford:

> Of one y^t had stolne much out of Seneca.
> Put of thy buskins Sophocles ye greate,
> and morter treade wth thy disarmèd shankes.
> for this man's heade hath had a happier sweate,
> whereof ye worlde doth conn him little thankes.
> Blush Seneca to see thy feathers loose,
> pluckt from a Swann stuck vpon a goose.
>
> J.H.20

There is always the unlikely chance that the poem was aimed as a genial satire at his friend Ben Jonson, the bricklayer's son, who would know how to "treade mortar."

Hoskyns is given credit for another poem in the Chetham MS that probably is from his Oxford days. On 22 September 1586, Sir Philip Sidney died in a surprise attack on a Spanish convoy following the battle of Zutphen. His knightly gesture of giving water to another wounded man with the classic phrase "Thy necessity is greater than mine" merely capped a career which already had won him the hearts of his countrymen and impressed all of the writers of his age. His Arcadia would form the basis for most of the remarks on rhetoric that Hoskyns was to make in Directions of Speeche and Stile; his Astrophel and Stella was to define the nature of the Elizabethan sonnet sequence; and his Defence of Poesie was to be recognized as the primary work of literary criticism of the age. His life spanned all of the literary and artistic currents of the period, from his friendship with Fulke Greville and William Camden to his acquaintance with Tintoretto and Veronese and his membership in the Areopagus, a club which undertook the typical 16th century task of making classical metrics useful in English verse (much as the Camerata of Florence was trying to use the elements of Greek music as they knew them in the early development of the opera).

When Hoskyns first felt his intense love for

the work of Sidney is not known. It is possible
that he knew something of Sidney through Camden, as
Sidney was, after all, only twelve years older than
Hoskyns. Closer to the truth is the chance that he
would have become acquainted with the famous man's
work as an undergraduate at Oxford, or even during
his later days at Winchester, where he may have
been as interested in contemporary literature as he
was the classics. One of the closest contacts would
have been Thomas Thornton. Thornton was made Vice-
Chancellor of Oxford on 12 July 1583, but he was also Canon of Christ Church in Oxford, where he had
been tutor to Sidney. Among his other positions he
was intimately connected with Hereford Cathedral as
Chanter and about this time was made Master of Ledbury Hospital. He died in 1629 and was buried in
Ledbury, at Dr. John's church. The Oxford and Hereford ties make it quite likely that Hoskyns knew
Thornton, and it may well have been that Hoskyns'
affection for Sidney as a writer came about because
of personal contact with the great poet's tutor.
Another connection would have been the Wotton family. Sidney speaks of his close friendship with Edward Wotton, Henry's brother, in the Defence of
Poesie, and Henry showed Sidney's translation of
Aristotle to John, as we learn from the Directions
(although that happened at a later date).

At any rate, the Chetham MS contains a poem
by Hoskyns which the Rev. Grosart tentatively headed as being about Sidney. It seems a reasonable
guess, especially as it is found next to other
poems about Sidney.

> Here the bodie of that man lyes
> whose accons all were histories;
> Noe Epitaphe can make him knowne,
> nor add one prayse more then his owne.
>
> J. Hoskynes.[21]

But if the poem is about Sidney, it was not
the only poem by Hoskyns on his great contemporary,
nor the best known. Most of the poets of the age,
including Spenser and the future King James I, were
quick to celebrate Sidney's memory in verse. In

Oxford, the young students and writers rose to the occasion of Sidney's death and made up the usual commemorative volume of verses which characterize so much of the poetry of the age and give it its strong occasional cast. As a matter of fact, two volumes of poems on Sidney issued forth from Oxford in 1587, the Exeqviae Illvstrissimi EQvitis, D. Philippi Sidnaei...., and Peplvs Illvstrissimi Viri D. Philippi Sidnaei.... Hoskyns contributed to the latter, which was dedicated to Henry Herbert, Earl of Pembroke, from New College in September. The Countess of Pembroke was Sidney's sister and one of the great patronesses of poetry of the Elizabethan age. The Herbert family was close to or included almost every poet of any notice of the late 16th and early 17th centuries. John Donne wrote several poems to or about the Herberts, and both Lord Herbert of Cherbury, the founder of Deism, and George Herbert were, of course, leading poets in their own rights.

Among the authors included in the volume are some of the group of friends we have discussed: Henry Martin, John Gifford, Thomas Bastard, and John Owen. But the longest poem by far of the entire volume is that by Hoskyns, occupying pages 14 through 27. It immediately follows that by Henry Martin. Hoskyns' "poem" is actually a collection of eight Latin poems of differing approaches to the death of Sidney, under the general title: Ph. Sidnaei Peplus.

The title of the volume (and Hoskyns' poem) refers to the cloak worn by Greek women in ancient days, but the reference is even more explicit to the garment placed on the statue of Athena during the Panathenaea, that celebration and procession immortalized by the frieze of the Parthenon now known as the Elgin Marbles. Its literary allusion is to a poem entitled Peplus, which was falsely attributed to Aristotle. That poem commemorated the fallen warriors at Troy. The volume came out on the anniversary of Sidney's death, and the title indicates an intention to continue a yearly celebration of his death, just as John Donne later intended with his <u>Anniversaries</u> on the death of Elizabeth Drury. Hoskyns takes an additional touch from the title, however, and, by using the figure of the Muse Thalia, he makes the peplus become the mourning garment of this figure of classical mythology. The entire first poem is dedicated to a conversation of the poet with Thalia, the Muse of Comic Poetry. Immediately the wit of the young poet becomes obvious. The irony of using the Muse of comedy rather than tragedy allows Hoskyns not only to identify himself and his reputation, but also to heighten the sense of grief by having Sidney's death affect even the most unlikely of the Muses.

Hoskyns begins by referring to his own "hoarse voice," to which the Muse is "always deaf, but at this time a little deafer to my prayers than she is accustomed to be." The description of the goddess is short but telling, for although she is a goddess of "youthful years," her slow steps reveal neither youth nor divinity. In reply to his questions as to why she did not speak sooner (it has, after all, been a year), for example, whether she now thinks his ability less, she answers,

> Ah, none of these held me back.
> "Sidney, Sidney," and having said this name
> twice
> Grief holds back any more words of speech.

She then explains that she knew what he wanted, and it was grief that made her late. After silencing him from saying more, she goes into some fifty lines of description of the details of Sidney's death, with which Hoskyns was obviously well acquainted. She explains that Sidney, of all the English, was determined in his aid to the Belgians, that after a short trip away from Belgium, he returned and raised up "the almost lifeless hearts of the Belgians with his eloquence." The Spaniards are described as fighting to destroy the "true worship of God" and keeping the Belgians from tilling their fields. "Sidney's virtue cannot bear to see Flanders oppressed," nor can he bear sacrilege.

59

"Filled with God, he puts on arms, and with the
hand that grasped learning, he drags me headlong
into battle." After a description of the details
of the battle events, always comparing them favorably with battles of the ancients, she recounts how
Sidney fell, wounded by a cowardly fellow who shot
him in the leg with a poisoned bullet. It is only
when Sidney tries to dismount that he notices his
injured leg, as it fails to "perform its normal office." He is angered, "not because your foot is
lost, but because the use of the foot is lost."
(For the knowing reader the dramatic irony of life
comes to the fore during this part of the poem because of the reason for Hoskyns' own death fifty
years later.) Thalia goes on to remark that Sidney
would have fought without the use of his body if
one could fight without his body. She then describes the slow spread of the poison through Sidney's body, which medical science could not stop,
and points out the many nights of pain which Sidney spent before his death. Then follows one of
the most effective parts of the poem, when Thalia
compares Sidney's death with Achilles'. Both were
wounded by flying missiles, Achilles in a temple,
Sidney in battle. The reference to Achilles is an
obscure one. In medieval legend, Achilles was just
about to marry Polyxena in a temple when he was
shot by Paris.22 Then the use of poison to send
people to heaven is documented, bringing in examples up through the Renaissance. Thalia puts a
curse upon the Spanish for this death:

> Behold, I prophesy: you will pay penalties,
> Spanish youth.
> And you will be badly covered under your
> leader shield.

The pun is brilliant, as the latin word for shield
is Parma, and the line also reads, "And you will
be badly protected by your Duke of Parma," leader
of the Spanish forces in the lowlands. Less than
a year later the prophecy turned true in the English Channel. Finally, Hoskyns' practice in the
epitaph form pays off, as he has Thalia report the
marble epitaph of the man who has been "carried

60

off above the stars":

> He who lies here, does not lie here, but has
> flown to the stars:
> This part wanted to follow, if it were not lame.
> It is well, Sidney, that you leave a part for
> the fatherland,
> That as you have not completely left, you have
> not completely died.

The second poem is not as effective as the
first. In 148 lines of trochaic tetrameter, Hoskyns bewails not only Sidney's death, but the effect that the death has had on the Muses, hair dis-
hevelled, faces covered with tears. He urges them
to banish their grief: "enough, more than enough,
has been given to the ashes of Philip"; both the
Greek and Latin Muses have been able to sing of no
one but Sidney; Italy, France, England, Germany,
and even Spain, all bewail Sidney in song. Sidney
has now achieved immortality, even divinity, and
further mourning is out of place. Hoskyns ends by
saying that if readers find fault with his "badly
conceived words," they must remember that the Muses
have been lost. The poem follows the traditional
lines of the elegy and is skillfully composed, but
lacks the intensity of some of the other sections
of this work.

The third poem is quite the opposite. An unrhymed sonnet, it in some ways prefigures Donne's
famous sonnet "Death, be not proud." If it lacks
the personal involvement of Donne's poem, it makes
up for that by a show of wit and poetic skill that
is lost in any attempt at translation. The inver-
sions of the lines, especially the repeated first
and last lines, the repetition of key words, antitheses of ideas, all are used to put Death in his
proper place.

> Mors grauis nimis, ah, nimis grauis mors,
> Quae cunctis animam suam Britannis
> Rapis, totque homines necas in vno:
> Quod crudele satis, satisque longum
> Facto supplicium tuo precabor?

An, qua tu reliquis sales nocere
Morte, illam capiti tuo precabor?
Vt fiat tibi poena talionis.
At mors non poterit nocere Morti,
Serpentem citius venena perdent.
Ergo (Dij iubeant valere vota)
Vitam perpetuam tibi precabor.
Vt sis ipsa tuae molesta vitae
Mors grauis nimis, ah, nimis grauis mors.

I have attempted to catch some of this, as well as
most of the five stress line pattern in the following translation, but the lack of success is only
too apparent in comparison with the original,

Death too heavy, ah, too heavy death,
You who ravish life itself from all
The English, and slay so many men in one:
What judgment cruel enough and long enough
Can I invoke against your deed?
Or shall I invoke upon your head that death
By which you're used to hurt those left alive
That punishment deservèd might be yours?
But death will not be able to injure Death;
The Serpent his poisons will sooner kill.
Therefore (may the gods decree that prayers pre-
                               vail)
Perpetual life I will invoke on you,
That you might be a burden to your own life,
Death too heavy, ah, too heavy death.

The fourth poem is reminiscent of some of the
conversations between the gods in the Iliad, and
the classical setting is brought to life with a
keen dramatic sense in the speech of Minerva which
makes up the body of the poem. Speaking to Mars,
she bewails their fate when men shall cease to worship them because they have failed to save the life
of one so dear to both, to learning and to warfare.
Obviously the gods cannot stop the work of the
Fates, "the sisters who do not give just times to
old age but are pleased to cut the immature thread
of green youth." The Fates cut short the life of
all valiant youth, but Death can destroy only Sidney's body; his soul will go to Olympus. Hoskyns

does not allow the goodwill of the goddess to have
the last say, however:

The Goddess spoke, but envious Clotho
took the spindle, and the other sought
the loom; scarcely did Atropos
allow her to draw out the thread,
but she broke the thread
in the spindle.

The reality of death is reasserted in the face of
mythologizing wish fulfillment.

The fifth section starts out in much the usual
way, with the gods looking at the mourning of the
people on earth, especially the princes and students. But the scene changes and narrows on one
woman, whom the reader would initially expect to be
someone like Sidney's sister. This becomes quickly
impossible, however, as the woman is emaciated and
self-destructive, her breasts filled with gall. It
is Envy, who does not lament Sidney's death, but
weeps "because you died so bravely." The picture
drawn and the situation described so well by Hoskyns reminds the reader of nothing so much as Botticelli's famous rendition of Envy. The shock of
surprise and the unexpected twist of the poem makes
a real experience out of what could have been just
another traditional description of one of the more
familiar seven deadly sins. In a volume of often
platitudinous reactions to death, this scene stands
out.

The sixth poem is directed to Philip himself,
showing how his death was greater than those of
many famous classical heroes. It does not particularly move the reader. Number seven returns to the
previous level of interest, however. Hoskyns considers what place Sidney will have in heaven. Does
he strum the strings of Orpheus' lyre? or has Jove
let him take over the role of the Thunderer? Hoskyns then allows some remarkable truth to enter in.
Although Sidney was more skilled than any poet a-
live to perform before Jove, he is not equal to
Orheus, "and the first place at the lyre should not

be given to him." Moreover, his soft hands are not
prepared to injure beloved lands with lightning.
With this admission, blended with praise, Hoskyns
can now return to a more typical approach and suggest,

Give him the sunbearing chariot, and fear not
the fire;
He knows the ways of the earth and heavens.

The final poem is a short piece tying the
first poem together with the others. Hoskyns apo-
logizes for Thalia's failing to sing the good songs
of which she is capable. Under the circumstances
she can sing nothing, and she has, therefore, sung
this nothing. It is a weak ending to some remarkably good Latin verse. From this time forward,
Hoskyns was to be in demand by many people of high
rank, as well as by his many friends, to write
poems and epitaphs on their deceased relatives.

The next call for his ability, at least as far
as we are aware, came about a year later. On 6
June 1588, Anne, Countess of Oxford, daughter of
William Cecil, Lord Burghley, the chief administrative figure in the council of Queen Elizabeth, died
in the palace at Greenwich and was buried in Westminster Abbey. Hoskyns was asked to write a commemorative poem for a collection to be presented to
Lord Burghley. Hoskyns' poem is the first in the
collection, the longest, and by far the best copy.23
The poem's form is a kind of anagram of the summary
of her life which prefaces it. Never has the "argument" of a piece been used more integrally with
its expression:

Anna / Vera / vxor Eduardi Veri Comitis Oxoniae, /
filia Guil. Burghlaei summi Angliae Quaestoris, /
mulier pietate, / prudentia, / patientia, / pu-
dicitia & in Coniugem amore singulari, / prin-
cipi, parentibus, fratribus & vniuersae Aulae
regiae admodum chara. / Abiit in Aula regia
Greenwici. / Tres filias superstites reliquit.

The ten poems are indicated by the divisions I have

64

inserted in the "argument" of the poem. There is
also a concluding eleventh poem.

The wit of the poem is more apparent than its
sincerity, but it more than satisfied those closest
to the late Countess, as it made all of the necessary erudite gestures to the classical world that
one could ask in such short form. Indeed, it is a
complete period piece, even to the shaped verse construction of the next to the last section, in the
form of an altar, which was to be used so extensive-
ly in the years to come by so many writers. The
most famous example was the poem of George Herbert
simply entitled "The Altar." In this poem as well
as in much of his writing (evidenced, as I have indicated, in the sonnet section of the Peplus, the
uneven line length epitaph, and the "horseback poem"
he wrote with Wotton), Hoskyns was a real leader of
poetic movements or fashions rather than a follower.
Here also we find many of the favorite tags of Hoskyns' Latin verse, such as the substitute choices
of metrically identical words or phrases to give
alternate choices of meaning, as in the second line

Dum fugit hostiles per $\begin{Bmatrix} \text{mare} \\ \text{freta} \end{Bmatrix}$ fratis opes:

where either "sea" or "straits" will do, the latter
following the more specific reference to the tale
of Anna, Dido's sister, fleeing to Rome, where she
would become the goddess of the suburbs. There are
the parody lines, as in the loathesome

Semibolosque pedes, semipedesque bolos

which the Cyclops spews forth, a line which is obviously based on Ovid's description of the Minotaur,

Semibovemque virum, semivirumque bovem
(Ars Amatoris, II, 24).

There are the puns of English names changed into
Latin words whose meanings carry the message of the
poem, as in the Latinizing of Anne Vere's last name
to Vera, or Truth, the pun which contains the central meaning of at least half of the poem. And

65

there is the usual excuse for poor writing at the
end, an excuse which in this case spoils the possibility of any really sincere reaction to the poem
as a poem.

But the cleverness and wit are everywhere apparent. The opening statement contains, as I have
said, the shifting subject matter of all but the
end of the poem:

> Anne Vere, wife of Edward, Earl of Oxford,
> daughter of William Burghley, high Treasurer
> of England, a mother pious, prudent, patient,
> and chaste and of singular love to her hus-
> band and completely beloved by prince, parents,
> brothers, and the entire royal Court. She
> died in the royal Palace at Greenwich. She
> left three surviving daughters.

The first section of the poem compares the contemporary Anne with "Anna sister, sister Anna dearest to her Elisa," who gained divinity by leaving
her home and travelling to Rome after Aeneas had
left her sister Dido to die of a lost love at her
own hand. Hoskyns goes into a neat twisting of
past attributes of this one goddess and makes the
names attributed to her into qualities which are
involved in Anne Vere. The neatest twist is to take
the name "Perenna," used in Rome as the second name
of the suburban deity, Anna Perenna, and to point
out that "Undoubtedly Anna is a Goddess, but Anna
is not yet Eternal." Six lines before, Hoskyns
uses the pun on Anne's married name for the most
effective tribute in the entire poem:

> The dreams of a prophetic poet did not give her
>   to me: she is Real Vera :
> (And that which is real is used to be eternal.)

Of course, the poet then states the usual conclusion,
that honorable death did grant eternal life, in this
case just as the Phoenician Anna found true joy
after being exiled from her fatherland.

The section Vera-Vere starts off with the nice
touch

> She was true: that is enough, nor is it right to
>   add anything;

66

Whatever you add to what is true, it will be
false.

The rest of the section, however, is a forced comparison with Penelope which mixes, in rather
strange ways, the experiences of Hercules, Odysseus,
and Hector. It also raises some unnecessary questions about the marital relations of Anne and her
husband which, at best, obscure the issue. The
reasons for Hoskyns' approach would have been clear
to members of the court, however.

Edward Vere, the 17th Earl of Oxford, had been
taken care of by William Cecil when Vere's father
died in 1562; the young Earl went to live in Cecil's
house in the Strand. He married Anne in 1571, but
after a trip to Italy in 1576, he and his wife were
estranged and were never very cordial afterwards.
He was hotheaded and argued with Sidney, who called
him a "puppy." He was a great favorite of Elizabeth because of his charm, but he squandered his
money and managed to get most of his friends in
trouble.

The section on Edward Vere is too forced to
be effective. Hoskyns states that the Earl gave
Anne the name of Athens, but that she added the
Attic strength of intelligence. Athens, the home
of the Academy, obviously stands for the seat of
learning, hence, the University of which Hoskyns
was a part, Oxford. This explains how the Earl of
Oxford gave his wife the name. But the reference
to Athens is, to say the least, far-fetched.

More successful is the tribute to Lord Burghley in the next section. As God has entrusted to
Burghley this land which is the treasure of the
world, so this land has entrusted him with its
treasure. Burghley is urged not to mourn the loss
of this precious gem, his daughter, for what belongs to God was not the Lord Treasurer's alone.

God gave this one and God took it away, and
each has acted fairly,

You because you are grateful [for the gift] ,and
               He because He exercised His right.

The sections on Anne's motherhood are quite ordinary, but that on her dearness to friends, family,
and the court has the somewhat questionable but
bold statement that she willingly and knowingly injured all her friends when "she died surely knowing
and willing it." On her death in Greenwich. he
points out that the place's fame would be established without a name since the Queen was born there
and now Anne has died there. However, since Hoskyns uses the name "Vera" for her, one is forced to
see the possibility of reading the line to mean
that the Queen was born at Greenwich and Truth died
there. The wits of the period would undoubtedly
have seen the double meaning in that. Hoskyns was
already beginning to tread the dangerous knife-edge
that wit provides when the object is a person of
high rank.

In the final section on the three daughters,
their number and their grief are compared to the
three Graces, the daughters of Jove and Eurynomia.
Since Eurynomia is dead, the Graces (which include
Thalia) are sad and provide no charm for song.
Hoskyns then breaks into the coda section of the
epitaph. Calliope, the muse of poetry in general,
is equated with Anne, and this explains why she is
not present in the verses Hoskyns has written. Fur-
ther--and we now enter into the shaped verse of an
altar--Anne is Merope, the invisible member of the
Pleiades and daughter of Atlas, the English Atlas,
who has borne the burden of the realm on his shoulders. The altar which is represented carries aloft
the final prayer of the epitaph. that Jupiter will
grant to the father the days he has denied to the
daughter, so that he can carry the burden of the
realm a longer time. The gesture to Lord Burghley
is a nice one, especially as it refers to the great
crisis of England which occurred between the death
of Anne in June and the date at which Hoskyns finished the poem, probably in the autumn. The death
of Anne is compared to her appearance as a herald
of the fall of Spain, which occurred in July when

the Armada was vanquished by a combination of speedy English ships and an unexpected storm. Had Hoskyns finished on this note, the death of Anne would have been placed in a framework which would have supported both the grief of her death and the glory of England in one. The altar would have been a symbolic or emblematic ending which would have heightened the emotion of the poem. But Hoskyns, perhaps aware that the shaped poem is still not accepted (as it would be in another forty years), ends with apologies for his forcing of line lengths into patterns and bemoans the faults of his verse. It is doubly unfortunate as an ending because it destroys the one section of the poem which has some real artistic merit.

The faults of the poem are many, but its show of wit and obvious praise of Burghley made it successful in the eyes of Hoskyns' contemporaries and added to his reputation and stature as a poet. From this point on, he was to be a friend of many of the members of the court, and he was to be used as an aid in the composition of Latin verse and prose by those who needed such help around Elizabeth. Not until his overt attacks upon King James in 1614 was he to weaken the contacts that helped to pave the way to his own advancement in the legal system of England and provided him with friends to aid his brothers through their school days at Winchester and Oxford.

Another of those brothers was born during these early days at Oxford. Some time before 29 September 1587, just after Hoskyns had written his poem on Sidney, his brother Charles was born.[24] Aubrey described Charles as follows: "Charles Hoskyns was brother to the Serjeant and the Doctor; a very ingeniose man, who would not have been inferior to either but killed himself with hard study." For John Hoskyns at this point, however, Charles was but a younger brother, some twenty-one years younger. Whether such a young child would be an embarrassment to the university student is difficult to know. The sense of humor of the day certainly tended to the bawdy, and remarks on the fer-

tility of his mother may well have come from the
witty associates of his college days. They might
also be mixed with admiration for the fifty-three
year old matron.

Death was more important to John than life in
the events of 1588, however. In March the Earl of
Rutland died, and on the 10th of that month, Hoskyns was named among those being provided black
outfits for the funeral ceremonies. The list of
the "Blacks required for the funeral" included
twelve yards for the young Earl and five yards each
for eleven knights. Then: "Item for Mr. Staunton,
Mr. Fleminge, Mr. Jegon, Mr. Wood, Mr. Bacon and
Mr. Hoskyns each a gown of 5 yards." He is also
in the list of those who will take part in the funeral procession.[25]

The entry is an interesting one for several
reasons. None of the volumes concerned with this
period of history, such as Stow's Annales or Camden's Annals... of... Elizabeth, mention the funeral, although they go into some detail about the
death of the third Earl of Rutland, Edward Manners,
the previous year. The third Earl had been one of
the Queen's wards especially under the charge of
Sir William Cecil. In one of those strange marriage
relationships of considerably older men with women
young enough to be at least their daughters (John
Donne's son-in-law, Edward Alleyn, was several
years older than Donne himself), Cecil was to marry
Rutland's daughter early in 1588, just before his
own daughter, Anne, died. Rutland had been a considerable favorite of Queen Elizabeth and flourished during her reign. He lived at a very high level
and died the same way. For two days before his
death on 14 April 1587 he had been Lord Chancellor,
following the death of Lord Bromley on the 12th.
As he had no son, his brother, John Manners, succeeded him, but lived for less than a year, dying
on 21 February 1588. It was John's son Roger, the
fifth Earl of Rutland, who is referred to in the
funeral accounts as the young Earl. The Mr. Jegon
who accompanied Hoskyns and Bacon in the list was
the tutor of the young Earl at Queens College, Cam-

70

bridge.   Later they were both to move to Corpus
Christi as Jegon began his upward move which even-
tuated in his becoming Bishop of Norwich.

Whether it was Hoskyns' friendship with Burghley or an acquaintance with young Roger Manners
that led to his being included in the funeral party, we do not know. It was probably not any great
closeness to Bacon. It may even have been that he
was asked to write an epitaph for the dead Earl.
Young Rutland was one of the group with which Hoskyns and Donne, as well as Wotton and all of the
rest of the friends we have mentioned were closely
associated. After a trip abroad in 1595 and the
following years, Rutland returned to Gray's Inn in
1598 and soon after accompanied the Earl of Essex
to Ireland. Unfortunately, he also joined Essex in
his unsuccessful plot against the Queen and escaped
death only on the payment of a £30,000 fine. The
set of close relationships we have been noticing
comes full cycle when, in 1599, Rutland married
Elizabeth, the daughter of Sir Philip Sidney. He
died 26 June 1612, but it appears from the poems
and documents in his collection of papers at Bel-
voir Castle that he kept up a close connection with
Hoskyns, Donne, Wotton, and the rest up to the end
of his life.

The reason for the death of John, fourth Earl
of Rutland, not being mentioned in the usual records is obvious. England was preparing for the
attack of the Armada, even while there were final
attempts to bring about a peaceful settlement, although the guile of the Prince of Parma seemed a
bit obvious:

About this time went Dale by the Queenes com-
mandement to the Prince of Parma, and mildly
expostulated with him about a booke lately set
forth by Cardinall Allen and Englishman, wherein he exhorted the Nobility and people of England and Ireland, to ioyne with the Spanish
forces under the leading of the Duke of Parma,
to execute the sentence of Sixtus quintus, Bishop of Rome, published already by Bull against

71

the Queene of England: wherein she was declared
an heretike, illegitimate, cruell against Mary
Queene of Scots, &c. and her subiects commanded
to ayd the Prince of Parma, against her. (And
indeed there was a great number of these Bulls
and Bookes printed at Antwerpe, to bee dis-
persed all over England.) The Duke denied that
ever hee saw any such booke or Bull, neither
would he undertake any thing in the Bishop of
Romes name: how be it he must obey his Prince.
But for the Queene of England, hee did so honour
her for her royall vertues, that next to the
King his master hee observed her most, and desired to doe her service. Thus hee had perswaded the King to condescend to this treaty of
peace, which would bee more commodious for the
English than for the Spaniards. For if the
Spaniards were overcome, they would soone recover their losse; but if you (sayd hee) bee
once vanquished, your kingdome is lost withall.26

No statement could have hurt the pride of the English commissioners more or guaranteed more certainly that a major conflict would occur.

    Meanwhile, all of England prepared and wait-
ed.27 It seems strange that the Universities were
not more disrupted, but apparently few of the students felt compelled to leave Oxford or Cambridge
for the camp at Tisbury or the ships commanded by
the Howards, Seymour, Drake, Hawkins, and Frobisher.
(Eight years later many of those now at University
would join Howard and Essex in the attack on Cadiz.)
Hoskyns was admitted to the degree of B.A. on 6 May
1588 and sometime within the first three months of
1589 went through the determination exercises which
put the conclusive touches to the awarding of the
degree.28 Wood says that a month after Hoskyns got
his degree in 1588, Wotton supplicated for his B.A.,
but Wood could find no record of his being admitted
to the degree.29 The third of the close friends,
John Donne, left Oxford rather than take his degree,
probably in order to avoid taking the religious oath
required of all degree candidates, as we have noted.

The situation of the Catholic student was not
an easy one during these days of high religious
tension, but we have already seen that religion
made no difference in the forming of University
friendships, and it appears that it did not keep
many people from their degrees either, at least for
another few months--until the arrival of a new
Chancellor of the University:

The Chancellor, Robert Dudley Earl of Leicester , in the Year 1584, by a letter sent at the
Queen's instance to the University, commanded
that no Person should be admitted to any Degree,
without performing the statutable Exercise for
the same, upon a Report made to her Majesty,
that Degrees were taken here by the Method of
Dispensations, without any Regard had to Learning or Merit; wherefore he commanded them, both
in his own and the Queen's Name, to see that all
Persons whosoever, did their Exercise for the
same, and that they staid their proper Time,
before they presum'd to take any Batchelor's
Degree in Divinity, Law or Physick, or any other
Faculty whatsoever, or sue for any Doctor's Degree, without reading their Cursory Lectures;
except the Sons of Kings and Noblemen, having
a Voice in the Upper House of Parliament; nor
shou'd any Dispensations be granted for the Doing of Exercise after the taking of such Degree:
which by giving of Bonds, and then forgeiting
the Conditions thereof, have suffer'd such infamous Blockheads to pass their Degrees, as
cou'd never have otherwise been conceiv'd to
have had the least Part of an University Education. Hinc illae lachrymae, etc. ... who Leicester coming to Oxford about the middle of
August, 1588, gave way to Fate soon after at
Cornbury in Oxfordshire, and was succeeded in
the office of Chancellor of this University by
Sir Christopher Hatton, Lord High Chancellor of
England. Yet notwithstanding what has been said
of the Earl's Conduct and Government of this
celebrated Mart or Staple of Learning, it must
be acknowledg'd, that some Dissensions and Im-
moralities were rather owing to the Chancellor's

73

Tyranny and Indiscretion in Point of Government,
than to the License of the Times.
Whatsoever the Earl of Leicester had been defective, about reforming the University, was
this Year in some measure accomplished by his
Successor, who took care, that all Persons to
be admitted to any Degree, should first give an
account of their Faith, which thing had been
hitherto much neglected by his Predecessor and
was complain'd of by the Bishop of Hereford,
finding many Heterodox Divines living in his
Diocess. He not only detected many Romanists
lurking in the neighbourhood of Oxford, and se-
ducing the younger Students to go to foreign
Universities, but also restrain'd the Scholars
Excess in Apparel, chastising all other Vices
in them.30

One has to admit that at least on the face of
it, the students at University in these momentous
days of mid-summer 1588 were more concerned about
their life at the University and at home than they
were with the prophetic battle in the narrow seas
separating England from the continent.

Back at home the Hoskyns family was again ex-
tending its holdings and becoming involved in legal
suits. Now John definitely was involved, which indicates that he was not totally immersed in his
studies at Oxford. On 8 October 1588, John Hoskyns
leased several acres of a section called Broad Meadow from Henry Prittfoote and Henry Hancock for 99
years.31 The Meadow belonged to the great estate
of the Mynde which lay to the northwest of Monkton.
It is impossible to tell whether the Hoskyns involved is the father or son, but it seems likely
that it is the father, who still had twenty active
years ahead of him and whose virility obviously e-
qualled his wife's fertility. Two years later, on
28 October 1590, the father brought two of his sons
with him into legal conflict against one of his in-
laws, Thomas Jones. Jones, a lawyer, had been using
his training to put the Hoskyns family at a disad-
vantage. We may well conjecture that if John had
not yet decided on his future, it was just such a

74

case as this that helped him decide. Certainly his father would see the practical advantage of supporting his son for a still longer period of time in order to have a lawyer in the family.

There is a letter addressed to Sir Richard Shuttleworth, knight, from the Privy Council meeting in the Star Chamber:

Whereas John Hoskins exhibited unto their Lordships in the name of himselfe and of divers others dwelling in the county of Hereford a complaint against one Thomas Joanes, a councellour at law and a practiser in the Court of the Marches, conteyning manie matters fowle and disordred, besides divers particuler vexacions offred to Hoskins and the rest in a matter of suite for tithes for the which he hath sued the complaynauntes in divers Courtes at one time. He is required with such others of the Court of the Marches as he shall call unto him to consider of the complaint and the articles annexed, and to give order by commission for the examining of the misdemeanures, and if due proofe shalbe made of the same, to see the offendours punnished according to the lawes, or to certifie the proofes to their Lordships that they may take such order therein as shall appertein. Injoyning the said Joanes that if he shall proceed in the tryall of his pretended tytle concerning the said tithes that the same be done in some one Court onely.[32]

Mr. Jones seems not to have been any more foul and disordered than Hoskyns, however, as the father and his two sons, who are now identified, made sure that one of the commissioners was a friend. The Privy Council, meeting at Richmond on 15 December, reacted to complaints from Jones and wrote again to Shuttleworth:

Wheras upon complainte heretofore made unto us by John Hoskins th'elder, John Hoskins the younger and Oswald Hoskins conteyninge certeine misdemeanures committed by Thomas Jones, esquire,

councellor at lawe, mencioned unto you in October... that you should joine with you therin
Edmond Walter and Fabian Phillips, two of the
Councell in the Marches of Wales... Forasmuch
as wee are informed that the said Fabian Phillips doth much favor the said petitioners, and
therfore no indifferent proceedinge can on his
parte be expected in the cause, wee have thought
good to exempte him from further dealinge therin... (and get someone else for the hearings
(viva voce)....33

It all seems downhill from there. From the
tone of this and the last letter in the series, it
seems that Jones had made his point somehow. On 13
March 1591, the Privy Council again wrote to Shuttleworth saying that the Hoskyns group had petitioned again, this time for

further examinacion of witnesses in the said
cause, which thoughe of your self we know in
your discretion you would doe, neverthelesse
the suite being so reasonable we have thought
good to requier you to favor the suppliant so
fare forth therein as shalbe agreable to justice and for the better manifestacion of the
truthe.34

We have no record of the final outcome of this
case, but two things seem clear: the Privy Council
of England could be made to act wherever the possibility of uneven justice seemed apparent, and the
Hoskyns family needed good legal advice in their
handling of law suits. It was a world with which
the graduate student at Oxford was to become extremely well acquainted, especially the world of
the Council of the Marches of Wales.

A little over a year remained of school and
university life for Hoskyns. Fourteen years had
been a long time considering the fact that school-
ing had only begun when he was twelve years old.
And there were to be another seven years of law
training ahead in London. But Hoskyns was never to
regret his long education; one of his most telling

76

Comparisons in the Directions is that "Hee that prferrs wealthy Ignorance before chargeable studdy preferrs contempt before honnor, darkenesse before light, Death before life, and earth before heaven".35

During his final days at New College he would be writing at least two more Latin epitaphs, but each has a touch that is far different from the longer poems that had previously made his reputation.

Late in 1590 one of his friends, Peter Woodgate, died and was buried on November 4th in the chapel at New College. Hoskyns wrote an epitaph which still stands on the walls of the cloisters. Aubrey lists it as one of John's best known, and Camden introduces it thus: "In the Cloyster of New Colledge in Oxford, this following is written with a coal, for one Woodgate, who bequeathed 200 pound to one, who would not bestow a Plate for his memorial."

HEVS.PERIPATETICE
CONDE TIBI TVMVLVM.NEC.FIDE HAEREDIS AMORI
EPITAPHIVMQUE.COMPARA
MORTVVS.EST.NEC.EMIT.LIBRIS.HAEC.VERBA.DVCENTIS
WOODGATVS.HIC.SEPVLTVS.EST.36

Camden's note explains what otherwise would be a very obscure in-joke of the friends of Woodgate. It explains why one should build his own tomb without trusting to the love or affection of an heir. The one who is dead did not purchase this epitaph with two hundred pounds, the amount left to his heir. Hoskyns' friendship was all the price that was necessary. The bitterness of the attack is nicely controlled by the precision of the Latin verse, and it becomes a lasting tribute from Woodgate's college friends to their attachment to him, as well as their attack on ungratefulness.

On 20 November 1591 the Chancellor of the University Oxford and Lord Chancellor of England, Sir Christopher Hatton, died. His career was hardly one to endear him to the hearts of many people. He went to Oxford but took no degree, attended the

Inner Temple but was not called to the bar. He
rose quickly in the court as a favorite of the
Queen because of those elements of the courtier
that were most superficial: he was handsome, tall,
a graceful dancer, a good jouster, and he was always willing to do the Queen's will, even in so
shady a business as the final trial of Mary Queen
of Scots (who, incidentally, accused her cousin of
taking Hatton as her paramour). His tendency to
pettiness revealed itself most clearly when he pout-
ed over the rise of Ralegh, but he himself soon returned to favor and on 25 April 1587 became Lord
Chancellor. Camden shows the reaction of members
of the legal profession to the appointment

> Sir Christopher Hatton, a man in great grace
> with the Queene, was made Lord Chancellour from
> out of the Court, which the great Lawyers of
> England tooke very offensively. For they euer
> after the ecclesiasticall men were put from this
> degree, had with singular commendations for equi-
> ty and wisedome, borne this highest place of
> gowned dignity, bestowed in old time for the
> most part upon Churchmen and Noblemen. But Hat-
> ton was aduanced thereunto through the cunning
> Court practises of some, that by his absence
> from Court, and troublesome office of so great a
> magistracy, for which they knew him to be insuf-
> ficient, his fauour with the Queene might be a-
> bated. Yet bare he the place with the greatest
> state of all that euer wee saw, and what was
> lacking in him in knowledge of the law, hee
> laboured to supply by equity.[37]

Camden's judgment is more fair than many of
the time would have been willing to admit, and it
appears from many sources that Hoskyns sided with
the legal community both at that time and later.
Some of the Serjeants even refused to plead cases
before Hatton, and it is interesting that none of
his decrees have been preserved. We have already
seen the lack of enthusiasm with which the students
at Oxford, especially the clever and witty ones,
would have greeted his new reign of hard discipline.

Early in 1592 appeared the usual memorial volume, Oxoniensivm Στεναχμός, Siúe, Carmina ab Oxoniensibus conscripta, etc. This Mourning of Oxford, or Songs composed by Oxford students... on the passing of their Chancellor is a very strange volume. There is only one volume extant, and most of our knowledge of it comes from Falconer Madan's Oxford Books.[38]

It appears never to have circulated publicly. Although there are fifty-six writers involved, none of the group one would expect to find present is there except for Hoskyns, and at this point he apparently did not care what he said. There is plentiful evidence that his wit was leading him into awkward situations and would soon cause his forcible removal from the University. The poem is ambiguous at best, and it seems to include, for all who knew the story, the rumor of the day about the cause of Hatton's death (which apparently was the result of kidney stones). Camden states it clearly:

he dyed... of a Flux of his Vrine, and griefe of minde, for that the Queene had somewhat more bitterly exacted a great summe of money collected of tenths and first fruits, whereof he had had the charge, which he had hoped in regard of the favour he was in with her, she would have forgiven him....[39]

All the double meanings of Hatton's situation are in Hoskyns' poem. The over-favoritism of the Queen is contained in the first two lines, where Hoskyns overtly says that Hatton cannot be just a thin and naked shadow if the Prince's mind, virtue, or gratitude can adorn him; but John tacitly raises the question as to whether Hatton existed as anything but the Queen's creature. The picture of Hatton's death as being caused by his kidneys consumed by a burning or raging stone is a powerful one to say the least, but it seems a bit too strong for a memorial poem. The play of words that follows, putting Hatton to blessed rest under a pile of stone is too nasty after the cause of his death. The conclusion may be considered wit, but I think any

79

young reader of the time would have seen it as sarcastic:

When a stone grows inside the viscera of a man
Who is able not to remember the tomb?

Even the position of the negative in the line raises
some question as to the meaning it is supposed to
carry.

The mention of the tomb raises another issue.
In the Directions Hoskyns mentions to his youthful
reader a speech which he expects that reader to be
acquainted with. It is on "D.H." Every indication
is that the person referred to is Dominus Hatton,
or Lord Hatton, a Latin phrase that would fit the
rank of the late Chancellor, either at Oxford or at
the Court. Hatton died and was buried with a flourish. Stow describes the funeral:

On the sixteenth of December, hee was honourably
buried in Saint Paules Church at London, one
hundred poore people hauing gownes and Cappes
giuen them, going before him, of Gentlemen and
Yeomen in Gownes, Cloakes, and Coates, more then
three hundred, with Lords of the Counsell, and
other, besides fourescore of the guards that
followed, a most Sumptuous Monument is since for
him raysed in Paules Church.[40]

In the Directions, Hoskyns writes:

for example in reprhending the prodigallitie of
monumts in the speech of D.H. I begin wth the
excesse of Alphonsus on his fathers funerall.
thence to Alexanders profusion on his freinds
toombe, then to Vrbinus towards his servaunt
thence to Caesar on his horses buriall. After
that to the Molossians on their Doggs, thence to
the Aegiptians that charge themselues wth the
sumptuous buriall of a Crocodile, so seeming in
some sort to admitt the first but lesse the second, and soe growing weaker and weaker in the
excuse of every one, as I proceed the last will
seeme most ridiculous, yf not odious. (f.14v.)

80

On 26 February 1592, Hoskyns was licensed Master of Arts[41] and was made terrae filius in the Act following the awarding of the degrees. The Terrae Filius was, according to the O.E.D., "An orator privileged to make humorous and satirical strictures in a speech at the public 'act'." In 1669 John Evelyn was to describe the acts of one terrae filius thus:

> ... the terrae filius, the university buffoon, entertained the auditory with a tedious, abusive, sarcastical rhapsody most unbecoming the gravity of the university and that so grossly that unless it be suppressed, it will be of ill consequence, as I afterwards plainly expressed my sense of it both to the Vice-Chancellor and several heads of houses, who were perfectly ashamed of it and resolved to take care of it in the future. The old facetious way of rallying upon the questions was left off, falling wholly upon persons, so that it was rather licentious lying and railing than genuine and noble wit.[42]

It seems that Hoskyns had been one of those who had changed the nature from the rallying on the questions to the attack on persons. Clark, in his notes to Aubrey's Brief Lives, records the official judgment of the University on the event and says Hoskyns was expelled "propter dicteria maledica sub persona Terrae filii."[43] Wood goes into more detail, although he is wrong in saying that Hoskyns did not finish his degree.[44] It is true that he was forced to resign his fellowship for any further study.

> ... he had the Degree of M. of A. conferr'd upon him, and being Terrae filius in the Act following, he was so bitterly satyrical, that he was not only denied the completion of that Degree by being admitted ad regendum, but was expel'd the University.[45]

Apparently there were limits to the humor and satire allowed, and Hoskyns was always one to stretch those limits.

81

I believe we can reconstruct the events from
our knowledge of the circumstances and from Hoskyns' writings. We know certainly that Hatton was
a fit subject for satire and that his appointments
as Lord Chancellor and Chancellor at Oxford met
with a good deal of opposition or criticism. We
know that the circumstances of his death gave vent
to much criticism that might otherwise have remained unsaid. We also know that his expensive funeral
did not help matters. We can guess that news of
his adopted son's plans to erect a huge monument in
St. Paul's was already spreading. What better subject for satire than this for a graduating M.A.
whose flare for wit made him known to the whole
University? It is apparent that Hoskyns had already written a questionable poem for the memorial
volume on Hatton, and he apparently thought that
his office of _Terrae Filius_ would give him leave
to murder a reputation that already was tarnished
among his friends. He misjudged the world and
political pressure. You do not attack the dead so
soon after burial, especially when the dead has
powerful friends. If Hoskyns had planned a University career in classics, he had now effectively
killed those plans, just as in 1614 he was to kill
his political career by an equally untactful speech.
Then he was to face a year in prison; now he was
merely to be rusticated--and no one has been more
effectively rusticated than he, banished to the
plains of Somerset.

Footnotes for Chapter III

1. The exact date on which Hoskyns went to Oxford
   is quite difficult to ascertain. The facts as
   far as they are ascertainable are these: Anthony
   Wood says that Hoskyns was made a Probationary
   Fellow in 1584 and a Verus Socius two years later (Athenae, p. 614). Andrew Clark, who also
   edited the Register of the University of Oxford,
   remarks in a footnote to the life of Hoskyns in
   his edition of Aubrey that Hoskyns "was admitted
   probationer of New College June 22, 1584, and
   Fellow 1586." (p. 424) In Part III of the Register (1888), Clark inserts an explanatory note
   on Hoskyns: "Scholar of New C. in 1584." None
   of these are official entries. Clark's Register
   shows that Hoskyns matriculated from New College
   on 5 March 1585 (Part II, p. 141). The Liber
   Successionis et Dignitatis of Winchester College
   indicates that Hoskyns entered New College on 22
   June 1586, but this is probably the date on
   which he was made a Fellow. It may well be that
   Hoskyns was in Oxford as early as June 1584, but
   the records and the wording of the Statutes of
   Winchester would tend to support the idea that
   he was accepted at Oxford by that June and therefore could stay at Winchester right up to the
   end of his 19th year, when he then moved north
   to University.
2. Registrum Primum, p. 101; Liber prothocollorum...
   Feb. 29. 1596.
3. The dates given here are from the Winchester
   Liber Successionis.
4. p. 450. The volume was edited in 1665 by Milton's
   nephew and pupil, Edward Phillips.
5. See Baird Whitlock, "Donne's University Years,"
   English Studies, XLIII, 1, February 1962.
6. D.N.B.
7. MSS Add. 15,230, f. 27v.
8. The Dr. Farmer Chetham MS (Chetham Society, Vol.
   XC, 1873), ed. Alexander B. Grosart, II, 186.
   Camden, Remains... 1674 (Library of Old Authors,
   1870), p. 418, carries the final line in an enlarged form as an epitaph by W. Lambe for him-

83

self. It is probable that he used Hoskyns as a source.

9. Camden, Remaines... Concerning Britaine (1605), p. 56. Other versions are in Harley 1107, f. 10v; Sloane 1792, f. 113v; Harley 5353, Manningham's Diary, under October 1602, f. 46; MSS Add. 15,227, f. 15; Egerton 923, f. 8v; Farmer Chetham MS, II, 182; MSS Add. 30,982, p. 170; Rawlinson Poetry 172, f. 15v; and Rawlinson D, 1372, f. 9.
10. Remaines (1605), pp. 56ff.; 1870 ed., pp. 429ff.
11. Osborn also includes as an epitaph by Hoskyns in Camden's list a latin one on the actor Tarleton, who died in 1588, but Camden's note "Vpon merry Tarlton I haue heard this" seems to separate it from the others. She also includes three others (pp. 298-99) that either because of their style or the manner in which Camden introduces them do not seem to be by Hoskyns.
12. Chetham, II, 183. Osborn mistakenly locates the poem in Camden. She lists an anonymous version in MS Malone 19, p. 150.
13. Chetham, II, 186.
14. See my "Donne's University Years"(n. 5 above).
15. II, 182. It is likely that Hoskyns' original began "Here lyes..." as that is his usual form and is better metrically.
16. II, 184.
17. II, 185; MS Lansdowne 104, f. 11 and MSS Add. 15,227, f. 11v, both anonymously; Camden (1605), p. 56, also includes a variant of this epitaph among Hoskyns' other poems; Osborn also gives references to MS Ashmole 38, p. 172, and MS Tract Dd. v. 75, f. 15v, in the University Library, Cambridge.
18. II, 185. Although without attribution in the Ms., it is included in the group of poems by Hoskyns and is certainly by him.
19. I, 84. A pasquil or pasquinade was a piece of libel or satire which was originally placed on an antique statue erected in the Piazza Navonna in Rome (O.E.D.). This verb form is not noted in the O.E.D., but it is typical of the kind of word coinage that Donne and other members of this group of wits indulged in, perhaps following Hoskyns' lead. See Reynold's use of the

form in his translation of the Convivium (Chap. 12): to "Ratcliffize."
20. I, 84. Osborn did not attribute the poem to Hoskyns because it was printed in Henry Parrot's Laquei ridiculosi (1613). But its position among the poems definitely written by Hoskyns and attributed to him argues strongly for his composition, as does its appearance in a ms. owned by D.A.S.W. Rosenbach and examined by Osborn, where it is placed next to the epitaph on a Bellows-maker. As we have reason to see later, a great many writers were given credit for Hoskyns' poems and prose through the years.
21. II, 181.
22. Hyginus, Fab. 110. I am indebted to Kenneth Fleissner for this obscure medieval reference.
23. MS Lansdowne 104, ff. 195-198.
24. Registrum Primum, p. 103.
25. Historical Manuscripts Commission, Duke of Rutland, Vol. II (1889), p. 243.
26. Camden, Annals... of... Elizabeth (1635), p. 364.
27. For an example of how the impending attack affected one family, that of John Donne, see Baird Whitlock, "The Family of John Donne, 1588-1591." Notes and Queries, October 1960.
28. Oxford Register, Part III, p. 148.
29. Fasti Oxoniensis, col. 135.
30. John Ayliffe, The Antient and Present State of the University of Oxford, Vol. I (1714), pp. 196-98.
31. NLW, Lease Book of the Mynde, #41.
32. Acts of the Privy Council, N.S. XX, 1590-91 (1900), pp. 60-61.
33. Ibid., pp. 117-18.
34. Ibid., p. 353.
35. MSS Add. 15,230, f. 12.
36. Camden has a copy in his Remains, p. 54.
37. Camden, Annals, p. 357.
38. Vol. II, 1450-1650 (Oxford, 1912), pp. 31-32. The copy of the poem used here is a transcription made from the unique copy of the book in the Lambeth Library by Osborn, p. 188.
39. Camden, Annals, p. 406
40. Stow, Annales, p. 764. It is ironic that Hatton's sumptuous monument was consumed when St.

Paul's burned to the ground in the great fire of London while John Donne's simple statue survived.
41. Oxford Register, Part III, 148.
42. Witherspoon and Warnke, Seventeenth-Century Prose and Poetry (2nd ed., 1963), p. 486.
43. p. 424.
44. Clark includes the notice of his incorporation as M.A. in 1592 in the Oxford Register, p. 148.
45. Athenae Oxoniensis, col. 614.

CHAPTER IV

Inner Barrister of the Middle Temple

Aubrey recounts Hoskyns' fall from grace and subsequent activities:

> When he came to New College, he was Terrae fi-
> lius; but he was so bitterly Satyricall that he
> was expelled and putt to his shifts.
> He went into Somersetshire and taught a Schole
> for about a yeare at Ilchester. He compiled
> there a Greeke Lexicon as far as M, which I have
> seen. He maried (neer there) a rich widowe, by
> whome he had only one sonne and one daughter.[1]

Aubrey's account is interesting for at least two reasons. It indicates where Hoskyns met his future wife, or at least relatives of her husband, and it shows how he occupied himself in what must certainly have seemed a condition of near exile.

Ilchester, some twelve miles south of Glaston-bury in Somerset, was "an auncient Citty that flourished in ye Brittaines Saxons Romans Danes and Normans times,"[2] but by 1592 it was certainly "almost wholly decayed." Even today it is little more than a few houses on the road from Yeovil to Glastonbury. Except for an excellent inn, it does not offer anything to the visitor, in spite of its historic past, when it was an important Roman town. Even all of its town records have been taken away for storage at Taunton. Unfortunately, there is no mention in those records of Hoskyns' presence during his brief stay. There are several Bourne families mentioned, however, and it is almost certain that he met Francis Bourne and his wife at this time at some local or nearby party or celebration. Bourne's home in Writhlington was less than twenty-five miles north along the old Roman Fosse Way running from Ilchester to Radstock and on to Bath. But his father also owned a manor in Long Sutton, less than three miles from Ilchester, and had given the manor of Sutton Saint Cleares to Francis and his wife on their marriage.

87

The question arises, of course, as to why this
brilliant scholar of Winchester and Oxford, tact-
less though he might be, would end up in such an
out-of-the-way place. The answer may well be found
in the history of Ilchester. It had been for centuries, and would continue to be for some time, a
town with a tradition of good education. There was
a Dominican School in Ilchester before 1260. In
the 17th century the Quakers were to found a school
there for about seventy scholars. And in the 18th
century the corporation of the town was to take responsibility for the school, a rather remarkable
event for such a small village at that date. Forced
suddenly to find something to do, Hoskyns apparently accepted a position in a town that had a long
tradition of studies in the classics and in theology. He was certainly not the first person of national reputation to be connected with Ilchester.
Roger Bacon had been born in Ilchester in 1214, and
the birthplace of so reknowned a forerunner of the
new science, a man whose work may well have been a
major influence on Copernicus, would likely have
had some attraction for the Oxford graduate. The
whole tradition of the Grail and the Holy Thorn of
Glastonbury would have added a more romantic flavor
to the area. Furthermore, a short boat ride from
Bristol across the Severn to Chepstow would have
put him on the main road north to Hereford through
the Wye Valley, past the still new ruins of Tintern
Abbey and the estates of his friends in Monmouth,
the Nevilles, whom he would later serve as Steward
and with whom he would share the king's wrath in
1614.

He may also have had family connections of his
own in the area. In 1600 there is a case in Chancery concerning a John Hoskyns and Peter Hoskyns
and some lands in Wincanton, only ten miles east of
Ilchester.[3] Although the man is not our John Hoskyns, the entry does indicate possible family relationships

More important to us is the knowledge that he
continued his work in the classics. The compila-
tion of a Greek lexicon through Mu, put another way,

88

through more than half of the known words in Greek, is no small task. The fact that it was still extant at the end of the century reveals how important it was considered by his family. Unfortunately I have not been able to find the manuscript.

Hoskyns' reputation was kept alive among the wits during this year by the publication of Ulysses Redux, a tragedy written by William Gager especially for performance at Christ Church College, Oxford, on the Ides of February 1592, in other words at the same time that Hoskyns was getting into trouble as Terrae Filius. The play was publicly recited by students of Christ Church and was then published later in the year. Hoskyns wrote commendatory verses for the published volume, and since he left Oxford in a considerable hurry, it is probable that the Latin poem was written soon after he arrived in Somerset.[4]

The ten-line poem is a slight one but a graceful compliment to Gager, who had graduated from Christ Church in 1580 and received his Bachelor of Law degree from the same college in 1589.[5] Hoskyns says that Homer has been saved from the spurning which the modern proud stage would give an "unadorned old man," for Gager has woven a golden tragic boot. There is always the chance that there is some irony in this praise since it implies that Gager has written according to the demands of what is obviously a debased age, an age which would censure Homer as "unadorned." Under the circumstances, however, the compliment seems to be sincere. The second stanza plays on the idea that Socrates went more gladly to death in the knowledge that he would see the Ithacan leader, Ulysses, in the Elysian fields. But now he would wish to be alive and to return from the Elysian fields in order to see the Ithacan leader on the stage. One is tempted to remark that on the evidence that only one small edition of Gager's book went to press, Socrates would have been rather lonely in his desire to see the presentation.

But writing a commendatory verse on an obscure

play and composing a Greek lexicon could not make
up for the loss of the company of John's poetic circle and the life of the court which he had tasted
at Oxford. He found that teaching was not his
forte, and the friends he was making in Somerset
were in training for the law at London. So, in
just a little over a year after his departure from
Oxford, John was back in civilization in London. On
13 March 1593 he was admitted to the Middle Temple,
paying the entrance "fine" of £3 and being bound,
as the custom was, with two members of the Middle
Temple, one his old friend John Davies and the o-
ther James Kirton.[6] Under the regulations of the
Temple, seven years of preparation were required
for admission to the Utter Bar,[7] and Hoskyns served
the full term.

    We have seen that Hoskyns used to say that all
who went to London were either carrion or crows. He
also compared the capitol to a tennis game, "for in
both all the gaines goes to the hazard."[8] At times
he showed a considerable contempt for the intellectual abilities of many of the young men studying
law at the Middle Temple. To a young friend entering the Temple in 1599, he said that he hoped the
young man would "make somewhat more of you then one
of my young M^{rs} of the Temple." At the same time he
pointed out his own reputation among the other students both at the Temple and at the University:

    I value not my paynes in Collecting theise ob-
    servacions, I will forgett y^t I denied the ear-
    nest entreaties of many kind of Gent. that sued
    mee for such helpes I am loth to tell you they
    are notes of whome yor M^{rs} of the Vniversities
    haue thought the Author as great a reader and a
    greater obseruer then themselues

    But that he felt a part of London life is all
too clear. Aubrey, after repeating the error of
the date of John's marriage, says of his life in
London,

    After his mariage he admitted himselfe at the
    Middle Temple, London. He wore good Cloathes,

90

and kept good company. His excellent Witt gave him letters of Commendacion to all ingeniose persons. At his first comeing to London he gott acquainted with the Under-Secretaries at Court, where he was often usefull to them in writing their Latin letters.

Knowing John's relationship with Lord Burghley, we have no reason to question Aubrey's statement. Sections from the Directions indicate his social skill and aptitude. Describing the intelligent speaker, he says, he uses

... a sporting wisedome, and eloquent pratling: but wth Matrons of better respect and lesse Curiositie his Duty their kindnesse, their common acquaintance, the occasion of his Comming, the remembrance of his last Conference, the place, the time, the last news of forraine lands, the Court, the Countrye, the Cittie, fedd his invention, satisfied their eares.

He also knew how to flirt with various kinds of young women:

... he would take any occasion of discourse wth a gentlewoman. first wth younge wittie ladies, from their behavio^r yf she said nothinge, hee would pretily quarrell wth her silence, yf she smiled hee would gather out of it some inter-p^rtacion of her praise and favo^r, and of his owne ioye and good fortune; yf she frowned hee would both moue her to mirth and deny that she would bee angry in earnest, yf she were scornefull hee wald conforme his speech and action in that sobernesse to her humo^r as might beguild her passion by way of false Confederacye; yf she walk't or play'd the secrett praise of her face, her eyes her haire her voice her body, her hands her gate wth the applicacion of other conceipts what ever gaue the ground of them yet wth such dissembled arte as yf forgetfullnesse or loue aluded in them not cunning or want of varietie.

He knew the faults of poor dancing as well: "It is

91

a badd grace in Dauncing either to shrinke much in o^r sinke farr downe that you may rise the higher Caper." But above all he was at home in the satiric humor of the Court and with the sophisticated wits of his acquaintance, where his flare for description would always be appreciated. Of a man who had grown too fat, he said, "hee is growne from a body to a Corporacion." "Againe fo^r a litle man on horsebacke (as the tale is) hee was mistaken fo^r a hatt riding on the pummell of a Sadle." Or of the disputatious person with whom all lawyers come into contact, he was "soe honest a wrangler, that his nose being betwixt was the onely cause that his eyes went not to law."

The descriptions of life at the Middle Temple in the 1590s that have come down to us are a strange mixture of an extremely fine education in the legal system of England, entertainments for the Queen and court, social life of all kinds, and plain tomfoolery. Ben Jonson, in Every Man Out of His Humour, referred to the Inns of Court as "The noblest nurseries of humanity and liberty in the Kingdom." Sir Henry Chauncey, Treasurer of the Middle Temple in 1685, stated quite accurately the place of the Inns in English society: "these societies were excellent Seminaries for the education of youth, some for the Bar, others for the seats of Judicature, others for the government and others for affairs of State."[9]

The Inner Barristers, "which are the youngest men, that for lack of learning and continuance are not able to argue and reason in their motes,"[10] were subject to rules of discipline and fines that were obviously more honored in the breach than the observance. Previous to the 17th century, the term Inner Barrister was synonymous with Student. Actually, there seem to have been fewer students in the Middle Temple than boarders, for the Inns of Court were considered the best place for young courtiers to keep apartments while in London. Some, like Ralegh and Wotton, appear never to have taken any part in the study of law. Others, like John Donne, did study law, but with no purpose of being called to the Bar. William Dugdale said that there were so many non-students in the Middle Temple that "the Students may as quietly study in the open streetes, as in their Studies."[11] As a result, they apparently worked in the Temple Church, which in turn became terribly noisy.

The year was divided into court Terms, during which students were expected to visit Chancery, where civil causes had been heard since the time of Edward I; King's Bench, which handled criminal actions; and Common Pleas, where cases "Civil betwixt part and party" were tried. There were four such Terms: Hilary Term began 22 January and ended the Saturday after Septuagesima Sunday; Easter Term began two days after Quindena Pasche and ended five days after the Ascension; Trinity Term began the Friday after Corpus Christi and lasted nineteen days, usually ending about July 15th; Michaelmas Term began the day after St. Michael's (September 29th) and lasted three weeks.

During two of the vacation periods between Terms there were Readings at the Inns of Court. These were the real learning sessions of the law schools, and only the best Barristers were chosen as Readers for these occasions. Following their appointment as Readers, these men became members of the governing Parliament of the Temple and were first in line for appointment to the offices of Judges and Serjeants-at-Law picked by the King. The Easter Reading began on Monday in "cleane Lent" and continued three weeks and three days. The Autumn Reading began the first Monday after Lammas day and continued for the same period. Fines were particularly heavy for missing the readings, both for Barristers and Students, as part of the responsibility of being a Barrister was to continue the high level of legal training which was a part of the Inns of Court. We shall have reason to examine the readings more closely later on, but it is worth noting briefly what happened during these sessions. A learner pled a doubtful legal matter in homely Law French: then an Utter Barrister "doth argue and reason it in Law-french"; then another Utter Barrister reasons the contrary in Law French; finally the three

93

Benchers "declare their myndes in English."

The term Utter-Barrister derives from these Readings:

> Utter Barristers are such that for their learn-
> ing and continuance are called by the Readers to
> plead and argue in the said house doubtful cases
> and questions, which among them are called Motes,
> at certain times propounded and brought in be-
> fore the said Benchers or Readers, and are call-
> ed Utter-Barristers, for that they, when they
> argue the said Motes, sit uttermost on the form-
> ers, which they call the Barr.[12]

As is apparent from merely looking at the a-
bove school year, there was a good deal of time for
doing many things besides attending court, reading
law books, and attending the Readings. And the students and others living at the Middle Temple took
full advantage of the time. The records of the
Middle Temple and other sources are full of regulations concerning dress and behavior. For example,
the dress rules of the Middle Temple stated that no
great Ruff was to be worn; there was to be no white
color in Doublets or Hose; there was to be no facing of velvet in the Gowns; also, that no gentlemen were to walk in the streets in Cloaks, but in
Gowns; "No Hat or long, curled hayr worn"; and, perhaps the most distasteful to the color-loving Elizabethan youths, "No Gowns but of a sad color."[13] In
term time the student was to wear a round cap in
both the Hall and the Church.[14]

As we have seen, Hoskyns was "bound" with
James Kirton and John Davies when he arrived at the
Middle Temple. There were two categories of entering students at the Temple: the "general" student
paid five marks (a mark was 13s 4d, or two-thirds
of a pound), the "special" student paid five pounds;
that is, unless he had already attended an Inn of
Chancery, which many of them had. If the student
had spent a year at an Inn of Chancery, he would
only pay forty shillings as a "special" student
and twenty shillings as a "general" student. On

his entry, "two others formerly admitted of the House, enter into Bond with him, as his sureties, to observe the Orders, and dischardge the duties of the House." It was something like a big brother system in a fraternity. The difference between the general and special students was that the general student was bound to continue in Commons for two years' vacations or receive a fine of twenty shillings. The special students, in other words those who really were not law students intending to be called to the Bar, were not bound to any attendance.[15]

As we have done for the days at Winchester and Oxford, it would seem helpful to indicate once again the group of friends and associates that were at the Middle Temple at the same time as Hoskyns. Some of the previous group, like John Donne, were at other Inns of Court. Donne, for example, had entered Thavies Inn in 1591 and moved to Lincoln's Inn in May of 1592. There he became a very close friend and roommate of another young poet, Christopher Brooke, who was to be an active member of the Mermaid Tavern group and a fellow MP with Hoskyns in many years of service in Commons. Donne was also making his early contacts with the Egerton family, whom he was later to serve as secretary, and it may be that it was he who brought Hoskyns into that circle as well.

At the Middle Temple there were famous personages of the court whose lives were intertwined with Hoskyns' for one reason or another. Sir Fulke Greville, close associate of Sir Philip Sidney, had entered in 1581; Sir Walter Ralegh had entered in 1574; Donne's intimate friend and weekly correspondent, Henry Goodyer, another of the Mermaid group, had been there since 1589.[16]

Closer to Hoskyns in his days at the Temple were the two who were bound with him upon his entry; James Kirton, who had entered the Temple in 1585, was the second son of Robert Kirton of Wells, Somerset,[17] just over fifteen miles north of Ilchester. Perhaps he was influential in getting Hoskyns to

95

move to London and the study of law; later they were to serve together in Parliament. The second was his friend from as far back as Winchester, John Davies, who had entered in 1588.[18] Also already there was Richard Martin, who had entered from New Inn in November 1587.[19] These latter two were to get into considerable conflict later on.

Both had already been in some difficulty before Hoskyns arrived. Martin had joined with others on Candlemas 1590 and caused a riot, "making outcries, forcibly breaking open chambers in the night and levying money as the Lord of Misrule's rent." He was threatened with expulsion unless he paid a fine of £20. The next year he did it again, and this time with Davies involved as well, and both were expelled, although they were both allowed to return.[20]

Benjamin Rudyard had arrived in April 1590, and his activities may have been slightly curtailed as he was bound with his father. Just previously, Francis Bourne had entered on 23 February 1590. This, of course, was the first husband of Benedicta Moyle, who was to marry Hoskyns almost immediately after Francis died. He was from Writhlington, Somerset, and, like Rudyard, had spent the previous year at New Inn. We have already noted the probable connections of Francis Bourne with Ilchester, and it may have been Rudyard who introduced Hoskyns to young Bourne, as Rudyard and Bourne were not only close friends but shared chambers.

At the end of 1590, on December 1st, Walter Pye of The Mynde, the large estate north of Monkton, entered. It could not by any stretch of the imagination be asserted that he and Hoskyns were friends, but they were associates from Hereford in Parliament, and Hoskyns wrote one of his most popular and sarcastic epitaphs on the man at his death. As Rudyard was one of those bound with Pye, one wonders if it was anything in the interrelationships of this trio which led to the duel between Rudyard and Hoskyns.

Then, in March 1593, two people entered who would share the rest of their legal and parliamentary careers. James Whitelocke, from London, entered on March 2nd, and John Hoskyns, noted here as the second son of John Hoskyns of Monkton, entered on the 13th.[21] Whitelocke was the fourth son of Richard Whitelocke, who lived in the parish of St. Dunstan-in-the-East. He had been educated at the Merchant Taylor's School and then went to St. John's College, Oxford. He was called to the bar in 1600, made Recorder of Woodstock in 1606, created Serjeant-at-Law in 1620 and knighted. He was a member of Parliament from Woodstock in the Addled Parliament of 1614, and it is from his journal, the Liber Famelicus, that we learn much of his friend Hoskyns' tribulations at that time. He was a Judge of the King's Bench under James I and Charles I and remained a close friend of John until his death at Fawley Court in Buckinghamshire in 1632.[22]

Hoskyns was the only one of those we have listed who did not spend the previous year at New Inn. This explains why he paid the "general" fine of £3 rather than the 20s required of the rest. From the date of his entry until he moved to Serjeants' Inn in 1628, we have a long series of records dealing with Hoskyns' life at the Middle Temple, some of them very important, some considerably less so.

For example, we can trace some of his influence and reputation by noticing those new students who were placed in his care, or bound with him at entry. Most of the entries are those that one would expect, young men entering from Herefordshire. But there were others from many different parts of England. To understand this process better, it might be worth noting that whereas the Middle Temple used the term "bound" to show the relationship of the older students with the new ones, Lincoln's Inn used the term "manucaptores," indicating that the new student was taken in hand by the older ones. John Hoskyns was obviously the man both the Middle Temple and parents at home thought proper for their young law students to be taken in hand by. Oddly enough, the first person for whom Hoskyns was bound,

97

along with John Davies, was a Robert Moorton, son
and heir of George Moorton, "late of Esteward, Kent,
esq. dec. [deceased]" on 25 March 1595, New Year's
Day under the old calendar. It would seem that
through his friendship with Francis Bourne and his
Kentish wife, as well as through his friendship
with Henry Wotton, Hoskyns was already known and
respected by families in Kent. On September 24th
of the same year, Gilbert Searle of "North Warn-
borrowgh," Hampshire, was bound with Hoskyns and
Benjamin Rudyard. As Rudyard was from Winchfield,
Hants., we can understand his part in the bond.
Hoskyns was probably playing the part of a friend
to Rudyard, as there are no other records which
link the individuals involved.

During the summer in between these two entries
two events in which Hoskyns would have been interested took place. John Davies was called to the
bar on July 4th, and on 12 August 1595, Henry Wotton was brought into the society on a "special"
basis.[23] Wotton had gone overseas in 1589 on the
first of the journeys that were to make him one of
the most respected travellers in all of English society, one to whom John Milton would later go for
advice before his visit to the continent. Wotton
returned just before the end of 1594 and went almost immediately into the service of the Earl of
Essex. The Middle Temple, with its many courtiers
in residence and with close friends like Hoskyns
and Martin in training, was the most obvious place
for Wotton to seek lodgings for attendance upon Essex while in London. It was in 1599 at the Middle
Temple that John remarked that he had seen the Sidney translation of Aristotle "in the hands of the
noble studious Henry Wotton lately."[24] The old
clique from Winchester and Oxford were now all together again except for John Gifford, who was still
working on his medical degree at the University.

Almost a year went past before Hoskyns and
Rudyard were once again bound together, on 12 August 1596, with a young man named Thomas Wayte,
from London, whose father had died. There may have
been some connection between Wayte and Hoskyns'

98

brother Oswald. At any rate, young Thomas was obviously of special interest to Hoskyns, and John kept watch over his lodgings, roommates, etc., for several years. Still another year passed, and then Hoskyns became quite busy looking after new students. On 4 November 1597 he and Walter Pye were bound with a Mr. Henry Kyrle, who was entering from Much Marcle, Herefordshire, a small town some six miles northeast of Ross and just about ten miles away from both the city of Hereford and the village of Llanwarne. Twelve days later, on the 16th, Hoskyns and a man named James Walwyn were bound with William Vaughan, who was coming up from Winforton, Herefordshire, fifteen miles west of Hereford, not far from John's uncle's lands in Shobden or from the manor of Titley, which John was soon to lease from Winchester College. A week after that, on the 23rd, he joined Rudyard once again in being bound with David Urrey of the Isle of Wight.[25] The joint entries with Rudyard make it all the more difficult to figure out the exact date of the duel between these two friends. When all of the dates of their friendship are put together, one is forced to admit that whenever the unpleasantness occurred, neither one held it against the other for too long a period. Since Rudyard both called for the duel and was the one who was wounded, reconciliation was made easier.

Such was not the case with two of their friends. At some time between June 1594, when it was presented to the Stationers' Register, and 1596, the date of the earliest extant edition, John Davies published his long poem Orchestra, with a dedicatory epistle to Richard Martin. Hoskyns gives as a prime example of the rhetorical device of Division, Davies' poem: "This only tricke made vpp J: Ds. poeme of Dauncing. All Daunceth. the heavens, the elemts. mens minds common wealths. and soe by parts all daunceth."[26] We have seen that Davies and Martin were involved together in the illegal games connected with the yearly celebration of the Lord of Misrule. Rumor has it that Martin had, perhaps untactfully, said some unkind things both about Orchestra and even more about Davies' Gulling Sonnets, a group of poems that Donne also took to task for their abominable overuse of legal metaphors in

99

love poems. Whatever the reason, Davies felt himself insulted by Martin and reacted violently. The Middle Temple Records for 9 February 1598 read:

> While the Masters of the Bench and other fellows were quietly dining publicly in the Hall, John Davyes, one of the Masters of the Bar, in cap and gown, and girt with a dagger, his servant and another with him being armed with swords, came into the Hall. The servant and the other person stayed at the bottom of the Hall, while he walked up to the fireplace and then to the lower part of the second table for Masters of the Bar, where Richard Martyn was quietly dining. Taking from under his gown a stick, which is commonly called "a Bastianado," he stuck Martyn on the head with it till it broke, and then running to the bottom of the Hall he took his servant's sword out of his hand, shook it over his own head (super caput suum proprium quatiebat) and ran down to the water steps and jumped into a boat. He is expelled, never to return.[27]

Actually, he was allowed back in October 1601, after he submitted to the Masters of the Temple and received Martin's pardon.

As we might expect, this incident also appeared in Hoskyns' Directions, two years before Davies' readmission, but while it was being considered:

> Shall a Souldier, for a blow wth his hand given in war to a Captaine bee disgraced, and shall a a Lawyer for the bastinado given in an hall of Court to his companion bee advanced. Shall wee that professe lawes maintaine outrage, and shall they that breake all lawes yet in this obserue civilitie.[28]

Hoskyns obviously sided with Martin on this event; indeed, it would be hard to do otherwise.

Just before this outburst, on 15 January 1598, James Walwyn and Hoskyns once again joined together in a bond, this time for John Vaughan of Clerewood,

Herefordshire.[29] Although I have not been able to
establish the location of the manor of Clerewood,
it is possible that Vaughan was related to Rowland
Vaughan, another acquaintance of Hoskyns, and came
from the region around the Golden Valley, where
Hoskyns made his final residence and died. At any
rate, Hoskyns and Vaughan soon joined in bond together for the admission of a real Welshman, Richard Phillips of Rushmore, Carmarthenshire, on 10
May 1598. Earlier, on 16 March 1598, Hoskyns joined with John Chapman, another of his Kentish
friends, who had entered the Temple in 1592, to act
as bond for John Manningham, of Fenne Drayton, Cam-
bridgeshire. It was from the diary of Manningham
that much of our knowledge of this period of English history, especially of some of the royal entertainments, was to come.

From this time on, most of the students from
Hereford would be bound with Walter Pye. There are
two more of these entries involving Hoskyns before
he was called to the bar, however, both on the same
day, 24 October 1599. One was Christopher Jones,
from Wraxall, Somerset, just to the west of Bristol,
and the other was Robert Harley, "son and heir-apparent of Thomas Harley of Brampton Castell, Herefordshire." The latter is the best claimant for
the young man to whom Hoskyns addressed his <u>Direc-
tions of Speeche</u> & <u>Stile</u>, to which we will return
at length in the following chapter.

The infrequent times in the future in which he
was to act as bond all seem to have some sentiment-
al or close ties for Hoskyns. On 26 March 1604 he
was bond for Marmaduke Lloyd of St. David's, Pembrokeshire, who was to give us a personal and on-
the-spot description of Hoskyns' final sickness.
On 16 June 1613, Hoskyns acted as bond for his own
stepson, John Bourne, and on 11 June 1619 he took
in hand Thomas Cockes, of Castleditch, Herefordshire.

There are a great many other entries in the
Middle Temple records that help us know the kind of
life and daily activities that Hoskyns was involved

101

in. Like all other segments of life in London in
this period, the students at the Temple constantly
had their lives broken into by the plague. There
was, for example, no reading at the Middle Temple
during the first summer of Hoskyns' life there because of the plague. As a matter of fact, there
were no commons kept at the Temple from 7 July 1593
until 19 January 1594.[30] Many young students stayed
in their lodgings and made arrangements for meals
elsewhere, others simply went home, and others seem
to have visited their wealthy friends on their
large estates.

During the summer of 1593 the plague reached
its full height. On July 19th, the Court of Assizes was held in Saint Georges Field. "This assise was ended the same day, which was thought
would haue beene three dayes worke, for the Justices (all duties being paid) made hast away, for
feare of being infected with the pestilence." There
was reason to be afraid:

The whole number deceasing this yeere in the
City, and suburbs adioyning, from the nine &
twentieth of December, in the yeere 1592. vntill
the 20. of December, 1593. was within the walles
of all diseases 8598. whereof the plague, was
5390. without the walles, and in the liberties,
9295. of the plague 5385. so that within the
Citie, and liberties of all diseases died, 17893.
whereof the plague was 10675.[31]

Even St. Bartholomew's Fair was cancelled.

If Hoskyns did stay in the city, he was not
the only one of his group that did. John Donne,
whose brother was in prison for sheltering a semi-
nary priest, was there for financial reasons, his
inheritance just then coming due. He wrote to one
of his friends, Everard Guilpin, who was up the
hill in Highgate,

Even as lame things thirst their perfection, so
The slimy rimes bred in our vale below,
Bearing with them much of my love and hart,

102

Fly unto that Parnassus, where thou art.
There thou oreseest London: Here I have been,
By staying in London, too much overseene.
Now pleasures dearth our City doth posses,
Our Theaters are fill'd with emptines;
As lancke and thin is every street and way
As a woman deliver'd yesterday.
Nothing whereat to laugh my spleen espyes
But bearbaitings or Law exercise.
Therefore I'le leave it, and in the Country strive
Pleasure, now fled from London, to retrive.
Do thou so too....^{32}

Donne's family lived in London, and that may
have been the reason he felt "too much overseene."
Hoskyns, on the other hand, may well have wanted to
stay with his older brother Oswald in London. Certainly he was on affectionate terms with the London
branch of the family and spent the last years of
his life worrying about their welfare.

In 1594 activities at the Temple were back to
normal, and John returned to his regular schedule
of court sessions and Readings. At Christmas he
probably went home for the usual three week vacation break. Christmas day at the Middle Temple was
not kept solemnly according to an order on 22 November 1594. Some of the Templars did stay around,
however, as "A cartload of coals and 40s. for the
minstrels shall be allowed to those who remain."[33]

In this age of religious controversy, there
was the usual need to restate the religious rules
of the Middle Temple: on 7 February 1594 "The orders for conformity in religion, requiring attendance at communion shall be put in execution." And
the clothing regulations needed constant reinforce-
ment: "Gentlemen coming into the Hall or buttery to
breakfast, dinner or supper in boots or cloaks
shall ipso facto be out of commons until they pay
the Treasurer 10s...."(21 November 1595)

Not only the clothing regulations were being
violated in the fall of 1595, however. The reader
for the Autumn vacation was fined £10 for not fi-

103

nishing his reading, for calling unfit people to
the bar, and for excesses in diet during the reading. Attendance at the readings was also dropping
off. On 6 February 1595 it was ordered that "every
Utter Barrister who has not served all his vacations,
shall be in commons five weeks every Lent and four
weeks every Summer till he has served six vacations
after being called to the Bar... on pain of a fine
of 20s." In 1609 the fines were raised markedly: to
40s the first time and £3 thereafter. The reason
was clear to everyone: "The smallness of the fine...
has made them careless, so that the Reader is dis-
couraged for want of company." If the record of
Hoskyns and most of his friends is any indication,
a great many of the barristers found it more fruit-
ful to pay the fine than to stay around. The period of the Readings was the same as many of the local sessions in cities around the country, where
the young lawyers made much of their income. It
paid John to miss a reading if he could handle at
least two cases back in Hereford.

And the Records are filled with the problems
of room accommodations. There was an incredible
amount of moving around, as older members of the
Society looked for better living quarters. By following some of these changes, we can discover the
rooms of John Hoskyns for a major part of his stay
at the Temple. In February 1596 Francis Bourne and
Benjamin Rudyard moved into a chamber on the west
side of the two lower chambers in Mr. Sandis building in le Vine Court and paid a fine of £13 6s 8d;
the amount indicates that it was a very fine lodging. This move also gives some indication of the
wealth of Francis Bourne, which his wife was to inherit before her marriage to Hoskyns. In March
1599 Bourne moved in with Francis Ashley, replacing
Walter Moyle, of Boughton Allow, Kent, who was his
wife's cousin.

Bourne's move was not a great one; the Ashley-
Moyle chamber was "the upper chamber with the gar-
ret on the north side of the second floor of Sandes
new building." John Tynte was to replace him in
Ashley's chambers on 21 February 1601, just three

days before Bourne died in Bristol. In May 1596
Tynte's brother Edward, who had been admitted from
Wraxall, Somerset (only a few miles from Bourne's
home),in 1594, moved to a chamber with William Burdett, "the lower chamber on the south side of Sandis' new buildings in the Garden." On January 27,
1598, Thomas Wayte, Hoskyns' young friend, replaced
William Burdett in this pleasantly located set of
rooms. Just over two months later, on April 4th,
Hoskyns moved into the chambers, displacing Wayte
and paying a fine of 20s. On 30 October 1598 Hoskyns' friend John Chapman replaced Tynte, and this
stopped the game of musical chairs for a while.

It was not until a year after his call to the
Bar that Hoskyns was to change chambers again, and
then he made what is a very difficult move to explain. On 5 February 1601 he moved in with William
Copley, who had entered the Temple in 1595, from
Bredon, Worcestershire. When Copley had entered
the chamber of John Wilson, "late Steward" of the
Society, to join William Mackreth, he had paid a
fine of only 10s "because the chamber is ruinous."
It was still apparently ruinous when Hoskyns replaced Mackreth, for he also paid only a 10s fine.
This move allowed Thomas Wayte to return to his
former chamber, now with Chapman as a roommate. One
is forced to speculate that Hoskyns' financial re-
sources were sorely strained in the year following
his call to the Bar. Yet ten years later Hoskyns
will comment to his wife that he still owes £10 for
his part of this chamber transaction. That remark,
while it makes more cloudy the condition of the
chamber itself, certainly supports speculation on
Hoskyns' financial condition. One is also forced
to face the possibility that this was one reason
that he married the newly-widowed Benedicta Bourne,
whose husband died in this same month of February
1601. Perhaps it was this sequence of events that
led Aubrey and Wood to equate John's marriage to a
wealthy woman with his entry into the Middle Temple.

But life at the Temple was not made up of re-
formulation of rules or constantly changing chambers. Nor were Martin and Davies the only rule-

breakers. Other young and not-so-young Inner Barristers continued their practical jokes and general
hell-raising. On 30 June 1598 it was orderd that
as

> Divers grievances are daily committed by reason
> of water, chamberpots, and other annoyances cast
> out of gentlemen's chambers to the great offence
> of gentlemen of good worth passing by, as well
> as of the House and others; in future the owner
> of a chamber where such an offense is committed,
> shall be fined 40s.

As late as 1610, the Parliament of the Middle Temple was forced to change the casements of the over-
hanging windows because a John Dashfield and his
wife had suffered injuries by chamberpots, etc.,
being tossed out the windows. Two members of the
estimable Lewknor family were the ones involved in
that affair. Hoskyns, of course, in his lower
chamber, was not one of those in trouble in any of
these events. His sense of humor was largely literary, and a good deal more dangerous.

He was still writing humorous epitaphs, and he
was still skirting the edge of disaster with them.
In 1596 Bishop Fletcher, father of the playwright
John Fletcher and uncle of the two poets Giles and
Phineas Fletcher, died. Hoskyns soon wrote his
epitaph, which was popular enough to show up in several manuscript collections, meaning that it circulated widely. The Bishop had married the widow
of the uncle of one of the group of friends at Oxford, Sir Richard Baker, and it is this marriage
that Hoskyns plays with in his epitaph:

> Of the B. of London.
> I was the first that made Christendome see
> a Bishop to marry a Ladie, Lady;
> the cause of my death is secrat and hid
> I cryed out I dyed, and soe I did.[34]

Stow merely chronicles the Bishop's death with no
remarks of any rumors: "In this meane space, to wit,
on the 15. of June **Rich. Fletcher**, Bishop of Lon-

106

don deceased at his palace in Paules Church-yard, and was buried in his Cathedrall Church."[35] But William Camden was ready to give the more complete story: "Richard Fletcher Bishop of London, a Courtly Prelate: who while by immoderate taking of Tobacco, he smothered the cares he tooke by means of his unlucky marriage, and by the Queene misliked, (who did not so well like of married Bishops,) breathed out his life."[36]

If Hoskyns wrote the poem immediately upon the death of Fletcher, several of his friends, like Donne and Wotton, would have had to wait a while to see it, for they and most of the youth of England-- at least that is sometimes the way it seems--were off with Essex, Ralegh, and Howard to attack Cadiz and raise the national temper and Elizabeth's treasury by the act. It is in some ways strange that Hoskyns who, in almost every way, reflected the entire range of activities of his age apparently had no desire to leave England, either to take part in any of the battles in which the nation was engaged or simply to travel on the continent. Of course, he was a good deal older than many of his associates, and he must have felt the pressure of time. He was thirty and still getting his education. Even without an interruption of the sort that was leading Donne this year and the following into events which provided him with imagery that was to give far greater power to his poetic expression, Hoskyns still had four years before he could be called to the Bar. Still, it would have been interesting to see what kind of epitaphs he would have written had he seen the naval battle at Cadiz.

It seems likely that about this time, while he was associated so closely with people about the court, he wrote the charming

Vppon on of the Mayds of Honor to
Queen Elizabeth

Here lies, the Lord haue mercy upon her,
One of her Majesties maids of Honour:
She was both young, slender and pretty,
She died a maid, the more the pity.[37]

107

It would be ridiculous to try to work out which specific lady it might be.

Probably also by Hoskyns is another epitaph found in Camden and in Egerton 2421 on the same folio (2v) with other poems by Hoskyns:

> A zealous Lock-Smith dy'd of late,
> And did arrive at heaven gate,
> He stood without and would not knock,
> Because he meant to pick the lock.[38]

Two other poems attributed to Hoskyns in the Chetham MS cause some real problems, but if they do nothing else, they show the similarity of poetic efforts among the group of friends we have been tracing. The Chetham MS copyist clearly identifies the author of the first as "Mr Hoskynes: medij Templi.":

> An Epitaphe on Mr Sandes.
>
> Who wo'ld live in other's breath
> fame deceaves the deade man's trust:
> When o^r names are lost by death:
> Sandes I was and nowe am dust.[39]

Camden included this epitaph in all his editions, but like the one on Woodgate it appears earlier in his collection than the group specifically described as by Hoskyns.[40] It also appears in three other manuscript collections in close proximity to other poems by Hoskyns, although it is not specifically assigned to him.[41]

The Chetham MS also specifically attributes the following verse to Hoskyns:

> Of a Cosener
>
> And was not death a lusty strugler
> in overth cominge James the Jugler;
> his lyfe so little truth did vse
> that here he lies: it is noe newes.[42]

Besides the attribution to Hoskyns, its position in

108

the middle of the group of poems that are definitely by John argues strongly for his authorship.

Yet in 1598 Thomas Bastard published a book of poems entitled Chrestoleros, all of which he claimed to have written. Epigram #29 of Book 6 of that volume is a couplet:

And was not death a sturdy strugler,
In ouerthrowing Iames the iugler?[43]

Later in the book there is a version of the quatrain on Sands with the title "On Johannis Sande."[44] Ordinarily such an inclusion in a printed work would be sufficient evidence to credit Bastard with the poems, but in this case the evidence for Hoskyns' authorship is so strong, the fact that the "James the Jugler" verse is found only in couplet form in Chrestoleros is so strange, and the reputation of Bastard even among his friends for poetic thievery was so widespread that I think we can claim the poems for Hoskyns.

Another epitaph certainly by Hoskyns would seem to date from John's Inner-Barrister days. Henry Herbert, the second Earl of Pembroke, instituted the Salisbury races and gave the money for the gold bell prize. In 1600 he won the bell at his own races. It is probable that Hoskyns addressed the following humorous epitaph to him:

Of one y^t kepte runinge Horses.

Here lyes that man whose horse did gayne
the bell, in race one Salisburye plyane;
Reader, I knowe not whether nedes it,
you or the horse rather to reade it.[45]

As might be expected, John also wrote satiric verses about other lawyers. The only surprising thing is the small number of such poems that have survived, as the composition of this genre was one of the favorite indoor sports of Inner Barristers with any talent. Two of Hoskyns' quatrains and a couplet, certainly written at an early date, appear in Malone 19,[46] but their sophomoric quality ex-

109

plains why they are found only in one manuscript.

Also probably from this period comes a short verbal duel of versifying that gives us some idea of the openness in conversation between the sexes during the Elizabethan period. Once again, the poem is a weak one, characterized by nonsense elements. One can imagine a dinner conversation at which one of the ladies present asked for a poem in a jesting way. Hoskyns would have tossed one off that night or the following morning and sent it by a messenger to the lady, and within a day or two she would have sent her reply. If Hoskyns seems rather bawdy under the circumstances, it is clear from her reply that she not only was not offended but could pay him back in kind.

John Hoskins to the Lady Jacob

Oh loue whose powre & might non euer yet wthstood
thou teachest me to wright, come turne about Ro-
in Hood.
Sole Mistresse of my rest, lett mee thus farre
presume
to make this bolde request, a black patch for ye
Rume.
yor tresses finely wrought like to a golden snare
my louinge harte has caught, as Moss did catch
his Mare:
yor eyes like starrs diuine make me renew this
arrant
in my most silent speech a Buttock or a Warrant.
o women will you nere beleiue but I doe flatter?
I vowe I lou'de yow euer but yet tis no great
matter.
what is it I shoulde doe to purchase yor good
smile?
bid me to Chyna goe & i'le stand still the while
I know that I shall dye loue so my harte be-
witches
it makes mee howle and crye oh how my elbow
itches.
teares over flow mine eyes wth floods of daily
weepinge
that in the carefull night I take no rest for
sleepinge.

110

Cupid is blinde men say & yet mee thinks he seeth
hee hitt my harte today a T̲_̲_̲_̲ in Cupids teeth.
my M^{rs} shee is fayre & yet h̲e̲r̲ ̲l̲a̲t̲e̲ disgraces
haue made mee to despayre a pox of all good faces
but since my simple meritts her louinge lookes
                                        must lack
Ile stopp my vitall spiritts wth Claret & wth
                                        Sack.
regarde my strange mishaps Joue father of y^e
                                        Thunder
send downe thy mighty clapps & rend her smock in
                                        sunder
but since that all releif & comforte doe forsake
                                        mee
Ile hange my selfe for greif, nay then ye Diuell
                                        take me.^{47}

Why either Hoskyns or the copyist should be afraid
to write out the word "Turde" when the pun on gon-
orrhoea is so blatant at the end of the poem is not
clear. The Lady Jacob, after a nice reference to
the Imp carved into the triforium of the Angel
Choir of Lincoln Cathedral, returns the heavenly
fire in full measure.

              The Lady Jacobs Answer
Yo^r letter I receiu'd bedeckt wth florishinge
                                        quarters
yor meaning I conceiue, go hange yo^w in yor
                                        garters
I cannot chose but pitty yor restlesse mourninge
                                        tears
because yor plaintes are witty yo^w may goe shake
                                        yor eares.
to purchase yor delight no labour yo^w shall leese
yor paines I will requite wth a peece of Tosted
                                        cheese.
tis yo^w I faine woulde see, tis yo^w I onely
                                        thinke on
my lookes as kinde shalbee as ye Diuells ouer
                                        Lyncoln
if euer I returne great Queen of Lightninge
                                        flashes
send downe thy fyre & burne his Cods peece into
                                        ashes.

111

There is only one extant poem in Latin which might conceivably date from his Inner Barrister days, and even that may well come from later years, when he returned to Latin composition. On 24 April 1597 Aegremont Thynne entered the Middle Temple and was called to the Bar the usual seven years later in 1604.[48] In 1623 he would be one of those who, along with Hoskyns, were made Serjeant-at-Law. At some time during that acquaintanceship, Hoskyns wrote a mock epitaph[49] on him, much in the same spirit as the one to the Earl of Pembroke. Aubrey notes that the subject was one of Hoskyns' close friends. Unlike many of his longer Latin poems, his short ones, such as this, often come across just as directly and effectively in English translation:

> Here lies Egremundus Thynne
> Brilliant at defending paradoxes.
> He is dead, as it appears,
> But if he could speak, he'd deny it.

It is worth pausing for a moment to consider why the change from Latin to English verse took place on Hoskyns' part. At the University his reputation was gained largely as a classical scholar, and the occasions called for his exercise of this ability. In London, although all of his old friends were around, the setting was considerably different. At Oxford everyone could be expected to understand Latin; at court, no. Of course, Elizabeth could and did. As a matter of fact, in the summer of 1596, she berated the Polish Ambassador for three quarters of an hour in extempore Latin.

Besides, all of his friends were changing to writing their poetry in English. Donne was making his great splash as a writer of "strong lines" in the years following 1595 with his satires and elegies as well as the early songs and sonnets. Bastard and Davies were publishing their poems. Everyone was getting into the act, and the act was in English. Hoskyns had little choice but to switch rather than fight the trend.

112

And he began to write a different kind of poem
as well. Like his contemporaries, he moved to the
longer lyric and to the love poem. We have four
that seem to come from the late 1590's. The first,
"on Dreames", is reminiscent of Donne's poem on the
same subject; indeed, as in so many cases at this
time, there may have been a small contest as to who
could write the better poem on a given subject, as
in the famous debate over the relative merits of
the city and country. We would, of course, have to
admit that Donne is more successful. He addresses
the girl directly, whereas Hoskyns addresses the
personified Dreams. The verbal twists and turns of
Donne's poem lead to an obscurity which draws the
reader into the personal drama of a relationship
which is never really clarified, but which ends with
a kind of sadness and pathos that belies the sexual
play of the poem. Hoskyns is all clarity; he is
also more direct in his sexual intentions. He wants
to act out his mistress' dream "iust in the place
where I would bee." He is witty, but not dramatic.

On Dreames

You nimble Dreames wth cobwebb winges
that flie by night from braine to braine
and rep^{r}sent a world of thinges
wth much a doe and little paine

Yow that finde out the easiest wayes
through eury strongest gate and wall
that none yor passage spies or stayes
not Jealousy that watcheth all.

You visitt Ladies in their bedds
and are most busie in their ease
You putt such fancies in their heads
that make them thinck on what you please.

Howe highelie am I bounde to you
(Safe Messengers of secresie)
that made my M^{r}s thinke on mee
iust in the place where I would bee.

O that you would mee once preferr
to bee in place of one of you,

that I might goe to visitt her
and shee might sweare here Dreame was true.^{50}

The next poem is entitled in the <u>Chetham</u> <u>MS</u>.
"His Melancholy."

Loue is a foolish melancholie
    Leading mens Minds w^t false persuasion
Else why should I not see my folye
    That loose whole times to gain occasion

Cupid is stronge forsooth they say,
    his strength is but imagination.
y^t doth mistake for reason's sway
    the rash commande of idly passion.

My loue is almost Lunacy
    Mee thinkes my hart is so on fire
That though my mistrisse sent for mee
    I dare not for my life com nye her.

Mee thinkes loues sparkles so would starte
    And at her sight giue forth such flame
That standers by would see my hart
    And by the light cleare read my name.

Then best to single her alone
    Though to encounter shee be loth
The match is equall one to one
    And solitud will right us both

But having her alone I finde
    some greater thing then speach to doe
though y^t perhaps would ease my minde
    were it not losse of time to wooe.

Alone or elsewhere all's in vaine
    For evrye time that yet wee met
Was but a cause to meet againe
    for some what that I did forget.

I will not loue and yet I will
    for feare lest I leaue off a looser
I will not let my sute lye still
    lest man speed besyde that wooes her.

114

Let loue the God or Loue the Boy
Make her to loue me if he can
Let God or Boy teach her that Toy
Ile say at least he is a Man.[51]

Again Hoskyns loses the dramatic impact of Donne's
poetry by failing to put his own into the form of
direct address. At the same time, however, he nicely catches the indecision of the lover who knows
what he wants and yet is put off by the beauty of
the girl, fear of social comment, and inability to
put the question. He is, in a real sense, a sensu-
al J. Alfred Prufrock. Perhaps the greatest poetic
fault of the piece is its lack of metaphor. Only
in stanza five does John work with the image of single combat, using the technical language of the duel
to make his point. Instead of metaphor he once a-
gain retreats to the wit of the final stanza, the
play or contrast of God, Boy, and Man. One could
strain to call it something like a Renaissance
statement, and certainly he plays with the two icon-
ographical portrayals of Love which the sixteenth
century constantly used,[52] but it would be straining.

    The third poem of the group is "The Dying Lou-
er," found only in one manuscript in the British
Museum, Harley 3991, ff. 120v-121v, with "J. H." at
the end. It follows a group of poems by Beaumont
and Donne:

                    The Dying Louer

Some powers Regard me or my hart will burne
Till it conuert my bosome to an vrne.
I call for no physitians; how you Spread
You fatall Carryons of a Sick mans bed--
Stand from mee; hearbs nor mineralls Can
Cure ye Consumption of a loue-sick man.
You Climbing waues if happly at this hower
you haue Some New Leander in y^r power,
Oh let his Voyage Calmer fortunes try;
T'is pitty ye belou'd againe should die.
But well you may my Scorn'd breast ouerflow,
yet would my heart make yor Cold billowes glow;
you Rude winds, troublers both of Seas & Skies,
before whose wrath ye white wing'd Vessell flye's,

115

leaue persecuting wretches on ye maine
and Coole mee wth a Storme--but t'were in Vaine:
I Sprinkle Teares & wth full Sayles I breath,
Doe fanne flames only to bee quench'd by death.
And See hee Comés how pale?   how far vnlike
to her y^t sent him to mee?   wouldst thou strike?
T'is done allreadie: Look upon my hart.
Alas!   Thou knewst not when Shee threw y^t Dart.
Shee makés both Loue & you not as you will
but as Shee guides y^r hands to saue or kill;
perhaps you raign'd in times past but in mine
her Smilés were Loue's darts & her frowns were
                                        thine:
I'ue Seen her mix a Sad look wth a Sweete,
Then Life & death All Ioyes All torments meete
like twilight, as her Louer Could not Say
whether his feares brought night or hopes brought
                                        day.
Which I must see no more--tis her decree
That add's one Sister to y^e fatall three,
Another to y^e Muses: if Th'enquire
What wonder this may be, please yor desire:
It is a beauty such as might giue breath
to Senseless pictures and to me giues death.
Muses farewell: Your friendes $death^h$ deplore
whom you are not Medeas to restore.
Loue let me kiss thy hand by whom I fall,
Yet thou hast kill'd mee wth a Cordiall.
Death Cry thee mercie, Loue's Commands extend's
soe farre I Saw not thine; yet wee'l meete friends.
I feele thee, in my marrow, Thy Shaft lurkes
wth a cold poyson Typt; now now it workes.
What Ague's this?   but now my heart did glow,
AEtna was not soe fiery; no^w I grow
more Cold then are ye Alpes; I am like one
Toss'd from ye torrid to ye frigid Zone:
A winter's in my blood, my Veine freeze ore,
It Snows upon my heart, I Can no more
moue my contracted Sinewes.   If there bee
mongst those y^t in theyr teares would burie mee
Some poore forsaken Virgin y^t did meane
All faith & found no Iustice, let her gleane
The ruines of my hart, ye rest Conuey
Into Some Sad groue where ye Turtle may
Mourn out my Elegie.   write on my Tombe

116

I had a faire Iudge but a Cruell Doom
                    J. H.

I have punctuated the poem for ease in reading but
have tried to keep within the conventions of 16th
century punctuation. Dr. Osborn is right in crediting the poem to Hoskyns, although scarcely because
of the reason that she gives, that its "light, whim-
sical, satirical vein is not unlike Hoskyns'." Lines
like "I feele thee, in my marrow" or "A winter's in
my blood" are not typical of his other poetry. However, the poem appears in the type of collection
that most of his poems do, and in association with
poems of Donne, which is usually the case. In all
other such cases, the initials "J. H." stand for
Hoskyns rather than for someone like John Harrington
or any other possible poet of the day with those initials. Furthermore the allusions to Leander, the
three Fates, Medea, etc., are those we meet with
some regularity in Hoskyns' other verse, especially
his Latin verse. The one keynote of Hoskyns which
is relatively missing is the obvious play of wit,
but even that is partially present in the play between the beauty of the Loved one who has killed
the poet and the ugliness of Death, who is her messenger. When all is said and done, the allusions
and figures of speech are relatively commonplace.
What is at all different is the extreme complexity
of the syntax, which makes the lack of punctuation
in the manuscript version even harder to understand,
and the frequent use of enjambed or run-on lines
that were to become far more common in the Baroque.
One is tempted to say that Hoskyns was attempting to
write the "strong lines" which Donne and Chapman
were making famous, and that he really failed in his
attempt.

    If there are difficulties with the previous
poem, the circumstances of the fourth are even more
awkward. But it is also a far finer poem.

                    Absence.

        That time and absence proves
        Rather helps than hurts to loves.
    Absence heare my protestation
        Against thy strengthe

                    117

```
        Distance and lengthe,
  Doe what thou canst for alteration:
     For harts of truest mettall
     Absence doth joyne, and time doth settle.
```

Who loves a Mistris of right quality,
   His mind hath founde
   Affections grounde
Beyond time, place, and all mortality:
   To harts that cannot vary
   Absence is present, time doth tary:

My Sences want their outward motion
   Which now within
   Reason doth win,
Redoubled by her secret notion:
   Like rich men that take pleasure
   In hidinge more then handling treasure

By absence this good means I gaine
   That I can catch her
   Where none can watch her
In some close corner of my braine:
   There I embrace and there kiss her,
   And so enjoye her, and so misse her.[53]

In collections of Donne's poetry in the 18th and
19th centuries, this poem was attributed to John
Donne, and there are good reasons for doing so. In
at least one collection it is specifically credited
to "J. D." and in such manuscripts as Lansdowne 740
and Stowe 962 it appears among poems which are definitely by Donne. In one other, the Hawthornden MS
which we have used as the source for "Loue is a
foolish melancholie," it is assigned to "J. H."
Ever since Sir Herbert Grierson's great 1912 edition of Donne's poetry--in which he decided to assign the poem to some one other than Donne on the
basis of the various manuscripts and the fact that
no editor had assigned the poem to the famous poet
until the 18th century--the poem has been given,
obviously with some hesitation, to Hoskyns.[54] I
think that we can be reasonably sure that this is
the case. The verbal play, especially of the last
two stanzas, resembles the usual witty play of words
which Hoskyns enjoyed. The complexity of line
lengths and metrical patterns, as well as the care-

118

ful construction of the whole poem relate quite well
to Hoskyns' Latin verse, although the approach to
love is much more like Donne than Hoskyns. The latter seldom preferred an imaginary love object to a
physical. And the entire poem is characterized by
a greater sense of command than most of his English
poetry. I think we can take "Absence" as an example
of Hoskyns at his very best as a late Elizabethan
poet. If it is representative of many of the poems
lost in the complete collection of his poetry, "bigger than those of Dr. Donne," then our loss has been
great indeed.

The years at the end of the century were also
the period at which Hoskyns achieved his finest work
in prose, both of a humorous and a serious nature.
The best example of the former is an ex tempore
speech given during the performance of Le Prince
d'Amour as part of the Christmas festivities of the
1597-98 holidays at the Middle Temple.[55] Aubrey
made himself a memorandum while he was compiling
the life of Hoskyns: "collect his nonsense discourse, which is very good."[56] Aubrey's opinion of
the work is echoed by Hoskyns' contemporaries as
well, and it appears both in manuscript collections
and printed versions of the Christmas performance.

That Hoskyns himself felt it was a worthy performance is evident in his Directions of the following year. He defines Symploce, or Complexio, as
"when seuerall sentences haue the same beginning
and the same ending."[57] After some examples, he
says, "This is the wantonest of repetitions, and is
not to bee vsed in matters too serious, You haue an
example of it in the fustian Speech about Tobacco."
In describing Antimetabole, he says,

And notwithstanding that this is a Sharpe and
Wittie figure, and shewes out of the same words
a pithy Distinction of meaning very convenient
for schoolemen yet Mr. P. did wrong to tyer
this poore figure by vsing it thirtie times in
one sermon. for vse this or any other point
vnseasonably, it is as ridiculous as it was in
the fustian oration horsemill, millhorse &c.[58]

119

Finally, he sums up both the figure of <u>Occupatio</u>
and all of the figures of speech he has been discussing,

> This figure cannot bee out of season but of
> purpose, as was in the fustian speech, you
> listne to my speeches I must confesse it, you
> hearken to my words I cannot Deny it, you looke
> for some sence I partly beleiue it, but you
> find none I doe not respect it. And yf you
> will read over that speech you shall find most
> of the figures of Rhetoricke there meaning nei-
> ther harme nor good but as idle as yor selfe
> when you are most at leisure.[59]

No better description of how to take the speech is
possible. It is a sheer exercise of rhetorical wit
displayed for the amusement and entertainment of his
fellow Templars. More specifically it is aimed at
Sir Walter Ralegh in a very friendly way. Although
Ralegh did not introduce tobacco to England, he certainly was the one that popularized it, and Hoskyns
used tobacco as one of the main satirical thrusts of
his speech. The immediate reason for Hoskyns' attack is that during the speech preceding that of
Hoskyns, "the Orator took Tobacco." We learn this
from Benjamin Rudyard's account of the festivities
as quoted in Hoyt Hudson's edition of the speech.[60]

The play is a description of life in the myth-
ical kingdom of the Prince of Love. It starts with
a description of the offices, duties, etc., in the
kingdom; for example, the "Lord Treasurer is to receive all the Revenews of the Corown; as Sighs, Sonnets, Tears, Vows, Protestations, &c... Lord Chamberlain to keep all Roomes voide of Spies, sweetly
perfumed, the Couches made all for advantage, that
the Windows admit but twilight, to cover Blemishes,
and discover perfections...."[61] The Clerk of the
Council, the part played by Hoskyns, is described
also. "The <u>Clerk</u> of the Councils note of the duty
of the Officers shall help furnish some that are out
of discourse."[62] In the 1660 version of the play we
have the following introduction to Hoskyns' speech:
"The Princes Orator having made a ridiculous and

120

sensless speech unto his Excellency, the Clerk of
the Council was requested to make an Answer therunto
at ex tempore, which at the first he refused; but
being importuned, he began and said:" In the manuscript version in the British Museum at least one of
the personalities present is further identified:
"Refused to answer at ex tempore beinge importuned
by yᵉ Prince [played by Richard Martin] & Sʳ Walter
Raleigh began." If it really was completely extem-
poraneous, Hoskyns was cleverer than even his own
writings give him credit for. It is extremely difficult to speak for so long, using every rhetorical
device in the book, without deviating into sense:

The Fustian Answer made to a
Tufftaffata Speech[63]

   Then (Mr. Orator) I am sorry that for your
Tufftaffata Speech, you shall receive but a Fustian Answer. For alas! what am I (whose ears
have been pasted with the Tenacity of your
Speeches, and whose nose hath been perfumed with
the Aromaticity of your sentences) that I should
answer your Oration, both Voluminous and Topical,
with a Replication concise and curtal? For you
are able in Troops of Tropes, and Centuries of
Sentences to muster your meaning: Nay, you have
such Wood-piles of words, that unto you Cooper is
but a Carpenter, and Rider himself deserves not a
Reader. I am therefore driven to say to you, as
Heliogabalus said to his dear and honourable servant Reniger Fogassa, If thou dost ill (quoth he)
then much good do thee; if well, then snuffe the
candle. For even as the Snow advanced upon the
points vertical of cacuminous Mountains, dissol-
veth and discoagulateth itself into humorous liq-
uidity; even so by the frothy volubility of your
words, the Prince is perswaded to depose himself
from his Royal Seat and Dignity, and to follow
your counsel with all contradiction and relucta-
tion; wherefore I take you to be fitter to speak
unto stones, like Amphion, or trees, like Orpheus,
than to declaim to men like a Cryer, or to ex-
claim to boyes like a Sexton: For what said
Silas Titus, the Sope-maker of Holbornbridge?

For (quoth he) since the States of Europe have
so many momentary inclinations, and the Anarchi-
cal confusion of their Dominions is like to ru-
inate their Subversions, I see no reason why
men should so addict themselves to take Tobacco
in Ramus Method; For let us examine the Com-
plots of Polititians from the beginning of the
world to this day; What was the cause of the re-
pentine mutiny in Scipio's Camp? it is most evident it was not Tabacco. What was the cause of
the Aventine revolt, and seditious deprecation
for a Tribune? it is apparent it was not Tabacco. What moved me to address this Expostula-
tion to your iniquity? it is plain it is not
Tabacco. So that to conclude, Tabacco is not
guilty of so many faults as it is charged with-
al; it disuniteth not the reconciled, nor re-
concileth the disunited; it builds no new Cities, nor mends no old Breeches; yet the one and
then other, and both are not immortal without
reparations: Therefore wisely said the merry-
conceited Poet Heraclitus, Honourable misfor-
tunes shall have ever an Historical compensa-
tion. You listen unto my speeches, I must needs
confess it; you hearken to my words, I cannot
deny it; you look for some meaning, I partly believe it; but you find none, I do not greatly
respect it: For even as a Mill-horse is not a
Horse-mill; nor Drink ere you go, is not Go ere
you drink; even so Orator Best, is not the best
Orator. The sum of all is this, I am an humble
Suitor to your Excellency, not only to free him
from the danger of the Tower, which he by his
demerits cannot avoid; but also to increase dignity upon his head, and multiply honour upon his
shoulders, as well for his Eloquence, as for his
Nobility. For I understand by your Herald that
he is descended from one of an Ancient house of
the Romans Calphurnius Bestia, and so the generation continued from beast to beast, to this
present beast. And your Astronomer hath told
me that he hath Kindred in the Zodiack; therefore in all humility I do beseech your Excellency to grant your Royal Warrant to the Lo. Mar-
shal, and charge him to send to the Captain of

the Pentioners, that he might send to the Captain of the Guard to dispatch a Messenger to
the Lieutenant of the Tower, to command one of
his Guard to go to one of the Grooms of his
Stable, to fetch the Beadle of the Beggars, _ut
gignant stultum_, to get him a stool; _ut sit
foris Eloquentiae_, that he may sit for his Eloquence. I think I have most oratoriously insin-
uated unto your apprehension, and with evident
obscurity intimated unto your good consideration,
that the Prince hath heard your Oration, yea
marry hath he, and thinketh very well of it, yea
marry doth he.

There is one element of unintentional pathos
in the speech. It was not the Orator who was to be
in danger of imprisonment in the Tower, but the
speaker of the Fustian speech, who in 1614 joined
Ralegh in the Tower of London.

In the British Museum manuscript, the speech
is identified as by Hoskyns and there addressed to
"his deere & hono^{bll} seruant Remiger Fogassa if
thou doste ill (quoth hee) then much good doe thee,
if well, snuffe the candle." This repetition from
the speech itself may help to identify the collect-
or of this manuscript, who would be willing to have
been addressed jokingly as Hoskyns' "seruant." The
large number of Hoskyns' poems in this manuscript
adds to the supposition.

Charles Best, the Prince's Orator in the play,
was Hoskyns' friend and entered the Middle Temple in
April 1592, from Cotheridge, Worchestershire. Best
was fined for not fulfilling his duties as Reader in
1618 and three years later was referred to as "one
of the most ancient masters of the Utter Bar." He
had some of his poems published in Davison's _Poet-
ical Rhapsodie_ in 1612, and John Davies of Hereford
devoted one epigram to him in the _Scourge of Folly_
and referred to him as "my kind friend."[64] His
father was named John Best, and there is a real possibility that he had a brother with the same name
who, as a Canon of Hereford Cathedral, depended on
Hoskyns for legal counsel. Either one of them would

123

have been interested in collecting Hoskyns' poems
as well as the Fustian speech, and neither would
have been insulted by Hoskyns' jest about being his
servant.

John's relationships with Ralegh are the more
interesting ones for us, however; yet Ralegh was
not the only influential person with whom Hoskyns
was close at this period. To see his other acquaintances we must back up before finishing his days as
an Inner Barrister.

While Hoskyns was busily engaged in his law
training and writing, his younger brothers were
growing up, and two of them were leaving the farm
at Monkton. Naturally they went to the same school
at which their brother had made such a reputation.
On 25 July 1593 Dr. John was admitted to Winchester
College at the age of 11, the same age at which John
had entered from Westminster. He took the oath on
Wykeham's statutes on 29 February 1596.[65] While he
was still there, the third Wykehamist Hoskyns entered; Charles was admitted on 5 July 1598, aged 10.
He took the oath on 29 November 1601.[66] But Dr.
John was eager to get on to New College, and he appealed to his older brother in London to help him.
This meant having influence put on the two Wyke-
hamite institutions by members of the court.

In August 1598 three of the highest ranking
members of the Elizabethan court came to the support of the young boy. Between July 7th and October 1st each year, the Warden and two Fellows from
New College, one of whom had to be a Master of Theology or Philosophy and the other a Bachelor or Doctor of Canon or Civil Law, visited Winchester to
hear and investigate complaints but primarily to
elect scholars for both Winchester and Oxford.[67]
The three letters arriving that August were directed to the Warden and visiting team, and there is no
possible explanation for them other than that John
Hoskyns had enough influence to bring about the writing of the letters. The first we can understand
well enough. It is from Thomas Egerton, Lord Keeper of the Privy Seal, but more important for stu-

124

dents of English Literature, the employer of John
Donne. Donne had returned from the two Essex es-
capades against the Spanish in 1596 and 1597 and
gone almost immmdiately into service as secretary
to the father of his friends and fellow students at
Lincoln's Inn, the Egerton brothers. It would be a
nice added touch if the letter had been in Donne's
handwriting, but it appears that Egerton jotted
this note off himself, addressed "To my lovinge
ffrindes m^r Doctor Colepepper, and m^r John Harmer,
and the rest of the Electors for the Colledge of
Winchester." It is immediately evident that he
does not know the young man he is writing about.

> After my harty commendacions. I ame informed
> that ther is at this tyme one John Hoskins a
> child of yor Colledge of Winchestr. wch hath
> been long since, for his learning and manners
> fitt to be chosen to New Colledge in Oxon. And
> that at yor last eleccion he had yor approbacion
> and testimonye, to be of the best meritt of his
> company, but was stayed there one year longer,
> for the good of others, wch stood vpon the has-
> ard of ther p^{r}ferment, and for no defect of his
> owne. I earnestly intreat y^w to favour his de-
> servings, and accordingly to place him in this
> yor eleccion at this tyme, the rath^r because (as
> I ame informed) his age, his honest conversation,
> and knowledge are such as may ill be putt back
> any longer. And so I bidd y^w hartily ffarewell.
> At Yorkhouse. the xixth of August 1598.
>
> > Yo^r lovinge ffrind
> > Tho. Egerton. C. S.[68]

Two days later another letter went off to the electors of Winchester, this one from the Lord High Admiral of England, Thomas Howard, Earl of Nottingham.
His letter is less detailed as to the circumstances
of the situation, but it reveals the same request
made for his influence:

> ... I am enformed that there is one John Hoskyns
> a chyld of yor College whose towardlynes in
> learninge and good behaviour may well deserve

125

yor favour in this yor next election. I therefore earnestlie intreate y^u to respect hym w^{th}
the first ꝑ let hym loose no part of the reward
wch in yor iudgement$\underline{es}$ y^u have vsed to bestow
vpon so good deserviṉge, wch I shall acknowledge
as a favour, ꝑ be ready to requitt it in all
thanckefulness... from the courte att Greenew^{ch}
the 21 Awgust 1598

Yo^r verie lovinge freind

NOTINGHAM

It would seem that the support of two such highly
placed men would be enough, but Hoskyns sought out
still another support for his brother, Sir William
Knollys, Controller of the royal household and
Privy Councillor. Knollys was still on his way up
in the peerage of England, finally being made Earl
of Banbury in 1626. But as Privy Councillor, his
position in the kingdom was already high. His letter is much the same as the other two, although he
is more explicit about his reason for writing:

... I haue bin entreated to commend vnto you the
Suit of one John Hoskyns a Chyȴde of yor Colledge for such a place in yor next Election to
Oxford as in yor fauourable censure he shall be
worthy of. I am informed that he comes not
short of anye of his companye in learninge ꝑ
good behaviour, and I entreete you that he may
be not further behynde them in his place....

your lovyng ffrend

W. Knollys

Although the letter is not dated, it is safe to assume that it was written during the same month of
August, 1598. Besides the testimony that these letters give us as to Hoskyns' influence at court,
they show something rather praiseworthy about Winchester College and New College, Oxford. The political pressure simply didn't work. Dr. John was
not admitted to Oxford until 2 November 1599 and
was not made a fellow at New College until 24 August 1601. Once at Oxford, he stayed around longer

than his older brother, getting his B.C.L. on 27
January 1606 and his D.C.L. 28 April 1613, when he
resigned his fellowship.[69]

Hoskyns' relations with Winchester were not
only those of an alumnus and brother of two students, however. As he drew near to his calling to
the Bar, he began to prepare for his own economic
future in other ways as well. On 11 January 1600
he leased the manor of Titley from Winchester College, no doubt borrowing money from his father to
do so. His father also helped him stock the farm
with cattle. Titley is just two miles south of the
Welsh border at its furthest penetration into the
borders of Hereford, a little over fifteen miles in
a direct line northwest of the city of Hereford,
but a good deal further by road. It is only two
miles from one of the better preserved sections of
Offa's Dyke. Moreover, it was less than five miles
over the hills to the property of his uncle and
cousins in Shobdon and Byton.

Titley Court is still one of the best preserved houses in that section of Herefordshire and has
an overmantel dating from the period of Hoskyns'
lease,[70] although most of the building was altered
in the late 17th, 18th, and 19th centuries. It
was a two storey house with cellars and attics and
was at least as impressive a structure as the family farm at Monkton, although it was not as grand
a place as either Bernithen Court or Morehampton,
where John set up his own family.

The indenture is worth noting as it indicated
both the size of the holding that was to occupy
much of Hoskyns' attention for the rest of his life
and the duties that went with the manor. The indenture is "Betwene John Harmar Clerke Warden of
St Marye Colledge of Winchester... and the schol-
lers Clerke of the same Colledge... And John Hoskyns of the Midle Temple london gentleman." The
language is standard for such a document: "for
diuers good causes and consideracons" the College

Haue demysed grannted and to farme letten...

127

vnto the said John Hoskyns, All that the Manno^r
or Pryorye of Titley in the marshes of Wales ꝫ
in the Countie of Hereford togeather wth all manner of landes Tenements leasures, pastures,
comons, commadities ꝫ proffittes whatsoeuer...
And also all the Rentes of all the Tenementes
theire and all and allmonnies of Tithes obla-
cions and obvencions whatsoeuer of all the pa-
rishoners of Titley and all that the Dovehowse
theire, And all fines herryottes amerciam^tes
and all other proffittes and perquisittes of
courtes rightes commodities and appurtenances
whatsoeuer... Except and always reserved out of
this presente lease demyse and grannt vnto the
said Warden... All wodes vnderwoodes trees and
Copices... wth free ingresse egresse and re-
gresse into and from the same woodes.

Hoskyns was "To haue and to holde" the property
"from the feast of St Michaell tharchanngell next
ensuyng... vnto thend and terme of tenn yeres."
Actually he and his son renewed the lease for more
than thirty years. He was to pay a rent

> Yealdinge payinge and deliueringe therefore yere-
> lie... vnto the said Warden and Schollrs Clerkes
> ... six poundes thirtene shillinges and foure
> pence... and in steed of other three poundes
> sixe shillinges and eight pence beinge the third
> parte of the olde and accustomed rent of the be-
> fore demysed premisses sixe quarters of good
> sweet well wynnowed and merchanntdizable wheat
> and five quarters three bushelles of good sweet
> well dryed and merchanndizable malte Amountinge
> to the said some of [£3 6s 8d]... after the rate
> of sixe shillinges and eight pence for a quarter
> of wheat and five shillinges for a quarter of
> malte... The said money wheat and malt to be
> paide and deliuered at the feast of St Michaell
> Tharchangell yerelie.

There were other requirements besides simple
rent for the Baron of Titley Manor, however. Hoskyns had to

128

Covenant and graunt... to and wth the said Warden... that... at his... owne proper costes and
Charges shall and will yerelie and from tyme to
tyme when and as often as nede shall require...
well and sufficientlie repaire maynteyne and
sustayne all howses barnes edifices and walles...
and also the Channcell of the parishe Churche of
Titley... And also all the hedges ditches and
enclosures... And the same... at thend of the
said terme... shall leave and yeld vppe.

In another section of the indenture, however, it is
made clear that the Warden had to provide the necessary wood for the repair of such objects as the
hedges, ploughs, and carts. Moreover Hoskyns also
had to "provide and fynde... one sufficient Chaplen
or minister to serve the sacram^{tes} and to reade and
saye dyvyne service in the parishe Churche of Titley
aforesaid at the proper costes and Charges." He
also had to "beare paye and discharge all quitt
rentes costes paym^{tes} dueties and Charges... to
oure soueraigne ladye the Quenes Matie... and to
the lorde of Stepleton." He also had to "kepe and
maynteyne... a sufficient or convenyent howseholde
or fammlye there to be resiant dwellinge and inhab-
itinge." As we shall see, he had a little trouble
with his choice of Steward for the manor.

He had two further obligations outlined in the
indenture: he had to give to the Warden or his substitute

good and suffycyent meat drincke and lodginge...
and sufficient hey litter and provender wth stable rome for there horses and geldinges by the
space of two dayes and two nightes once euerye
yere... when they shall come to kepe courte or
to survey or viewe the state of the premisses...
and... paye... betwene the feastes of St Luke...
and all S^{tes}... fortie shillinges... in leiwe
satisfacion and consideracion of all fynes
heriettes amerciem^{tes} and all other proffittes
and perquisittes of courtes.

He had to deliver "true copies of all courtes and

129

co^rte rolles,... w^thin sixe monethes after request."
The indenture ends with the usual restraints: he
could not transfer any of the land without the Warden's permission, and he had a grace period of thirty days each year for payment of rents and three
months for making repairs before the Warden would
"reenter" the property.[71] On the same day, however,
they gave him a license of "free libertie and ly-
cence to demyse grannt sell assigne or sett ouer
the premisses... or any parte thereof."[72] The indenture is actually a very generous one considering
the size of the estate. And although Hoskyns was
fairly regular in his yearly payment of £8 13s 4d,
there were years, particularly late in his life,
when he and his son fell far more than a month behind in their payments.

     Although the manor of Titley with its Court
Baron rights was certainly not the largest property
farmed out by Winchester College, it was a good-
sized one. There is no way of knowing how much
Hoskyns had to pay for the original indenture, but
the wording of the lease, along with other evidence
of Hoskyns' financial situation at the time, would
lead us to suspect that they let their former prize
student have the property for a very small amount.
Although it gave him a comfortable return, we shall
later see that it was not a great money maker for
him. It did, however, start him on the road to
becoming a major landholder.

     And within two months he was also a Barrister.
During the Lent Reading, Hoskyns and his friend
John Chapman were called to the Bar by the Reader.
There was no ceremony, except that after dinner one
day they were called to the Cupboard, where they
took the Oath of Supremacy from the Treasurer of
the Temple.[73] The Records for 2 May 1600 carry the
entry: "The calls of Messrs. John Chapman and John
Hoskins to the degree of the Utter Bar by Mr. Man
during his reading are confirmed.[74] Finally John
Hoskyns was out in the world with his formal education completed.

Footnotes for Chapter IV

1. Wood continued Aubrey's error of having Hoskyns marry Benedicta Bourne before he entered the Middle Temple, Athenae Oxoniensis, p. 614.
2. J. Stevens Cox, A History of Ilchester (Ilchester, 1958), p. 234. The following information on Ilchester is taken from this volume.
3. P.R.O. Chancery Cases, F 29/17.
4. The poem, found in Osborn, p. 188, is on Signature A₄v of VLYSSES REDUX / TRAGOEDIA NOVA / IN AEDE CHRISTI OXONIAE / PUBLICE ACADEMICIS RE- / CITATA, OCTAVO IDVS / FEBRVARII, 1591. It was dedicated to the Countess of Pembroke.
5. Wood, Fasti, Cols. 120, 137.
6. Middle Temple Records, Vol. 1, 1501-1603. ed. Charles H. Hopwood (1904), p. 333.
7. J. Bruce Williamson, The History of the Temple, London (1924), p. 189.
8. This and the following quotations from Hoskyns are from Directions, ff. 10-10v, 2v, 17, 13, 12v-13, 14v, 14.
9. Sir Lynden Macassay, Middle Templars' Associations with America (pamphlet), pp. 8, 9.
10. Alexander Pulling, The Order of the Coif (1884), p. 175.
11. Origines Juridiciales (1666), p. 195. The following information on Terms and Readings is from pp. 38, 90-91, 194.
12. Pulling, p. 175.
13. Dugdale, Origines, p. 191.
14. Ibid., p. 202; Williamson, p. 206.
15. Dugdale, p. 202.
16. Register of Admissions... Middle Temple, Vol. I, Fifteenth Century to 1914, ed. H. A. C. Sturgess (1949), pp. 48, 59; Williamson, p. 221.
17. Hopwood, I, 279.
18. Sturgess, p. 58.
19. The Middle Temple Bench Book (2nd ed., 1937), ed. J. Bruce Williamson, p. 98.
20. This and the entries from the next two paragraphs are from Hopwood, I, 318, 326, 312, 317.
21. Ibid., p. 333; Register of Admissions, I, 64.
22. Middle Temple Bench Book, p. 101.

131

Chapter 4 footnotes

23. The entries on Moorton, Searle, Davies, and Wooton are in Hopwood I, 351, 354, 355.
24. Directions, f. 23.
25. The entries in this paragraph are from Hopwood, I, 368, 378.
26. Directions, f. 12v.
27. Hopwood, I, 379-40.
28. Directions, f. 12.
29. This and the entries in the following three paragraphs are in Hopwood, I, 380, 383, 382, 396; II, 444, 571, 638. Osborn also lists a Hoskyns' bonding entry on p. 420 of Hopwood, Vol. I, but she apparently misread the entry on Thomas Fettiplace, who was bound with William Copley and Henry Norwood and moved into the apartments of Hoskyns and Copley, in the latter's place.
30. Hopwood, I, 334, 335.
31. Stow, p. 766.
32. The Poems of John Donne, ed. H.J.C. Grierson (1912), I, 208-09.
33. Entries on activities at the Middle Temple in the following seven paragraphs are from Hopwood, I, 347, 350, 359, 365, 361; II, 536; I, 362, 393, 347, 411, 363, 381, 389, 353, 402, 410, 386; II, 545.
34. Chetham MS, II, 183. Lansdowne 740 has a sonnet with a side note, "Verses vpon Bp Fletcher, who maried a Woman of il Fame." f. 94. It was not the character of the widow Baker that seems to have been the problem, however, but the age and rank of the Bishop. Queen Elizabeth was outspoken in her disapproval, which some took to be the reason for the Bishop's speedy demise. There are two versions of the epitaph in MSS. Add. 30,982, on f. 28 and f. 57, neither a very good copy. Both versions are credited to R.C., however, who would seem to a man named either Clark or Corbet from other poems in the collection. Richard Corbet was one of Hoskyns' scholarly friends. The attribution to Hoskyns in the Chetham MS would seem to carry more weight than either of these, however. MSS. Add. 10,309,

132

Chapter 4 footnotes

which contains quite a few Hoskyns' poems, has
this one on p. 277; another version is in Harley 1107, f. 11. Both are anonymous. Osborn
also notes versions in MS. Rawl. Poet. 172, f.
15v, which I have not seen, and MS. Add. 5832,
f. 205. The latter is inaccurate. That manuscript is a record of Herefordshire business.

35. Stow, p. 777.
36. Camden, Annals, p. 469.
37. Camden added this epitaph to his list of Hoskyns' poems in his 1614 ed. of the Remaines,
beginning on p. 382. I have used the title
from Osborn's citation from MS. Ashmole 38, p.
181, where the verses are specifically assigned
to "Serj^tHoskins."
38. Remains (1870), p. 433. The poem also appears
as Epitaph #22 in Wits Recreations (1640), and
in Egerton 2421, f. 2v.
39. II, 181.
40. 1605 ed., p. 53.
41. Stowe 962, f. 201v; Egerton 923, f. 9; MSS.
Add. 15,227, f. 94v. It is also listed as #70
in Wits Recreation.
42. II, 185.
43. Reprinted by the Spenser Society (1888), p. 148.
44. Ibid., p. 177.
45. Chetham MS., II, 184; also listed among the
Hoskyns' poems in the 1605 edition of Remaines;
Osborn also gives references to MS Rawlinson D.
1372, f. 9v, and MS. Ashmole 38, p. 170.
46. p. 148. In Osborn, p. 211.
47. MSS. Add. 25,303, f. 70v; also in MSS. Add.
24,665, f. 81v; Osborn notes its presence in MS.
Rawlinson Poet. 172, f. 14v. She also says it
is in MSS. Add. 22,601, but it is not. Only in
MSS. Add. 25,303 is the poem attributed to Hoskyns. Osborn does not assign the poem to Hoskyns because she has seen a manuscript belonging to Dr. A.S.W. Rosenbach in which it is headed "Mr. Poldens delight of New Coll: Oxon:"
But MSS. Add. 25,303, put together for Hoskyns'
close associate in Parliament, Robert Bowyer,
and containing a number of Hoskyns' poems as

well as the Fustian speech. all clearly and cor-
rectly assigned to Hoskyns, is an almost unim-
peachable source. It also contains Lady Jacobs
Answer on f. 71.

48. Hopwood, I, 373; II, 448.

49. Brief Lives, ed. Clark, I, 424. Osborn also
notes its appearance anonymously in Malone 36,
f. 121.

50. The main text I have used is that of Sloane
1446, ff. 28v-29, but I have added the second
verse which is found in MSS. Add. 25,303, f.
138v; MSS. Add. 10,309, p. 91, and Chetham MS.,
I, 85. I have used the stanza as it is found in
the first of these three. There is another version of the poem in Sloane 1792, f. 6v, which,
along with MSS. Add. 25,303, changes "makes"
to "make" in line twelve and places the "mee"
(which is missing in Sloane 1446) in the first
line of the last stanza. I have also changed
"about" in Sloane 1446, line 2, to "by night"
on the authority of both the Chetham MS. and
MSS. Add. 25,303. There is another version in
MSS. Add. 22,603, but it is inferior throughout.
Sir Herbert Grierson also noted another version
which he had consulted in the Trinity College,
Dublin, Library, which he refers to as TCD
(Second Collection), Donne, II, cix. The Chetham MS. adds a final couplet which is found nowhere else and seems spurious because it does
not follow the stanzaic pattern of the rest of
the poem,
     Yea trewe indeede, constant & suer
     that truth it self shoulde not be trewer.
                                        J.H.

51. I have followed Osborn in using Hawthornden
MSS, Vol. 15, ff. 8-9, as the principal source,
but I have added stanzas two and six from the
Chetham MS (I, 86-87) both because of the authority of that MS on Hoskyns' poems (it is there
described as by "Mr Hoskins.") and because the
two additional stanzas sound very much like
Hoskyns, especially stanza six. I have also
adopted the reading "all's" instead of "else"

Chapter 4 footnotes

in the first line of stanza seven from <u>Chetham</u> because of the meaning of the line.

52. Panovsky treats the dual treatment of Cupid in Renaissance and Mannerist painting in <u>Studies in Iconology</u>.

53. <u>Grierson, I</u>, 428-29.

54. Ibid., II, cl-clii. Osborn summarized all of the history and sources of the poem (pp. 285-87) with one slight error in stating that it appears in <u>Lansdowne 740</u>, ff. 99v-100. It actually is on f. 107.

55. Hopwood, I, 379, notes that the Christmas celebration was to be "solemn not grand." Commons was to be continued throughout the holidays.

56. Clark ed., I, 424.

57. f. 8.

58. f. 8v. "Mr. P." was identified by Prof. Hudson as Thomas Playfere.

59. f. 28.

60. <u>Directions for Speech and Style</u>, ed. Hoyt H. Hudson (Princeton, 1935), p. 109. There are many stories about Ralegh's use of Tobacco. Perhaps the most interesting is found in Lansdowne 702, "Rawlins's Notes, etc...", ff. 90v-91.

It was brought into England by S^r Fr: Drake's Seamen, but first into repute by S^r. W. Rawleigh. By ye caution he took in smoaking it privately, he did not intend it sh^d be copied. But sitting one day in a deep Meditation wth a pipe in his Mouth, inadvertently call'd to his man to bring him a Tankard of small Ale; ye ffellow coming into ye Room, threw all ye Liquor in his master's fface, & running down stairs, bawl'd out ffire! Help! Sr Walter has studied till his head's on fire, & ye Smoak bursts out of his Mouth & Nose. After this Sr Walter made it no secret, & took two pipes just before he went to be beheaded.

61. <u>Le Prince d'Amour or the Prince of Love with a Collection of Several Ingenious Poems and Songs By the Wits of the Age</u> (London, 1660), p. 25.

62. Ibid., p. 35.

135

Chapter 4 footnotes

63. Osborn's reference to Hoskyns' speech as the "Tuftaffeta Speech" misses the point made in the play. The orator's speech was the Tuftaffeta, an ornate speech whose title comes from a luxurious cloth of taffeta with a pile or nap arranged in tufts (O.E.D.). Hoskyns' answer was Fustian, made of coarse cloth of cotton and flax, or, as it was used of language, inflated, turgid, or inappropriately lofty language; bombast, rant. (O.E.D.) It also contained the earliest known Latin equivalent of "Fractured French" in the final two quotations. For the text, I have used the Le Prince d'Amour (1660) version with variations from MSS Add. 25,303, ff. 184v-185v. (The manuscript made for Robert Bowyer). The speech also appears in MS. HM 1338 in the Huntington Library and in Malone 16, ff. 74v-75.

64. Details on Charles Best are from G.C. Moore Smith, "Charles Best," Review of English Studies, I, 1925, pp. 454-56.

65. Registrum Primum, p. 101; Liber prothocollorum.

66. Reg. Pri., p. 103: Liber protho.

67. Kirby, Annals, p. 71.

68. The three letters are found among the Winchester MSS. Letters, 223B, 223C. 224.

69. Liber Successionis; Oxford Register, Part II, p. 237. Part III, 268.

70. Royal Commission on Historical Monuments, England, Herefordshire, Vol. III (1934), pp. xxxvii, 191; plate 52.

71. Liber Registarij Collegij 1596-1613, ff. 51-51v.

72. Ibid., f. 52.

73. Dugdale, p. 203.

74. Hopwood, I, 403.

Chapter V
Directions of Speeche & Stile

A year before he became a Barrister, John Hoskyns produced his most important literary work. It
is too long to treat in any context except itself
and deserves a separate chapter. There is little
reason at this point to repeat the detailed arguments given by both Professors Hudson and Osborn
for dating the composition of the work on rhetoric
at some point around the summer 1599. The reference to the Earl of Essex' being in Ireland at the
time is clear enough: "The Speciall for the par-
ticular as the Earle is gone to Ireland for E. $\overline{\text{E}}$."
(f. 6v) The occasion for the work also seems ap-
parent. Robert Harley, son and heir-apparent of
Thomas Harley of Brampton Castle, Herefordshire,
was to come up to the Middle Temple and be bound
with Hoskyns in October. Brampton Castle was less
than five miles north of John's uncle's home in Byton, and the Hoskyns and Harley properties touched
at some points. From internal evidence we quickly
discover that the work was as much a gesture of
friendship and respect for the father as it was affection for the son. The Harleys were an important
family in Herefordshire, and young Robert was to
become one of the most important landowners and
legislators of the area, as well as a co-worker
with John's son Benedict during the struggles between Parliament and Charles I. That young Harley
was introduced by Hoskyns to the group of friends
in London is indicated by a letter from John Donne
to Harley in 1613, loaded with the rhetorical devices that Hoskyns prescribes for letter writing:

> ... But, Sir, as I was willinge to make thys
> paper a litle bigger than a physician's receit
> lest that representation should take your sto-
> make from yt, so I wyll avoyd to make it very
> longe or busy, least your physician chide me as
> much as your patient would have done. It shall,
> therefore, onely say that which if I were goinge
> to my grave should be the honorablest piece of
> my epitaph, that I am your humble and affection-

ate servant.[1]

Whether Harley recognized the value of the work Hoskyns addressed to him is hard to know, but the number of manuscript copies of such a long work indicate that it was generally recognized as being of great worth. As should be familiar enough to all students of Ben Jonson by now, the entire section on letter writing and a section of the opening epistle were lifted by Ben and placed bodily in his Timber. Thomas Blount was to use even larger sections of the work in his Academie of Eloquence (1654). Neither was to acknowledge his debt to Hoskyns, although we have seen that Jonson was quick to acknowledge Hoskyns' "polishing" of him.

There are several reasons for paying close attention to the Directions. Aside from Thomas Wilson's published The Art of Rhetorique (1553), it can be considered the major work on prose style in England in the 16th century. This fact gains special significance when we recognize the role of rehtoric in the composition of this period. We have become so used to considering writing from an 18th century grammatical point of view that we have often been blinded to the fact that during the greatest period of English prose, that of the late 16th and 17th centuries, the approach to writing was not grammatical but rhetorical. Moreover, those elements which until the last few years have been central in college composition courses, spelling, punctuation, logical connectives, etc., played little part in what was considered the best writing. The writers were far more interested in gaining the emotional and intuitive response of the reader, and for this the elements of rhetoric were far more important. Bacon, in the Advancement of Learning, described the function of rhetoric as "to apply Reason to Imagination for the better moving of the will."[2] Professor Morris Croll summed up the spirit of the age and its writing style best in his 1929 article "The Baroque Style in Prose."

In the latter years of the sixteenth century a change declared itself in the purposes and

138

forms of the arts of Western Europe for which it is hard to find a satisfactory name. One would like to describe it, because of some interesting parallels with a later movement, as the first modern manifestation of the Romantic Spirit; and it did, in fact, arise out of a revolt against the classicism of the high Renaissance... It would be much clearer and more exact to describe the change in question as a radical effort to adapt traditional modes and forms of expression to the uses of a self-conscious modernism; and the style that it produced was actually called in several of the arts--notably in architecture and prose-writing--the "modern" or "new" style. But the term that most conveniently describes it is "baroque"....

Expressiveness rather than formal beauty was the pretension of the new movement, as it is of every movement that calls itself modern. It disdained complacency, suavity, copiousness, emptiness, ease, and in avoiding these qualities sometimes obtained effects of contortion or obscurity, which it was not always willing to regard as faults. It preferred the forms that express the energy and labor of minds seeking the truth, not without dust and heat, to the forms that express a contented sense of the enjoyment and possession of it. In a single word, the motions of souls, not their states of rest, had become the themes of art.

Croll goes on to distinguish between two different kinds of prose that he regards as baroque, the Curt Style and the Linked Style. He finishes with the most concise statement possible of the relationship of our own tradition of good prose and that of the period under discussion:

This is not the place to consider what we have gained or lost by this literary philosophy, or whether the precision we have aimed at has compensated us for the powers of expression and the flexibility of motion that we have lost; we have only to say that we must not apply the ideas we

139

have learned from it to the explanation of
seventeenth-century style. In brief, we must
not measure the customs of the age of semicolons
and colons by the customs of the age of commas
and periods. The only possible punctuation of
seventeenth-century prose is that which it used
itself. We might sometimes reveal its grammar
more clearly by repunctuating it with commas or
periods, but we should certainly destroy its
rhetoric.[3]

This is not the place to indulge in an argument with Prof. Croll as to whether both the Curt
and Linked Styles are good examples of the Baroque.
His general point is certainly valid, and any study
of the prose of the 1590's and succeeding period
must be based ultimately on his discussion. For
our discussion of Hoskyns' Directions, however, it
must be said that John was writing in an age in
which only the characteristics of the Ciceronian
prose of the century and the beginnings of the Curt
or anti-Ciceronian prose are obviously present.
The Linked Style is still in the future.

Another way to approach Hoskyns' discussion of
prose is to quote him on the great diversity of
style both of the age and of his own style, for he
makes one of the great statements for understanding
any of the artistic movements of the decade of the
1590's, and indeed of the period up to about 1620.
This age of the Counter-Renaissance[4] contained within it as diverse elements as slavish adherence to
Ciceronian rules of composition and the purposely
antagonistic elements of the anti-Ciceronian sentence. In between the extremes it tolerated almost
every conceivable experiment. Hoskyns puts it wittily but truly:

Sententia if it bee well vsed it is a figure
yf ill and too much it is a stile wherof none
that writes humerously or factiously now a dayes
can bee cleere for now there are such scismes of
Eloquence that is enough for any tenn yeares that
all the bravest witts doe well imitate some one
figure wch a Criticke hath taught some great per-

140

sonæge; Soe it may bee within this 200^e yeares
wee shall goe through the whole body of Rhetoricke

   It is true that wee studdy according to the
p^{r}dominancy of Courtly inclinacions. Whilst
Mathematickes were in requist all our similitudes came from lines circles and angles Whilst
Morall Phylosophy is now a while spoken of it is
rudenesse not to bee sententious, and for my part
Ile make one. I haue vsed and outworne sixe severall stiles since I was first fellow of Newcol-
ledge, and am yet able to beare the fashion of
writing company. Lett our age therefore only
speake morally, and lett the next age liue morally.(f.21)

His prophecy on the following two hundred years
could not have been more correct. But it is pre-
cisely the tremendous experimentation in all of the
arts that makes the 16th century so attractive to
our own with its similar experimentation. In fact,
our own return of interest in rhetoric rather than
grammar is merely a part of that experimentation,
and we have been driven back to such writers as
Hoskyns to discover the power of the rhetorical approach. Whether such a return can be possible in
an age of science requiring precision of expression
is yet to be seen.

   Although Hoskyns must certainly be placed a-
mong those pursuing a middle road, he criticizes
those elements of Ciceronian style which we today
feel were the least satisfactory elements of 16th
century writing. He was as aware as any modern critic is of the faults of writers like John Lyly.

   Paranomasia is a pleasant touch of the same letter sillable o^r worde wth a different meaning as
for the running vppon the word (More) This very
litle is more then too much. Sr P. S. in Astrophell and Stella calls it the Dictionary methode,
and the verses soe made rimes running in ratling
rowes, wch is an example of it... In those dayes
Lilly the author of Euphues seeing the dotage of

141

the time vppon this small ornam^t; invented vari-
eties of it for hee disposed the Agnominations
in as many fashions as repetitions are distin-
guisht by the authors Rhetoricke. Sometimes the
first and last, Sometimes the midle and last,
Sometimes in severall sentences, some times in
one, and this wth a measure, Compar, a change of
contentio o^r Contraries, and a Devise of a similitude in those dayes made a gallant shewe, but
Lilly himselfe hath outlived this stile and
breakes well from it. (ff. 8v-9)

It is of interest that he does not completely con-
demn Lyly but notes his change of style in later
life.

Today we look upon Bacon as one of the chief
instigators of the new style, but in 1599, two
years after the publication of the first edition of
the Essays, he appeared to his contemporaries as
one of the most obvious examples of the older followers of a too-balanced style, and Hoskyns attacks
him several times, although only once by name:

The second way of Amplificacion is Division
wch Bacon in his fift colonye tooke out of y^e
Rhetoricians A way to Amplifie any thinge
(quoth hee) is to breake it and make an Anotomy
of it, into severall parts and to examine it,
according to severall Circumstances. Hee said
true, it is like the show that Pedlers make of
their packes when they display them contrary to
the German Magnificence that serues in all the
good meate in one dishe, but whereas hee saith
that this arte of amplifying will betray it
selfe in method and order, I thinke y^t it rather
adorneth it selfe. (f. 12v)

He also attacks Bacon for his overuse of Sententia,
the piling up of moral statements suitable for quotation:

It is very true that a sentence is a pearle in
a discourse, but is it a good discourse that is
all pearle? it is like an eye in the body: but

142

is it not monstrous to bee all eyes? I take Cyclops to bee as hansome a man as Argus, and y^f a
sentence were as like to bee a hand in the text
as it is commonly noated wth a hand in the marg.
yet I should rather like the text that had noe
more hands then Hercules then that wch hath as
many as Briareus.... (ff. 21-21v)

Hoskyns also takes to task the overuse of the three-
fold division commonly known as the Ciceronian tri-
colon. For any contemporary, the allusion to Bacon's
Essays would be unmistakable.

... The tast of former times hath termed it sweet
to bring in three clauses together of the same;
As yor beautie sweet Lady hath conquered my reason subdued my witt and Mastered my iudgem^t how
this will hold amongst our curious successo^{rs} in
their time I know not, hee that lookes on the
wearing of it, will find it bare, how full of
stuffe soever it appeareth. fo^r it passeth fo^r
parts of a division when indeed it is but Varia-
tion of an English. Yet notwthstanding the practise of it will bring you to abundance of phrases
wthout wch you shall never haue choice the mother
or perfeccion. Cicero in his orations vseth it,
oft, some others follow it to fowre clauses. but
hee seldome exceedeth three; but it hath this
Certaine effect. that it will sufficiently testifie yor vaine not to bee drye and spent. (ff.
13v-14)

As Hoskyns was known as perhaps the leading wit
of his day, it is interesting to see his own attitude towards the quality which we accept as the typical exemplification of that word in the late 16th
century. The O.E.D. defines wit at that period as
"That quality of speech or writing which consists
in the apt association of thought and expression,
calculated to surprise and delight by its unexpectedness." The definition of the "conceit" or "con-
cetto" was almost identical. Giovanni Marino, the
Neapolitan author who influenced poets throughout
the continent, said that "The aim of the poet is the
marvelous... He who knows not how to astonish de-

143

serves the cudgel."

Hoskyns, after he has shown how to draw Comparisons between like things, remarks that such comparisons are not as forceful "as when things seeming vnequall are compared, and that in similitudes as well as examples as in my speech of a widdowe [compared to a ship], both aske much tacklinge and sometimes rigging, and you shall most of all profitt by inventing matter of agreem^t in thinges most vnlike." (f.10)   But he also recognized the limits that such comparisons should observe: "The rule of a Metaphore is that it bee not too bold, no^r too farr fetcht; and though all Metaphors goe beiond the true significacion of things, yet are they requisite to match the Compassing sweetnesse of mens minds...." (f.5)   He would probably have shared Samuel Johnson's feeling that some of Donne's conceits, written at the same time as the Directions, went too far.

But it is not only the perceptiveness of Hoskyns' criticism against the writing excesses of his contemporaries or his analysis of rhetorical figures that makes the Directions so fascinating. There are the many references to his own experiences, even his own writings;[5] there are remarks on famous people of the day, like Essex--and Elizabeth: "This figure [Contentio] Ascum [Ascham] told Sturnius that hee taught the Queene of England and that she excelled in practise of it, and indeed it is a figure fitt to sett forth a Copious stile." (f.19v) There is a really remarkable section on the comparative daring and ability of Sir Francis Drake and Vasco do Gama in which the latter comes off as a far more heroic figure than the idol of the English nation:

As y^f a man would compare Vastus Gama wth Sr Francis Drake hee might say Sr Francis Drake indeed travaild round about the world in two yeares, saw diverse nations, endured many perills at Sea, and returned laden wth great treasure and Vastus Gama. first searched the Coast of Quiloa Moramba and Calicute, and opened a passage to the East

144

Indies. But as it was easie for Drake to proceede farther in discoveryes, when hee had an entrance made by Columbus, soe was it most Dangerous and Difficult for Gama to adventure a Course without example and direccion. Drake scoured the coasts wth sufficient company of Shipps, made pillage of others and thereby furnished his owne enterprises, Gama went but weake at first, lost most of his small fleete, and mett nothing at Sea but Tempest and famine. Drake invaded vppon opportunities, hazarded but his owne fortune and retired to sea vppon all advantages Gama had in Charge an expedition of his soveraignes commaundmen^t, was constrained to victuall himselfe amongst barbarous nations, and not only to buy provision in their continent land, wth the price of his, blood, but Durst not depart wthout leaving his king proclaimed and possessed in their territories Diverse places of strength established and fortified to his vse, soe that yf Gama had beene to peruse the example of Drake, as Drake had the light of Columbus and Magellus travailes. Vastus Gamaes spiritt was as likely to haue conquered the Whole World as Drakes fortune was to Compasse it. (f. 11)

There is an interesting comment on foreign travel which may partially explain why he did not participate in the pastime that was such a favorite occupation of his friends:

... travaile in forraine countreyes, setleth a young mans humors, yf it bee taken in this sort that it will inforce him to warinesse, and secrecy and restraine him from powring forth his counsailes it is very profitable, for hee shall haue few freinds to putt confidence in, and few companions to pratle [wth] vppon whome hee might bestowe his idle time, or idle thoughts, but yf you intend that by travailing all vanities should bee taken away, it seemes not soe likely and admittable, because hee shall walke through many ill examples, and great libertie (ff. 24-24v)

And there is also the charming quality of his manner of slipping in advice to his young friend under color of rhetorical forms:

It is lamentable y^t a young man should bee offended wth the advise of his experienced freind tending to his profitt. First it is a hard case that counsaile should bee neglected but harder that it should offend, it is woefull to see any man displeased wth good admonitions, but more woefull to see a youth soe affected. who would not greiue to haue his advice ill taken but who would not greiue to see his owne experience controlld. vnhappy is that youth that listens not to good exhortacons of his skilfull freinds hee is miserable and vnfortunate that quarrells wth the sound p^{r}cepts of his Discreet freinds, but more miserable and vnfortunate that mislikes dirreccions given for his owne good advantage. (f. 15v)

... you must bee content, Nay you must bee Desirous to take paines yf, you will write well, it is the only qualitie, wch in all actions in yor shire will winn you praise. praise (quoth I) nay honno^r and admiracion. (f. 16v)

... I vrge not to you the hope of yor freinds though that should animate you to answer their expectation I lay not before you the necessitie of the place wch you are to furnish, wherin to bee defectiue & insufficient were some shame. I omitt then envious concurrencies and some prepared Comparisons in yor Countrey wch haue some feeling wth young men of foresight. I only say how shall our owne promises giue iudgem^t against vs, how shall wee discharge o^r owne ingagem^t to yor father, yf this time hath not taken full effect and profitt in o^r labo^{rs} and endeavo^{rs} (ff. 17-17v)

The core of the entire work is a series of analyses of Sir Philip Sidney's Arcadia, which Hoskyns generally praises but sometimes criticizes for weaknesses. Sidney is not the only figure from Hoskyns'

early poetry that plays an important role in the
Directions, however. Lipsius is perhaps Hoskyns'
most direct source for much of his discussion, although it must be admitted that Hoskyns is more dependent on this rhetorician than he acknowledges in
the text. Cicero, naturally enough, is the most
quoted authority, but Hoskyns does not adopt a slavish attitude towards the man he refers to as "The
Philosopher." He reserves his highest praise for
Aristotle:

> The perfect expressing of all qualities is
> learned out of Aristotles tenn bookes of morall
> Phylosophy, but because (as Machiavill saith)
> perfect virtue or perfect vice is not seene in
> our time wch altogether is humerous and spirtinge
> therfore the vnderstanding of Aristotles Rheto-
> ricke is the directest meanes, of skill to de-
> scripe to moue to appease to p^{r}vent, any motion
> whatsoever, whervnto whosoever can fitt his
> speech shall be truely eloquent. (f. 23)

He is remarkably free from sticking to any one
set approach to style, and in his own prose style
he moves with considerable freedom from parallel
constructions in the classical mode, to asymmetri-
cal, hovering progression of clauses and phrases,
to what can only be considered forerunners of the
linked, wandering constructions of the loose style.
The Directions is, therefore, not only a first-rate
description of the writing styles of the period; it
is itself an example of the varying styles under
discussion.

The headpiece describes accurately the main
intent of the work:

Directions of Speeche & Stile[6]

Of the meanes to.
{
Penn letters
Vary
Amplifie
Illustrate.
}
otherwise then ever
any p^{r}cepts haue.
taught.

147

<u>Conteininge</u> all the figures of Rhetoricke,
and the art of the best English. Exemplified
either all out of Arcadia. wch it censureth
or by instances, the matter whereof may
benefitt Conversation. (f.1)

The Dedication contains one of the best statements
ever penned on the importance of good written or
oral expression:

To the forwardnesse of many virtuous
hopes in A Gent. of the Temple, by
the author./

The Conceipts of the mind are pictures of things,
and the tounge is interp^rter of those pictures;
The order of Gods creatures in themselues, is
not only admirable and glorious, but eloquent;
then hee that could ap^rhend the consequence of
things in their truth, and vtter his app^rhen-
sions as trewly, were a right Orator. Therefore
Cicero said much when hee said, Dicere recte
nemo potest, nisi qui prudenter intelligit. The
shame of speaking vnskillfully were small, yf
the tounge thereby were only disgraced. but (as
the Image of the Kinge in a seale of waxe ill-
rep^rsented is not soe much a blemish to the waxe,
o^r the signet that sealeth it, as to the King
whome it resembleth) soe disordered speech is
not soe much iniury to the lipps which giue it
forth, or the thoughts which putt it forth, as
to the right proportion and coherence of things
in themselues, soe wrongfully expressed; yet cannot his mind bee, thougt in time whose words doe
iarr, no^r his reason in frame whose sentences
are p^rposterous, no^r his fancy cleare and <u>perfect</u>
whose vtterance breakes it selfe into fragments
and vn<u>cert</u>ainties. we<u>r</u>e it an hono^r to a mightie
Prince to haue the Matie of his Embassage spoyl-
ed by a carelesse Embassador: and is it not as
great indignitie, y^t an excellent conceipt, and
Capacitie, (by the indilligence of an idle
tounge) should bee defaced? Carelesse speech
doth not only discreditt the person^age of the
speaker, but it doth discreditt the opinion of

148

his reason and iudgm^t: it discrediteth the truth, force, and vniformitie of the matter & substance. Yf it bee soe then in words, which fly and escape censure, and where one good phrase beggs pardon for many incongruities and faχlts, how shall hee bee thought wise, whose penning is thinn and shallow? how shall you looke for witt from him whose leasure, and whose head assisted wth the examinacion of his eyes could yeild you noe life and sharpenesse in his writing? (f. 2)

The opening section on letter writing is divided into two parts on Invention and Fashion.

Fo^r the Invention, that ariseth vppon yor buissinesse, whereof there can bee noe rules of more certaintie, or p^{r}cepts of better direccon given, then Coniecture can lay downe of all the severall occasions of all mens particular liues and vocations....

When you haue invented (yf yor buissinesse bee matter and not bare forme, not meere ceremonies but some earnestnesse) then are you to proceede to the ordering of it and the disgestion of the parts, wch is sought out of Circumstances. one is the vnderstanding of the person to whome you write; the other is the coherence of the sentences... Fo^r the consequence of the sentencs you must see that every clause doth as it were giue ye Q. to the other and bee, (as it were) bee spoken, before it come. (f. 3)

Fashion is covered under four subheadings: brevity, perspicuity, plainness, and respect. As for brevity,

letters must not bee treatises, or discourses except it bee amongst learned men, and [eaven] amongst them there is a kind of thrift o^r saving of words. therefore are you to examine the clearest passages of yor vnderstanding, and through them to convey yor sweetest, and most significant English words that you can devise, that you may the easier teach them the readiest way to another mans conceipt... (yf you write to

149

a man whose estate and sences you are familiar
w^th, you may bee the bolder to sett a taske to
his braine; If to yor superior you are bound in
him to measure three further points. Yo^r interest in him his capacitie of yor letters, and his
leasure to p_ervse them... Brevitie is attained
by the matter in avoiding idle complem^ts, p^r-
faces, p_rotestacions, parenthesis, superfluos
and wanton circuits of figures and digressions.
By the Composition in omitting coniunctions,
both the one and the other; not only but also,
whereby it commeth to passe, and such idle par-
ticles that haue noe great buissinesse in a serious letter. By breaking of sentences; as oftentimes a long iourney is made shorter by many
baits: but as Quintillian saith there is a
breifnesse of parts sometimes that make the
whole longe... this is the fault of some latin
writers within this last hundred yeares of my
reading and p_erhapps Seneca may be appeached of
if I accuse him not. (ff. 3-4)^7

Perspicuity is achieved by careful writing:

Perspicuitie... is oftentimes indangered by the
former qualitie (brevitie), oftentimes by affectation of some witt ill angled for, or osten-
tation of some hidden termes of arte; few words
they darken the speech and soe doe too many, as-
well too much light hurts the eyes as too litle,
and a long bill of Chauncery Confounds the
vnderstanding asmuch as the shortest noate...^8
first minde it well, then pen it, then examine
it, then amend it and you may bee in ye better
hope of doing reasonable well.... (f. 4)

The rule for Plainness is

not to bee curious in the order... But both in
methode and words to vse (as Ladies doe in their
attire) a kind of dillig^t negligence: and though
wth some men you are not to ieast o^r practise
trickes; yet the delivery of most weightie and
important things may bee carryed w^ith such a
grace, as that it may yeild a pleasure to the

150

conceipt of the reader. There must bee store
(though not excesse) of termes, as yf you are to
name store, Sometimes you may call it choise,
sometimes plentie, sometimes copiousnesse or
varietie, and soe that the worde which comes in
liewe, haue not such difference of meaninge as
that it may put the sence in hazard to bee mistaken. (f. 4)[9]

Respect is the ability

to Discerne what fitts yor selfe him to whome
you write, and that wch you handle... and that
must proceed from ripenesse of iudgement w^{ch}
(as an author truely saith)[10] is given by fowre
meanes God, Nature, Dilligence, and conversa-
cion. Serue the first well and the rest will
serue you. (f. 4v)

The section on Varying takes up ten folio
pages and contains a full list of rhetorical phrases
or figures of speech. It is in this description of
rhetorical devices that Hoskyns uses Sir Philip
Sidney's Arcadia as his main source, quoting from
it over fifty times.
1. Metaphor. "A Metaphore or translation is the
freindly and neighbourly borrowing of one worde to
expresse a thinge, wth more light, and better noate
though not soe directly and properly...." (f. 5)
2. Allegory. "...the continuall following of a
Metaphore... throug the sentence o^r through many
sentences."

...to delight Generally take those termes from
ingenuous and severall professions from ingenious arts to please the learned of all sorts,
as from the Meteors, Planetts, and beasts in
naturall Phylosophy. from the Starrs, Spheres,
and their motions in Astronomie; from the better
part of husbandry, from the politique governm^t
of Citties, from Navigation, from Militarye profession, from Physicke, but not out of the depth
of theis misteries;[11] But ever (vnlesse yor purpose bee to disgrace) let the worde bee taken
from a thinge of equall or greater dignitie.(f.5v)

151

3. Emblem.

An <u>Embleme</u>, an Allegory, a Similitude, a fable,
and a Poetts tale differ thus. An Embleme is
but ye one part of the similitude, the other
part (viz) the aplicacion expressed indifferently
and iointly in one Sentence wth words some proper
to the one part, some to the other; A Similitude
hath two sentences of severall proper termes Compared. A fable is a similitude acted by fiction
in beasts A Poetts tale for the most part by
Gods and men. (f. 6)

4. Metonomy.

...an exchange of a name when one word comes in
liewe of another, not fo^r Similitude but fo^r
other naturall affinitie and Coherence. As when
the matter is vsed for that wch therof Consist-
eth As. I want silver, fo^r money. When the
Efficient o^r author is vsed fo^r the thinge made.
As my blade is a right Sebastian fo^r of Sebas-
tians making. The thinge conteyning fo^r the
thing o^r person conteined, as the Cittie mett
the Queene fo^r the Citizens. The Adiunct, pro-
pertie, qualitie, o^r badge fo^r the Subiect of it,
as Deserts are p^{r}ferrd, fo^r men deserving; Giue
roome to ye quoife fo^r the S^{r}iant.[12] (ff. 6-6v)

5. Synechdoche. "...an exchange of the name of
the parte fo^r the whole o^r the whole for the part."
(f. 6v)
6. Catachresis.

<u>Catachresis</u> in English abuse is now growne in
fashion as most abuses are; it is somewhat more
desperate then a Metaphore. It is the expressing of one matter by the name of another wch is
incompatible wth it and sometimes cleane contrary... This is an vsuall figure wth the fine
Conversants of our time when they straine for an
extraordinary phrase, as, I am not guiltie of
theise phrases. I am in danger of p^{r}ferrm^t I
haue hardly escaped good fortune. (ff. 6v-7)

152

7. Epizeuxis.

The eares of men are not only pleased wth store
and exchange of words, but feele great delight
in repetition of the same wch because at the
beginning, in the midle, and in the ende and in
sundry correspondencies of each of theise places
it happeneth. therfore it hath purchased severall
names of figures. As, a repetition of the same
word o^r sound immediatly o^r wthout interposition
of any other is called Epizeuxis... this figure
is not to bee vsed but in passion. (f. 7)

8. Anadiplosis. "a repetition in the ende of the
former sentence, and beginning of the next. As.
Shall Erona dye. [Erona dye?] oh heaven &c." (f.7)
9. Climax. "a kind of Anadiplosis, leading by
degrees and making the last worde, a stepp to a
further meaning. Yf it bee turned to an argum^t it is
a Sorites. A young man of great beautie, beautified
wth great hono^r honored by great valour... This in
pennd speech is too Academicall but in discourse
more passible and plausible." (ff. 7-7v)
10. Anaphora. "...when many clauses haue the like
beginning... This figure beats vppon one thinge, to
Cause the quicker feeling thereof in the audience
and to awake a sleepy o^r dull person." (f. 7v)
11. Epistrophe. "...contrary to the former, when
many clauses ende wth the same words... This rather
is a figure of Narration o^r instruction then of
motion." (f. 7v)
12. Symploce or Complexio. "...when seuerall
sentences haue the same beginning and the same ending... This is the wantonest of repetitions, and is
not to bee vsed in matters too serious, You haue an
example of it in the fustian Speech about Tobacco."[13]
(ff. 7v-8)
13. Epanalepsis.

...the Same in one Sentence wch Symploce or Complexio is in severall sentences As, severe to
his servuants, to his Children severe; o^r the
same sound reiterated first and last in a sentence as his superio^r in meat in place his inferior... This is a milde and sweet figure of

153

much vse. (f. 8)

14. Epanados. "...when the midest and the ende or
the midst and the beginninge are the same... This
kind of repetition and the former Epanalepsis, are
most easilee admitted into discourse and are freest
from the opinion of affectation, because words receaved at the beginning of many sentences, o^r at
both ends of the same are more notorious." (f. 8)
15. Antimetabole or Commutation. "...a sentence
inverst o^r turn'd backe, as yf any for loue of
honno^r o^r honno^r of loue, that as you are Childe of
a mother soe you may bee mother too a Child." (f.8)
16. Paranomasia.

...a pleasant touch of the same letter sillable
o^r worde wth a different meaning... Sr P. S. in
Astrophell and Stella calls it the Dictionary
methode, and the verses soe made rimes running
in ratling rowes, wch is an example of it. Ther
is a Swinish poeme made thereof in latine called
pugna procorum and L: Lloid in his youth tickled
it in fashion of a Poetts dictionary
    Hector Hamo Haniball dead, Pompey Pirrhus spild
    Cyrus Scipio Caesar slaine, and Alexander kild[14]
Not only Mr Lillye whose poesie at the beginning
of his booke was stampt wth this cognizance,
Commend it o^r amend it, but even wth Doctor Mat-
hew[15] this figure was of great accompt, and hee
lost noe estimacion by it. O^r paradice is a
payre of dice, o^r almesdeeds are turn'd into all
misdeeds, o^r praying into playing our fasting into
feastinge: but that kind of breaking words into
another meaning is prettie to play with among
Gentlewomen... See to what p^{r}ferm^t a figure may
aspire, yf it once growe in creditt in a world,
that hath not much true Rhetoricke. (ff. 8v-9)

17. Poliptoton or traduction. "...a repetition of
words of the same linnage that differ only in term-
inacion, as exceedingly, exceeding, that exceeding-
nesse... This is a good figure and may bee vsed wth
o^r without passion. but soe as the vse of it come
from some choice, and not from barrennesse." (f.9v)

154

Hoskyns introduces the remainder of the Directions by saying,

To Amplifie and Illustrate are two the Cheifest ornaments of eloquence, and gaine mens minds to two the Cheifest advantags, admiracion and beleife. For how can you commend a thinge more acceptably to our attention, then by telling vs it is extraordinary, & by shewing vs that it is evident. There is noe looking at a Comett yf it bee either litle or obscure, and wee loue and looke on the same aboue all starrs, for theise two excellencies his greatnesse, and clearenesse such in Speech is amplificacion and illustration. (f. 10)

The section on Amplification covers fifty-two folio pages and includes most of the passages that are quoted elsewhere in this book. Hoskyns used his own life and thoughts as illustrations of how to Amplify. The main methods he outlines are: "Comparison division Accumulation, intimacion, and progression." (f. 10)

Comparison is either of things contrary, equall, or things different   Equall as Themistocles and Coriolanus, both great statesmen both of great deserts to their countrey, both banished, both dead at one time... But this is not soe forcible an Amplificacion of things equall indeed... as when things seeming vnequall are compared... (f. 10) comparison of things different is most commendable where there seemes to bee great affinitie in the matter Conferd as in the King of Spaines assisting ye Irish the Queene of Englands ayding the Neitherlands. The Spanyard prpared helpes for a people vntrue, in their treatises vncivill in their manners; for them wch haue traiterously rebelled wthout provocacion, and fledd out contrary to their owne submission, broake their owne peace and wasted their owne Countrey. The Queene did but lend some few Voluntaries to the protecion of a nation, peaceable in their liues, free by their priviledges a people denying noe claime of any true Prince, ex-

155

cept perpetuall servitude in their bodyes and importable exaccions in their goods... (f. 11v) Comparison of Contraryes is the third way and most flourishing way of Comparison. (f. 12)

He introduces his example of the Davies-Martin feud by saying: "There is another way of ordering them wth interchangable Correspondencies in sentences, that though each touch not the other, yet each affronts the other." (f. 12)

The second way of Amplificacion is Division wch Bacon in his fift Colonye tooke out of ye Rhetoricians... (f. 12v) The Third kinde of Amplificacion is Accumulation wch is an heaping vpp of many termes of praise or accusation importing but the same matter without Descending to any part, and hath his due season after some argum^t o^r proofe, otherwise it is like a schoolem^r. foaming out synonomaes o^r words of one meaninge and will sooner yeild a Coniecture of superfluitie of words then of sufficiencie of Matter... (f. 13v) The fowrth Way of Amplifying is by Intimacion that leaues the Collection of greatnesse to o^r vnderstanding by expressing some marke of it. it exceedeth speech in silence, and makes o^r meaning more palpable by a touch then by a direct handling. As. hee that should say you must liue many yeares in his Company whome you shall account fo^r yor freind, saith well, but, hee that saith you had neede eate a bushell of Salt wth him saith more and giues you to reckon more then many yeares.., (f. 14) This fashion of Amplificacon I terme Intimacion, because it doth not directly agravate but by Consequence and proportion and intimateth more to yor mind then too yor eares. (f. 14v)

The last method is Progression, "wch by stepps of Comparison scornes every degree till it come to the topp and to make the matter seeme the higher advaunced sometimes descends the lower." (f. 14v) His chief example is Hatton's funeral.

This is a most easie, cleare, and vsuall kind

of Amplificacion, for it guies more light and
force out of ever Circumstance   The Circumstances are theise. The persons who and to
whome, the matter, the intent, the time, the
place, the manner, the consequences, and many
more, out of every one of wch any thinge may bee
made more notable, and egregious by way of Comparison. And because I would leaue it fresh in
yor memory, lett this bee yor last charge to enquire in every Controversie for theise Circumstan-
ces and compare them wth other lesse matters,and
you shall hardly faile of Discourse o^r bee left
on ground for want of good invention. (f. 15v)

   Hoskyns then moves to a long discussion of
"Figures serving fo^r Amplificacion." He begins with
Hyperbole: "Sometimes it expresseth a thinge in the
highest degree of possibilitie beiond the truth that
it Descending thence may find the truth. Sometimes
in flatt impossibilitie that rather you may conceaue
the vnspeakablenesse then the vntruth of the relation... this figure is more creditt to yor witt
then too yor speech." (ff. 16-16v) Correctio is a
figure in which "Having vsed a word of sufficient
force yet p^rtending a greater vehemencie of meaning refuseth it and supplies the place wth a greater... This figure is to bee vsed when you would
make the thinge more credible it selfe then in the
manner of yor vtterance. It is sometimes vsed vppon passion wth an intent to Amplifie." (f. 16v)
Irony "expresseth a thinge by Contrary by shew of
exhortacion when indeed it dehorteth... Milo had
but a slender strength that caried an oxe a fur-
longe on his backe, and then kild him wth his fist
and eate him to his breakefast." (ff. 16v-17)
Paralepsis "is when you say you lett passe that
which notwthstanding you touch at full." (f. 17)
John's example is his own preparation of the Directions: "I value not my paynes in Collecting theise
observacions." (f. 17) He then describes two figures to which he does not attach names: "The first
is a round dispatching of much disiointed matter
not plainly and simply the same in sence yet tending to the same ende." The second "is a wild and
Dissolute repetition of all that went before...

157

theise two figures doe not only make your cause
seeme better but skilfully and fitly vsed doe amaze
and adversary of meane conceipt." (f. 17v)

Interrogation "is but a warme proposition, and
therefore oftentimes serues more fitly then a bare
affirmation, wch were but too gentle and harmelesse
a speech... It is very fitt for a speech to many
and vndiscreet hearers..." (ff. 17v-18)

Shall hee bee a bad husband who having all his
wealth abroad in stockes doth not oftentimes
survey it? and shall hee bee a discreet gent
whose creditt consisting in acquaintance, doth
not often visitt them, since they accompt it
their honno^{rs} to bee visited? I could heere
write a whole life of Interrogatories. but lett
it suffice that it is easie and sweet to re-
create the flatt stile of affirmations to a
downeright telling of tales. (f. 18v)
    Exclamation is not lawfull but in extremitie
of motion... in my booke of Charitie and resignation in the Chapter; that the truest mor-
tificacion is ye studdy of Cosmographye. Oh
endlesse endeavo^{rs} and vainglorious ignorance!
Dost thou desire to bee knowne? Where? In Europe
how canst thou bee famous, when Asia and Affrica
that haue thrice as many people heere not of thy
actions; art not thou then thrice as obscure as
thou art renowned? Dost thou looke that all the
World should take notice of thee, when for 5
thousand yeeres theise three parts of the World
tooke noe notice of the fourth? But Europe is
the house of fame because it is the nursery of
arts and bookes wherin reports are p^{r}serued Oh
Weake Imagination! oh selfe pleasing fancie!
canst thou expect in theise parts from 40 degrees
to 90 Northwards such praises and honno^{rs} for
thy name, when every mapp on every wall shewes
the as much space from 40 to 90^{tie} Southwards
inhabited wth nothing but silence and forgetful-
nesse. (f. 18v)
    Acclamation. is a sententious clause of a
discourse or report, such as Daniell in his

poemes concludes wth perpetually... Such notes
are theise scrapps of pollicie wch men now a
dayes gather out of Polybius and Tacitus, and
not vnlike are theise moralls that hang vppon
AEsopps fables... Yet yf this bee too much vsed,
it is like a noate booke gathered out of Histories.
Contrary to Amplificacion is Diminution and
descends by the same stepps that Amplificacion
ascends by and differs noe otherwise then vphill
and downe hill which is the same way begunn at
severall times. (ff. 18v-19v)

Next Hoskyns moves to figures of speech that
aid in Amplification and once more gives many examples from Sidney's Arcadia. Indeed, he will make
specific references to that work over 80 times in
the remaining pages of the Directions.

Synoikeiosis is a Composition of contraries
and by both words intimateth the meaning of
neither p^rcisely but a moderation and medioc-
ritie of both as brauery and raggs are contrary
yet somewhat better then both is meant by braue
raggednesse... This is a fine Course to stirr
admonition in the hearers and make them thinke
it a strange harmony wch must bee exprest in
such discords... Contentio is contrary to the
former. That was a Composition of termes dis-
agreeing. this is an opposition of them... Hee
is a swaggerer amongst quiet men but a quiet
man amongst swaggerers, earnest in idle things
idle in matters of earnestnesse... indeed it is
a figure fitt to sett forth a Copious stile...
Compar. is an even gate of sentences, annswering
each other in measures interchangeably. Such as
is in St Augustine but oftener in Gregory the
divine, such as are in the byshopp of W.[16] in
his bookes wch hee hath written in English, and
many places of Euphues, but that Austine Bilson
and Lillie doe very much mingle this figure wth
Agnominatio, and similiter cadens. it is a smoth
and memorable stile for vtterance, but in penning it must bee vsed modestly and moderately...
my yeares are not soe many but that one death

159

may conclude them, nor my faults soe many but that
one death may satisfie them... This is an excellent figure in noe place vntimely, yf not too
often. it fitts well the even pauses and inter-
p^{r}tac_ions of an eloquent tounge seemes to bee
rich and wise and Conteines many parts wherof
each wth a tedious man would make a sentence
sticke in the hearers sences thereof. I called
it smooth and memorable, it hath beene in request ever since the dayes of Isacrates whose
orations are full of them. (ff. 19v-21)

Next Hoskyns deals with Sententia, giving examples
we have already quoted earlier in the chapter. He
ends with a strong admonition to the reader:

    Theise examples may make you beleiue that a
sentence may bee courst through the whole figure booke, and it shall appeare in a sett treatise, that many figures may easilie assemble in
one clause and any figure may consort wth any.
a slender reason to ground vppon any one figure
the frame and fashion of yor whole stile. In
o^r profession there are not many (yf two were
many) whose speeches rely vppon this figure, and
in my iudgm^t sententia is better for the bench
then the barr. Then (of all others) why would
the writers of theise dayes imprison themselues
in the straightnesse of theise maximes. it
makes their stile like arena sine calce as one
saith of such a writer; and doth not hee vouch-
safe to vse them that called them poesies for
rings. Yf it bee in matter of short direccion
for life and accion or notes for memorye I intend not to discredit this new tricke. but
otherwise hee that hath a long iourney to walke
in that pace is like a horse that overreacheth
and yet goes slowe. St Ambrose sanctifies this
figure. (f. 22)

    The final twelve folio pages contain a dis-
cussion of Illustration: "Illustracion consists
in things o^r words. In the description of things
living or dead, of things living, either reaso^{ble}
as of men and of personages and of qualities of
    ^

vnreasonable as of horses shipps Ilands Castles &c."
(f. 23) His examples are still largely from Arcadia.
He introduces other figures of speech and sprinkles
pieces of advice among them:

> There are other sparkes of figures, first yf
> there bee any doubt o^r ambiguitie in the words
> it is better left out then distinguished. but
> yf you are to annswer any former speeches, you
> may disperse all clouds and remoue all scruples
> wth Distinction... But as Ambiguitie is not only
> in words but in matter, soe both waies it is
> taken away by Distinction... Distinction of Am-
> biguitie in matter is a Determinacion of the
> truth of generall propositions to tell wherin
> they are certaine wherein they are not. (f. 24)

as in his discussion of foreign travel.

> Next. followes Definition wch is the shortest
> and truest exposicion of ye nature of any thinge;
> heeof you haue examples of virtues and vice in
> Aristotles moralls, of passions in his Rheto-
> ricke... Of seven or eight wayes of deffinition
> you may reade Valerius Logicke, but to bee most
> perfectly instructed reade the sixt booke of
> Aristotles Top:... Sometimes Parenthesis makes
> yor discourse faire and more sensible..

but

> all Parenthesis are in extremities either gracs
> o^r disgraces to a speech. Yf they bee long they
> seeme interruptions.... (ff. 24v-25)

> Division is a severing of the whole into parts
> as of time into that past p^rsent and to come...
> Out of Division arise three severall inforcem^ts
> and manifestacions of yor purpose, w^ch (though
> they are by Rhetoricians Diversly termed, yet)
> are in effect grounded vppon one art of distri-
> bution

> The first is expedition, w^ch (reckoning vppon
> diverse parts) destroyes all but that one w^ch

161

you meane to rest vppon...

The second of this sort is Prosopoesis, that overthrowth noe part of the division but return-eth some reason to each member... The last is Dilemma wch proposeth two sides and overthrowes both. You must haue both abilitie and will to write well for to say I cannot is childish, and to say I will not is Womanish. (ff. 25-26)

Then he moves to the double subject of Peri-phrasis and Paraphrasis:

There is in the best writers sometime a vaine of speech wherin the Vulgar conceipts are exceed-ingly pleased, for they admire this most that there is some excellencye in it, and yet they themselues suspect that it excells their admira-cion... What plainer meaning then, Sleepe a-mongst theeues and verely sleepe, life, trust, and theifes, are common english words, yet it is not common fashion of speech to say trust a sleeping life, amongst theiues: in the same sence when they had slept a while is ordinary; but when they had awhile hearkned to the per-suasion of sleepe is extraordinary. though all the words of it by themselues are most knowne and familiar, yet the bringing in and fetch of it is strange and admirable to the ignorant wee therfore call it a Periphrasis or Circumlocution and it is much helped by metaphors... Yf a short ordinary sence bee odly exprest by more words it is (periphrasis) but yf by as many other, it is Paraphrasis... fo^r kill any maried man make his sword accursed by any Widdowe.... (ff. 26-26v)

Apostrophe is a turning of yor speech to some new person, as to the people when yor speech be-fore was to the iudge to the Defendant to the adversary to ye witnesses... But to animate and giue life is Prosopopoeia as to make dead men speake, as yf yor auncestors were now aliue, and saw you defacing soe goodly a principallitie by them established would they not say.... (f. 27)

162

The Directions ends with a short treatment of
Occupatio and subiectio, neither of which he defines;
he simply gives examples, including a general reference to his fustian speech. His final statement
gives evidence that he was tiring of his work:

There is another figure that hath been called
by the name of Concessio but I meane to mistake
Occupatio and Concessio one for another till I
know them better The forme of Concessio is this.
I admitt you are resolute I grant yor determina-
cion is [im]moueable, but [it] is in things a-
gainst yor freinds iudgm^t, and things against
yor owne praise and profitt (ff. 28-28v)

It is no wonder that his attention to detail
was flagging. He had worked hard and diligently at
this long work that was not intended for publication
but was certainly written with an eye to his friends
and associates. Its continued influence during the
next century more than justified his effort.

Chapter V Footnotes

1. HMC, Duke of Portland, at Welbeck Abbey, Vol.
   III, 14th Rept. App., Pt. II (1894), p. 6. For
   the rest of the letter, see Chapter 10.
2. Bacon, Works, III, 409.
3. Prof. Croll's article is reprinted in its entirety in Witherspoon and Warnke, Seventeenth
   Century Prose and Poetry (2nd ed., 1963), pp.
   1065-77.
4. See Baird W. Whitlock, "The Counter-Renaissance,"
   Bibliothèque d'Humanisme et Renaissance, February 1958, and "From the Counter-Renaissance
   to the Baroque," Bucknell Review, Vol. XV, No.1,
   March 1967.
5. Besides those already mentioned, such as the
   speech on Chancellor Hatton and the Fustian Oration, he mentions works that we can well wish
   we still had: a book on Charity and resignation (f. 18) and a speech of a widow (f. 10).
   These, along with the Greek lexicon, the anthem
   written for Hereford Cathedral, a latin poem in
   praise of ale, and an autobiography written
   after 1623, all appear to have been lost per-
   manently.
6. MSS. Add. 15,230, purchased of Thomas Rodd 19
   June 1844. Bright's Sale Lot 217. There have
   been two printed versions of the Directions, by
   Hudson in 1935 and by Osborn in 1937. Neither
   of these writers was aware of another major
   manuscript in the British Museum which appears
   to antedate both of their versions. It is more
   complete and more accurate than either of the
   other two, as evidenced by the fact that most
   of the words that Prof. Hudson had to supply
   for continuity of sense occur in this manuscript, MSS. Add. 15,230. Although it would
   seem clear from faults in the manuscript that
   this is not the original, it is interesting
   that the signature on the dedicatory epistle,
   one of the best concise statements on style
   ever penned, is so much like that of Hoskyns
   himself that if he did not write it, the scribe
   made a conscious attempt to imitate the original. Where a word or a phrase is missing that

can be supplied from one of the other manuscripts, I have supplied it in brackets. I have not attempted to collate the various mss. or editions. Osborn used Harley 4604 and noted the incomplete version in Harley 850. She also collated differences in the version found in MS. Ash. Mus. d.1. It is worth noting that this ms. does not include "Pronounce" among the list of activities to be described as it does in Osborn's version. There is, of course, no attempt anywhere in the Directions to deal with Pronunciation. A later copyist (Osborn's version is from a 1680 source) apparently thought such a manual would naturally deal with the subject.

7. Hoskyns here shows both his appreciation of the values of the Curt Style which was gaining in popularity and of its weaknesses. The fact that he ties his example to Seneca indicates his awareness of the popular (and still current) judgement that Seneca was the model for such writing. As a genuine classicist, however, he realized that the attribution was unfair to Seneca as a stylist.

8. This is such a superb example of the Curt Style that it is unfortunate that Prof. Croll did not know of it to include in his article.

9. Some critics of prose style claim that the use of "copia" went out with the advent of the Curt Style. Hoskyns shows clearly that this was not the case. It just appeared in a slightly different guise.

10. Angel Day, in The English Secretarie (1586), noted that three things were to be observed in Epistles: "Aptness of wordes and sentences respecting that they be neat and choicely picked, orderly laid down & cunningly handled," next "brevity of speech according in matter," lastly "comeliness in deliverance." Hoskyns is probably referring to Day in this passage.

11. This passage is a valuable antidote to those critics who claim for Donne the individuality of his use of metaphors from just such fields as Hoskyns lists as proper for any writer. Ben Jonson also felt that Donne erred in going too

far into the "depth of these misteries" in his
love poems.

12. One wonders if Hoskyns remembered this sentence
in 1623 when he was created Serjeant-at-Law.

13. Osborn has the additional words "in derision
of vayne Rhetoricke." This would appear to be
a later addition explaining what would have been
an obvious reference to Hoskyns' acquaintances.

14. Hudson discovered the quotation in Lodowick
Lloyd's "An Epitaph vpon the death of Syr Edward Saunders" in The Paradise of Daintie De-
vises. Lloyd was a well-known figure around
the Elizabethan court and referred to himself
as the Queen's Serjeant-at-Arms. He is perhaps
best known as the person who provided the debt-
ridden Edmund Spenser with an elegant funeral.
(D.N.B.)

15. Tobie Matthew, who was born in Herefordshire.
As we have seen, his son was the close friend
of Donne and Henry Goodyer as well as of Sir
Francis Bacon.

16. Thomas Bilson, author of The True Difference
Betweene Christian Subiection and Vnchristian
Rebellion (1586), was well known to Hoskyns
both as an author and preacher. He had been
Warden of Winchester College during John's days
there.

Chapter VI
Marriage and Hereford City

While Hoskyns was gaining his education and legal training, his major interests obviously had to lie in the towns and cities where he was living. As soon as he became a barrister, however, he showed how intense his love and attachment to his home shire were. For the rest of his life, no matter how involved he might be in business in London, much of his attention was focused on his family and property in Herefordshire. He seems never to have made any attempt to set up more than bachelor quarters in the city where he and his sons who were studying at the Middle Temple lived.[1] It is true that until 1618, his brother Oswald was living in London and provided a residence for any of John's family while they were in the city. Oswald Hoskyns was a very successful merchant tailor with a large family, all of whom came under John's care and guidance after Oswald's death. But even after that death occurred, John moved most of this brother's family back to Hereford as soon as possible and placed them on his various land holdings. Never did he attempt to be known as a resident of the metropolis but took special pride in his role as a citizen of Hereford. There is every indication that whenever his duties in London allowed, he left for his home in the west.

We do not know what his activities were during the year following his call to the bar, although he maintained a close connection with his friend Francis Bourne and the Bourne family, which was soon to become his own. Like many other young barristers, John missed the Readings immediately following his own call. On 24 October 1600, he was fined along with such friends as Francis Bourne and John Chapman for missing Nicholas Overbury's Reading, at which his other friends James Whitelocke and Benjamin Rudyard were called to the bar.[2] Indeed, Hoskyns was so careless of the fine of 20s that he missed all six of the required readings

167

after his call, as did Chapman and Rudyard.[3] The
only activity in which we know he took part at the
Temple during these two years was religious in nature. On 18 June 1602 the governing body of the
Temple ruled that

> Every Utter Barrister, or other fellow of this
> House, lying within the House or in the Parson's
> Buildings, or being in commons at any time with-
> in the year, shall receive the communion in the
> Temple Church once a year at least, on pain of
> 40s. fine or loss of his chamber. If the of-
> fence be repeated two years, he shall be expel-
> led the House and Fellowship.[4]

Lack of conformity in religion, however, was one
problem from which Hoskyns never suffered. It is
unlikely that he was much bothered by some of the
other regulations passed during this period either,
such as the fact that no hawks were to be kept in
the house or that no one was to eat oysters in the
Hall. Nor was anyone allowed to wear a beard above
three weeks. Strong feelings against the Irish
were still running high as well: "Non Irishe men
shalbe admytted."[5]

The usual reason for barrister's missing the
readings was that they were busy at their own practices or personal business. As we have noted, the
Assizes in Hereford coincided with the Readings in
London, and John needed the income from the legal
practice he was now able to undertake. But during
1601 Hoskyns also had very important personal business to attend to. Some time early in the year his
close friend Francis Bourne fell very sick. He
died in February after writing out his will on the
11th, "being of perfect memorie thoughe sicke in
bodie," and was buried in the church at Bath on
the 24th.[6] Bourne was apparently aware of his own
critical condition, as were his friends, for the
will ends: "This will was made by the abouewritten
Frannces Bourne and written by me Richard Meredeth
Parson of the Parrishe in great haste..."[7] Although Bourne was married to a very competent woman, there was need for haste and for help, for

168

Benedicta Bourne was not only the mother of two
small children; she was carrying a third still unborn. It is no wonder that she put a great deal of
trust in her husband's friend, John Hoskyns.

Benedicta Bourne was the daughter of Robert
Moyle of Buckwell, Kent, and brought with her as
her marriage dowry the manor of Dover Court in
Essex.[8] In 1621 she still had two sisters and one
brother living in Kent. She also seems to have had
a sister, Elizabeth Kempe, who lived with her and
her new husband when Mr. Kempe died. Benedicta's
family was well-to-do when she married Francis
Bourne, and she became even wealthier by that marriage. Bourne left her almost all of his estate
for her use during her lifetime. It was then to
descend to his male children.

His will is detailed in its bequests in spite
of the haste in its execution. The Manor of Sutton
Saint Cleares was given to her, as well as all of
Bourne's other lands "in Bristowe ⟨ Samforde or els
where... for tearme of her life." From later letters we know they included property in Churchill
and Banwell in Somerset. They were then to revert
to his son Walter for the rest of his life. He
left £100 in security for his daughter Frances, to
be paid to her on her seventeenth birthday or her
day of marriage, whichever came first. He did the
same for his posthumous child "yf yt please god the
childe my wife goes withall be daughter," which it
was. Elizabeth Bourne was christened at Bath on 15
March 1601.[9] If it were a boy, he was to have the
reversion of Baintons Tenement in Long Sutton after
the death of his mother. He then named his son
Robert as the inheritor of thirty pounds a year
from the Parsonage at Dover Court in Essex, the
deeds of which were in his study at the Middle Temple. This entry causes a bit of trouble. There is
no further evidence of a son Robert, but Benedicta
brought with her to her new husband a son, John
Bourne. It can only be assumed that this is the
same child with the full name of John Robert Bourne.
Benedicta was to be the sole executrix if she lived
forty days after her husband's death. He then lis-

169

ted all of the places where property belonging to him was located, such as furnishings and books in his chamber at the Middle Temple, a pair of virginals in Norton, two instruments of music at Mr. Denman's in the parish of Little Saint Bartholomew in London, etc.

All of Bourne's possessions became part of the Hoskyns' estate in the following months and years. Francis' eldest son, Walter, was buried next to him in the Abbey Church of SS. Peter and Paul less than two months later, on 17 April.[10] His daughter Frances married Dr. John, the brother of her own step-father. His son John was brought up and watched over by the same step-father until the young man's death in 1627. The still unborn Elizabeth became the manager of her step-father's home when her mother died and then married her step-cousin, William, son of Oswald Hoskyns. Although Hoskyns is not mentioned in the will, it is not stretching the imagination too far to suppose that Francis asked his close friend of the Middle Temple to look after his family; and if that is the case, never has a friend followed out such a request more fully. He adopted the family quite literally lock, stock, and barrel, and he treated them all with love, affection, and care for the rest of their lives. There is no indication that he ever showed his own children more consideration than he did those he gained by marriage.

With the wooing of Benedicta Bourne and the activities connected with his marriage, it is not surprising that he found other activities more improtant than the Readings at the Middle Temple. Francis Bourne's will was probated on 9 May 1601, and less than three months later, on 1 August, John Hoskyns and Benedicta Bourne were married in the same church in which Francis was buried.[11] Lest one too easily think of Hamlet's charge that the marriage feast followed too quickly upon the funeral ceremony, it is important to remember that in Elizabethan times it was a regular custom for women to remarry soon after the death of husbands. The legal position of women was nothing like the situation today, and there were always plenty of people ready to take advantage of an unmarried woman. As

170

a holder of property which was subject to many legal entanglements, Benedicta Bourne was showing uncommon good sense to marry a man who would not only provide a home for her small children and affection for herself, but also had a good legal mind and training to protect her holdings.

Aubrey was only really aware of one facet of this marriage relationship when he wote his biographical sketch of Hoskyns: "He maried... a rich widowe, by whome he had only one sonne and one daughter." As we noted before, Aubrey thought that this influx of wealth allowed John to enter the Middle Temple on a firm financial basis. Just the opposite is true. He had now finished his legal training and was in a good position to support a family, and there was much he could do to return the benefits which Benedicta obviously brought in a financial way.

There is no reason to consider the marriage simply one of convenience, however. Hoskyns was a fascinating and congenial fellow, noted for his wit and good humor. His wife had the same reputation, and they would seem to have made a perfect pair. It is true that he was no young man: he was already thirty-five years old, nine years older than she was. But then, at twenty-six, with three children, she was no young virginal creature either. In fact, he would outlive her by thirteen years and marry again. We know from his Directions that he knew how to speak and write in such a way as to attract and win over women of many different ages, and even if we did not have that treatise, we have his own letters to Ben, which is the pet name by which he usually addressed her, to prove the point. On 13 November of this year he wrote the first of the many letters to her which are still extant, and it shows the warmth of their relationship better than any description could possibly do.[12]

To mrs Hoskyns at her
house in Widmarshe streete
in Heref giue these
wth speed

171

midle temple
   13 Nov: 1601

    My very good m^{rs}/.
I would intreate y^u to thincke a little vpon the
solytary passions of y^r servaunt./ Yf I fynd
not my patience, to be from y^u six weeks, to
grow to greater strength hereafter I must geue
over my profession. For I sweare might I dissemble my habit I had rather be in your skullion
boys place then where I am: for soe should I be
a creature, whereas now I am but a shadow devided from myne own lyfe & essence, I am lyke
an owld pryest that commes to church to reade a
chapter and hath lefte his spectacles at home so
am I comme to behold the practise of the Law
and have lefte myne eys of my mynd in your bosom
O send me those eys that they may tell me how
little y^u remember me, how much gladder y^u are
to be kyndely intreated by som other then by my-
selfe, and how sory y^u are that my returne shall
soe soe soone interrupt y^r libertye, Let them
make relation of y^r slight regarde of my earnest
affeccion, of y^r secret smyles at my folly, y^r
setled resolution to feede me wth shows, & make
a fidlers bridge of my hart, over wch the musique
passeth to others eares, but it selfe hath neyther
sence nor share in it.
    Let those eys of my mynd wch I left wth y^u
comme and make report to me of som thinge true
or false that may be a persuasion to me that it
is in vayn for me to loue you, for till then I
shall neuer leue louinge over much, wch wilbe
but lothsom to y^u and thancklesse, troblesom to
me and endlesse.
    But o sweete troble that hast wthin these ⟨ ⟩
weekes assured me that the only ⟨ ⟩ absence is
gryef w^thout intermission ⟨ ⟩ proccedes from my
imperfeccion, for y^r ⟨ ⟩ hath taken order to the
contrary: ⟨ ⟩ hath neyther sent letter, nor message, ⟨ ⟩ geuen any demonstration of longinge
f⟨or⟩ me, wch had ben only fuell to mayntain the
passions of loue, the only wynd that would fild
the sayles of those thoughts wch might loose
themselues in an Ocean of sighs, teares, throbs,
and tempests, that poore louers endure./ but

172

y^r discretion hath forborn all such occasions, and y^r silence hath pleaded agaynst my vanity: whoe yf I be asked, why doe y^u loue her soe much I cannot say so much for myselfe as She would haue m̄e doe soe./ No No fayr, witty and worthy mistresse I haue to longe deceaued myself bycause when I was wth y^u my hart was soe fixed vpon you that I could not looke into myselfe, Now I comme to pervse my disordred study from that survey I came to behold my distempered selfe; I fynd neyther noblenes nor richesse, nor government, nor knowledge, nor eloquence, nor commelynesse nor any thinge loue worthy in me, for my welth y^u may disdayn me for my behaviour y^u may shunne me, for my witt y^u may laughe at me, for my speech y^u may reprehende me, for my letters y^u may be weary of me, and for my face y^u may most iustely hate me, and therefore I am I must be

y^r most vnworthy outcast

J:H

It is easy to see how easily the rhetorical figures described in the Directions came to Hoskyns when he wrote his own personal letters. It is also easy to see how difficult married life was for families living in the distant parts of England when the husband's business lay in London. Three months after their marriage Hoskyns was forced by his profession to be away for six weeks. It is no wonder that letter-writing became a study in itself.

As we shall be placing our main attention on the character of John Hoskyns rather than his wife, it would be well to notice the few small pieces of information about Ben that are not directly gained from him. We hear of her as a wit and sometimes even as a poet, although the latter may simply be a misunderstanding of some of the events during Hoskyns' imprisonment in 1614. From Hoskyns letters we can draw the conclusion that she had a very strong mind of her own and a genuine sense of independence, partly attributable, perhaps, to her financial independence. There is another story recounted by Aubrey which tells us a good deal about

173

Ben's superstitious nature. Oliver Dick describes it in his edition:

> But Aubrey, in his isolation, was surrounded by these tales. "Our Country-people would talke much of Faeries," he said. "They swept-up the Harth cleane at night: and did sett their shoes by the fire, and many times should find a three-pence in one of them." In this belief the rustics were not alone, for later in life Aubrey reported that "Mris. Markey (a daughter of Serjeant Hoskyns the Poet) told me, that her mother did use that Custome and had as much money as made her a little Silver-cup of thirtie shillings value."[13]

Unless one also believes in such faeries, one is forced to see the gentle affection which Hoskyns had for his wife, humoring her in her fancies.

Benedict Hoskyns, John's son, had a story of a similar nature which he recounted, but he did not claim it about his own family:

> Not far from Sir Bennet Hoskyns there was a labouring man that rose up early every day to go to work, who for a good while together found a ninepence in the way that he went. His wife wondering how he came by so much money, was afraid he got it not honestly, at last he told her; and afterwards he never found any more.[14]

It seems that the mother's beliefs in the supernatural found some response in her children.

In later years Ben's gullibility and independence would at times strain the relationship of husband and wife, but in these early days there seems to have been little but mutual harmony.

In picking their home in Hereford, Hoskyns chose not to settle down among his parents and brothers. Not only had he married a family complete with children, but he had married into considerable money as well, and there was no need to live in any

174

cramped quarters. Benedicta was used to life in
towns also rather than on old farms like Monkton.
It is likely that John already had his eye on legal
affairs in his home county, and for that, he would
need a headquarters in the main city itself, Hereford. He therefore rented a rather large house and
grounds from Roger Phellpotts just off the main
square on Widemarsh St., the same street where David
Garrick was to be born in 1717.

Eventually this property would consist of approximately a quarter of an acre of houses, land,
stables, gardens, etc., but it is not likely that
Hoskyns started off with such a large establishment.
By 1605 he would still be listed next to last on the
election list for the city of Hereford,[15] but from
the time of his purchase of this property which he
formerly rented, he would be listed third, immediately behind the incumbent mayor and Sir John Scudamore,
the leading peer of the district. This purchase
took place in 1609, when he bought from Phellpotts
three separate pieces of property, all of which "are
in the tenure of the sd John Hoskins or John Clarke
or theire Assignes and were heeretofore by me mor-
gaged to the said John Hoskins."[16] The three parcels included "all that my late messuage or Tenemte
& of and in all houses, buyldinges, Chambers, loftes,
sellers Roomes Stables Curtellages[17] backsides with
thappurtenances... in Wigmor Streete... and a garden adioyning between the lands of George Hurdman
William Page and the said John Hoskins and Phillip
Trehearne... and one Stable and one backside thereto and the easte side."

The size of this property in comparison with
other holdings in the city is made clear in a 1624
subsidy list.[18] In that list Hoskyns is numbered
among the commissioners and pays £5 20s "in terris,"
which gives us a good idea of the relative value
of his land: his tax is over £2 more than anyone
else in the city. None of the commissioners, such
as James Clarke or John Warden, paid more than £3
12s. On the assessment for the first fifteenth,
paid the same day, Hoskyns was once again the leading taxpayer. Although his final purchase of the

Widemarsh property lies in the future, there can be
little doubt that Hoskyns made clear in his renting
of a sizable home in 1601 that he intended to become an active citizen in Hereford affairs.

And the city reacted favorably. By 15 April
1602, Hoskyns had been appointed Justice of the
Peace and Deputy Steward for the city of Hereford.[19]
The Deputy Steward was an appointed officer who assisted the Mayor at the Mayor's Court. His qualifi-
cations were that he was to be a "man learned in
the law." As the office of High Steward seems to
have been more or less of a sinecure (the Earl of
Essex had occupied the position), the appointment
indicates that Hoskyns was the chief legal advisor
of the City. His signature appears with the desig-
nation of Deputy Steward from this time until 1609.
As Justice of the Peace he could also hold his own
court, as he did on July 16th, the first day of the
General Session of 1606.[20] In December 1604 he is
called "Clerk," which means that he was City Clerk
for a period.[21] In a 1616 letter to which we will
refer later, King James refers to Hoskyns as once
being Recorder of the City, which would be still
another position. That Hereford turned much of its
legal work over to him and that he served the city
well in various capacities cannot be questioned.
It is no wonder that the citizens chose him automatically as their representative in Parliament
until he fell into disfavor with the King.

Most of his duties seem to have been routine
in nature, which is not surprising in a local court.
It was his task to sign various recognizances or
bonds taken in the Mayor's court for required duties or payments.[22] But there were interesting
cases as well, such as that in which he first took
part as Deputy Steward:

> William Reade [later to be High Sheriff of Here-
> ford] of the Cittie of Heref baker haveinge ar-
> rested William Parrye gent Henrye Perryne and
> Roger Davies of murder viz for the supposed mur-
> deringe of Anne Wilcoxe wieffe of James Wilcoxe
> this ex^{tes} syster... deposeth as followeth that

he did arreste the said persons by the consente
of James Wilcoxe whoe will prosecute the same
and cannott saye any thinge of his owne knowledge
savinge that aboute three weeckes before the said
Anne Wilcoxe died she... reported to this ext
in the presence of this extes brother that she
was beaten ⅋ throwne one a carre and plowe and
Rudges by the said William Parrye Henrye Perryne
Roger Davies and others and sayd ffurther that
she did knowe that she shoulde never recouere
the same and prayed this ext and his brother and
her husbande to ffollowe the same... the said
Anne Wilcoxe did then reporte to this ext that
the said Roger Davies called for a roope to bynde
her vppon the said carr and that Mrs Parrye
wieffe of Lewis Parrye gent byd them throwe her
the said Anne over the hedge And... she did
laye the cause of her death vpon them yf she did
dye....23

There were three other men hearing the case with
Hoskyns: Thomas Clark, the Mayor; Richard Bromwich
and Walter Hurdman, both Justices of the Peace and
Aldermen named in an Elizabethan Charter for the
city in 1597. These four felt that the case was
important enough to be turned over to the King's
Law at the Assizes and so bound the defendants.

    John also helped to protect the interests of
the city against the favoritism sometimes shown by
members of the peerage in county and city affairs.
On 22 August 1603 he and Walter Hurdman, the new
Mayor, wrote "To the eight worshipfull the Comis-
sioners of Sewers assigned for the Countie of
Heref." They said that they had word from the King
that there was to be an alteration for the best in
the situation of private owners of weirs who were
ruining private fishing and river commerce, changing channels, etc., in the river Wye. They asked
that the Commissioners consider the city's plea.24
It is then that the manuscripts reveal the intelligence of the City of Hereford in appointing as
Deputy Steward a man with close connections with
the court in London, especially with the Lord Chancellor, Thomas Egerton. For on 27 September the

Lord Chancellor wrote to the Commissioners saying
that he had heard that they had been playing favorites in their task and that they were to stop it
immediately.[25] He singled out Sir James Scudamore
especially, and it may well be that the obvious an-
tagonism between Hoskyns and the Scudamore family
dates from this time. It is pretty clear that thirteen years later it was the Scudamores who prevented
Hoskyns from being elected Mayor of Hereford after
many years of service to the city.

In a case in either 1604 or 1605 we see Hoskyns
performing the special task for which a Deputy Steward was appointed: handing down a legal decision
in a case brought before the court. Richard Powell
and his attorney Thomas Powell asked for dismissal
of a case because of "insufficient matter." Hoskyns agreed with them and wrote at the bottom of
their case:

Causes of demurrer
There is noe oyer[26] of the band nor Condicion
demanded which ought to be.
There is not de verbo in verbum pleadinge of the
Convenannts and agreements in the Condicion wch
ought to be before the conclusion of the condi-
cell et agreementa per implebit.

J. Hoskyns[27]

Throughout his legal life, Hoskyns was to be a
stickler for detail in legal proceedings and often
won his best cases by arguing such details. It is
for that reason that it is strange that Aubrey described him as "worst" at the law of all of his
abilities.

One of the rather strange facts of the various
records of Hoskyns' life is that in almost none of
the documents relating to his work and land dealings is there mention of the sums of money that he
handled or earned. It makes it rather difficult to
estimate the size of his income at any time in his
life. In all of his records in the Sheepskin Bags
in the City Clerk's Office in Hereford, there is
but one which indicates the kind of money that he

178

made as Deputy Steward for the city. In September
1604 there was a case in which Thomas Curle was the
complainant against John Turnor, and among the papers is a set of charges of the plaintiff. Among
the items, which include the usual pay for Juries,
is the following: "Item to Mr John Hoskins esqr
for his ffee for Conncell in makeing the declar --
v^s."[28] This is the largest item on the bill. It
is also a quite large amount of money for the time.
As he had a hand in many of the cases brought before the Mayor's Court, he undoubtedly made a tidy
income from his position.

    But his main source of income was always in
the city of London, arguing cases in one of the
three branches of the courts there. It was probably only during the vacation Readings that he could
afford to be away from the Middle Temple. And during the Lent Reading of 1602 he missed one of the
great events on record during his time at the Temple,
the performance of Shakespeare's Twelfth Night at
the Reader's Feast on February 2nd, recorded so fully in the diary of his former charge, John Manningham.[29] He also was absent when a new roommate was
assigned to him in place of William Copley. On 12
February Thomas Fettiplace of Barkshire entered the
Middle Temple and moved into Hoskyns' apartments.
But there was a more politic event for Hoskyns taking place in Hereford, and he undoubtedly remained
in that city for it. Robert Benet, the Dean of
Windsor and Master of St. Cross Hospital in Winchester, was consecrated Bishop of Hereford on 20 February.[30] Benet was obviously a close friend of
Hoskyns, perhaps from the days at Winchester, but
certainly from the period when they were both established in the city of Hereford. John's first son,
Benedict, was a godson of the Bishop and was referred to both familiarly and often legally as Bennet.
John himself carried on many of the legal affairs of
the Cathedral Chapter, a result, at least in part,
of his friendship with the Bishop, who died on 25
October 1617.

    But the usual pattern of his life reasserted
itself, and he was soon back to commuting between

179

his home in Hereford and his lodgings in the Middle
Temple. There he was caught up once more in the
events of the court and the activities of his
friends. He undoubtedly was brought up to date on
the eventful marriage of John Donne and Anne More,
the daughter of the worthy Sir George More, one of
the more conservative members of Parliament and future co-committee worker with Hoskyns. Walton's
famous summary of that marriage: "John Donne, Anne
Donne, Undone," was unquestionably common fare for
gossip around the Inns of Court, especially among
the group of Oxford friends. But Hoskyns would perhaps be less than fully sympathetic, for he had already, two years earlier, warned against just such
a marriage as this. Anne More had been the house-
keeper for Sir Thomas Egerton, and John Donne was
but a secretary in the household. For him to aspire to such a family as that of the Mores, especially when Anne was still a minor of seventeen or
eighteen years, was a considerable social error.
And it cost him dearly. Hoskyns, in the <u>Directions,</u>
had warned:

> As a Story of one who being a servaunt of a
> famely and of many qualities wonne the doating
> loue of a Wittie Ladie in the house, whereas she
> never lookt vppon the suits the Cunning insin-
> uations, the worthy deserts of many lovers of
> higher Degree but wth free iudgm^t and carelesse
> censure. this close may follow, Soe hard en-
> trance hath liking into a heart p^{r}pared to sus-
> pition especially in the weakest natures, whose
> safeguard is mistrust. Soe easie is the increase
> of loue by insensible stepps when the service you
> offer seemes to yssue out of the goodnesse of
> yor owne disposition, wch Woemen expect to bee
> permanent and not out of the necessitie of yor
> sute wch may frame you for a time to vaine dif-
> ference from yor proper honno^r.[31]

Another friend, Christopher Brooke, who was a member of all of the literary and political groups of
which Hoskyns was a part, had played an intimate
role in Donne's marriage and was thrown into prison
along with Donne at the urging of Sir George More.

The marriage had occurred in January 1602, but Donne and the Brookes were not imprisoned until early February. Donne was released by the 13th, but Christopher probably did not get out until the end of the month. Donne claimed in a letter to his father-in-law that he and Anne had been married in early December. Unfortunately the records of the case do not bear out that claim. So the group of friends may also have been discussing the reasons for Donne's attempt to predate the wedding.[32]

If not much in the way of extraordinary events followed for the rest of 1602, the early months of 1603 made up for it. In March Queen Elizabeth fell sick at Richmond, and all of England waited to see if she would survive. On the last day of the old year, which until the adoption of the new calendar in the 18th century was the twenty-fourth of March, she died, and perhaps the greatest reign in the history of England came to an end. It is true that in her last years she had become a querulous old woman, and her tendency to change her mind had warranted her the description of the Moon goddess among the poets. But under her leadership the country had flowered and attained a position of world leadership which it was never to lose. Stow's Annales contains as good a one paragraph summary of her character as any:

Shee was tall of stature, strong in euery limbe and ioynt, her fingers small and long, her voyce lowd and shrill, shee was of an admirable ready wit and memory, very skilfull in all kind of Needleworke, had an excellent eare in Musicke, played well vpon divers Instruments, shee spake the Greeke, Latine, Italian, and French tongues well, and vnderstood the Spanish, she was resolute, and of vndaunted Spirit, of all which speciall vertues apparantly approued, and publiquely knowne to the whole world, during all the time of her owne raigne, and besides her wisdome and great discretion shewed in preventing and escaping many imminent daungers, wherewith shee was strongly environed during her sisters Raigne, holding this (Maxime) firmely in her

181

minde; beeing a subiect, she would obey obedient-
ly, and being a Soveraigne, she would be obeyed
accordingly.[33]

The execution of the Earl of Essex had disillusion-
ed many of the poets and courtiers around Elizabeth,
and the mood of the court had been such that many
critics and historians have found in the situation
in London the source for the malaise in the court
of Denmark in the play Hamlet. But with all of her
faults, Elizabeth was clearly one of the greatest
women in the history of the world, and her contemporaries knew it.

Oxford, as usual, lept immediately into print
with a memorial volume in Latin. And one of those
submitting poems was "Io. Hoskins Nov. Coll. Socius."[34] It is difficult to determine fully whether this is John or his brother, Dr. John. Certainly the latter was the only member of the family
presently a fellow of New College. We also know
that he was capable of writing a Latin poem, which
he did for a volume presented by Oxford University
to the King and Queen in 1613, on the marriage of
their daughter, Princess Elizabeth.[35] However,
later in 1603, John was to write another poem, this
time to the incoming monarch, James I, and he is
there identified as "Ioannes Hoskins Iurista Novi
Coll. Soc."[36] The fact that he is identified as
both a jurist and fellow of New College clarifies
the situation enough to allow us to attribute the
former poem to him as well.

The volume for Elizabeth. Oxoniensis Academiae
Funebre Officium... In Memoriam... Elisabethae, includes many poems by various Doctors of Theology
and students whose names are not among the usual
set of poets associated with Hoskyns. One of three
things seems to have happened: members of the University who remembered Hoskyns' previous contributions to memorial volumes once again requested a
work from his pen fit for the occasion; or Dr. John
asked his brother to submit a poem as part of the
offering of New College; or a relative of his new
wife saw fit to seek his participation. The last

possibility is raised when it is noted that Hoskyns'
poem immediately follows one by Richard Boorne.
There would seem to be more than chance to the fact
that in the following volume on James, Hoskyns'
poem once again follows immediately a poem by Richard Boorne.

The poem is stanzaically free with an opening
stanza of 10 lines followed by three stanzas of
four lines each, another stanza of ten lines, and
a final stanza of six lines.[37] The differentiation
of stanza length provides the four principal elements of subject matter of the poem: the gifts of
the gods at Elizabeth's birth, her feminine strength,
her ability at languages, and her goal of founding
heaven on earth through the establishment of true
worship.

If there is not quite so much obvious wit in
this poem as in his earlier ones, it may be attributed to his relatively long period of inactivity
in writing Latin verse. Many of the same elements
of the earlier poems are still present, however.
He introduces Lucina, the goddess of childbirth, as
one who looked with favor on Elizabeth's birth, thus
bringing in one of the lesser-known classical dei-
ties immediately. To have Minerva give the gift of
intellect is more usual. But then Hoskyns jumps
into the most difficult task in praising the Queen:
what to do about her looks? By no account was
Elizabeth a beautiful woman. As we have already
seen, she was tall and strong. The only really
feminine thing about her was her hands. So Hoskyns
picks his language with care. He says that Venus
wished her body, as it grew, to be lovely or graceful, "a form fitted to your fortunes."

And Fortune, taking pains not to seem blind,
    Placed nothing but the best in the best hands.

Mars, of course, added spirit and Apollo the gift
of many languages. Then the poet returns to lesser
known and somewhat witty examples, explaining that
with these various gifts she would be able to be
called Pandora except that Libitina, the goddess of

183

corpses, gave nothing.

In the second section he asks the reader whether he is amazed that the Britons were filled with so much peace for so long a time under a fragile woman. The answer is that he should be amazed that she should be thought of as a woman who was womanlike in nothing but her body. The third stanza is perhaps the most unusual. Once again Hoskyns goes to the cause of death and explains that the illness was clever enough to block her throat and tie her tongue so that the tongue could not bend nor change the mind of Almighty God. The fourth stanza is more usual in its statement that whereas with some people, we shed tears only once at their death, every time we think of Elizabeth, it seems that she dies again.

In the second long stanza Hoskyns returns to his favorite practice of speaking to the Fates who cut the thread of life. He explains that Elizabeth could plead with Fate in English, Italian, French, Greek, and Spanish. Fate, though, is a barbarian who speaks only with the knife. Then he finishes the poem with a tribute to Elizabeth's care for divine worship, and for her wish to found heaven on earth. It is a fitting tribute to the monarch who managed to bring her nation through the throes of the reformation compromise without chaos. Her successors were less fortunate and far less skilled.

King James VI of Scotland was duly notified of his succession to the throne of England, and in the following month he made his progress south through the cities of Newcastle, Durham, York, Doncaster, and Newark, and on May 7th reached London, to be greeted by "an eloquent and learned Oration vnto his Maiestie" by Hoskyns' close friend and companion at the Middle Temple, Richard Martin.[38]

Then began a summer of events connected with the accession of the new monarch. Scores of new knights were dubbed,[39] celebrations such as the naming of the Knights of the Bath were held; but all of these events took place under the shadow of

184

the plague. The summer Reading at the Middle Temple was cancelled, as well as that of the following Lent,[40] and the regular term of the Courts was moved to Winchester. The usual public panoply connected with such events as the Knighting of the Order of the Bath had to be sharply curtailed:

Also by reason of Gods visitation for our sinnes, the Plague of Pestilence there raigning in the City of London, and Suburbes, (the Pageants and other shewes of Triumph, in most sumptuous manner prepared, but not finished) the King roade not from the Tower through the Citie in Royall manner as had beene accustomed, neither were the Citizens permitted to come at Westminster, but forbidden by Proclamation, for feare of infection to be by that meanes increased, for there dyed that weeke in the City of London, and Suburbs, of all diseases, 1103. of plague, 857.[41]

The poets were at their usual occupation of turning out Latin poems of celebration, however, and the usual Oxford volume appeared: Academiae Oxoniensis Pietas... Iacobvm. Not only the usual faculty and student poems appeared, but now Hoskyns was joined by other Oxford graduates like Henry Martin; and Sir Walter Ralegh and others added their tributes.

Hoskyns' contribution was relatively short and quite different from his previous poems. He was more concerned with the person who did not succeed than the one who did. James is seen as Jacob who succeeded Isaac (Elizabeth), the younger son who received his father's blessing. Hoskyns says that James stands for true religion against the Papist Esau who claimed "the names of antiquity" and plotted to take the throne. The reference is, of course, to Arabella Stuart who was first in line to the succession and an Englishwoman, but who had the strong support of Spain and the Spanish party in England. It was due to his supposed support of Arabella Stuart that Ralegh was later to be beheaded by James.

185

The final stanza of the poem is strangely re-
ticent. It is true that in the second stanza Hoskyns addresses James as the most holy of Kings and
says that his honor will rise higher as his true
nature becomes better known. But then he finishes:

Great King, great things will be written about
                                        you,
    Nor will the world be able to write in such a
            way that more might not be added:
Read what others write about your particular mer-
                                its and love;
    I will be silent about them.

It is almost a foreboding of the strained relationships between these two men. Perhaps Hoskyns was
already worried about the influx of Scottish favorites which the new King brought with him from his
native country, along with his hunting dogs. But
whatever the cause, this poetic silence was unlikely to endear him to the monarch who was to become
known as the wisest fool in Christendom.

Footnotes for Chapter VI

1. There is an undated record in the token books of the Liberty of the Clink, on the south side of the Thames in Southwark, which indicates that a John Hoskins with a family of 3 persons lived there and took communion. This is the same section of the London suburbs where John Donne's mother lived for some years and was brought to task as a Catholic who did not take communion. There is no reason, however, to identify this John Hoskins with the subject of this biography.
2. Hopwood, I, 407, 408.
3. Ibid., I, 413, 416, 422, 426; II, 440.
4. Ibid., I, 424.
5. Ibid., I, 434-35.
6. The Registers of the Abbey Church of SS. Peter and Paul, Bath, ed. Arthur J. Jewers, Vol. II (1901; Harleian Society, Registers, Vol. 28), p. 338. Francis' father, of the same name, died in 1599 and left the income of his lands in Bristol, Sanford and Churchill to his wife Edith. Rev. Frederick Brown, Abstracts of Somersetshire Wills, 1st Series (1887). p. 29.
7. Probate Registry, Somerset House, 30 Woodhall.
8. Vowchurch epitaph among Harewood Mss; Wood, Athenae Oxoniensis, Col. 614; Charles J. Robinson, The Mansions of Herefordshire (1872), pp. 133-34. Add. Mss. 24,291, ff. 202v-203v, says she was the daughter of John Moyle. Considering the genealogy of the Moyles in A Visitation of the County of Kent... 1663 (Harleian Soc., Vol 14, 1906), it may be that his name was John Robert. Bourne received the lease on Dover Court parsonage for the length of three lives, on 28 December 1596, which may indicate the year in which he and Benedicta married, although that seems late. SPD-Elizabeth, 1595-1597 (1869), CCLXI, p. 323.
9. Bath, Register, I, 13.
10. Ibid., II, 338.
11. Ibid., I, 205.
12. The letters are preserved in the Muniment Room of Sizergh Castle in Kendal. They are usually

quoted here from the transcripts made by Henry
Hornyold-Strickland, the father of the present
owner, Thomas Hornyold-Strickland. Although
there are errors in transcription, they are
minor, such as substitution of "u" for "v", un-
italicized spelling out of contractions, such
as "you" for "yu", and occasional capitaliza-
tion of lower case letters, such as "Mr." for
"mr." But these are minor. For those who wish
to check the difference, I have given an exact
transcription of the first two letters and then
have used Mr. Hornyold-Strickland's copies for
the rest. Osborn used his copies throughout.
Mr. Hornyold-Strickland was so helpful, so generous of his time and energy, so hospitable to
visiting researchers, that to quibble over minor points would have been silly. His son has
shown the same warmth and friendliness since
his father's death in 1976.

13. Dick, p. xxix.
14. Anecdotes and Traditions, ed. W. J. Thoms,
    Camden Society 5 (1838), p. 115; quoted from
    Aubrey.
15. Uncatalogued records in the Sheepskin Bags in
    Hereford Town Hall Muniment Room.
16. Local Collection of Deeds 2045, in the Here-
    ford City Library. A complete summary of Hos-
    kyns' property in Hereford is in B. W. Whitlock,
    "The Hereford City Properties of John Hoskyns,"
    Transactions of the Woolhope... Club, Vol.
    XXXVII, 1961, pp. 62-66.
17. A Curtilage is a small court or yard attached
    to a dwelling-house and forming one enclosure
    with it. O.E.D.
18. Hereford City MSS., Vol. 4, f. 40.
19. Sheepskin Bags 1600-1602.
20. Ibid., 1605-06.
21. Ibid.
22. Two such recognizances for the year 1602, on
    17 August and 10 October, occur in the Sheep-
    skin Bag in the City Clerk's Office for 1600-
    02. These records give us one way of finding
    out the periods of time he spent at his home in
    Hereford rather than in his lodgings at the
    Middle Temple.

23. Sheepskin Bag 1600-02. I cannot find any de-
    finition for the word "Rudges." It may be that
    it stands for "Rucks," which would be a pile of
    hay or any combustible material, or "Ridges,"
    which might refer to a part of the cart and
    plow.
24. Add MSS. 11,053 (Scudamore Papers), f. 71.
25. Ibid., f. 72.
26. The hearing of some document read in court;
    esp. of an instrument in writing, pleaded by
    one party, when the other "craved oyer" of it.
    O.E.D.
27. Sheepskin Bag 1602-05.
28. Ibid.
29. Manningham's Diary is found in Harley 5353.
30. Thomas Blount's Collection, Vol. II (Hereford
    City Library Mss.), List of Bishops of Hereford,
    #72; also in Aubrey, Clark ed., p. 418. The
    D.N.B. gives the date of consecration as 20
    February 1603, and that may be correct, depend-
    ing on when Blount, at some point after 1675,
    began his new years. It would be surprising
    for Clark to make an error of this kind, how-
    ever.
31. ff. 19-19v.
32. R. C. Bald, in his standard biography of Donne,
    accepts Donne's word about the marriage date,
    although he knew of the wording of the official
    document in the Loseley papers. He felt their
    ambuity was sufficiently indecisive to allow
    for the usual interpretation of a December mar-
    riage. Prof. Edward Le Comte, in Etudes An-
    glaises, 1968, and "Jack Donne," in Just So
    Much Honor, ed. P. A. Fiore (Penn State UP,
    1972), has argued persuasively for the January
    dating, however.
33. p. 813.
34. Oxoniensis Academiae... In Memoriam... Elisa-
    bethae, Oxoniae, 1603, pp. 140-41.
35. Epithalamia (Oxford, 1613),
36. Academiae Oxoniesis Pietas... Jacobvm, Oxoniae,
    1603. p. 168.
37. This is another reason to link it with the po-
    em in the volume to James, for that is a three
    stanza poem, with stanzas of ten lines, six

189

lines, and four lines, in that order.

38. Stow, p. 823.

39. Godfrey Davies, in The Early Stuarts 1603-1660 (1937), p. 1, observes that James in two months created as many knights as Elizabeth had during the entire last ten years of her reign, which included the incredibly large number she dubbed knight following the 1596 voyage to Cadiz. Sir Francis Bacon was one of those elevated by King James at this time, but on 3 July 1603 Bacon wrote to Cecil, "For this almost prostituted title of knighthood I could now without charge by your means by content to have it; both because of this late disgrace, and because I have three new knights in my mess in Gray's Inn commons, and because I have found out an alderman's daughter, a handsome maiden, to my liking." He was not exaggerating. On July 26th, "all the Aldermen of London were sent for, to come to Westminster, there to bee Knighted by the King." (Stow, p. 828).

40. On 8 July 1603 it was ordered that "All gentlemen of this House, clerks and serving men, shall depart and not be suffered to continue in their chambers until such time that it shall please God to cease the sickness." (Hopwood, II, 441). On 10 February 1604 the order was less stringent: "There shall be no reading in Lent next, and no vacation. Notwithstanding, Utter Barristers and gentlemen of the House lying within the House or in the town are to keep commons of the House." There is a marginal note of explanation: "By reson of the daunger of the plauge." p. 442.

41. Stow, p. 827.

Chapter VII

The 1604 Parliament: Round One

There is, of course, no reason at all to take
for granted that King James noted the curious reti-
cence of one short poem in the memorial volume addressed to him.[1] (He would certainly have paid
closer attention to the poem by his suspected opponent, Ralegh, for example.) But it would not be
long before he would be disturbed by the words and
actions of the member of Parliament from the City
of Hereford who had written that short poem. In
fact, he would be disturbed by the actions of the
whole House of Commons, who seemed, from his point
of view, simply to be out to frustrate all of his
plans and to keep from him the necessary funds to
run the government as he thought it should be run.
As a firm believer in the Divine Right of Kings for-
mulated in France at the end of the previous century
by Jean Bodin, James was constantly at war with a
Parliament which was fighting for its rights as a
constitutional body. During Elizabeth's reign, the
Parliament had been swayed by the personal magnetism
of the monarch, and even then they had increasingly
shown their irritation at the way she handled them
and the finances of her day, especially in the matter of monopolies bestowed by the Crown. With James,
there was no personal magnetism to curb the unruly
elements in the House. Nor did James show the good
sense to insure that a large number of his privy
councillors would be members of the House of Commons,
as Elizabeth had. Even the few that were there seldom exercised leadership in the debates.

Yet there is every reason to see John Hoskyns
as the kind of person who could have been won over
to the King's side, providing the kind of support
that the new monarch needed. He had entered Parliament with ideas that certainly favored the monarchy rather than leaning towards popular government through an elected Parliament. In the Directions he had stated, "you could not enioy yor good-
nesse wthout governm^t, noe governement wthout a

191

Magistrate, noe Magistrate wthout obedience, and
noe obedience where every one vppon his private
passion doth interprett the doings of the rulers."[2]
It is true that this is not a statement of Divine
Right; rather it is an interpretation of the kind
of social contract envisaged at the middle of the
century by Thomas Hobbes. But it certainly indicated that Hoskyns, and probably a large majority
of the Commons, were prepared to follow and support
a monarch who used his power with discretion. And
discretion was not James' strong point. As a result, within ten years Hoskyns was to be one of the
leaders in the opposition against the King. But
that was still in the future.

Early in 1604 John Hoskyns and Walter Hurdman,
his fellow Justice of the Peace, were elected by
the citizens of the City of Hereford to represent
them at the first Parliament of the new King. As
we shall have reason to note later, Hereford elected only its own citizens to Parliament.

The first session of the Commons began on Monday, 19 March 1604, and Hoskyns' very close friend,
Edward Phelips, was chosen as Speaker that same day
after some initial difficulty.[3] It was not until
the 22nd, however, that Parliament actually got
under way with the opening speech by the King. One
of his chief goals for this Parliament became immediately apparent: the union of England and Scotland into one nation under his monarchy. In this,
as on almost every other point, he was to meet with
failure. One reason for his failure was also apparent in that speech, for he stressed peace with
Spain and Leniency towards Roman Catholics, neither
position being popular at the time. In the early
days of the session, before a recess at the King's
pleasure from 4 April to 11 April, Hoskyns took
little part in the activities, serving his appren-
ticeship as a fledgling member of the Commons; but
this inactivity was not to last long, and by 14
April he became involved in the debates.

The Commons had gotten off to a fast start,
and it was clear on the day after the King's speech

192

that his plans for a first Parliament were going to
have rough sledding. On 23 March, Sir Robert Wroth,
a strong Puritan and M.P. for forty years, had submitted a set of seven proposals for consideration
by the Commons, the first four of which were of special interest: 1. Confirmation of the Book of
Common Prayer; 2. The Wardship of Mens Children,
as a Burden and Servitude to the Subjects of this
Kingdom; 3. The general Abuse and Grievances of
Purveyors, and Car-takers, &c.; 4. Particular and
private Patents, commonly called Monopolies.[4] Numbers two and three, both feudal privileges of the
Crown, were to be the main bones of contention of
the session.

It is rather typical that the debate in which
Hoskyns first took part was one of the hottest of
the first session of this Parliament. It was on
the matter of Purveyors and their abuse of their
position. The right of Purveyance was a medieval
right still used by the monarch for raising money
and supplies to support the royal household and
establishment. Under the system, the crown could
buy whatever it needed for the royal household at
a price fixed by the Purveyor, and could requisi-
tion horses, carts, etc. for any of the king's
journeys. Sir Francis Bacon himself informed the
King that "There is no grievance in your kingdom
so general, so continual, so sensible, and so bitter unto the common subject."[5] Obviously such a
custom was subject to considerable abuse, and it is
to that abuse that Commons turned its attention.

The first question to be raised was the correct
procedure in attacking the problem, whether by Petition to the King or by a Bill of Parliament. Four
men spoke up: Richard Martin, Lawrence Hyde, John
Hoskyns and Sir Henry Jenkins. Martin set the tone
immediately: "Let us proceed by way of Act, not by
way of Petition. All good Kings will submit themselves. Nothing ordered here, to a Resolution, but
may be renewed, upon better Advice."[6] Hoskyns wanted to focus on the nature of Purveyance. His speech
is noted as "Prerogative of Purveyors. The King
hath Pre-emption. In every Beef, 3 1. in every

193

Mutton, <u>10 s</u>. in every Quarter of Wheat, <u>13s</u> 4d."
What appears to be conciliatory to the crown actually may not be. Hoskyns does not question the right
of the King to first choice in the purchase of food;
<u>that</u> is the prerogative of the Purveyor. But he
wants a fixed price, not one to be determined by
the Purveyor, which is the abuse that is under question. Mr. Hyde followed, seconding Martin's proposal that they proceed by Bill rather than Petition: "Rather let us be denied Justice, than not
to dare ask it." Sir Henry Jenkins then rose to
speak, but it was not to the point at hand. Rather
he spoke to another question that was bothering the
whole House: the interference of the King in the
elections of Members of Parliament. He said the
"Liberty of Election [was] the greatest Liberty"
of the House. Important though the issue was, it
was not to the point.[7] So they returned to the
question of Purveyance, and following the dispute,
the House decided to take the more politic path at
this early stage and ordered the Committee studying
Sir Robert Wroth's proposals to prepare a Petition
to be submitted to his Majesty.

The Commons then turned its attention to a request from the House of Lords for a meeting that
afternoon in the Painted Chamber to discuss "the
blessed and happy Union of these Two Kingdoms."
Hoskyns was among the 100 members appointed to the
Committee. On Monday April 16th, Sir Henry Mountague, Recorder of London, reported on the meeting
to the full House of Commons. He said all of the
proper things, such as the fact that it was not a
new idea, but added that this King had brought to
pass what "no Wit, no Policy, no Art of Man could
ever bring to pass." It appears that the major
discussion was over the question of a name, as nothing but the name would be decided until after the
subject had been argued and concluded in Parliament.
He personally suggested that the name ought to be
Great Britain. The question of the Union had obviously gotten off to a very slow start.

During the rest of this session of Parliament
these two topics of Purveyance and the Union re-

194

bates. On 19 May 1604, Toby Matthews, the son of
the Bishop of Durham and an arch-conservative,
wrote to John Donne, who was in retirement at Pyr-
ford as a result of his marriage:

> The vild Speakers are, Hoskins, Fuller, with an
> & caetera of an hundred men. And surely, saving
> that Sir George Moor is your father in law, and
> not in conscience, he speaks as ill as ever he
> did, saving that he speaks not so much... The
> choise and usuall Speakers are, Bacon, Edwin
> Sands, Yelverton, Martin, with some few more. I
> am content to tell you, that Sir Maurice Barkley
> hath done exceeding well, and, so that you be-
> lieve me, you shall have good leave to wonder at
> it with me.[11]

Matthew was M.P. from St. Albans, having received
that position from Sir Francis Bacon, who chose to
represent Ipswich, thus allowing his young friend
a seat in Parliament.

On 2 June Sir George More moved that it would
be better "to give an annual Composition to his
Majesty, and not to continue longer subject to Purveyance," and Hoskyns once again argued against
Composition. Unfortunately, the person taking
notes of the debates often shortened Hoskyns' speeches so much that it is difficult to discover what he
actually said. What obviously impressed everyone
(except Toby Matthew) listening to his speeches was
John's wit, and when wit is taken in a kind of
shorthand, it is sometimes difficult to reconstruct.
This time, however, we have a clue to what impressed one of the recorders. He noted Hoskyns' speech
as follows:

> Mr. Hoskins,---against the Composition.---
> Quod fecimus hiis, fecimus tibi. Our thankful-
> ness to the King,
> Naturalizing the Scotts.

(or, as another record explains, "We had shewed our
Thankfulness to the King in naturalizing the
Scotts.")[12] There is one point that Hoskyns was

196

consistent on from his first session of Parliament until he was thrown into the Tower of London in 1614: he did not like King James' obvious favoritism towards his Scottish followers, and he did not like the obvious drain of English money which was the result of this favoritism.

James had had the courts proclaim a rule of Post-nati, which said that anyone born in Scotland after James ascended the throne of England became a naturalized citizen of England. But James wanted more; he wanted all the Scots to be considered naturalized subjects of his new nation. The English, for various reasons, national and financial, were opposed to this, and this opposition was at the root of their dislike of the proposed Union. What Hoskyns is doing is mis-applying the Biblical parable with a vengeance. "What we have done to these, we have done to you." Had not God said that what you have done to one of the least of these my brethren, you have done it unto me? It is indeed witty--and dangerous.

The Commons and the King were not able to settle their differences on the touchy subject of Composition in any satisfactory way during the opening months. On 28 April the House had duly submitted its bill of particulars on the Abuses of the Purveyors, especially the Cart-Takers for moving the King's goods: that there were too many for the job needed, that they took too long, went too far, etc.; that there was much cheating in the purveying of victuals, wood, coal, etc. The Purveyors were not showing their licenses, which the law required, they were cutting too much wood in one place, taking too much hay, requiring unfair amounts of corn, and engaging in a great many other activities bound to raise the ire of local farmers.[13] The King answered the Petition in a rather typical paternal speech, but nothing really happened except that the offenses listed were labelled Felonies and Misdemeanors and were to be prosecuted in the country Assizes. As long as the Commons and Lords remained as far apart as they did on the amount of Composition, the possible resolution of the problem

197

Another of the touchy issues of the session was
the matter of financial aid to the King in the form
of a Subsidy from the Parliament. Later on in this
first Parliament of James, the issue of Subsidy
would be a major one. During the first session,
however, there was nothing but talk. Hoskyns seems
only to have taken part in the debate once, on 19
June. Often the method of Subsidy was to grant two
sums during a given year, which required local governments to collect the given sums at two separate
times. This is the point to which Hoskyns spoke--
and in the negative; he said "That we have no Sheep,
that yields Two Fleeces in the Year."18 Once again
the unstated implication is stronger than the stated. Parliament would be a flock of sheep in granting the Subsidy. James could see the way things
were going in the discussion of Subsidy, however,
and on 26 June he sent a letter to the Commons saying that he didn't want any Subsidy as it would be
a burden to the people. He then got to the real
point: he knew that discussion was going on, and
he didn't want the matter brought to a vote, for if
it went against the Subsidy, it would look bad for
him as a new monarch. He then reiterated, in very
strong terms, that he did not want any further discussion of the matter. He added that he was sure
the House would find a better way of supplying money, "least hurtful to our Subjects." The House
charged the Speaker with thanking the King for his
gracious letter.19 They did not, however, find a
better means of supply.

Hoskyns also took part in debates on two matters
close to the hearts of all members of Parliament,
freedom of elections and freedom from arrest during
the Parliament. These and freedom of speech formed
the core of the famous "Apology" drawn up by this
Parliament although never actually submitted to the
King. John certainly had no idea that he was to
suffer from royal abuse of all of these freedoms
later on. In the debate of election, Hoskyns' participation was minor, and it was not on the case
which made the most stir, that of Sir Francis Goodwin, in which the King had become involved. Other
cases, in Cardigan and Shropshire, were those in

which the Sheriff of the shire had sent men other than those actually chosen by the towns.[20] In the debate on 17 April as to whether the Serjeant of the House should be sent to bring the Sheriffs to appear before the House or whether there should be a writ of Attachment, in other words, an order of arrest for contempt of the court of Parliament, two men, Mr. Winch and Mr. Hoskyns, spoke up, in favor of sending the Serjeant and not issuing the writ of Attachment. Their advice won the day, and the record reads, "resolved, upon Question, to be sent for by the Serjeant or his Deputy."[21]

The second abuse of Parliamentary privilege was the arrest of Sir Thomas Shirley for debt and his incarceration in the Fleet Prison. On 14 May most of the day was taken up with a debate about how to get Sir Thomas out of prison, and on the 15th he was released, but not until the Warden of the Fleet was threatened with the dungeon of the Tower of London. On that same day Shirley was sworn into the House.[22] But that did not satisfy the members. On the 17th the Warden submitted himself to the House, and his letter was read and registered as part of the record. It was at that time that Hoskyns spoke up. His point seems small at first, but again it has important implications, for it asserted the rights of Parliament in a particular way. Hoskyns moved that the Warden should not get away with simply a letter but should submit himself by Petition to the House.[23] This action would place Parliament in a position somewhat like that of the monarch himself, who could be appealed to by petition. Feverish tempers were raging, however, and they wanted more overt action; so Hoskyns' suggestion was over-ruled in favor of making the Warden come in person and "humbly pray Favour of the House upon his Knees." On the 19th, he duly appeared, "got down on his knees and apologized and was let go with Fees."[24]

One of the twenty committees on which Hoskyns served during this session was for an "Act to disable Outlawes also termed ["Utlaries"] to be of the Parliament," obviously in response to the

201

it is agreed, that it shall not exceed One hundred; and is thought will be little more than Eighty.

For the Manner of the Relief; by Money collected, and given as a Donative, by a gross Sum.

For the Time of levying it; presently, or with as much Expedition as may be, considering their present Wants.

For the Subjects of and from whom it is to be levied; it is agreed, that it shall be out of the Alehouses, Inns, Taverns, Tipling-houses, and Cooks Houses, in this Manner; viz. of every Alehouse, Tipling-house, Cook, or other, selling Ale or Beer by the Quart, or less Measure, Two Shillings and Six-pence; of every Inn, Three Shillings and Four-pence; of every Tavern, Four Shillings; if this House like the Proportion.

The Authority by which it should be levied; the Levy not to be made by Act, but by Letters from his Majesty to the Justices of several Shires and Liberties; willing them to take a Review of the Licences of such Persons aforesaid, and to make them new Licences for **** for the which those Persons shall pay the several Sums before-mentioned.

The whole being levied, and returned hither into some certain Hands, to be given by Divident equally to the said Number of Captains.

That the House will recommend the said Persons by Names, and this Project, together with their Opinion, both of the Captains, and of the Manner of Relief, unto the King.

One speaker said that he thought it wrong to take money from so base a group; he suggested that Commons recommend that the King pay it. Considering the fact that Commons was so hesitant about giving the King any financial relief, the latter recommendation is almost as funny as the reason given to support it.[30]

The House did nothing with the proposal until 12 June, when the Speaker was forced to move the suggestion again. It appears that the King had urged that the Parliament commit itself with an

204

Act to cover the Captains' needs. The discussion
centered on various sources of money, and then the
Committee was ordered to return to the Star Chamber on Saturday the 16th to consider it further.[31]
On the 20th Hoskyns once again reported back to
the House the Committee's deliberation. Once a-
gain they had refused to take the responsibility
upon themselves and turned it over to the King:

> That, upon his Majesty's gracious Recommenda-
> tion, the Cause being often debated, and seri-
> ously treated of, both in this House, and at
> several Committees;
> It was resolved, that our humble Report should
> be made back to his Majesty;
> That we could not think it fit, they should
> be relieved by Act, enacted, or otherwise con-
> cluded, as an Act of this House:
> But what Course soever his Majesty should take
> for their Relief, we find their Cause so exceed-
> ingly well affected in every Man's particular,
> that their particular Opinions are, that if it
> should come unto them, not as to Parliament-men,
> in the Country, where their respective Powers
> and Friendships stand, it were like to receive
> as effectual and earnest Furtherance, as ever
> might be expected amongst his Majesty's Subjects,
> in Matter of this Nature.[32]

It is unlikely that any of those voting would be
among those hurt by the assessment. At any rate,
the House divided, and the Project was approved,
104 to 84, and was entered in the record.

Hoskyns spoke up in the House on the subject
of three other Committees of which he was a member,
and from other sources we can reconstruct more
fully what his position might have been in at least
two cases. The first of the Committees that drew
his comment was one of the hottest of the session,
and one which grew out of an unexpected event. In
the middle of the session the Bishop of Bristol
published a book scoring the Commons for its proceedings on the matter of the Union. This understandably stirred the wrath of the House, and they

I take it not indifferent, that both should by
ye abrogation of the same law bee equally repealed. The one hath his living Casuall by his
temporall paines; the other his maintenance Certaine by ecclesiasticall provision. The one
may purchase by his annuall revenues, and soe
may raise a patrimony lawfully to maintaine his
posteritie the other can by noe thrift vppon
the Common good gather a living f^{or} Wife and
Children wthout imbeseling from ye poore, de-
ducting from hospitallitie, defrauding the intent of the giver o^r defrauding his successor.
Lastly the one hath all to the vse of his office,
the other is owner of nothing but to his owne
behoofe and disposition.[38]

But actually in the Directions he was arguing a
technical point that was no longer in dispute.
Marriages had been allowed, and under the newer
circumstances, he sided with the Masters with whom
he had associated. Hoskyns was conservative on
legal matters, but when a law had been changed, he
was liberal in the interpretation of the new situation. But he and Martin were not able to change
the mind of the House, and the Bill passed. Before it did, however, it was suggested that Eton
and Winchester be added to it. Here the two Wyke-
hamists were more successful, and it was decided
that if anyone wanted to include these two schools,
they would have to submit a new Bill.

Near the end of the session Hoskyns was put
on another Committee in which as Deputy Steward of
Hereford he had already shown an interest: an Act
"For the Abating, and to restrain, the new Erection of all Weres, Kiddells, Stanks, and other Ob-
structions in great and navigable Rivers." Those
whose interests lay in constructing weirs naturally spoke up against the Bill. Hoskyns is named
as one of those supporting it, but nothing of what
he said is noted.[39] His earlier letter to the Commissioners about the situation on the Wye leaves no
doubt as to what his arguments might have been.

Hoskyns appears to have been a hard-working

member of Parliament, taking his duties both on
the floor and in committee quite seriously. He
served on twelve Committees besides the ones already mentioned, ranging from personal inheritance
matters to restrictions on trade and support of
local industries.[40] He was not what George Herbert would term "a morning man":

> When there is a Parliament, he is to endeavour
> by all means to be a Knight or Burgess there;
> for there is no School to a Parliament. And
> when he is there, he must not only be a morning
> man, but at Committees also; for there the par-
> ticulars are exactly discussed, which are
> brought from thence to the House but in gen-
> erall.[41]

The Committees on which he served had a remarkably
good record for successful bills. Only that on
Skinners was completely rejected, while ten were
passed. Moreover, as one of the Committee members,
Hoskyns became closely associated with a powerful
group of men who in the succeeding years would
more and more direct the destiny of England as the
Stuarts showed increasing inability to deal with
Parliamentary government. Among those who almost
daily shared committee assignments with Hoskyns
were Francis Moore, Sir George More, Nathaniel
Bacon, Henry Yelverton, Sir Charles Cornwallis,
Sir George Carew, Sir Robert Wroth, Sir George Vil-
liers (father of the future royal favorite, the
Duke of Buckingham), Sir James Scudamore, Sir
Richard Lovelace, Sir Edward Lewknor, Nicholas
Fuller, Sir John Thynne (brother of John's friend
Aegremont), Robert Bowyer, Sir Edward Greville,
Sir Thomas Hoby and his brother Sir Edward, Sir
Henry Beaumont, Sir Edward Stafford, Sir Hugh Beeston, Sir John Bennett, Sir Francis Bacon, Sir
Henry Neville, Toby Matthew, and John's long-time
close friend Richard Martin. Most of these men
would be immortalized by John's bawdy pen before
the first Parliament of King James was through,
but that was not to be before Hoskyns had gotten
to know them well and they had gotten to know his
particular kind of humor, which, it must be ad-

209

Footnotes for Chapter VII

1. Hoskyns' poem was the 253rd entry in the collection.
2. f. 7v.
3. Journals of the House of Commons, from... 1547 ... to... 1628, Vol. I, 141. The king's speech is on pp. 142-146.
4. Commons Journals, I, 151.
5. Quoted in Davies, The Early Stuarts, 1603-1660, p. 4; found in Bacon's Works, X, 183.
6. C.J. I, 946.
7. C.J. I, 172.
8. C.J. I, 202.
9. C.J. I, 978.
10. C.J. I, 223.
11. Bald, John Donne, pp. 144-45. Bald also quotes the Earl of Strafford on More, that he "had the annoying habit of rising up in Parliament 'about Eleven of the Clock,... [to] make Repetition of all that had been spoken that Day.'"
12. C.J. I, 984, 231.
13. C.J. I, 190-92.
14. C.J. I, 949.
15. C.J. I, 176.
16. C.J. I, 952. Once again, the second recorder placed the final statement among the contra speakers, p. 179.
17. C.J. I, 180-81.
18. C.J. I, 242, 995.
19. C.J. I, 246-47.
20. C.J. I, 170, 945.
21. C.J. I, 175, 948.
22. C.J. I, 210, 972.
23. C.J. I, 212, 974.
24. C.J. I, 976.
25. C.J. I, 948, 176, 183, 185, 957, 212, 974.
26. C.J. I, 184, 956.
27. C.J. I, 961, 966, 206, 969.
28. C.J. I, 185, 957, 190, 960, 202, 966, 206.
29. C.J. I, 221.
30. C.J. I, 224, 979.
31. C.J. I, 237, 991.
32. C.J. I, 243, 995.
33. C.J. I, 981.

34. C.J. I, 230, 983.
35. C.J. I, 232-33.
36. C.J. I, 234.
37. C.J. I, 238, 991, 243, 244, 996.
38. f. 11v.
39. C.J. I, 245, 997.
40. Restraining of frivolous Actions (C.J. I, 182, 954, 956, 959); the Jointure of the Wife of Martin Calthrop, Gentleman (187, 958, 961, 193, 962, 211, 973, 224, 245); Against the Turning of Coppices, or Underwoods, into Pasture or Tillage (This same Committee considered another Bill at the same time: "For the Preservation of Wood and Timber." 189, 960, 964, 198, 964.); To prevent the Overcharge of the People, by Stewards of Court Leets, and Court Barons (200, 965, 212, 974, 215, 976); for the Making of Sail Cloths, called Poll-davies, and Mildernix (205, 968, 221, 977, 244, 996); for the Relief of such, as use the Handicraft of Skinners (214, 975, 235, 989, 237, 991); for the Confirmation of a Decree, made in Chancery, for the Payment of 505 l. 10 s. 6 d. and Resignation of a Lease, after Sixteen Years Suit (231, 984); for the establishment of manors of the late Duke of Somerset (237, 991); to encourage Seamen of England to take Fish, whereby they may increase, to furnish the Navy of England (243, 995, 244, 996, 250, 1000); Concerning Attorneys and Clerks in the Courts of King's Bench and Common Pleas (244, 996); Concerning Tanners, Curriers, Shoemakers, and others, occupying Cutting of Leather (247, 998, 250, 1000, 251); and For Explaining of a former Act made Anno 43 Eliz. intituled, An Act for the Enabling of Edward Nevill, of Birling in the County of Kent, and Sir Henry Nevill, his Son and Heir apparent, to dispose of certain Copyhold Lands, Parcel of the Manor of Rotherfield in Sussex, and the Manors of Allesley and Filloughley, in the County of Warwick (210, 238, 991, 250, 1000).
41. Joseph Summers, George Herbert (1954), p. 47. Herbert, in A Priest to the Temple, lists this activity among the proper callings for men.

Moreover, on December 22nd, he was in Winchester signing a renewal of his lease on Titley for ten years.[4] Actually it was renewable every four years. In 1601 and 1602 he had paid his regular £8 13s 4d to the Bursar, but in the year 1603 he had missed a payment. This year, 1604, however, he paid for two years and for renewal of the lease, to the amount of £25.[5] The Titley account was a drain on his finances throughout his life, and even now he was having some trouble making the annual payment. There is no question that he wished that Hereford paid its representatives the 2s per day salary after each Parliamentary session instead of waiting until the entire Parliament was over. Unfortunately, it would be fourteen years before he was paid for even the opening year of this Parliament.

Until at least two months before John arrived at Winchester to renew his lease, his youngest brother, Charles, had still been there. John would have visited him each autumn when he went to Winchester to pay his rent to the College. Charles had been admitted as a probationary fellow at New College on 26 July 1604 and had matriculated from there on 26 October. Two years later, on 22 July 1606, he was admitted as a regular fellow of the College, and was admitted to the B.A. on 13 April 1608, completing his determination exercises in 1609.[6] We have already noted Aubrey's statement about Charles' ingenuity and the fact that he killed himself with hard study. We really know very little about Charles except that he wrote two memorial poems in Latin while at Oxford,[7] in 1605 and 1606, neither of which is up to the level of his elder brother, and that the epigrammatist John Heath celebrated Charles as well as John in his Two Centuries of Epigrammes in 1610. We shall also see that Charles shared an interest with John in the Virginia Company. Aubrey may be very nearly right about the cause of Charles' death, for he died in 1609, immediately after leaving Oxford. Heath blamed Charles' weak body, however.

This same month of December 1604 saw sickness

216

and near death back in Hereford. John's brother
Thomas, "being sicke in body," wrote out his will
on the 11th. It indicates already some of the
friction between himself and John that is to be
apparent in John's letters for years to come.
There can be little doubt but that John treated
this brother more as a servant than an equal.
Thomas describes himself as "of Dydley" a geographical attribute that seems to have resulted
from an indenture of 1596 in which Thomas' father
leased Monkton for a period to cover the lives of
three of his sons, Thomas, Dr. John, and Charles,
if they were to let him use it for the rest of his
life and his wife's. The same appears true of the
property in Didley. At any rate, Thomas willed
his rights to Monkton to his father and mother during their lifetimes and then to Dr. John and
Charles. He left his brother Phillip all his lands
in Orcop and Didley, as well as "all the reasidue
of my goodes Cattles and Chattles whatsover vnbe-
queathed." Phillip was to be the executor, and
after he had paid all of Thomas' debts, legacies,
and funeral expenses, he was to share "anie ov^r-
plus" with Dr. John and Charles "in some reasonable
sorte." All that he left his barrister brother was
£3 3s. There is more to the sentence designating
this legacy, but the entry is too stained to be
legible. But there is no question that the size
of the gift indicates a real coolness between the
brothers.[8]

This coolness at home certainly did not de-
tract from the other event of this interim year
between sessions of Parliament. In 1605 John's
efforts as a writer of humorous epitaphs received
wide public attention. William Camden published
his Remaines of a Greater Worke... and, as we have
already seen, brought his collection of antiquarian
items to a close with "a few conceited, merry, and
laughing Epitaphs, the most of them composed by
Master John Hoskins, when he was young." Now all
of England was acquainted with the lighter wit of
the Member of Parliament from Hereford. The fact
that the volume was dedicated to Hoskyns' fellow
member of Parliament Sir Robert Cotton, the other

217

Footnotes for Chapter VIII

1. Aubrey, ed. Dick, p. 145.
2. Sheepskin Bags, 1602-05, 1605-06.
3. Hopwood, II, 450.
4. Liber Registarij, f. 110v; Upper Muniment Room, Drawer 30.
5. Bursars Accounts 1599-1600 to 1623-1624.
6. Liber Successionis; Aubrey (ed. Clarke), p. 416; Oxford Register, Part II, 276; Part III, 277.
7. MS King's 12. LXIV, ff. 44-5; Funebria, Wood, 460 (the latter noted in Osborn, p. 250).
8. Early Hereford Wills, Hereford City Library.
9. HMC Marquis of Salisbury... at Hatfield House, Pt. XVII (1938), p. 360.

Chapter IX
Rounds Two and Three

At the beginning of December 1604, five very misguided Roman Catholics started to work digging a hole through the basement wall of a house adjoining the upper House of the Parliament. King James had managed, during his first year as monarch, to lose the affection of people from a great many walks of life. Just as he had angered the puritan element within the Church of England by failing to attack the Catholic Recusants with the spirit that they wanted, so he had failed to gain the following of the Roman Catholics, who felt he should have gone much farther in allowing them back into full citizenship in England. Moreover, unlike his predecessor, James did not walk a steady middle course but wavered from side to side, angering everyone in the process. But no one was angrier than one Robert Catesby and his four associates, Thomas Percy, Thomas Winter, John Wright, and Guido (better known as Guy) Fawkes.

Catesby understood that under the present circumstances, with James making overtures to both France and Spain, no foreign prince was about to invade Britain to better the condition of English Catholics. His only chance lay in reducing Britain to a state of near paralysis and then having his Catholic friends provide the new leadership. Today the whole plot reads something like a good French burglar film. The conspirators hired the house closest to Parliament, expecting the new Parliament to meet in early February. They even brought in enough food and wine for twenty days so that they could work undisturbed and unseen during the vital last fortnight. Guy Fawkes changed his name to John Johnson and posed as Thomas Percy's servant. This gave him a reason to stay near the door and act as sentinel for the diggers, giving them "warning vpon the least signe of suspition, when to cease, and when to worke againe."[1] They kept guns and powder with them at all times so that

221

Star Chamber, convicted, fined £30,000, and recommitted to the Tower for life. The charges against him were obviously trumped up, including the first item: "For endeuouring to bee the head of the English Papists, and to procure them Tolleration."[2] Henry Garnet, the head of the English Jesuits in England, had been tried in March and then executed on the charge that he knew of the plot and had not reported it--the same charge implied but not actually stated against Northumberland.

More probable an explanation of Cecil's role is that he knew just enough from messages from the continent to realize that something was definitely planned, and he kept putting off Parliament until someone else discovered the plot. The results would be the same.

And in some ways he got what he wanted. This was no Parliament of Love, but it did end up in May having achieved two major goals of the King: Parliament willingly and almost graciously voted Subsidies for James, and they agreed to set up a Commission to make recommendations on the Union. But the main subjects of debate remained the problem of the Purveyors and the subject of Grievances to be submitted to the King for reform. Moreover, the growing structure of a self-directing Parliament was beginning to become clear. Three times during the spring all of the lawyers in the Commons were required to be present. That it was considered an important move is indicated by Robert Bowyer's comment for 5 February 1606, "Note the Serieant was sent into the hall to requier the lawyers which are members of the howse to come up and give ther attendance and he tooke his mace."[3] The Commons was increasingly becoming aware of the fact that much of its power lay in the ability of its lawyer members to argue from past precedents in setting limits to the prerogatives of the monarch and claiming its own privileges. It was not until the next session that the House would begin to realize how to use the power of the Committee of the Whole, when no official records would be kept but when all members could share in the stat-

ing of positions on proposed bills, especially
those of greatest interest. Twice during this
session, however, the Committee on Grievances was
opened to any member of the House who wished to be
present. On 11 March, "the howse ordered that the
former committees appointed to consider of greavances should consider farder therof, and likewise
what is fit to be doon for supplie of the Kings
occasions, and at this Committee anie of the howse
to be present and every man present to have a
voice as a Committee."4 On 24 April the Committee
took a further step (but the importance of the Committee of the Whole had obviously not yet taken
hold):

> The Committees for the Matter of Grievances or
> so many of them as were present, and such as
> offered and arose voluntarily to accompany them;
> went up into the Committee Chamber to Marshall
> these Grievances, during which tyme being a
> full hower the House did sitt idle without doe-
> ing anything; after which long pawsing, the Com-
> mittees sent word that they would come downe in-
> to the House (if so it pleased the House) and
> conferr with the Company, not as in the House,
> but by way of Committee: This the Speaker hav-
> ing received from them by the Sergeant, did de-
> liver to the House, and the House alloweing
> thereof; The Speaker added, that himself in
> this Case was to departe the place, which with
> allowance he did, and the most of the Company
> departed with him....5

Committee membership and the chairmanship of
the Committees remained the same as before, a somewhat haphazard arrangement which, although it did
not lead to the sense of purposeful direction
achieved later in planned committees, also did not
allow for very strong governmental direction in
either the choosing or direction of the Committees.
Committee members were chosen from those who stood
up and volunteered or from those names shouted out
by other members. Nicholas Fuller tried to bring
a little order to this system on 28 January 1606,
when he moved that "no man shoulde name above two

225

of legislators. As the daily records drone on,
they show ever more clearly that the House became
more and more suspicious of Bacon as being merely
a tool of the King. Even in the matter of the
Union, Bacon changed from making early speeches
against the proposal to supporting the King's position completely. Rather, Hoskyns was one of the
new leaders who sprang up in this Parliament, for
many of them their first, to take on the responsibilities of committee work and chairmanship, of
speaking up at crucial moments, of putting on the
brakes when the King's party tried to move the Commons too fast, of looking for precedents for their
actions and for consciously making precedents with
their actions in order to establish the power of
the body in which they were working. During this
second session Hoskyns was fourth among the top
ten speakers in the House, according to a study
made by Williams Mitchell of the rise of the revolutionary "party" in the Commons. In the fourth
session he was fifth.[9]

It was indeed a busy few months for John.
Parliament had met on the afternoon of that fate-
ful day of November 5th and again on the 6th, but
the excitement surrounding the plot that had almost done away with the lives of all of those
gathered in Parliament was too much for any business. Besides, there was still the threat of further danger; so, on the 9th, after statements of
appropriate thankfulness of the House to God for
their deliverance and the deliverance of the King,
Parliament was prorogued until 21 January 1606.
On that day the Commons returned to its discussion
of the plot and set up a Committee to insure severe
proceedings against Catholics, Popish agents, etc.
All of the early business was of an emergency,
anti-Recusant nature. On the 22nd the usual sorts
of bills began to be sent to Committee, including
a Bill for the better Execution of penal Statutes;
and with the Committee for that Bill, Hoskyns'
activities began.[10] Also on this early Bill, Sir
Edwin Sandys started to exert his quiet leadership
very clearly in the new alignment of forces: "Sir
Edwyne Sandys moved that the same Committees, manie

of them being learned in the Law, might allso consider what penall lawes are needelesse and fitt to
be abrogated: this mocion was allso allowed."11

Hoskyns spent the following five months in almost constant activity in Parliament. He served
on at least 41 committees and spoke at least
thirty-two times. He was committee chairman, or
at least reported in the bills, five times. He
was deeply involved in the three main items of discussion for the session: the continuing criticism
of the activities of the Purveyors, the discussion
of when and how much to give the King in the way
of subsidy, and the drawing up of a set of Grievances to submit to the King for remedy.

For the Purveyors, on 29 January 1606, "An
act for the better execucion of sondry statuts
against Purveiors and Cartakers" was first read
and submitted the following day to a Committee
which included Hoskyns with such men as Sir George
More and Sir Edwin Sandys. The Bill indicates
that Hoskyns' argument in the previous session had
won the support of Commons. There was not to be
any composition for the right of Purveyance, but
there was to be regulation of the abuses now present among Purveyors. Some of the abuses were
listed in the Bill: that present commissions made
to Purveyors "containe divers matters contrarie to
the statuts of Purveiance now in force" and leave
out things which should be there according to the
laws; that people are called up "before the officers of the Greenecloth" on the pretense that some
of the matters in the statutes are not in force
against the King, "wherby the subiect cannot know
how to give his obedience in case of Purveiance"
and is often wrongfully imprisoned without knowing
the law which would protect him.

The act first confirmed all former statutes
touching Purveyance and Car-Taking. Then, among
other items, it provided that no warrant should be
made in the King's name but one which was warrant-
able by the statutes and which omitted nothing in
the statutes. It required that cash be paid for

228

the hiring of carts and carriages according to the
rates set down in the act. The Justices of the
Peace in every county were to rate the fees for
hiring the carts and carriages each year "at the
Quarter cessions next after easter." The act also
went into detail as to how the owner was to be
paid by a customary official, such as the bailiff,
head constable, or "Coferer of the King's howse."
Appraisers of things to be taken were to be appointed and sworn to deal honestly between the King
and his subjects. And perhaps most important of
all, the Purveyor was to be forced to swear before
the Lord Steward or Treasurer or Controller as to
the truth of any complaint he was making against
any subject before the subject was called or sent
for to appear before the officers of the Greencloth
(the Lord Steward's court for the Royal Household).
The accused was also to have two days' notice before he had to appear in court, "to the ende he
maie come upp prepared with witnesses to iustifie
himselfe." If the complaint of the Purveyor was
found false, he was to be punished according to
the laws for perjury. Moreover, the law was to
hold for at least the period covered by either six
years or until after the end of the following Parliament.[12]

On the day the Bill was committed, Hoskyns
recommended that it be extended to include Salt-
petre men, and this was left up the Committee.[13]
On 13 February the Committee revealed its plan of
action to the House: first, they will set forth
their grievances and inform the Lords of the Bill
that did so. If the King directs the Lords in
some other course of action, they will then examine that. If the Lords suggest some Composition,
then they will listen and deal further with that
issue at that time.[14] Discussion on the Bill went
on almost daily through the middle of March, and,
at the request of the King, there were meetings
with a Committee from the House of Lords. For one
such meeting, on 19 February, the Committee on Purveyors agreed to go prepared "as well to annsweare
what might be obiected in defence of Purveiance as
to obiect or complaine of Purveiors." Among the

229

principal points under debate was the fact that a
statute of the time of Henry VI had included in
its statement on purveyance the phrase "savinge to
the King his prerogative of and to the premisses."
The House's answer was to be that suggested by Hoskyns in the previous session, that the King's prerogative was that of pre-emption, namely the right
to be "first to be served for his money."[15] On
18 March the Bill was passed and sent along to the
House of Lords two days later.[16] But that did not
end the debate on Purveyance, and on 12 April both
Houses wanted to discuss the issue once more,[17]
this time as one of the Grievances to be sent to
the King. Finally, on 10 May, the Bill was passed
and sent up to the Lords.[18]

But Purveyance was just one of the numerous
grievances which Parliament wished to lay before
the King before they granted the monarch the money
to run his government. And Hoskyns was a busy member of the Committee assigned the task of drawing
up the grievances. On 12 February the Committee
was assigned its first meeting on the 14th, the
same day on which the King was to call a joint Committee meeting at which the "Commens might according to his Majesties most gracious invitacion ac-
quaint the Lords and by them the King with their
greavances wherof they might have redresse and from
their Lordships understande the Kings occasions."[19]
The move on the King's part was intelligent but too
open. It was clear that he did not wish a lot of
time spent compiling grievances instead of working
out the Subsidy. At the same time he made the mistake of acquiescing in connecting the grievances
with the granting of the Subsidy, which was the
precedent that Parliament was striving for. Hoskyns argued that what they were doing was not only
reasonable but of long practice. On 12 March he
spoke at some length on the subject, pointing out
that "Greavances weare aunciently sent upp to the
King." However, it was clear that it now entailed
some danger because "to treate of them att Conference or Committees doth butt disclose our harts
and make our selves to be singled out." That did
not keep him from going further, however. He

230

showed the weakness of arguing that the King's
wants should lead to the Commons voting money without checking the possible misuse of that money:

> And as touching the matter, I must say that be-
> tweene theis proposicions: 1. A Kinge may not
> waunt; 2. Subiects ought not to examine how it
> is spent: A supply may easily be spent so may a
> resupply, and so the Fortunes of the crowne may
> runne a circle and whatsoever wee give, wee can-
> not give that [which] may suffice.[20]

Pushed very far, this sentiment could call for a
line-item budget, but, of course, Hoskyns was not
pushing so far. He just wanted guarantees that
Parliament's money was not to be spent in the very
activities against which there were grievances already.

On March 15th, Fuller brought in a collection
of Grievances and especially urged the first,
which concerned the restoring of deprived Ministers. The day before, a Bill had been submitted
to attack this grievance with the title, "An act
for inablinge deprived Ministers to sue and prosecute their Appeales."[21] In the debate that followed Fuller's speech, which represented the more
puritan side, such men as Sir William Morrice, who
was openly known and described as a Roman Catholic,[22] supported the Bill, as did Hoskyns. John
argued that anyone would have "a dull Spirit, that
hath no Feeling in this Cause." He then made his
usual kind of witty twist, that "We ought to be
Intercessors for such as are Intercessors for us
to God." But it was clear that he did not want
Commons to act alone on religious matters. He
urged the House "To confer with the Bishops, before we offer it to the King." His motion carried.
All through his life Hoskyns was to fight for the
position that religious acts were the combined
business of the monarchy, priesthood, and laity,
and not the business of any one of them alone. On
17 March the House returned the Grievances as a
whole to the Committee to work on.[23] On 5 April
Fuller reported the Committee's action on the

231

Grievances touching Ecclesiastical Matters, but
noted that nothing was to be done in the way of
submission to the King until the Committee met with
the Lords, as the House had directed. There were
four grievances under this general heading. The
first was

> ... in Effect To restore Ministers deprived,
> Suspended, or Silenced by force of the Cannon
> in the last Synode for want of Subscription to
> their Appeale. The 2d. To give remedy, and re-
> dresse to the Multitude of Spirituall Commis-
> sions, Commonly called High Commissions, where-
> by diverse Bishops have, and all may have more
> Authority then appertayneth to the ArchBishop
> in his ordinary Iurisdiction; Therefore it is
> desired, That there may be only two such Com-
> missions, vid. The one to be executed and set
> on in London, or within 10.miles thereof for the
> Precinct of Canterbury: The other at Yorke or
> within 10. Miles thereof for the Province of
> Yorke; The third requiring That in the Summons
> against any Person should be contained the mat-
> ter to be obiected against him. Fourthly, That
> Excommunication be not used for triffling Caus-
> es.24

The struggle against the Bishops that John Milton
was to join in so valiantly had begun.

In a joint meeting with the Lords on 3 May,
Henry Yelverton carried the fight a good deal further. He spoke for the House, and his chief point
was

> that the Statute in the first Session of the
> King doth repeale the Statute of Queen Mary
> which did repeale the Statute of E[dward] 6. the
> Effect of which Statute of E. 6. is, That all
> Bishops and Archbishops shall make their Pro-
> cesse in the name of the King, and themselves,
> viz. The Bishop is to be but Testis; And said
> Mr. Yelverton, your Lordships my Lords of the
> Bishops having continued Proces in your owne
> names, the Proceedings are Coram non Iudice,

232

and voide.

Further witness bore this claim out, much to the
Bishops' displeasure.[25]

On April 7th Fuller brought in seven more
grievances that were under debate in Committee and
not agreed on. These were a group to be submitted
to the King by Petition rather than by Act. They
included such items as an imposition on Currants
"and other Merchandise after long Journies." The
complaint was an obvious one but one which the
House could not handle by Bill. All agreed that
the right to impose duties on goods coming into
the country was part of the King's prerogative.
All they could do was decry the immense jump in
that Imposition, from 18d. to 5s. 6d. They claimed
that it was killing foreign trade and ship building, "Yea the best Marchant of London is determined to sell foure great Shipps, and doth offer
in them to lose diverse thousand Pounds."[26]

At this point the Speaker, seeing the problem
that the House was getting itself into, moved that
the grievances should be divided into two groups,
those against the law and those, although warrant-
able by law, which ought to be redressed. In the
Committee meeting that afternoon in the Exchequer
Chamber, Hoskyns addressed himself to the kind he
was most interested in, those against the law.
There were certain men given commissions by the
King to deal with persons who had been given Crown
lands and who were willing to pay a fee to have defects in the title to the property set right. Hoskyns brought a complaint against one of these men,
who

now is easily perspicuous, for that he rideth on
horseback, doth prevent the Kings Subiects of
the Benefitt of his Majesty Grace, whereby they
may establish, and have their Estates amended
upon Composition with Certaine Commissionors.
And his Course is, First he sendeth for the
Party by a Letter from the Commissionors, when
such Partie cometh to him, he telleth him to

233

this Effect, You hold such Lands, That Tytle is
defective, This is the Case, and then he delivereth him such Cases he thinketh good, and with
all he requireth to see the Parties Evidence
and upon Sight thereof, and notes taken out of
it, or having such Evidence left with him, he
then seeketh how a Quirke may be found in the
Tytle, and for this Purpose he hath obtayned
Warrants for Sight of the Kings Records in diverse Offices, as namely in the Augmentation
Records which he hath soe handled, That a man
may tracke him easily where he hath bene (and
note here, Mr. Hoskyns used plaine words signi-
fying that this Fellowe hath blotted and falsi-
fied many Records there) yea said he, he hath
gotten a lease of 40. or 41. Mannors and when
the Tenants or Owners of them come up to compound, they come too late: And all this he doth
upon Promise to bring one hundred thousand
Pounds to the King in fyve yeares; And for reward, he and an other have the fourth Part of
all they shall soe bring in: But hitherto he
hath not brought to the King, I thinck one thousand Pounds.   In Conclusion his name is Tipper.[27]

Mr. Tipper was well known around Parliament, and
even that evening had a conversation with the man
who took the above notes, Robert Bowyer. Bowyer
says that he mentioned the proceedings that day in
an around-about way and that Tipper immediately
said he knew that it was probably a lease by Mr.
Pelham that was being discussed.

    But Mr. Tipper's activities were well known to
any member of Parliament with a decent memory--and
Hoskyns had more than a decent memory. Tipper had
been the principal agent of the poet-courtier Sir
Edward Dyer, under a monopoly given by Queen Elizabeth for the searching of concealed property.[28] On
5 May 1604, in the previous session of Parliament,
it was disclosed that Tipper had taken £100 to insure the passage through Commons of a Bill for the
making of Hats and Felts and had been called to the
bar for this early piece of lobbying.[29] Mr. Fuller

made the charge after hearing of Tipper through
Sir Edward Mountague and Sir Edward Hoby. Tipper
argued, on 7 May, that he used all of the money
for expenses to get the bill through, and the
charges were dropped. Obviously members of the
House were involved and wanted the issue squelched.
But on 11 May the issue came up again and was sent
to Committee.30 That satisfactorily stopped any
further action. Actually, William Tipper had been
accused of misusing his office as Commissioner for
concealed lands back in 1600 but instead of being
punished had been rewarded by the Crown.31

This time Hoskyns, who by now knew his way
around land dealings, was not to be put off so
easily. On 16 April he submitted the Grievance in
writing to Fuller, who gave it to the Speaker, who
then read it out:

Many Cathedrall Churchs, Colledges, Hospi-
talls, Corporations and Foundations erected to
charitable uses, infinite Numbers of the Kings
Tenants are grieved with the uniust vexation and
subtill Practices of Tipper, he pretendeth himselfe to be an Officer authorized to deale with
all such as have defective Tytles and Estates
derived out of the Crowne, and by Color thereof
carrieth a great Port and Countenance Keepeth
an Office without Warrant, and he and his Clerk
takes unlawfull Fees, and Extorts of the Kings
Subiects great Summes of Money; He hath accesse
to the Kings Records, perswadeth the Clerks of
the Court of Augmentations and the Exchequer
that they suffer not the Subiect to have sight
of the Records for strengthning their Tytles;
And since his Accesse, the Records are mis-
placed, unperfect, and imbezelled: He hath procured to himselfe Grants of the whole Estates
of Cathedrall Churches, and other Corporations,
and of particular Persons, and vexed them without Cause: He hath now a Grant of 41. Mannors,
with diverse other Granges and Fermes to his
use, for the Consideration of 20£--only paid by
Clerck and Clerk: And when the Kings Tenants
and others called up to compound for defective

235

Tytles by his Majesty honorable Commissioners
authorized to make them good Estates, doe offer
Composition, after such tyme as the said Tipper
hath by long Molestation discovered their Tytles, then he interposeth his said lease betwixt
them, and his Majesty favour intended by the
said Commission, in fraud of his Majestyes Grace,
and dishonour of the Commission, he first giveth
false Coppies to such as come to Compound, then
searcheth their Evidences, and either taketh
bribes, or multiplieth Endlesse Suites. He and
his Partaker hath convenanted to bring into his
Majesty 100000£--in few yeares by discovery of
Tytles, and is to have together with his Partaker either a fourth part of the same 100000£
--and what ever else he shall bring in in money,
or a fourth part of the Lands so evicted in
lease for 90 yeares at his Election. And hath
undertaken debts due to the King, but little or
nothing is brought in by this Course to the King,
infinite Number of Subiects troubled and Scan-
dall raysed by this Course, which in Common Persons is Barretry and Maintenance. It is humbly
desired that his Majesty Service be supplied by
a man of honnor, Reputation, and by the direction of his Majesty Judges or learned Counsell,
and that they be not referred over to such a
person to worke upon them by undirect Sleights
to their great Charge and Grievance.32

The House ordered Tipper to appear on April 28th
with his lawyers. This was after Hoskyns announced
that Tipper was "desirous to be heard."33 For the
next few days the Grievance Committee was busy, at
the request of the House, framing the different
Grievances. Hoskyns is one of those specifically
designated to help in this work, along with The
King's Learned Counsel, Sir Henry Neville, Sir Edwin Sandys, Christopher Brooke, Fuller, and a few
others.34 Brooke recommended that "these Committees should meete as soone as might be, and devide
the Articles so as no Man to be burthened with more
then one Article."35 On the 26th these men were
sent out from the regular morning meeting of the
House to work on the Grievances some more in the

236

Court of Wards.[36] On the 28th Tipper was heard in the Committee, and Hoskyns, Fuller, and Mr. Winch were ordered to frame the Article against Tipper and to present it on Friday morning, May 2nd. That afternoon Tipper and his counsel were to be heard, "if he require it."[37]

The confrontation took place on Saturday, the 3rd.

After dinner Councell came to the Barr to shew Cause, and satisfy the House, why the Article and matter exhibited into the House should not be exhibited to the King as a Grievance. Tipper desired to be discharged in particular, and he would answer thereto particularly; Generally he said, that 50. E.[dward] 3. untill the tyme of H.[enry] 4. there went forth almost yearely Commissions to enquire of Concealements, and that in the late Queens tyme diverse Bookes of Concealement were granted: All which by this Commission of amendement of defective Titles, wherein he is imploied, are avoided; Then he shewed the Course holden in this Commission.[38]

During the discussion, Hoskyns complained "That Mr. Typper singled out the Preferrer [of the Grievance] by the Name of the Gentleman." Tipper was reprehended for using this vague description and was asked who it was. He replied, "Mr. Hoskins." When told that he was in error for his action, he "craved Pardon."[39]

Against Tipper it was inter alia alledged, that he did threaten some that heretofore kept the Records in the Tower, for shewing them to Suitors. Tipper said he never had but 3. Suites, viz. One with Mr. Dutton, an other with Mr. Pelham of Sussex; The third with Mr. Tirwitt of Lynconshire.

And he claimed that the one with Mr. Tirwitt had been settled with a fee, or compounded.

After Tipper withdrew, there was a full-scale

237

description of his past activities, and I think
that we can take for granted that Hoskyns was the
one who did the describing:

To this after he was withdrawnen, it was answered That the Commission proceeded from a
gratious minde in the King, and was performed
most honorably by the Lord Commissioners after
that the Parties came to them, but Tipper being
employed in the Execution hereof, doth grieve
the People, as in the Articles is set downe.
And therefore out of the Tower was vouched a
Record mentioning a Petition of the Commons to
the King, that he would please to use Serieants
at Law and other Persons of good fame, in
searching out and enquiring his concealed Titles: And shewed that Tipper is a Person Notorious for his Evill Courses; for he was sued
from two Colledges, and 40. Churches in Wales,
whereof he tooke a lease for 40s. per Annum of
Queen Elizabeth: And in that Suite it appeareth that the Queen had 100 Marks yearely out of
the Premises for tenthes... and in that Suite a
decree passed against Tipper and Dawes defendants it is mentioned thus, viz. In detestation
of the Wicked, Odious, and Ungodly Practises of
the Defendants and these words were reade out
of the Exemplification of the decree.40

Hoskyns, who was doing a good deal of record-
searching for the Commons at the time, had used
his time well in building his case against Tipper.
The House referred the whole matter back to the
Committee for Grievances. On 10 May Hoskyns asked
that a special Committee be appointed on the Tipper case.41 Four more members of the House were
to give evidence at that time, the 12th, at the
Temple. As no more is heard, it may be taken for
granted that on the 15th, when Sir Francis Bacon
delivered the full Petition of Grievances to the
King, in the presence of the entire House, who had
gone along for the occasion, the Grievance against
Mr. Tipper was among them.42 Bacon had merely
wanted to read the Grievances to the King, but the
House demanded that they be handed to James; and

238

the reason that so many went--the most in the history of Parliament--may have been that they wanted to see that Bacon carried out their wishes.[43] This may be unfair, of course. Obviously the overt purpose of the grand concourse was to present to the King, along with the Petition of Grievances, the Bill of Subsidy which the King had waited through the whole session to receive.

There was one other grievance that Hoskyns spoke to during the long debates that took place in this session. It would seem at first to be an unimportant one, and indeed it was only included in the list by a vote of 109 for to 104 against.[44] The small total vote is due to the fact that Parliament was at this point very low in attendance. At a roll call on 9 April only 299 of the potential membership of 500 were present in the House, and at the best estimates, only 367 were anywhere around London.[45] Earlier in the month the King had said that it was not a good idea to go on with any final business of any importance until everyone was back in Parliament, but that he did not want orders from Parliament recalling members to go out through his sheriffs. It was a precedent he did not feel was warranted. He offered to send a message if they wanted him to, but the House decided it would be better if they handled such matters on their own.[46]

The Grievance under consideration was a Patent giving to Sir Roger Aston

all the Fynes, Amerciaments, and... other Penalties and Forfeitures Knowen under the Name of the Green Wax, rysing within the Dutchy of Lancaster, which is or may be of very great yearely value... under a small Rent of 48£--by the yeare, which preventeth those Subiects of the Dutchy from such Mercy and favour as alwaies heretofore hath bene used to good and loving Subiects, and giveth to private men to dispence with great faults, which is hurtfull to the Common Wealth, and may be the undoeing of many.[47]

239

Aston's defense, of 9 April, was that there was no
difference between the King's imposing amerciaments, or fines, at a rate set by the one imposing
them or the Duke of Lancaster, if there now were
one, or any other subject disposing of them instead of the King. Hoskyns was one who spoke a-
gainst the Bill, but in partial jest. Bowyer records him as introducing the lighthearted observation that the word standing for pity or mercy had
been changed, through Latin alterations, into a
word standing for the imposition of fines and penalties: "Mr. Hoskyns merrily said of this et
huiusmodi, that Misericordia, in latine is by this
meanes come unto Americiaments."48

There had been little humor in general in the
handling of the Grievances. The intention of the
House had been clear from the moment that discussion had started until the day that Bacon delivered
the Grievances and the Subsidy together to the
King. One was not to go until the other was ready.
Subsidy was tied to the King's reception of the
Grievances. It was not to be a much further step
to the position that the King would have to get
rid of the object of the Grievances before the money would be forthcoming. But Commons was still
feeling its way at this point.

On 10 February there had been a long initial
debate about Subsidies, including the usual line
that they indicated the mutual love of the King
and his people, that there were many needs of his
followers, etc. Hoskyns got right to the point,
however. It was the wrong time for the Subsidy.
That should be at the end of the session. He urged
the Commons "Not to knit the Two Ends of a Parliament together." He then suggested that they go
about the matter the proper way: "No Subsidy without a Bill; therefore a Committee."49 The entire
tone of the debate changed immediately, and when
the question was called as to whether to submit
the matter to Committee, it was so resolved. Moreover, it was put that the question was whether the
amount of money to be given was to be Two Subsidies and Four Fifteens, a rather traditional figure,

240

not taking into consideration the large needs presented by the King. (A Subsidy was a tax on land
while a Fifteen was a tax on movable property.)
The next day the King sent a message of congratula-
tion on the House's swift action on the matter of
Subsidies and their general agreement in open discussion. The irony of that message is that at the
end of the day the House deferred action "to a
Time uncertain."50

On the 19th, during a joint meeting with the
Lords over Purveyors, the Lords made it clear that
they were shocked by the attitude of the House.
They intimated that the lower House was spoiling
the nice relations of Parliament with the King:
Commons knew that the King had a desperate need of
money and they were just being petty. The representatives of the House answered back quite clearly that the House required freedom of movement in
its actions, that there was a need for remedy in
the abuses of the Purveyors and in other Grievances.
Mr. Hare, the leader of the House Committee, who
had been criticized by the Lords for his handling
of the House's position, was given a vote of confidence by his fellow M.P.'s.51 It is interesting to compare a statement made by Hoskyns twenty-
two years later, even when he was a Serjeant-at-
law, with the position the House was now taking:
"That knowing our own rights, we shall be better
enabled to give. Two legs go best together, our
just grievances and our supply; which he desires
may not be separated, for by presenting them together, they shall be both taken or both refused."52

The debates on Subsidy went on through the
early part of March, with Speaker Phelips trying
to get the House to make up its mind. On the 14th
he called for the Question, but had to put off the
decision when the nays had it.53 On the 18th a
message came from the King urging the House to a
decision and indicating that he would pay attention to their grievances. Even this just barely
brought the members to action. First the Speaker
proposed: "As many as thinck it fit and convenient to give any more to his Majestie then hath ben

241

already given say yea: and the econverso: and
uppon division of the howse, the Yea, was 140, and
the Nay 139." This could hardly be considered a
major triumph by the royal party, but it was all
they needed. The next question was whether to
make that further help in the form of Subsidy and
Fifteens, and the margin this time was 26. Then
the Speaker tried to see if he could force a further grant by proposing that they see how many extra Subsidies and Fifteens the Commons wished to
grant, but Sir William Skipwith lept to his feet
and said that issue had already been decided in the
previous vote: it was to be one Subsidy and two
Fifteens. The Speaker put it to the vote, and the
House agreed immediately.54 So the King had his
three Subsidies and six Fifteens in principle, but,
as we have seen, he didn't receive the official
Bill from the House until the end of the session,
along with the Grievances.

On the 22nd all of London was aroused by a
rumor that the King had been slain at Oking, about
ten miles west of the city. The rumor, which
started about 7 a.m., took such strange forms as a
charge that the deed had been done by a group of
Jesuits, or a group of Scotsmen dressed in women's
clothes, or by Spaniards, or Frenchmen. Most a-
greed that a poison-tipped dagger had been used.
The rumor reached Parliament at 8 o'clock, with
Sir George More carrying the message. All regular
business was dropped immediately, and at 11 a.m.
the House broke up. The arrival of James in the
city that afternoon brought an end to the uproar.55
It is possible that the rumor was started to bring
Commons to some action on the Subsidy Bill, but
there is no proof of that. If that was the purpose, it did not work.

On the 25th, however, the King sent a message
thanking the House for its action, and they then
debated on when the money should be paid. Hoskyns
urged that it should not be too fast because of the
penalty it would impose on the people. After all,
"The King [is] in Possession of the Subsidy."
Since that had been decided, their care should be

for the people who had to pay the money: "He
would not have the Sheep to say, the Bramble was
more merciful then the Shepherd."56 The King, who
had spoken of not wanting to be too much of a burden to his people, had given Hoskyns his opening.
The House then voted "that the first payment was
to be the first of August, the second the first of
May. The second Subsidy, the first payment in November Twelve-month, the second in May come two
Years. The Three in Two Year, from May to May."
Even with this schedule the King was to have to
complain in less than a year at the slowness with
which the money was coming in. Also, during this
session the slowness in finishing off the Subsidy
Bill was obvious, as it was not passed in its final
form until 9 May. Sir Anthony Cope and others opposed even the final reading of the Bill until the
Grievances were read on the basis that it would be
capitulation with the King.57 And the House did
not allow the Bill to pass up to the Lords until
the Grievances were ready.

The Subsidy Bill was not the only money bill
that the King was interested in during this session.
There remained the possibility of achieving a fixed
"Composition" for getting rid of the Purveyance
system completely. But if the Composition were
high enough, James would have had a yearly income
that would have removed his necessity of coming to
Parliament with hands outstretched, asking for support. For some, the matter of Composition was
merely a matter of how much, and the King wanted
far more than the Commons were willing to consider.
But for Hoskyns, just as it had been in the first
session, there was no question what the position of
the House should be. He simply opposed the whole
principle of Composition. On 25 February he gave
a short but telling speech based on past history.
His argument was that gradually the country was being caught in taxes that remained from medieval
trade relationships but was losing the services
that those early relationships had also provided:
"Tonage and Poundage [import duties on wines and
other commodities] remaineth; Safe-conduct and
Waftage [convoy protection] is gone." Moreover he

saw Composition as an act which entailed the decisions of future generations as much as their own:
"Our Ancestors passed Bills: --Never an Imposition of Inheritance demanded." Then he added a
real warning to those members of the House who saw
themselves gaining a new power for Parliament by
this act: "The Horse and the Hart did strive; the
Horse got the Victory; the Hart [is] at Liberty in
the Forest; the Horse inherits the Saddle and Bri-
dle."58

On 5 March once again "the howse entered into
dispute whether a composition for Purveiance should
be yeilded unto." And again Hoskyns joined the
contra, along with Nicholas Fuller. As in his previous statement, he made comparisons with the past;
for example, that in the Duke of York's case in 6
Edward III, the "Merchants granted Two Shillings
upon every Ton." But he was not going to agree to
the King's position of the rights of purveyance as
such. He argued that "Inter alia to prove the King
had no such valuable right in purveiance as might
be woorth much he disproved that which the Lord
Archbishop did speake att the last conference, uppon this text Hoc est ius regis: for quoth he in
the booke of Samuell [I Samuel 8] from whence this
text is drawen God spake of an evell King whom he
would sett over the people who should oppresse them
as there appeareth." a king that was given "To People, that God had rejected" because they had rejected Him. But, "quoth he in the 17 of Deuterono-
my wheare a good King is described there is not
such power saied to be in the King as that he could
take the goods of the subiects." Indeed, he was to
be "A King, that is not lifted up above his Brethren [17:20]." Hoskyns did not say it, but if anyone bothered to check his reference, he would find
the even more fascinating injunction that the people should not choose "a stranger over thee, which
is not thy brother." [17:15] At the time of the
discussion over Union, this was not the most politic of references. But Hoskyns unquestionably had
outpointed Richard Bancroft, the Archbishop of
Canterbury, on his own Biblical ground, for his
analysis of the sources is unquestionably accurate,

and he was using the Biblical context to excellent advantage. However, he left the debate with a light touch: "He concluded merily: viz. that if wee proceeded in a composicion he feared wee should do like unthrifts who begin with a Rent charge, then proceede to a Mortgage, and in conclusion departe with the lande itselfe." The figure of speech was extremely apt on the matter of Composition. He ended with his usual witty twist of word-meaning: "No Composition, but some other Composition."[59] Somewhere in his speech he had emphasized the perpetual nature of the planned Composition, saying that it would last till Doomsday. Two days later he was verbally slapped on his hand by the King's leading mouthpiece in the Commons, Sir Francis Bacon. On 7 March, while he was speaking for Composition, Bacon said,

> It is obiected that hereby wee shall bring a perpetuall taxe on the Realme. To which it is aunswered, that it is not desiered it should be perpetuall nor other than a probation for a tyme so as Doomesday (herin he glaunced at Mr. Hoskyns who two dayes before had used that woorde) is not to be expected before the Inconvenience hereof be founde, except the next parliament be saied to be the day of doome, if for anie inconvenience it take away and censure this composicion.[60]

If Hoskyns had been a bit hyperbolical, Bacon was being a little less than honest. In the end, no Composition was voted by the House, and the problem of Purveyance continued.

Hoskyns was on two other committees in which the King had special interest, one on a Bill of Attainder which would take away all of the civil rights, including the ability to pass on property to their children, of those who had been involved in the Gunpowder Plot. The Bill had been introduced on April 3rd as "An Act for the Attainder of of diverse Offendors in the late most Barbarous, most Monstrous, Detestable and Damnable Treason."[61] It had been sent down from the Lords by the Lord

245

Chief Baron, Sir Thomas Fleming, and

> was specially recommended by the Lord Chief Baron from the Lords unto the House with declaration that it was Matter of great moment, in which it was desired that Expedition Might be used.
> Mr. Speaker moved the House That this being a Matter of much consequence, they would advise what Course is to be holden therein; And for that diverse Offendors named in the Bill are absent, he wished the House to consider if it be not fitt to heare Counsell at the Barr to prove the Parties guilty: The House seemed to incline to that Motion, and the rather for that Mr. Alford affirmed That the same Course was herein held by the Lords. In Conclusion it was ordered and directed, That the Clerke should seeke and search what Presidents had bene in like Case.

There was considerable debate the next day as to whether the Bill should be read immediately, and Hoskyns joined people like Sir Edwin Sandys and Robert Bowyer in opposing it, partially because of the small number of members present in the House. However, the majority wanted it read, and it was. From the debate and the line-up of speakers, this was apparently a power-play by the forces of the King. On the 10th the Commons, realizing that the court forces were applying too much force, applied some legal restraint,

> In handling the Bill of Attainders, in which Case Councill was to deliver Evidence at the Barr, it was ruled, That the Kings Councell being Members of this House (viz) Mr. Sollicitor and Sir Francis Bacon) cannot, nor may not at the Barr for the King deliver Evidence to prove the Treasons, and so in all other Cases, for every Member is a Judge and cannot therefore give Evidence as Counsell at the Barr; Neverthelesse in such Case, the Kings Counsell as any other Member may deliver what he thinketh good, as well to informe the House in the Matter of

246

Fact, as by way of advise, Keeping his Place
but not at Barr.62

On April 29th, the King sent in a Message that
he felt the Bill needed strengthening, and the Committee was set up to include all Members of the
Privy Council, the King's Learned Counsel, and all
lawyers of the House.63 This same Committee, on 3
May, was given the other Bill which remained central to the King: "explaining a Branch of an Act
made in the first Session of this Parliament, intituled, An Act authorizing certain Commissioners
of the Realm of England to treat with Commissioners
of Scotland, for the Weal of both Kingdoms."64
This Bill had been sent down from the Lords on the
1st. If James could not get Parliament to act, at
least he could get them to appoint a Commission
which would make recommendations. Both Bills from
this Committee ultimately passed.

There were four bills with which Hoskyns was
closely associated because of being from Hereford
on the borders of Wales. On 20 March he was appointed to the Committee on a "Bill for the better
Maintenance of Husbandry and Tillage in the County
of Hereford" with men like Sir Henry Neville who
were also interested in the farm lands of that
shire. Nothing happened to this Bill following a
committee meeting on the 27th, but it was brought
back in the following session, and Hoskyns' associate from the City of Hereford, Mr. Pembridge, was
made Committee chairman.65 Another Bill for the
western counties was that given a second reading
on 31 March, "for the Making up and Keeping in Re-
paration of Chepstowe Bridge."66 On 11 April Sir
Robert Johnson argued against the Bill and offered
a proviso which apparently excluded Monmouth from
paying the necessary money for the repair. As a
representative from that shire, his motion was obviously one of self interest. Hoskyns spoke up
immediately and said that he wanted another proviso
first: "that none of Monmouth may pass over that
Bridge." Then, he said, he would vote for Johnson's proviso.67 That put everything back into
perspective, and the House simply ignored Johnson's

247

motion. The Bill passed. A third Bill was one "touching Welsh Cottons" introduced on 10 March. There was apparently no problem connected with it, and it passed, with no difficulty, ten days later.68

Of far greater importance was a Bill introduced on 21 February, "For the better Explaining of a former Act made 34 et 35 H. [enry] VIII. concerning Ordinances for Wales, and Establishing the Government of the Lord President and Council there."69 It received a rather surprising reaction:

At the first the howse cried away with it, but Sir Herbert Croft [one of the Herefordshire representatives] stoode up [and] in a verry long speache declared the importance of the bill, he shewed that the fower shires viz. Hereford Gloucester Woorcester and Salop weare neaver in the marches: Then he declared how by encrochment those shires weare drawen in: and lastly how much they are hurt and oppressed with that gouvernement: in which he shewed manie wrongs and oppression: to the number of 100: and about all which he said himselfe and certaine other gentlemen had putt under their hand would Justifie....

It is no wonder that the House requested that he submit his notes to the Committee which would consider the Bill. Hoskyns wanted to make a legal point to the increasingly law-minded Commons.

After him Mr. Hoskyns spake to second him: and among other things he affirmed that they which labored to free those 4 shires from that arbitrable or commissionary governement do not impeach the Kings prerogative, but quoth he they which will against Law imprison the Kings subiects and not deliver them uppon a Habeas Corpus they stand against the prerogative, for they will not suffer the King to free the person of a subiect whome they have iniustlie imprisoned.

248

After a long debate, these two won their point,
and the Bill was committed to a very large Committee of all those interested in it.

There is a record of the debate that took
place in the Committee in <u>Cotton Vitellius</u> CI, ff.
132ff. in the British Museum. The Statute under
discussion said that

> There shalbe and Remayne a Presid^t and Councell
> in the sayd 〈 〉 Dominion and Principality of
> Wales and Marches of the 〈 〉 wth all Officers,
> Clerckes and Incidents to the same in mann〈er〉
> and forme as heertofoer hath beene vsed and ac-
> customed 〈under?〉 wch Presid^t and Councell
> shall haue Power and Authority 〈to〉 heare and
> determyne by theer wisdomes and discretions
> 〈such〉 Causes and Matters as be, or hereafter
> shall be assigned them by the kyngs Matie as
> heretofore hath beene accusto 〈med〉 and vsed.

All told, there were twenty-four points raised in
favor of removing the four counties of Gloucester,
Worcester, Hereford, and Shropshire from the jurisdiction of the Council, but the important ones were
those raised over and over through the years: the
counties had always been English, not Welsh, and
the statute had been concerned with Welsh counties;
and the rights of the English citizens in the four
counties were suppressed because of their inclusion
under the Council. There were basically two arguments for leaving the situation as it was: it was
more efficient in dealing with relationships with
Wales and there was precedent for the arrangement.

After a good deal of discussion, the Bill was
brought up a vote on 10 March, with Fuller and Hoskyns ending the final debate. Fuller spoke "In Defence of the Bill, and the Proceeding of the committee." Hoskyns, certainly now acting as the Deputy Steward of the City of Hereford as well as a
Member of Parliament, discussed "the Certificate
from <u>Hereford</u>, under the Seal of the Mayor." The
Bill passed.[70] On 10 April Sir Herbert Croft moved
that some of the words in the Bill, which had been

passed up to the Lords, should be removed. He
called them an error of abundance. But the House
took the position that when a Bill had been passed
up to the Lords, it had to stand as it was.[71] It
appears clear that the Lords rejected the Bill as
it was, and on 14 May a substitute Bill was entered.
But on the following day,

> Sir Herbert Crofts moveth, touching the Bill of
> Wales; that, sithence his Majesty, in his Speech
> Yesterday, would be always ready to give Execu-
> tion to any Law; desired, that the Bill might
> sleep, and he would rest upon His Majesty's
> Grace for Execution of the Law. --The House
> assented.[72]

The Bill had, in spite of Hoskyns' disclaimer, attacked one of the real sources of power of the
King, his extra-legal jurisdiction over the two
Marches of England, the shires facing Scotland and
Wales. That they were a carry-over from past wars
and now only faced territories equally under the
rule of the King did not take away from the monarch's desire to maintain his own sway in those re-
gions. At least the Bill had forced the King into
a statement that he would see that the laws of the
nation were uniformly enforced in the counties involved.

The four Bills that Hoskyns reported out of
Committee to the House were not leading ones, and
they all came relatively late in the session. On
2 May "The Bill for the Relief of such as lawfully
use the Trade and Handicraft of Skinners" was giv-
en its second reading, and the Committee was to
meet the following afternoon. The Bill was passed
with the proviso that it was to be continued till
the end of the following session of Parliament and
was duly sent up to the Lords on the 10th.[73] On
May 9th he reported in two Bills, one "to reform
the Multitudes and Misdemeanors of Attorneys and
Solicitors," and the other "Against the Delay and
the Defeating of the Course of Law and Justice, by
Writs of Error, in Cases of Trials by Verdict." He
had been given the latter on 6 May.[74] On 12 May

the Lords had asked for a discussion on "An Act for Transportation of Beere" which had been sent up to them earlier from the House.[75] On the 16th Hoskyns was placed on the Committee for that Conference in the afternoon and reported the Conference to the House on the 19th. On the 26th he was one of those who argued on the Bill before it was passed with the amendments sent down from the Lords.[76]

There was one Bill that he chaired, however, that was close to his concerns throughout this session and later, that of proper copies of laws, bills, records, etc. On 30 April was read "An Act to reforme the Abuses touching writing of Coppyes in Paper in English words in many Courts of Record or Offices belonging to those Courts in or about Westminster hall to reduce the great Charges which the Subiect often payeth for one Coppy, to a more reasonable rate."[77] Fees for records made up a good deal of the source of income of lawyers of the day, and one can imagine that neither Hoskyns nor his fellow lawyers were going to rush into the matter too hurriedly. And so it appears. Hoskyns was added to the Committee on May 5th, along with Sir Edwin Sandys; the Committee met the following day; and on the 8th, Hoskyns reported back to the House:

> That more than 20. Committees appeared; That it was resolved by them, that it was not fitt for them to deale with the Matter of Fees; nor to alter the Rates now and heretofore taken, but to leave that Point as it is, for if they be iust Fees, the Committees thought no reason to diminish them, and if encroched, it is Extortion, and remedy lyeth in that Case by Lawe. Also such as prosecuted this Bill, thought not good further at this tyme to deale in it.

He also said that other Bills offered during this session dealt with similar problems. He and the Committee recommended that the Bill should sleep until the next session, which the House agreed to.[78] The clerks who would have been affected by any

251

change in the Bill would have been those on whom
the lawyers depended for accurate work. And, of
course, the Lawyer would not be hurt if a person
did bring a suit against any given clerk, as a
lawyer would have to be hired to prosecute the
suit. This Bill stood no chance in a House domi-
nated by lawyers.

We have no record of his having spoken in
twenty-one of the Committees in which he took part,
but they represented a very wide range of interests and backgrounds: inheritances, legal problems,
grievances, business practices, and taxation.[79]
Undoubtedly his associates in Commons found him a
valuable co-worker for him to be on such a large
number of Committees.

In three other Committees we at least know the
position which he supported. On 7 February a second reading was given to a new Bill "for the Abate-
ment, and to restrain the new Erection of Weares,
Stanks, Kiddles, &c."[80] That he was for such leg-
islation we have already seen. On 12 March his
friend and future co-judge on the Welsh circuit,
Nicholas Overbury, brought the Bill in, but as
there were so many amendments to it, the House decided to put off final debate until the next day.
During the debate on the 13th, Sir Robert Johnson
once again offered a proviso, and once again Hoskyns opposed it, but not, apparently, in witty
enough terms to lead the court recorder to quote
him. Once again Hoskyns' point won, and the proviso was rejected.[81]

On 22 May Hoskyns, Fuller, and Christopher
Brooke got into a debate over a new Bill before it
was even given its second reading: "For the Avoiding of certain Doubts and Inconveniences which
might otherwise happen and arise, touching Sanctuary, and Wines, by reason of certain Clauses in a
Statute, and intituled, Act for Continuing and Re-
viving of divers Statutes, and for Repealing of
some others."[82] The section on wine had to do with
price controls. One Bill had come down from the
Lords, and the Committee, which met that afternoon

252

in the Middle Temple and included people like Sir
Francis Bacon, Fuller, and Richard Martin along
with Hoskyns, did not think it was worth pursuing.
The next day they recommended that the Lords' Bill
be allowed to sleep, and they then pushed through
their own double Bill containing both Sanctuary
and Wines.

A third Bill had to do with a subject on which
Hoskyns had spoken before in the first session. On
25 January a Bill "prohibiting the Resiance of married Men with their Wives and Families in Colleges,
Cathedral Churches, Collegiate Houses, and Halls
of the Universities of Oxford and Cambridge" was
given its second reading and assigned to a very
distinguished Committee in which Hoskyns joined Mr.
Secretary Herbert, the two Lewknors, Dr. Daniel
Dunne, Sir Thomas Lake, Sir Edwin Sandys, Sir
George More, Sir Edward Hoby, and Sir Henry Ne-
ville.83 After several Committee meetings, the
Bill was brought into the House ingrossed. Then
began one of those humorous debates which has characterized the Commons at its best throughout the
ages, and there can be little doubt that Hoskyns
took his part, debating on the side of Oxford. Ev-
en level-minded Robert Bowyer got in his oar. The
triggering of the debate lay in the fact that although in the body of the Bill it was always written with Oxford before Cambridge, on the outside
the endorsement put Cambridge before Oxford. Here
was a matter of honor to be decided between the
alumni of those institutions. Bowyer records the
general order and outcome of the verbal skirmish:

> it was much insisted whether University should
> be first named, for which purpose divers statuts
> weare produced in which Oxōn was first named
> and one wherein Cambridge was first mencioned:
> Mr. Camdines booke was vouched Pro et Con: One
> viz. Sir Fra Vane affirmed that the iunior Mas-
> ter of Arte of Cambridge had precedency before
> the senior Master of Oxōn being both of one
> yeere, who afterward declared the mystery of
> his meaning viz. for that the Act or Commence-
> ment in Cambridge is before that in Oxō: An

253

other viz. R. B. [Bowyer himself] alleaged that
in Oxo two Kings had found two severall Colleges
whereas only one had found a college in Cambridge: Also that Oxon̄ was dignified with a
Cathedrall church and the See of a Bishop, which
Cambridge had not: afterwards it appeared that
when the bill was readde in the howse and when
the Clerke delivered it to his servant to be en-
grossed, the same was endorced Oxon̄ and Cambridge and that two ministers cambridge men being without by him caused him to endorce it Cambridge and Oxon: how beit it was agreed to put
it to the question, which being doon Oxon̄ pre-
vailed and the endorced was [to] be amended and
made Oxon and Cambridge.84

King James must have been thoroughly convinced that
he was dealing with a bunch of madmen. His government was in great need of money, he had pled with
the Commons to work on his ideal of Union, and instead they were spending hours carrying on an undergraduate feud. But then the Scots and the English have never really been at their best in trying to understand one another.

When the Bill was brought in for final vote
on 3 March there was a great deal of debate, and
Bowyer notes that so many spoke against the Bill
that it would be too long to set down their arguments in particular. Hoskyns then spoke for the
Bill, and he returned to the position he had taken
in the Directions. He used three points to justify the Bill, two of which might seem to be more in
place in a theological discussion than in the House
of Commons: "Virginity [is] a virtue: Marriage
[is] not of necessity." Since these are true and
the men involved have freedom of choice, then "Vol-
untas donatoris observetur," the wish of the founder should be observed, "and the founders would
that the heads of their howses should be single
and unmaried." Arguments against the Bill continued, including some by Bowyer, but the Bill passed.
It seemed to be a good Bill to pass in a traditional way, so the House divided for the first time
of the session, physically getting up from their

254

seats and going out different sides to be counted.[85]

Whether Hoskyns was on the Privileges Committee is difficult to ascertain. This important Committee was busy with a number of items during the
session, especially trying to keep enough members
around to make carrying on business worthwhile.
On 26 March John took part in a debate over the
fact that a Mr. Brereton had left without license
of the House, and it looks as though Hoskyns was
assigned to the Committee to study the case.[86]
Brereton had been told as early as 13 February to
report to the House. On that earlier date Hoskyns
was involved in an even more important point of
order. One of the privileges which the House protected most zealously was the freedom of arrest af-
forded its members. Hoskyns called the House's attention to a striking violation of that privilege
which had happened to his friend Christopher Brooke
immediately after the first session of the Parliament. Brooke explained the situation further: that
he "was arrested veary dispitefully in westminster
hall in the last Michaelmas terme within 3 daies
after the adiornement of the parliament by the
meanes of Andrew Mallory and his servaunt Hol-
borne." The Commons acted quickly, as it did in
all such cases, and the following day Mr. Mallory
was brought to the Bar. Mallory's defense was that
he did not know that Brooke was a member of Parliament, nor did his servant. Brooke claimed that he
wrote to him of that fact, however. The House commanded Mallory to withdraw the action against
Brooke, but they let him off the hook by accepting
his statement that he didn't know the facts.[87]

One of the most interesting points connected
with Hoskyns' whole activity in the House is that
he seems almost always to have been on the winning
side on any Bill. Besides the cases we have already considered in which his more telling arguments seem to have won the day, there are lesser
cases, such as on March 24th, when he supported the
passage of a Bill "For the Transportation of col-
oured Cloths undressed," which he was later to

255

champion even more strongly. The Bill was passed.[88]
Or on 1 April, when he argued against a Bill
"touching Inmates" and it was defeated.[89] There
is no question that his opinion, often clothed in
the wit for which he was famous, was respected by
the House as a whole.

On 27 May all of the major business before
the House had been settled, and the King was ready
to have the House stop its deliberations. Although
he had accomplished some of his principal aims, he
had seen the House assert its own prerogatives in
opposition to many that he claimed for himself, and
it was dangerous to have the members continue sitting longer than absolutely necessary. The lawyers
in the House felt the need for getting about their
own business as well, and there was the increasing
danger, as there was almost every summer in London,
of the plague. Therefore, that afternoon, at about
five o'clock, the Speaker and the rest of the Commons went up to the House of Lords, where, after
the usual formalities, the Lord Chancellor announced the prorogation of the Parliament and set
the date for reconvening on 25 November.[90] It is
unlikely that anyone present disagreed with the
action.

* * * * * * * * *

It was a very different session that followed
on 18 November as far as Hoskyns was concerned.
For some reason he stopped speaking up as often,
perhaps recognizing that his statements in the previous session had brought him to the King's attention in the wrong way. Bowyer, who had obviously
been impressed with Hoskyns' way of expressing himself, found nothing worth reporting by Hoskyns in
this session. In the Journals of the House it
would appear that John spoke only nine times, four
of those in reporting Bills from committee. Even
the number of Committees on which he served dropped
to twenty-five. It is possible that he recognized
that the strength of the Commons was to be achieved
best in the new ways of exerting itself, for the
importance of lawyers in the discussions of the

256

House and in the Committees was made perfectly
clear in this session. The Commons also discovered
the power of calling for a Committee of the Whole
on important issues such as the Bill on the Union.
Or he may have discovered that his warning in a
previous session that speaking up in Committee
brought one too much notoriety was all too true.
If he was already a close friend of Northumberland,
he may have been worried about being tagged with
guilt by association. There is another possibility
as well. We simply do not know how close John was
to his father, although it is likely that his interest in the family lands indicated at least a
common bond of interest. At any rate, during this
session, John the Younger of Monkton died, and Hoskyns would have been concerned with the welfare of
his mother as well as of the family holdings.

This does not mean that John became one of the
absentee members of the House. His activities indicate that he was present throughout the session,
at least when the House was actually meeting. We
also know that his sense of humor was not failing,
for during this period he wrote what was certainly
his most famous poem during his own life time.
Other records indicate that his life was going on
as usual. On 26 July 1606 he had been in Hereford
working as Deputy Steward and Justice of the Peace,
even holding his own court during the general sessions there.91 On the day Parliament had broken
up, he had gained a new roommate at the Middle Temple, when William Copley had moved in, replacing
Fettiplace. And during the new session, on 11
February 1607, Copley moved out and Christopher
Jones, a young Inner Barrister who almost certainly was connected with John's mother's family, moved
in.92 In the Autumn he made his annual visit to
Winchester to pay the rent on the manor of Titley.

There really is no fully satisfactory explanation for the alteration in Hoskyns' participation
in Parliament at this period. He certainly did not
change to a position of supporting King James. During the long debates on the Union, which stretched
from the monarch's opening pleas in November for

257

action on this Bill nearest the royal heart to the beginning of July, Hoskyns spoke twice. Both times he urged the House to slow down. On 15 December there was a long discussion over Escuage, the feudal requirement of forty days of military service from subject. The question which was raised was a natural one: if the two kingdoms are joined, what military service is now to be performed, what proclamations will be required, and so on. Hoskyns spoke up to remind the House of a statement of the King: "This to be revived by Message, and therefore to be deferred till after Christenmas."93 That would seem an innocuous enough statement, and it could even be taken as supporting the King's power to direct the debate. Such a position gains support when one notices that the general debate is to accept at its face value the King's statement the Escuage was to be taken away by the uniting of the two kingdoms, something the King might not quite want to be done. But Hoskyns' voice had been heard; the decision of the House was "to pray a further Time." Again on 2 March 1607, this time on the vital issue of Naturalization, which caused the King more headaches than any issue of the session, Hoskyns spoke up, this time even more cryptically. Once again he went to the historical precedent. "This Point being in Question in E. [dward] III. Time, it held Seven Years, before it received a Decision; therefore [it is] no Marvel --."94 The recorders stopped at that point, but it is not difficult to reconstruct the rest of the sentence: therefore it is no marvel that we can not and should not come to an easy or quick answer. The House of Commons certainly did not need any historical precedent for dragging its feet in any matter of the Union, but that was exactly what Hoskyns was supplying. But restraint is often a two-edged affair, and once again, a reader could interpret Hoskyns as urging the Commons not to go the way they were tending and to infuriate the King by declaring null and void the Judges' decision that those born in Scotland after the King's accession to the throne of England were automatically citizens of England.

Hoskyns' restraint is all the more remarkable

258

because of his later statements as well as his already clear lack of affection for the Scots. Moreover, many of his friends and associates were anything but restrained. The normally sober Nicholas Fuller gave a long and very anti-Union speech employing the usual argument that Scotland was not really an equal in commerce with England and using Abraham and Lot as examples: each should go his own way.[95] It is not recorded who was to choose the cities of the plain, but then Fuller was not as apt a quoter of scripture as his friend Hoskyns. That same day, 14 February 1607, Kit Piggott turned loose a diatribe against the Scots which resulted in his being dismissed from the House (and, incidentally, helped to date one of Hoskyns' poems). He urged the House:

> Let us not join Murderers, Thieves, and the roguish Scotts, with the well-deserving Scotts. As much Difference between them, as between a Judge and a Thief. They have not suffered above Two Kings to die in their Beds, these Two Hundreth Years. Our King hath hardly escaped them: They have attempted him. Now he is come from amongst them, let us free him from such attempts hereafter.[96]

Piggott's knowledge of Scottish history exceeded his good judgement. But it is rather surprising, as the King was quick to note, that no one in the House was bothered by the speech. It was only after the King himself complained that Piggott was dismissed and sent to the Tower.

All through the session the King was forced to call the House into personal confrontation in order to keep them moving. On 18 November 1606, the day on which the session began, he had questioned some of the positions which they had taken in the last Parliament, but he had concerned himself mainly with the matter of the Union and the recommendations of the Commissioners which the House had agreed to the previous May.[97] On 31 March 1607, he called the Commons to him in the great Chamber of the Palace at Whitehall and urged

259

them to get on with the Union. He also spent a
long time discussing the ever-tender subject of
naturalization.98 On 2 May, he called them all
once again to Whitehall and said that although they
had all said that he had delivered a fine speech
the last time, no one seemed to have done much a-
bout it. He ended up with a severe warning:

That you beware of all fanatical Spirits, all
extraordinary, and colourable Speeches; that
there be no Distractions, nor Distempers, among
you; that you breed not Contempt to the great
Work so well begun, and Discouragement to others
that wish well; that you tempt not the Patience
of your Prince; and finally, that, with all
Speed, you proceed with as much as can be done
at this Time, and make not all you have done,
frustrate.99

It took the House over a month after that speech
to pass even the part of the Union concerning hos-
tile laws, which was introduced on 4 May, two days
after the King's speech: "For the Continuance and
Preservation of the blessed Union of the Realms of
England and Scotland, and for the Abolishing and
Taking away of all the hostile Laws, Statutes, and
Customs, that might disturb or hinder the same."100
Even then it took the rest of June to work out the
differences between the version of the Bill passed
by the House and the one passed by the Lords.101
By the time the next order of business on the Union was taken up, a Bill "Whereby the Counterfeit-
ing of the Great Seal of Scotland, or Privy Seal of
Scotland, is made High Treason," Parliament was
just one day away from being prorogued.102 But
throughout this long passage of time as a member of
the Grand Committee, Hoskyns apparently said little
except to counsel slowness of action.

It was a relatively strange session in another
way. Although ostensibly it met from mid-November
until the beginning of July, it by no means occupied all of that time. On December 18th the King,

considering the great Travel of the Knights,

260

Citizens, and Burgesses, Committees employed in
this Matter of Union; and that the solemn Feast
of Christenmas approaching, it were fit the
Gentlemen repaired into their several Countries,
to solace themselves, comfort their Neighbours,
and perform other Duties in their several Places... And because this Business might be no
Hindrance or Impediment to the Course of common
Justice of the Realm, in the Term-time

(Hilary Term), adjourned Parliament until 10 February 1607, nearly a full two months.103 On 18
March, the supposed illness of the Speaker caused
a postponement until the 23rd, and the celebration
of the anniversary of the King's coronation on the
following day caused a further adjournment until
the 26th. On 31 March, after the King had spent
the morning urging them to some action, the Speaker announced that His Highness' Pleasure was that
Parliament should be adjourned until April 20th, a
break which would have been for the Easter session.
Because so few people returned on that day, the
Speaker adjourned the session for another week, to
the 27th. Now over three months had been spent in
adjournment out of the five. On May 13th Parliament was adjourned for two more days, until the
15th, and on the 20th the Speaker announced at nine
o'clock in the morning that the King wished them to
adjourn until the 27th, which they did. Finally,
there was a short adjournment from June 23rd till
the 25th. So almost exactly one half of this third
session of James' first Parliament was spent in adjournment.

Another strange element was the sudden sickness of the Speaker in mid-March. It was not the
first time that Hoskyns' friend Edward Phelips had
suddenly contracted a politic illness. On 26 February 1606,

The Speaker wrote unto the clerke being in the
howse that he shoulde excuse him to the companie for that having taken pills over night
which did not woorke as was expected he had not
ben well all night, but woulde attend betweene

261

9 and 10: at which tyme he came accordingly: in
the meane time the opinion of the howse and the
ordinary speache was that he had taken a pill
from the purveiors.104

That had occurred during a particularly tricky part
of the House's discussion over the Grievance on the
Purveyors, when the King had been under attack.
Now, in March 1607, a far more difficult matter
was being discussed. The King had failed to win
the Commons' agreement to vote full citizenship
for the Scots. As a result, he had had the Judges
rule that at least all those Scots born after his
English coronation, the so-called Post-nati, automatically gained such citizenship. Individual
cases of Ante-nati Scots still had to be voted on
by the House, and Hoskyns was often a member of the
Committees which considered such cases. During
March he was on two Committees, those for John Rams-
den105 and James Desmaistres.106 It became quite
clear during the House debates on naturalization
that not only were the Ante-nati not going to be
given automatic citizenship, but that the House was
about to overrule the Judges' decision on the Post-
nati. Thus the King decided to halt debate by
causing the absence of the Speaker. The ultimate
irony of his action, however, is that the continued
absence of the Speaker caused the House to move ev-
en more strongly in the direction of establishing
the principle of the Committee of the Whole. At
the time of the Speaker's sudden attack of illness,
the House was also having a full debate on a matter which they had discussed and passed during the
previous session, a Bill "for the Abuses of the
Court of Marshalsea."107 The Committee for the
Bill had had new members added on 3 March, with
Hoskyns named first, along with all of the other
lawyers of the House, and a man with whom Hoskyns
began to share a great many committee assignments,
Sir Oliver Cromwell.108 On 16 March, because of
the Speaker's absence, a special order was worked
out:

Upon a former Order of the Commons House of Parliament, made by special Motion, on Saturday

262

last, the Counsel on both Parts, in the Bill
touching the Abuses of the Marshalsea, were appointed to be heard this Day publickly at the
Bar: But Mr. Speaker being absent, by reason of
his Sickness, and the said Counsel being ready,
and attendant (as they had been many Times before, to the great Charge of the Parties inter-
essed) it was considered as fit, by sundry Members of the House there present, that the next
sitting Day the House should be eftsoones moved,
for the Hearing of the said Counsel the same
Day, at Eight a Clock in the Morning; and the
Clerk of the House directed to enter a Note of
Remembrance in his Book, to that Purpose.109

On the 18th, Sir Francis Hastings informed the
House that the Speaker's sickness was "a great Pain
in his Neck and Head,"110 and it was an equally
great pain in the neck to the House. By Monday the
23rd, with the Speaker still missing, Fuller advised the House to get going on matters that could
be accomplished without the Speaker, and all agreed.
They then set up a Committee to work out procedures to follow in the Speaker's absence.111 That
brought the Speaker back just in time to urge adjournment for the Coronation anniversary. But the
House had not forgotten its intention. On 7 May
the Speaker went to the King early in the morning
and stayed until 9 o'clock. That was just long
enough; for that day, after a long discussion on
the Union, the House passed a motion that said,
"If the Speaker be not here, all the House may be
a Committee." Moreover, they decided to commit the
Union Bill the next afternoon to a Committee of the
Whole House, the Speaker excepted.112 The principle had been established, but it was not to reach
its fulfillment in this session. Already the government recognized that Parliament was working for
a principle of self-direction which was a danger to
the King's direction of affairs. So, on 26 June,
when it was moved that the discussion of amendments
sent down from the Lords on the Hostile Laws Bill
should be discussed immediately in a Committee of
the Whole, with the Speaker to depart, the government forces argued that it was not fit and without

263

precedent, "carrying with it no Decorum, in respect of Mr. Speaker's ordinary and necessary Attendance upon the House till Eleven a Clock." So the House moved that they should meet that afternoon at two o'clock instead.[113] Although the Parliamentary forces had not yet succeeded in forcing the Speaker from the chair, they had thoroughly established the principle of the Committee of the Whole to discuss important issues.

And, as we have seen, the lawyers were gaining an ever more powerful position in the House. Strangely enough, the King seems to have concurred in this rise in power, somehow thinking that the presence of lawyers would increase his chance of winning his way. It was to be a mistaken judgement on his part. Besides the Bill on the Abuses in the Marshalsea, to which all lawyers were assigned several times during the sessions, they were named as a group to three Bills,[114] none of which got past the first Committee meeting. Of more importance were the orders for the attendance of lawyers. On 29 November the House moved that no lawyer who was a member of the House was to leave London without the permission of the House. The same day all lawyers were appointed to meet the next Monday in the afternoon "to peruse, debate, and consider of, the Act of the Commissioners for the Union; thereby to be better prepared for a Conference intended with the Lords of the Upper House."[115] On 27 February it was decided that at the meeting with the Lords that afternoon, every lawyer was to attach himself to one of the Judges,[116] which seems to be one of the better counterploys of Parliamentary history. The same day the King ordered that no lawyers were to leave the meetings of the House, and on the 4th of June, while the final debates were being held on the Hostile Laws Bill, all the lawyers were commanded to be present at the eight a.m. session the following morning.[117] Clearly the House was striving to establish its legal base of power, which is also evidenced by its increasing searching of the records for precedents.

There was another Bill concerning the copying

264

of court records this session, "To reform the A-
buses of wide and wastful Writing of English Copies
in Courts of Record," and once again Hoskyns served
on it. But in spite of the meetings of the Committee, the Bill apparently was lost in the shuffle
during the waning days of the session.[118]

Hoskyns had gotten off to a fast start in his
Committee activity. On 21 November 1606 he had
been added to the Committee for the Bill "To make
good Grants, and other Conveyances and Assurances,
made to Corporations, notwithstanding the Misnaming
of the same Corporations," which had been the first
item of business of the new session on the 18th.
The Committee submitted the Bill for ingrossing after only one committee meeting in the Middle Temple
Hall, on the 24th. When it was submitted for ingrossing on the 28th, Fuller, who acted as Committee Chairman, spoke for the Bill, and Hoskyns spoke
against it. On 2 December, when it was brought up
for final vote, the Bill was defeated.[119] Then
John pulled what appears from the records to be the
neatest trick of this or any session of Parliament.
On 26 November he was assigned to two Committes,
one on an "Act to enable all his Majesty's loving
Subjects, of England and Wales, to trade freely into the Dominions of Spayne, Portugall, and France,"
which had been introduced during the last session,
and the other on a Bill "for the better Enabling of
William and John Evelyn, Esquires, to make Sale of
certain Lands, for the Payment of Debts."[120] Both
were to meet the following afternoon at 2 p.m., the
first in the Middle Temple Hall, the second in the
Exchequer Chamber, at least three miles apart. On
the 29th, John reported in both Bills, and both
were ingrossed.[121] This usually means, as we have
seen, that he was chairman of both Committees, and
the membership of the Committees, although slightly
overlapping, was certainly not the same. As to the
Evelyn Bill, Hoskyns said "that it is as honest and
just a Petition, as ever was preferred in Parliament: [it] Delivereth in a Conveyance made of Land
made to his Children"; and when it went up to the
Lords, he made sure that it carried a covering note
"that as much Land is given in Recompence to his

265

Children, as is here sold by this Bill." The Free
Trade Bill was seriously impugned and disputed,
but it too was ingrossed. On 2 December both Bills
were passed, and on the 10th both were sent to the
House of Lords.122

It is not until 26 February 1607 that John's
name reappears in the Parliamentary records. Like
most of the other members of the Lower House, he
probably took the King at his word and returned to
his home. And like most of the lawyers of the
House he may have returned to London for the usual
business attendant upon the Hilary term. But there
are two reasons for doubting it. The storms in the
west of Britain would have worried any landholder
in the area and would have made him want to check
on all of his property; and some time during February John's father died, which made John all the
more concerned with the family property. Stow's
Annales carries a full description of the terrible
weather.

The 20. of January, it pleased God to send a
mighty West winde, which continued full sixteene
houres, and with extreame violence and rage
brought in the Sea, by reason whereof, and of
the spring tides, both which furiously encountred
the Land waters, presently after a great rayne,
and caused the riuer of Seauerne, beginning as
farre as S. Michaels Mount in Cornewall, to ouerflow the bankes, and bounds, all along on both
sides vp into Somersetshire , and Gloucestershire , in some places fiue foote, and in some
places the water ouerflowed their bankes three
foote in some places fiue foote and in some
places almost eight foote, and ranne into the
land in some places almost twenty miles in
length, and foure miles in breadth, and in all
places wheresoeuer it ran, it came so fiercely,
that it was hard for man or beast to escape by
flight, at the very first comming in of the waters, besides the horror of the noyse, and the
terrour to the eye, to behold the swift outrage
of waters, comming vpon them like great mount-
aines, which of many were more seene then sus-

266

pected to approach vpon them, and their habita-
tions so hastily, and thereupon stayed and attempted to remooue and set things as they
thought in order, and more safe in their houses.
Others stayed to haue their horses sadled, and
then to ride away: others taking the first aduantage of the time, and being onward on their
way to escape, some a flight afoote, some more,
some lesse, would needes returne home, vpon hope
to saue their wiues, children, friends, iewels,
or euidences of their lands, &c. in which space
the flouds came violently vpon them, and ouer-
whelmed many of them, and their houses, and
their cattell, for the waters in diuers Townes
and Villages, vpon the suddaine in respect of
time, grew higher then the tops of their houses,
trees, and Churches, and in many places, many
saued themselues by climing into trees, vpon the
tops of houses, and Churches, others by swim-
ming, and some by sitting vpon the new ruines
of houses floating vpon the water, many heards
of cattell perished: in this great extremity,
there were some that with shew of pittie, made
out Boates pretending to relieue the distressed,
but performed no such charitie, for they went
onely a boot-halling and made a prey and spoyle
of all they could lay hands on: and among other
things of note, it happened that vpon the tops
of some hilles, diuers Beastes of contrary nature had got vp for their safetie, as Dogs, Cats,
Foxes, Hares, Conies, Moales, Mice, and Rats,
who remained together very peaceably, without
any manner of signe of feare, or violence one
towardes another. There were drowned in the
parts of Somerset-shire, fourescore persons,
and damages done vnto the value almost of twenty thousand pound, in twentie Townes.[123]

Once back in Parliament, Hoskyns would serve on a
Committee to relieve the victims of the flood.

Not only was the storm damage felt in the Wye
valley as well as the Severn, but John's wife
owned considerable holdings in the Churchill and
Sanford area most directly affected by the flood

and tidal waves. It is unlikely that he would
have returned to London, or remained there in term
time, instead of checking out his lands and the
damage to them. It is even possible that it was
pressure on his part which led his friend Edward
Phelips, as Speaker of the House, to appoint a Committee to study the results of the flooding and
make recommendations to the House. This Phelips
did on 3 March 1607, in a motion "touching the
manifold Wants and Miseries fallen upon sundry his
Majesty's Subjects, by reason of the late great
Overflowing of Waters in the Counties of Devon,
Somersett, Glocester, Monmouth, and Glamorgan."
The House decided to name a special Committee 'with
Direction and Authority to consider of all convenient and likely Courses for the Repair and Relief of
the Losses and Calamities occasioned by so extraordinary an Accident, whereof the like hath not
been heard of in many Ages."124 Hoskyns was put
on the Committee as a burgess of Hereford. On 27
March, Sir Maurice Berkeley reported in the Committee's action, which consisted of suggesting to
the House one of three possible actions: 1. a
limitation, or set period of time of two years,
within which Parishes would pay a small set assessment, some of 2d., some 6d., but none over a shil--
ling; 2. a Subsidy in which no man with an income
of under £5 a year would pay anything, and those
above would pay one shilling on the Pound; 3. a
voluntary contribution. The Committee thought the
last was the most plausible suggestion, as is often the case, unfortunately. They then suggested
that a sum of money be agreed on and distributed,
part voluntary, part by constraint. "Justices of
Peace to be authorized to demand the voluntary; if
that would not serve, then such Power to levy it,
as shall be fit."125 However, on the day the Committee was to deliberate further, the House was
preparing to meet with the King and to be dismissed
for the next month, and there is no further indication in the Parliamentary records that any final
action was taken. However, in June the Privy
Council was stirring up various shire commissions
to report their progress in collecting money for
"the Aid."126

268

Perhaps it was a result of ill health due to the bad weather or work in restoring property in and around Monkton that John's father died. We do not know the exact day of his death, but it was probably rather late in February, as the will was proved on 3 March. The will itself was written a little less than two years before, on 6 June 1605, when the writer was approximately 75 years old. His son Thomas had been sick and was better by then, and it probably occurred to the old man that Thomas' will would have to be clarified by his own, since he was in possession of most of the property. The will is a very fair one in many ways when the entire family situation is considered. John and Dr. John had been given the best education that England offered at the time and were both either fully established or well on their way to being. Dr. John was working on his Doctor's degree, which would practically guarantee a good position in the church. John was a successful lawyer, leading citizen of Hereford, and married to a wealthy woman. The eldest son, Oswald, was a wealthy merchant tailor in London, well-established in his business and quite prepared to leave his own family comfortably well-off at his death. Charles was still in University as an undergraduate and had not made up his mind what to do for a living. That left two sons who were still at home, unprepared for anything in life except farming, and it is to them that the bulk of the estate of John the Younger of Monkton was to go.

The first real legacy is to Phillip, the brother we know least about. He is to have all of his father's property in Didley and St. Devereux, which apparently Thomas had been farming the year before. That gift did not cover one piece of property which was to go to Oswald. The reason for this legacy to his older son is explained in the will. The father had borrowed money from his son, and this bequest was to cancel the loan, which otherwise would have fallen upon Thomas. The Monkton farm was to remain in the possession of his wife until her death, and then it was to go entirely to Thomas. He asked that Dr. John and

and Charles sign over their rights in Monkton to
Thomas. If they did, then he left them £5 a year
each for the next three years. If they didn't,
they received no money at all. To Thomas he also
left his lands in St. Weonards, Tretire, and Michaelchurch. All these lands were given to Thomas
and his heirs if Thomas would let his mother live
at Monkton without any trouble for her lifetime.

The rest of the will, although the language
is found in many such documents, indicates a possible split among the sons, with Thomas and Phill-
lip on one side and Oswald, John and Charles on
the other. Oswald is given a meadow in the parish
of Much Dewchurch provided he doesn't fight the
will, or have anyone (John?) fight it in his name.
If Oswald shall "molest sue troble or vex my executors," then the meadow will go to those executors,
Thomas and Phillip. Charles is given a parcel of
land in Tretire and Michaelchurch called Tretires
Broom, if he doesn't fight the will. Finally John
is mentioned, and we find the reason for his not
receiving any previous bequest: "Item I geve and
bequeath to John Hoskins the elder my sonne all my
goodes and Cattalls wch I have now remayninge vpon
the farme of Titley in the said Countie of heref
and wch I had at any time there," unless, of course,
John tries "to impeache disanull or make void this
my last will and testamt" or to "vex sue molest or
troble his said Brothers." If he does, he wants
his executors to "sue and implede" him for all the
"goodes and cattalls wch he had of myne at Tytley."127 Apparently John's father stocked the Titley farm for his son while John was busy in the
Middle Temple training as a barrister. This certainly helps to explain why John is otherwise not
mentioned in the will. And yet there is a nagging
suspicion in the very wording of the document that
the father was afraid that John would use his legal
training to take over some of his brothers' portions. There is no question that in later years
John treated Thomas more as the overseer of his
lands than He did as a brother. There are no documents to show it, but the general feeling that one
gets reading the whole set of papers dealing with

the family is that John was much closer to his
mother than to his father, and that his gradual
assumption of the lands held by the family was
made through his mother's good will.

* * * * * * * * *

The third session of Parliament reconvened on
10 February 1607 and tried to make up for lost time
by requiring that the House assemble each morning
at 8 and get to major business at 9. The Speaker
also summed up the state of various Bills as they
had been left in December. But, as I have said,
there is no evidence of John's presence in the
House until the 25th. At that point he became
deeply involved, for he was put on six Committees
in three days. One Bill, "To convert the Manor
and Prebend of Cutton, in the County of Devon (being a Prebend sine Cura) to the Maintenance of a
Free-school." found Hoskyns back at work with his
usual associates, Sir George More, Richard Martin,
Christopher Brooke, and Nicholas Fuller.128 Hoskyns was made Committee Chairman and reported in
the Bill, with amendments, on 3 March, when it was
ingrossed. Two days later it was passed.129 John
wasted no time on any Bill furthering public education wherever possible. On 26 February he was assigned to the Committees on the Ramsden Bill--al-
ready mentioned--and three others.130 None of the
three Bills fared very well; one was defeated and
the other two simply disappeared.

The other Bill from these three days was much
closer to Hoskyns' heart, and one can imagine his
fighting for it for all his worth. It took until
the middle of June to accomplish it, but the Bill
was finally passed, amended by the Lords, and
passed again by the Lower House by 11 June. The
Bill was "For the better Provision of Meadow and
Pasture, for necessary Maintenance of Husbandry
and Tillage in the Manors, Lordships, and Parishes
of Marden, alias Mawarden, Bodenham, Wellington,
Sutton St. Michael, Sutton St. Nicholas, Murton
upon Lugg, and the Parish of Pype, and every of
them, in the County of Hereford."131 His associate Anthony Pembridge shepherded the Bill through

271

Committee and debate to its successful conclusion.
All of the lands described bordered on the River
Lugg in an area four miles north of the city of
Hereford. It is about the only area anywhere a-
round Hereford where Hoskyns could not be accused
of promoting his own self-interest.

During the remaining months there were eight
more Committees on which John served. Three of
them concerned the church in one way or another.
One Bill "against Pluralities, and Non-resi-
dence,"132 sought to remove abuses which had been
under attack since the days of Langland's Piers
Plowman and before. Another concerned "certain
Disorders in the Ministers of the Church."133 The
Committee for the third Bill, "For the more assured
Execution of Justice in Ecclesiastical Courts and
Causes," apparently never met.134

There were two "private" bills on which he
served,135 and two city Bills in which he took
part, one for Southampton and one for London.136
There was also "An Act for the Confirmation of certain Lands of the Warden and College of the Souls
of all faithful People Deceased, of Oxon" and other
lands to Sir William Smyth, Knight, which caused a
full-scale debate with Hoskyns arguing "pro Billa."
After being returned to Committee, the Bill
passed.137 But it was the last Bill of the session which Hoskyns was to report in that caused the
greatest difficulty aside from the major Bills on
the Union. And if Hoskyns had remained rather quiet during the third session for the purpose of a-
voiding conflict with the King, he certainly
spoiled the impression as the session came to a
close.

On 11 May, the Committee handling a Bill "For
the true Making of Woollen Cloths" reported in the
Bill for a third reading. Among those speaking to
the matter was Hoskyns, who favored the Bill. The
recorder of the debate notes that those who took
part were largely those "Burgesses of Clothing
Counties, and Towns," which certainly included
Hereford. Both Sir Herbert Crofts and Anthony Pem-

272

bridge also got into the debate for Hereford. The
debate led to the suggestion of an amendment in
the last Proviso of the Bill, and the only way out
seemed to be by recommitment.[138] The next morning
Hoskyns reported back from the Committee that they
disliked the entire final Proviso, and the House
got into a technical battle over whether a Proviso,
once the Bill was ingrossed, could be put to the
question without dashing the entire Bill. They
finally decided that it could, voted against the
Proviso, and ordered it to be scratched out of the
Bill. The Bill then was passed.[139] At this point
in the records of the Commons there seems to be
little reason for all of the fuss. Then it all becomes stranger when the Bill came back from the
Lords with amendments and an additional Proviso--
over a month and a half later! Even the adjourn-
ments do not explain this long lapse. By the 30th
of June it was perfectly clear that the session was
within a very few days of prorogation, and the obvious explanation is that the Crown did not wish
the passage of the Bill. But the Committee and the
House were not prepared to bow to royal pressure
on this or any other item when their interests were
involved. As a result, the next day, 1 July, they
read the Bill with its amendments twice, committed
it to the former Committee, and ordered them to
meet "presently" in the Committee Chamber.[140] The
Committee then reported back to the House, but were
put off till the next day. On the 3rd the Bill
went back up to the Lords. It was not until the
final day of the Session that the situation finally came clear:

> About One a Clock, Mr. Speaker was sent for to
> Whytehall, to the King, about the great Bill of
> Clothing, which was said to be much opposed; yet
> was it so strongly defended, as the King was
> pleased to give it Passage with the rest of the
> Bills, presented in the House for his royal As-
> sent.[141]

Later that afternoon, at four o'clock, the
whole of the Commons went to attend His Majesty,
and prorogation was announced until 10 February

273

1608. The reason for the long hiatus was that

> as the Infection of the Plague is now in some
> Parts of our City of London, so that it is to
> be feared, that, if the Term and Parliament
> should meet together, and thereby draw a double
> Concourse of People from all Parts of the Realm
> thither, it might give Occasion both to increase
> the said Sickness thereabouts (where our most
> Abode is) and to disperse it into other Parts
> of the Realm.[142]

The King had obtained very little during this session. Commons had gone very slowly on the Union,
only doing away with laws hostile to that Union.
They had threatened the whole idea of automatic
naturalization of the Scots. It is no wonder that
he was not eager to have them gather again. So
there was little surprise when, on 10 January 1608,
he prorogued the Parliament until 27 October "for
divers special Causes, us moving." When the plague
began to spread again that fall, he prorogued it
again until 9 February 1609. On 4 January he prorogued it once again, this time until 9 November,

> forasmuch as the Dearth and Scarcity of all kind
> of Victual is at this present great, and, if it
> should draw so great a Concourse of People hith-
> er, as the Parliament will bring, it would not
> only more increase the Prices of all things
> hereabouts (which are already high) but also
> draw many Gentlemen out of their Countries where
> there Hospitality will give much Relief to their
> poor Neighbours.

There was to be still another prorogation that fall,
until 9 February 1610, because of the plague, which
was so bad that it canceled most of Michaelmas term
in 1609.[143]

Hoskyns was probably quite happy when the
third session came to an end in mid-summer 1607.
There is even a possibility that after the middle
of June he had left the meetings. At least from
then on there is no positive evidence of his pres-

ence. Sir Henry Mountague reported the Bill of
Clothing out of Committee on 1 July. John's law
interests called him back to Hereford, as did the
settling of his father's estate. And an event
during the spring session had triggered his wit
into producing a long and very irreverent poem a-
bout his colleagues in the House of Commons.

Footnotes for Chapter IX

1. Stow, p. 875.
2. Ibid., p. 884.
3. David Willson, The Parliamentary Diary of Robert Bowyer 1606-1607 (1931), p. 25. See also. C.J. I, 277 (4 March), 306 (8 May).
4. Bowyer, p. 76.
5. Ibid., p. 136.
6. Ibid., p. 9.
7. For a good coverage of the growth of the committee system and the increasing power of the House of Commons, with Hoskyns one of those often mentioned, see Williams M. Mitchell, The Rise of the Revolutionary Party in the English House of Commons 1603-1629 (1957).
8. Bowyer, p. 158.
9. Mitchell, p. 44.
10. The Bill is mentioned in the Commons Journals or was discussed in Committee in the Chequer Chamber 22, 25 January; 1, 15, 18 February; 4, 7, 27, 31 March, 17 April; pp. 258, 260, 268, 277, 290, 299. The Bill passed.
11. Bowyer, p. 3.
12. Ibid., pp. 10-11.
13. C.J. I, 261.
14. C.J. I, 267.
15. Bowyer, p. 47.
16. C.J. I, 286, 287.
17. C.J. I, 297.
18. C.J. I, 307.
19. Bowyer, p. 38.
20. Ibid., pp. 77-78.
21. Ibid.
22. On 31 January Sir Robert Wingfield publicly accused Morrice of going ordinarily to mass. He couldn't make the charge stick, but only because of a technicality. C.J. I, 262.
23. C.J. I, 285.
24. Bowyer, pp. 102-3.
25. Bowyer, pp. 145-46.
26. Ibid., p. 105.
27. Ibid., pp. 106-7.
28. For a full account of Dyer and Tippers' activities, see Ralph Sargent, The Life and Lyrics of

Sir Edward Dyer (1968), Chap. VIII.
29. C.J. I, 965, 199; 200.
30. C.J. I, 206.
31. Bowyer, p. 107n.
32. Ibid., pp. 132-33. Tipper's Partaker was Dyer.
33. C.J. I, 299.
34. C.J. I, 300.
35. Bowyer, p. 135.
36. Ibid., p. 137; C.J. I, 301.
37. C.J. I, 301.
38. Bowyer, p. 147.
39. C.J. I, 305.
40. Bowyer, pp. 147-48.
41. C.J. I, 307.
42. C.J. I, 309. But the King paid no attention
    to the Commons. In 1606 Tipper was rewarded
    for his service to the King, along with Sir
    Edward Dyer. See Sargent, p. 139.
43. C.J. I, 308.
44. C.J. I, 298.
45. C.J. I, 295; Bowyer, p. 114.
46. C.J. I, 293.
47. Bowyer, p. 126.
48. Ibid., p. 114.
49. C.J. I, 266.
50. C.J. I, 267.
51. C.J. I, 271-72.
52. Ephemeris Parliamentaria... Parliament, in the
    third and fourth years of... King Charles
    (1654), p. 140.
53. C.J. I, 284; Bowyer, p. 78.
54. Bowyer, pp. 84-5; C.J. I, 286.
55. Ben Jonson even wrote a poem on the subject
    that month.
56. C.J. I, 289.
57. C.J. I, 307.
58. C.J. I, 274.
59. Bowyer, p. 59, with additions from C.J. I, 278.
60. Bowyer, p. 65.
61. Ibid., pp. 100-101. Debate noted in C.J. I,
    293.
62. Bowyer, p. 116.
63. C.J. I, 302.
64. C.J. I, 304; Bowyer, p. 142.
65. C.J. I, 287.

66. C.J. I, 291.
67. C.J. I, 297.
68. C.J. I, 281, 285, 287.
69. C.J. I, 272; Bowyer, p. 49.
70. C.J. I, 281-82.
71. Bowyer, p. 115.
72. C.J. I, 309.
73. C.J. I, 303, 306, 307.
74. C.J. I, 305, 307.
75. Bowyer, p. 157.
76. C.J. I, 310, 312.
77. Bowyer, p. 140.
78. Ibid., p. 152. C.J. I, 305, 306.
79. "Confirmation of Leases against Patentees of
the Inheritance" (which stated that leases of
lands by Elizabeth or James remained good a-
gainst any new assignee to whom James had
granted the lands) (C.J. I, 258, 261, 263, 268,
273, 276, 277, 279; Bowyer, p. 5.); "the Relief of the Parson of Radipoll, in the County
of Dorsett" (Bowyer, p. 5; C.J. I, 258, 261,
268, 273); "for the better Assurance of Copyhold Lands" (that bonds might be assigned to
purchasers of such lands (Bowyer, p. 9; C.J. I,
260, 273, 283, 292); "touching upon the Assurance and Conveyance of Lands and Tenements"
(261); "for the better impaneling of Juries at
Westminster and the Assizes" (262); "for the
better Execution of One Act of Parliament, made
in the 31st Year Eliz. intituled, An Act a-
gainst the Erecting and Maintaining of Cottages"
(to avoid a proviso whereby Corporate towns
were exempt so that no Cottages could be e-
rected in any such town except as certain lands
were specifically set aside for that purpose)
(269, 273, 277, 283, 287, 300, 302; Bowyer,
p. 87); "for the Performance and Execution of a
Decree in the Chancery, made between Wm. le
Grys, Plaintiff, and Robert Cottrel, Defendant"
(269, 273, 275, 288); "For the further Explanation of the Statute made in the Nineteenth Year
of King H. VII. for the due Execution of Ordinances made by Guilds and Corporations" (a Bill
in which his brother Oswald was no doubt interested) (275, 282; Bowyer, p. 77); "For the

278

better Conforming of Recusants, their Wives, Children, and Servants to the true Religion" (284); "for Confirmation of Letters Patents made to the Governors of the free Grammar School at St. Bees in the County of Cumberland" (285, 287; Bowyer, p. 87); "for the Naturalizing of Sir James Areskin Knight, his Wife and Children" (286, 287); "To restrain many Abuses of Players" (286, 293, 294, 300); "To take away all Excuse of not coming to Church"; "concerning Taxes and Impositions upon Merchants, and other Subjects of the Realm, and upon their Wares, Goods, and Cattles" (287); "For the Reforming of the Abuses of the Marshalsea" (284, 288, 299, 301, 305, 307, 310); "Bill of Restitution of Roland Merrick, Son of Sir Gilley Merrick Knight" (291); "concerning the Election of the Members of the Commons House of Parliament" (that no servant or retainer of any member of the House should be elected, nor anyone chosen by "Letters Mandatory or Request," nor for Money or any other gift) (Bowyer, p. 100; C.J. I, 293, 303, 306); "Touching the Assize of Fewel" (295, 300); "for the Draining of certain Fens and low Grounds within the Isle of Ely and Counties adjoining, subject to Hurt by surrounding, being Three hundreth thousand Acres at the least" (298, 301, 303, 305, 306, 308, 311, 312; Bowyer, p. 149-50); "for the Settling of the Manor of Rye, in the Counties of Glocester and Worcester, upon Wm. Throckmorton, Esquire, and his Heirs" (307); and "Against Forestallers and Regrators" (those who bought up goods before they reached the market and raised prices) (300, 305, 306).

80. C.J. I, 265.
81. C.J. I, 283, 284.
82. C.J. I, 311.
83. C.J. I, 260; Bowyer, p. 8.
84. Bowyer, p. 55; C.J. I, 274.
85. Bowyer, p. 58; C.J. I, 276. The Bill passed 169 to 104.
86. C.J. I, 290.
87. C.J. I, 267, 268; Bowyer, p. 35.
88. C.J. I, 288.

89. C.J. I, 292.
90. C.J. I, 313.
91. Sheepskin Bags 1605-6.
92. Hopwood, II, 465, 475.
93. C.J. I, 1011.
94. C.J. I, 345, 1024.
95. C.J. I, 334.
96. C.J. I, 1014. On 27 February Piggott asked to be released from the Tower because of sickness, but the House found that it could only sentence a man to the Tower, not also release him. The following day the King relented and Piggott was released, but not restored to the House. pp. 343, 344, 1022.
97. C.J. I, 314.
98. C.J. I, 357-63.
99. C.J. I, 368.
100. C.J. I, 368.
101. C.J. I, 389.
102. C.J. I, 390.
103. C.J. I, 331, 1011. Other notices of adjournment are on pp. 353, 354, 1032, 363, 1035, 364, 375, 1046, 386, 1054.
104. Bowyer, p. 54.
105. C.J. I, 342, 1021, 1027, 352, 1030, 354.
106. C.J. I, 351, 1029, 352, 1030.
107. C.J. I, 346, 1025, 1027, 350, 1029, 351, 1031, 353, 354, 1032, 1034, 364, 1035, 365, 1038, 366, 1040, 368, 369, 371, 1043, 372.
108. The uncle of his famous namesake.
109. C.J. I, 353.
110. C.J. I, 353.
111. C.J. I, 354.
112. C.J. I, 370, 1042.
113. C.J. I, 387-88, 1054.
114. "For Amortysing of Lands to poor Churches, and for better Serving of Cures" (1045, 374); "For Reformation of One Branch of a Statute made in the first Year of the late Queen Eliz. for restoring to the Crown the ancient Jurisdiction over the State spiritual and ecclesiasticall, and abolishing all foreign Power repugnant to the same" (387, 1054): and "For the Continuance of One Act, intituled, An Act against unlawful and rebellious Assemblies" (389, 1056).

115. C.J. I, 326, 1006.
116. C.J. I, 1021.
117. C.J. I, 379, 1048.
118. C.J. I, 373, 1043, 1049, 1051.
119. C.J. I, 318, 1003; 326, 1005; 327, 1006.
120. C.J. I, 325, 1004.
121. C.J. I, 326, 1005-6.
122. C.J. I, 327, 1006; 329, 1009.
123. Stow, p. 889.
124. C.J. I, 346, 1025, 1026.
125. C.J. I, 355, 1033, 357, 1034.
126. SPD James I, 1603-10, XLV, 122, p. 519.
127. The will is among the Early Hereford Wills
     (catalogued in alphabetical order) in the
     National Library of Wales.
128. C.J. I, 340, 1021.
129. C.J. I, 346, 1025; 349, 1026, 1028.
130. "To make Jointuresses of an Estate in Tail,
     apres possibilitie del Issue extinct, punish-
     able for Waste" (342, 1021, 1026, 1028, 1042);
     "To avoid the Wasting of Wheat, by Making of
     it into Starch" (342, 1021, 1026, 1028, 354,
     1032, 376, 1047); and "For the better Satisfy-
     ing of due Debts." (342, 1021, 1027).
131. C.J. I, 343, 347, 1025, 1028, 351, 352, 1030,
     355, 1033, 365, 1038, 372, 378, 1048, 382,
     1051.
132. C.J. I, 347, 1025. 348, 1026, 350, 1028.
133. C.J. I, 350, 1028, 353, 1031, 366, 1040, 372.
134. C.J. I, 374, 1045.
135. "Restitution in Blood of the Sons and Daugh-
     ters of Edward Wyndsor, Esquire" (374, 1045,
     1047, 380, 1050, 386, 1054); and "For the Sale
     of certain of the Lands of William Essex Es-
     quire, for Payment of his Debts" (382, 1052,
     386, 1054).
136. "For the Confirmation of some Part of a Char-
     ter granted by King H. [enry] VI. to the Town
     of Southampton" (365, 1039, 372, 1043, 1046,
     376, 1047, 379, 1049, 380, 1050, 382, 1051,
     390) and "For the Securing and Confirming of
     the Lands, Tenements, and Rents, granted, de-
     vised, or conveyed to several Companies of the
     City of London, and to the Mayor and Common-
     alty of the said City." (368, 1040, 370, 1042,

372, 1043).
137. C.J. I, 371, 1042, 373, 1043.
138. C.J. I, 372, 1043.
139. C.J. I, 373.
140. C.J. I, 389, 1056.
141. C.J. I, 390, 391.
142. C.J. I, 391.
143. Prorogation announcements are in C.J. I, 391-92.

Chapter X

The M.P. as Poet

On the morning of 11 March 1607, while the debate on the Union continued, "In the midst of the Dispute came down Sir John Crook... with this Message from the Lords"[1]; as the venerable Serjeant-at-Law, speaker of the House of Commons in 1601, and chief Messenger from the House of Lords to the Commons started to speak, Henry Ludlow, M.P. from Ludgershall Borough, Wiltshire, farted loudly.

Such a social faux pas may not seem to a twentieth-century audience worthy of remark except perhaps for a suppressed smile. But the early seventeenth-century found it uproariously funny. There is a great deal of scatalogical humor which runs through the literature of the time (and up through the work of Jonathan Swift). Much of it is extremely witty, as for example, an anonymous poem published in the same volume as Hoskyns' description of Harry Ludlow's moment of embarrassment:

Well Madam, wel, the Fart you put upon me
Hath in this Kingdome almost quite undone me.
Many a boystrous storm, & bitter gust
Have I endur'd, by Sea, and more I must:
But of all storms by Land, to me 'tis true,
This is the foulest blast that ever blew.
Not that it can so much impaire my credit,
For that I dare pronounce, "twas I, that did it.
For when I thought to please you with a song,
'Twas but a straine too low that did me wrong;
But winged Fame will yet divulge it so,
That I shall heare of't wheresoe're I goe.
To see my friends, I now no longer dare,
Because my Fart will be before me there.
Nay more, which is to be my hardest doom,
I long to see you most, but dare not come;
For if by chance or hap, we meet together,
You taunt me with, what winde, Sir blew you
                                        hither?

If I deny to tell, you will not fayle,
I thought your voice, Sir, would have drown'd
                                    your Taile;
Thus am I hamper'd wheresoe're you meet me,
And thus, instead of better termes you greet
                                    me....2

It was this same volume that Aubrey referred to in
his mention of Hoskyns' poem: "His verses on the
fart in the Parliament house are printed in some of
the Drolleries." Aubrey also noted an earlier but
more embarrassing moment of the same kind which
happened to Edward de Vere, the Earl of Oxford and
husband of Anne Vere, whose epitaph John had written: "This Earle of Oxford, making of his low
obeisance to Queen Elizabeth, happened to let a
Fart, at which he was so abashed and ashamed that
he went to Travell, 7 yeares. On his returne the
Queen welcomed him home, and sayd, My Lord, I had
forgott the Fart."3

In her edition of Hoskyns' works, Miss Osborn
did not reprint the poem that Hoskyns wrote on the
occasion of Ludlow's unhappy slip, although she
stated that she had met up with the verses in some
twenty sources. Her reason was that Ben Jonson,
in The Alchemist, refers to the authors of the poem,
and in one manuscript, Hoskyns is named as one of
four authors of the work, the others being his
close friends Inigo Jones, Richard Martin, and
Christopher Brooke.4

Although both of these statements are true,
there seems to be no real question who the principal author of the poem was. Moreover, it is clear
from the various manuscript sources that if the
other three were involved in the poem in any way,
it was in the subordinate role of adding extra verses. No two copies of the poem are the same as
far as the number of verses are concerned. It is
also true that the poem was so popular that members
of later parliaments kept adding to it, which may
be the cause of a remark some ten years later that
Hoskyns was in danger of action by the Privy Council for his poetry. He avoided the difficulty,

whatever it was, and it appears that he managed to prove to the Council that he was not responsible for the offensive verses, whatever they were.

That the poem was indeed extraordinarily popular is obvious. It is very long, far longer than most of the poems that were included in manuscript collections in general. Yet it appears with a regularity achieved only by some of the shortest epigrams and lyrics. Ballads of the day were sometimes set to the music which was written for this poem.[5] It may well be that John wrote his own musical setting for the verses. There is good reason for its popularity. Everyone who counted in public life and who was in Parliament at the time shows up in the poem in couplets that capture the personalities, attitudes, and often the occupations of these figures as succinctly as possible. It is obviously not a literal rendition of what happened; it is an imaginative reconstruction of what each member would have said if he said anything, and, once again, the poem's popularity reveals how clever and accurate these couplet portrayals are, whether they show Sir Robert Cotton's interest in old manuscripts and public records, Sir George More's conservative view of the prerogative and conduct of Parliament, or the gruff profanity of a lesser-known M.P. from Wales.

Probably even those who are named in the poem took the jest in good spirit. After all, Parliament was in many ways an extension of the group of friends we have been following, all of whom were part of a clique of poets and wits, and of their friends and associates in the Inns of Court. In this session of Parliament Hoskyns' poetic friends included Henry Goodyer, Richard and Henry Martin, Christopher Brooke, John Harrington, Lewis Lewknor, Edward Phelips, Arthur Ingraham, and William Hackwell. Other close friends or associates included all those from Hereford, Robert Cotton, George More, Henry Neville, Heneage Finch, Robert Hitcham, Tobie Matthews, John Egerton, and all the Bowyers. And there were at least twenty-five members of the Middle Temple, including friends like James Kyrton

285

and Nicholas Overbury.

An indication of how wide a range of jesting
was allowed within the group is the story told a-
bout Hoskyns by Nicholas L'Estrange, in his Merry
Passages and Jests (Harleian MS 6395, #336, f. 53):

Hoskins vs'd to call Serieant Hecham Sir Robert Hitcham his Ape, because of his writhen
Face, and sneering looke; and one day the Lawyers being merry together, one ask't his Brother Hecham when he would marry? Neuer sayes
he, I had rather leade Apes in Hell: Nay 'faith
sayes Hoskins, if it comes to that once, I am
sure thou wilt pose all the Diuells in Hell, for
there will be such gaping and enquiring which is
the Man which is the Ape; and they can neuer
distinguish, vnlesse thou goest thither in thy
Sergeant's Robes.

If such joking on personal appearance could take
place after Robert Hitcham had been made Queen
Anne's Attorney General in 1603 and been created
Serjeant-at-Law in 1614 (and King's Serjeant in
1616), we can imagine what was allowable in earlier
days of their acquaintance.

Reconstruction of the poem in its original
form is difficult, to say the least. The only way
to do it with any certainty is to take only those
stanzas which are present in most of the best copies. For our purposes this would also mean that
the basic structure of the poem should follow those
copies which clearly attribute the poem to Hoskyns.
The first of these is the version contained in a
manuscript in the possession of Sir Geoffrey Keynes,
a copy of which he kindly sent me. It was that of
Sir Henry Rainsford, the friend of William Shakespeare and most of Hoskyns' circle. In the summer
of 1619 at least, Hoskyns spent some time with Sir
Henry's son in the company of James Whitelocke and
other close friends in the Middle Temple. There
is but one reason to question its final form, which
is that this version dates from after 1628, for it
is headed "Verses giuen mee of m^r St John Hoskins

Composure." and has the explanatory head note that
the event took place in 1628 (3° Car), when Hoskyns
was both a Serjeant-at-Law and an M.P. from Hereford once again. But he was certainly not writing
potentially libelous verse. Rainsford would have
been in the position to know the correct authorship of the poem, however. An equally good source
is Stowe 962, in the British Museum, which is extremely accurate in its crediting of poems to
friends of Hoskyns such as Donne and Wotton. The
Rainsford version runs 57 couplets in length, while
the Stowe, which ends "per Jo: Hoskines," runs to
92 couplets. Add. Mss 4149 has the poem clearly
placed with Hoskyns' other work and separated from
the following poems by other authors by a break of
several pages, but it adds nothing to the other
versions. Other copies tend to place the poem
close to other verses by Hoskyns, but not in all
cases. As Miss Osborn indicated, one version, in
the Conway papers, attributes the poem to four
authors, including Hoskyns, but it is this version
which includes twelve persons not mentioned in the
other major versions. This same manuscript contains two versions of the poem, one much shorter
than the other and a great deal rougher in its
metrics.6

Much the same situation confronts us when we
try to date the poem exactly. There is no question
that it was written during the first Parliament
under King James. The fact that it is mentioned in
Jonson's Alchemist places it in or before 1610.
The only problems raised are in the names of all of
the M.P.'s mentioned. Some simply do not appear in
any extant Parliament lists. Some appear in lists
for different sessions of the one Parliament, and
sometimes the rank of the person, as either Mr. or
Sir, does not agree with the timing of the rest of
the list.7 Yet it is clear that the incident involved happened during the third session of James'
first Parliament. First, by far the greatest number of names can be accounted for in the lists for
that session. The titles given agree more closely
with that session than any other. In the poem,
Sir Christopher Piggott has already been expelled

from the House, and this event took place on 16
February 1607. Edward Peake, M.P. from Sandwich,
who is alive in the poem, died at some time after
the end of the third session and was replaced by
John Griffith on 11 January 1608. Because of various prorogations, Griffith did not take his seat
until 1610, but he was officially the representative of Sandwich from the beginning of January 1608.
Sir John Acland did not enter Parliament until 27
January 1607, and Sir Thomas Knevet moved to the
House of Lords at the end of the third session, on
4 July 1607. There is no way of placing the exact
date within the third session, however, except the
verbal similarity of the poem and the official Parliamentary record mentioned at the start of this
chapter.

In the following version I have used the Rainsford and Stowe copies as the base, with the first
determining the order of the couplets, and the latter supplying further material. Where noted I have
used other versions when better line wording or
regularity of metrics was indicated. If the humor
seems a bit heavy-handed or earthy to the modern
reader, it might be good to remember that Hoskyns
was able to use as a reference by one of his speakers, Sir Roger Owen, a story by one of the greatest of all English poets, Geoffrey Chaucer, who
took at least equal delight in the same subject.

The Censure of a Parliament Fart[8]

Downe came graue ancient S[r] John Crooke
and read his message in a booke.
Ferry well (quoth S[r] William Morris)[9] soe:
But Henry Ludlows tayle cryed Noe.
Vpstart one Fuller, fuller of devotion[10]
Than Eloquence, and sayd a very ill motion.
Not so neither quoth S[r] Henry Jenkin[11]
The motion were good but for the stinkinge.
Quoth S[r] Henry Poole[12] tis a very bold trick
To fart in the nose[13] of the body Politicke.
Indeed I confesse too quoth S[r] Edward Grevill[14]
The matter it self was somewhat vncivill.
Thanke god quoth sir Edward Hungerford,

that this fart proued not a turde.[15]
Then S[r] Ierome in Folio[16] swore by the Masse
This fart was enough to haue broken my glasse.
q[th] sir Jerom the lesse, there was noe such abuse
Ever offered, in Poland, or in Pruse.[17]
Indeed q[th] sir Jo: Trevor[18] it gaue a foule
                                                    knocke
as it launched forth from his stinginge docke.
I q[th] another it once soe chaunced,
that a greate man farted as he daunced.
Well then quoth Sir William Lower[19]
This Fart is no Ordnance fit for the Tower
Quoth S[r] Richard Haughton[20] noe Justice of Quorum
But would take it in snuffe to haue a fart let
                                        before 'um.
If it would beare an action quoth S[r] Thomas Hol-
                                            craft[21]
I would make of this fart a bolt or a shaft.
Then spake S[r] John Moore[22] I think it be fitt
That wee this fart to the seriant comitt.
Not so quoth y[e] Seriant[23] bent lowe on his knees
Farts often breake prison but neuer pay fees
Then S[r] Walter Cope[24] said this fart was well lett
I would it were sweeter for my Cabinett.
Such a fart was never seene
Quoth the learned Council of the Queene[25]
Yet quoth m[r] Peake[26] ther's precedents in store
His father farted th'last Sessions before.[27]
Then said m[r] Noy[28] this might lawfully bee done
For this fart was intayled from y[e] father to th'
                                        sonne.[29]
[Well quoth Kit Brooke[30] we'll give you a reason,
though he had right by descent, he had no livery
                                        and seisen.
Well saith Moore[31] let's this motion repeale,
What's good for the private is ill for the Com-
                                        monweal.
A good yeare on this fart quoth gentle sir Har-
                                        rie,[32]
It hath caus'd such an earthquake y[t] my cole
                                        pitts miscarry.[33]
Yes q[th] Laurance Hide that we may come by it,
Wee'l make a proviso, time it, and tie it.[34]
q[th] Harry the hardy[35] looke well to each clause,
As well Englands libertie, as her lawes.

289

Now then the knightly Doctor[36] protests,
This Fart shall be brought in the Court of Re-
                                        quests.
Nay rather qth sir Edwine[37] I'le make a digres-
                                        sion
and fart him a proiecte y^t shall last him a Ses-
                                        sion.
Quoth Sir Edward Hoby[38] alledged with the spig-
                                        got,
Sir, if you fart at the Union, remember Kit Pig-
                                        gott.[39]
Quoth Sr Roger Owen[40] if bookes bee not lyars
I read y^t a fart was divided amongst 12 fryars.[41]
Graue Senate quoth Duncomb[42] vpon my salvation
This fart wanteth greatly some due reformacion.[43]
Quoth the Country Courtier[44] vpon my Conscience
It would bee reformed wth a litle frankincense.[45]
Then spake Sr Thomas Chaloner[46] I'll demonstrate
                                        this fart
To bee ye voice of his belly not the thought of
                                        his heart.
Quoth sir Hugh Beeston,[47] 'twas a dissembling
                                        speech,
Our mouth hath priviledge, but not our breech.
Quoth Sr Roger Ashton[48] it would mend well y^e
                                        matter
if this fart were well shauen and washt wth Rose-
                                        water.
Than Sr Thomas Knevet[49] said sure ther may lurke
Vnder this vault some more powder worke.
No quoth Sr John Parker[50] I sweare by my rapier
This Bombard was stopt with vile coppy paper.
Sir Robert Cotton[51] well read in old stories,
Conferringe his nots wth graue Mr Pories
Can witnes well y^t these are no fables,
And yet it was hard to put the fart in his Tables.
Each of y^m concluding they thought it not well
To store vp this fart so odious in smell.
Yet sayd a good friend ere it bee transacted
Wee must haue this fart heer surely enacted.[52]
And wee shall haue (nay do not abhorr it)
a fart from Scotland reciprocall for it.[53]
A very good jest it is by this light,
Quoth spruce Mr. Iames of the Isle of Wight.[54]
Quoth Sr Robert Johnson[55] if you will not laugh

Ile measure this fart wth my Jacobs staffe.^56
No y^t must not bee quoth Sr John Bennett^57
Wee needs must select a Comittee to pen it.
Why said Dr Crompton^58 I think none can drawe
This fart w^thin the Compasse of the Civill lawe.
No quoth Sr William Pady^59 assured I am
Though praeter modestiam non contra naturam.
Then gann sage Munson^60 his silence to breake
And said y^t this fart would make an image to
                                        speake.
Yes quoth Mr Daniell^61 this young mans too bold
The priuiledge of fartinge belongs to vs old.
Then sd Mr Tolderburie,^62 I like not this passage,
A fart interlocutory, in ye mid'st of a message.
Then Sr Richard Buckley^63 that Anglesey lad
Rose swearing Cogs wounds <u>and</u> sate downe half
                                        madd.
Quoth Sr James Parrott^64 it greeves mee at y^e
                                        heart
To heare a private man sweare at a publique fart.
Then Sr Thomas Lake^65 said if this howse bee not
                                        able
To censure this fart wee'le to the Counsell table.
Before god q^th m^r Brooke^66 to tell you noe lie,
This fart befo^r law is of the Post-nati.
Upstarts Ned Wymarke^67 the pasquill of Paules,
And thought this fart fitter for ye chappell of
                                        ye Roules
And merry m^r Hoskins swore twas but a stale
To put the plaine seriant out of his written tale^68
Fy Fy I thinke you never did see
Such a thing as this quoth Sr John Lee.^69
Then Oxenbridge^70 said tis a great suspicion
That this fart doth proceed from popish super-
                                        stition.
Then presently rose vp Sr Anthony Cope^71
And prayd god it bee not a bull from ye Pope.
Nay q^th Mr Goode^72 <u>and</u> allsoe some other,
It should by its libertie be a reformed brother.
In all y^r Eloquence quoth Richard Martin,^73
You canot find out of the figure of fartinge.
Now sayd m^r Lewkner^74 wee haue heer such a thinge
as never a tale bearer can carry to the king.
 Quoth Sir Lewis^75 his Brother, if it come of
                                        Embassage,

The Master of Cermonies must give it passage.
I quoth Sir Robert Drury,[76] that were your part,
If so it had been a forrein Fart.
Nay quoth sir Richard Lovelace,[77] to end the dif-
                                        ference,
It were fitt with the Lords to have a conference,
Hark, quoth Sir John Townsend,[78] this Fart had
                                        the might,
To deny his owne Master to be dubbed knight.
For had it ambition, or orationis pars,
Your Son[79] could have told him, quid est Ars.
Then soe qth sir Rich: Gargraue[80] by and by,
This mans arse will speake better then I,
It were no great grievance, qd. M. Hare,[81]
If the Surveyour herein had his share.
Be patient then qth sir Francis Bacon,[82]
Ther's non of vs all but may be ouertaken.
Phillipp Gawdy[83] strakt the old stubble of his
                                        face,
Said, the Fart was well penn'd, and squat downe
                                        in his place.
Then modest Sir John Hollis[84] said, on his word,
It was but a Shoo that creak'd on a board.
Not soe qth sir Jo: Acland[85] that cannot be,
the place vnderneath is matted you see.
Then up start Sir John Young,[86] and swore by gods
                                        nayles,
Was nere such a Fart let in the Borders of Wales.
Well sayd the Clarke[87] I smell y^t a fee
of the private motion a fart is for mee.
Then Sr George Moore[88] in his wonted order
Said I rise to speake of the howse's disorder
And me thinks that mocion wth noe reason stands,
That a man should be charg'd wth y'^{ts} not in his
                                        hands.[89]
With many men more whom heere I omitt
in censuring this fart y^t busyed their witt.
Here silence quoth Bond[90] tho all words be wind
Yet I must mislike of these motions behind
Vpriseth the Speaker that noble Ephestian[91]
And saith gentlemen Ile put it to th' question.
The Question beeing made the Yeas did it loose
for the maior part went cleare with the no'es.[92]
Come come quoth the kinge libellinge is not safe,
Bury you the fart, I'll make the Epitaph.[93]

There are many other couplets to be found in various manuscripts, some of them merely different in attributions or wording from those already included, others describing M.P.'s of different sessions of Parliament.[94] There is no question that most were added to an original poem that found particular favor among the society which surrounded the court and Houses of Parliament. That original poem was undoubtedly by the M.P. from the city of Hereford.[95]

But earthy jokes against his associates in Parliament were not John's only poetic efforts in 1607. That year his friend John Owen published the third edition of his epigrams: Epigrammatum Ioannis Owen Cambro-Britanni. Aubrey not only included the following note in his sketch of Hoskyns: "I thinke John Owen and he were schoole-fellowes," but he also included one of Owen's poems dedicated to his friend Hoskyns.[96] As we have seen, the two had been classmates not only at Winchester but at New College as well. Their friendship remained strong throughout their lives, and in 1622 Hoskyns was to write one of the epitaphs on Owen at the latter's death.

There was good reason for Hoskyns to write an introductory Latin poem or two for the new edition of Owen's work; there are four epigrams on Hoskyns and two on Winchester College contained in the volume. The earliest had been written on New Year's Day, 1603, as a strena, or new year's gift. It is a graceful gesture to his friend, with whom he has wandered through the changing years, as a boy at Winchester and a youth at Oxford, the friend whose love he has tested and found without deceit or fraud. That love which "joins you to me, conquers me for you."[97]

The second is a couplet filled with the verbal play that Hoskyns himself enjoyed:

Ad D. I. H. Poetam ingeniosissimum.
Egregius non sum vates; tamen è grege vatum:
E grege tu vatum non es; at egregius.[98]

293

It would appear that Owen felt that Hoskyns was from a higher social class than himself, as he labels himself as a poet of the common people who is not "uncommon" or extraordinary, while Hoskyns is not of the common people but is "uncommon" or distinguished.

Joined to the third edition of the epigrams was the first edition of a collection of Latin epigrams called <u>Liber Singularis</u> and dedicated to Arabella Stuart, the pretender to the throne who was backed by Sir Walter Ralegh. Book I, 152, of this collection is to "D. Ioan. Hoskins Iuriscons."99 The poem is a bit ambiguous. John says that friendship is limited to two people; love is multiplied to many. No matter which way this is taken, it is obviously a poem in praise of their relationship.

The fourth poem is one of the dedicatory epigrams of the volume.100 It is difficult to tell whether one of Hoskyns' poems stirred Owen's pen or vice-versa; but, as we shall see, one obviously influenced the other. In 1628, Robert Hayman found Owen's epigrams popular enough to translate in a separate volume, <u>Certaine Epigrams Ovt of the First Foure Bookes of... Iohn Owen. Translated into English... By R. H.</u> One of the ones that he chose was this:

To <u>Master</u> Iohn Hoskins <u>of his Booke</u>.

My Booke the World is, Verses are the men,
You'll finde as few good here, as amongst
them.101

Hoskyns wrote two Latin dedicatory epigrams for Owen's volume. One is the second of the dedicatory poems. It is a strangely straightforward statement on a publishing adventure: that nothing stands in the way of publishing the book; that either Hoskyns is no judge of poetry or the age, if it is wise, will read the book; that Owen thinks his own reputation is in great danger, but that, for Hoskyns, nevertheless, "the die of my judgement is cast."102

The second poem is more interesting. It is a
dedication for the third edition and is linked, as
I indicated before, in some way with Owen's own
epigram to Hoskyns, based on the opening phrase,
"Hic Liber est Mundus."[103] Each edition of Owen's
work showed considerable alteration, not only in
the addition of new material, but in the alteration of many of the epigrams themselves. These
changes Hoskyns compares with the Heraclitean flux
of the universe: "This book is the world;[104] it
changes and is changed endlessly." Then there is
the nice touch, "Even if you keep quiet, the book-
seller approves." Owen's epigrams have kept the
press perpetually at work and three times have returned to the "tired type." There is no question
of the close and continuing friendship of these
two men, and yet in these two epigrams of Hoskyns
there is still that faint touch of pride on the
part of the man who has not stooped to print, who
has maintained his social position by keeping his
poetry--except for the rare occasion of a memorial
poem on a famous person or an occasional dedicatory epigram--in manuscript form, circulated among
the elite of those who are themselves practicing
poets.

* * * * * * * * * *

The following year seems to have been spent
in a quietly normal way. There is a slight indication that all was not going as well as possible,
however. For the year 1607-08, John fell over £22
behind in his payments on the Titley lease. But
by the next year he was in better financial shape
and made up for the previous year.[105]

From about this time there is a document that
gives us a rather pleasant indication of life at
the Hoskyns' menage in Widemarsh St., Hereford. It
is not possible to date the document exactly, but
it is probably before 1609, the date of the birth
of Hoskyns' first child, Benedict.[106] Although the
young clerk involved would obviously not have had
charge of a small baby, there would have been some
mention of the presence of the heir apparent in the
household in any set of instructions following his

birth. For one reason or another, John and Ben
had decided to wait eight years before having
children of their own. Perhaps they decided that
it would be best to allow the Bourne children to
grow to youth before introducing new infants into
the family and causing the usual competition and
jealousy.

The document, found among the letters in the
collection of Thomas Hornyold-Strickland, at Sizergh Castle, was written by John for the instruction of his young clerk, William Taylor.[107] Taylor
wrote his own heading to the instructions: "A note
to instruct me in my vocacon." Hoskyns obviously
required of others many of the personal habits that
he himself practiced: rising at 5 a.m., paying
close attention to his wife's tastes and idiosyn-
crasies and fulfilling her needs, keeping his
clothes neat and pressed, his house clean and in
order, and probably smoking a pipe or two a day.
The daily life of the household before the arrival
of young Benedict is clear. Dr. John had a room
with the family and seems to have spent a good deal
of his time with them while finishing his work at
Oxford for his Doctor's degree. He also helped
tutor John Bourne in the afternoon. Ben seems to
have had few duties or worries. She received visitors and looked after the general running of the
household, giving permission for servants to come
and go, etc. Her three children were well looked
after by William Taylor. The oldest of the three,
John Bourne, was taken off to school to learn Latin, and in the evening he and Taylor studied law
together. It is interesting to note that young
Bourne was given the opportunity to "teach" Taylor
the Latin Bourne himself learned each day. Hoskyns was centuries ahead in education theory. During the day, Taylor gave lessons in writing to
Frances and reading to Elizabeth. But he was a
good deal more than a tutor. Apparently Hoskyns
left him more or less in charge of the major activities of the household when he was not at the May-
or's Court. At the Court he would no doubt keep
track of activities for his master, the Deputy
Steward, as well as learn the vocation of law.

There was prayer in the morning and prayer at night.
By 9 p.m. the house was well locked, the windows
closed against the night air, and the family asleep
to prepare for the early arising the next day.

In 1609 the regular rhythm of daily life must
have changed abruptly, as young Benedict arrived.
He was never to have the same educational opportunities as his father, as he went directly into
legal training as an eleven year old boy, but he
was to share many of his father's positions as he
grew older, and he was to achieve a far higher distinction than his father ever reached: a baronetcy.
In 1609, though, he was just a very much doted upon
infant who added a new touch to the household in
Hereford.

In 1609 also occurred an event that still
raises critical battles over what John Hoskyns did
or did not write.   It might be well to review the
historical situation first.   Parliament had been
prorogued in July 1607 because of the fear of the
plague.   The Commons had agreed to a Subsidy which
would meet the King's needs for several years, but
they had been intransigent enough otherwise to keep
James from calling them back into session unless it
was absolutely necessary, which, considering the
rate at which he spent money, was sooner than he
would wish.   The continuation of the plague, or at
least its threat, and the lack of food in London
allowed him an excuse to keep proroguing the next
session through 1609.   That these delays often were
mere excuses seems clear from contemporary records.
All the churches in the city except St. Paul's were
in the process of being cleaned and repaired; the
King pulled down the old banqueting hall at Whitehall, site of the performance of many of Shakespeare's plays, and raised a new one; so many new
buildings were being constructed for the influx of
new residents in the general area of London that
orders had to be proclaimed about the kind of materials used.   And the weather in January and February was such that the danger of plague seemed far
away.   For two months an intense frost hit London
and froze the Thames for the longest period since

297

1564.[108] But the King and his advisors wished to
keep Parliament from getting together as long as
possible. His opinion of that group is clearly
shown in an anecdote collected by Sir Nicholas L'-
Estrange about the monarch whose favorite pastime
was riding to the hounds: "Kinge James mounted his
Horse one time, who formerly vsed to be very sober
and quiet, but then began to bound and Prance: The
De'le o my sol Sirrha sayes He, and you be not quiet, Is'e send you to the 500 kings in the lower
house of commons; They'le quickly Tame you."[109]

In the spring nothing of great importance was
happening around London, but out in Hereford a
celebration was going on which became known all o-
ver the country and was memorialized by a tract
published later that year by John Budge in London,
"to be sold at his shop, at the great south doore
of Paules."[110] The title begins in a slightly mis-
leading way, but as it goes on, it explains most of
the tract: Old Meg of Herefordshire for a Mayd
Marian and Hereford Towne for a Morris Daunce or
Twelve Morris Dancers in Herefordshire of Twelve
Hundred Years Old. According to the author of the
tract, who is anonymous, the event was the result
of a horse race in May of 1608 just outside of
Hereford. The "Knights, Esquiers, and Gallants (of
the best sort) from many partes of the land" had
such a good time that they agreed to "a more fresh
and liuely meeting in the same place, to be performed this yeare of 1609." The agreement was that
every man present should bring with him running
horses for the race, game cocks for fighting, and a
good deal of money for betting. Then we find out
something about the person who suggested the whole
thing:

> He that first gaue fire to this sotiable motion,
> was charged to stand to his tackling, and to
> come well prouided, who thervpon (whilest the
> mettle of his braines were hot and boyling) vn-
> dertooke to bring a Hobbie-horse to the race,
> that should out-runne all the Nags which were
> to come thither, and to hold out in a longer
> race, then any would be there.[111]

298

The outstanding question is, was this man John Hoskyns? There can be no question that Hoskyns was present during the celebration. He was acquainted with many of the courtiers who came to his town for the meeting, and his place in the city government would insure that he would at least help to welcome the influx of members of the King's Court whose presence turned Hereford into one of the fashion centers of England for a short period. The chronicler of the event says that Bath temporarily lost its position as the leading resort of the country as between two and three hundred of its visitors moved north to Hereford. There, "Innes were lodgings for Lords: Baucis and Philaemons house (had it stood there) would haue beene taken vp for a Knight. The streetes swarmed with people, the people staring and ioyfully welcomming whole brauies of Gallants, who came brauely flocking on horsback, like so many lustie aduenturers."[112] Whoever made the suggestion of the meeting certainly was a friend of the city, as the influx of courtiers assured the citizens a considerable amount of trade. Where so much money was passing hands in betting, it would be certain that a good deal would be spent around the town on food and drink, or just trifles. The payment for housing would be far more than normal, and tips would be large for the housekeepers and servants.

The source of the tradition that Hoskyns was the man responsible for the entire affair lies in Thomas Fuller's The Worthies of England:

There cannot be given a more effectual evidence of the healthful air in this shire, than the vigorous vivacity of the inhabitants therein; many aged folk, which in other countries are properties of the chimneys, or confined to their beds, are here found in the field as able (if willing) to work. The ingenious Serjeant Hoskins gave an entertainment to King James, and provided ten aged people to dance the Moorish before him, all of them making up more than a thousand years, so that what was wanting in one was supplied in another: a nest of Nestors not

299

to be found in another place.[113]

So clear a statement about Hoskyns' part in the affair would seem to leave no doubt, especially written by a man about whom Aubrey said, "His naturall
memorie was very great, to which he added the Art
of Memorie: he would repeat to you forwards and
backwards all the signes from Ludgate to Charing-
crosse."[114]

The difficulty is that King James was certainly not in Hereford for the event; in fact, he never
visited Hereford at all. One way around this difficulty is provided by a William Gibson Ward, in a
letter to the Ross Gazette in 1875:

That Serjeant Hoskyns offered, literally offered, an old English welcome to the King, and
that he accepted the offer, are beyond doubt;
for the learned Serjeant prepared a costly
carved mass of woodwork to serve as a canopy to
a throne by day, and cover to a bed at night for
his use, is so certain, that the woodwork was
seen for years in Ross by numbers of people.
But, after all, the event never came off.[115]

Ward then quotes from the tract and shows that it
was not James, but

Ye seruants of our mightie king,
That came from court one hundred mile
To see our race, and sport this spring....[116]

Such local traditions are shaky at best, but
there must have been good reason for Fuller to have
named Hoskyns as the man connected with the famous
Morris Dance. There is certainly nothing within
the tract itself to indicate him. Only the leading courtiers are named, and the tract purposely
hides the name of the man who suggested the whole
idea. There is every reason to believe that Hoskyns was that man, however. His connections in
London covered Parliament, the courts of law, the
business world, and the royal court. He was known
for his wit and witty ideas. His poem on the Par-

300

liament Fart would have endeared him to the younger courtiers of the time. He had known men like
Henry Herbert, the second Earl of Pembroke, who
were the leaders in the horse-racing world. Hoskyns himself was an excellent rider. Aubrey gives
one example of his prowess: "He was a very strong
man and active. He did the pomado in the saddle of
the third horse in his armour (which Sir John Hoskins haz still) before William, earle of Pembroke."
William Herbert had succeeded to the title in 1601.
The maneuver described certainly does require a
strong man. The pomado was the one-handed vault
over a moving horse achieved by grasping the pommel
of the saddle and leaping. To do this while fully
armed would be a major task in itself; to do it
three times in a row would indeed require "a very
strong man and active."

Hoskyns' relationships with the Herbert family were quite close. For one thing, his friend
Benjamin Rudyard was a close friend of William Herbert, and they composed several poems together.
The shield of arms of Hoskyns' family also seems to
be a variant of the Herbert family, and there may
well have been a family connection which was kept
alive.117 It is for that reason that the list of
the leading figures at the race meeting in 1609 is
especially interesting, for it begins with Lord
Herbert of Ragland. Lord Herbert of Ragland was
actually a member of a branch of the Herbert family.
He was Henry Somerset, second son of Edward Somerset, fourth Earl of Worcester. Born in 1577, he
was called to the opening Parliament of James I as
Baron Herbert of Chepstow. His home, however, was
Ragland Castle, and his son Edward was styled
"Lord Herbert of Ragland" from 1628 to 1644. Henry
was not to become fifth Earl of Worcester until
1628 and Marquis of Worcester until 1642. He was
always a favorite of the Stuarts, and Charles I
visited him at Ragland during the Civil War. Like
all of the Somersets, he had a penchant for racing
and hunting, which was one of the reasons for his
closeness to James I.

Amongst many of the better rankes, these marched

301

with the foremost.

Lord Herbert of Ragland	Sir Ed. Lewes
Sir Thomas Somerset	Sir Francis Lacon
Charles Somerset	Sir Iames Scudamore
Count Arundels 2 sonnes	Sir Thomas Cornwall
Sir Edward Swift	Sir Ro. Boderham
Sir Thomas Mildemay	Sir Thomas Russell
Sir Robert Yaxley	Sir Bascaruile
Sir Ro. Carey	Sir Thomas Conisby
Sir Iohn Philpot	Sir George Chutel18

The list of those present does not include the greatest names at the court of King James by any means, but it does include the kind of people that James willingly associated with and whose activities drained the royal purse and injured the ruler's reputation. Sir Robert Carey, for example, was the youngest son of the first Lord Hunsdon. It was he who incurred the intense displeasure of the court of Elizabeth by hurrying north to tell James of the imminent death of the Queen and of his succession. Naturally he was a great favorite of James, and under the Stuarts he served well and faithfully, becoming the Earl of Monmouth in 1626, under Charles I. In all ways he was a typical courtier and reaped the rewards of his service. Thomas and Charles Somerset were younger brothers of Lord Herbert of Ragland and sons of the 4th Earl of Worcester. Thomas became a Viscount in 1626 and Charles was later knighted and made a Knight of the Bath. The double marriage of their sisters was the occasion for Spenser's Protholamion. Sir Thomas Mildmay was to be created Baronet in 1611; he was the great grandson of Sir Walter Mildmay, who had been Chancellor of the Exchequer and founder of Emmanuel College, Cambridge. Sir Francis Lacon was M.P. from Bridgenorth, Salop, and thus a Parliamentary associate of many of those present.

Most of the courtiers involved were connected with Herefordshire in one way or another. Sir Roger Bodenham lived close enough to Hoskyns for his widow, in later years, to be a possible source for a coach when the then Serjeant-at-Law needed

302

transportation for his second wife. Sir Thomas
Coningsby was the owner of Hampton Court in Herefordshire. An intimate friend of Sir Philip Sidney, he had been an M.P. from Hereford in the last
three Parliaments under Elizabeth, and he was also
a member of the Council of Wales. In 1614 he
founded a hospital farther out Widemarsh St. from
Hoskyns' home, for the benefit of superannuated
soldiers and servants. We know of his closeness to
Hoskyns from a later letter. One of the Baskervilles was present at the races, and all of the
records note that the Baskervilles were an ancient
Hereford family. Sir Thomas Baskerville, one of
Elizabeth's great generals, was born in Hereford,
and Sir James Baskerville was one of the early owners of Hoskyns' Morehampton estate. Sir Thomas
Cornwall, Baron of Burford, married Katherine Harley of Brampton Bryan Castle. He died in 1615, and
his widow was still a good friend of Hoskyns in
1625. Katherine was the sister of Robert Harley,
to whom the Directions was addressed. There are
any number of Philpotts in Hereford, and Sir John
was undoubtedly a knight of that family. And, of
course, Sir James Scudamore was one of the leading
peers of Hereford.

When the races had been completed as planned,
everyone waited for the promised hobby-horse that
was to outdo the racers. Here the wit shown points
to Hoskyns. Who else would have dreamed up such an
entertainment? The hobby-horse was one of the central characters in the ancient Morris Dance. While
the dancers went through their figures, one dancer,
wearing a costume with a horse's head, took part in
the merriment. It is obvious that his actions often took a salacious turn, as the term "hobby-horse"
also stood for a prostitute in the common parlance
of the day.

The writer of the tract, about whom we know
nothing except that he was very well acquainted
with both the people of Hereford and the city of
London, and also that he had an excellent background
in the classics (and who in Hereford had more claim
to those characteristics than John Hoskyns himself),

303

sets the scene better than anyone else could:

> The exercises of this <u>Olympian</u> race, required
> strength, speede, lustinesse of courage, and
> youthful blood, none but able and actiue bodies
> could climb ouer such labors. But to performe
> a race of greater length, of greater labor, and
> yet in shorter time, and by feeble vnexercised,
> and vnapt creatures, that would be an honour to
> him that vndertooke it, that would be to Here-
> ford-shire a glorie, albeit it might seeme an
> impossibilitie.
> What man would not wonder to see fire struck
> out of yce? to see dead Ashes kindled againe,
> and to yeelde fire? to see Saples trees in the
> depth of Winter laden with mellow Apples, and to
> see those Apples when they are pluckt and cut,
> to grow againe. This wonder was as great, the
> accomplishment of it as strange.
> Age is no bodie (in trials of the bodie) when
> youth is in place, it giues the other the buck-
> lers: it stands and giues aime, and is content
> to see youth Act, while Age sits but as a spec-
> tator, because the one does but studie and play
> ouer the parts, which the other hath discharged
> in this great and troublesome Theater. It was
> therefore now plotted to lay the Sceane in Age,
> to haue the old Comedie presented, Fathers to
> be the Actors, and beardlesse boyes the Specta-
> tors. <u>Sophocles</u> (because he was accused of im-
> becilitie and dotage, should rehearse his <u>Oedi-
> pus Coloneus</u>, while the Senate and his owne wild-
> brain sonnes stoode by, and were the audience:
> and to set out this Sceane with mirth, as well
> as with wonder, the state of the whole Act, was
> put into a <u>Morris-daunce</u>. To furnish which ful-
> ly and rarely, a <u>Bill</u> of names able to impannell
> three or four Juries was giuen and read, but
> onely 18 were sworne, and had the charge de-
> liuered to them... The running horses being too
> light of foote for vs to follow, be content I
> pray to stay with vs, and to march along with
> our Infanterie of <u>Hereford</u>, which thus brauely
> came on.[119]

304

He then lists the performers in this antique dance.
A squire of Hereford "tickled a trebble Violin...
the diuision hee made on the strings, being more
pleasing then the Diapason. In skill he outshines
blind Moone of London, and hath out-played more fidlers then now sneake vp and downe into all the
Tauerns ther." He was 108 years old. The chief
musician, to whom the whole tract is dedicated,
was "old Hall," the tabor player; he was a mere 97.
Then there were four Marshals, who took the part
of Whiflers, who kept the dancing area clear of
spectators, looking very martial with their official chains and staffs: Thomas Price of Clodacke,
"a Subsidie man" of 105 years; Thomas Andros of
Begger Weston, another Subsidy man of 108; William
Edwards of Bodenham (who had a young wife and a
six year old child), 108; and John Sanders of Wal-
ford, an Ironworker, 102. Then came the dancers:
James Tomkins, Esq. of Langarren, 106 (who was
father of an eight year old child); John Willis of
Dormington, a bone setter, 97; Dick Phillips of
Middleton, 102; William Waiton of Mardon, 102; William Mosse, 106; John Lace of Madley, a Taylor and
"a special good codpiece maker," 97; John Careless
of Home Lacy, 96; William Maio of Egelton, an old
Soldier who was wounded forty years before, 97; and
John Mando of Cradley, 100. Finally, there were
the principals, John Hunt, the Hobby-horse, "wanting but three of an hundred, twere time for him to
forget himselfe, and sing but O, nothing but O, the
Hobbie-horse is forgotten," all in the manner of
Sterne's Uncle Toby, and last,

> ...old Meg Goodwin, the famous wench of Erdi-
> stand, of whom Maister Weauer of Burton, that
> was fourescore and ten yeares old, was wont to
> say, she was twentie yeares elder then he, and
> he dyed ten yeares since. This old Meg was at
> Prince Arthur's death, at Ludlow, and had her
> part in the dole; she was threescore yeares (she
> saith) a Maide, and twentie yeares otherwise,
> thats what you will, and since hath beene
> thought fit to be a Maide-marrian.[120]

There were, then, eighteen people involved, with a

305

grand total of years of 1837. But the writer feels
his point about Hereford is not yet quite established: "And for a good wager, it were easie to
finde in that countie foure hundred persons more,
within three years ouer or vnder an hunder yeares;
yet the shire is no way foure and twentie miles
ouer." The costumes for the dance were not the
grotesque ones that often were used in the Morris
dance, but "long coates of the old fashion, hie
sleeues gathered at the elbowes, and hanging
sleeues behind: the stuffe, red Buffin, stript with
white, Girdles with white, stockings white, and
redde Roses to their shooes." Half wore "a white
Jewes cap with a Jewell, and a long red Feather:
the other, a scarlet Jewes cap, with a Jewell and
a white Feather." The Wiflers carried long staves,
white and red. "After the daunce was ended, diuerse Courtiers that won wagers at the race" took
the feathers and wore them in their hats.

Before the dance got under way there was an
opening speech in verse, and it is probable that
Hoskyns wrote it, although he purposely assumed the
rustic pose called for under the circumstances:

The Speech spoken before the Morris.

Ye seruants of our mightie king,
That came from court one hundred mile
To see our race, and sport this spring:
Ye are welcome, that is our Country stile,
And much good doe you, we are sorie;
That Hereford hath no better for yee.
    A Horse, a Cocke, Trainsents, a Bull,
Primero, Gleeke, Hazard, Mumchance:
These sports through time are growne so dull,
As good to see a Morris dance.
Which sport was promised in iest,
But payd as truly as the rest.
A race (quoth you) behold a race,
No race of horses but of men,
Men borne not ten miles from this place,
Whose courses outrun hundreds ten.
A thousand yeares on ten mens backs,
And one supplies what other lacks.

306

THE LENUOY.

This is the Lenuoy (you may gather
Gentlemen, Yeomen, Groomes, and Pages,
Lets pray, Prince Henrie, and his father,
May outlive all these ten mens ages.
And he that mocks this application,
Is but a knaue past reformation.

The description of the dance itself moves from
homely observations of Hereford, to Will Kemp's
famous 1599 Morris Dance from London to Norwich,
to the blindness of Homer, to a quotation from Tul-
ly, to a remark on the chronicler John Stow. It
has many of the rhetorical devices which Hoskyns
described in his Directions, some of his twists of
vocabulary, and a good number of his turns of
phrase. There is no proof one way or another of
its authorship, but as a description of an event
at which he was present, it is worth reading. As
we shall see by a later poem by a family friend,
John Heath, Hoskyns was not only present but was
indeed, as claimed by Fuller, the man who staged
the whole celebration.

And howe doe you like this Morris-daunce of
Hereford-shire? Are they not braue olde youths?
Haue they not the right footing? the true tread?
comely lifeting vp of one legge, and actiue be-
stowing of the other? Kemps Morris to Norwich,
was no more to this, then a Gaillard on a common stage, at the end of an old dead Comedie,
is to a Caranto daunced on the Ropes.
Nestor makes a bragging in Homer, (a kind of
blind Poet, that could not see when he did well)
of his owne praises, and especially keepes a
prating of his Age. But I would faine read if
euer a Homer of them all, if Nestor at that age
(whatsoeuer it was) was able to haue made one
in such a Morris-daunce...
A Taylor at fortie yeares, is glad to trust
to his yard, and walkes leaning vpon that. A
Fencer at thirtie (by reason of his knocking)
takes any foyle, to be a staffe to his age. A
waterman at fiftie yeares, falles from water to

307

drinking of Ale, onely to keepe life and soule
together. A Vintner at threescore, has legges
no bigger then a Crane, they are so wasted with
running. But here is a doozen of yonkers, that
have hearts of Oake at fourescore yeares: backes
of steele at fourescore and ten, ribbes of yron
at a hundred, bodies sound as Belles, and health-
full (according to the Russian proverb) as an
Oxe when they are trauelling downe the hill, to
make that one hundred and twentie.

These, shewed in their dauncing, and moouing
vp and downe, as if <u>Mawlborne</u> hilles, in the
verie depth of Winter, when all their heades are
couered (in steade of white woollie cappes) with
snow, had shooke and daunced at some earthquake...

A dishonour were it to Poets and all Pen-men,
if acts of this worth should not Encomiastically
be celebrated and recorded. For heereby the
Vertuous are heartned: if you will not believe
me, I will prooue it by strong reasons. Whore-
mongers, drunkards, and such like fellowes, (who
are euery hower wrastling with Vices and Vil-
laines, which are harder to be tripped downe
then the Guard) that in their youthfull dayes
spend more at a Tauerne reckoning, or in a
Vaulting-schoole, in one houre, then their Great
Grandfathers did (among all their neighbours) in
a whole Christmas. These (I say) drew out a
short, a blacke, a rotten, and gowtie threed of
old age. But it is therefore an argument, that
these white-bearded youths of <u>Hereford-shire</u>
were neuer given to wine or to <u>wenches, both</u>
which are sharper then the destinies Sheeres, to
cut in sunder the very bottome of the soundest
life.

Old age is to all men for the most part a disease; It is to some the cough; they do nothing
but spit; to some, the Palsey: If these were
rotten, they would shake themselues to peeces:
to others, it is the Gowte, they haue not a good
legge to throw at a Dogge, and were ill to be
cowardly souldiers, because they could not runne,
vnles the running Gowte set them forward: But
old age in <u>Hereford-shire</u>, neither spits nor

spawles, feeles no aches, nor oes in his bones...
Alas! what doe I see? Hold Taborer, stand Hobby-horse, Morris-dancers, lend vs your hands,
behold one of the nimble-legd old gallants, is
by chance falne downe, and is either so heauy,
so weary, so vnactive of himselfe, or else fiue
of his fellowes are of such little strength,
that all their Armes are put under him (as Leau-
ers) to lift him vp, yet the good olde boyes
cannot set him on his feete. Let him not lie
for shame, you that have (all this while) seene
him daunce, and though hee bee a little out of
his part, in the verie last Act of all, yet
hisse at nothing, but rather (because it is
beg'd for God's sake.)

Summi <u>Iouis</u> <u>causa</u> <u>plaudite</u>.

* * * * * * * * * * * *

When all of the crowds had left after enjoying the show, Hoskyns stayed on in Hereford, going
about his business as Deputy Steward. Following
orders from London, he and the mayor, Thomas Ste-
phens, sent out orders to three of the city's wards
on Saturday, 5 June: "To bring all victuallers and
keepers of alehouses in ward to come to Guildhall,
with their names in writing, as per order of Privy
Councel. Monday 7 June 1609."[121] On the 15th they
and the other "Commissioners for the Aid" of the
county of Hereford reported their proceedings to
the Privy Council and requested further time on
account of the plague. This was undoubtedly the
"voluntary aid" the Parliament had called for as a
result of the storm damage of the previous winter.[122] On 25 September 1609 he was also in the
mayor's court, but this time as a witness rather
than a member of the court. His testimony on a
recognizance is in an almost illegible latin script,
and the entire entry is crossed out, but his signature is clear.[123] If he had been planning to go up
to London soon after for the opening of the next
session of Parliament on 9 November, he must have
changed his plans when on 26 September, the King
prorogued the Parliament until 9 February 1610.
The cause of the prorogation was the plague in Lon-

309

don, which also cancelled most of the Michaelmas
term. This gave him more time for his own affairs,
and he used it to clear up the ownership of the
home in which he had been living, right next to the
Guildhall of the town.

On the last day of October, 1609, Roger Phellpotts did "demise release and quitclayme... for
euer all my ferme estate Right Tytle interest vse
behoofe condicion of Redemcion vnto John Hoskins of
the said citie and countie esquior" all the property which John had been renting since his marriage.
As I have noted earlier, this purchase established
John as the largest property holder in the city of
Hereford and increased his reputation and standing
in the community. It was a fitting follow-up to
his chamber-of-commerce activities in the spring.

But it was not alone in Hereford that Hoskyns"
position and reputation were increasing. As he returned to London early in the new year, three volumes of poetry were either off the press or were
in the process of being printed which were to contain a poem by Hoskyns or one to him. The first
was by a native of the Golden Valley in Herefordshire, the valley which was before long to be the
main residence of John and his family. Rowland
Vaughan was a nephew of Blanche Parry, one of the
attendants of Queen Elizabeth, and he lived for
three or four years at the court as a child. He
came into possession of the estate known as Newcourt by marriage, and by 1607 he had built up an
estate of at least 1500 acres directly across the
river from John's future home. Here he tried out
many of the ideas of irrigation which are the subject of his 1610 volume, Most Approved, and Long
Experienced Water-Workes. Containing, The manner
of Winter and Summer-drowning of Medow and Pasture,
by the aduantage of the least, River, Brooke, Fount,
or Water-prill adiacent. Hoskyns would have been
keenly interested in Vaughan's ideas because of his
own concern with proper drainage, etc., and it is
not at all surprising to find him writing commendatory verses for his friend. The fact that the volume was dedicated to William Herbert only indicates

once again the tight group of relationships which
characterized life in this period.124

To Rowland Vaughan

In praise of the VVorke

and Author.

My little ROWLAND, you may looke that I
(All things considered) MUCH should say of you:
Then, this your WORKE (to say that MVCH in few)
Shall worke the Workers endlesse Praise: and why?
A worldly WITT, with Heau'nly Helpes indow'd,
Getts Ground, and Glory of the Multitude.125

The closeness of the two writers is obvious in the
address to "My little ROWLAND." The wit that follows is typical of the short poems of Hoskyns, but
the last statement may also be a comment slyly hidden from all but his friend about the way Vaughan
managed to build up such a large estate in so short
a space of time.

Then his old friend and schoolmate John Davies
of Hereford published his collection of epigrams,
The Scourge of Folly, some time during 1610. The
collection has the usual rakish approach to women
and tobacco; rather dull and contrived to the modern eye. Epigram 96, to Richard Martin, is so
flowery as to be nothing. #97, to John Donne, is
considerably more witty:

Dvnne is the Mouse (they say) and thou are Dunne:
But no dunne Mouse thou art; yet art thou one
That (like a Mouse) in steepe high-waies dost
                                                runne,
To finde foode for thy Muse to prey vpon.....

Many men have poems addressed to them, and most are
people with whom Hoskyns was either a close friend
or associate: Thomas Bastard, Sir Thomas Coningsby, Ben Jonson, Inigo Jones, Shakespeare, King
James, Sir Thomas Egerton, the Earl of Northampton,
Sir Francis Bacon, Sir John Davies, John Owen. A-
mong these is one

311

To my beloued Mr Iohn Hoskins.

Iohn of all Iohns, if I should Stile thee so
Thou might'st except against it; sith it points
But at some Sott. Then, art thou such a one? No:
Thy witt (good Iohn's) too nimble in the Ioynts
To stand for such: but, for witt, thou maist
                                            bee
Iohn of all Iohns; at least, so held of mee.126

The pun, of course, is on the large bottle which
held the cheaper hard liquor of the day. Partially
from that and partially from the fact that the name
"John" was given to servants, messengers, etc., as
a common title or nickname, the name became attached to drunks as a group.

    Another of Davies' epigrams may have been ad-
dressed to Hoskyns: "To my dry friend Mr I. H.
Epigrammatist, for a farwell to him and his remembrance." But if it is not addressed to Hoskyns,
if may well have been addressed to the other author
who celebrated John this same year. At about the
same time the other two books reached the book
stalls around St. Paul's, a volume of epigrams by
a fellow of New College, John Heath, also appeared.
One of Heath's epigrams, in his Two Centuries of
Epigrammes, is a helpful discussion of wit and the
epigram during this period. The epigram, I, 42,
is addressed "Ad modernos Epigrammatistas," and is
directed at the first great English epigrammatist,
John Donnes' grandfather, John Heywood:

Heywood, th'old English Epigrammatist
Had wit at will, and art was all he mist:
But now a daies we of the moderne frie
Haue art, and labour with wits penurie.
Wit is the substance, art the polishment:
Art does adorne, and wit it does inuent.
Since then they are so ioyntly link't, that
                                            neither
Can well subsist without the helpe of either:
I gladly could haue wisht with all my hart,
That we had had his wit, or he our art.

312

Heath had, like the Hoskyns' brothers, gone to
Winchester (at the age of 13 in 1600) as well as to
New College, Oxford (at the age of 19 in 1605). He
was made a Fellow and got his B.A. on 2 May 1609
but remained to take his M.A. in 1613. He finally
resigned his fellowship in 1619. Among his epigrams Heath memorialized John, Dr. John, and their
younger brother Charles. We have already noted
Aubrey's remark that Charles might well have proven
the brightest of all the Hoskyns' brothers had he
lived longer. But unfortunately, he died the previous year, in 1609, soon after getting his B.A.
from New College. We have two Latin poems of his,
and they indicate considerable ability, if not the
wittiness of his older brother.[127] Heath says of
his college friend Charles,

That thou wer't witty, if I tell thy name,
I know there's none will contradict the same.
Oh had thy body answer'd to thy minde,
Thou would'st (or els affection makes me blinde)
Haue beene one of the mirrours of our dayes,
Borne both thine owne, and countreyes name to
                                        raise.
Pitty it was (but that it was Gods will)
That so diuine a wit did dwell so ill. (II, 71)

The epigram on Dr. John (II, 63) indicates that
Heath knew this middle brother's theological and
philosophical positions well, and it sets them
forth in a dialogue on Stoic and Christian resolution in the face of tyranny. It is a nice gesture
of understanding a friend's thoughts and feelings.

But the greatest interest in Heath's book for
us lies in the epigram addressed to the oldest of
the three Hoskyns' brothers, the established leading wit of the Oxford graduates. Heath was close
to the whole family, and it is all the more important that he takes as the subject of the epigram to
John the event with which most people would associate the witty barrister at the time. The entire
epigram would be meaningless unless John had been
the promoter of the Morris Dance in Hereford in
1609. Thus Fuller's statement on Hoskyns' role re-

313

ceives support during the very year of the event:

128

Ad M. Iohannem Hoskins I. C.

The yonkers which of late did trot and praunce,
Frisking it nimbly in the morrice daunce.
Vpon a new aduenture now are bound,
The like not to be seene aboue the ground:
To warres forsooth: and whether mought it be?
To the low Countries, where they all agree,
Vnder the Graue, when time serues to stand too't.
And thence till doomes day not to moue a foot.

So the credit for the Morris Dance of Hereford must
certainly return to Hoskyns, and with it almost
certainly goes the attribution of the opening poem
for the ceremony. None of this proves that the entire tract is by Hoskyns, but even that seems quite
likely under the circumstances. The fact that it
does not bear his name should not be surprising as
he never published anything else on his own and
clearly kept his creative life separate from the
printed page except in tributes to other people.
An event as public as the Morris Dance was in some
ways different, which may have caused him to write
the tract, but it would not be different enough to
cause him to attach his name to it.

And so, with a new measure of fame for his a-
bilities and wit, John returned to his seat in Parliament, ready to take part in the increasing opposition to King James. The King had managed to
increase the number of his own supporters by this
fourth session of his first Parliament, but they
were still much smaller and less organized than the
group who were gathering around Sir Edwin Sandys to
further the strength of the House of Commons and
their opposition to both the Union and the Scottish
courtiers who surrounded the King.

Footnotes for Chapter X

1. <u>C.J.</u> I, 1029. As a matter of fact, the event could have occurred on any one of a number of days during this third session of the Parliament, as the messages from the Lords were consistently brought by Sir John. That the official recorder of the House should use the exact terminology employed by Hoskyns in his poem for this specific occasion is a partial indication that this date does apply. Naturally, the recorder did not find it fit to describe the ensuing event.

2. <u>Facetiae</u>. <u>Musarum Delicae</u>: <u>1656</u>...., ed. Sir John Mennis, 1817, 2 vols., p. 55.

3. Dick ed., p. 305.

4. Osborn, p. 300. Why she gives a folio reference to the play rather than Act, scene, and line is beyond me, unless it is to protect the reader from Jonson's remark. Jonson has Sir Epicure Mammon name as his choice of poets:

    ... and then my poets
    The same that writ so subtly of the fart,
    Whom I will entertain still for that subject.
    (II, i, 11. 101-3)

5. In <u>MSS</u>. <u>Add</u>. <u>23,299</u>, f. 19, there appears the title "A proper newe ballad intituled the duel of dogs to the tune of downe came graue auntient Sergeant Crooke."

6. <u>Add</u>. <u>Mss</u>. <u>23,339</u>. The first version, ff. 15-15v, is divided into two hands, the second that of a very poor copyist. The second version, entirely in one hand, begins on f. 16 and runs through f. 17v. The last four lines read:

    Ned Jones Dick Martyn, Hopkins, & Brooke
    The fower compilers of this booke.
    Fower of like witte, fower of like arte.
    And all fower not worth a farte.

7. One reason to question the version in the <u>Le Prince</u> d'<u>Amour</u> (pp. 93-99) is that it contains four names not usually included. The fact that a given name is not to be found in the Parliamentary Returns does not in any real way indicate that he was not present. There are only

315

408 members listed in the returns, which leaves almost one hundred members unnamed. Many of these can be identified in the lists of committees and debates, although their constituency often can not be determined.

8. The Rainsford Ms. has the full title "A censure of a fart that was lett in the Parliament howse 3º Car by a worpᶠˡ Jury each speaking in their order as followeth;" Add. Mss. 4149 attributes the windy deed to Henry Ludlow, but follows the Rainsford note otherwise. Add. Mss. 23,229 labels the poem: "The Parliament Libell," which may explain the trouble that Hoskyns was in about 1615 or 1616. Le Prince d'Amour has the opening couplet:

> Never was bestow'd such Art
> Vpon the tuning of a Fart

9. Morris often spoke with little reference to what was going on, and on occasion had been ruled out of order by the Speaker. Sir William represented Carnarvon County. Henry Ludlow of the Inner Temple represented Ludgershall Borough, Wilts., with James Kirton, Hoskyns' friend in the Middle Temple.

10. Nicholas Fuller, Hoskyns' close associate on so many committees, and a leading member of the opposition to the King, but undoubtedly one of the less inspired speakers of the House, was M.P. from London. He was an outspoken Puritan.

11. from Hutton, Yorkshire.

12. Represented Cricklade Borough, Wilts.

13. Facetiae: "in the Face."

14. M.P. for Warwick County. Stowe reads "Sir Henry Greevill."

15. The couplet is not in Rainsford. Also there is no record of Sir Edward in this Parliament. He represented Wiltshire County in 1601, and there were three other Hungerfords from Wiltshire in this session. Sir Edward also served in 1614.

16. Rainsford: "the longe."

17. Prussia. The two Jeromes seem to have been Sir Jerome Bowes, for Reading Borough, and Sir Jerome Horsey, for Bossiney Borough, Cornwall. Both had been to Russia as envoys of Queen

316

Elizabeth and caused quite a stir there. Horsey had, finally, rescued Bowes from the Czar's displeasure.
18. Represented Bletchingly Borough in Surrey. The following pair of couplets are not in Rainsford.
19. Neither Rainsford nor Facetiae have this couplet, but both Stowe and Prince do. Facetiae later on has a different couplet for Lower:

It is hard to recall a Fart when tis out,
Quoth Sir William Lower with a loud shout.

There is no record of a return for Sir William Lower in this Parliament. He was the pupil and correspondent of the mathematician Thomas Hariot and kept up with all of the discoveries in astronomy of the period. In 1614 he was sending pursuivants after Sir Henry Goodyer (Gosse, John Donne, II, 67).
20. M.P. for Lancaster County.
21. M.P. for Chester County. As Sheriff of Cheshire he had taken part, with John Donne, in the funeral of Sir Thomas Egerton, son of the Lord Chancellor, on 26 September 1599.
22. Recorder of Winchester. In Stowe this is given to Sir George More. Facetiae also gives it to Sir George, but as part of a longer speech. The Recorder of Winchester would certainly fit the sentiment here expressed.
23. The Serjeant for this session was Roger Wood, Esq.
24. Sir Walter Cope was elected for Westminster in February 1604. In another list he is mentioned as M.P. from Stockbridge, Southampton. He was Salisbury's secretary and Chamberlain of the Exchequer in 1601. He was also a well-known antiquary. He and John Pory, also named in this poem, were linked by John Donne in his satirical The Courtier's Library: "11. Believe in thy havings, and thou hast them. A test for antiquities, being a great book on very small things, dictated by Walter Cope, copied out by his wife, and given a Latin dress by his amanuensis John Pory." From E. Simpson's edition of The Courtier's Library (1930), pp. 45-46.
25. Sir Robert Hitcham, M.P. from King's Lynn, Nor-

folk. He is noted in the Returns as the Queen's Attorney General. As we have seen, Hoskyns was a close friend and jesting associate of his.

26. Edward Peake represented Sandwich, one of the Cinque Ports, but died before the fourth session of this Parliament.

27. A Henry Ludlow did represent Andover, Southampton, in the 1601 Parliament.

28. William Noye represented Grampound Borough, Cornwall.

29. Rainsford has a couplet following this of Noye which is not in the other major versions:

> Yet it comes not wthin the statute de donis
> Because a fart seemes to bee de Nullius bonis.

30. Christopher Brooke, one of the inner circle of Hoskyns' friends, represented the city of York. He is also credited with having written some of this poem, as already noted. This and the following eight couplets are not in the Rainsford Ms. and it may be that they are additions by a different author, such as Brooke or Richard Martin. Henry Goodyer was certainly closer to Brooke and Donne than to Hoskyns, although they were both members of the Middle Temple.

31. Probably Francis Moore, representing Reading, who was one of the ablest lawyers of his day. He was a Reader at the Middle Temple this same year and was made Serjeant-at-Law in 1614.

32. Sir Henry Goodyer, the close friend and correspondent of John Donne, held the very important coal monopoly of the Crown. He represented West Looe, Cornwall.

33. Stowe next adds the couplet attributed to Lower in Facetiae (n. 19) but gives it to Sir John Frogmorton, who is not listed in the Returns. It could be John Throckmorton, who replaced Sir Richard Barkeley from Gloucester in May 1604.

34. Lawrence Hyde represented Marlborough, Wilts. He was one of Sir Edwin Sandys' kinsmen and a troublemaker for the Crown in 1601 as well as later. MSS. Add. 23,229 contains the variant

> O wofull tymes, quoth Lawrence Hyde.

yf once ou^r freedome of speech be denyed.

Facetiae contains couplets on Hyde. The one
approximating the above ends, "That these our
priviledges are deny'd."

35. No identifiable reference is to be found in the
Returns.

36. Dr. Daniel Dun represented Oxford. In 1598 he
was appointed Dean of the Arches and Master of
Requests.

37. Almost certainly Sir Edwin Sandys, whose delaying tactics were the despair of King James.

38. M.P. for Rochester. He was a nephew of Lord
Burghley and married the daughter of Lord Huns-
den. More important at the moment was the fact
that James had made him a gentleman of the
Privy Chamber in 1605. He held several monopolies from the Crown, but he was also one of the
leading translators of the day.

39. Piggott was expelled from the House on 16 February 1607 for his extreme language against
the Scots.

40. Roger Owen represented Shropshire in 1601 and
was in both the 1603 and 1614 Parliaments, but
his name is not listed in the 1603 Returns. He
is certainly given credit for wide reading,
however, in his reference to Chaucer's Sum-
moner's Tale.

41. Facetiae has the totally different

In compasse of a thousand miles about
Sir Roger Owen said, such a Fart came not out.

42. M.P. from Tavistock Borough, Devon.

43. Mss. Add. 23,229 has a completely different
context which links it with the generally more
libelous nature of that version:

Naye quoth Sr Rodger, I went from this place,
And reported it worde for worde to his grace
You did so, quoth Duncombe, but wth an ill in-
tent
You left out the sense precedent and the sente
subsequent

44. Mss. Add. 23,229 identifies the speaker as Sir
Robert Wingfield, M.P. for Stamford, Lincoln.

Like Hyde, he had been rebellious against the
Crown since Elizabethan days.
45. Stowe: "It would be well mended."
46. There are no records of Sir Thomas in the Returns.
47. M.P. for Stafford Borough. Mss. Add. 23,229
is quite different:

Then quoth Hugh Beeston with a stammeringe speach
Though you[r] liberty for you[r] tounge, you haue
none fo[r] yo[r] breeche.

Prince also has a second couplet on Beeston:

Nay, quoth Sir Hugh Beeston, and swore by the
Mass,
It's rather the braying of some Puritan Ass.

48. There is no record of a Roger or Robert Aston,
Acton, or Ashton in the Returns. The couplet
appears with all these names. But the holder
of the "Green Wax" Patent in Lancaster, Sir
Roger Aston, was certainly in the House. Sir
Roger was the brother-in-law of Donne's and
Henry Goodyer's close friend Mrs. Thomas Co-
kayne. In Facetiae, Stowe and Prince, the
couplet is joined with a second:

Why, quoth Sir Roger Acton, how should I tell it.
A fart by hearesay, and not heare it nor smell it?

49. M.P. for Westminster. The Gun-Powder Plot was
still very much alive in the minds of all present. Knevet, of course, had been the man who
discovered the explosives under the Parliament
House. On the final day of this session Knevet was made a Baron and took his seat in the
House of Lords.
50. M.P. from East Looe Borough, Cornwall. Mss.
Add. 23,229 assigns the couplet to S[r] John
Parder.
51. Sir Robert Cotton, perhaps the most famous collector of historical manuscripts in English
history, and the chief source of records of the
Parliamentary Party, represented Bridgewater,
Somerset. For more information on Pory, see
note on Sir Walter Cope (24). Pory attended
Cambridge at the same time as Goodyer, was

granted an M.A. at the same time as John Donne, and carried letters to and from Donne while the latter was on the continent with Sir Robert Drury in 1612.

52. Only Mss. Add. 23,229 assigns this couplet to any specific person: Sir Edward Hoby.
53. This is the kind of remark that Hoskyns was quite ready to make and that got him into such trouble with the King.
54. Richard James represented Newport Borough on the Isle of Wight.
55. Johnson was M.P. from Monmouth.
56. The Jacob's staff was a surveying instrument. The meaning is made clear in an added couplet in Stowe and Prince:

And though it be hard, Ile bend my intentions,
To survay it out equall into severall dimen-
cions.

It is almost impossible not to read the double entendre of these four lines. Hoskyns is no kinder to Johnson in his verse than he was in debate in the House.
57. Not listed in the official returns, but we know he represented Oxford.
58. Dr. Thomas Crompton represented Oxford University, along with Dr. Dun.
59. M.P. for Thetford Borough, Norfolk. Stowe calls him "Doctor" and uses "praeter" in both places. Facetiae uses "contra" in both. Both miss the distinction of something which goes beyond modesty yet is not against nature. Dr. William Paddy was knighted in 1603 after being made King's Physician. He was President of the College of Physicians in 1609, 1610, 1611, and 1618, and was on Archbishop Laud's side against the Puritans.
60. Sir Thomas Monson was M.P. from Castle Rising Borough, Norfolk. The entry is extremely ironic as Monson was no sage. He was a great favorite of James, who made him Master Falconer for his hunting abilities. He was Keeper of the Armoury in the Tower and was later accused of complicity in the murder of Sir Thomas Overbury.

321

61. The identity of the speaker is not clear. In Stowe he is "sir Daniell," in _Prince_ "Sir Dannet." Mss. Add. 23,229 has "Damnet." Add. Mss. 10,309 has "Dauenant." Neither Daniel nor Davenant appears in the Returns, but there is a Thomas Damett (or Dannett) from Great Yarmouth, Norfolk, and he is undoubtedly the one meant.

62. The person involved seems to be Christopher Tolderrey, representing the Cinque Port of Hythe.

63. Only _Rainsford_ has his proper title.

64. Sir James was another Welshman, representing Haverfordwest, Pembroke. In both _Stowe_ and _Prince_ these Welsh references lead right to John Hoskyns' remark and the end of the poem.

65. M.P. from Launceston, Devon; a well-known courtier with a future in trading companies. In 1603 he was named Latin Secretary and knighted by James. He was a royal favorite because he championed the interest of the Scottish courtiers. In 1612 he was named Secretary of State and was made a Privy Counselor in 1614. To show the inter-relationships of the various personalities involved in the circles we are studying, it should be noted that Sir Thomas's son, Sir Arthur Lake, was the second husband of Penelope Devereux's (Sir Philip Sidney's Stella) daughter Lettice. When she died, Chamberlain wrote to Carleton, "Since the death of Sir Arthur Lakes Lady there is a daughter of hers come to light (thought to be Dicke Martins, or rather a greater mans) that by helpe of goode frends layes claime to Sir George Caries [her mother's first husband] land because she was borne in wedlocke." (_Letters_, II, 247) John Donne wrote a long and fulsome poem of praise to this young lady and her sister from Amiens in the winter of 1611/12.

66. Giles Brooke was an Alderman of Liverpool and represented that city in Parliament.

67. Edward Wymarke represented Peterborough, Northampton. Obviously he was better known as a writer of lampoons based on the social interchanges of Paul's Walk, the much-frequented

main aisle of the old St. Paul's Cathedral. For an example of Wymarke's cause of complaint against the practices of the day worthy of satirizing, see his letter to Lord Egerton in R.C. Bald, John Donne, p. 101n.

68. At this point the reader may have forgotten that Sir John Crook, Serjeant-at-law, was going to read a message from the Lords. Osborn quotes another couplet on Hoskyns from a version of this poem for which she does not give a reference:

> Well quoth Mr Hoskins, I dare pawn my nose
> The gentleman meant it noe further then's
> hose. (p. 305)

69. Sir John Leigh represented Helston Borough, Cornwall. In Facetiae, Stowe, and Prince there is a second couplet credited to Sir John Lee:

> Swooks quoth Sir John Lee, is your Arse in dot-
> age?
> Could you not have kept this breath to cool your
> pottage?

70. Sir Robert Oxenbrigg represented Southampton County.

71. Sir Anthony probably represented Banbury, Oxford, as he did in 1601. He and his brother Sir Walter were well-known Puritan sympathizers, but this did not keep them from making a handsome profit on the sale of rectories in 1609.

72. John Good was M.P. from Camelford Borough, Cornwall.

73. M.P. from Christ Church, Southampton, and one of those credited with the joint authorship of this poem. Obviously the wording of this speech is directed squarely at the author of Directions. In Prince and Stowe there is a further couplet

> Nor what part of Speech, save an Interjection,
> This fart can be in Grammatick Perfection.

74. There are no unknighted Lewkenors in the Returns. This is probably Sir Edward, M.P. for Maldon, Essex.

323

75. Sir Lewis Lewkenor represented Bridgenorth,
    Shropshire. As might be surmised, he was Mas-
    ter of Ceremonies. The following twelve coup-
    lets are not found in Rainsford, but are found
    in Stowe, Prince, and Facetiae. There is noth-
    ing which sets them apart from the rest as be-
    ing potentially more libelous or scurrilous,
    nor are they about a group less close to Hos-
    kyns and closer to the other suggested writers.
    I think we must consider them part of the ori-
    ginal poem. It is interesting that this group
    of couplets shows practically no variation be-
    tween mss.
76. Sir Robert Drury, the close friend, fellow
    traveler, and landlord of John Donne, was M.P.
    from Suffolk. Drury had made his reputation
    at any early age in military service abroad and
    took part in the peace embassy to Spain in 1605.
    On the morning of 11 March 1607, he was allowed
    to leave Commons because of the illness of his
    wife and daughter, Elizabeth. The latter, of
    course, did not die until 1610, when she became
    the subject of Donne's Anniversaries.
77. Not the poet, who was born in 1618, but a dis-
    tant relative, who represented Abingdon Borough,
    Berks. Like so many opposition leaders in this
    Parliament, he was a kinsman of Sandys.
78. M.P. from Chipping Wycombe, Bucks.
79. It would be nice if "your son" were the poet
    Richard Lovelace, but that is not the case.
    The closest connection between the two was that
    Sir Richard's daughter-in-law was the poet's
    "Lucasta."
80. M.P. for York County; he did not enter the
    House until after 7 April 1605.
81. John Hare was returned from West Looe, Corn-
    wall, in 1601. Although he is not listed in
    1604 returns, it is possible he was one of the
    missing members from Cornwall, as, for example,
    from St. Mawes. He was Clerk to the Court of
    Wards under Elizabeth.
82. Bacon, who represented different Boroughs in
    different Parliaments, this session represent-
    ed his own home, St. Albans, Hertford.
83. M.P. for Sudbury, Suffolk. The following three

324

unsavory couplets are in a group separated
from the previous eight.

84. Not listed in the Returns, but represented a
constituency in Nottinghamshire. Bacon considered him one of the leading opponents of the
Crown. Prince gives a second reading for Hollis:

Then swore Sir John Hollis by the Mass,
Such a Fart would not I let pass.

As usual Mss. Add. 23,229 gives a worse version:

Quoth Sr John Hollis I beshrow his hurt,
They looke vpon mee as if I lett the farte.

85. Sir John Acland replaced Sir Thomas Ridgeway
in the House on 27 January 1607, when the latter was appointed Treasurer in Ireland. The
appointment apparently was made to rid the
House of one of the independent men who were
part of the opposition to James' plans.

86. A John Young represented Rye in this Parliament, but he was not knighted. The speaker
more likely came from the west. In the very
short and awkward version in Add. Mss. 30,982,
the couplet reads:

Know time quoth Sr Young had he thus slipt
Ith' marches of Wales he should haue been whipt.

87. In Prince and Stowe the present couplet is attributed to an Evans who is not listed in the
Returns.

88. John Donne's father-in-law always represented
Guildford Borough, Surrey.

89. Facetiae attributes this couplet to the Serjeant of the House. In Prince and Stowe another couplet follows:

In his hands quoth Price? Noe, that fault was in
his breech.
Some Taylor should have given the hose another
stitch.

Facetiae has a Price couplet in a different
place, with different wording:

Then, quoth Mr. Price, it stinks the more you

<u>Naturam</u> <u>expellas</u> <u>furca</u>, <u>licet</u> usque <u>recurrit</u>.

> stir it,

<u>Stowe</u> and <u>Prince</u> have this couplet but attrib-
ute it to <u>Bond</u>. No Price appears in the Returns for this session, although three came
from Wales in 1601.

9.0. No Bond appears in the Returns. It is possibly
Thomas Bond, secretary of the Lord Chancellor,
who succeeded to that job when John Donne was
sacked as a result of his marriage to Sir
George More's daughter. <u>Prince</u> and <u>Stowe</u> attribute this couplet to Anthony Cope's brother.

91. Edward Phelips was M.P. from Somerset. To refer to him as a noble "Domestic" was a bit
rough on the King's Household.

92. <u>Prince</u>, <u>Stowe</u>, and <u>Facetiae</u> say "nose," which
is the clearer way of writing what is an oral
pun. <u>Rainsford</u> has the more witty way of expecting the reader to understand.

93. Not in <u>Rainsford</u> or <u>Facetiae</u>. <u>Prince</u> and <u>Stowe</u>
both end with this couplet, as do other mss.
As it immediately precedes "per Jo: Hoskines"
in <u>Stowe</u>, it is difficult not to include it.
<u>Facetiae</u> ends with the quite different

> But all at last said, it was most fit,
> The Fart as a Traitor to the Tower commit;
> Where as they say, it remaines to this houre,
> Yet not close prisoner, but at large in the Tower.

94. Many of the additional couplets describe M.P.s
that are more closely connected with the Addled Parliament of 1614: Anthony Dyott, William Wade, Sir Thomas Shirley, Sir John Fortescue, Sir John Sheffield, Sir Thomas Freke, and
Sir Michael Hicks. There are also couplets on
Sir Maurice Barkeley, Sir William Strowde, Henry Yelverton, Richard Berry, Sir Thomas Horseman, and Dudley Carleton, the great letter
writer. We might end with one that links to
similar humor in John Donne:

> Much a doe quoth S[r] Peter Manwood for a stenche
> My Father lett a hundred in the benche.

Manwood, although a native of Kent, represented Saltash Borough, Cornwall. His father, Roger Manwood, was one of the judges of the Common Pleas and was charged with "deliberate perversion of justice in his later years." John Donne's reference to him in The Courtier's Library is not much more subtle than the present couplet: "A Manual for Justices of the Peace, comprising many confessions of poisoners tendered to Justice Manwood, and employed by him in his privy...." (Simpson, pp. 49, 69).

95. It is possible that Hoskyns was also responsible for the shorter poem that is often found close to the present poem on the fart. The ending of the main poem certainly called for something further: an epitaph by the King. That epitaph was provided by someone, but it is anonymous in all the versions that I have seen: Stowe 962, f. 219; Egerton 2421, f. 2v; Sloane 1792, f. 95; Add. Mss. 30,982, f. 157v; and Add. Mss. 15,227, f. 79. The number of classical references certainly makes it possible that Hoskyns was the author, but there is little other evidence. The cross-reference found in Stowe 962 points out the location of the epitaph just at the same point that it identifies Hoskyns as the author of the longer poem. In Egerton 2421 the Epitaph is found directly between two other epitaphs by Hoskyns. The following version is from Stowe.

Epitaph of the parliament fart.

Reader, I was borne and tride
Crackt soe, smelt soe, and soe died
Like to Caesars, was my death
He in Senate lost his breath.
And alike inter'd doth lie
The ffamous Romulus and I.
At last like Flora Fayre
I left the Commonwealth my heire

The final, very bad pun is certainly one that Hoskyns might have written.

96. Clark, ed., pp. 417, 418.
97. Taken from the 3rd ed. (1607) of the volume, Book I, 96. Osborn, p. 6, uses the 1620 edi-

tion for all of the epigrams in the Owen volume.

98. Book II, 5. Not noted in Osborn.
99. Osborn version, p. 221.
100. A$_3$/3. Osborn, p. 221.
101. P. 1, #3.
102. A$_2$. Osborn, p. 209.
103. A$_2$v/7. Osborn, p. 209.
104. There is a double meaning to the phrase; it may also read, "This book is elegant."
105. Winchester Bursar's Accounts 1599-1600 to 1623-1624; WCM 19040.
106. The Middle Temple Benchbook records Benedict's birth as 1609 (p. 119).
107. Another writer has added a heading "Instructions By Serjeant Hoskyns For The Regulation Of The Conduct Of His Clerk Mr W. Taylor." Osborn prints the instructions, as transcribed by Henry Hornyold-Strickland, pp. 65-66.
108. Stow, pp. 891-92.
109. Harley 6395, #437.
110. Old Meg of Herefordshire for a Mayd Marian and Hereford Towne for a Morris Daunce, reprinted in Miscellanea Antiqua Anglicana, Vol. I, 1816.
111. Ibid., p. 2.
112. Ibid.
113. Thomas Fuller, The Worthies of England, ed. John Freeman (1952), p. 217.
114. Aubrey, ed. Dick, p. ci.
115. Mss. Add. 35,280. f. 5.
116. Old Meg, p. 9.
117. See Osborn, p. 224, n. 77.
118. Old Meg, p. 3.
119. Old Meg, pp. 3, 4.
120. This and the following quotations are from Old Meg, pp. 8-12.
121. Sheepskin Bag 1606-1609.
122. SPD James I, 1603-10, XLV, 122, p. 519.
123. Sheepskin Bag 1606-1609.
124. Vaughan died in 1629 and was buried in St. Dunstan's-in-the-West, where John Donne was the parish priest.
125. Sig. D$_2$v.
126. P. 223.
127. Information on these poems and a copy of

Heath's epigram are in Osborn, p. 250. The
poems are much easier to translate than the
similar classic verse of his elder brother.

128. Osborn notes Heath's epigram on Hoskyns (II,
32) on p. 218 but makes no comment on it.
Nor does she include it in her discussion of
the Morris Dance tract on pp. 300-01, which
is very surprising.

Chapter XI
Rounds Four and Five

In his study of the growth of opposition to the Stuarts, The Rise of the Revolutionary Party in the English House of Commons 1603-1629 (1957), Williams Mitchell remarks that "one is baffled by finding contradictory evidence, as in the case of George Cotton, John Hoskins, and Sir John Sammes, who appeared to speak now on one side and now on another."[1] Actually Hoskyns represented the shifts of Parliament as a whole. We have noticed a lessening of his negative comments during the third session of the Parliament. That shift was a reflection of a corresponding willingness of the Commons to come to a working agreement with James in 1607. John also was on quite friendly terms with a large number of courtiers around King James during the next couple of years. When Parliament reconvened, he continued to hold to his major ideas that Supply to the King should go hand in hand with redress of grievances by the King, but he was more than willing to take a conciliatory position whenever possible. As James continued to press his demands, however, and when the integrity and basic authority of the Commons was called into question, Hoskyns once again began to shift into a position of outspoken opposition.

Whatever his stance on particular issues, John was one of the real leaders of the final two sessions of this first Parliament of James I. He spoke at least 35 times, often at great length.[2] He served on at least 42 Committees besides those to which all lawyers were named. And he chaired or reported in eight Bills. As usual, he served on a number of Committees studying private Bills, most of which concerned members of the House.[3] And there were the customary Bills concerning specific towns and ports, and protection of wildlife and nature,[4] Bills on various businesses,[5] Bills on courts, prisons, and penal laws,[6] and miscellaneous other Bills.[7] He also took part in Committees on

331

which all lawyers were supposed to sit and sometimes got into the debate on such Bills.[8] For example, on 24 May a Bill concerning the Statute on
Recusants was submitted to a Committee containing
all the Lawyers of the House. The following day
the Bill was discussed in the House, and claims
were made that young gentlemen were "seduced" while
in prison and became converts to Roman Catholicism;
also that the various Ambassadors' houses were
filled with English people at the time of Masses.
Hoskyns joined the discussion by remarking that
"Licet haereticum principem occidere," a prince is
allowed to kill a heretic. (But never was John
more dangerously ambiguous. The statement may also
be translated, "It is allowable to kill an hereti-
cal king"!) Others suggested that all condemned
Jesuits and Seminaries be hanged; those not condemned should be punished. One speaker suggested
that all Recusants should be made to leave the city
of London. Sir Edward Montague turned the discussion by urging the Commons not to be so severe,
"but to send, To-morrow, to confer with the Lords;
and jointly to petition to the Lords, for some present Care for his Majesty's Safety."[9] The irony
of the final speech was that the Montagues were
probably the leading Roman Catholic family in the
city of London, and many of the men sitting in the
Commons during the debate were known recusants.
As a matter of fact, just one week earlier, on 18
May, someone moved for a Committee to know the religion of Sir John Davies. They decided "to take
Satisfaction of him first, before a bill," however.[10] On the 4th of June the King issued a Proclamation for all Roman Priests, Jesuits and Seminaries to leave the Kingdom within the month and
for all Recusants to leave London and not to come
within ten miles of the Court.[11]

Hoskyns also undoubtedly attended some of the
committee debates on Bills which were simply opened
to all who wished to come.[12] One of these, A Bill
on Highways, introduced on 26 May, is of more than
special interest because one of the people particularly interested in the passage of this Bill, "for
the better Repayre of the highe waies and amend-

inge diuers defectes in the Statutes alredy made,"
was William Shakespeare.[13]

But of more interest to John were those Bills
which were committed to his charge, and for which
he was responsible to report the results to the
full House. A letter from John to his wife on 25
March indicates the sense of responsibility he felt
for these Bills and for his general role of service
in the Parliament.

To my lovinge Mrs. Ben. Hoskyns.
Ben: I could easily condemne myselfe for an vn-
kynd husband yf I knew one hower wherein I
thought not vpon y^u. my fellow Mr. Pembrug[14]
steales away: both cannot possiblie; and I worse
than he; such is the reward of a mans service as
is among carters for horses and oxen; he that
draws well shall nev^r out of the plow or teeme:
Good sweete hart yf I knew that it touched y^r
hart wth such impatience as it doth almost teare
myne to be thus asunder: had I an horse heere I
would leve all & comm to thee but then must I
be discredited for euer: for there are div^rs
bills of the parliament committed vnto me w^{ch}
are to be sate vpon, som to morrow som on munday.
O deere Ben the longer I love thee the more
impotently & infinitely I love. now my little
Mr. Pembrug angers me that he lets me know his
parting but on the instant. I have receaved no
rent or debt. I have payed fiue pound that the
taylor tooke vp at the mercer in searge &c. and
ranne away wth it: I have bought a filthy blacke
suiet & worn it out. I have payed my commons I
know y^u may want I have sent you 8^l in gold, I
have a little left, I have yet liued by my la-
bours: though now out of terme publique paynes
make mee weary wthout fees. Tell my brother
John on this suddain I could not speake with
Doctor Lake.[15] Much wranglinge I have wth my
brother aboute a cloake, but shall have it & I
will sett it on makinge presently. I will send
by the next messeng^r what D. Lake hath done.
Thus in hast I could wish I might carry m^r Pembrug cloakebagge so that I might but comm by

the doore and see y^u. I have spoken to Sr Henry Williams for Morgan,16 but he is gone on a suddain. I have spoken to Wotton but he coms not down I feare: tell m^r Wallwyn17 I relye on him to goe to the Judge y^f neede be. Let Thom Gwillim18 return my recognisances & examinations taken before me to the Judge carefully. God blesse thee, sweet, lovinge excellent Ben, & John, franke, Bess & Ben, & god be m̄^{r}cyfull to us all & ever.
Mid: temp 25 Mar: 1609 [10]   y^r J. H.
     My humble duty to my Lord19
& most harty & thanckfull remembrance
   to Mr. D. Bradshaw & his wife.20

It is impossible to discover the specific Bills that Hoskyns is referring to in this letter as the Parliamentary records do not give a full account of all of the meetings of the various Committees by any means. We do know that he reported out eight Bills to the House. The first was a private Bill "For the Sale of the Lands of William Essex," given its second reading and assigned to Committee on 16 February, one week after the session began. The Committee met on the 22nd in the Middle Temple Hall, and the following day Sir Henry Poole said that "one Robinson, that is indebted, and dare not come, desires Protection." The House ruled that he could send his Counsel, as there is "No Protection in Matters of Execution." As that is a position that Hoskyns took in other cases of privilege, we may take it for granted that he was the one who suggested the action. He and Sir Henry often crossed swords during this session, even though they were both on the side of the Commons in its struggle with the King and were close friends outside Parliament. After other committee meetings, which are not recorded, Hoskyns reported in the Bill with Amendments on 1 March. However, action on the Bill was stayed until counsel could be heard. In the debate that followed, Hoskyns took Essex's side. On the 7th Mr. Essex let it be known that he assented to the Bill as it now stood, but the Bill was recommitted, with some Amendments to be made. The next day the Bill was brought in as amended and passed, and on the 13th it was sent up to the House of Lords. That was not the end of the Bill, however, as the Lords sent it back with further amendments on 3 May, and Hoskyns was on a smaller Committee which was to consider the Bill the following morning at 7 a.m. They appear to have acted quickly as the Bill was sent back up to the Lords on the 8th.[21]

Four other Bills which he reported were passed by the House: "For the Repairing and Maintaining of the Port and Harbour at Mynhead, in the County of Somersett";[22] a Bill to relieve the "Horners of London," those who made their living by making objects out of horn (When he reported the Bill in, on 9 March, John described the Horners as "A Trade of Antiquity, Singularity, Honesty" for the past 400 years. He said of their work, "None made in any Part." Moreover, there has "Never [been] any Complaint against them.-- 200 1. will buy all their Stuff." They are now in poverty, and the former Bill was "Unwittingly repealed.");[23] a Bill for a Mr. Elrington which was challenged both on the floor and in Committee by a Mr. Cage;[24] and a Bill concerning Milicent Smyth which Hoskyns managed to shepherd through the House in the last difficult month.[25] It is not possible to discover what happened to the three other Bills that he reported: "Kembers and Spinsters";[26] "a Bill against Weares"; [27] and "Debts due by simple Contracts, &c."[28] The last-named Bill is not clearly distinguishable from a Bill named earlier, that on Confirmation to the Contractors, and Hoskyns may have been responsible for both. The Bill obviously caused special problems as John was forced, on 10 July, to ask "for Opinion from the House whether all other Subjects Estates, upon Compositions for defective Titles, shall be confirmed." He also wanted to know whether there should be "A several Bill, or inserted in this Bill." The House decided that all of the subjects should, "upon good Consideration" be inserted.

But he was not only busy on Committees. Once again he was involved in searching for records in

335

support of the Grievances that the Commons were submitting to the King. On 6 June, he moved that his old co-searcher, "Mr. Robert Bowyer, and other Clerks, to give their Attendance at the Tower, in the Place where his Majesty's Records are kept; and further the foresaid Search, by all such Directions, Notes, or Calendars, as they have in their Keeping."29 And he was involved in the intensive search for records on Grievances in the waning days of the session.

His letter home on 25 March had indicated something of the problem of attendance, both of lawyers and "civilian" members of the House. Hoskyns' active participation in this session should not be taken as an indication of the way most of the M.P.'s behaved during the same year. The Journals are filled with references to the poor attendance. On one vote on 24 May, only 144 members of the House were present. The problem had begun almost immediately: on 21 February they decided to "call" the House, in other words have attendance taken by name, the next week. But on 1 March some weakened and tried to put the call off until after the meeting of the Assizes, and they then agreed "That no Man shall depart without open licence... All departed, sent for... all the Lawyers of the House, absent, be sent for." It didn't work. On the 3rd, they had the first call. There were obviously a number missing and the Committee on Privileges was asked to consider what action to take; meanwhile, they issued another call for a fortnight later. They discussed the problem further on the 12th, and on the 17th, after another roll call, decided on a further call in two weeks. On 30 March, they realized that there was no use in having a call so close to the Easter break and decided to have it on the Thursday after they returned instead. By 14 May the situation had become so bad that Martin moved, "That all Lawyers, and other Members of the House, do attend here this Afternoon; and if any neglect, then the Party offending to be called to the Bar." The members present agreed, but there is no record of anything having been done. It was not until 26 June that

336

the Bill on better attendance, on which Hoskyns served, was passed. On 6 July they decided to call the House every week, and finally, on 12 July, they put some teeth into their decision by voting that anyone absent at a roll call should be fined twenty shillings.[30] By then, however, it was less than two weeks to the end of the session, and it is doubtful that anyone actually received a fine.

The main offenders were the lawyers, and that is easy to understand. They depended for their livelihood upon the activity in the law courts during the two main terms that occurred during the long session of Parliament, as well as on the trials at the Assizes in their home shires. Their pay as members of Parliament in no way made up for the loss that they incurred from their absence in the courts. The fact that we can trace John's activities on a day-by-day basis through the session indicates how seriously he took his role as a Parliamentarian, for we know what it was costing him financially. Once again, we must keep in mind that he did not receive the money for his service in Parliament from 1604 through 1610 until 1618.

At the same time, the Commons continued to realize the importance of the lawyers, especially as it drew up the Grievances against the King and sought to find the legal precedents for its own power. Unwilling to accept the Stuart claim to absolute monarchy, the Baroque divine right of kings, they needed to base their claims to a constitutional monarchy on the precedent of law in the absence of any specific Constitution. In this task, lawyers played a major role. They were aware of the dangers of conflict of interest, however, and a week after the session opened, they decided that the lawyers could not plead any of the cases in either House.[31] Yet they were needed in committee discussions, and at least sixteen Committees included "all of the lawyers" of the House.[32] With the attendance problem what it was, the record is filled with special attempts to get the lawyers into the debates and committee meetings.[33] On 24 April, when the real discussion on Grievances be-

337

gan, a special plea was made: "all the Lawyers to
attend specially;--as a Time appointed for the
greatest Matters." By 14 May it became necessary
to order the Lawyers "to attend, upon Pain of calling to the Bar." And one month later, on 18 June,
the House decided, "The Lawyers of the House to be
put in Writing, and to be noted, if they be absent."
The next day they read out the names of all missing
lawyers, but the list was not put down in the records. Finally, the lawyers came under the same
danger of a fine as the rest of the House in July.

This session also arrived at a clear and working concept of the Committee of the Whole. We have
seen the early developments of the concept in the
previous sessions, but now, on 15 March, it was decided that there should be "A Committee of the
whole House:--To sit every other Day." Its first
task was to consider the matter of Wards, one of
the touchiest of the Grievances; the Committee was
"to begin at Seven, or Eight; to sit till half an
Hour after Nine." The House would then "sit till
half an Hour after Eleven." In the afternoon the
Committee for Grievances, which eventually turned
into a Committee of the Whole, would meet, followed
by private bills until three o'clock. On the 23rd
this neat schedule already began to break down, as
the Committee of the Whole sat the entire morning,
"till half an Hour after Eleven; the Speaker, from
Nine, sitting in the Clerk's Chair; the Clerk
standing at his Back; and Mr. Recorder, the Modera-
tor of the Committee, sitting on a Stool by him."
By 1 June, the situation had become even more fluid,
with the House deciding at any given moment to
shift into a Committee of the Whole, whereupon the
Speaker would leave the hall, and one of the M.P.'s
would take over as chairman.[34]

At the same time that the House was developing its new rules of order, it was spending a good
deal of time protecting its privileges, and as a
member of the Committee on Privileges, Hoskyns was
playing his usual role. We have already noted his
part in the Bill concerning attendance at meetings
of the House.[35] As usual the Committee reacted

quickly to the arrest of any members of the House or their servants. Sir Thomas Denton had been arrested at the Gloucester Assizes by a man named Brugge, and they moved to stay the trial. On the same day, 2 March, they handled a case in which Pages of members of the House had been pulled downstairs forcibly by a vintner because they had been buying wine and building up debts, for which they had pawned their cloaks. Although the vintner was not there, Hoskyns and four other M.P.'s were sent to examine the vintner's servant, Thomas Reely. They brought in a report from their examination a little while later, and apparently an amicable settlement was arranged.[36] A somewhat similar case arose on 5 March, when a servant of Sir James Scudamore, Eustace Parry, was reported arrested at the instigation of a man named Wayte and placed in Aylesbury Gaol. On 15 March the case was referred to the Committee on Privileges when the Sheriff who had done the arresting appeared. After considerable discussion, the House agreed to pardon Mr. Wayte when he had paid the fees connected with the arrest. The interesting part of this small interlude was that Hoskyns seems to have continued his feud with the Scudamores; he argued in favor of the arrest, saying that there is "No Privilege in Matter of Peace." The servant was apparently breaking a curfew by "Walking late"; therefore, "No Privilege."[37] Sometimes the debates on matters of privilege could become quite petty, as on 31 March, when most of the day seems to have been taken up with a debate over what to do about a young man named Craford who came in, stood a while, and then walked out. After much parliamentary rule haggling, they called Craford back, made him kneel at the bar, and the Speaker admonished him for his contempt.[38]

Only one contested election return caused any difficulty in this session, that of Bridgenorth, Salop, represented by Sir Lewis Lewkenor and Sir Francis Lacon. The struggle was between Sir Francis, Hoskyns' friend at the Hereford Morris Dance, and Sir George Howard, both of whom claimed they were elected. On 7 March they appeared with counsel, and the House referred the matter to the Committee on Privilege. On 9 March the question was raised as to whether the Writ from the House had been sent, delivered, etc. Hoskyns, Fuller, and Sir Roger Owen reported that there had been an erasure on the Writ, "No good Seal," and "No Bailiff's Hand." Others argued that the Bill was legal even if a little questionable. The next day they decided that the Return was "good in Law," but that any misdemeanor should be examined by the Houe. After a week of haggling over legal details, Hoskyns suggested that the House ought first to examine the abuse and then to issue an Order for the Bailiffs involved to return, which is what was decided.[39] They then apparently dropped the whole thing.

More important issues concerned the proper way of handling material which involved relations of the House and the King. Hoskyns was always interested in the matter of freedom of speech within the House, and on 7 May, during a debate on Grievances, he quoted a Statute from the reign of Henry VII, "That no Man should be impeached for speaking in Parliament freely." He referred to that law as a "Proclamation," for freedom of speech was "The Freehold, the Conscience, the Life of Men."[40] He did not realize how much that issue of freedom was to involve himself later on. Earlier that day the House had decided how to handle a touchy situation concerning a Bill sent down from the Lords: "An Act for Confirmation of a Grant made to the high and mighty Princess Anne, Queen of England, Scotland, France." On the 5th, when the Bill arrived, there was a motion to send it to the Committee on Privileges, but Sir George Carew argued against that, obviously intending that the House act upon it immediately in favor of the Queen. Wentworth and Hoskyns, however, joined the opposition and argued for its submission to Committee, which is what happened. On the 7th the Committee reported that the Queen's Bill should be received because there was a precedent, but that there should be an "Order to be conceived, that none be received hereafter, of that Form."[41]

340

On 11 May the Speaker found himself caught between the upper and nether millstones of the Grievance controversy. That morning he reported that the King was in general agreement with Parliament's course of action, but that he had some questions about the legal aspects. Wentworth immediately argued that he was sure "That it is not his Majesty's Meaning, that we should not consider what is fit to be done." Hoskyns, Fuller, and Mr. James joined together to argue that the Commons was well within precedent. Then the debate grew hot. Several members asked the Speaker if he had gotten that message from the King or someone else. He retorted that Speakers had never been pressed like this before. Sir Herbert Croft said that "it hath grown into too much Custom, that the Speaker should bring any Message from the King, but when he was sent by the House." Others argued that the Speaker should not go to the King but by leave; that he should always go in company, not singly. Then Hoskyns brought the debate into some kind of order by suggesting that the House decide what should be committed to the Committees, then just "How far to treat of Impositions." Finally, "How far our Speaker may deliever from the King, or to the King from us." And the House agreed that these points should be put into an order to be penned by the Committee on Privileges, which was done the following day.42 In that short debate, John made sure that the Commons had recaptured the office of Speaker as their representative rather than as an agent of the King.

At the same time the House recognized its need for keeping its own procedures in order. On 27 March Sandys tried to keep the number and kind of Grievances to be considered by the House in some reasonable form; he moved that the Committee for Privileges "consider how to prevent the Preferring of Grievances, like Pasquils, and yet to preserve the Liberties of the House."43 On 20 June an extreme case of this kind was reported when the Speaker told of finding certain pacquets at the door of the House which claimed knowledge of treason. Before they voted that the Speaker should

341

burn the papers, they decided "that if any Stranger prefer any Grievance, he must stand by at the reading."44

At the end of the session there was a small problem of M.P.'s giving in to outside pressure in what today would be referred to as a conflict of interest. On 19 July Hoskyns reported to the House that someone "hath brought good Manufacture of Spanish Cloth" into the House for the purpose of having some of the "Clothiers of this House" examine it and give some encouragement for it, "the Party pretending, that it will make it more vendible."45 It was too late in the session to do anything but note the infraction.

Two cases introduced potential struggles for power between the King and his Commons, but in both the King finally agreed with Parliament. One was the case of Sir Stephen Proctor, who was involved both in Grievances and in matters of Privilege. On 8 March 1610, Sir Edwyn Sandys brought up a new commission given to Proctor as one of the real Grievances of the kingdom, and Sir John Mallory offered to draw up particulars against Proctor. On 25 April, Mallory charged that Proctor "had given out that Sir John had a Purpose to murder him, because he informed against him." After the Committee on Privileges had met, the House heard that Proctor had "Abused every Commission"; he had kept back money he collected, frightened landholders into paying graft, used the King's Commission to break open chests of money in private homes. The House wanted to take him out of the King's hands and punish him themselves for the breach of Privilege. On 2 May the King promised never to employ him again, but that did not satisfy the Commons. On 12 May the Speaker suggested that for "Abuses to the Commonwealth, to petition to the King; for slandering a Member, to commit him to the Tower: That within the Jurisdiction of the House." On 14 May they discussed the method of handling him further, and on 15 May had him imprisoned; the King claimed him as his own prisoner. Under some pressure from the Lord Chancellor, the King agreed that

342

Proctor should be sent to the Parliament, and they
then tried to decide what to do in regard to the
prisoner's actions, "in Matter of State, the Punishment to be left wholly to his Majesty or else
to proceed by Bill." They decided in favor of a
Bill, and Hoskyns was one of a small Committee to
frame it. Meanwhile they sent Proctor to the Tower because of the "wrong done to the Dignity of the
House."46 The Bill was reported in on 6 June, re-
assigned to Committee, and finally passed on 3
July. It is clear that Proctor had friends in the
House of Lords who wished to tone down the Bill,
and on 19 July they asked for a conference on the
Bill. Hoskyns was assigned to a small Committee,
including the Privy Council, to consider what to
say at such a conference, and they decided to "defend the Bill generally." As the session ran
quickly to its close, there was a last minute attempt to table the Bill on the 21st, "to let the
Stephen Proctor Bill sleep." But it was turned
down, and in the last minutes of the sesion, the
Lords finally sent down word that they had left
Proctor's name out of the Pardon list that accompanied the end of Parliament. It had taken a good
deal of waiting, but the House had finally won its
point.

The second case was one brought up by John
within two weeks of the opening of the session, and
it got right to the heart of the Parliament's
struggle with the Stuarts. As suggested earlier,
Hoskyns began the session really trying to find
some solutions to the King's problems. He even
gave a little on his former stand that Parliament
should not substitute payments of money for the doing away of burdensome feudal rights of the King.
But he would not budge on his position about the
nature of the monarchy and the power of Parliament.
On 23 February he delivered a long speech obviously
aimed at the upcoming meeting of the Committee on
Grievances, on which he served. The shorthand version of the keeper of the Commons Journal does not
always allow for a clear interpretation of his
speech, especially as it dealt at length with precedents from previous statutes, but most of his

343

argument can be deciphered.[47] He started by suggesting that many of the Commons' Grievances were improper. The question on matters of Composition lay in what specific matters there might be a basis for Exchange with the King. Magna Carta provided a base for such exchange, where a Fifteen was given to do away with the misuse of Wardships.[48] The principle of Contracts was "Do, ut des; do, ut facias; facias, ut des." I give as you would give; I give as you would do; you should do as you would give. In the twenty-fifth year of Edward III, some Tenths and Fifteenths went back again into "Fines, Issues, and Amerciaments of Labourers." Six years later in the same reign there was "A Pardon of all Escapes of Felons Goods, not estreated, -- Amerciaments not offered." In the fourth year of the reign of Henry IV there was a confirmation of "Privileges to the Clergy." Under it the King was proclaimed "no Traitor, nor Felon." The subjects agreed to a payment of a Fifteenth. In the seventh year of Henry VII there were "Grants to all that will go into the Wars, Liveries of their Lands and Wardships." This is similar to present grants. Therefore, the business of the Commons was "To consider whether Things [were] exchangeable." For example, Silenced Ministers and Alum are "not Symbolizantia"; they do not have any qualities in common that would allow one to substitute for the other. Smalt, a cobalt-blue glass, is "Not exchangeable: Not fit for a Retribution."

Then the speech takes a sharp turn. Hoskyns brings up a book published nearly three years earlier in Cambridge by a Dr. John Cowell, who was "the Kings Maiesties Professour of the Ciuill Law in the Vniversitie of Cambridge."[49] The book, entitled The Interpreter, Hoskyns argues, says "That the King gives us Leave to make Laws of Favour." He then names the offensive passages as the "Titles -- Subsidy, Parliament, King." There has been much "Preaching against Prohibitions," but at the same time there are obviously "Books in Print against the Common Law." "These Opinions in print will" clearly lead to abuse. He then moves, "That some may be appointed to censure the Books that are

344

touching the Common Laws." The House agreed immediately to "refer this Matter of Mr. Hoskins Motions, to the Committee for Grievances." For the next month the debate over this volume was to take up a very considerable amount of the time of both Houses of Parliament. Hoskyns had touched a raw nerve of the body politic, and only the cauterizing of the book by the express command of the King was to restore the normal processes.

On the face of it, the book does not seem to be worth the controversy: The Interpreter: or Booke containing the Signification of Words: Wherein is set foorth the true meaning of all, or the most part of such Words and Termes, as are mentioned in the Lawe Writers, or Statutes of this victorious and renowned Kingdome, requiring any Exposition or Interpretation. A Worke not onely profitable, but necessary for such as desire throughly to be instructed in the knowledge of our Lawes, Statutes, or other Antiquities. It is a dictionary with historical derivations. Moreover, Cowell's forward to the Readers is very humble. He claims only that "my true ende is the advauncement of knowledge." He does not claim to have the ultimate truth but to be searching. No one could be offended by definitions such as "Almond (amygdalum) ... it is the kirnell of a nut or stone, which the tree in Latine called (amygdalus) doth beare within a huske in Maner of a walnut...." Nor generally for that of the Lord Chancellor: "the cheife man for mater of iustice (in priuate causes especially) next vnto the prince. For whereas all other Iustices in our common wealth, are tied to the lawe, and may not swerue from it in iudgement: the Chanceler hath in this the kings absolute power, to moderate and temper the written lawe, and subiecteth himselfe onely to the lawe of nature and concience...." But contained in the latter definition is the kernel of a harder nut than the almond, the phrase "the kings absolute power." Cowell makes his point quite clear in his definition:

King (Rex) is thought by M. Camden... to be contracted of the Saxon word Cyninge, signifiing

him that hath the highest power & absolute rule
ouer our whole Land. and thereupon the King is
in intendment of Lawe cleared of those defects,
that common persons be subiect vnto... he is a-
boue the Law by his absolute power... and though
for the beter and equall course in making Lawes
he doe admitte the 3. estates... vnto Councell:
yet this, in diuers learned mens opinions, is
not of constreinte, but of his owne benignitie,
of by reason of his promise made vpon oath, at
the time of his coronation. For otherwise were
he a subiect after a sort and subordinate, which
may not bee thought without breach of duty and
loyaltie. For then must we deny him to be a-
boue the lawe, and to haue no power of dispens-
ing with any positiue lawe, or of graunting especiall priuiledges and charters unto any, which
is his onely and cleare right... For hee par-
doneth life and limme to offendours against his
crowne and dignitie, except such as he bindeth
himself by oath not to forgiue... And though at
his coronation he take an oath not to alter the
lawes of the land: Yet this oath notwithstanding, hee may alter or suspend any particular
lawe that seemeth hurtfull to the publike estate... Thus much in short, because I haue heard
some to be of opinion, that the lawes be aboue
the king.

The lawyers of the Commons were quite correct in
seeing that passage as an attack upon the basic
validity of the Common Law system. As members of
Parliament as well, they would be doubly incensed
by parts of Cowell's definition of that body:

In England we vse it for the assembly of the
king and the three estates of the Realme, videl-
icet. the Lords Spirituall, the Lords Temporall,
and commons, for the debating of maters touching the common wealth, and especially the making and correcting of lawes. which assembly or
court is of all other the highest, and of greatest authoritie... And of these two one must
needes be true, that either the king is aboue
the Parlament, that is, the positiue lawes of

346

his kingdome, or els that he is not an absolute
king... And therefore though it be a mercifull
policie, and also a politique mercie (not alter-
able without great perill) to make lawes by the
consent of the whole Realme, because so no one
part shall haue cause to complaine of a partial-
itie: yet simply to binde the prince to or by
these lawes, weare repugnant to the nature and
constitution of an absolute monarchy.

Cowell simply writes off anyone who disagrees with
this point. In his definition of the King's Prerogative, which had been a central issue during
this whole first Parliament of James, he is even
more explicit. Prerogative "is that especiall power, preeminence, or priuiledge that the King hath
in any kinde, ouer and aboue other persons, and a-
boue the ordinarie course of the common lawe, in
the right of his crowne." He makes light of a
statute on which the Commons had based much of
their argument: "the statute of the Kings prerogatiue made, an. 17. Ed. 2. conteineth not the summe
of the Kings whole prerogatiue, but onely so much
thereof, as concernes the profit of his cofers...
for it is more then manifest, that his prerogatiue
reacheth much farder: yea euen in the maters of
his profit, which that statute especially consist-
eth of." After giving some examples in law, Cowell
goes right back to the heart of his argument:

Now for those regalities which are of the higher
nature (all being within the compas of his prerogatiue, and iustly to be comprised vnder that
title) there is not one that belonged to the
most absolute prince in the world, which doth
not also belong to our king, except the custome
of the nations so differ... that one thing be in
the one accompted a regalitie, that in another
is none. Onely by the custome of this kingdome,
he maketh no lawes without the consent of the 3.
estates though he may quash any lawe concluded
by them. And whether his power of making lawes
be restreined (de necessitate) or of a godly
and commendable policy, not to be altered without great perill, I leaue to the iudgement of

347

wise men. But I hold it incontrowlable, that
the king of England is an absolute king. And
all learned politicians doe range the power of
making lawes, _inter_ _insignia_ _summa_ _&_ _absolutae_
potestatis....

Were Cowell's view to gain hold, all of the
rights and power that Parliament had been arguing
for would have been lost. And their main lever had
always been in the granting of subsidies, which
Cowell also sought to undermine:

... a taxe or tribute assessed by Parlament, and
graunted by the commons to be leuied of euery
subiect, according to the value of his lands or
goods after the rate of 4. shillings in the
pound for land, and 2. shillings 8. pence for
goods, as it is most commonly vsed at this day.
Some hold opinion, that this subsidie is graunted by the subiect to the Prince, in recompence
or consideration, that whereas the Prince, of
his absolute power, might make lawes of himselfe, he doth of fauour admit the consent of
his subiects therein, that all things in their
owne confession may be done with the greater in-
differencie... Subsidie is in the statue of the
land, sometime confounded with custome....

The sub-committee read the book that afternoon and reported back the next day, calling it
"very unadvised and undiscreet; tending to the Dis-
reputation of the Honour and Power of the Common
Laws."50 It became clear that the best way to
handle the matter was to join with the Lords in
punishing Cowell. Even Sir Francis Bacon rose to
speak on the matter, but carefully avoided criti-
cizing the specific claims of the book. He blamed
all the trouble on "The Licence of the Pen, Disease
of the Time," "Poisoned Opinions" are a "Disease in
Spirits." He urged that not Cowell's "Error; but
Presumption; to be handled." They should act with
proportion: their object should be "not this House
alone, but the King, and the whole Body." They
should not "Induce Misunderstanding between the
King and his People." Then Hoskyns tried to show

348

that the problem was much greater than simply the book by Cowell; he "Produceth many other Treatises containing as much as D. Cowell." But by now the King's forces had pretty much gotten the situation in hand: the Speaker sent the matter back to the sub-committee, Mr. Attorney Hobart made sure that the charge should be to the whole body of Parliament rather than just the House, and Bacon was added to the sub-committee. In the month that followed Hoskyns was busy in the sub-committee that prepared the arguments for the conferences with a similar Committee from the House of Lords and then reported back to the House of those conferences.51

The passages that they considered "scandalous and dangerous matter against the authority of the Parliament" were those we have already noted. Perhaps the most interesting speech in the joint conferences was that on 8 March when the Lord Treasurer, Salisbury, delivered the King's message on Cowell's book. The King had read the book, "and he doth conceave and acknowledge that that booke is too bold with the Comon lawe of the Land; holdinge yt a greate presumcion in any suject to speake or write against those Lawes under which he must live." Cowell has also misunderstood the basis of Parliament. In the matter of Prerogative, he has gone farther than is fit for a subject: "this man in theise things hath offended both against the Kinge and Parliament in regard of that union of interest which all of theym have in the lawes of the Kingdome...." If the King had known of the book before Parliament began, he would have suppressed it, which he now intends to do. Then James tried to find a middle way out of the controversy, but he was forced to go farther than his previous and later statements on the power of the King, a power which he saw personally as deriving from Divine Right:

...That for his Kingdome he was beholden to noe elective power... and yet he doth acknowledge that, though he did derive his tytle from the loynes of his ancestors, yet the lawe did set the Crowne upon his head, and he is a Kinge by

349

the comon lawe of the land... He said further
that yt was dangerous to submit the power of a
kinge to definition. But withall he did acknowledge that he had noe power to make lawes
of himselfe, or to exact any subsidies de jure
without the consent of his 3 Estates; and therefore he was soe farre from approvinge the opin-
yon as he did hate those that beleved yt.52

The King followed this up with a proclamation on
the Cowell book on 26 March. The House was understandably overjoyed, and the Committee on Privileges prepared an order touching the proclamation.
On the 27th, Chancellor Egerton took the thanks of
the House directly to the King and returned with
the answer of his Majesty that he was "Very glad,
the eucharistique Days were not yet ended.--As
great Comfort in Thanks, as you in Love and Favour."
He even went further, assuring them "That whatsoever he spoke to themselves, or to Mr. Speaker, he
will ever stand to in publick which he spoke in
private." So an amicable conclusion was achieved
in a matter of extreme importance for the position
of Parliament. Once again, it was John Hoskyns
who had set the action in motion in his own quiet
way.

The Cowell case and all of the other committee action which we have so far looked at were actually peripheral not only to Hoskyns' main activities during this session, but to the main business
of the Commons. The major problems were a continuation and sharpening of those that had been building since 1604. One, that of Union with Scotland,
was brought up on 10 February, the second day of
the session, by Sir William Morris, and for all
practical purposes simply disappeared.53 On the
15th a Committee of 120, which included Hoskyns,
met with the Lords to be told the reasons for calling this session; they were supposedly two: "1.
The creation of the Prince, Prynce of Wales, and
Earle of Chester and Flint. 2. To demand some supplie of treasure."54 The first was strictly a
formality; the second was bound up with the usual
questions of Subsidy, the redress of Grievances,

especially Impositions, and the whole unresolved
problem of the Composition of feudal rights. Each
of these problems was assigned to a general Committee and sub-committees, and Hoskyns' name appears
on almost all of them.

Of all of the Grievances, the one with the
greatest explosive potential was that of Impositions. Since the previous session of Parliament,
the Lord Treasurer had received a legal ruling
which, if stretched beyond the intent of the Judge
involved, Chief Baron Fleming, could potentially
allow the King to impose import duties on products
at such a high level that the King would conceivably be free from dependency upon the Subsidies
voted by Parliament. The Commons wanted to make
sure that such a wide interpretation of the ruling
would not go unchallenged.55

But the first Grievance to appear was one of
the last to be mentioned in the previous session.
On 14 February, Sir Herbert Croft once more spoke
up for the freeing of the four western counties
from the jurisdiction of the President of Wales,
and the House immediately reactivated the old Committee on the subject. The next morning Hoskyns
asked more specifically for the appointment of a
Committee on the matter and pointed out that it was
"An old Rule:--The King of England cannot foreclose
his Subjects of a Trial at the Common Law." Sir
Edwyn Sandys was obviously looking ahead to the
general method of attack for the session, however,
and he moved that the general Committee for Grievances be set up and that they then establish the
sub-committees. That general Committee included
the Privy Council, the first Knight of every shire,
all the lawyers, the first burgess of every Borough
(hence John), and Sir Edwyn Sandys. Then they
added anyone who wished to come.56

On the 17th the Attorney General and Sir Francis Bacon reported a joint conference with the
Lords on the 15th and explained the financial situation of the King. His Majesty had done all he
could on the basis of past grants to get rid of

351

previous debts, such as those incurred by the state
funeral of Queen Elizabeth, but he was still
£300,000 in debt. Moreover, current revenues fell
short some £50,000. Parliament should remedy the
situation and keep the ship afloat as other Parliaments had done in the past. Sandys answered calmly but strongly, asserting that the people had
rights as well. The King was never so great that
he could "demand at Pleasure;" nor should "Subjects
deny, out of Humour... The true Scale of the King's
Prerogative was, when in Concurrence with the public Good." He summed up by saying the House should
"Proceed in Love and Fear to our Prince:--Proceed
in tuto et commodo," which meant that grievances
should go along with the monetary provisions.57
On the 19th, Hoskyns issued his usual call for
caution:

> Neither was it thought yet tyme to enter into
> consideracion of subsidies, for that the former
> were not yet payd, and to grante subsidies in
> reversion was not usuall, nor warranted by any
> president, especially considering that His Maj-
> estie did declare in his proclamacion for the
> parliament, that he did not call that parliament
> for any private benefite to hymselfe, but for
> the good of the Comonwealth. And that also it
> was sayd in the last grante of subsidy, that
> that grante was without president, and should
> not be drawne into example in after tymes.58

That same day, in the general Committee for Grievances, he tried to sweeten his stand a bit by moving, "concerning wardships, that the whole benefite might come to the King's purse, and not unto
the committee's, but that motion was not seconded
by any other."59 There were many, like Wentworth,
who felt far more strongly about the state of the
King's finances: "For his part... he would never
give his consent to take money from a poore frize
jerkyn to trappe a courtier's horse withall."60

On the 21st, Sandys suggested that there be
another joint conference to find out exactly what
the King and the Lords were willing to discuss and

how much they were asking. When that meeting was
reported back on the 27th, the House was told just
how much the King was asking for the relief of
many of their grievances, such as the doing away of
Purveyance: at least £450,000, with another
£100,000 really needed; indeed, the request was for
a total Subsidy of £600,000 and a support or composition of £200,000. The next day the debate became understandably hot. Sir George Carew argued
that since the grievances were just, the people
shouldn't pay anything to have them removed. Fuller pointed out that more was "demanded than ever
was in Parliament." It was true that a person,
like a country, might wear gold on the head and
leather on the feet, "but to go bare-foot--"! Sir
Robert Cotton argued that there was never any dispute about the King's needs, and that Kings were
often granted subsidies for ten years in a row.
Then Hoskyns tried to build a bridge between the
positions: it was "Like a Contract of Marriage:--
No betrothing as good." He argued that trying to
meet individual, wandering needs was "A dangerous
Point." Finally the House agreed to send a message that they had "taken Knowlege of the State of
his Majesty's Wants; and, for Supply therein, will,
in due Time, take Consideration of it; and doubt
not, but, like dutiful Subjects, to give his Majesty
good Satisfaction." But they also made it clear
that they wanted an answer on such Grievances as
Tenures and Wardships. The next day they changed
the message to make it a bit clearer: they saw no
other way of answering the problem of Supply than
by their usual Subsidy, which they would consider
in due time; as for Support, that would depend on
the answers given by the Lords.[61]

The number of problems that arose during the
rest of the session led to at least fourteen joint
meetings with the Lords at which Hoskyns was present.[62] They covered such issues as the Grievances
on Tenures and Wardships, the Cowell case, the matter of Impositions, and the problems of Subsidy and
Support. The Lords wanted to speed up the processes of such meetings and on 3 May suggested that
since discussions on Tenures and Wardships had

"been carried with a sweet Correspondence, and
their Lordships must participate in the Good, or
Ill, made manifest and clear by the Arguments; that
either might know others Minds:--That the Committees might have Liberty to hear Propositions, and
Questions, and to make Answers; as also to ask
Questions; not concluding any thing on either Part."
The House immediately saw the danger of the Lords
exerting pressure on individual committee members
on such central grievances. Christopher Brooke
argued precedent: "no such Liberty.--To hear what
they will say, and then report nothing." Sir
Nathaniel Bacon argued that they were "not wise
alone, but together." Hoskyns added the warning,
"We may mistake in answering: The wisest have mistaken." And the House agreed and refused to let
their representatives do anything but report the
action of the House and to listen to what the Lords
had to say.

When the men did report back on the 5th, they
reported that the Lords were quite put out over the
reply of the House and that they also suggested ten
demands that the House "thought not worth accepting." Then there was a request to know what else
had been said as they had heard that some of the
speeches by the Lords had been against the Commons.
Hoskyns, after making sure that he was reporting
accurately by having the comments put into writing
and checked by the others, reported that three individual members of the Lords had spoken. One, an
old man, had said that he had been in many Parliaments and that there were always conferences. Never had there been more need, but the method was
"one Day Tongues, another Ears.--As the primitive
Church, not collationes, not contentiones." The
Archbishop of Canterbury was "Sorry that Things
were not carried. The King's Necessity had been
notably, plainly delivered unto us." In his reading of the situation, the Kingdom was in trouble.
"The King may want shift for himself," but there
were "Millions of men" involved, which made it different. Certainly he "can help himself," but "In
speculative Divinity he took it for a Ground that
a Kingdom must support the King." John also re-

354

ported that "Some fine Wits made Orations:--being
dismembered, and disjointed, would prove nothing
but Froth."63

     The issue of Wardships continued throughout
the entire session, as it had in earlier sessions,
when it had been the subject of the important Apology to the King. This feudal right of the king to
act as ward over any land-owner who was a minor was
as much a matter of concern of the highest peers of
the realm as it was of the middle classes, and almost everyone was willing to pay the King a given
Composition for the right, if he would only give it
up. The question was really how much. The major
part of the debate took place in March. After a
joint meeting with the Lords on the 12th about a
number of different Grievances, Sir Henry Hobart
reported back the King's position. On the matter
of Tenure, which concerned the services of landholders to their landlords, in this case the King,
James was willing for them to discuss the matter
and to clear up any faults. He was willing to
"part with Purveyance on basis of just Complaint."
But "On Wards he asked they not blast the Flower of
his Prerogative." This was a good deal calmer
statement than he had made in the first session of
the Parliament, and members of the House vied with
each other in thanking their Monarch. The question
arose as to whether they should send their thanks
directly or together with the Lords, and Hoskyns
argued that they should join with the Lords, to
show "That we have tender Care." When Sir Edwyn
Sandys took the same position, the point was
really decided, and they so moved.64 The next day
they began their daily sittings of the Committee
of the Whole to consider the question of Tenures
and Wards, beginning each morning session with
Prayers. By the time of the Easter recess, which
ran from 3 April to 16 April, the House was ready
to take action on the question, but the Lords were
dragging their feet, undoubtedly at the behest of
the King. On 2 April the Upper House sent word
that "the Particulars with great Advisement propounded by this" were "so great in general,--so
weighty,--the Time so short, and designed for other

355

Cogitations of higher Nature," that they were not
yet ready, but that by their next meeting would be
"neither remiss, nor forgetful." They kept their
word and on the 19th called for a meeting the next
day, at which they reported that the King agreed
to most of their requests, and they now sought to
return the practice to its original use. They all
agreed that "The King [is] constant to himself:--
In all Messages, excepted Point of Sovereignty, or
Regality; and, in return, we professed not to med-
dle with it." Shortly after this date the main
discussion on this subject ended until the actual
amounts of money to be given were discussed near
the end of the session.

Grievances of all kinds were handled throughout the session. The matter of the Four Shires,
which had been brought up as the first issue, was
still being debated on July 18th, when Hoskyns
joined in the discussion over whether it should be
made part of the Composition. The majority felt
that it should not be a necessary part, but that
it should be simply a Petition to the King.65

After the matter of the Cowell book had been
taken care of in early March, the Grievance Committee set itself another set of guidelines, one of
which was that all of the sub-committees were to
sit from one till three in the afternoon, after
which they were to report back to the Grand Committee. Moreover, they were to meet at Westminster
rather than in various rooms around the city so
that they could be called for whenever it might be
necessary.66 On 19 March Sandys did not feel that
things were moving quickly enough, so he got the
House to agree to a full week of all-day meetings
of the Grievance Committee, with the sub-committees
meeting at two o'clock. It apparently worked, for
by the 23rd he felt that all of the Grievances
could be "rough-hewn" in one more day of meetings,
and then general discussions could start. One
month later, Sandys reported in the first part of
the Grievances, which had to do with Ecclesiastical
Matters, and a real debate ensued. At the end of
the session the King was to make it quite clear

356

that he felt that Parliament had no real right to
interfere on ecclesiastical questions.[67] In later
Parliaments, Hoskyns was ready to argue the matter,
but not at this point. Sometimes, as on 9 June,
debates on Grievances were delayed by the failure
of search committees to bring in their reports from
the Tower; on other occasions rescheduling of the
Grand Committee was made necessary in order to carry on other business. Finally, on 7 July, the
Grievances were ingrossed, although they did not
contain many items that had been discussed. These
were to be kept in the Clerk's Hands until the
next session. The Grievances were sent to the King
and finally discussed by the House in a retrospec-
tive session on the 17th. The King was to discuss
the Grievances individually in his last speech, but
the last few weeks of the session were mainly given
over to discussion of Impositions and of the amount
of Subsidy and Support.

As I have said earlier, the subject that was
at the heart of this session of Parliament was the
matter of Impositions, for it lay at the root of
the King's argument over Prerogative, and it had
enough legal basis stemming from the Magna Carta
to be a thorn in the side of Parliament. As early
as 1599 Hoskyns had given an indication of the popular antipathy to these taxes: "all men exclaime
vppon theise exactions, Nobles Gentlemen Communal-
tie, poore rich Schollars Merchants Pesants, young,
old, wise, ignorant, high, lowe, and all cry out
vppon the hard impositions of theise burthens...."[68]

The King and the Lord Treasurer saw Impositions as a way out from under the restraining influence of the Commons. It is no wonder that the
debates were long and increasingly hot. On 18 May
Commons agreed to send a message to the King, "to
give him Satisfaction for Matter of Impositions,"
which he knew they were discussing. On the 21st
the Lord Chancellor took the message to the King,
who immediately summoned them all to an afternoon
meeting at Whitehall. If he was angry at the way
the House was talking about Impositions, it was
nothing compared to the anger of the House at what

357

he had to say to them. The next morning the cauldron bubbled. Sir Francis Hastings said, "His Majesty made a publick Claim of Matter of Impositions, to his Court of Parliament," and that according to that claim, "His Majesty then hath a Power in all our Properties." He urged that a Committee be formed "to consider of some Satisfaction between the King and the Subject," but "to do it dutifully, carefully, and strongly." Hoskyns' close friend James Whitelocke said that "The King made a Claim of his Right:--Not de quanta, sed de quota parte." It is not a matter of how much, but of what part. The people of England are "Masters of their own." Their property "Cannot be taken without Consent"; there cannot be laws without their consent. "Parliament a Store-house of Liberty." He acknowledged that there was some support in the civil law for the position that the pleasure of the Prince had the strength of law, but there should be specific regulations, such as a tax on tonnage, that would make "Satisfaction of arbitrary Impositions." Sir George More tried to pour a little oil on the waters by suggesting that they sit down and compare notes to find out exactly what the King did say, and they decided to have a Committee to do that as well as draw up a Petition.

The next day they edited the Petition carefully and, unlike the earlier Apology, entered it into the record in full. The key passages of their argument read:

[We] have received first by Message, and since by Speech, from your Majesty, a Commandment of Restraint from Debating, in Parliament, your Majesty's Right of Imposing upon your Subjects Goods exported or imported, out of, or into, this Realm; yet allowing us to examine the Grievance of those Impositions, in regard of Quantity, Time, and other Circumstances of Disproportion ... we hold it an ancient, general, and undoubted Right of Parliament, to debate freely, all Matters which do properly concern the Subject, and his Right or State... we have no Mind to impugn, but a Desire to inform ourselves of, your

358

Highness' Prerogative in that Point, which, if
ever, is now most necessary to be known....

They then strongly requested that he withdraw his
objection to their debating the issue. This Petition was sent directly to the King, and he granted
access of a small Committee to meet with him the
next morning. As they reported back on the 25th,
the King withdrew his objection to their inquiry,
hoping that "Mistaking may not breed." For the
moment any further clash was avoided, but they decided that from then on Impositions and Support
would be discussed together.[69]

On 31 May the time came for one of the stated
reasons for the calling of the Parliament.

This Day the Lord Mayor, with the Citizens of
London, in the Liveries of their several Companies, went to Putney, in the Way to Richmond,
and waited upon Prince Henry, coming down to
Whytenhall; the Duke of Brunswick, Earl of
Shrewsbury, Earl of Penbroke, Earl of Marre, in
the Barge with him.
At Nine a Clock in the Morning they went. The
Drums and Fifes were so loud, and the Company
so small, as Mr. Speaker thought not fit, after Nine a Clock, to proceed in any Business;
but to arise, and depart.[70]

And on the 4th of June, which was the day of the
Prince's Creation, all of the members went together
to the House of Lords for the ceremony.[71] The
admiration for the young Prince seems to have been
genuine, and he was considered one of the great
patrons of the arts in this period, as well as the
great hope of the strong anti-Catholic party. The
irony is that just over two years later, in November 1612, he died before he could show whether or
not he would live up to the expectations.

From the beginning of the session, the King,
had been trying to get some action on the question of Supply, which had been the real reason

359

for the calling of Parliament. But after the message in early March in which they had told the King that they would certainly do something about a Subsidy, the House had avoided the subject as much as possible, building up their case on Grievances and Imposition. At a meeting on 5 March the Lords had reported that the King had many times been pleased with Parliament, but also many times been displeased, "with Passion." If they denied him any Supply, "which rested in theire owne power and freewill to give him," he would not be angry. No matter what Man wanted favour with the monarch, still he could "be sure of Justice." They pointed out how fortunate all were to "have a Man in our King," that the country was in a _via lactea_ (the equivalent, no doubt, of a land flowing with milk and honey), and no one was in danger of losing anything.[72] The King himself talked with them on the morning of the 21st, at the same time that he submitted three of his own Bills. And on the 24th the whole House went to a sermon at Westminster Abbey, preached by the Chaplain of Lord Stanhope, Mr. Grant, who used as his text, "Render unto Caesar the things that are Caesar's."[73] But even the news of the assassination of the French King which they received on 8 May did not spur them to any quicker action in the support of their own.[74] On 25 May after they had decided that Impositions and Support would go together, the King tried once again to get them moving and called for a meeting with their representatives on the 28th. Finally, on 11 June, a Committee from the House joined with the Lords to discuss messages from the King and hear once again a request for money. Hoskyns was one of the small group that was asked to make the report on that conference.[75]

The report, made on the 13th, brought on considerable debate. The Lord Treasurer had used the death of the French king as reason for the need for a vote on Supply and for immediate action. The King had promised that there would be no new Impositions until Parliament met again. What the King desired now was "A Suspension of the rest of the Business of the Parliament" until a Bill of

360

Support and a report on Grievances were drawn up.
Salisbury emphasized that Parliament had to get his
Majesty out of debt; the country was in a miserable
condition. Sir George More tried to work both sides
of the controversy by suggesting that they vote a
Subsidy or two but keep it until the Grievances
were ready. Mr. Tay urged that "having sate so
long, if wee should now retorne into our contry
with nothing for the good of the comon wealth, they
would say that we [have bene] all this while like
children in ketching butterflies," and Hoskyns was
among those that agreed with him. John also added
that "If we shall now press One, and not stay a
Time for more, [it were] little Service to the
King." It is not likely that James would have a-
greed. It was pointed out on the other side that
the country could not last until October. But in
the end the debate reached no conclusion or suggestions for action.[76] The next day the King tried
again and sent a message by the Lord Chancellor
that he promised "to answer all and every of the
Grievances before we depart." He said, rather log-
ically, that he could not give a figure in the matter of Support until he had seen a copy of the
Grievances to be met by composition. Meanwhile,
"His Majesty, not forgetting his Honour, referreth
it, whether it shall not be fit, first to express
our Love in the Supply." The House flatly refused,
and Martin proclaimed, "This is the fairest Day
that ever he saw in Parliament." Sandys suggested
a more tactful approach and moved a message to his
Majesty that the House would put all other business
aside "and endeavour, within a short Time, to give
his Majesty Satisfaction."[77]

First they spent until the 21st gathering records from the Tower, translating them, and reading
them before the Grand Committee. On the 21st,
eighty-six documents were read. On the 22nd Sandys
reported in the Preamble to the Grievances and the
first four of those Grievances, and on the 23rd
the full-scale debate on Impositions got off to a
very slow start. Fuller spoke first, followed by
"A great silence." At some time during the long
debate that followed, probably on the 25th or 26th,

361

Hoskyns gave a major speech, summing up various
precedents and attempting to make a fair evalua-
tion of those precedents. His main point remains
that the King of England is not an absolute monarch: "unlimited power is contrary to reason."
Earlier in the debate Sir Francis Bacon had argued,
"An universal negative position. It appeareth not
by any record that any imposition sett by the King's
absolute power was ever adjudged to be voyd." Hoskyns retorts that no authority can be validated by
a negative argument: "No judge ever gave judgment
in the like case." The speech, which was clearly
considered an important one by the recorder, is
worth quoting in full, even in its fragmentary
state from the recorder's pen. Some of the points
are clarified by a second copy, found in the State
Papers:

> Expectation a great adversary; and I will free
> myself of it as soone as I can.
>   He will remove the impediments and arguments.
>   Argument 1. Custome is the King's inherit-
> ance. The King may improve his inheritance,
> [ergo he may improue his Custome.]
>   He denies the _major_ _in_ _genere_; and in particu-
> lar deny.
>   Also he denies the _minor_ [vpon this reason,
> if he may improue his inheritance, he may im-
> proue Escuage wch cannot be.]   3 E. I, escuage
> 19 H. 6, 9 H. 4. Quinzime called the King's
> inheritance, and yet cannot be improved.
>   Divers inheritances not improvable. If a
> tenant be putt in a ...? for the repayring of a
> comon way. It must be affayred by the homage,
> and yet it is an inheritance.
>   [What a common body an incorporacion may doe,
> the K. may doe. but they may impose therefore
> the K. may. answ. They can do no more then Law
> allowes.]
>   Case of Chamberlayne of London. Charters of
> London to make by-lawes confirmed by act of Par-
> liament, and so is not the King's power to im-
> pose.
>   Jeffrey's case proves an imposition may be
> made where the Comon lawe gives authority.

11 H. 4, et 18 H 8. Generall and comon customes are but the Comon lawe of England. So,
if it be proved that by the Comon lawe the King
may impose, then that argument is of weight:
aliter non.
Bacon's ob. In answere of ye vniuersall neg-
atiue, wherein it was obserued by the Sollicitor, that no Judgment hath euer past against
the K. in this case, therefore he may do it.
Ab authoritate non valet argumentum negative.
No judge ever gave judgment in the like case.
The cases of cards &c. was betweene subject and
subject.
   2. Charta mercatorum grants iii d. per libr.
[imposed by ye merchant,] but the merchants being
no corporation cannot grant. [The marchant hath
no autoritie but by the King.] and there the
strength of that comes from the King's power.
1 Mar. Dy. 100. 12 H. 7, fol. 28. [therefore
the K. may impose.]
   Temp. Joh. Regis. The grant of the Townsmen
of Newcastle of i d. per chaldron: good.
   3. The King's answer has that he would take
away all impositions unreasonable; igitur he
would not reasonable.
Stat. 27 H. 8. nules unreasonable customes.
Also reasonable is certayne. Rationabilem dotem.
   4. The King accepts not that as a guift which
is due unto hym by prerogative.
   5. 25 E. 1. Ayd a general word. The Kinge not
bound by generall words. [Which (?) generall
words are confirmed by course of statutes.]
   6. 14 E. 3, et 15 E. 3. After Michaelmas next.
Ayde there named.
   7. The King may inhibite, igitur he may impose. 8 H. 6, 19; 33 H. 6, 14; 11 H. 4, 2; 12 H.
4. The Kinge may restrayne me from suing in one
Courte; therefore he may take money to release
me... So the Lord Chancellor may injoyne me
from suing; therefore he may take money to sett
me at liberty.
   8. Judges may judge the excesse, if the imposition be unreasonable.
Neither the Judge nor the Jury can judge what
gaynes is reasonable for a merchant his aventure.

363

If it be excessive then voyd, say they. But it is voyd for want of power or knowledge. I should be loth to say the King's power is above his knowledge, or that he should borrowe knowledge of his subjects when he hath power of his owne.

His opinion, custom a tolle.

No good tolle, if the subject receave no benefit by it. 22 Ass. p. 63. Toll traverse justifiable. [To be, potestas emendi et vendendi in terra aliena, this is liberty.

maltolt is restrayne of this libertie.]

The regal power from God, but the actuating thearof is from the people.

To have this power illimitated is contrary to reason, 11 H. 7.

5 H. 7, prescription to distrayne and to keepe till the owner redeeme theyme at the lord's will is void.

So an unlimited power is contrary to reason.

2 H. 3, fo. 42. The King cannot discharge of security of peace,--from a nusance. 6 E. 3, fo. 220, grant taste of wynes, but cannot of beefe and mutton. So the Kinge cannot doe any thinge against the comon peace or common proffit.

Customes due to the King by Comon law. Magna Charta: <u>antiquas</u> et <u>rectas</u> <u>consuetudines</u>. It was a statute in <u>temp</u>. John. Math. Paris, 247.

<u>Temp</u>. R. 1. Customes of Bristow mencioned, fo. 158, <u>temp</u>. <u>Lucii</u>. He built in Dover Castle a churche, and indowed it by the tolle or custome of the Haven. Toll in Edw. Conf. because.... is an exemption of toll.

If toll be due whense comes the lymitation? Thoe he have custom <u>de jure</u>, yet the lymitation is <u>de pacto</u> by Parliament. 25 E. 1, <u>et</u> 14 <u>et</u> 15 E. 3, <u>ut supra</u>, &c.

3 E. 1, aydes lymited; for conscience then grew past lymitts, &c. And 25 E. 3, the safest way for the Kinge and the subjects.

President of questioning judgments in Parliament, a° 2 H. 4, num. 109. Judgment in <u>Scacc</u>. 16 <u>et</u> 17 R. 2, yet they pray in Parliament that it may be sett downe in Parliament what prisage they shall pay.

364

[Greater peace, greater securitie, when the K.
is limited by Parlament and the rates allowed,
Conclusion., That notwithstanding the Judgmt of
ye Exchequer, we should desire we might enjoy
our auncient Liberties, and that Custome should
be rated and allowed by Parlament] 78

On 18 June the House had asked the Lords to
tell them what the "lowest Price, for those Things
for which we are to compound" was. On the 27th,
Sandys reported the King's price-tag for a monetary
Support in place of the feudal rights, although as
he "would not sell us Justice, so he would not buy
our Love." For general Support, he wanted £140,000;
then he wanted £40,000 to give up Wardships and
£40,000 for giving up Purveyance, for a grant total
of £220,000 beyond the Subsidy. Moreover, he was-
n't really sure about the Purveyance. He questioned "Whether the King must not needs purvey."
According to the figures of the Lords, a tax of
four shillings in the pound would bring a £200,000,
which was the usual Subsidy figure. That led to a
few days in which little was done except to debate
the matter of Impositions. And on 3 July a Committee was set up to frame the Petition on that subject. After two readings, it was voted, and the
Committees went back to work on the Grievances.

Meanwhile there were frequent meetings with
the Lords on individual Grievances, and Hoskyns was
a member of all but two of these joint Committees.
Everyone knew that the King was about to bring the
session to an end, and the death of a Mr. Glasior
from the plague on 7 July made everyone ready for
imminent departure. That very afternoon the Grievances were delivered to the King by a Committee,
and on Monday morning the 9th, James announced that
he wished to speak to the whole House the next day.
The House went right ahead on its study of Impositions, and on the 10th assigned Hoskyns and a few
others to "digest the Dispute on both sides." On
the 11th Egerton urged "That all Counsels in the
Name of God ought to begin... The Plague increasing,--the Time threateneth.--Little done in Six
Months; nothing but Matter of Grievances--etc."

That finally brought them to the point, and the
debate began on the Subsidy. Sandys tried to keep
it to just one Subsidy and no Fifteenth because it
was not a time of war, but by a bare majority the
House voted a Fifteenth. They refused to vote two
Fifteenths, however. It was hardly the figure that
the King had hoped for. The very next day the King
announced that Parliament would adjourn on the
20th, and the Commons slowed down. The gesture
was too obvious. The following day the Grand Committee reported a mere two shilling in the pound
tax on Support, and the House agreed, "upon a per-
emptory Resolution" on a total of Support of only
£180,000, "no Penny to be offered more." Hoskyns
led off the following debate with what seems to be
even greater restraint: he urged the House "To confer with the Country. Without Reference to the
Country:--without Reference to the major Part, that
are absent" they would be making a mistake. "We
are declaimed against in both Universities; in Pul-
pits.--The Groans of the People [are even] a greater Accusation." But they decided to give the
£180,000 "for Tenures, &c. the Incidents, and all
other Matters of Ease propounded" (which is the
common term for removal of Greivances).

On the 14th he was put on another joint Committee with the Lords, this one on Purveyance and
Impositions, and joined in the debate on who should
pay the Subsidy. The two Universities had, as usual, been excepted, but there had been reports that
"scandalous Words [were] uttered by some of them."
Martin and Hoskyns had received a letter of a questionable nature from a Mr. Fotherby from Cambridge,
but as neither of them knew the man, they suggested
that the Attorney-General write to him for satisfaction.[79] Two days later the House let the matter
drop. At the same time, on the 16th, they passed
the Subsidy Bill, and on the 17th they did the same
with the Petition on Impositions. That same morning Hoskyns went up to the Lords with the rest of
the Impositions Committee to receive the message
from the King. James yielded some points but denied others. Then he ended: "If this Offer succeeded not, then this would be an End of this Par-

liament." Part of the offer was that he required
a Support figure of £200,000, and the House grudg-
ingly granted it after Egerton called it "A divine,
a sacred Offer: Let not our Posterities curse us
that we have refused."

On 19 July, in preparation for a meeting with
the Lords, a Committee which included Hoskyns,
Martin, Neville, Oxenbridge, Berkeley, George More
and several of the Privy Council met in the Court
of Wards to consider the Heads of the Conference.
Later More reported back to the House that the
Lords agreed "to join with us as parties, not fur-
therers only" and that the plan was to offer an
additional £200,000 and hope that the King would
"admit the other projects."80

Then the Proctor affair kept everyone busy for
a few days. There was more desultory conversation
about what had been said at Cambridge, discussion
of the collection of the usual gift for the Poor,
the passing of a Subsidy Bill for the Clergy at
six shillings in the pound, and more talk of how
to guarantee payment of the Support. Hoskyns took
part in that debate, but what he said is not recorded. What the Commons was really looking for
was a direct statement on what Grievances would be
removed so that they could publish them at the same
time that the Subsidy was announced. But at the
final meeting of the Parliament with the King, on
the afternoon of the 23rd of July, all that James
would do was to say that he would consider each
point carefully. If the Commons had made him back
up several times during the session, now he had the
last word, which was that although Parliament had
the right to submit Grievances to him, it would
have to leave the way he treated them up to his own
royal judgement. Then the Lord Chancellor pro-
rougued the Parliament until the 16th of October.

* * * * * * * * * *

There is no doubt that the members of Parliament were ready to leave. Tempers were on edge,
those who had taken an active role were worn out by
meetings that had lasted from six or seven in the

367

morning until into the early evening nearly every
day for six months, and the plague was in the city.
John's associates in Parliament scattered quickly.
For example, Sir Robert Drury was at the Spa and in
Paris by August. Sir Edward Herbert joined the
Lord Chandos at the siege of Juliers, where John
Donne sent him a verse letter that month. Meanwhile the threatened plague did not occur, and London was filled with news of the English and Scots
troops under Sir Edward Cecil who were helping out
the Protestant forces in Germany in the preliminary struggles leading to the Thirty Years War.[81]

John, of course, headed for Hereford as quickly as possible to look after his lands and his family, whom he had not seen for over half a year.
For one thing, his colleague in Parliament, Anthony
Pembridge, had died. This provided a way for Hoskyns to increase his own holdings in the city of
Hereford. Pembridge had leased his house from Sir
Herbert Croft. John obtained the lease of that
house from Croft for his immediate neighbor, John
Clarke. This then freed the Clarke house for Hoskyns' use. On 4 September 1610, it was moved in
the local justice's court

> that the day & yeare abovesaid we Tho: Clarke &
> John Clarke of the citie of heref gents. in con-
> sideration that John Hoskins of the said Citie
> procureth to the said John Clarke a graunt or
> demise of the house wherin Anthonie Pembrug esqr
> deceased lately dwelt from Sr Herbert Croft for
> yeares to comme & in consideration the said John
> Hoskins shall pay such summes of money to the sd
> John Clarke as hereafter... meantime the sd John
> Clarke & Thomas Clarke doe agree & contract to
> assure to the sd John Hoskins such estate as we
> or eyth^r of vs ... hath in the house next ad-
> ioyninge to the house of the sd John Hoskins in
> heref... wherin the sd John Clarke now dwelleth
> the sd John Hoskins payinge,... somuch money as
> shalbe appoynted by John Warde and Thomas Manne
> gent and at such days as they shall sett....[82]

Herbert Croft and Edward Price were the witnesses.

The amount set for the house was the relatively
large sum of thirty pounds. There was some trouble
with the transfer, as correspondence the next year
was to show, but Hoskyns had now completed his
property dealings within the city. From now on he
was to concentrate on his country estates.

On Tuesday, 16 October, he was back in London,
living in his rooms at the Middle Temple and once
more deeply involved in the activities of Parliament. In this session his fellow M.P. from Hereford was John Warden, the Mayor of the city in
1604; Warden, however, apparently did not take up
his duties until 6 November. The final session of
the first Parliament of James was doomed to failure
before it ever started. The King had been disappointed in the amount of money that Commons was
willing to give in the way of Composition for his
feudal rights, the Lords were caught between the
monarch and the lower House and felt that the Commons were not being entirely open with them (which
was certainly true), and the Commons had received
no real satisfaction on the matter of Grievances
and Impositions. All they had managed to obtain
was the King's agreement to consider their Petitions. No one was willing to give in on what he
considered essential points. The official Journals
contain no information on the fifth session, and
the Debates edited by Samuel Gardiner do not cover
many of the events that took place. For example,
on 23 October the Lords asked for a joint Conference on the Great Contract on the 25th, but no account of that Conference exists.83

On the 31st the King called Parliament to
meet with him at Whitehall,

...at what tyme he made a speech unto us, blam-
ing us for our slacknes and many delayes in the
greate matter of contract; by meanes whearof
his debts did dayly swell, and his wants increase upon hym. And therefore he requyred us
upon our next meeting to reviewe the memoriall
agreed upon the end of the last session... and
to send hym a resolute and speedy answer whither

wee would proceed with the contract: yea, or
noe... because then he might resolve upon some
other course to be taken for supplie of his
wants; for, he sayd, he was resolved to cutt
his coate according to his cloathe, which he
could not doe till he knewe what cloath he
should have to make it of.84

On 5 November he sent another message, saying that
he expected to receive £500,000, although it would
not meet his needs, and he ended up indicating that
he expected £200,000 de claro. On the following
day, during the debate in the House, it was made
clear that he wanted the money from a tax on the
land only, which most of the House felt was not
possible. There was the usual suggestion that they
work out the problem with the Lords, but this Hoskyns felt was not the right way. He argued, "Not
fitt to conferre with the Lords, for the mene matter of supplie ought to proceed from us. No danger to proceede to the question, for it may please
His Majesty to recommend it unto us agayne in the
same state as it was." The House, by a unanimous
voice vote, followed his suggestion.85

The debate on Supply went on, but it was not
the only subject of interest during this last session. It is clear from many sources that the members of Parliament were increasingly interested in
the matter of Impositions because of their own interest in business trade. Many of them were looking into the various trading companies that were
trying to extend the commerce of England. That the
Hoskyns family was involved in such interests is
not at all strange with the eldest brother, Oswald,
a successful merchant tailor. A list found in the
Minutes of the Court of Assistants of Merchant
Taylors' Company for 29 April 1609 showing the
"particular brothers of the Company" who "have adventured with the Virginia Company in the name of
themselves and theire friendes or children" contains the name of Charles Hoskyns,86 and another
list of the same time, of the "Batchelers Company,"
includes Oswald Hoskyns and John Donne. This was
a somewhat different kind of group, for they "have

370

agreed that the gayne thereof (if any be) shall from tyme to tyme be given and bestowed upon the poore of the said Batcheler's Company."87 In November 1610 a list was circulated among the members of Parliament for the Virginia Company. It contained "The names of such as have signed with the somes of money by them adventured on 3 yeares towardes the supply of the Plantation begonne in Virginia," and it seems as though everyone in the Commons is included. Among them is "John Hoskyns £37 10 0."88 Although the sum is a large one, it is the typical amount. The official list is dated 20 February 1611, but we know that it was made up while Parliament was in session. And Hoskyns' name, along with the rest, duly showed up on the Third Charter of the Virginia Company as a contributor.89 So although John did not show the usual interest of his contemporaries in travel, he did share their interest in trade to the new colonies.

Meanwhile the struggle over financing the kingdom went on, with a big fight on Supply on 13 November, and a meeting with the King on the 16th, in which "they fell to treate of the four greavincis, Prohibitions, Proclamations, Wales four shyres, Impositions. In the three first they receyved good satisfaction, but for impositions, none...."90 On the 21st the King sent another message, this one indicating the final limits of his action:

First, concerning impositions, his finall answer is that he wilbe contented to passe an act to restrayne hym hearafter from imposing upon merchandises, his heyres and successors; but not to take away those that be. Otherwise then by leaving theyme to our consideration to transpose as we think fitt, if any be unduly rated, or in lieu of theyme to rayse any other benefite of equall benefite.
2. Prohibitions and proclamations and 4 shyres. 4 shyre, never had any intention to deny justice. He suspends his consideracion till the end of Midsomer terme next. From which tyme forward he will leave theyme to the course of lawe and justice.

371

The speakers that followed the reading of that message, including Hoskyns' young friend Sir Robert Harley, were not satisfied. Moreover, the House was understandably incensed at the King and Salisbury's action in calling certain members of Parliament to them and asking them to act as private men rather than Parliament men.91 It is not at all surprising to find the remark on 23 November, "divers free speackers why rebus sixtantibus [sic] we should not give as Lukenors, Fullers, Wentworth, and Hoskinges the i [sic] sent for by the Lord Tresorer."92 Salisbury had obviously picked the leaders of the opposition. It was also on the 23rd that Hoskyns brought together, with colloquial Latin, apt classical allusion, and pejorative metaphor, many of the complaints of the opposition: how to change things for the better with a king that was throwing money away on his Scottish favorites.

The question whither wee will give, rebus sic stantibus, is like to be with childe with another. Quomodo possunt res mutari in melius.?
Henry the 7th and Tiberius bothe rich, but not taking all from the people. Tacitus.
Cato had a double revenue: frugality is one. Well governing of revenue hathe bene a meanes used by princes to supplie his revenue.
The falt of those that so presse upon the Prince as to hold his Parliament to sitt 7 yeares together to fynde meanes how to supplie the King.
1. Theise not English. They were wont to spend theyre owne revenue in the King's service.
2. Not Irish; they will be costermongers rather then want.
Not Dutch; for they are ingenious and industrious.
They be such as hold a consultacion how to draw out of this cesterne as fast as wee fill it.93

The King's reaction was what one might expect: "the more he was desirous to give theyme contentment, he did perceave the lesse it was regarded, and that new greevances and complaints were raysed to his dishonor." So, on the 24th, he adjourned the House till the next Thursday, then till 9 February 1611, and finally, on that date, he dissolved the Parliament. And to show his contempt for the criticisms leveled by Hoskyns and the others, "He now scattered £34,000 among his favourites, mostly fellow countrymen, and created Robert Carr Viscount Rochester, thereby for the first time enabling a Scot to sit in the house of lords."[94] That gesture was to cost him dearly at the next Parliament that he was to call. And Hoskyns' stand against the Scots was also to cost him dearly at the same time.

1. P. 41.
2. Mitchell lists Hoskyns as fifth ranking speaker of the final sessions with 22 speeches. I cannot account for his low number even though he appears to use only the Journals as his basis.
3. "For the Confirmation of the Sale and Conveyance of divers Manors, late Henry Jernegan's, Esquire, to Sir Jo. Heveningham Knight, and Dame Bridgett his Wife" (C.J. I, 397-8, 405, 408-9. Passed.); "To enable Humphrey Mildmay Esquire, and the Heirs Males of his Body, to make Jointures to their Wives, of certain entailed lands" (397, 408-10, 413-17, 419, 425, 432. No final action.); for "Sir Henry Crispe" (409. Disappears.); for "Sir John Wentworth" (413, 418. Passed.); for "Mr. Davison" (415, 442, 445, 448. Hoskyns contra the Bill. No final action.); for "Sir Rob. Drury" (415, 423, 434, 436, 441. Passed.); for "Jenison" (416, 428, 438, 441. Rejected.); for the naturalizing of "Sir Geo. Keere" (Hoskyns is first on the Committee list which was assigned on 24 April. Although there is no record of action, these specific Bills of naturalization for Scottish favorites of the King usually passed quickly; C.J. I, 42. The Bill for the naturalization of Sir Robert Carr had taken just two days to reach ingrossing earlier in the month.); Mr. Rous (432, 438, 444-46. Passed.); and Hubberd (447).
4. A "Bill touching Leistoft and Yarmouth" (410, 412, 420, 427, 442-3, 445. Disappears.); "Disuniting of the Parsonages of Ashe and Deane" (445-6, 448, 450. Passed.); "Supply of Timber in Devon, for Shipping" (443. Disappears.); "Preservation of Woods" (413, 417-8, 422-3, 427, 430, 437, 444.); "Preservation of Game" (413-4, 417-8. No final action.); "Fens" in the Isle of Ely (414, 417. 419-20, 423. No final action.); "Moor-burning" (415, 419, 423. Disappears.); "Hawking, Pheasants, and Partridges." (416, 418, 427, 432-3, 436. No final action.)
5. "The Consideration of Clothing" (398. The Bill disappears.); "For the Securing and Confirming

of certain Lands and Tenements, &c. to the Companies of Salters and Brewers of <u>London</u>" (397-8, 403-4, 413, 415, 417-9, 421. Passed.); "Abuses of Silk Dyers" (416, 424, 443, 450. No final action.); "Deceits in Dying" (416, 434. Rejected.); "Traders of Butter and Cheese." (419, 423, 428, 433. Passed.)

6. On Marshalsea (416, 423. 432. No final action.); "Keepers of Prisons" (426, 430, 432, 436, 443. No final action.); "Rogues, Houses of Correction" (429. Disappears.); "Copyholders" (417, 421-2. Passed.); "Warrants of Attorney" (416, 419, 423. Disappears.); "Delays of Executions." (432, 444. Disappears.)

7. "For Reformation of Disorders and Abuses amongst Commoners, concerning their Commons" (also called "Better Attendance of the Commons," 396, 423, 443. Passed.); "Confirmation to the Contractors, &c." (445-6, 449. No final action.); "Oath of Allegiance" (The Committee met on the last day of the session (23 July) to consider amendments sent down from the Lords. It was reported out by Fuller and passed immediately.); "Residence of Provosts, &c." (418. Disappears.)

8. "Lands entailed, liable to Debts," (398, 423); the "Great Charter" (404); "Ambassadors Children" (422-3, 428, 440, 445, 448); "Sutton" (444, 445); "Shipping and Mariners" (426, 432, 444).

9. <u>C.J.</u> I, 432, 433. Hoskyns joined in debate on 3 April as to whether a Bill on the Prerogative Court should be sent to Committee, but the record does not show which side he was on (probably in favor, along with Fuller). The Bill was rejected. <u>C.J.</u> I, 418.

10. <u>C.J.</u> I, 429.

11. <u>S</u>tow, p. 995.

12. For example, 16, 18, 24, 26 May, 7 June; <u>C.J.</u> I 429, 432, 435.

13. G. E. Bentley, <u>Shakespeare</u>, <u>A</u> <u>Biographical</u> Handbook (1961), p. 49. Shakespeare paid his subscription to the expenses of prosecuting the Bill in September 1611. Apparently Bentley thought that Parliament was still in session at that time.

14. Anthony Pembridge, the other M.P. from Hereford,

was not only lax in his duties; he was also not terribly well. He died before the next session of Parliament convened.

15. Arthur Lake was another Wykehamist who had been made Dean of Worcester in 1608 and in 1616 would become Bishop of Bath and Wells as well as Vice-Chancellor of Oxford. Dr. John was obviously seeking preferment from this rising cleric.

16. Probably the father of Mary Morgan of Howton, who married John's brother Phillip in 1634.

17. James Walwyn was the Hereford lawyer who joined with Hoskyns in being bound with two new students at the Middle Temple.

18. The Gwillims were a Langarren family that intermarried with John's cousins.

19. Bishop Benet, young Benedict's godfather. Dr. Bradshaw was a close friend of the family mentioned again in a letter to Ben dated 6 Nov. 1611.

20. Sizergh MSS.

21. The Bill is mentioned in C.J. I, 394, 396, 398, 403, 404, 405, 406, 407, 409, 424, 426.

22. In Journals of in Committee in the Exchequer Chamber, on 23 Feb., 1, 12, 28 March, 28 Apr.; C.J. I, 398, 399, 403, 409, 416, 422.

23. The Bill was assigned on 23 Feb. to a Committee to meet 1 March in the Star Chamber, reported out on 9 March, passed and sent up on 13 March; C.J. I, 399, 408, 409.

24. In Journals or in Committee in the Exchequer Chamber, on 1, 2, 17, 18 Apr., 7, 12, 18, 19, 21, 24 May; C.J. I, 417-19, 425, 429-30, 432.

25. In Journals or in Committee on 18, 21, 25, 26, 30 June, 3, 10, 14 July; C.J. I, 440, 443, 444, 447, 450.

26. This Bill on Wool combers and spinners was reported in by Hoskyns and ingrossed on 24 May; C.J. I, 432. It probably passed.

27. It is possible that the entry on 6 June means that John introduced this Bill rather than that he simply reported it. C.J. I, 435.

28. In Journals or in Committee in Chequer Chamber on 27 June, 2, 10, 12, 13 July; C.J. I, 444,

447, 449.
29. C.J. I, 435. Sir Edward Sandys had earlier
    moved for a search of the Parliament records
    with Sir Robert Cotton assisting (30 Apr.; C.J.
    I, 422), and the next day Sir Edward Hoby re-
    ported in the Statute that they had found
    which gave Parliament the right of access to
    all records (p. 423).
30. References to attendance problems are found in
    C.J. I, 398, 403, 405, 409, 416, 428, 443, 447,
    448.
31. 19 Feb. 1610; C.J. I, 396.
32. 15, 22 Feb., 3, 8, 9, 22, 29, 31 March, 21, 27
    Apr., 8, 10, 14, 24, 25, 30 May, 12, 29 June,
    10 July; C.J. I, 393, 398, 404, 408, 413, 416,
    417, 420, 422, 426, 428, 432, 434, 437, 444,
    448.
33. References to the attendance of lawyers are
    made 1, 14, 17 March, 24 Apr., 14, 18 May, 15,
    18, 19, 22, 27, 28 June; C.J. I, 403, 410, 412,
    420, 429, 440-42, 444.
34. C.J. I, 411, 414, 434. Also 29 June, 20 July;
    C.J. I, 444, 453.
35. The Committee was given the charge to draw up a
    Bill on the subject on 3 March; C.J. I, 405.
36. C.J., 403, 404.
37. C.J. I, 412. Other references to the case are
    C.J. I, 406, 416.
38. C.J. I, 417.
39. C.J. I, 407, 408, 409. 410.
40. C.J. I, 425.
41. C.J. I, 425.
42. C.J. I, 427. The Speaker had several hard days
    before the end of the session. Just before the
    end, on 18 July, Sir Edward Herbert, the famous
    poet and founder of Deism, said he meant no of-
    fence to the House by an earlier action. Ap-
    parently, according to the Speaker, Herbert had
    kept his hat on, "put out his Tongue, and plopt
    with his Mouth." Everyone tried to get the
    Speaker to let it drop, and that only made him
    madder. Finally Sir Edwyn Sandys said some-
    thing that calmed them all down, but what it
    was is not recorded. C.J. I, 452.

43. C.J. I, 415. He reported out the Committee order on 30 March; C.J. I, 417.
44. C.J. I, 442.
45. C.J. I, 452.
46. Referer.. es to Proctor are on 8, 15, 27 March, 25 Apr., 1, 2, 5, 7, 9, 10, 12, 14, 15 May, 6, 15, 20, 22, 23, 25, 26 June, 3, 5, 19, 21, 23 July; C.J. I, 407, 412, 415, 421, 423-27, 435, 440, 442, 443, 445, 452-54.
47. C.J. I. 399.
48. Hoskyns made specific reference to Cap. 37. Magna Carta, which reads, "If any one holds of us by fee-farm or by socage or by burgage, and of another he holds land by knight service, we will not have the guardianship of the heir or of his land which is of the fee of another, on account of that fee-farm, or socage, or burgage, nor will we have the custody of that fee-farm, or socage, or burgage, unless that fee-farm itself owes knight service. We will not have the guardianship of the heir or of the land of any one, which he holds of another by knight service on account of any petty serjeanty which he holds of us by the service of paying to us knives or arrows or the like." It made clear that the King did not have the preroga-tive of seizing lucrative wardships. This translation is from William F. Swindler, Magna Carta (1965), pp. 314-15.
49. The volume was "Printed by Iohn Legate. Anno 1607." and dedicated to the Archbishop of Can-terbury on November 3, 1607.
50. C.J. I, 399-400.
51. The Cowell case is mentioned in the Journals or was discussed in Committee 23, 24, 26, 27 Feb., 2, 3, 5, 7, 8, 10, 26, 27, 30 March; C.J. I, 399-401, 404-5, 407, 414-16.
52. Samuel R. Gardiner, Parliamentary Debates in 1610 (Camden Soc. No. 81, O.S.; 1862), pp. 19, 22-23.
53. C.J. I, 392.
54. Gardiner, p. 2; C.J. I, 393; Add. Mss. 48053, f. 2v.
55. For a brief and clear treatment of the whole problem of Impositions stemming from the case

of John Bate, see Davies, The Early Stuarts,
pp. 9-12.
56. C.J. I, 393-94. All of the Grievances, Petitions, Compositions, and Major Acts of the 1610
Parliament are contained in A Record of Some
Worthie Proceedings: in The Honorable Wise, and
Faithfvll Hovse of Commons in the Parliament
holden in the yeare, 1611 (London, 1641).
57. The report and discussion are on C.J. I, 394-96.
58. Gardiner, pp. 9-10.
59. Gardiner, p. 11.
60. Davies, p. 11.
61. C.J. I, 398, 401-3.
62. 2, 8, 12, 26 March, 20, 26 Apr., 4 May, 11, 26
June, 5, 6, 13, 14, 23 July; C.J. I, 404, 409,
414, 418-19, 421, 424-25, 436, 437, 441-42,
444-47, 449-52, 454.
63. C.J. I, 424-25; Add. Mss. 48053, f. 71.
64. C.J. I, 410-11. Further mention of activities
on Tenures and Wards are on 15, 17, 23, 30
March, 2, 19, 21, 23 Apr., 3-5 May, 27 June,
9, 12, 13 July; C.J. I, 412, 414, 417-20, 424-
25, 444, 447-49.
65. C.J. I, 451-52. Other references to the Four
Shires are on 27 Apr., 5 May; C.J. I, 422, 425.
66. 12 March 1610; C.J. I, 409. Other references
to the Committee for Grievances not already
mentioned are 19, 23, 28 March, 18, 21, 23-26,
28, 30 Apr., 7 May, 9, 22, 25, 26 June, 5, 7,
10, 14, 17 July; C.J. I, 413-14, 416, 419-21,
425, 443, 446-47, 450-1.
67. Hoskyns was on a Committee named 5 July to join
in a joint conference with the Lords on the
next day concerning the Bill of Canons. C.J.
I, 446.
68. Directions, f. 17v.
69. C.J. I, 429-32.
70. C.J. I, 434.
71. C.J. I, 435. A full description of the ceremony is in Gardiner, pp. 48-9.
72. Reported 10 March; C.J. I, 409; Gardiner, p. 24.
73. C.J. I, 413-14.
74. C.J. I, 426.
75. C.J. I, 436; Add. Mss. 48053. f. 77.
76. C.J. I, 437-38; Gardiner, p. 55.

77. C.J. I, 438-39.
78. Gardiner, pp. 75-77. Bracketed entries from SPD James I. Addenda 1611-1616, Vol. 40, #60, ff. 139-139v. The debate is incorrectly labeled as May or early June 1614. Osborn, who quoted parts of the speech (pp. 34-5), followed the incorrect dating.
79. C.J. I, 449.
80. Add. MSS. 48053, ff. 89v-90; C.J. I, 449-52. There is some discrepancy in the two accounts.
81. Stow, pp. 996-97.
82. Hereford Library, 2045 L.C. #10.
83. Gardiner, P. 126.
84. Ibid.
85. Gardiner, pp. 128-30.
86. Alexander Brown, The Genesis of the United States (1890), I, 303.
87. Ibid., pp. 304-5.
88. Ibid., pp. 466-67.
89. Ibid., II, 546.
90. Hist. Mss. Comm., Duke of Rutland, Vol. I (1888), p. 425.
91. Gardiner, pp. 137-38.
92. H.M.C., Rutland, I, 425. Osborn, p. 232, placed this incorrectly on the 13th.
93. Gardiner, pp. 144-45.
94. Davies, p. 15.

Chapter XII

The Company of Wits

For ten years Hoskyns had been engaged in establishing himself as head of a family, building a law practice and reputation in both London and Hereford, and taking part in the many activities of the first Parliament of James. With the dissolution of that Parliament, he had more opportunity to enjoy the various events in the city, help the future plans of his younger brother, and even further the affairs of his alma mater of Oxford. He had as a group of friends in the city both the large number of associates that had kept together since their early days in Winchester and Oxford and a new group of fellow-workers and companions in the Parliament. By at least 1611 these had coalesced into one or two companies that met on a somewhat regular basis and enjoyed the play of wit which they all valued so highly. It is not always possible to keep the groups separate, nor is it ever possible to establish them as essentially the same society; but at the center of whatever groups there were was the figure of John Hoskyns, the acknowledged wittiest of them all. There was something about the almost erudite spoofing of which he was capable that drew together various kinds of people, from the somewhat scatter-brained Thomas Coryat and Dick Martin to the basically serious John Donne, Henry Wotton, and Ben Jonson. Moreover, it appears that Hoskyns and his friend Martin were the force that held together the literary and business communities which made up the Mitre and Mermaid tavern society of wits.

As central as Hoskyns and Martin (perhaps even more so) was the merry-minded Thomas Coryat. Coryat shared the travelling propensities of men like Henry Wotton and the love of public display of Will Kemp--only instead of dancing his way to Norwich, as had Kemp, Coryat hiked by foot to Venice and back, a distance of 1975 miles, in about five months. That feat must have impressed even a man

381

who could do saddle vaults in full armor. By 1611
Coryat not only had put together an account of his
trip, entitled Coryats Crudities, but had managed
to get most of the wits of the city of London to
write introductory poems for the work (which was
dedicated to Prince Henry). He insisted that he
had not solicited any of the poems, but that is
hard to believe, since the tone of many of them indicates that there had been some kind of pressur-
ing. He published these poems first in a separate
volume, The Odcombian Banquet (Odcombe being Coryat's home town in Somerset), early in the year,
and then prefixed them to the longer book as well.
Still together after all these years were Dick Martin, Hugh Holland (with poems in Greek, Italian,
Welsh, Latin, and English), John Gifford, John
Owen, Thomas Bastard, William Baker, and John Davies of Hereford. John Donne was there along with
his close friends Christopher Brooke and Henry
Goodyer. Michael Drayton (a close friend of Goodyer), the great song writer and M.D. Thomas Campion, John Harrington, and Inigo Jones lent their
talents, as did Coryat's friends Lawrence Whitaker
(with poems in Greek, Latin, French, and English)
and Ben Jonson, who wrote the opening poems of the
book. And from Parliament came Sir Henry Neville,
Lewis Lewknor, Henry Poole, Robert Phelips, Dudley
Digges, and Lionel Cranfield. All of them were
caught up in the spirit of good fun that Coryat
seems to have engendered. Even John Donne, coming
out of his years of enforced retreat at his "hospital" at Mitcham, wrote a poem that could be described: "Not since the period of the fourth Satire had Donne given such a brilliant display of
wit and high spirits."[1] Nor had Hoskyns opened up
with such rhetorical flourishes since his fustian
speech in Le Prince d'Amour.

Incipit Johannes Hoskins[2]

Cabalistical verses, which by trans-
position of words, syllables, and letters,
make excellent sense, otherwise none,
In laudem Authoris
Even as the waues of brainelesse butter'd fish,
with bugle horne writ in the Hebrew tong,

382

Fuming vp flounders like a chafing-dish,
That lookes asquint vpon a three-mans song:
Or as your equinoctial pasti-crust[3]
Proiecting out a purple chariot wheele,
Doth squeaze the spheares, and intimate the dust;
The dust which force of argument doth feele:
Euen so this Author, this Gymnosophist,[4]
Whom no delight of trauels toyle dismayes,
Shall sympathize (thinke Reader what you list)
Crown'd with a quinsill tipt with marble prayse.

Encomiologicall Antipasticks[5]con-
sisting of Epitrits, the fourth in the first
syzugie, which the vulgar call Phaleuciac
hendecasyllabes; trimeters Catalecticks, with
Antipastic Asclepiads, trimeters Acatalectics
consisting of two dactylicall comma's of some
learned named choriambicks, both together di-
coli distrophi, rythmicall and hyperrythmicall,
amphibologicall, dedicated vnto the vndeclin-
able memorie of the antarkisticall Coryat, the
only true trauelling Porcupen of England.

Admired Coriat, who like a Porcupen,
Dost shew prodigious things to thy countri-men.
As that beast when he kils doth vse his owne
                                            darts,
So do thy pretty quils make holes in our harts.
That beast liues of other company destitute,
So wentest thou alone euery way absolute.
That beast creepeth a foote, nec absque pennis,
So didst thou trot a iourney hence to Venice.
Liue long foe to thy foe, fierce as a Porcupen.
Liue long friend to thy friend, kind as a Porcu-
                                              pen.
Hencefoorth adde to thy crest an armed Histrix,[6]
Since thy cariage hath resembled his tricks.

Hoskyns then moves into an eight line stanza which
he labels "The same in Latine" but which is actually a very free paraphrase of the previous six
lines. Then he returns to English in rollicking
tetrameters:

No more but so, I heard the crie,

383

And like an old hound in came I
To make it fuller, though I find
My mouth decayes much in this kind.
The cry was this, they cride by millions,
Messengers, Curriers, and Postillions,
Now out alas we are vndone
To heare of Coryats paire of sho'ne;
There is no newes we are more sory at,
Then this strange newes of Rawbone Coryat.[7]
Who like an Vnicorne went to Venice,
And drinking neither Sacke nor Rhenish,
Home in one paire of shoes did trample,
A fearefull and a strange example,
But what's the news of learned people
In Pauls church-yard and neere Pauls steeple?
Hang vp his shoes on top of Powles
Tyed to his name in parchment rowles,
That may be read most legibly
In Tuttle fields and Finsbury.
Fame is but wind, thence wind may blow it
So farre that all the world may know it:
From Mexico, and from Peru
To China and to Cambalu:
If the wind serue, it may haue lucke
To passe by South to the bird Rucke.
Greater then the Stymphalides
That hid the Sunne from Hercules.
And if Fames wings chance not to freeze,
It may passe north ninetie degrees,
Beyond Meta incognita,
Where though there be no hollyday,
Nor Christian people for to tell it,
Horrible Beares and Whales may smell it.
Thence may it on the Northern seas,
On foote walke to the Antipodes,
Whose feet against our feet do pace
To keepe the center in his place.
But when those fellowes that do wonder
As we at them, how we go vnder
From clime to clime and tongue to tongue,
Throughout their Hemispheare along,
Haue tost these words as bals at tennis,
Tom Coryate went on foote from Venice,
This trauelling fame, this walking sound
Must needs come home in comming round,

384

So that we shall cry out vpon him,
His fame in trauell hath outgone him.
When all haue talked, and time hath tri'd him,
Yet Coryate will be semper idem.

Hoskyns finishes with another eight line Latin
stanza comparing Coryat with figures from Greek
myth and history. After all his busy years of public life, John could still play classical allusions
with the best of them and misuse rhetorical terms
as only an expert can. The balances and antitheses
of the Latin finale are as sure as they had been
over a decade before. Moreover, following the introduction to the second stanza is our only extant
example of Hoskyns' musical composition, although
we know he wrote at least two other longer pieces:

> Also there is this tune added to the verses,
> and pricked according to the forme of Musicke
> to be sung by those that are so disposed.

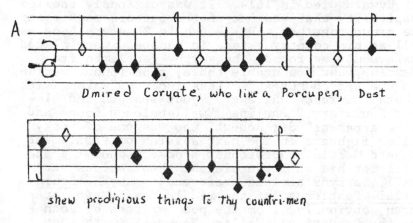

But more important in many ways than the poems
that appeared in these volumes of Tom Coryat is the
set of associations which they reveal. During
these years around 1611, a consistent group of
friends had come together to enjoy one another's
company. We learn about them, not only in their

common task of publicizing Coryat's work, but in a
group of letters written by that indefatigable
traveller in the following years. Before the end
of 1612 Coryat was on his way again, this time as
far as the court of the great Mogul in India. He
never was able to get back to England, but luckily,
before his death, he addressed three letters[8] to
his friends in London which were published in 1616,
the year after they were written, as Thomas Coriate
Traveller for the English wits: Greeting. As he
had not been in contact with his friends since he
left England, the company he describes is certainly
one that gathered together in the years we are discussing. The first letter, "wrote from Asmere on
Michaelmas Day 1615," is addressed to Sir Edward
Phelips, who, in 1611, at the age of 53, had just
finished his rather unhappy task as Speaker of Parliament.[9] In that same year he was appointed Master of the Rolls. Indication of how out of touch
Coryat was by the time he wrote the letters is that
Sir Edward died in 1614. It was obviously Phelips'
hospitality that was one of the factors in keeping
the group together. His house in Chancery Lane as
well as his country estate in Wanstead were places
where could be found "the worthy gentlemen fre-
quenting your Honourable table, that fauour vertue,
and the sacred Muses." These included, along with
others, Lawrence Whitaker, "your learned and elegant Secretary," Phelips' "well-beloued Sonne and
Heire-apparent" Sir Robert, who was one of Hoskyns'
fellow fighters in the next session of Parliament,
Richard Martin, Christopher Brooke ("whom I thanke
still for his no lesse elegant then serious verses"), Hoskyns himself, referred to as "M. Equin-
octiall Pasticrust of the middle Temple" (a phrase
taken, obviously, from the poem written by John
for the Crudities), William Hackwell (with whom
John had served on over 15 committees during the
last session of Parliament), and the wives of both
Sir Edward and Sir Robert. Most of those mentioned
in the letter were members of Parliament, and all
were moderate Parliamentarians with a tendency to
move against the King when the rights of Parliament were called into question. It is interesting
to see them clustered about the Speaker of the Par-

386

liament himself. It would seem that the criticism
levelled against the Speaker as being a tool of
the monarch misread the real situation. But Whitaker, Martin, Brooke, and Hoskyns were also poets.
Hackwell was not only closely associated with Hoskyns in Parliament, but was connected in some not
very clear way with John Donne, in that the two of
them were listed among those possessing a governmental code having to do with many sensitive events
in 1615-1616, including the poisoning of Sir Thomas
Overbury. But there is no evidence of Hackwell's
being much of a poet. This, then, provides one
core group, gathering at Sir Edward's house regularly enough for a letter to be addressed to them
there.

The second letter is addressed to Sir Edward's
secretary, Lawrence Whitaker, who was also Coryat's
assistant in putting together the verses in The Odcombian Banquet. Coryat, after describing his trip
from Jerusalem to Asmere and mentioning, for their
envy, that he only spent £3 between Aleppo and Asmere, ends the letter with greetings to Sir Edward
and Sir Robert, "once my Mecaenas", and their
"right vertuous Ladies," to Richard Martin ("though
at a mans house in woodstreet, he vsed mee one
night verie peruersly before I came away: but you
see that my being at Ierusalem dooth make me forget many iniuries."), Hugh Holland, and Inigo Jones.
Perhaps more important are the postscripts: in one
he asks to be commended to "M. Protoplast and all
the Sireniacall gentlemen to whom I wrote one Letter from Aleppo... and another I intend to write
before my going out of Asia" (he also suggests that
Whitaker read some enclosed verses about Coryat to
his friends, "especially to the Sireniacall gentlemen; for they are elegant and delectable."). In
another postscript he asks to be remembered to "M.
Williams the goldsmith and his wife (who may be his
"uncle Williams") and to Beniamin Iohnson as well
as to a m. Elizabeth Balch, who apparently was a
friend or relative of Mrs. Whitaker.10 Neither
Miss Osborn nor any of the other scholars who have
dealt with the letter have been able to come up
with a definite identification of M. Protoplast,

but I think that we can assume that Hoskyns best
fits the bill. In the first place, we know that
since 1599 he was known for his "nonsense" language,
and none of the other wits fit that category. We
also know that Coryat liked to talk about him in
nonsense names. Although it is true that in the
other two letters Hoskyns is referred to as "Pasti-
crust" rather than "Protoplast," there is no reason to doubt that Coryat would be willing or even
eager to shift the denomination of his jesting
friend. Protoplasm is, of course, the first-made
thing, the original or archetype, "that which is
first formed, fashioned, or created."[11] If we go
back to the passage which Coryat used as the basis
for his jesting name for Hoskyns, we get a picture
drawn by John of a particularly strange form of
the creation:

> Or as your equinoctial pasti-crust
> Proiecting out a purple chariot wheele,
> Doth squeeze the spheares, and intimate the
>   dust...

If to Coryat, John was the equinoctial pasti-crust,
he would certainly also be the protoplasm which
formed the basis of the spheres and dust.

        If indeed M. Protoplast is Hoskyns, and there
is certainly more reason to believe it to be him
than anyone else in the groups mentioned, then he
would be listed once again as a member of the group
which we have been following for three decades--
with the addition of Whitaker, who was another link
between the poets and the political figures around
the two Phelips and their ladies. The point is,
however, that Hoskyns was a primary link through
his work in Parliament. The fact that Ben Jonson
is listed with Inigo Jones, his set designer for
all of his major masques, and John Hoskyns, his
literary "father," should surprise no one. The
core of the two groups so far is the friendly duo
of Martin (to whom Ben Jonson had dedicated his
Poetaster in 1601) and Hoskyns, along with the
Phelips family.

The third letter moves us out of the Phelips'
household and into the taverns of London. It is
addressed, on 8 November 1615, "To the High Seneschall of the right Worshipfull Fraternitie of Si-
reniacal Gentlemen, that meet the first Fridaie of
euery Moneth, at the signe of the Mere-Maide in
Breadstreete in London." These "Right Generous,
Iouiall, and Mercuriall Sirenaicks," so-called no
doubt not only because they were all sweet singers,
but also because the Mermaid was traditionally a
siren, were, before Coryat left, presided over on
at least one occasion, by their "quondam Seneschall
of the noblest society," Mr. Lawrence Whitaker.

As Coryat mentions in a previous letter, one
of the acts of bandinage of the group was to present him with a mock safe-conduct passport: "that
incomparable elegant safe-conduct, which a little
before my departure from England, your Fraternity
with a general suffrage gaue me for the security
of my future peregrination." He indicates that he
has had no need of it as he has been in Mohammedan
countries, but he will put it to use once he returns to the dangers of Christian nations. The
letter does acknowledge that he has learned of the
death of Prince Henry. And it ends with a desire
that they befriend the Rev. Peter Rogers, who was
preacher to the English merchants in Asmere and who
carried the letters back to England, "to entertaine
him friendly for my sake, to exhilarate him with
the purest quintessence of the Spanish, French and
Rhenish Grape, which the Mermaid yeeldeth... Farewell noble Sirenaicks." The postscript begins,
"Pray remember the recommendations of my dutifull
respect to al those whose names I haue here expressed, being the louers of vertue and literature."
In the list of over twenty persons that follows it
is obvious that more than the Sirenaicks are included. As in the first letter, what they all seem
to share is the love of vertue and art. Some of
the list can be immediately dismissed from the
title of Sirenaicks: "the two Ladeis Varney the
Mother & the Daughter, at Boswell house without
Temple Barre"; William Forde, "Preacher to our Nation at Constantinople, if you happen to meete him

in any part of England"; Iohn Williams, who is always listed in these letters in a separate category; "all the Stationers in Paules Churchyard"; and Doctor Montacute, Bishop of Bath and Wells, who is mentioned in a separate postscript.

This leaves us with a working list of seventeen potential members. Among these are Sir Robert Cotton, the antiquarian and fellow records-searcher with Hoskyns in the Parliament (Coryat has collected an antique head for him); "M. George Speake my generous & ingenious countriman, the Sonne and heyre apparant of Sir George Speake in Sommersetshire:[12] him you are like to finde in any Terme, eyther at the middle Temple, or in some Barbers house neere to the Temple"; "M. John Donne, the author of two most elegant Latine Bookes, Pseudomartyr, and Ignatij Conclaue" (which indicates, as Prof. Bald pointed out, that Coryat had certainly not read the first of these and also that he did not know of Donne's entering the priesthood) "of his abode either in the Strand, or elsewhere in London; I thinke you shall bee easily informed by the meanes of my friend, M. L. W."; Richard Martin "Counsellor, at his chamber in the middle Temple, but in the Terme time, scarce else"; Christopher Brooke "of the city of Yorke, Councellor, at his chamber in Lincolnes Inne, or neere it."; "M. Iohn Hoskins, alias Aequinoctial Pasticrust, of the citie of Hereford, Counsellor, at his chamber in the middle Temple"; George Garrard, "of whose beeing you shal vnderstand by Master Donne aforesaide," who was a member of one of the leading business families of the time; William Hackwell "at his chamber in Lincolnes Inne"; Ben Jonson "the Poet at his chamber at the Blacke Friars"; John Bond, "my countreyman, chiefe Secretarie vnto my Lord Chancellour" and one of the characters in Hoskyns' Censure; Docket Mocket, "resident perhappes in my Lord of Canterburies house at Lambeth, where I left him"; Samuel Purchas, "the great collector of the Lucubrations of sundry classical authors, for the description of Asia, Africa, and America"; Inigo Jones "there where Maister Martin shall direct you", Hugh Holland "at his lodging, where M. Martin shall

390

direct you"; Robert Bing "at Yongs ordinarie, neere
the Exchange" (he may be the M.P. who was to be the
last recorded speaker in the Addled Parliament);
and William Stansby, "the Printer of my Crudities
and Crambe, at his house in Thames street: also
his childlesse wife."

From these letters and poems we have a good
idea of the relationships within the group--who
knows the addresses of whom, for example. We also
know the group that Coryat feels free to jest openly with: Martin, Hoskyns, Brooke, the young man
George Speake (whose father was a Knight of the
Bath and ex-sheriff of Coryat's home shire), and
the publisher Stansby (who undoubtedly had a covey
of children). Using Coryat's Crudities, the three
letters from India, and the poem we are about to
examine, we find that the central group contains
Coryat (5), Martin (5), Hoskyns (5), Brooke (4),
Holland (4), Jones (4), Robert Phelips (4). Whitaker (4), Donne (3), and Jonson (3). All of these,
plus Hackwell, Garrard, and Bond (and perhaps Robert Cotton and Samuel Purchas) make up the clearly
identifiable Mermaid Tavern group.

We have some idea of what the gatherings might
have been like from Ben Jonson's Leges Conviviales,
or rules for his own followers' meetings at the
Sun: each paid his own bill, except for guests;
sad, tasteless, lewd, and ignorant people were not
allowed; erudite, urbane, witty, and honest were;
choice women guests were not disbarred; offensive
odors or scents were; the food was to be prepared
on the basis of delectation rather than cost, and
the cook was to keep in mind the tastes of the
group; there was to be no arguing about seating;
the waiters were to be ready with glasses and wine
and to be vigilant but silent in their work; the
wine was to be of pure varietals, unmixed--or the
host would be whipped; drinking was to be in moderation; any contests were to be about books, not
wine; the members were to be neither mute nor too
noisy; once everyone had eaten and drunk fully,
there was to be no discussion of serious or sacred
topics; there was to be no music unless specially

called for; mirth, wit, dancing, and singing were
allowed; jokes were to be without malice; dull
poems were not to be read; there was to be no extempore versifying; there was to be no loud or
noisy arguing; lovers were to find some corner in
which to do their sighing; breaking of windows,
drinking glasses, or furniture was against the
rules; anyone who published what was said or done
at the gathering would be banished from the society; and no one should take advantage of another
because he has been drinking.[13]

Obviously the Mermaid Tavern group described
in Coryat's letter is not the one that has come
down to us in poetry and song, mentioned by Fuller
and Beaumont and then memorialized by Keats. Beaumont's famous Letter to Ben Jonson about the meetings at the Mermaid contains no mention of participants other than themselves:

> ...what things have we seen
> Done at the mermaid! heard words that have been
> So nimble, and so full of subtil flame,
> As if that every one from whence they came
> Had meant to put his whole wit in a jest,
> And had resolv'd to live a fool, the rest
> Of his dull life....[14]

Whatever conversations Beaumont had heard and seen,
they were not those of the regular group that met
there the first Friday of every month. Professor
I.A. Shapiro is probably wrong in using the information in the Coryat letters and in the poem which
we are about to examine to destroy Beaumont's
story and the long tradition of the Mermaid Tavern
group of playwrights, but it is equally wrong to
try to add to Beaumont's potential group any of the
poets, like Donne, who were part of the more regular sirenaicks.[15] At any rate, as a regular patron
of the Mermaid, Hoskyns would have become well acquainted with William Johnson, the host of that
tavern, who was a close friend and business associate of Shakespeare.[16]

Somewhere between 1608 and 1612 most of Hos-

kyns' group met together with other friends at the
Mitre Tavern in Fleet Street, near both the Middle
Temple and the church of St. Dunstan's-in-the-West,
where Donne was later to be parish priest (he often
met with his vestry in the Mitre). In this poem we
discover what appears obvious from all other sources: that Coryat's role was as a butt of the jokes
of the others. He served as a target for their
wit and took it all with genial good nature. But
the poem is more than simply a listing of the group
or a description of Coryat's role; it shows the
kinds of topics of conversations that came up when
this mixed group of poets, courtiers, and business-
men got together. Until Professor Shapiro raised
serious doubts as to the authorship of the poem,
it was credited generally to John Hoskyns, and I
would argue that that accreditation still stands,
in spite of the always persuasive arguments of
Professor Shapiro, and Professor Bald, who followed him in his line of reasoning. Andrew Clark
first published the poem in his edition of the
Brief Lives, based on a version in an old commonplace book in Lincoln College, Oxford. He attributed the work to Hoskyns on the basis of a manuscript shown him by Falconer Madan which was headed
"Mr. Hoskins, his Convivium Philosophicum" and
noted at the end "per Johannem Hoskins, London."17
Professor Shapiro argues that the copy of the poem
which should be used is that among the Chamberlain
papers in the Public Record Office, SPD James I,
Vol. 66, No. 2. It is headed:

> Conuiuium (a) Philosophicum teneŧ in clauso
> termino michis in crastino festi Sti Egidij in
> campis. Authore Domino Radulpho Colphabio:
> AEneo=nasensi.
> (a) quidam legunt (phoolosophicum) sed nequi-
> ter credo vt patet per ipsum catalogum conviva-
> rum in fine.

Clearly, the author is described as a man named
Colphabius who graduated from Brasenose College.
The trouble is, of course, that neither Shapiro
nor anyone else can find anyone named Colphabius
or any combination thereof in the lists of Brasen-

ose College--nor anywhere else, for that matter.[18]
Obviously the name is some kind of cover-up, but
it is not possible to work out what the root name
is. I would suggest that the clue lies rather in
the bronze nose, aeneo-nasensi. We have already
had reason to notice Hoskyns' comments on and his
self-portrait of his long and large nose.

But even if that is not a satisfactory answer
to the puzzle, it remains true that the poem is
written by an inside member of the group rather
than an outside observer, and no one comes closer
to meeting that description than Hoskyns. And
"Colphabius" does not connect with the name of any
other member of the group we have been able to assemble. Moreover, all of the Latin tricks of the
poem are ones which we can most easily connect with
the wit of John Hoskyns.

But there are two other perfectly good reasons
for attributing the poem to Hoskyns. The best copy
is in the Rainsford Ms. in the possession of Sir
Geoffrey Keynes and directly follows the copy of
the "Censure" poem as one of the "Verses giuen mee
of Mr St John Hoskins Composure." We have already
discussed the trustworthiness of that manuscript.
As the copyist, who clearly knew his latin, had the
Colphabius introduction to work with, it is important to recognize that he did not think that that
attribution in any way raised a question of Hoskyns' authorship. More important is the fact that
on 26 February 1612, not more than a few months after the poem was written, Samuel Calvert, secretary
to the Lord Treasurer and intimate friend of the
"court" of Prince Henry, in a letter to William
Trumbull, included the poem, "A Banquet of the Wits
by Hoskins of the Temple."[19] There can be no doubt
then that the poem is by our man, who would, after
all, be the one best suited to write it.

The specific date of the meeting, which, it
must be remembered, could have been 1608 just as
well as 1611, is not possible to set. The "day after the feast of St. Giles" would be September 2nd,
but there is, of course, no such saint as "St.

394

Giles in the Fields." Moreover, the Michaelmas
Term for 1611 ran from 6 October to 28 November, so
that a feast at the end of the term would be in
late November. But whatever the date that autumn,
the gathering was to be great sport. Clark printed
a contemporary translation of the poem by one John
Reynolds,[20] which not only helps the modern reader,
but also indicates the difficulty, even at the time
the poem was written, in trying to make sense in
English out of Latin nonsense language.

> Whosoever is contented
> That a number be convented
> Enough but not too many;[21]
> The Miter is the place decreed,
> For witty jests and cleanly feed,
> The betterest[22] of any.

Then follow four stanzas of Latin-English puns on
the names of those present: Christopher "Torrens"
(Brooke) will come "running slowly"; John "Factus"
(Donne); "Gruicampus et Arthurus" (Cranefield and
Arthur [Ingram]);[23] Robert "Equorum amicus"
(Φίλ-ίππους - Phelips); Henry "Ne-vile" (Neville);
"Cuniculusque quercitanus" (and cony oak - Richard
Connocke);[24] John "Caligula" (little-boots--Hos-
kyns); Richard "Guasta-stannum" ("Destroy" or "mar"
tin); Henry "Bonum-annum" (Goodyer); John "Occi-
dens" (West); Hugh "Inferior-Germanus" (Holland);
Ignatius architectus (for anyone in early 17th century England, Inigo Jones was "the" architect);[25]
and finally Thomas "Coriatus," the "quarry" of all
their jests, without whom the company would be incomplete:

> For wittily on him, they say,
> As hammers on an anvil play,
> Each man his jeast may breake.
> When Coriate is fudled well,
> His tongue begins to talke pel-mel
> He shameth nought to speake.
>
> A boy he was devoid of skill
> With white-pots and oaten-cakes at will
> Somersetizated.[26]

And is a man with Scots and Angles
With silken scarfes and with spangles
    Fitly accommodated.

Are you in love with London citty?
Or else with Venice? he will fitt ye;
    You have his heart to prize it.
Or love you Greeke--of tongues ⟨the⟩ chiefe,
Or love you Latin? hee'le in briefe
    Sir Edward Ratcliffize itt.[27]

This orator of Odcombe towne
Meaning to civilize the clowne,
    To parlé 'gan to call
The rusticks and the Coridons,
The naturalls and morions,
    And dis-coxcombde them all.

To pass the sea, to pass the shore,
And Fleet-street it all Europe o're,[28]
    A thing periculous.
And yet one paire of shoes, they say,
And shirt did serve him all the way,
    A thing pediculous.

Whoso him exouthenizeth,[29]
Garretating swaberizeth.
    And for this injurie
He shall walk as disrespected,
Of good fellows still neglected,
    In city and in curie.[30]

Hoskyns then refers to the freedom of speech
allowed at the meetings and turns to the topics of
conversation that they pursue.

The king religion doth out-bear,
The people doe allegiance sweare,[31]
    Citizens usurize it.
The soldiers and the merchants feare,
The boyes and girles do love their paire,
    And women cuculize it.

Prince Henry cannot idly liven,
Desiring matter to be given
    To prove his valour good.
And Charles, the image of his father,

Doth imitate his eldest brother,
And leades the noble blood.

The Chancellour relieveth many,
As well the wyse as fooles, or any
     In humble-wise complayninge.
The Treasurer doth help the rich,
And cannot satisfy the stitch
     Of mendicants disdayninge.

Northampton, seeking many wayes
Learning and learned men to rayse,
     Is still negotiated.32
And Suffolke, seeking, in good sorte,
The king his household to supporte,
     Is still defatigated.

The noblemen do edifye,
The bishops they do sanctifie,
     The cleargie preach and pray:
And gentlemen their lands doe sell,
And, while the clownes strive for the shell,
     The fish is lawyers' prey.33

Thus every man is busy still,
Each one practising his skill,
     None hath enough of gayne.
But Coriate liveth by his witts,
He looseth nothinge that he getts,
     Nor playes the fool in vayne.34

It may be of value to look at the names added
to the group that we have been following. Most
important by far is one of the contributors to The
Odcombian Banquet, Lionel Cranfield, later raised
to the position of Earl of Middlesex for his financial acumen. On the way up he was Master of
the Wardrobe, and his somewhat shady business dealings led to his impeachment as Lord Treasurer.
His latest biographer35 has described him as both
clever and unscrupulous. As a young merchant he
made the beginnings of his fortune in marketing
cloth, and it would seem likely that a combination
of his business acquaintance with John's brother
Oswald and the fact that John was always on the
Parliamentary Committees involved with cloth-making
and the cloth trade would account for their friend-

ship. Certainly in 1619 Hoskyns was using his friendship with Cranfield, now knighted and Master of the Wards and Liveries, to further his brother's business interests.36 Richard Martin was, next to Ingram, Cranfield's closest friend and was deeply in his debt. That the friendships of these days continued well into the future is evidenced by a letter from John Donne to Cranfield, then Earl of Middlesex, on 18 November 1628, telling him of Donne's current bout of sickness.37 One 17th Century description of Cranfield reveals a major difference between Cranfield and the other members of this group of friends: "a man of no vulgar headpiece, yet scarce sprinkled with the Latin Tongue."38 Nevertheless, for the help he rendered to an entire generation of poets and artists, Cranfield well deserved to be buried in the poet's corner of Westminster Abbey when he died in 1645 at the age of 70.

Arthur Ingram was also a financier and Secretary of the Council of the North. He and Cranfield were the closest of friends and were often involved in business together, sometimes bringing others of the Mitre Tavern group into their dealings.39 Richard Connock was Auditor of Prince Henry's Revenues, having been appointed with the rest of the group of household officers when the Prince set up his court at St. James, in December 1610.40 John West also held a financial post in the government, being secondary to the King's Remembrancer in the Exchequer. With this group of wits, M.P.'s, and financial experts, it is no surprise that the topics of conversation included what they did.

As we have already noticed, all of the young poets and artists of the day looked to Prince Henry as their royal patron, and they were concerned with his activities--or lack of them. Having set up his court, the young Prince still did not have more than titular duties, which must have depressed him as well as his hangers-on. The note in the Convivium on the activities of his younger brother, Charles, is even more important in view of Henry's approaching but unexpected death. All of the group

398

were connected with Sir Thomas Egerton in one way
or another, and the comment in this poem reflects
in many ways the respectful attitude shown by Donne
towards his then-employer in Satire V. We have already noted Lord Treasurer Salisbury's difficulties
in making ends meet for his sovereign during these
last few years of his life. Suffolk was the father
of Frances Howard, wife of the Earl of Essex, who
was to get an ill-fated divorce to marry the rising
Viscount Rochester. Suffolk was to take over as
Lord Treasurer and then to be convicted of taking
bribes at the moment at which the King's financial
crisis was deepening. Hoskyns was to be involved
as a lawyer in that case. And Northampton was
Frances Howard's great-uncle and leader of the pro-
Spanish element in the government.

Hoskyns' poetry was having a resurgence of interest at this time. Two weeks before Calvert sent
a copy of the Convivium to Trumbull, John Chamberlain sent a copy of another poem of Hoskyns to Dudley Carleton: "This inclosed paper is of Hoskins
doing, though I have no great tast in yt myself,
yet perhaps you may find more: for the wittes of
this age esteem yt very much."41

It is also possible that it was during this
fall, or perhaps the following summer, that Hoskyns
joined Henry Wotton on one of their trips out of
the city. There is no date on the poem that they
wrote while riding together, but this period of
their lives seems to be the most fitting for its
creation. The fact that Hoskyns is referred to as
Serjeant-at-Law seems likely to be the result of a
title added at a later date. It is always a possibility that the poem actually does date from the
years following 1623, but Wotton seems to have
cooled in his friendship with Hoskyns after they
served together but in opposing camps during the
1614 Parliament. It is, however, true that by 1625
the two apparently were friends again.

Sir Henry Wotton, and Serjeant
Hoskins, riding on the way.

Ho. Noble, lovely, vertuous Creature,
    Purposely so fram'd by nature
      To enthrall your servants wits.
Wo. Time must now unite our hearts;
    Not for any my deserts,
      But because (me thinks) it fits.
Ho. Dearest treasure of my thought,
    And yet wert thou to be bought
      With my life, thou wert not dear.
Wo. Secret comfort of my mind,
    Doubt no longer to be kind
      But be so, and so appear.
Ho. Give me love for love again,
    Let our loves be clear and plain,
      Heaven is fairest, when 'tis clearest.
Wo. Lest in clouds, and in differring,
    We resemble Seamen erring,
      Farthest off, when we are nearest.
Ho. Thus with Numbers interchanged,
    Wotton's Muse and mine have ranged,
      Verse and Journey both are spent.
Wo. And if Hoskins chance to say,
    That we well have spent the day,
      I, for my part, am content.[42]

    The summer and autumn of 1611 were busy times
for John. Not only was he involved with his poetic
and political friends, but he was also engaged in
lawsuits and care of his Herefordshire property.
On 1 August, his wedding anniversary, he wrote "To
my most lovinge wyfe Mr Ben: Hoskins":[43]

Good sweet hart--I was not very well vpon my
travayll. Mrs. Richard came one Jorney to this
house under color to fetch fier & saw me not,
then when I came furth again into the fold to
see my horse she came wth the lett[r] inclosed
from my lord president.[44] I told her before she
spake anything I knew her arrant bid her wellcom
& desired her to deliv[r] me the letter. I re-
ceyued it as from a lord that I had just cause
to honor & when I had done wth my horse I would
goe in & read it & repair to my lord or otherwise accomplish what he should expect of me: she
would had the matt[r] put to frends: I told I knew

400

her husbands disposition, the matt^r betwixt hym
& me was known in the best courts in England,
and when I had satisfied my lord president then
let her husband vse his discrecon. she would had
me reade the letter in her presence. I told her
my lord had other matt^{rs} heretofore wch he communicated with me it may be som such are in the
letter also wch concern her not nor her husband,
so she departed & I turnd my backe & reade the
lett^r. I had a should^r & vmbles the vmbles I
send you none heere can dresse them, the sholder
I keepe for Mr. Delehays[45] supper yf he comms.

I have som pills from filly[46] who was heere
yesterday when I was at Goodrich.[47] I am promised halfe a bucke agaynst sunday wch I will
keepe in steed of our marriage day for wch I am
to thancke God above all his worldly blessings,
& therefore doe more rejoyce in this title then
any mortall dignity.
Y^r true louinge husband

1611.   J. Hoskyns.
         1 August our marriage day
full ten yeares since
         god be blessed.

The letter appears to have been written from Bernithen Court, in Langarren, and can be explained as
a pleasant gesture from a busy landowner who could
not make it home to Hereford for his wedding anniversary, but who wanted his wife to know he was
thinking of her and planning for their celebration
the coming Sunday instead.

The fact that he was in Bernithen rather than
Hereford on the first was obviously not a simple
matter of choice, for he and his brother Thomas
were trying to get clearance on property in Bernithen of one messuage, three gardens, and ninety
acres of land. The next day, 2 August, Thomas appeared in court in Hereford to get a final ruling,
for the case had been decided at Westminster on 8
May that year.[48] As John's name does not appear
as a witness, it may well be that he did not make

it to Hereford until Sunday the 5th.

On 14 October John was back in London for
Michaelmas term, but he was still concerned with
his property in Hereford. On that day John Clarke
wrote Hoskyns a long letter concerning the house
he had sold him the previous year. Hoskyns wrote
a note at the top of the letter:

"Mr John Clark_es_ lettr of Recognig how he was
payd for my le_ss_er lease in hereford."49

The letter itself is addressed

"To the wor; m^r John Hoskins esq^r at his chamber
in the Middle temple London this be _delivered_."

Good m^r Hoskins I forgate to move yo^w before
yor goinge vpp for the v^{li} behind of the xxx^{li}
for the house, but sythence yor departure lately
I repayred to m^{is} Hoskins & acquainted her there-
wth, who answered me that as she thought there
was nothinge behind for as she sayd she vnderstood that there were certein reckoninges betwene yo^w and me abouts that value, as xx^s or
thereabouts yo^w disbursed for the writt of ex-
com Cap..., xl^s for procuringe the Composicion,
and the rest for rent, I hope yo^w meane not to
deale soe wth me for as for the xx^s yo^w knowe
the writt was soe longe Comminge that before it
cam the woman was gon foorth of the house, and
sythence cannott be app^{r}hended & nowe the retorne
of the writt is out, soe that I must either renue it or els loose all the chardges already,
but howesoever I meane not that yo^w should be a
looser a fa^{r}thinge therein only I desyer yo^w because y^t these troubles happeninge vnto me to
forbeare for a tyme vntill my matters are ended
or the woman app^{r}hended, and for the xl^s as I
told yo^w allwaies soe doe I nowe <then a line
lost because of a crease in the paper> of the
composicion when I am satisfyed of my desburse-
m^{ts} out of the gaines yo^w shall have it and for
any rent I littell dremed of any such demaund
for I was to have my goodes foorth before yo^w
were to have it, and it was the most parte in my

402

hands in the sicknes tyme, at wch tyme yo^w beinge
foorth of towne I knowe lettell wold it have
pleasured yo^w, and I am suer that at those tymes
yo^w Could have noe rent, I pray yo^w m^r Hoskins vse
me as yor frend, yo^w knowe partely the troubles I
have sythence I cam to this house, I assuer yo^w
all the money I had of yo^w on way or an other only in these troubles in kepinge possession,
Chardges in lawe, rydinge vpp and downe, ε repara-
cions have I whole spent, besydes the losse of
gaines vnto me in followenge the same, and the ne-
glectinge of my other busynes, almost out of my
way as much, therefore I pray y^u take me not at the
worst, yo^w shall not loose any thinge by me, I am
nowe ⌊undecipherable contraction⌋ the vjth of November to goe to the councell at Shrewsbury wth vj
at my chardge, ε howe longe to tarry there I
knowe not, therefore havinge such occacons I pray
yo^w prevent me not of that w^{ch} [? blotted] I ever
made account of to have at my occacion and the
key at yor pleasure I am ready to deliver, m^{is}
Hoskins alsoe wished me to write vnto yo^w that
she alsoe might vnderstand yor mind herein. And
soe expectinge yor answer hopinge of yor health
I doe for this present wth my hartiest commenda-
cions I committ yo^w to gods proteccion.
restinge Hereff. the xiiijth of October i6ii
                    Yo^r ever lovinge frend to Commaund
                              John Clarke

Hoskyns used the letter that Clarke had written as stationery for his own letter to his wife. In
it we discover the roots for later dissatisfaction
over financial matters between John and Ben, but we
also discover the long friendship and quiet agreements between John and the Clarke family. It is not
possible to discover what the specific cause of discontent the city of Hereford had with Hoskyns over
these dealings, but we can surmise that it had something to do with the Mrs. Richard mentioned in the
August letter to Ben. The greatest problems that Hoskyns was to face in legal matters were with difficult women.

I pray y^u deliver m^r Clarke/ 5 pound vpon his
acknowledginge to y^u that he will performe what

403

he writes in this letter & I will haue no-rent
of hym he payinge me in convenient tyme hereafter the charges of the writ of excommunicato
cupiendo: & the other money wch he promised the
writ of excomm Cap: cost xxix^s. wch I had no
cause to disburse but vpon his letter & it was
ready money out of my purse.

And tell hym it is reason I should loose no
money in eyther these causes for in the one I
lost Breynton & a plump^{50} wth a chayn worth xl^s
in the other I lost allmost the loue of all the
town. yf he deale as constantly wth me as I doe
wth hym & his father we shall never haue occasion
to differ & for such a matter as this he shall
not be disappoynted. therefore let hym have 5^{li}
vpon deliuery of the key for he hath kept the
house this halfe yere when we called for it for
the oth^r matter he promised me xl^s when I procured Justice Yelvertons^{51} hand & for that it is
denyed that the Maior ev^r consented to the composition is his only falt & not myne but thereby
I beleeuinge hym am drawn into question & ill
will wch notwthstandinge that I will defend a-
gaynst others yet let hym & I betwixt vs acknowledge the truth. I am to exchange the lives
wherin his father & he must shew their forward-
nes & in som othr things as I doe for them therfore for this tyme I will part wth my money in
hand & forbeare the other though my occasions &
necessities be greater then his. & let him reade
my awnswer yf y^u please not lettinge any man know
of any agreem^t betwixt hym & me for the xl^s. And
sweetehart in this y^u must be contented to be
overrated as I am by y^u in greater matt^{rs} yf y^u
have the money deliver hym v^{li} & keepe this
lettre

                                        J H

The fact that these letters are now in the local
collection of deeds of the city of Hereford indicates that at some later date, they became factual
witness of the bargains involved, and John's desire for secrecy of the arrangements was lost.

A little under a month later, on 6 November

1611, John wrote to his wife again. Even Aubrey's
description of Hoskyns as an early riser does not
prepare us quite for the postscript which John
added.

To Mrs. Ben: Hoskyns at Hereford.[52]
Sweethart: I have agreed to sell the parsonage
for 830^l and 10 angells[53] for you I could get
no more possibly for parsonages are at xij yeres
purchase & this price comes to above 13 yeares
purchase. Sr James Freere calls for his money,
& Seymores wydow being married to a needy fellow
her husband haunts me by hymselfe & others every day for 80^l so doth one kinge likewise for
50^l that I ow for morse[54] pt of the money for
Dydley. And the Taylor to whom I ow 72^l for
Rawlinges[55] and some 10^l more for myself yf he
forbeare requires use. Bacon calls for 10^l that
I undertooke 8 yeres since for Colipep part of
the price of my chamber.[56] I must be out of
debt heere or else I may give over my pracktise
wch I hope wilbe in London better then 200^l a
yeare and I would be loth it should goe to pay
use & the principall undischarged. this day my
gaignes this term commes to 23^l I hope the terme
will make it above xxx^l. I have rcccyved of
kattle three pound for Rent of Churchehill &
Bemwell[57] lands. I have sent you a letter or
warrant inclosed to receyve it of Mr. Clarke to
whose sonne James I lent it as Mr. Clarke usually desires me & hee had occasion therefor. J.
assures me he will not fayle you or allow it Mr.
John Clarke. I receyved no other rent of Somersetshire nor the 10^l yet of Mr. Whitson though
he evry day he sayth he will send it. my rent
to Tomchester this yeare came to 25^l wch was all
the rent of Dover Court[58] my lease of Titley
expires at Michaelmas next therefore I must sue
to renue it as I have written. So that now I
have payd the seven pound 10^s to the Kinge for
Dover Court out of my poore gaignes.[59] I accoumpt I must pay in debts above 300^l heere besides I must lay out above 20^l for John Delehay
to gett the cause heard the next terme wch he
promiseth to allow or pay me by his letter writ-

ten wth Morgan Delehays hand. If I could so
compasse it that I owed nothinge but to Thomas
Webb & John Delehay I would thincke myselfe happy for Clement expects his money & yt Doctor
Bradshaw or his wyfe will have any money payd
heere send me word. I thincke I must send down
one of my men to take a fine of y^u for it must
be sent up & the money receyved before I can
comm down. the commission shalbe directed to my
lord Byshop⁶⁰ to whom I will undertake to make
you what estate you will in Dydley & Bernithen.
I have receyved all this terme but xx^l in gold
wch I send you by this messenger my Cosen Bevan
of Garway. So having many grievous conflicts
evening & morninge betwixt me & my debts I am in
hope to conquer the mayn battle of them this
term & skatter the rest as I can single them
within a yeare or 2 and then I hope to live mer-
rylie with my 2 Bens & provide for y^r 2 girles.⁶¹
I will bringe down every penny that remaynes
above the forsaid debts discharged that must of
necessity be discharged heere in London. my
deare lovinge kynd earnest resolute weake mighty
desperat tender harted brave miserable dayntie
bountyfull carefull cruell godly sweet honest
Ben: god keepe y^u & your daughters & y^r little
boy whom I pray you doe not breed a clown. Send
word whether I shall bring John Boorne down wth
me. pray god I may finish this bargain for yet
it is but a spech write to me where you will
keepe y^r Christmas & what small provision I
shall heere make for it & as you will it shall
be. God keepe you sweet deere hart.

                              y^r J. H.

Mid. Temp.
4 of clocke in the morning
        vi Novemb:
            1611.

    Hoskyns was not overstating his financial
problems, as the sums of money mentioned indicate.
The letter is particularly interesting because it
gives us one of the few explicit statements on Hoskyns' income as a lawyer. The mention of the prop-

406

erty at Didley is the key to the other problems. About this time a man named Warren, who had the mortgages on the estate of Didley, some six miles southwest of Hereford on the Pontrilas road, died. In his will he ordered his executors, Morse and Atkins, to sell the manor for £600. One of John's cousins and his close friend, Richard Hoskyns, son of Thomas Hoskyns of Shobden, intended to buy the property but could not come up with the £730 necessary for the final purchase. In 1611 John began to buy up the title of the land to clear the way for final purchase, which occurred the following year. He already knew the full amount he would need to clear the property. Didley was a major landholding; just one section of it, Willock's Fields, was over eight acres.[62] In some way that is not totally clear, this case linked with his "loss" of Breinton mentioned in the last letter. In 1603 Richard Hoskyns, who had taken possession of the manor of Sugwas, which included parts of Breinton, in a lease from the Dean and Chapter of Hereford Cathedral, was involved in a lawsuit with one Thomas Brugge. John appears to have been caught in the middle of that battle somehow.[63] Ben's part in all of these transactions is, however, clear. It was her money, or the money from the sale of her property, which was being used for the clearing of debts and the purchase of the new property in Didley and the addition to Bernithen Court. Walter and John Delehay had bought Bernithen originally for £1500 and in 1611, at the time of this letter to Benedicta, were attempting to sell all or part of the manor to John for the sum of £700. Unfortunately because of a marriage contract that involved a Thomas Jones, Jones claimed the Delehays had no claim to the title. On 6 February 1612, Thomas Egerton, Lord Chancellor and John's acquaintance for many years, decided in favor of the Delehays and Hoskyns.[64] So Benedicta apparently agreed to use her money for investment in Bernithen.

At the same time John was using some of his own money to pay off debts connected with Ben's property, as at Dover Court. Moreover, he was looking ahead, as he knew that his first lease of Titley was to come up for renewal in just a year, and he had to be prepared for that. With all of his financial worries, however, there is still a very sure note of optimism about the letter and a sense of caring for his family as a proper husband and father. He had even introduced his step-son John Bourne to life in the big city, although the boy was not to be admitted to the Middle Temple for another two years. John himself would be unable to make it back to Hereford for Christmas, however, and tried to make up for his absence by sending the proper food for the celebration to whichever house Benedicta chose for the occasion.

The next record we have of his activity is half a year later, and once again he is concerned with food, but this time on a much grander scale. He was one of four who, on 26 June 1612, were "appointed to provide the Reader's feast."65 Although this assignment was an indication of his rise in reputation at the Middle Temple, it also meant an outlay of a considerable amount of money. In 1619, when Hoskyns' close friend James Whitelocke was doing his Summer Reading, John gave him a gift of a buck worth 13/6 and further gifts in money for food and entertainment of £3 6 0.66 Those entrusted with providing the major feast of the Reading were under a much greater financial burden. Before the Summer Reading, however, he was back in Hereford for the assizes and mayoral elections. On 27 July 1612, he is listed as Justice of the Peace for both Widmarsh and Eigne Wards to put into execution articles drawn up by the Justices of the Assizes. And in the list of elections for the year, he is third, following the Mayor--Thomas Williams--and Sir John Scudamore; as usual he is listed as Deputy Steward.67

In the fall he found himself more than usually busy with the affairs of his younger brother. Dr. John was about to leave Oxford and had set out to make a position for himself in the ecclesiastical world. Although he was not to get his Doctor's degree until the following spring, he set about

establishing himself in a parish and diocese. Not
surprisingly, he decided to stay in his home shire,
not far from his brother's house where he had a
room of his own and a close friend and supporter in
his sister-in-law. His brother's closeness to the
Bishop of Hereford only insured a more successful
future. As there was no opening within the city of
Hereford itself, Dr. John decided to accept the
parish of Ledbury, fifteen miles due east of Hereford. It was the premier parish church of Herefordshire and thus a rich prize. Besides having a
fine church, blending excellent examples of various
early periods of architecture, from early Norman
through late Perpendicular, the town had a good old
Grammar School and a new church house, a fourteenth
century hospital and chapel, and what must then
have been an even more beautiful set of sixteenth
century houses and inns than are still present today.

The Dictionary of National Biography entry on
Dr. John is filled with minor inaccuracies, as, for
example, saying that in 1612 he was made Chaplain
to James. That was not to happen for some time.
However, on 24 October 1612, John Hoskyns, Bachelor
of Civil Law, was "admissus ad vicarium de Ledbury
in comitatu Hereford."[68] It is interesting that in
the entry for this admission and for his admission
to the Prebendary of Puttston Minor on 23 March
1613, there is merely the note "Comp" but no fee
registered. Dr. John's is the only entry of this
kind; all the rest note the required fees paid.
It would appear that Bishop Benet was already showing some favoritism and allowing a period of monetary grace to the young Oxford man. Anthony à Wood
may be correct in his note that Dr. John was made
Chaplain to Benet at this time. Even stranger is
the fact that there is no entry in the Bishop's
Certificates for Dr. John's admission as Prebendary
of Nonnington, which he apparently held at some
time in 1612, but there is a Mandate for his induction as Prebendary of Nonnington on 25 July 1612
in the Vicars Choral Library of the Cathedral of
Hereford.[69] In the Institutions of the same library, an entry indicates he was made Prebendary

of Nonnington as a B.C.L. and gave it up the same
year.[70] The Institutions also note that he was
Prebendary of Norton in 1612,[71] but that is not
entered in the Bishop's Certificates either. As
both of these institutions were made before he became a priest in the diocese, they seem rather ir-
regular.

The Composition Books in the Public Record Office, indicating the payment of First Fruits for
church offices, help clarify the official record
somewhat. On 12 February 1613, Dr. John paid the
tithe of 23/3 on his composition as vicar of Ledbury, agreeing to pay the remaining £13 3 2 over a
two year period on the first of each August and
February. Oswald Hoskyns, of the parish of St.
Augustine's in London, merchantaylor, and John Hoskyns, citizen of Hereford, stood as his bond. The
same day these two stood bond for Dr. John's entry
into the Prebendary of Norton, which amounted to a
total of 43/2.[72] But by May 1st, a John James was
made Prebendary of Norton. Then, on 25 June 1613,
Dr. John finally paid the first fruits on Putteston
Minor, for which his elder brothers again stood
bond.[73] Some of the complications of all of this
churchly infighting show up in a letter written by
Dr. John to his sister-in-law on 10 May 1613, as he
prepared to take part in the Act connected with the
awarding of the Doctors degree:

Good Sister,[74]
God in heaven grant y^u health. Before I tooke
a foolish degree I could visit y^u easily and a-
lone, but nowe I have made myselfe vnfitt for
such a duty except I had both horse & man. I
pray y^u thinke not y^t I love y^u the lesse because I com not to y^u. When I am furnished y^u
shall have enough of my companie, & vntill then
& for ever my prayers. I desire my brother
should vpon his first arrival make som meanes
to deale with Clement[75] about my prebend, for
there is noe reason I should still pay for others fruites & enjoy noe profitt, these first entrances into spiritual livings if they be noe
more then first entrances will soone vndoe a man:

410

my brother considers not y^t I have paid tenths
& fees for ye former prebend, whereas (except he
had accepted the rent) I might have stood vppon
ye forfeiture of Mr. Sebornes lease as Dr. Best
& Dr. Kerry would have donn. I write not this
to make eyther of those doctors my rules, for I
followe none but Christ in all things... If it
please my brother soe to conclude y^t I may be
sent for in ye visitation-weeke (know he must
send me horse and man or else I can hardly com)
I may be installed otherwise I must keepe Trinity tearme in Oxford and then there may be som
danger of ye commodities of this yeare for y^e
prebend if not of ye prebend it selfe. When I
keepe horses I shall have lesse vse then he, &
soe may somtymes steed him. I shall much desire
y^{ur} presence at Oxford at ye Act, if y^u can
bringe y^{ur} sicke body thither I trust it shall
not be more sicke at y^{ur} returne. I must enter-
tayne som, there is none livinge whom I would
more willingly entertaine then y^u, I will provide a convenient place for y^u if y^u can com:
but of this when I see y^u next.
Meanewhile god keepe y^u.
I am god helpe me
   A Doctor wthout men or horses, a purchaser
  wthout money, and a Vicar without meanes Of
  hospitality, but god will provide....
      Once more ye Lord preserve y^u for ever
         y^{ur} brother in love and
           good affection ever
                    J. Hoskyns.

The duties of the Prebendary were to oversee
the affairs of the Cathedral. It appears that although he had done the duties of the Norton Prebendary, he had clearly not been officially installed or received any of the financial benefits.
As the Prebendary of Putteston Minor was considerably more valuable than that of Norton, Dr. John
eventually received a better position than he had
started with a year earlier. What is even more
clear is that John had been willing to act quickly
in the time of his brother's need but was indicating an unwillingness to make a practice of it. He

had, after all, been supplying a home for Dr. John for some time, and he probably felt that the now D.C.L. should start meeting his obligations on his own.

At the same time that Dr. John was setting himself up in the diocese of Hereford, John's lease on the manor of Titley was approaching, with its obligations, and on 27 November 1612, he was back in Winchester signing a lease of Titley for another ten years with John Harmer, the Warden of the College.[76] Although the Bursar's Accounts for the following years indicate that he regularly paid the annual rent, he had to pay £5 for defaults when he renewed the lease again.[77]

Even though we do not have many specific records of John's activities in the fall and winter of 1612-1613, we know that he was busy with the activities at the court in London, for all of the active wits were involved in one way or another. King James was consolidating his own household and trying to establish a foreign policy in the tried and true fashion of his ancestors: marriage of his children in such a way as to establish foreign power balances. The Spanish had suggested that both of James' children should marry into the Spanish aristocracy, but James had seen that was a foolish waste of children. Early in 1612, however, he had sent Wotton on a fishing trip to Turin to see about a marriage for Elizabeth; this had fallen through, and an earlier plan for her to marry the Elector of Palatine, one of the most eligible of the young leaders of the Protestant faction of Europe, was renewed. James also wished to repair the damage done to the reputation of his mother, Mary, Queen of Scots.

In the autumn of 1612 he managed to achieve both of his goals, but at the same time he lost his, and England's, major hope for the future. On 8 October, the body of Queen Mary was brought into the Royal Chapels of Westminster Abbey, at night, and buried in state, in the south chapel, parallel to the tomb of Elizabeth in the north chapel.

412

Eight days later Prince Frederick, Count Palatine, arrived in England and began a series of public functions all leading up to the anticipated marriage. But one guest was missing at the great banquet in the Guildhall on 29 October: Prince Henry. The young Prince had contracted a malignant fever which was sweeping the city, and on 6 November he died, to the consternation of all of the artistic group that had gathered around him. He was a young eighteen years, eight months, seventeen days old. It is rather surprising that in the glut of verses that poured out in the next few months, none seem to be by Hoskyns. It has to be admitted though that there was a strange quality to the verses that appeared. Donne's famous remark about his contribution is symbolic. He told Ben Jonson that "he wrott that Epitaph on Prince Henry Look to me Fath to match Sir Ed: Herbert in obscurenesse."

The court also recovered with remarkable rapidity, and two days after Christmas, the Elector and the Princess Elizabeth were betrothed. On Valentine's Day 1613 the marriage took place, once again with many of the poets lending their praises in the form of epithalamia; but once again Hoskyns was silent. The night after the wedding, the lawyers of the Middle Temple and Lincoln's Inn joined together to put on a masque at Whitehall by George Chapman which added considerably to the festivities:

> Upon Shroue-munday at night, the gentlemen of the Middle Temple, and Lincolns Inne, with their Traine for this businesse, assembled in Chancery-lane, at the house of Sir Edward Phillips, master of the Roles, and about eight of the clocke, they marched thence through the Strand, to the Court at White-hall... First rode fifty choyce Gentlemen richly attyred, and as gallantly mounted, with euery one his footemen to attend him... Next... marched an antique or mock-maske of Baboons, Attired like fantastique trauailers, in very strange and confused manner, riding vpon Asses, or dwarfe Jades, vsing all Apish and mocking trickes to the people, mouing much laughter as they past... After them came

413

two Chariots triumphal, very pleasant and full
of State, wherein rode the choyce Musitians of
this Kingdome, in robes like to the Virginian
Priests with sundry deuives, all pleasant and
significant... Then came the chiefe Maskers with
great state in white Indian habite, or like the
great Princes of Barbary... the horses for rich
shew equalled the Maskers... euery of these
horse had two Moores to attend them, attired
like Indian slaues with wreathes of gold... the
Torch-bearers carryed Torches of Tirgin ware,
the staues whereof were great Canes guilded all
ouer, and their habites were likewise of the Indian Garb, but more extrauagant then those of
the maskers... And thus they marched through the
Strand to White-hall, where the King, the Prince,
the Bride and Bridegroome, and the chiefe Nobility stood in the gallery before the Tilt-yard,
to behold their approach....[78]

The next night the Inner Temple and Gray's
Inn put on a similar display, this time going to
Whitehall by way of the Thames. After the royal
couple had left the country on 25 April, the lawyers took time to see what it had cost them, and
they were unhappy. The cost to the Middle Temple
for its part in the one night performance had been
£1086 8s 11d. By 11 June they were still more than
£600 in debt and they had to levy a tax of £3 on
each Master of the Bench, 40 shillings for each
Utter Barrister, and 20 shillings for all of the
others. That proved too high for the members to
accept, and on the 16th it was decided "In consequence of the unwillingness of the gentlemen to be
taxed such great sums, the taxation order on 11
June is reduced to 50s. for Masters of the Bench."
For Utter Barristers it went down to 30 shillings
and for the others, 15 shillings.[79] One of "the
others" was now Inigo Jones, who had joined Hoskyns
and his other friends in rooms in the Middle Temple
on 21 February.[80]

About the only event causing any excitement
during the summer of 1613 was that on 29 June, St.
Peter's Day, when the Globe Theater burned down

414

during a performance of Shakespeare's Henry VIII, as one of the cannon started a fire in the thatched roof. Considering the importance of drama at this period of English history, it was one of the major events of the year. On 29 September a far more important event for the city of London occurred, however, when the New River was completed, bringing in a supply of fresh water for the fast-growing metropolis. It had been the business project of one of Hoskyns' acquaintances, Sir Hugh Middleton, a merchant and clothmaker of Denbigh, which he had represented in Parliament in the previous session and would represent again in 1614 and all of the succeeding Parliaments through 1628.

Earlier in that month, on 24 September, Hoskyns became the recipient of what must certainly be one of the first alumni fund-raising letters in history. From Thomas Singleton, Principal of Brasenose College and Vice-Chancellor of the University of Oxford, and Thomas James, Librarian, came a request to Dr. Kerry, Treasurer of Hereford Cathdral, and "Jhon Hoskins Esquior at his house in Hereford," asking them to aid in the current building project at the university, which "is both knowen vnto your selues, and reported vnto you no doubt by others." The letter has an uncannily modern air about it, even to a promise to put donors' names on a permanent record at the University and a hint that their children will be admitted when they come of age. We have already seen Hoskyns' concern for the Universities in debates in Parliament, and it was only reasonable that he would be one of the graduates from Hereford who would be approached for a fund drive. Gone were the memories of the days when he had been so satirical a student that he had been banished from the sacred halls. The letter continues:

Where vppon, wee are bolde to presume vppon you two, (as being both most sencible of ye Vniuersities perpetuall good and welfare), to intreat your furtherance of ye common cause... according as time and occasion shall yeelde you fittest opportunitie you cannot doe a worke more

acceptable, nor to a body Politique y^t will be
more thankefull vnto you for your paynes. How
ruinous and dangerous ye former schooles were,
your selfes best know wch haue left so good
testimonies of your worth in them: but these
wch wee intend... doe ayme at nothing but at y^e
Vniuersities honour, and ye students safetie and
incolumitie. Neither is ye buylding of y^e
Schooles all our care but ye raising of competent and annual stipends for ye alotting of sufficient rewards for ye readers in eache of y^e
faculties of Arts; for wch purpose, (yf we be
not deceaued) there will be giuen willingly
500 li per annum. Thus much we thought good to
impart vnto you, knowing how ready you will be
to instill ye same into ye eares of all true Oxford men; ye Lesser motifs, as of recording
there names vppon our Register, to be layed vp
for all eternitie in our Publique Librarie, y^e
benefit y^t is to redounde vnto there ofspring
and posteritie we leaue vnto your wisedomes to
be enforced as occasion shalbe timely offered.
Wee knowe you haue beene both in your seuerall
faculties accompted good orators, here is matter
for you to discourse abundantly, and (yf we be
not deceaued) you will in this cause truly manifest both your unfained zeale, vnto your mother
ye Vniuersitie, and your best skill in oratorie.
But we will forbeare, because this is but cur-
rentes incitare....
Oxford from Brasennose Coll. 24 Sept 1613[81]

Apparently, however, they were deceived, and
the alumni did not respond with the alacrity or
fullness that they expected. On 1 March 1614 Singleton was forced to write again, this time adding
Dr. Griffith, Archdeacon of Hereford, to their list
of potential fund-raisers. The tone is much more
urgent.

... the charge of ye rebuylding of our common
schooles of Arts increasing dayly more and more
beyond y^t wch as yet we haue receaued already,
of men piously affected vnto ye Vniuersitie of
Oxford; we are compelled to make vse of all such

416

as are able any wayes to bee helpefull vnto vs
in this our extremitie, and knowing none in y^e
Countie of Hereford y^t can better perswade or
sollicite ye Cause of ye Vniuersitie, whether it
be amongst ye gentlemen of ye Country, or y^e
Clergie of y^t Diocese then you three, wee doe in
most earnest manner desire you all ether iointly
or seuerally, to perswade ye riche and well
able... to contribute vnto so pious a worke.
wherein as they shall follow ye example of others y^t haue traced them ye way, so they shall
no doubt drawe on and inuite others to doe y^e
like in other sheeres, and Counties thereabouts
and to striue to be ye first and formost in so
good an Action is (as you know) a godlie kinde
of contention and ialousie....[82]

As usual, the first thing to go had been the increase in faculty salaries. The only thing that
seems to have been missing was a class or shire
prize for the group contributing the most. There
is, indeed, nothing new under the sun.

Hoskyns' past was still alive not only in the
minds of Oxford officials. In 1613 Richard Zouche
published a long poem called The Dove and ended the
work with a closing section "To the Reader":

There is, who hath vndertaken to illustrate by
places of the Arcadia, all the points of the Art
of speaking: I will adde (which is as much as
Achilles his Father desired Chiron should teach
his Sonne) hee is rude that cannot discerne, or
exceeding austere that scornes to obserue therein worthie behaviour and carriage both in priuate and common businesse.[83]

So the Directions was still making its way around
England in manuscript form and still being admired as a pedagogic tool.

One of the young men who had undoubtedly read
the Directions was John Bourne, Hoskyns' eldest
step-son. His earlier stay with his step-father at
the Middle Temple now changed into a formal arrange-

417

ment: 4 November 1613, "Mr. John, son and heir of Francis Bourne, a Master of the Utter Bar, deceased, specially; bound with Francis Ashley and John Hoskyns; fine, 3 1. 10s.[84] Apparently the young lad was being given a chance to decide for himself whether or not he wanted to pursue the study of law and so was brought into the Temple on a special status rather than as a full-time student. It was not the best time for a young boy to be entering the Temple. For the next two years discipline was out of hand, as indicated by numerous entries in the Temple Records. It all started on 7 January 1614, when some of the young lights pulled the usual kind of Lord of Misrule mischief and were fined heavily on the 28th. Sir Edward Phelips mediated for them and managed to have the fines pardoned and the young men restored to the Temple on a full-time basis.[85] But from then on things got worse. Benchers broke up Readings with nasty remarks, there were many cases of excessive drunkenness, students were breaking windows all over the place. It may well be that the breakdown in behaviour denoted a general malaise in London and England at the time which was to reach its peak in the Addled Parliament of 1614.

Other troubles were brewing for Hoskyns, for which he was not prepared. The winter of 1613-1614 was exceptionally bad, and John was undoubtedly worried, as were the rest of the farmers of England, about his crops. The previous late fall and early winter had also been bad, but luckily there had been a good crop in the summer of 1613.[86] This winter, however, the bad weather continued right through March, almost to the day that the new session of Parliament opened.

At some time during this winter also, Hoskyns gave help to an Alice Williams who was to plague him for years. She asked him to take into his care a sum of £29 14s, and to give her the money at intervals upon request during the following year. This he did, but she continued her claims against him until the case was finally thrown out of court in 1637.[87] We shall see the problems that this

418

raised for Hoskyns later on; it was to be one of
his worst legal experiences. Early in 1614 Dr.
John received the mastership of St. Oswald's hospital, near Worcester, according to the D.N.B.
This also was to lead to a number of legal tangles
in which John would be his brother's attorney in
an attempt to guard Dr. John's rights in the position.

But for the moment John and the rest of his
Parliamentary friends were getting ready for their
next confrontation with King James. It was to be
the worst confrontation yet for both, and as it
turns out, both sides were preparing for the contest in their own ways. The opposition was lining
up its arguments and its plan of attack, while the
King was doing all he could to pack the Commons
with his own supporters or "Undertakers." As we
have noted, there was a general sense of breakdown
in customs and behavior this year. Not since the
death of Essex had a similar malaise been so ramp-
ant; all in all the Parliament was doomed before
it started.

Footnotes for Chapter XII

1. Bald, p. 193.
2. The Odcombian Banqvet, Sig. H. to Sig. H 3.
   with some obvious spelling improvements from
   Coryats Crudities, Sig. e 5 to Sig. e 6v. 59
   people wrote dedicatory poems for Coryat.
   Whitaker and Ben Jonson also contributed poems
   to another 1611 volume of Coryat, Coryats
   Crambe.
3. This became a popular name for Hoskyns among
   his jesting friends.
4. "This word gymnosophist is deriued from two
   Greek wordes γυμνος and σοφιςης which signi-
   fie a naked Sophister. And he therefore cals
   the Author so because one day he went without
   a shirt in Basil, while it was washing," Coryat's note.
5. In the margin next to Antipasticks is following scansion pattern:

   _ _ _ ᴗ ᴗ _ _ ᴗ ᴗ _ ᴗ ᴗ

   _ _ _ ᴗ ᴗ _ _ ᴗ ᴗ _ ᴗ ᴗ

   _ _ _ ᴗ ᴗ _ _ ᴗ ᴗ _ ᴗ _ ᴗ

   _ _ _ ᴗ ᴗ _ _ ᴗ ᴗ _ ᴗ

6. The generic name for porcupine.
7. "A great Gyant swift on foot of whom mention
   is in Polychronicon." Hoskyns' note.
8. There were four letters in the volume, but the
   fourth was simply addressed to his mother.
9. Phelips' father was Coryat's godfather.
10. The third postscript announces the arrival of
    Sir Thomas Roe as Ambassador to Shah Selim,
    the "Great Mogul."
11. O.E.D.
12. Speake was a young man who had matriculated
    from Magdalen College, Oxford, on 28 March
    1607 and entered the Middle Temple on 23 Janu-
    ary 1611 without having taken his degree.
13. The original Latin set of rules is in Herford
    and Simpson, Ben Jonson, VIII, 656.
14. The Works of Francis Beaumont and John Fletcher,

Vol. X (1912), pp. 199-201.
15. I. A. Shapiro, "The 'Mermaid Club'", Modern
Language Review, Vol. XLV, 1950. Shapiro's
remarks concerning the "Convivium philosophicum," quoted in the following paragraphs, are
all from this article.
16. Bentley, p. 85.
17. See Clark, I, 50, 53.
18. The closest parallel I can find is Hoskyns'
title of "calphurnius" given to Edward Best in
the Fustian speech. Since Best is not among
the group of friends involved in this or the
other poems, this possible connection is not
very helpful.
19. HMC, Marquess of Downshire, Vol. III (1938),
p. 250.
20. Printed in Osborn, pp. 288-91.
21. Literally "Just as we have promised."
22. Literally "The bestest."
23. Reynolds was misled into thinking that the line
referred to only one person: "And Arthur Mea-
dow-pigmies'-foe."
24. Reynolds stretched the Latin to "Rabbit-tree-
where acorn grows."
25. Reynolds worked far too hard for these last
four: "Pewter-waster," "Twelve-month-good,"
"Hesperian," "Inferior Germayne," and "Inego
Ionicke-piller."
26. Reynolds avoids Coryate's skill in mixing fabis
et fartis, but almost any school child knows at
least one poem that links beans and farts.
Hoskyns certainly would have. Odcombe, of
course, was a Somerset town. The syntax of
the stanza is "as a boy... as a man."
27. The shift in line length led Reynolds to over-
do his paraphrase. "If you love London, if
you love Latin, he will love you. Or if you
love Greek, he will Sir Edward Ratcliffize with
you." Ratcliffe was a physician who was the
butt of many jokes of the period, although obviously a favorite of King James, who knighted
him in 1605.
28. One of Hoskyns' best coinages, indicating that
Coryat walked to Venice as easily as he walked
the street outside of the Mitre Tavern in which

421

they met.
29. To "exouthenize" means to show contempt; to
swabberize is to act like a low sailor.
30. Probably the court, but it could be more literally the Parliament House where many of this
group gathered together.
31. These two lines bear the mark of the summer of
1610 when the King was indeed "caring for religion" and everyone was swearing allegiance.
The entire stanza is far more straightforward
than Reynolds makes it. The citizens are over-
charging on loans (as Hoskyns was to quote
Cranfield a few years later), the soldiers and
merchants are clamoring (as John had said in
the last Parliament), boys and girls are making love, and wives are committing adultery.
32. Reynolds may have had some knowledge of an inside joke. The line merely says he was delighted.
33. Literally "The lawyers grow rich." An interesting comment for Hoskyns to make, true as it
was. Henry Goodyer was one of the gentlemen
who was being forced to sell lands.
34. Another good reason for putting the date of the
poem after the publication of Coryat's two
books.
35. Minna Prestwich, Cranfield Politics and Profits
under the Early Stuarts (1966). She discusses
the whole Mermaid-Mitre group pp. 93-104. Unfortunately she sees them only in terms of sy-
cophants to Cranfield as a rising financial
star. She has many inaccurate entries on Hoskyns which raise questions of fact in other
directions. For example, she keeps referring
to Hoskyns as a bright young lawyer in 1610-14,
when he was already at least 45, some ten years
older than Cranfield (pp. 92-3); and she says
that the Mermaid group dined in 1615, which can
certainly be disproved by internal evidence in
Coryat's letters (p. 97). The biography of
Cranfield is, in spite of its shortcomings, a
fascinating study of its major subject.
36. HMC, Earl De La Warr at Knole Park, 4th Report,
appendices 1 & 2, p. 315.
37. Bald, p. 512.

38. John Hacket, Scrinia Reserata, London, 1693, p. 51.
39. Prof. Bald cites the apposite letters in HMC, Lord Sackville at Knole, I, 100, 271.
40. Stowe, p. 997.
41. SPD James I, #68; in The Letters of John Chamberlain, ed. Norman McClure (1939), I, 335.
42. Reliquiae Wottonianae (1651), p. 517. Osborn has it pp. 211-12.
43. Sizergh MSS. In Osborn, letter IV, pp. 67-8.
44. Lord Eure, then Lord President of the Marches of Wales. Mrs. Richard could be the wife of Richard Hoskyns, John's cousin who was in the process of selling some land in Didley to John because of financial problems. This is the only "Richard" who was involved in any lawsuit "in the best courts in England" with John at the time.
45. See the following letter for more information on the Delehays. John Delehay was one of John's clients at the time and owed him a considerable sum of money. The Delehays were a Langarren and Hereford City family and were close friends and relatives of John, who later refers to John Delehay as his "Cosen." In 1612 John bought the estate of Bernithen from Walter and John Delehay.
46. Likely one of the rare references to his brother Phillip.
47. Goodrich is less than four miles from Bernithen and the town of Langarren.
48. Hereford City Library, Local Collection of Deeds. John Swan was the other party.
49. Clarke's letter with Hoskyns' letter to Ben is in the Hereford City Library, 2045 L.C. #9.
50. Breinton was a manor due west of Hereford. The "plump" was a plumb line.
51. John's fellow M.P. was made King's Solicitor in place of Sir Francis Bacon in 1613.
52. Sizergh MSS. In Osborn, letter V, pp. 68-9.
53. An Angel was worth approximately 10 shillings. The parsonage was the lucrative one connected with Benedicta's property at Dover Court, Essex, mentioned later in the letter.
54. Morse was one of the co-executors of the manor

of Didley who sold the property to John's cousin Richard. He worked for John for a period of four years about this time.
55. Mr. Rawlings was a Hereford Merchant tailor who is mentioned again in a letter of 12 May 1621 (see Chapter 15).
56. There is no available explanation for this debt. The only person that John would have owed any money to for the price of a chamber at the Middle Temple eight years before this letter would have been William Coppley, who moved in and out of chambers with John several times. The price involved would have been 10 shillings rather than 10 pounds. The only guess I can make involves the fact that on the day that Thomas Fettiplace replaced William Coppley in Hoskyns' chamber (12 Feb. 1602), the entry in the Admissions book is preceded by one in which a John Weld of London was admitted to the chamber of John and Thomas Culpeper "in expectancy of the former." The fine was 40s. (Hopwood, I, 420) It is possible that there was some agreement between Hoskyns and one of the Culpepers that allowed John to keep his chamber or choose his own chambermate.
57. The Churchill and Banwell lands were part of the Somerset holdings that Benedicta inherited from her first husband.
58. John's statement indicates that the income from Dover Court was less than the £30 per year that Francis Bourne had earmarked for John Bourne's annual maintenance from that property.
59. The amount was one-half the annual rent due for Dover Court. See SPD Eliz. 1596.
60. Dr. Benet.
61. Frances and Elizabeth Bourne, both later to marry into the Hoskyns family.
62. See Chancery Case C. 2. W 7/46 and Chancery Proceedings "Mitford," C 8/30/56.
63. Chancery Proceedings, James I, H 17/17. B 61/12 takes the case back to 1600. The Depositions on the case (C21/H 53/2) have the appearance of John's kind of interrogatories, which suggest that he was already assisting his cousin in law cases. The evidence of the Canon

of the Cathedral supports Richard's side.
64. Harewood MSS. Indentures.
65. Hopwood II, 552.
66. Liber Famelicus of Sir James Whitelocke, ed.
John Bruce, Camden Soc. 70 (1858), pp. 71, 73.
67. Sheepskin Bags 1609-1616.
68. P.R.O., Bishops Certificates Oct. 1609--Oct.
1614, Hereford E 331/5.
69. The same record notes his induction to Putteston Minor on 23 March 1613.
70. Institutions... Diocese of Hereford, p. 27.
71. Ibid.
72. Composition Book (First Fruits) 14, f. 221. Dr.
John paid an initial tithe of 4/4. He had the
same two years to pay the remaining 38/10.
73. Comp. Book 14, f. 321v. The total composition
was £4 9 10. He paid an initial nine shillings
and had the regular two years to pay the remaining £4 10d.
74. Sizergh MSS. In Osborn, pp. 254-55.
75. Who this Mr. Clement of this and John's previous letter was, I can not discover.
76. Register B 22998, ff. 5-5v. On 28 November
Hoskyns was given the freedom to "demyse grannt
sell assigne or set ouer the premisses... or
any parte thereof." f. 9.
77. Bursar's Accounts 1599-1600 to 1623-1624; Register B 22998, f. 84v.
78. Stow, Annals, p. 1006. For a full description
of the events, see E.K. Chambers, Elizabethan
Stage (1923), III, 260-62. The play is in The
Comedies and Tragedies of George Chapman (1873),
III, 87-122.
79. Hopwood, II, 565-66; J. Bruce Williamson, The
History of the Temple, London (1924), p. 273.
80. Hopwood, II, 561.
81. Hereford Cathedral Library, Archive No. 4558.
82. H.C.L., Archive No. 4557.
83. Reprint of the 1613 ed. in 1839, ed. by Richard
Walker, p. 50.
84. Hopwood, II, 571.
85. Hopwood, II, 575.
86. Stow, p. 1004. See account of winter storms
of 1613-1614 in Miscellanea Antiqua (1816), I,
13-20.

87. See Chancery Decrees & Orders 1636 B, C. 33/
172, f. 473v. The full case will be examined
in Chapter 18.

Chapter XIII
The Addled Parliament

By the end of 1613 King James was in dire
financial straits, but he left the decision about
calling another Parliament up to his Privy Council.
All of England was filled with rumours of the plans.
Primary among them was the obvious attempt to make
sure that the Commons had a majority in favor of
the King. "Undertakers" were attempting to force
local constituencies into voting for representatives who would be on the King's side. As we have
seen earlier in the case of Hereford, this was not
James' first attempt at such a maneuver, but it
was certainly the most obvious and widespread, and
the reaction was spirited. On 12 February 1614,
John Donne wrote to Henry Goodyer.

> The King at his going away left the debatements
> of the Parliament to his Council... It is taken
> ill, though it be but mistaken that certain men
> (whom they call undertakers) should presume
> either to understand the house before it sit,
> or to incline it then, and this rumour before-
> hand, which must impeach, if it do not defeat
> their purposes at last.[1]

Donne's prophecy was sound. There seems to be no
question whatever that whether or not actual "undertakers" were set on by the crown, the attempt to
sway the elections was certainly made, and the attempt to pack the Parliament was obvious to all.

Just before the Parliament opened, Sir Francis
Bacon wrote to the King:

> The opposition which was the last Parliament to
> your Majesty's business... I conceive to be now
> much weaker than it was, and that party almost
> dissolved. Yelverton is won; Sandys is fallen
> off; Crewe and Hyde stand to be Serjeants; Broke
> is dead; Nevell hath hopes; Barkeley I think
> will be respective; Martin hath money in his

purse; Dudley Digges and Hollys are yours. Besides, they cannot but find more and more the vanity of that popular course....[2]

Bacon was a very poor prophet in comparison with Donne, although he certainly had reason to take the position that he did. He simply did not understand that the motives of money and advancement can be extremely complex. He misjudged Sir Edwyn Sandys, and he also misjudged the nature of the opposition "party." In addition, his self-identification with Iago to Martin's Rodrigo lends a dark cast to the whole letter.

The supporters of the King had at least one good reason to feel that the new Parliament would be better than the last: according to Williams Mitchell, only twenty of the fifty-seven previous rebels were returned to Parliament; twenty-three had been defeated for re-election, and several had been converted. Three hundred of the 463 members were new.[3] But they had not taken two elements into consideration: first, that the very real Grievances that made up what Bacon referred to as "the popular course" were still present, especially the preferment of Scottish favorites and the spendthrift spending of a nearly bankrupt court; and second, that there was also a group, including the powerful Northampton, which were out to have Parliament destroyed as a decision-making body and who were willing to do almost anything to accomplish that end. Hoskyns seems to have been caught right in the middle.

Basically Hoskyns did not alter any major stand that he had taken in the previous Parliament, although he did become more outspoken. He took the position immediately, as he had in previous sessions, that any Subsidy should wait upon redress of Grievances; he argued for the rights of Parliament and for withstanding pressures from the monarchy against those rights; and he argued against the Scottish favorites. Unfortunately he also made a speech in which he warned the King of possible dangerous consequences if he continued in his pre-

428

sent path. It is that speech which raises questions of Hoskyns' exact role in the Addled Parliament, but many writers have failed to see the basic consistency of Hoskyns' position; instead they have emphasized his connection with Northampton.

As far as we can tell, something like the following happened: Hoskyns was known by all as a witty and effective speaker and supporter of Parliament's rights. By the end of the previous Parliament he had become one of the most outspoken critics of the Scottish favorites. Because of his legal ability and his special knack for searching precedents, he would be centrally involved in any drawing up of Grievances in the up-coming Parliament. And he was not one of those the crown had made special efforts to win over, even though they had worked on his friends Martin and Sir Henry Neville. He was openly friendly with Northampton and that Lord's circle, and they knew both his strengths and his weaknesses. Furthermore, we must remember that in the previous sessions, Hoskyns, unlike most of his fellow lawyers, had worked steadily and well in committees, obviously hurting his own law practice and endangering his own financial situation. In the intervening years, he had committed himself to even greater monetary burdens in his land dealings in Hereford and elsewhere and could not now stand to take the loss which constant attendance at a long Parliament would entail. On top of that we must continue to remember that Hereford had never paid him any of his salary for the entire first Parliament. Northampton, following his own plans, apparently simply offered Hoskyns, through Sir Charles Cornwallys or Dr. Lionel Sharp, £20 for sticking with his Parliamentary duties rather than taking time off to keep up with his various law cases. Northampton obviously hoped that Hoskyns would be a trouble-maker and would help to anger the King enough to have him dissolve the Parliament. Throughout most of the session Hoskyns did the first without accomplishing the second. Then a new element was added. Dr. Sharp, a minister and former Chaplain of the Earl of Essex and later to Prince Henry, suggested to Hoskyns that the situa-

429

tion was similar to that of the Sicilian Vespers.
There is no reason to doubt John's word that he did
not know much about the 13th Century event until
Dr. Sharp suggested it to him; it was not Hoskyns'
favorite period of history. The Civil War in Sicily in 1282 was, however, a nice warning to any
monarch who brought his own countrymen along to
rule a new realm. This outright threat, or so
James took it to be, was enough to move the King
to action, and the dissolution of Parliament and
the imprisoning of Hoskyns and others were the natural results.

But all of that was two months in the future
when, on 16 February 1614, the Privy Council finally advised James to call for elections for a new
Parliament. And on 5 April, the Parliament opened
in London, with Hoskyns once again representing
Hereford along with John Warden. At times it seems
as if nothing was destined to go right in this Parliament. After spending an hour the first day
swearing in the members in groups of ten and
twelve, the Commons sent 160 members to the House
of Lords to meet with the King; but there were so
many "Strangers, as that there should not be room
left for the Members of this House." The few who
did manage to get in returned at 4:30 in the afternoon, and then there was only enough time to elect
Randolph Crewe as Speaker. Two days later all the
members went up to present their new Speaker to the
King, at 1 p.m., and then returned for the reading
of one Bill and adjournment till the following
morning. Parliament was off to a slow start.

Then events began to bear out the negative
prophecies. On the morning or 8 April the debates
began with an argument over Privileges.4 It was
no mere issue of disputed election returns, however; it was the question of whether Sir Francis
Bacon should be allowed to sit in the House of Commons since he was the King's Attorney General. As
one unnamed speaker put it: his "Eye can endure
no Colours.--King's [Livery] hindereth their Sight."
William Hackwell, John's close friend and member
of the Phelips' circle, was open enough to admit

that he had "Searched the Precedents, and, as he remembereth, Mr. Attorney hath been of the House; yet wishes it were not so." Then Hackwell, James Whitelocke, Sir James Scudamore, Sir Edwyn Sandys and others were ordered to search the Precedents to see what they could find. If the King needed any sign of troubles ahead, this was it. In the previous session Henry Hobart, the former Attorney General, had represented Norwich City, and no one had raised the slightest problem. As a matter of fact, Hoskyns had served on at least ten Committees with Hobart.

Then they picked the general Committee on Privilege, and the Crown's attempt to get control is obvious. The Privy Council members were all on it, along with such sure men as Sir George More and Sir Oliver Cromwell; Sir Henry Neville and Sir Dudley Digges were now accounted safe men as well. But Hoskyns, Fuller, and Hackwell were also there, representing the Parliament side. The Committee was to get right down to work, at 2 p.m. that afternoon in the Court of Wards, and Sir Edwyn Sandys set the tone for what the Committee should study: "That this Committee may take into [their] Consideration the Liberties of the House; which--of Three Parts: 1. Freedom of Election.--If pressed by Power, Fear &c. not free. 2. Privilege for Persons. 3. In speech."

But Sandys had his eye on a greater task even than this. He moved a Committee "to be well chosen, of Lawyers, and other Gentlemen of Experience; and that this Committee may subdivide itself ... to consider of all Statutes, for Repeal of obsolete, unprofitable, and pernicious Statutes." He made it clear that not only whole Statutes ought to be considered, but separate clauses as well. Under his plan, Parliament would have been in permanent session for any foreseeable future. Gone was the King's rather limited intention of securing a Subsidy, naturalizing Frederick, Count Palatine, and having Commons give a Composition for the redress of the Grievance of Purveyance.[5] The Committee that was named was a huge one, including the

431

Privy Council as well as all lawyers. They were
to meet every Monday at 2 in the afternoon, in the
Parliament House. In effect, they were nearly a
Committee of the Whole. As a matter of fact, immediately after this action, the House did move a
Committee of the Whole for receiving Petitions,
which was to meet every Tuesday afternoon at 2.

The next morning, 9 April, Sir James Parrot
suggested a move to get everyone in the right mood:
all should take communion at the Abbey on Palm Sunday. His reasons? The King had said this Parliament should "be a Parliament of Love between the
King and us: Next, to free those that shall take
it, from unjust Suspicion: Thirdly, to keep the
Trojan Horse out of the House."[6] What looks like
a kindly gesture is really not when one considers
the number of practicing Catholics present, even
though their position was strictly illegal. The
figure of the Trojan horse was to be a recurrent
one throughout the session. Fuller, one of the
strongest of the Puritan element, jumped at the
suggestion, saying that this was "the best Means
for Love.--Difference in Faces, but Unity in Faith."
Once again the language of religious love was being used as a political device, but no one in the
alien camp dared to make his position public; the
House had already agreed "that anyone who did not
communicate could not come into the house until he
did." Even the Protestants could not act in con-
cert, however, as shown on the 13th, when the House
decided to take communion at St. Margaret's rather
than at the Abbey, "because they administer not
with common Bread" at the Abbey, which was contrary
to the Book of Common Prayer.[7]

Then they turned to the matter of election returns, which had at their heart the entire problem
of "undertakers." Some members, like James Whitelocke, had been elected in three constituences:
Woodstock, which he represented; Corfe Castle,
where he had been nominated by Elizabeth Coke, the
wife of the Chief Justice; and Helston in Cornwall,
which he gave to his brother-in-law, Henry Bulstrode.[8] They made their choices of which place

432

to represent so that there should be no difficulty with the Privileges Committee. As we shall see with Sir Charles Cornwallys, this matter of multiple elections could work both ways.

The real issues of the morning's debate on the 9th, however, were the "elections" in which Mayors or Bailiffs of cities had returned themselves. Fuller argued that neither a Mayor nor a Bailiff could be a member of the House, and the rest of the House agreed that no Sheriff could either. They finally decided to send the question to the Committee on Privileges. Whitelocke was then added to the Committee, which strengthened the hand of the Parliamentary forces. Meanwhile all Mayors and Bailiffs in question were sequestered until the House took action. There were those, especially of the Crown party, who felt that it was unnecessary to bring all of the Sheriffs to London to report on the disputed elections but to leave the contests open to handling by the law courts. Hoskyns spoke up for the first time in the Parliament, "contra." He was "for the Drawing of a Sheriff out of the Shire." Certainly, "If by no verbal Complaint, nor Affidavit, then no Sheriff shall be sent for." However, if there were such a complaint or affadavit, "If to leave them to the Law only, and not to send for him hither, a Gap open, to infringe all Liberty of free Election." Once again his arguments proved convincing to the House, as they moved to send for the Sheriff of Northumberland "with not above Three Negative Voices."

That afternoon they went to Whitehall to attend the King and heard James report on how he had removed grievances and had allowed Parliament the right to survey old Statutes, etc., as suggested by Sandys. He claimed that because of the Respite of Homage, his annual revenue was not above £600 while his expenses were £40,000. He was willing to allow Wales the privileges of English law. In general, he was "willing to grant whatsoever may be good for the Commonwealth, and shall be thought of by this House; hoping, nothing will be sought, tending to the Diminution of his Revenue, or Alter-

ation of his Government."[9] So the speech was reported two days later on Monday morning the 11th
by the Solicitor. Then, after some discussion a-
bout rules of order, including the decision that no
one should be allowed to speak in the general meetings more than once a day, they moved to a debate
on the King's two other desires: the naturalizing
of his son-in-law, Prince Frederick, and the allowing of Sir Francis Bacon to remain as a member of
the House. The Bill of Naturalization was given
its first and second reading immediately: "An Act
concerning the high and mighty Prince Fredericke,
Count Palatyne of the Rhene, Duke of Bavaria, of
the sacred Romane Empire... and... the Lady Elizabeth his Wife, Daughter to the King's Majesty, and
their Issues." Fuller didn't like the clause which
gave their issue citizenship for twenty generations,
for, as he argued, a child was "A mere Stranger,
after Five or Six Descents," but the Bill was sent
to a Committee of the Whole the next afternoon.

Then they moved to a consideration of Bacon's
case. Whitelocke told of his search of the records,
which, he said, do not support the Attorney-General
being in the House, but as he was now here and had
been duly elected, "Moveth, he may now stand; and
an Order, none at any Time hereafter." Both motions passed.[10] Bacon's place in the House was
never really in danger throughout the debate, but
the House had wanted to assert itself against manip-
ulation by the King and had succeeded in making its
stand in spite of the actions of the Crown party.
The new members of Parliament were given their
first training in opposition within the opening
week of the Session.

The debate on 12 April revealed the delaying
tactics in the House. The meeting began with general motions of various sorts, such as giving
thanks to the King for writing a book against Catholics and for marrying his daughter to a Protestant
Prince. Hoskyns rose to introduce a general discussion on ecclesiastical courts. He started by
saying that he was not offering a new Motion; he
just wanted to discuss a situation which should be

considered. "In the ecclesiastical Jurisdiction" there were two keys of power, "clavis ordinis, clavis jurisdictionis. In the first, ordaining of Ministers, &c. In the latter, the Proceedings in legal Course." The law does, with an accused person, "Take him Sheriff in the temporal, take him Devil in the ecclesiastical.--Stept to Hell with One Foot, standeth on the Earth with the other." An innocent person is "At the Common Law dismissed, at a common Person's Suit with Cost; contrary in the other.--Here the Penalty to the Informer, or King; there to the Party, that is the Judge." He urges the need for "Reformation; that Men may not be called for small Matters, and dismissed without Costs, if wrongful; and that Excommunication be not awarded so ordinarily, or upon so small Causes."[11]

The King's Secretary, Ralph Winwood, tried to get the debate back to the question of Subsidy and brought up the King's needs, mentioning various causes of Debt such as the wars in Ireland, the state of the Navy, and the marriage of Elizabeth. Fuller argued that discussion of how much to give the King should follow the passage of other Bills in order to find "a better Ground to give more." The Lord Chancellor countered with the pressing needs of the Navy, the fact that Dover Castle, as well as several in the Isle of Wight, were "like to fall down," and urged the appointment of a Committee to handle the subject. Then Hoskyns, breaking the rule about speaking only once a day in general meeting, took his usual stand at the beginning of any session. First he argued that not all of the members were yet present: "Divers not yet come. 2. The House not yet called." Then he too used the language of religion to stall debate. He pointed out that they should wait until after "The Receiving of the Communion.--As in the primitive Church, the Offering to come after.--Moveth a deferring of it."[12] That analogy was to provide others an excuse for putting off action. Sir Francis Bacon followed by saying that he was willing to abide by the decision of the House in his own case, but he urged them to consider the King's tremendous need of money and suggested a Committee of the Whole to

consider it. The debate went on and on and on,
with the two sides becoming crystallized. Whitelocke again introduced the subject of the Undertakers at the same time that he urged the House to
show that it was clearly going to give the King a
Supply; but first they should bring up Grievances.
Sandys tried to bring the matter of Undertakers into the discussion of Supply:

> Moveth a Message to the King... Grieved, that
> divers of the most worthy Members of the last
> and this Parliament, should be so unthankfully
> dealth with, as to be traduced as Undertakers,
> till their own Actions discover them--Moveth a
> select Committee to consider of a Message to
> clear this... Great Wrong done the last Parlia-
> ment, by misreporting the Speeches of many Mem-
> bers of this House.--Moveth the Deferring the
> Treaty of the Supply till after Easter....[13]

By the end of the day, all action had been deferred.

The next day the debates took on a distinctly
ridiculous air. Fuller introduced a Bill against
swearing that carried a 20s. fine. Chris Brooke
introduced Bills against gilding and the use of
gold and silver stuffs in apparel in a speech which
befitted a member of the Mermaid Tavern group.
This sort of thing went on until the Speaker had to
rule that "for the Dignity and Gravity of the House,
that no Interruption, till the Speech of the Party
speaking ended."[14] That brought them to more important matters, and Sir Roger Owen moved Sir Edwyn Sandys' suggestion: "for a Committee to consider of what Course fittest for a Message to the
King, to intimate the Protestation of the House a-
gainst Undertakers: and to let him know, whatsoever shall be done for him, shall be merely out of
the Love of the whole House to him." Hoskyns was
on the Committee to meet in the afternoon of the
15th in the Chequer Chamber. Sir Francis Bacon
then brought up the Bill for naturalizing Prince
Frederick and asked for direction for the iminent
meeting with the Lords. Hoskyns "agreeth, a Conference, but offereth something against the Confer-

436

ence.--The Danger of adding, 'by any other Husband.'
--Hopeth well, she will not match again, without
Consent of King, or his Successors.--Danger, in respect of the House of Austria, &c." Hoskyns' objection was overruled, however, and the amendment
"by any other Husband" was added to the Bill before
it passed.[15]

The following two days, 15 and 16 April, were
largely given over to the reading of new Bills, and
Hoskyns was put on two Committees.[16] Then all Committees were called off so that they could prepare
themselves for Communion the next morning, Palm
Sunday.

The Communion did not lead to greater love between monarch and subject, its intended purpose.
Instead it gave the Parliamentary party new zest
for their attack. On the morning of 18 April "An
Act concerning Taxes and Impositions upon Merchants"
was given its second reading and immediately became one of the central Bills of the session.
Berkeley, whom Bacon thought would now be "respec-
tive," said that "no Bill so acceptable as this:
None so grievous as this to the Subject." Fuller
reminded the House that in the last session the
Lawyers had resolved that "no Impositions might be
laid without Authority of Parliament, and a Bill
passed this House to that Purpose." Chris Brooke
urged all of the lawyers to look up their notes,
and Hackwell lectured the new members, many of whom
were young, that he "Desireth now, they may understand the true State of their Right, to leave it
for hereafter to Posterity." He also explained
that he had been against this Bill at the beginning
of the last session, but after seeing the Precedents, he would do his best to convert any like
himself. Then Hoskyns capped the discussion: he
moved that

before Consideration of Supply, the Issue of
this may be known; for that these Impositions
[are] the Cause of the King's Want. For,
1. Merchants cannot trade to make 10 in the
100 1.--Use therefore at 10 in the 100.

2. The People impoverished by Usury, by this Means of forbearing Trade.
3. Contractors for buying of the Crown Land, no Custom paid, gain a 100 in the 100.--Sell it at hard Rates to divers, by Parcels; at such Rates as undoeth them.[17]

The Bill was committed to the whole House, and all Lawyers were to attend. An "Act of Repeal of One Branch of the Statute 34 H. VIII. for Wales" was also sent to Committee, including all of the Knights and Burgesses for Wales and the four shires of Gloucester, Worcester, Hereford and Monmouth. In one morning the House had returned to the issues and grievances of the previous Parliament which had never been resolved.

The following morning the Parliamentary party felt strong enough to push further. Sir Francis Goodwyn reported that there was "a Bruit divulged, that the Commons House hath already too much Power ... Moveth for a Bill, to contain Matter of Regularity amongst ourselves." And Sir Dudley Digges urged a special committee to draw up an Oath if the Committee on Privileges could not find a Precedent. There was now a definite sign of collusion: although the Oath was assigned to a Committee of the Whole House, a specific list of names followed; Brooke, Crewe, Hackwell, Finch, Sandys, Sir George More, Whitelocke, Hoskyns, Neville, Wotton, and Fuller. They were to meet on the Thursday of Easter Week in the Temple Hall, while the House was recessed for the holidays.[18] More and Wotton, (as supporters of the King), were hopelessly outnumbered, and Neville would not speak too strongly against his drinking companions. On the morning of 20 April, after some desultory business, the House finally made clear what had already been apparent: they moved that "Consideration of his Majesty's Supply shall not be meddled in, till Thursday after Easter Week, the Fifth Day of May; and then to be treated of." Then they adjourned for a week.[19]

By the time they returned to work, a month of the Session had gone by and nothing had happened.

438

It is true that the Bill for the naturalizing of Prince Frederick had met no opposition, but Parliament was really no farther ahead than it had been four years earlier, and the Parliamentary "party" had regained almost complete tactical control of the House.

Once again, the recess only seemed to add fuel to the fires of discontent. After the introduction of some new Bills to Committee,[20] a bitter debate began over the question of Undertakers. Sir Roger Owen began by reminding the House that they had previously passed a rule that no one should confer with the King about Parliament business but the Speaker; "That Undertakers, if any, be worse than the Powder Traytors...."[21] Sir Robert Phelips suggested that to avoid further "Contention and Heat" they send a "Protestation to his Majesty, upon the general Voice and Rumour" rather than examining the particulars in the House. Then Hoskyns spoke up: "That this proceedeth from a rotten Foundation of Popery: Wisheth therefore, it may be examined. This the Argument that brought in the <u>Trojan</u> Horse, and overthrew the City.--Moveth a Re-commitment."[22] Sir Dudley Digges lept to his feet, explaining that Hoskyns' statement about the Trojan Horse was one that someone said he had made, and "He feareth that some false Rumour, spread to hinder the great Businesses now in hand." The whole debate angered Sir Francis Bacon so much that he said he "Wisheth himself, not only in the upper House, but in the upper World, because of this Discord." He took the usual administrative position that you can't discuss individual names in the House and that the matter ought to be discussed in a Committee of a few people. No one paid any attention, for they referred the whole matter of examining Undertakers to a Committee of the Whole House.

The morning's arguments are important for trying to understand Hoskyns' role in this Parliament. If there was any Catholic who was interested in using the matter of Undertakers or, for that matter, any other argument as a Trojan Horse to destroy the Parliament, it was certainly Northampton. This was one of the "bones" which he had thrown in to set the dogs fighting one another. If Hoskyns was in any way a "client" of Northampton at this point, it seems a strange speech to make, to say the least.

After two days of debates on Impositions, patents, and monopolies,[23] the House met with the King, whose patience was wearing thin. Although his words were conciliatory, he was clearly telling them to keep their hands off some subjects and to get on with the matter of Supply.

> ...when he came to the Crowne he chaunged no Counsellor Judges o^r other of Q Eliz., and he was perswaded by the one that ympositions were a greate flowre of his p^{r}rogatiue, and by the latter of the Lawfullnes therof, as also by a iudgment in the Chequer Chamber [against Bates], that therfore he woulde dye a 100 deathes before he woulde infringe his p^{r}rogatiue, yet not wth- standinge that he woulde if a writ... shoulde be brought, stand to the opinions of the iudges, and in anye matter of importance that the lower house coulde desire he woulde giue his consent. he added that although his vrgent necessitye mooued him to desire relief of his subiectes. yet he hoped this shoulde be the last time, for herafter he woulde call a parliament eyther to make good lawes o^r els to execute those that are alreadie enacted: that he woulde not like a merchant contract and demande anye summe of his subiectes, but did referre himself to their loues: and althoughe he had don her to fore for priuate men, yet herafter his whole endeuor shoulde be for the good of the common wealthe, all wch he protested verbo regio, and that he neuer desired anye vndertakers for him, but onlye relied on the loue of his people, that therfore he would in this his declaration of his minde free the lower house of debate and of sendinge anye petition to him o^r conferringe wth the lordes about the same.[24]

The House did not agree with His Majesty, at least by its actions. The next morning, 5 May,

after the House had sent two Bills to a Committee
including Hoskyns, Hackwell, Brooke, Crewe, Whitelocke, Fuller, Owen, and Sandys,[25] Sandys brought
them back to a debate on Impositions. It turned
very warm, and the Speaker had to reprimand some
hissing of the members.[26] Finally they decided to
follow Whitelocke's advice and set up a Committee
to prepare material for a conference with the Lords
the following day. Hoskyns, Sandys, Fuller, Hackwell, Whitelocke, and Brooke joined the Privy
Council and Sir George More, along with More's son-
in-law, John Donne. Donne, who had served in the
last Parliament of Queen Elizabeth, had returned to
the House after having missed the first Parliament
of King James. From other sources we can tell that
he was certainly of the King's party, but he was
abnormally quiet in the House and served on so few
Committees that it is hard to think that he accepted any assignments except under pressure. The Committee, which eventually contained all the lawyers,
was to meet the next morning in the House.

It was then suggested that discussion of Supply could go on at the same time as the debate on
Impositions, and Hoskyns disagreed: "That some"
people are "like interfyring Horses, that the faster they go, the more they lame themselves--That no
Subject (not consiliarius natus) should forestall
Parliament Businesses." Then he moved to his favorite tactic of taking the King's diplomatic language at face value. He pointed out that the King
said he had "Called [them] to give Counsel, not
give Money; no such Thing in the Writ," even though
there had been "Papers of Project cast abroad. Another, that if you give not, no more Parliaments;
and that the King's Prerogative shall be extended."
But, he urged the Commons, "That this House never
[acted] in Fear." Besides, there was "No Cause of
Fear of not calling of Parliament: The King gaineth
by them, not the Subject. If the Prerogative [was]
too far extended, then [this was indeed] the Time
for calling a Parliament of Love."[27] They decided
to put off any action on the Subsidy. On top of
that, the afternoon was given over to a long debate on Undertakers, finally getting down to spe-

441

cific names.[28] The King's speech had had no effect
whatever.

It had been a tense week,[29] and Saturday morning, the 7th, everyone relaxed during the introduction of a Bill "for the better observing and
keeping holy the Sabaoth-day, or Sunday." The
whole discussion has a decidedly hilarious cast a-
bout it, with members joining in with activities
that should be done away with, such as football.
One member suggested that he was against doing any
work on the Sabbath, "wherein the Lawyers most
faulty."[30] Then they all left the chamber to celebrate the Sabbath.

The next week got off to a deceptively slow
start. After some private Bills were introduced,[31]
the Committee on Privileges reported on election
problems in Stockbridge. The Chancellor of the
Duchy, Sir Thomas Parry, had written to a Mr. St.
John, urging the election of Sir Walter Cope, "wth
these words that if he did resist he should face a
greater power then he could resist and that it
would be ill taken of the state."[32] Although the
case was a simple one of misuse of power by an individual, it smacked of the general problem of Undertakers, and the House decided to meet at 7 a.m.
the next morning to look into it further.

Francis Moore began the defense of the Chancellor that morning, reminding the House of Parry's
old age, that he had to be helped around by a servant, that he had served his shire all his life, and
that his service as well as his age should be considered. Hoskyns was not about to let this obvious
piece of electoral skullduggery go by unpunished or
unexamined, however. He reminded the House that
there was "A Prescription of the Chancellor's Power
in Election." and what he had done was "against the
Right of this House and Kingdom." He then drew
their attention to the language of the letter: that
the "State" had been named and a "Greater Power
than able to resist." He wished them to savour the
possible meaning of that. Then he urged that the
"Elected, not to be received." Moreover, he argued

442

"That these Letters were brought to the Chancellor ready written." He moved that the House discover if "his Man may justify whether he had Instructions from his Master in these Points."[33] Hoskyns had hit a sore point, and Bacon spoke up immediately, supporting the House in its care of its own prerogative but urged mercy. The King also had offered to punish Parry. The House sent a message of thanks to his Majesty, but said they would proceed in their own censure.

The next morning Parry did not show up, and the House excluded Sir Thomas as well as Cope and Sir Henry Wallop, ordering new writs for another election. The King also sent a message that he was punishing Sir Thomas by removing him from the Privy Council. "the answar from the house was that they haue a double satisfaccon, in their owne punishment and the kinges and that they desire to proceede no further but rest contented."[34]

After some preliminary business on the morning of 12 May, the House finally got down to work preparing their report against Impositions. Sir Edwyn Sandys reported from the Committee that they recommended a two-fold approach: a search was to be made for all precedents concerning Impositions, and the House was to ask for a joint conference with the Lords for a discussion of the whole matter. He also read a speech which was to be delivered to them, explaining the House's position. It included such key statements as that, from an original Imposition on currants, there were now 1341 Impositions; "That the Kinge cannot ympose but by act of Parliament"; "That merchantes of the west loose their whole stock by reason of impositions in one yeare"; "Wheras the kinge affirmed that he had a Judgement in the Chequer Chamber for him, that there the Barons haue not proceeded more maiorum, for they shoulde haue asked aduise of the Parliament, because this case was aboue their commission." Sir Henry Mountague, who was Recorder of London, was to show why they wanted the conference. Sir Francis Bacon was to introduce the business and set the question. Sir Edwyn Sandys was to show that

443

the King's imposing without assent of Parliament
was contrary to the constitution and policy of the
kindgom. Thomas Crewe was to show "That to ympose
is against the common lawe and statutes." Whitelocke was to start the evidence between the King
and Parliament, reporting on the Statutes from Edward I to the end of Edward III. "The time from
50 Edward III. to 3 et 4 Ph et Mariae"   .

> during the Reign of Ten great Princes; during
> all which, a Cessation from Impositions: During
> which Time, the Statute of Tonage and Poundage
> granted by Parliament; first for Years; after,
> temp. Ed. IV. granted for Life: Which hath con-
> tinued ever sithence. Which produceth Two memor-
> able Points.
> 1. That if those great Princes, and warlike,
> had had Right to impose, they would never have
> taken them by Gift from the People:
> 2. The good Disposition of the Subjects here;
> that, when the Kings forbear to impose, they
> give more than Kings have before required.
> was assigned to Thomas Wentworthe of Lincolns
> In, and to John Hoskins of the Middle Temple,
> leaving them to divide, as they shall please.
> From Queen M. till now, upon Mr. Hyde.

Sir Roger Owen was to show that "no foreyne state
did as the king did," and Sir Dudley Digges was to
discuss the inconvenience to the common profit.[35]

After the House had agreed on the action, Hoskyns moved "for a Warrant, from this House, for
Search in the Tower, and Exchequer, and to any
other, that hath any Records; and to have Copies of
any such of them whereof they have not Copies under
the Officers Hand already.--That he hath many Records very material, that have not been examined.--
Desireth these may be copied out, at the Charge of
the House."[36] Then the men involved met immediately,
in the Committee Chamber. It was these reports and
the copies of the records that the King would destroy at the end of the session, as they were a
direct threat to his major source of income. It
was probably at his decision as well that the joint

444

conference with the Lords never took place.

Tempers began to flare and patience wear thin.
On the 13th a bitter argument took place in which
Sir William Herbert was accused of claiming that
Sir Roger Owen was biased. The Committee studying
the case reported back the next day that Sir Roger
Owen told of a piece of writing which supposedly
came from some undertaker. The villain of the
piece turned out to be Sir Henry Neville, who "affirmed it came from him self, that there was a communication beetweene the kinge and himself at Wind-
sore that they talked of a Parliament, and that his
intent was to breed a loue betweene the kinge and
subiect that he was no vndertaker to leake a parliament &c." The House accepted his excuse, and the
whole matter blew over.37

On the 14th also "An Act against Continuances
of Liveries, and bringing in of Evidences into the
Court of Wards; and returning of the Counterpanes
of Offices and Inquisitions into the said Court"
was introduced, and Chris Booke objected to the
second part. Hoskyns had even more to object: he
claimed

> That no such Title read by my Lord Chancellor.--
> This Corvan, to take from the Priest to give to
> the Pharisee.--
> That the Petty Bag maketh all the Summons, and
> other Proceedings, for Parliament--All the Sub-
> poenas special, Diem clausit extremum, &c. taken
> already from them, and yet they must be returned
> thither, and they have nothing for it. No Char-
> ity to add this to the Clerk of the Wards.--
> Danger to the Subject, to take away from the
> former Provision of retaining one.--
> A Clerk's Clerk's Clerk Escheator; and hath
> attended, and pulled off the Feodary's Boots.--
> That his Majesty would not, if he knew it,
> rob Peter, and pay Paule.38

All the lawyers, with many others, were put on the
Committee to consider the Bill in the Middle Temple
Hall on the 18th.

445

The following week was relatively mild, except
for an impassioned speech by Richard Martin, who
"vndertooke to teache them howe they were to proceede in parliament" about aiding the Colony in
Virginia. The House resented his approach and
forced him to apologize, but he continued to urge
their assistance and care.39 The Mermaid group
rallied round ("others who were his frendes moued,
to haue the rigor mitigated"). Sir Robert Phelips
tried to excuse Martin because of his affection for
the Virginia Colony, and his previous service in
the House, and Hoskyns was caught in a bind between
his membership in the House and his friendship with
Martin and support for the Virginia venture: "That
speaketh with as much Perplexity, as if he himself
arraigned there.--_Peccatum_ punished _cum_ _peccato_."

It was also a busy week for Committee work.
Hoskyns reported in the Jernegan Bill and was assigned to five new Committees40. Meanwhile the debate on Impositions went on. On the 16th Sir Edward Hoby urged a message to the Lords on Impositions. Hackwell stalled by saying that he had heard
that there were records during the period covered
by Wentworth and Hoskyns that were against the
House's position and asked for information. Hoskyns then moved, "no Message, till a Conference [of
the sub-committee] , and till all the Committees
have thought it fit."41 Either he or Hackwell also
moved that the Attorney, Serjeant, and Sollicitor
show the Committee "what recordes they haue seen on
the Kinges behalf, because it were a follye to proceed farther if they could showe... recordes that
the Kinges of Eng. maye lawfully ympose wthout consent of Parliament."42 The House then decided on a
meeting of the Committee Wednesday afternoon, the
18th, in Lincoln's Inn, to find out where they
stood. In that afternoon meeting, Whitelocke,
Hackwell, Jones, and Hoskyns reported their findings, "that the kinges learned Counsell concluded
an assented that the kinge coulde not ympose on
anye thinge wthin the land." Hoskyns ended the
discussion by saying "directlye that the kinge cannot ympose, that layinge ympositions is makinges
lawes in the highest degree, because they defined

446

it to be a restraynt, of thinges lawfull and nec-
essarye vppon a penaltie."[43]

The rest of the week was spent in debate on
Impositions and record searches. Hoskyns moved
that Sir Robert Phelips be the Messenger to obtain
a letter from the King to the Master of the Rolls
during the last Parliament (which was, of course,
Sir Robert's father), and also to search for a petition from the grand Jury of Herefordshire. The
House also received a letter from Sir Robert Cotton, "wherin is contayned his seruisable dutye to
the house and that he beinge sicke at Cambridge had
sent the keye of his studye to Sr Edward Mountague
and his brother to searche for suche recordes as
shoulbe for the benefit of the common wealthe,
wherto it was order Sr Roger Owen $\overline{M}^r$ Hackwell and
Mr Hoskins shoulbe assistant."[44]

Then, on Saturday, the 21st of May, a start-
ling event happened: Parliament actually passed
some Bills. The "first act that passed the lords
house was an act for the keepinge of the Saboathe,
to restrayne moris dance beare baytinge on the said
daye."[45] They also passed the Bill on Debts to the
Crown, the Bill on Wales, and a naturalization Bill
for Horace Vere's daughter. If anyone read this
flurry of activity as a sign of change in the House,
however, they were terribly mistaken. It is true
that on Monday the 23rd, they kept up their work,
passing the Bill on the "vain wasting and consuming
Gold and Silver" and sent six Bills up to the Lords.
That, however, ended the action, for the next Bill
introduced was for the naturalization of Stewart
and Ramsey, and Sir Robert Phelips asked for a Committee to "consider of some Course, that neither
these, nor any other of that Nation, that shall be
naturalized hereafter, may be of this House."[46]
The Parliament of Love of the Scottish monarch had
turned distinctly sour.

There was to be one more day of relative quiet
before Hoskyns blew the lid once again. On the
24th, they divided up the various Statutes to be
considered and agreed on the best way for all mem-

bers of the House to study them. Hoskyns was put
on two Committees for new Bills.[47] And the Sheriff
of Northumberland, Sir Ralph Selby, was brought in
for holding an election in which he asked for votes
from only those people who he knew were in favor of
Sir George Selby.[48]

The next day business came to a standstill.
Various members reported that outsiders were saying evil things about the House, and the Lords were
not meeting with them. Different courses of action
were suggested, and then Hoskyns stood up. He
"Asketh Pardon, if transported with the Zeal of the
Liberty of England." Then he made a comparison
with "That Bishop Stafford, in R. II. Time." The
object of John's attack was Bishop Neale, Bishop of
Lincoln, who had spoken out in the House of Lords
against the scandalous behaviour of the House of
Commons. Hoskyns defended the actions of Commons:
"That all Men have here spoken with a plain Declara-
tion" of their rights and freedoms. His next statement is a bit unclear in the recorder's shorthand:
"Tenants for Life, when but One Life remaining, the
Lords Means in the West to get.--That he maintained
only by the Sweat of other Mens Brows.--" But it
would appear that Hoskyns knew something of the
Bishop of Lincoln's dealings in real estate. Then
he made a direct attack on the Bishop's position,
and other Bishops as well, in words that would have
warmed John Milton's heart: "That Scotland and
Germany hath swept away greater Myters than his.
That we have maintained them.--" It could be argued that Hoskyns went too far, but tempers were
high as shown by the whole meeting that morning.
He let loose with a fine Hoskynsian rhetorical
flourish: "Knoweth nothing in him, except it be
infinite.--Admireth nothing in him, but his Ignorance." And then he made probably the best ironic
motion of the entire session of Parliament: "To
pass a Bill to seize his Bishoprick for Seven
Years, for his Majesty's Supply." After further
debate, the whole matter was referred to Committee,
including all of those who had spoken, along with a
sprinkling of members from both sides of the House.
All other Committees were put off for the afternoon,

as this matter took precedence.

The next day, 26 May, events grew worse.
Hackwell reported the findings of the Committee on
Neale: "He mayntayned that the matter of ympositions & dispute of them in the lower house was No-
li me tangere. That whosoeuer hathe taken the
oathe of alledgennce maye not dispute the kinges
prerogatiue, for it strikes at the roote & ymperi-
all Crowne. And diswaded for Conference wth the
lower house, for he affirmed that the spirites of
the lower house, woulbe vndutifull and seditious."
Those who look to a plot of Northampton or others
for the breakdown of the Parliament often fail to
note the importance of such an event as Neale's
speech. In each of the sessions of the earlier
Parliament, Hoskyns had directed the attention of
the House to statements, spoken or written, which
called into question the prerogatives and actions
of the Commons. None had been as overt or calculated as this. Northampton need not have done anything to interrupt the action of the Parliament,
for Bishop Neale had sealed the fate of any positive action with his speech. The House of Lords
was understandably caught. They could not well impeach so honored a member of their own body, and
yet there was nothing they could say in justification of his statement. They were also hoist on
their own petard of having failed to meet with the
Commons when a joint conference had been requested.

The Commons made three decisions: to find out
the truth about the statements made by Bishop Neale
from the Lords; to complain to the Lords of the
abuse and to state that they would have acted if
such a complaint had been brought against one of
their own members; and to seek redress of the King.
Meanwhile, they decided to cease discussion of any
other matters until satisfaction was obtained.[49]
While the discussion was going on, a message was
brought back from the Lords concerning the Commons'
request for a joint conference on Impositions. It
did little to calm the storm. The Lords answered,
"They will ever be willing to hold a mutual Corres-
pondency with this House; but that, having entered

into Consideration of the Cause and Circumstances thereupon, they hold it not fitting to confer with this House about it, at this Time." This answer only spurred the Commons on; Hoskyns argued, "Though we fail of Justice with the Lords, (as feareth we shall) yet thinketh fit we go to the Lords.--That the Course" of action to take. The House followed his lead and further added that they would "forbear" any further action until they received an answer from the upper Chamber.[50]

The next morning the Speaker read a letter from the King about their stopping the business of the Parliament. Hoskyns spoke up in answer that it was "fit to answer the Letter, in all Obedience; but that some, not knowing the Parliament Courses, do misinform the King. That it hath always been a Privilege to Parliament, to chuse in what Business we will proceed. That Yesterday an honourable Person" had reported the statements of Mr. Secretary about the Commons, which were apparently not to the Commons favor.[51] Mr. Alford was apparently the one who had done the reporting, and he asked not to be misinterpreted. Everyone joined in saying that the speeches had been misreported to the King, and they agreed to hold a Committee of the Whole that afternoon to discuss the matter further, and to decide on a message to the King.

The next day, 28 May, they sent Sir Edward Hoby to the Lords to find out what their answer was about a conference; he received a polite rebuff. At the afternoon Committee of the Whole, word came that the King would meet with a small group the next afternoon. The group chosen was a rather strange one, and neither Hoskyns nor most of the opposition leaders that one might expect to be included were there. Monday morning, the 30th, the House received two messages. The first was from the King, and it was quite strong. Among other things he said that "he was full of the Word "Forbearance'; could not in his Judgment, put a Difference between that, and Cessation;" but he wished the Commons to know that he was truly informed about the proper word. He admonished them "not to

be so young in our Judgments, as to do nothing."52
The second message was from the Lords, saying that
"they haue seriouslye considered the nature of the
Commons message, and doe not thinke that they ought
vppon a fame wthout anye farther proofe to punish"
Bishop Neale. At this point everyone was being
slightly less than forthright. Sir Edward Hoby reported that the previous day he had met Neale, and
the Bishop had bowed and protested that he really
didn't mean any criticism of the House. The Bishop
had protested with tears in his eyes that he did
not use the words "undutiful" and "seditious" a-
bout the Commons in particular, but that he was a-
fraid that in a joint conference someone might have
made such a speech.53 No one in the House apparently was willing to accept that explanation, and
the select Committee worked on another message to
the Lords. Meanwhile the House got back to setting up Committees again, and the time of "forbearance" was over.

On the morning of the 31st, the Committee reported their message, which was to seek satisfaction of the Lords or to have them say that the
Bishop did not say what he was reported to have
said. Meanwhile, they went back to committing new
Bills as if the Session were to last forever. Hoskyns was assigned to five Committees, for example.
The last one, which was to limit the amount of Corn
used in producing whiskey, led him to object "because of the Limitation of Thirty Barrels"; but
Brooke was for committing the Bill, and the House
agreed.54 Meanwhile the Lords agreed to a Conference on Saturday morning, 4 June; the Commons immediately returned a message that they would be
there.

On 1 June there was still the appearance of an
ongoing Parliament, with various new Bills being
announced, including at least one--committed to all
the lawyers--that had been rejected during the last
Parliament. But most of the day was spent considering what to do about Bishop Neale and the House
of Lords. The Lords had sent word that the Bishop,
once again in tears, had protested that "he ment

451

not anye thinge he saide to the p^{r}eiudice of the
house," and further "that no member of their house
ought to be called in question where there is no
cause but a common fame." Because of his submiss
behaviour, they commiserated with him and said that
if they thought he had really done wrong, they
would have proceeded against him with severity.
Once again, no one in the Lower House was ready to
accept that kind of verbal play. Sir Walter Chute
said that "He woulde giue nothinge to the kinge
vnles satisfacion were made." He also urged them
to ask the King not to dissolve Parliament "till
he know our Griefs, and we consider his Wants." So
the imminence of the end was all too apparent. In
spite of this they called a recess for the next
day, being Ascension Day, and for the afternoon set
up the same select committee, including Hoskyns and
John Donne for the third time, to consider the matter of what to do about the Bishop of Lincoln.[55]

June 3rd arrived, destined to be the most fate-
ful day in Hoskyns' life. It began ordinarily e-
nough, with an assignment of a day for the Committee on Deane and Lake. But then the Speaker read
a letter from the King. He told them to bring together their Bill on Statutes and any other Bills
they thought right and then meet him in the upper
house for the dissolution of Parliament, unless
they were ready to consider his financial relief,
for which this "Parliament was principally summoned, and that to be speedie and effectuall." Sir
George More, who may well have been the only man
caught by surprise by this move, said he was per-
plexed by the message because of the state of the
country: "His Majesty's Wants, and the Subjects
Grievances; in both which the Commonwealth inter-
essed; which the Ship, wherein we all sail, and
must live, or die." He then suggested that they
move to consider the matter of Supply immediately.
Others saw the situation in a more drastic light:
Sir Thomas Rowe remarked that this was "a Dissolution, not of this, but of all Parliaments." He
had the right sense, but the wrong Stuart. In general, however, the debate began to favor a Committee for immediate action on Supply, and Hoskyns

452

rose for his first speech of the day. He argued
once again, that "This a Parliament of Love.--All
the Arguments now used, Arguments of Fear." He
countered those who spoke of such pressing needs
by explaining "That in H. VI. Time, all the Jewels
pawned, entered upon the Parliament Roll." Again,
in "26º H. VI.--The King One Million, and some
100,000 l. in Debt." This time his fellow M.P.'s
were not willing to go along, and the general agreement was that, fear or love, they had better do
something. The decision was to hold a Committee
of the Whole in the afternoon to consider a message
to the King.56

In that afternoon session four speeches were
made that angered the King above anything that had
been said so far. Hoskyns led off. He spoke out,
as he had at the end of the last Parliament, a-
gainst the King's fellow countrymen and court favorites, the Scots. He even used the same figure of
speech he had earlier. As Aubrey reported it, he
spoke "too boldly in the Parliament-house of the
King's profuse liberality to the Scotts. He made a
Comparison of a Conduit, whereinto water came, and
ran-out afarre-off. Now, said he, this pipe reach-
es as far as Edinborough." He told the House "that
wise Prices put away straungers, as Canute when he
meant to plant himself here sent backe his Danes,
and the Palsgrave had lately dismissed all the
English that were about the Lady Elizabeth."57
Then, for reasons which no one, including Hoskyns,
could later figure out, he applied "the Sicilianae
Vesperae to the Scots who consumed both king and
kingdom in insolency and all kind of riot."58

The reference to the events in Sicily in 1282
was certainly an unfortunate one and not really
apt except in the most superficial way. Charles
of Anjou, at the urging of Pope Clement IV, had attacked Manfred, the regent of Sicily, and killed
him in 1266. This paved the way for Charles to
rule Sicily and southern Italy and to set him the
goal of ruling all of Italy as well as creating a
Mediterranean empire. His rule of Sicily was so
oppressive, however, that the people of that island

453

drove Charles out and massacred all his French followers in a blood bath that was named the "Sicilian
Vespers." Although the idea of the English mas-
sacring James' Scottish followers was almost ludi-
crous, the threat was indeed one that bordered on
treason. The knife edge of wit and irony that Hoskyns had learned to tread throughout his life was
this time, as it had been once before when he was
Terrae filius at Oxford, too sharp, and he slipped.

Wentworth, whom Anthony à Wood described as
"a silly and simple Creature," used passages from
Ezekiel and the second chapter of Daniel as a warning against "imposing kings, and witnessed in the
persons of Philip the Second king of Spain, and
Henry the Fourth the last king of France, butchered
like a calf with a knife by that base fellow Ravil-
liac." Sir Walter Chute, "a Kentish Man, who had
lately been put out of his Place of Carver to the
King."59 spoke "against building of stately houses
and the fruit of impositions going to them and not
to the king who (till they were laid down) should
not with his consent be supplied." Christopher Neville, Sir Henry's younger brother, "who was newly
come from School, and made the House sport with his
boyish Speeches, wherein were these words reiterated, O tempora! O mores."60 gave the longest and
most violent speech. He "shewed the miseries of
the times and lamented them, compared the Bills of
Grace, as they came pared to us, to 'potticaries'
boxes, shewed by the civil lawyers' definition the
difference between free and bond men, in which
state impositions had cast us." He said that "Nunc
Principes ita grassantur ut potius sit mori quam
vivere: and spared not great personages about the
court calling them arrisores et arrosores, which he
Englished spaniells to the King and wolves to the
people."61 Other speakers joined in the general
tirade, but these were the four speeches that were
remembered.

Finally the House agreed on an answer to the
King. They acknowledged "that the summoninge &
dissoluvinge of a Parliament belonged onlye to his
supreme power," and they would, of course, agree

454

to whatever the King ordered, but "the ympositions
latelye layed on goodes and merchandise in so huge
a number wch none of his most royall progenitors
haue don before him, haue bin the occassion that
they coulde not so freelye giue as they intended."
Because the King had so openly claimed the right
of imposing, "therefore before these ympositions
were layed downe if they shoulde graunt the kinge
reliefe, it might in after ages be accompted a
reall confirmation of the kinges absolute power of
ymposinge." They also brought up the Lords' refusal to join in conference with them, "contrarye
to the manner and custume of all ages." They concluded, "Till therfore it shall please God to ease
vs of these ympositions wherwth the whole kingdome
dothe grone, we cannot wthout wronge to the Coun-
trye giue y^r Matie that releif wch we desire."
They still held out the offer that if the King
would listen to their complaints, they would grant
him a Subsidy--if they were given enough time.⁶²

On Monday, 6 June, while some of the Lords sat
in their robes the entire day, expecting the dissolution of Parliament, the King sent a message to
the Commons that he "did not meane to p^rscribe anye
thinge to the house," but that he had given a commission to certain lords to dissolve the Parliament
as it had done nothing for two months; however, he
was willing to put it off until the next day.
There was a flurry of activity for some compromise,
Sandys and others attempting a letter in "milder
and sweeter terms." But Serjeant Mountague still
stated that he and the "kinges learned counsell"
ruled that the King could not impose. The members
had also heard of possible actions by the Privy
Council against specific members of the House, and
they "put to the question whether anye member of
the house had spoken vnbeseeminge & scandalous
speaches wch was occassioned in regard there was a
rumor abroad that some would be troubled after the
Parliament for somwhat they had spoken." The
Speaker asked anyone who could make such a charge
to make it immediately or "euer herafter holde his
peace; wheruppon Sr Henrye Wootton desire Mr Hoskins to explaine himselfe what he ment by the

Sicilian Vespers. his answere I coulde not well heare but he was cleared by the question."63 The most charitable way of looking at the incident is that Wotton was giving his long-time friend a chance to clear himself before the King acted. All of the discussion was really to no avail, however, as the House was not about to give the King a Subsidy without some guarantee on Impositions, and the King was not going to give up what he considered his royal prerogative. Dissolution was put off until the next day, however, with the intent of allowing Sir Edwyn Sandys time to polish his proposal. The next morning that proposal was read, but the debate that followed indicated a distinct lack of trust in the King's word. Hoskyns had not had his final say either. But he only wanted to repeat a proposal he had made earlier:

> 1 Hen 6 2 Hen 6 Ed 4 there haue bin subsidies graunted wth limitations and prouisions to be employed in certayne vses o[r] els to be returned to the subiectes of those dayes, aledginge there was a bushopp of Worcester Collecter therof; wheruppon moued to giue 1 or 2 Subsedies, wth this prouision that if the ympositions be not layed downe betwixt this and October, the monye gathered to returne againe to the subiect.64

It was apparent, however, that the King would never agree to such an ultimatum, and at three o'clock that afternoon Parliament was finally dissolved.

Northampton was triumphant at the dissolution and rode in state from Greenwich to London "coached only with Sir Charles Cornwallis." The joy of this pair was to be extremely shortlived.

The King was not through with the opposition, and the rumors of his intense displeasure were only too accurate. On 7 June, even before Parliament was dissolved, the Privy Council issued warrants for the arrest of Sir John Savile, Thomas Wentworth, Christopher Neville, and Sir Walter Chute. There was a "Like Warrant unto William Beaufou, messenger,

456

to bring John Hoskins, esquier before their lordships."[65] The records show that Wentworth, Savile, and Neville showed up, but there is no entry about Hoskyns. The next day he did appear, however, along with all of those who had gained the King's displeasure. The fullest record of the events of 8 June 1614 are in Whitelocke's Liber Famelicus:[66]

On Wednesday following, in the morning, mr. Thomas Crew, and others, that wear assigned by the House of Commons to be agents in the conference desired by the Commons withe the Lords, concerning IMPOSITIONS, wear called to the counsell table to Whitehalle, whear having everye on delivered what part he was assigned unto, we wear all commanded to burn our notes, arguments, and collections we had made for the preparing of ourselves to the conference. I broughte myne to the Clerk of the counsell, mr. Cottington, the same afternoone, being 24 sides in folio, written withe my owne hand, and saw them burnt... after we had been withe the lords, thear wear sent to the Tower four parliament men; sir Walter Chute, mr. Christopher Nevill, yonger sun to the lord Abergavenye, mr. Wentworthe, and mr. Hoskins.

If the Parliament had sometimes acted childishly in the previous two months, it was now King James' turn. First he personally tore up all of the Bills passed Parliament. Then, "All the while the lords sate, the king was in the clerk of counsell's chamber. I saw him look throughe an open place in the hangins, about the bignes of the palm of one hand, all the while the lords wear in withe us."

After the burning of the papers, which really accomplished nothing but to make the work of future Parliaments more time-consuming in recollecting the precedents,

We wear all sent out of the chamber, and then mr. Wentworthe and mr. Hoskins wear sent for back againe into the chamber, and after sum speeche unto them by the lords, they wear sent

457

to the Tower. Sir John Savill knighte for Yorkshire, and sir Edwyn Sandys, wear called before
the lords and dismissed upon bondes, so was sir
Edward Gyles, of Devonshire, and divers others,
as sir Roger Owen.[67]

In the Acts of the Privy Council for 8 June 1614 is
the letter to Sir Gervase Helwys, Lieutenant of the
Tower, for the safe keeping in the Tower, as close
prisoners, of Chute, Neville, and Wentworth. There
is another letter for the committing of Hoskyns.
Savile, Owen, and Giles were ordered not to leave
town.[68]

Before the end of the day, Wotton was writing
the first of several letters to Sir Edmund Bacon
dealing with the events.

It pleased his Majesty, the very next morning,
to call to examination before the Lords of his
Council, divers members of the House of Commons,
for some speeches better becoming a Senate of
Venice, where the treaters are perpetual princes,
than where those that speak so irreverently are
so soon to return (which they should remember)
to the natural capacity of subjects.

After naming the four who were made close prisoners
in the Tower, Wotton goes on to say of Hoskyns,
that he

is in for more wit, and for licentiousness bap-
tized freedom. For I have noted in our House,
that a false or faint patriot did cover himself
with the shadow of equal moderation, and on the
other side, irreverent discourse was called honest liberty; so as upon the whole matter, 'no
excesses want precious names.'[69]

At no point does Wotton mention his own involvement in the debates and countercharges of the last
few days of the Parliament.

On the 9th, Chamberlain wrote his summary of
the events to Carleton, adding the information

458

which the official records bear out, that "Presently upon the dissolution pursuivants were redy to
warne divers to be the next day at the counsaile
table."[70] On the 12th, Sir John Throckmorton wrote
to William Trumbull, mentioning the suspicion of a
plot:

> The king on Tuesday morning last dissolved the
> parliament with no small discontentment on all
> sides. On Thursday he sent 5 of the burgesses
> of the Lower House to the Tower. I pray God
> hold his hand for our home affairs are in no
> small danger. Through the whole realms nothing
> but discontentment. This is the fruits of the
> seed from Spain long since sowed among us.

He ends with the hope, "All is out of frame. God
put it in again."[71] What Throckmorton had not
heard was that the Privy Council had examined Hoskyns again. He was asked "whether he well understood the consequence of that Vesper to which he
alluded. Whereupon making answer that he had a
hint thereof, and afterwards a general information,
from Dr. Lionel Sharp of Cambridge."[72] Dr. Sharp
then implicated Sir Charles Cornwallys, and on 13
June, both Dr. Sharp and Cornwallys were ordered to
close imprisonment in the Tower.[73]

The most important figure in the affair was,
of course, the Earl of Northampton, but he was soon
freed from any further worry. On the 15th he died,
following an operation on the 9th. If the Earl did
have a direct role in any plot, Sir Charles Cornwallys kept it a secret, much to his credit. The
next day, letters left London en masse. Wotton
wrote to Sir Edmund Bacon,

> The Earl of Northampton having, after a lin-
> gering fever, spent more spirits than a younger
> body could well have borne, by the incision of
> a wennish tumour grown on his thigh, yesternight
> between eleven and twelve of the clock departed
> out of this world... there went a general voice
> through the Court on Sunday last, upon the com-
> mitment of Dr. Sharp and Sir Charles Cornwallis

459

to the Tower, that he was somewhat implicated in
that business... John Hoskins (of whose imprisonment I wrote unto you by the last carrier) having at a re-examination been questioned, whether
he well understood the consequence of that Sicilian Vesper, whereunto he had made some desperate allusion in the House of Parliament, made
answer (and I think very truly) that he had no
more than a general information thereof, being
but little conversant in those histories that
lay out of the way of his profession. Whereupon, being pressed to discover whence he then
had received this information, since it lay not
within his own reading, he confessed to have had
it from Dr. Sharp, who had infused these things
into him, and had solicited him to impress them
in the Parliament; and further, that Hoskins
hereupon demanding what protection he might hope
for, if afterwards he were called into question,
the said Doctor should nominate unto him, besides others (whose names I will spare), that
Earl, who hath now made an end of all his reck-
onings; assuring him of his assistance by the
means of Sir Charles Cornwallis, with whom the
Doctor was conjoined in this practice. Thus
came Sir Charles into discovery; who being afterward confronted with the Doctor himself,
though he could not (as they say) justify his
own person, yet did he clear my Lord of Northampton from any manner of understanding with him
therein upon his salvation; which yet is not
enough (as I perceive among the people) to sweep
the dust from his grave....[74]

The same day Secretary Winwood wrote two letters; one was to William Trumbull. After discussing the end of the Parliament and the imprisonment of the first four, he said that "Sir Charles
Cornwallish and one Dr. Lionel Sharpe, a minister,
are sent to the Tower, both for animating others to
be sticklers in this business, Sharpe being the man
that furnished Hoskins with the Sicilian vespers
...."[75] His second letter went to Sir Dudley
Carleton, in which he claimed that

460

Yt [the Parliament] was the fyrst I ever did
see, and yf the kyngs service did not requyre
my personal attendance I wyshe yt might be the
last. for I confess I did never see in my experience eyther at home or abroad so much faction or passion, so little reverence to the Maty
of a king, or so little respect of the publick
good or welfare of the kyngdome.

As in his first letter, he then recounted the e-
vents leading to the dissolution.[76]

Then, on 22 June, Cornwallys submitted his
statement of what had happened to King James.[77]
First he explained how he had missed gaining a
seat in Parliament although offered three. He had
placed two men recommended to him by Dr. Sharp,
who had shown him letters of recommendation from
the Earl of Northampton. Then he had given notes
for a speech that he had intended to deliver in
Parliament to Mr. Hitchcock, also recommended by
Dr. Sharp, "one of the gentlemen for whom I obtained by my Lord of Northampton's meanes, a Burge-
shippe to be a fitt man for the delivery of it to
the howse by way of motion." He then recounts his
speech, which urged the House to get down to business and give the King all he needs, but also requested that his Majesty "take into consideration
somethinges of great consequence and of most contentment to his subjects." First, he urged the
stopping of any increase of Catholics into England
and further discussion of a proposed marriage of
Prince Charles with a Catholic princess. Second,
that he appoint more Englishmen to his chamber:
"wee are to beseech his Majestie to be gratiouslie
pleased to stoppe the current of the future com-
mers of the Scottish nation to reside within this
kingdome, other then such as shall be necessary for
his especiall service...." This, he claims, is all
he intended to say.

This beinge communicated to Doctor Sharpe, and
Mr. Hytchcocke failinge to performe the motion,
it seemes that he gott by some meanes corres-
pondencie with Mr. Hoskins who made as I have

461

heard a speech in parliament concerninge the
Scotts, but such as neither agreed with mine in
fourme or matter.

Yet is the Doctor content (out of his owne
apprehensions) soe farre to forgett himselfe as
to affirme that I should promise in regard of
Mr. Hoskins losse of his practise in the terms
to give him xx li. which I protest unto your
Majestie before almightie god I never did nor
intended. He moved mee I confesse and per-
swuaded with examples of others that he said
would give, but did neither name nor in anie
such sort point at anie, as either in honestie
or christianitie I can justlie name anie one
without perill to charge an innocent, which I
know your owne royall and pious hart would
rather condemne then allow in mee.

If anyone thought that the King was merely
making a gesture and would soon release the prisoners, he was sadly mistaken. On 24 June Wotton
wrote to Bacon, "Chute, Hoskins, Sharp, and Sir
Charles Cornwallis are still in the Tower, and I
like not the complexion of the place."78 Neither
did John; Aubrey recounts of the early part of his
imprisonment, "he was kept a close prisoner there,
i.e. his windowes were boarded up. Through a small
chinke he saw once a crowe, and another time, a
Kite; the sight whereof, he sayd, was a great
pleasure to him." By the end of the month, Chamberlain was able to send to Carleton all of the
news, rumor, and report about the month's activities:

...I gave you notice of the dissolving of the
parlement, and what succeeded for a day or two
after. Since which time divers have been called
coram for their cariage and speaches in that
house, and driven to explane themselves, among
whom Sir Edwin Sandes so demeaned himself that
he was dismissed without taint or touch, though
upon examination yt fell out there was a plot
discovered to overthrow all orderly procedings
in this parlement, and to make yt utterly voyde,
by insisting upon daungerous points as taking

462

away impositions, restoring of silenced ministers, and removing the Scotts, with other matters likelie to make the King loose all patience, and for this purpose Hoskins was em-
boucht, abetted, and indeed plainly hired with
monie to do that he did, and some other drawn
on by other meanes: for which practises... litle
Dr. Sharpe, and Sir Charles Cornwallis (though
none of them were of the house) were committed
to the Towre and there remain... Christofer Ne-
vile upon submission found some favor and is
removed to the Fleet, and Wentworth (because
his offence is found to be rather of simplici-
tie then malice) had leave this Whitsontide to
go home to his wife for five or sixe dayes, but
is now returned to the Towre, where he hath the
libertie of the place, and stayes more to satisfie the French ambassador then any thinge els.
The Master of the Rolles [Sir Edward Phelips]
that was in great favor with the King hath lost
his conceit about this busines, for there be
many presumptions that his hand was in yt, his
sonne beeing so busie and factious in the house,
and Hoskins one of his cheife consorts and min-
ions so far engaged, besides divers untoward
speaches of his owne, and a notorious envie that
any thing should succeed better under another
speaker then himself.[79]

     We will never know the actual truth of the
matter. Even if Hoskyns' autobiography were to be
discovered among some unsorted 17th century manuscripts, it is not likely that we would know much
more. The autobiography was written after 1623,
when John was once again in the King's good graces,
and memory would certainly have played its usual
tricks in explaining earlier events. At the time,
however, Hoskyns was just as willing to see his
situation as the result of his wit as Wotton did.
And that is certainly what the events of his earlier life would bear out. It is unfortunate that
in the process he became entangled in the plots of
the Northampton circle.

Footnotes for Chapter XIII

1. Edmund Gosse, The Life and Letters of John Donne (1899), II, 34.
2. Mitchell, The Rise of the Revolutionary Party, p. 40. The Brook referred to is Giles Brook of Liverpool. If, as seems likely, the Martin mentioned is Dick Martin, all that the money achieved was to keep him from serving in Parliament.
3. Ibid., pp. 54, 60.
4. C.J. I, 456-57.
5. Mitchell, p. 57.
6. C.J. I, 457.
7. C.J. I, 463.
8. Liber Famelicus of Sir James Whitelocke, ed. John Bruce, Camden Soc. 70 (1858), p. 40.
9. C.J. I, 458-59.
10. C.J. I, 460.
11. C.J. I, 461.
12. C.J. I, 462.
13. C.J. I, 463.
14. C.J. I, 464.
15. C.J. I, 465.
16. "An Act for Relief of the King's Tenants, in case of Forfeiture for Non-payment of Rent" (p. 465); "An Act against false Bail, commonly called Knights of the Post." (p. 466) Sir George More had argued that the Penalty was too great, but Hoskyns answered, "(for Blood,) Save a Soul, and lose a Body.--Wisheth the Jurisdiction of that Court wherein the Offence commited, may not be excluded."
17. C.J. I, 467.
18. C.J. I, 468.
19. C.J. I, 469-70.
20. Hoskyns was on one "for the better avoiding of Charge and Trouble of his Majesty's Subjects, upon Respite of Homage."
21. C.J. I, 470.
22. C.J. I, 471.
23. Hoskyns was assigned to a Bill "concerning Assignment of Debts to the Crown." (pp. 471-72)
24. Add. MSS. 48101, ff. 99v-100.
25. "An Act against the vain and wasteful Consump-

tion of Gold and Silver, in gilding or silver-
ing within this Kingdom," and "An Act concerning Apparel." Both were introduced 13 Apr., by
Brooke. Hackwell spoke against the Gilding
Bill, but Hoskyns urged "That the other Bill
be read, and Committed." C.J. I, 472.
26. C.J. I, 473; Add. MSS. 48101, f. 101.
27. C.J. I, 474.
28. Add. MSS. 48101, f. 101v.
29. Hoskyns was also assigned to a Bill "for admitting the King's Subjects to plead the general
Issue, and nevertheless to continue their Possession," which Whitelocke argued concerned all
of the freeholders of England. (p. 475) There
were complaints about the noise in the Parliament chamber (which led to the bad writing up
of Bills), and Lionel Cranfield apparently felt
under attack on a Bill concerning the Accounts
of Sheriffs as a former Receiver for eight
years; he offered "to bring in his Patent To-
morrow Morning; and, if it shall be found
either prejudical to King, or Subject, will
yield it be cancelled here, and he to be punished."
30. C.J. I, 476.
31. Hoskyns was once again assigned to a Bill "for
Confirmation of a Decree in Chancery" for Mr.
Jernegan.
32. Add. MSS. 48101, f. 102.
33. C.J. I, 478.
34. C.J. I, 481; Add MSS. 48101, f. 103v.
35. Whitelocke, pp. 41-2; Add MSS. 48101, ff. 104-
104v; C.J. I, 481.
36. C.J. I, 482. At the end of the next day he
moved "for a Letter from Mr. Speaker, to one
that hath special Records [undoubtedly Robert
Cotton] that the House may have the Use of
them." Both motions passed. p. 483.
37. Add. MSS. 48101, f. 105v; C.J. I, 483.
38. C.J. I, 484.
39. C.J. I, 487-89; Add. MSS. 48101, f. 106.
40. "An Act to confirm and enable the Erection and
Establishment of an Alms-house, a free Grammar-
school, and a Preacher, intended to be done and
performed by the Master and Four Wardens of the

Fraternity of the Art or Mistery of Haberdashers, within the City of London, at the only Costs and Charges of Wm. Jones, Merchant, a Member of the said Fraternity, and now resident at Hamboroughe, in the Parts beyond the Seas" (p. 486); "some fit Provision for Assise by Bakers, and for Measures." This was probably a result of a proposal by Hoskyns found in the Scudamore papers for the relief of the poor, "to avoid excessive charge for entertainment of high sheriffs at time of Assizes" (Add. MSS. 11,053, ff. 144, 146-47.); a Bill for Highways and Bridges (p. 487); "for Confirmation of a Decree in Chancery between Lake and Deane" (p. 488); "for pulling down, and against the Erection of, Weares; and for the Preservation of the Fry of Salmon, and other Fish" (p. 492).

41. C.J. I, 486.
42. Add. MSS. 48101, f 105v.
43. Ibid., f. 107.
44. Ibid., f. 107v; C.J. I, 491.
45. Add. MSS. 48101, f. 108v.
46. C.J. I, 493. Hoskyns was also one of many Parliament party men assigned to a Bill on Baronets which the royal party rightly said was within the King's prerogative (p. 494).
47. "An Act for Repeal of a politique Constitution, 5° Eliz. for packing of Fish" (p. 495) and "An Act for Limitation of Actions, and avoiding of Suits." (p. 496)
48. C.J. I, 495; Add. MSS. 48101, f. 109v.
49. C.J. I, 498; Add. MSS. 48101, f. 110.
50. C.J. I, 498-99; Add. MSS. 48101, f. 110v.
51. C.J. I, 500.
52. C.J. I, 501.
53. Add. MSS. 48101, f. 111v.
54. "An Act for Knights and Burgesses to have Places in Parliament, for the County Palatyne, City of Durham, and Borough or Town of Bernerdscastle, alias, Castle-bernerd"; "An Act against the Oath ex officio"; "An Act for Restitution of Possession, to be granted in certain Cases, upon Entries with Force, or holding with Force"; "An Act to restrain common Brewers, or Tiplers, to be Justices of Peace in any County,

City, Borough, or Town-corporate, within this
Realm" (Hoskyns was for committing it); and
"An Act for repressing the odious and loath-
some Sin of Drunkenness, and for preventing of
the inordinate consuming of Corn." C.J. I, 502-
3.

55. C.J. I, 504-5; Add. MSS. 48101, ff. 113-114.
56. C.J. I, 505-6; Add. MSS. 48101, f. 115.
57. Chamberlain to Carleton, Letters of John Chamberlain, I, 538.
58. H.M.C., Duke of Portland, Vol. IX (1923), p.
138; State Papers Venice 99/16. (P.R.O.) Unless
otherwise noted, the descriptions of the end of
Parliament are from Portland.
59. Athenae Oxoniensis (1721), col. 614.
60. Wood, col. 614.
61. Chamberlain, I, 537-38.
62. Add. MSS. 48101, f. 115.
63. Ibid., f. 116.
64. Ibid., f. 118v.
65. Acts of the Privy Council 1613-1614 (1921), p.
456.
66. The account of these days is on pp. 39-43.
Whitelocke had himself been sent to the Fleet
from 18 May until 13 June 1613 for his stand
against Impositions. Williams Mitchell, p. 62,
incorrectly includes Whitelocke among those
sent to the Tower in 1614.
67. Sandys was questioned "for his speech of elective and successive kings, and his rehearsing
two verses in Juvenal Ad generum Cereris sine
caede etc.,; and Sir John Savile for alleging
he had warning from some of his neighbours not
to give anything that should confirm the impositions."
68. A.P.C. 1613-1614, pp. 459-60. Sir John Hollis
notes a report that all of those whose notes
were burned were ordered to stay in the city.
HMC Portland, IX, p. 138.
69. Logan Pearsall Smith, The Life and Letters of
Sir Henry Wotton (1907), II, 36-7.
70. Chamberlain, I, 539.
71. HMC, Downshire, Vol. 4 (1940), pp. 425-26.
72. Wood, col. 614.
73. A.P.C. 1613-1614, pp. 465-66.

74. Wotton, II, 38-9.
75. HMC, Downshire, IV, 427-28.
76. S. P. Venice 99/16; S.P.D. James 1611-1618, LXXVII, 237.
77. Copies of Cornwallys' statement are in the 15th Report, Part II (1897) of the Historical Manuscripts Commission, pp. 36-40; P.R.O., S.P.D., James I, 77/42; Ms. Harl. 1221, ff. 96-99v and Harley 6038, f. 35 ff. Osborn quotes part of the statement, p. 38.
78. Wotton, II, 41.
79. Chamberlain, I, 540.

Chapter XIV

Life in the Tower

Hoskyns was in his forty-ninth year when the
King put him in prison, and it could not have happened at a worse time. John was on the verge of
establishing himself securely both in his law business and in his real estate ventures. His wife
was pregnant, carrying their second child; and his
younger brother, Dr. John, was no longer around the
house in Hereford to help out. Moreover, for an
active man who loved the countryside, close imprisonment in the Tower of London was a terrible blow.
John appears to have taken it rather philosophic-
ally, however, and in the best religious spirit.
He wrote a Latin distich on the window pane of his
cell, explaining the meaning of his imprisonment,
soon after being pent up:[1] "Thus I pay and so I
have deserved; but the punishment which I have deserved and the sins for which I pay, thou hast
washed away with thy merits, O Christ." In spite
of his situation, John was still able to turn out
as tight and witty a piece of Latin verse as he
had ever made. That he apparently scratched it
into the window with a diamond ring only adds the
right prisoner's touch.

At about the same time he wrote another distich, addressed to his six-year-old son Benedict.
He wrote it first in Latin and then furnished a
translation quatrain:

> Sweet Benedict whilst thou art young,
> And know'st not yet the vse of Toung,
> Keepe it in thral whilst thou art free:
> Imprison it or it will thee.[2]

His wife was certainly not making his imprisonment any easier for him. From 18 July through 15
August she sent him four letters[3] which, because of
his close imprisonment, he was not apparently able
to answer. But he did manage to send tokens of
his affection, probably the two rings that he al-

469

ways wore. The beautiful, clear printing of these
letters reveal something of the strength of character of the woman John had chosen as a wife.

good sir. I with my family doe continue our
prayers to god for the kings ma^{tie} and his most
honourable counsayle, I am persw^{a}ded that if I
were there I would so petitio^{n} to his maiestie
that I should sure obtay^{n} your liberty which I
doe more desire than any treasure this world can
afforde concerni^{n}ge your priuate affaires they
are all in good order as for settinge of tytley
I will referre that vntill your cominge home
which I hope will be shortly; your little sonne
is a great scholler and remembers his humble
duty vnto you: Julie this xviiith

                        your Ben
To Mr John Hoskins   Hoskynes
at the Tower
  give these

                * * * *

I pray you good Ma^{r} hoskynes come home: and commaund to do w^{h}at you plase: and I will obaye: I
rely one none in this world: it tis a bad husband that a wife and child ⟨ ⟩not miss: if I
shall be harte by none but such as ⟨ ⟩flater mee:
the dangear is not nere: for I am not com ⟨ ⟩
fayer wordes and kinde vsages where I haue de-
se^{r}ued⟨ ⟩and as for that Judgment and beauty
w^{h}ich you out of your loue thought I had had:
is now with age and siecnes decaed and cone: it
thinke the bearing of children the breding them
vp: the extrame griue I haue sufferred for your
misserye dese^{r}ues love: and this I will swere:
if I dye befoare I see you agane: I loue you
truly and no other in the worled; so well... I
receued to toknes ffrom you for w^{h}ich I thanke
you. and I haue sent you my wedding ring by M^{r}
gyellem: for a token... I know ther ar worse
husbands then you: and better wyffes then I: it
I se no cause but wee to may liue contentedly
to gether: if wee pray to god to bless our
loues: without the which blessinge: all our loue

470

is nothing and so I end: showing you by this
letter as litil wit as your plesuer is I sholld.

* * * *

deare hart I beg for gods sake: let peticion bee
made vnto his maiesty and the priuy counsayle
for your deliuerance, that euen as god of his
mercy hath miraculously delyuered the king out
of the traiterous hand of gowry and his bloudy
confederates, and from the damnable powder tre-
son: so hee in imitation of this diuine quality
of mercy would be so princely compassionate as
to grant your liberty to mee... therefore good
sweet hart if you loue mee use all possible
meanes to procure your enlargement: if you meane
to see mee aliue, for I growe weake and heauy
and therefore vnfit to trauell, or els all the
perswasions which you or any other could vse
should not keepe me from you so long....

* * * *

...surely there is great mercy in ye kinge and
we are now subiect to great misery and therefore we are fitt matter for mercy to worke vppon; when please ye Lord and him: we must expect still y^{ur} deliverance and pray for more
patience for we have spent a greate dele I beseech god give y^u comfort and all ye meanes y^u
shall vse to com vnto vs good successe.

Aug 15 1614
Your Ben
Hoskynes

It must have been difficult for John to convince
his wife, five months into her pregnancy, that
there was really nothing he could do to hasten his
own release. It is a sign of the strength of his
convictions that during this period he did not attempt to move the king by any false supplication.

The truth of the matter is that imprisonment
in the Tower was not without its blessings to a man
of as inquisitive and literary a nature as Hoskyns.
The select company occupying the Tower of London at

471

the time made it one of the intellectual centers
of England. Aubrey lists as one of his acquaintances "Sir Walter Raleigh (who was his Fellow-pris-
oner in the Tower, where he was Sir Walter's
Aristarchus to review and polish Sir Walter's
stile)." Aubrey apparently also wrote to Anthony
Wood that Hoskyns was "A great man wth Sr Walter
Raleigh while he was in ye Tower who committed
seuerall of his writings to his view."[4] Aristarchus was the great critic of the second century
B.C. from Samothrace who made his reputation in
Alexandria for his severe criticism. His most important work was his great edition of Homer. As
Ralegh's History of the World appeared in 1614, it
has usually been taken for granted that Hoskyns'
work for Ralegh involved lengthy criticism of that
great work, but Aubrey is not so specific, and it
could have been other writings, prose and poetry,
which Ralegh gave to John for criticism. Certainly other men were involved in the writing of The
History of the World. Ben Jonson always claimed
that the "best wits in England were employed in
making his [Ralegh's] History." He said that he
himself had written the section on the Punic War,
which Ralegh then altered and put into his book.
Anthony Wood credited Ralegh's chaplain, Dr. Robert
Burrel, Rector of Northwold, Norfolk, with doing
most of the drudgery for the book and "for Criti-
cising Chronology & reading of greek & hebrew
authors."[5]

Ralegh and Hoskyns were, of course, old acquaintances, and their friendship extended at least
as far back as their humorous interchange in the
Prince d'Amour, during the Christmas season of
1597. Sir Walter's troubles with King James went
back a long way. Aubrey described the situation:

...at a consultation at Whitehall after Queen
Elizabeth's death, how matters were to be ordered and what ought to be donne, Sir Walter
Raleigh declared his opinion, 'twas the wisest
way for them to keepe the Government in their
owne hands and sett up a Commonwealth, and not
to be subject to a needy, beggarly nation. It

472

seems there were some of this caball who kept
this not so secret but that it came to King
James' eare, who, where the English Noblesse
mett and received him, being told upon present-
ment to his Majesty their names, when Sir Walter Raleigh's name was told (Ralegh) said the
King, O my soule, mon, I have heard rawly of
thee.

It was a most stately sight, the glory of that
Reception of his Majesty...the Company was so
exceeding numberous that their obedience carried
a secret dread with it. King James did not in-
wardly like it, and... sayd that he doubted not
but that he should have been able on his owne
strength (should the English have kept him out)
to have dealt with them... Sayd Sir Walter Raleigh to him, Would to God that had been putt to
the tryall: Why doe you wish that sayd the King.
Because, sayd Sir Walter; that then you would
have known your friends from your foes. But
that reason of Sir Walter was never forgotten
nor forgiven.[6]

The immediate reason for Ralegh's long imprisonment
in the Tower, however, was his suspected
part in the plot to supplant James with Arabella
Stuart, who was next in line to the throne after
James at the time of his succession, but had the
advantage of being English. She had married William Seymour (who was descended from Catherine
Grey) against the demands of the Privy Council and
thus could claim a double line to the throne. She
tried to escape from England in March 1611 (Seymour succeeded) but was caught and imprisoned. She
died in September 1615. Sir Walter had been in the
Tower since 1603, living with his wife and son,
and would not be released for another two years to
go searching once again for gold, only to return
to yet another trial and his death in 1618. Aubrey's report on his attitude towards the Scots
would indicate that Hoskyns' reason for being put
in the Tower would only endear him to Ralegh the
more.

In 1606, Ralegh had been joined by another

473

man held in great suspicion by King James: Henry
Percy, the ninth Earl of Northumberland. As we
have seen, Percy had been named as a possible par-
ticipant in the Gunpowder Plot, and, although the
charges were almost certainly false, he spent the
next fifteen years in the Tower. Like Ralegh, he
had relative freedom in the Tower and simply set
up his own establishment there, with easy access to
friends on the outside. Aubrey continues his account of Ralegh's stay in the Tower, "He there (besides compiling his History of the World) studied
Chymistry. The Earle of Northumberland was prisoner at the same time, who was Patrone to Mr. Harriot
and Mr. Warner, two of the best Mathematicians in
the world, as also Mr. Hues, who wrote De Globis."[7]
Northumberland was the patron of most of the
scientists and many of the men of letters of the
day. Hariot was the principal correspondent in
England with Kepler in the early 17th century, and
Professor Bald has suggested that it was through
Hariot that John Donne received much of the knowledge of Kepler's astronomy which is apparent in
Conclave Ignati (1611)[8] Hariot had earlier traveled
with Ralegh to Virginia; then,

> When the Earle of Northumberland and Sir Wal-
> ter Ralegh were both Prisoners in the Tower,
> they grew acquainted, and Sir Walter Raleigh
> recommended Mr. Hariot to him, and the Earle
> setled an Annuity of two hundred pounds a yeare
> on him for his life, which he enjoyed... [he had
> already given Hues and Warner sixty pounds a
> year earlier] They had a Table at the Earle's
> chardge, and the Earle himselfe had them to con-
> verse with him, singly or together... [Hariot]
> made a Philosophical Theologie, wherin he cast-
> off the Old Testament, and the New-one would
> (consequently) have no Foundation. He was a
> Deist....[9]

This scientific community helps to explain why Hoskyns was to inscribe on the outside wall of his
house at Morehampton some years later a Latin poem
which is one of the most outspoken early accept-
ances of the Copernican theory in England:

Stat coelum, fateor, Copernice; terra movetur;
Et mutant dominos tecta rotata suos.[10]

It would be hard to be more explicit about the
"New Philosophy": "I admit, O Copernicus, the heaven stands still; the earth is moved." The rotating
houses, or signs of the zodiac in the heavenly constellations, change their lords or, in John Donne's
language, the intelligences of their spheres. Although the verses were not put up at Morehampton
until 1623, it is clear that Hoskyns came to this
intellectual position during his year in the Tower,
and his verses are far more open in their acceptance of the new astronomy than anything his friends,
like Donne, were willing to express.

It was also at this time that Hoskyns made the
acquaintance of the other leading mathematician of
the time:

> Mr. Nicholas Hill was one of the most learned
> men of his Time: a great Mathematician and
> Philosopher, and a Poet and Traveller. But no
> writer (that I ever heard of) or, if he was,
> his writings had the usuall fate of those not
> printed in the Author's life-time. He was (or
> leaning) a Roman Catholiq... Old Sergeant Hoskins the Poet (grandfather to this Sir John Hoskins, Baronet, my honoured friend) was well acquainted with Mr. Nicholas Hill....[11]

Hill was a Londoner who studied Chemistry after
graduating from St. John's, Oxford. "...he liv'd
wth ye E. of Northumberland in ye Tower ⟨ was his
Steward...."[12]

Meanwhile, as the summer wore on, the wits about town had not forgotten the men in the Tower.
On 17 August 1614, Charles Glenham wrote to the
Count of Arundell, in Genoa:

> Sir Charles Cornewallise is still in the tower
> for being thoughte to have made the laste
> speeche hoskins spake in the parlamente house
> againste the Scottes. It is sayed hee confes-

475

sethe to have made parte, but not all, it is
thoughte some great ones had a parte with him,
yet will hee confesse none, but takes all to him
selfe w^h hathe as it is written to mee gotten
him much love for his magnanimity....[13]

At some time during the late summer or early autumn
a short poem circulated through the town wittily
discussing the fate of the prisoners:

> The Court's full of newes,
> London's full of rumo^rs;
> Fower men in the tower
> Of eight severall humou^rs.
> Sharpe the divine is soberly mad
> Hoskins the lawyer is merrily sad
> Cornewallis ye Ledg^r is carelessly p^rcise,
> And Chute the Carv^r is foolishlie Wise.[14]

At about the same time, certainly before October, when Sir Walter Chute was released from the
Tower, Hoskyns also wrote a Latin poem of 18 lines
to his fellow prisoners: "Ad chutum & sharpum."[15]
As in the earlier two short poems, Hoskyns shows
complete control of his verse and lets us in on the
world of seventeenth century wits and poets better
than many of his other poems do. Locked in the
Tower, these men still set up a community of poesy.
They might be "unhappy companions" of a "common
sorrow," but they are writing poems to each other
and calling for poems in answer. John immediately
goes to a classical source and explains that the
Pegasian muses as well as the wrathful Castalian
muses could not endure prison or the houses of
slaves. There is the touch of the Hereford farmer
in the statement that hills and forests and fields
watered by the Tyrrhenian waters produce songs.
And he caps the thought with the wonderful line
that "Songs are the work of the tranquil mind."
Their life in prison is all too evident, with the
ever-present guards and brazen tower; and there is
the open awareness of their guilt: "the just wrath
of Caesar." A prose work would be more fitting
than poetry, or a "sad voice kept in time with no
lyre." But he is willing to fulfill their request,

"your better feeling," with bound hands, as he re-
collects their crimes. Words held in control by
meter please him, for uncontrolled words have made
their own feet captive. One of the most pleasing
aspects of the relationship of Hoskyns and Lionel
Sharp is that instead of feeling that each had in
some way used or betrayed the other, a real friendship that lasted through the years grew out of
their common trouble. One cannot help feeling that
Hoskyns, in spite of his obvious discomfort and the
dangers to his financial and vocational future,
enjoyed the chance for quiet and solitude which
allowed him to get back to his old love of writing
Latin verse and enjoying the leisurely conversation
of intellectual company.

The outside world continued to intrude, however. On 8 September 1614 a letter was sent from
the Privy Council to Sir Gervase Helwys,

Wheras humble suite is made unto us by John
Hoskins and Oswald Hoskins, brothers unto John
Hoskins, now prisoner in the Tower, that for the
better settling and managing of the estate of
the sayd prisoner, and also to treate with him
of such busynes as may concerne his wife, children and familye, accesse might be gyven them
unto the sayd prisoner: we... hereby require you
to gyve leave unto the sayd John and Oswald Hoskins to repaire unto him... at fytt and convenyent tymes, so that it be in your presence, or
in the presence or hearing of such as you shall
appoint.[16]

The King was beginning to relent a little. On 12
October, Chamberlain wrote to Isaac Wake, telling
him of the news of the death of Hoskyns' close
friend, Sir Edward Phelips, "whose heart was so
great that he could not indure some discountenance
and disgraces lately laide upon him." Chamberlain
goes on,

On Friday Sir Charles Conwallis is expected in
the Star-chamber; Sir Walter Chute was released
last weeke with these conditions to loose his

477

place about the King, to pay his owne charges
that come to better than 110^{li}, and not to depart at any time above three miles from his
fathers house. But yt is not the least of
theyre punishments that he and his fellowes are
flouted by waggish witts with a rime....[17]

He then quotes the rhyme on the eight humours.

By the end of November Hoskyns began to feel
that there was some hope of his being released,
but more important, he wanted his wife to know that
he was thinking of her as the time of her delivery
drew near:

To my lovinge wyfe
   Mrs. Ben Hoskyns at her house in Heref^d.
Good Ben: by my accoumpt y^u are not yet in
straw. I neuer prayde soe earnestly for any
thinge... as I doe that I might see y^u before
y^u lye in. notwthstandinge yf that may not be,
yet I pray wth assurance of fayth to obtayne...
that y^u & y^r chyld both may live & haue health,
& ioy in the companie of this poore prisoner
that now wrytes to y^u, I haue intelligence (god
graunt it be true) that there is a purpose to
deliver vs vpon som vnexpected day neere the
end of the terme... I haue endured a triall I
am out of feare of my offences, I feare nothinge now, but only pray that god & his maiesty
would testyfy theyr reconciliation to me by my
deliverance: and I patiently attende it: I pray
y^u thancke Mr James Clarke very hartily he
came twise very lovingely & kyndely to the Tower. Vpon the notice of his suddayn departure
I intreate yu to accept this short letter. God
strengthen & preserue yu & blesse all your
children.
                    Y^r true Joh: Hoskyns.

I thancke god, I never was in better health in
all my lyfe
   Then now I am,

      J H

Tower
23 Nov 1614.[18]

Unfortunately, he was wrong, and over half a year
remained for him to wait. He did not realize how
high-placed his opponents were (although his anti-
Scot statements might have given him a clue).

Meanwhile, his brother, Dr. John, continued to
advance in the church in Hereford. On 7 December
1614 he was made Prebendary of Bartesham, a position carrying with it a considerably higher income
than his previous appointments.[19] On 20 April 1615
the official entry of his admission to the new
Prebendary in December was made, with the added
note that Bishop Benet now considered himself Dr.
John's patron.[20] The close family ties of the Hoskyns with Benet were beginning to pay off.

It was becoming increasingly clear to Hoskyns
that something more was going to be needed than
simply being a good prisoner. In November he and
the other prisoners had submitted petitions to the
King. Now he tried a double approach. First, he
wrote a long English poem which he apparently had
his wife present to the King. In it he describes
his wife as pregnant with their second child. But
in that case she must certainly have waited until
Benedicta was born before she made the long trip
to London. Then, for New Year's Day, he wrote a
long poem in Latin addressed to the King. He also
wrote an English translation, but James, as a
Latin scholar, scarcely needed that. Moreover a
coda to the poem in English was clearly not addressed to James I.

The first poem, "A Dreame," was designed to
pull at any heart strings the King had, but it is
remarkably free of false penance. He does not deny
his actions in Parliament, nor does he really excuse
them so much as he argues his otherwise patriotic
and loyal position. The version in Harley 6947 has
a long introduction which sets the scene:

479

Mr John Hoskins of the Middle temple Counsellor at Law, being committed to the Tower by the
King for certaine speeches vttered in the Parliament house, not long after his Committm^t,
(wch was in the yeare of o^r Lord 1614). wrote
these ensuing verses, wch he caused his wife to
p^rsent to the Kings Matie entituling the same

A Dreame.[21]

Me thought I walked in a dreame
betwixt a Caues mouth & a streame
vpon whose banckes sate full of ruth,
three as they seem'd, but foure in truth.

ffor drawing nere I did behold
a Widowe fourscore winter old,
a wife wth Childe, a little Sonne
but foure yeares old,[22] all four vndone

Out of the Caues mouth Cutt in stone
a Prisoner lookes, whom they did moane,
he smild (they sigh'd) then smote his brest,
as if he meant, god knowes the rest.

The widow cry'd, looking to heaven
Oh Phoebus I thought I had seauen[23]
like Niobe doe now Contest
lend this thy light this sonne my best.

Taught for to speake & liue in light
now bound to silence & to night
why is he closd vp in this Caue
not basely bredd, nor borne a slaue.

Alas this caue hath tane away
my staffe, & all his brothers stay:
Let that be least, that my gray haires
goe to the graue (alas) wth teares.

I greiue for thee Daughter, q^th she,
thee, & that boy, that babe vnborne,
yours though not his, yet others three[24]
he loued as his, but now forlorne.

Tis not the rule of sacred hest
to kill the old one in the nest;
as good be killd as from them hidd,
they die wth greife (ô god forbidd)

480

True quoth the boy, for Tom my page[25]
did finde a birds nest, & we tried,
& put the old one in a Cage,
then my poore birds, poore birds they died.

My ffather nere was soe vnkinde
Who lett him then to speake his mynde,
to speake to me   not to misse,[26]
oh Mother, say, who can doe this?

Then qth the Wife, tis Caesars will,
Caesar can hate, Caesar can kill.
the worst is tolld, the best is hidd:
kings know not all, oh would they did.

He Caesars title then proclaymed
vndoubtedly, when others aymed
at broken hope of doubtfull state:
soe true a man what king can hate.

Caesar, in person & in purse,
he seru'd when better men did worse.
he sware men vnto Caesar's Lawes
by thousands, when false hearts did pause.

He frawd & violence did w[th]stand,
& helpt the poore w[th] tongue & hand:
but for the Cause he now lies here
the Cuntry knowes his soule is cleare.

Why is he now silent & sadd
Whose words make me & many gladd;
well could he loue, ill could he fayne,
it was his losse, it is my gaine.

If Kings are men, If kings haue wiues,
& know ones death may cost two liues,
then were it noe vnkinglie part
to saue two liues in me, poore heart

What if my husband once hath err'd?
men more to blame are more preferrd;
he that offends not doth not liue;
he errd but once, once King forgiue.

Caesar to thee I will resort,
long be thy life, thy wrath but short:
this prayer good successe may take,
if all doe pray for whom he spake.

481

With that they wept, the waters swelld,
the sunne grew darke, the darke Caues yelld,
it brake my sleepe, I did awake,
& thought it was my heart that brake.

Thus I my wofull dreame declare,
hoping that noe such persons are;
I hope none are, but if there be,
god help them pray, pray god wth me./

The poem contains one of the few references that we
have to John's continued care for his elderly mother, now eighty years old. What we know of his concern for his brothers justifies his claim of being
their "stay," and there is no reason to doubt that
he was also his mother's "staff." There is one
particular remark in the poem which indicates John's
continued strength of character and political
stance. In 1614, and with his stated objections
against the Scottish favorites around the throne,
it was scarcely the most politic thing for him to
remark that "men more to blame are more preferrd."

For his Latin "New Year's Gift" to James, Hoskyns plays on the rather remarkable coincidence
that January 1st was exactly two hundred days from
June 8th, the day he was sent to the Tower. He
plays upon the nature of his close confinement,
with boarded windows, which seems to have been his
greatest cause of sorrow. But as in the former
poem, he does not prostrate himself before the
King. He asks for pardon for his offense, but he
does not recant his position. Perhaps the clearest
note of despair lies in his allusion to Tantalus,
for we have seen in his letters that he had actually been led to believe in November that his imprisonment was about to end. The Latin verse shows
the same care and precision that he had regained in
his earlier poems of the year. It is entitled
"JACOBO MAGNAE BRITANNIAE REGI MAXIMO, CLEMENTIS-
SIMO"[27] and consists of 42 lines of unrhymed penta-
meters with varying feet. It ends

Britannorum
Minimus,

Miserrimus,

J. Hoskyns.

The same in English[28]

An hundred nights twice told are come & gone
vnwashed with teares, of all those nights not one
As many dayes adornd with glorious light
But vnto me (poor wretch) as blacke as night
No pardon comes though my complaints are tire[d]
And though my hart yts last hath neere expired
Losse of my place and creditt (wch in part
by this offence is lost) greiues not my hart
Whose vniust money iustly is his foe
That he doeth mine detaine breeds not my woe
That those wch haue no right & pay no rent
doe vse my lands tis not my discontent
Nor y^t my pastures entertaine the theife
Whose stollen cattell glory in my greife
My Wife & Childrens teares moue not at all
Nor moues my litle famylies great fall
That these my lipps wch I may say weere madd
Haue God & thee displeased that makes me sadd
Had I but kept you two vppon my side
Then might my mouth haue bynne X times as wide
And my estate though poore yet being free
Had brought contentment bringing Liberty
I greiue and sorrow but tis not the way
to lessen greife with such a long delay
As ti's my part in sorrow to lament
So from thy nature neuer to relent
pardon thy meanest subiect then this thing
O thou great Brittaines great & glorious King
pardon & doe not with our griefe contend
In vaine he greiues whose greife doeth know no end
If for my wordes my woe must last for euer
with Tantalus in paine I shall perseuer.
The more his lipps the apple striues to stay
by so much more they Swim & glide away
When after freedome greedyly I gape
Then most of all it hastens to escape
Those wch as slaues & prisoners did liue
At New yeares tide the Romanes did forgiue
O Greater then the greatest Romane Prince
fforgiue thy prisoner this his great offence

483

So many happy yeares to the succeed
stryuing therein each other to exceed
Long maist thou liue as many yeares to tell
As I haue nombred dayes within this cell./
                  (or rather hell)

                H:

Thou who dislikest & makest mouthes at mine
If thou darest write, Ile doe as much for thine./

    It may well have been February 1615 before
Benedicta was able to get to London to give "A
Dreame" to King James. Certainly it was in that
month that she finally was able to see her incar-
cerated husband. On 10 February, the Privy Council
ordered Helwys "to gyve leave unto the wife of John
Hoskins, close prisoner there, and some of his
counsell in lawe, to have accesse unto him, for
the settling of his estate...."[29] We can imagine
the joy of the two in finally being able to get together, and for Hoskyns to hear about his new
daughter. His wife may well have brought the
whole family to London and settled in for a time
with her brother-in-law Oswald's family, as she
did three months later. On 23 February, Chamberlain mentioned Ben's visit to London in his letter
to Carleton, "Hoskins and his comperes are still in
the Towre and no speach of theyre releasing, though
Hoskins wife that is a poetesse hath ben a longe
suitor, and presented the King with a petition in
rime which I here send you."[30]

    We know why John needed to talk with his wife
and with his lawyers. In Hilary Term 1615, which
began 22 January, one Ford, Plaintiff, charged that
Hoskins, the Defendant, who was a lord of a manor,
was refusing the right of Ford to a copyhold estate, even though the present copyholder had nominated him. He charged that the custom of the manor
was that each copyholder could nominate his successor, upon the usual payment of a fee. Ford
claimed that he had "tendered his fine to the lord
in Court, and prayed to be admitted, which he refused." The question before the King's Bench was,
would the case lie? Justice Dodderidge argued that

the case lay against the lord in this case because
custom had conferred this manner of passing copyhold. Justice Coke, however, argued that it was a
case of Caveat emptor, and the plantiff should have
written the agreement down somewhere. "The whole
Court (Dodderidge excepted) agreed clearly, against
the plaintiff, that the action upon the case lieth
not against the lord." Final decision was adjourned to be further debated, however. The lawyers obviously wanted to discuss the matter with
Hoskyns before it came up again. He apparently
gave them the right advice, for when the case was
brought up again in Easter term even Dodderidge
had changed his mind. The plaintiff argued that he
could not get the profits of the estate until the
lord admitted him; thus it was a "damnum et in-
juria." Dodderidge said he could "not see how the
lord can be compelled by the plaintiff, by way of
action, to do this against his will." And the
whole court decided strongly against the plaintiff,
fearing the consequence any other way.[31]

Ben went back to Hereford after visiting her
husband, and on 2 March 1615 he wrote a long letter to her, explaining the current state of affairs.

To my only comfort & only earthly joy
    my Ben: the mother of my Bens:[32]

My best deservinge Ben. I only write that y^u
may understand I am in health since he is returned without me who can tell y^u no reason for
it, but that wch I ever conceyved: that other
things must be determined of before my deliverance. that some new rumor & opinion must be
first fashioned fitt for the wearinge of vulgar
fancy, before this vayne cloake be cast of that
poore I was the impediment of those great matters expected. All my honest brothers hopes, to
prosecucion whereof I submitted myselfe, are
proved no other then Courtly delusions of the
tyme, & appropriatinge the successe of my suiet
to som certayn meanes yf it had falne right: &
in that it is deferd imputinge the delayes to
some feares as that I will not be a thankefull

485

man: that no obligacion will bynd my witt &c. I
am well contented and now leve pityinge myselfe
& fall to pytie those greate ones that are so
abused as to be misledde by colours that my conscience knows to be false. for no greate person by whom I benefitted ever found me ungrate-
full or presumtuous to taxe hym but rather em-
braced me for the contrary. Witnesse no less
then the greatest Judges of law and equity in
this kingdom, y^{r}selfe & the family of wch I com:
& all that ever I gaygned or receyved in this
world proceeded from no other meanes. And
towards these my conscience cries aloud: that I
was never unkynd in earnest or bitter in jest.
So then why should I be sorry? but yet alass
the poor honest gentleman informer of greate
ones, hymselfe no doubt of no greater degree
than myselfe or lesse, as it should seeme by the
smallness of his hart that he so much feares a
jest & desires to imprison witt... and suer he
hath reade little history: for no man ever suffered for mere witt: but yf he lived not to requitt it hymselfe, yet the witt of all posterity took penaunce on his name that oppressed
hym. Be cheerefull noble Ben I cannot be persuaded that any man that hath witt of his own
is afrayd of anothers witt as no good soldier
that hath a sword feares another mans sword.
and for my part I had rather dy with witt then
live without it... Now Ben yf I shalbe delivered
when I am a thanckfull man & will not abuse my
friends, I shall tarry very little. For speake
thou nurse of my love, mother of the experience
of all my thanckfullnes, thou mistresse of my
witt, when did I abuse thee? when did I deal un-
gratefully wth thee? you must com Ben & refute
them. In meane while take home y^r Doctor the
late rare example of suictors now made a greate
kinge of beggars, a Mr. of an hospitall... Forgive me Ben, & God forgive me for this idle letter & yf whereas I have somtymes wept & prayd,
I somtymes laugh & pray hereafter. howsoever I
will ever pray will remayn malitiouse to none
infinitely & eternally loving to y^u. God ever
preserve y^u John, Francke, Besse, Ben, dic & all

486

```
          yr family
        thyne only thyne all thyne ever
    2: March 1614  5                      J. Hoskyns.
```

Of all the letters that John was to write, this one
gives us the best view of his attitudes about life,
particularly his feeling of the importance of wit.
We do not know who it was that was reporting him to
the King as unreformed or unloyal, although we will
learn that one of his opponents was the King's favorite. We do have an idea that even that summer
he was writing verses that were later to get him
into trouble once again. But whatever the specific
problems were to which he refers, we see him here
at his very best, as a man who knew his own mind
and was not willing to compromise his own integrity.
And in spite of his own troubles, he can jokingly
congratulate his brother, Dr. John, for being appointed Master of St. Oswald's Hospital in Gloucester.

    Perhaps he had read the proofs or one of the
early copies of Dr. John's first book, which was
printed this year: Sermons Preached at Pavls
Crosse and Else-where, By Iohn Hoskins, Sometimes
Fellow of New-Colledge in Oxford, Minister and
Doctor of Law. It was printed by Thomas Coryat's
old publisher, William Stansby, and dedicated to
Sir Thomas Egerton, Knight, whose father had long
ago helped the young student at Winchester College.
The sermons reveal Dr. John's background in the law
and a tendency to be extremely legalistic in approach. But for his brother in prison, perhaps
the line of argument that was most interesting was
that concerning the difference in virtue and sin in
respect of the social standing of the person to
whom it is directed:

    If you bee bound in a Recognisance to the King,
    tis more dangerously extended, then if you bee
    bound to a common person... you haue heard for
    the generall, that offences being vnequall, take
    their degrees of inequality thence, whence they
    take their special kinde and nature, from their

                        487

obiects, not in materiall, but a formall consideration: more plainly, from their ayme; the
higher they ayme, the higher the offence.[33]

It may not be good Bible, but it was certainly good
politics in 1614, and the preacher's brother was
tasting the bitter consequences not too far away
from Paul's Cross where it was preached.

Finally, as the year in prison drew to an end,
the King relented. That he demanded a petition
from the guilty parties is not surprising, and we
have already seen Hoskyns' willingness to make a
supplication in poetic form. Now the Privy Council
revealed that they did have an official petition
from him, submitted in November 1614, after "five
months of close imprisonment." No wonder he had
told his wife that he expected to be released at
that time!

Out of the bitterness of an afflicted soule
and from the bottom of a most penitent harte,
not for his libertie's sake, but for his conscience sake, he acknowledgeth his imprisonment
to be just, his offence to be heaynous, in his
to inconsiderate speeches in the last Parliament, in medling with matters that became him
not, in alledginge impertinent histories and
that one of damned memory and detestable consequence, which, as God knows, he conceived not
when he spoke, nor intended to mencion when he
first stood up to speak.
He hath suffered five monethes close imprisonment, sustayned greate losses in his estate by
accidentes which his only liberty might have
prevented, and acknowledgeth the same to be the
just and woefull effectes of a most dreadfull
cause, the displeasure of God, and the King's
sacred Majestie.
Most humbly beseecheth your Honours to mediate
for him to his most gratious Soveraigne for his
mercy, where unto he wholely and most humbly
submittes himself, and whereon only he reposeth
himself, and most instantly desireth it next to
the mercy of God in another world.

Among the Hoskyns papers in the possession of Sir Benedict Hoskyns is the Act of the Privy Council concerning John Hoskyns on that 8 June 1615. Present were many friends of Hoskyns from previous years, and it is no wonder that he expected to be released earlier: The Lord Chancellor, Chief Justice Coke, the Earl of Pembroke, and the Lord Treasurer. His continued imprisonment had clearly been the result of the same kind of personal whim of James which had led to the long-term imprisonments of Ralegh, Grey, Arabella Stuart, and Northumberland.

> This day John Hoskins Councellor at Lawe Prisoner in the Tower was by his Ma^{tes}Comanndem^{t} called to the Boarde and his Peticion and Submission wch he had formerly made in acknowledgm^{t} of his greevious offence, was reade vnto him, wch he did avowe to be subscribed by his hand, and did acknowledg the same to proceede from the true sence and meaninge of his harte And therevpon it was signified vnto him, that his Matie in his singuler mercy and Clemency was gratiously pleased to accept of his Submission, and the acknowledgm^{t} made by him of his offence, and to give order for his enlargem^{t} out of the Tower of London, wch their llp^{s} thought fitt and soe ordered should be donn in this manner. That John Hoskins Councellor at Lawe might (haueing his wife and ffamylie heere) remayne in London this next Tearme, to be confyned to some such House as he shall make choice of w^{th}out repayringe either to his Chamber in the Temple or to Westminster hall or to any other publique place; And the Tearme beinge done to goe downe into the Country to remayne confined at his House there, and w^{th}in five Miles compasse thereof vntill his Ma^{tes} pleasure be further knowne....

At the same meeting of the Privy Council, Sir Charles Cornwallys and Lionel Sharp were present and were put through the same process, and then the Council issued letters of release to the Lieutenant of the Tower.[35]

　　Hoskyns, as his freedom finally arrived, then
wrote another verse in the window: "Non mente
seruare potes licet omnia claudas,"[36] which might
be freely translated, "when you can't willingly
serve anyone, shut up!" John apparently was more
recalcitrant than his more public statements indicate. And his public supplication did not hurt
his reputation as a defender of Parliament's rights.
Anthony a Wood's remark at the end of his account
of Hoskyns' imprisonment indicates that the punishment which he had undergone had obvious meaning
for later M.P.'s: "After our Author Hoskyns had
continued a Prisoner for a full Year, he, with
Sharp and Cornwallis were released and ever after
were held in great value by the Commons."[37]

　　A week after the release, Chamberlain wrote
to Carleton, that the three prisoners "upon theyre
acknowlegement and submission were delivered out of
the Towre, where they have lien a whole yeare...."[38]
And six months later, George Lord Carew, in his
summary of events during the year, listed under
June that Cornwallys, Sharp, and Hoskyns, "(whome
you lefte prisoners in the Tower) are enlarged,
and will no more Burne there fingers wth parliment
business."[39] But in spite of all of this protestation, there is certainly more evidence than the
second verse scratched in the Tower window that
Hoskyns was still being rather outspoken. As we
shall see later, he was in very bad trouble about
an action that took place this summer--a poem that
he supposedly wrote. We simply do not know what
the actual basis of the trouble was, but there is
a poem found in two manuscripts in the British
Museum which gives at least a clue. It is in the
spirit of the final line written in the Tower window, only much more explicit.[40]

　　He that hath heard a Princes Secrecy
　　hath his Deaths Wound, & let him looke to dye
　　For Princes Hearts cannot Endure Longe
　　to be obnoxious to a Servants Tongue.

490

                   Noe Counsell but mans life will some way
                                                    show it
              then in some Case as good Doe ill as Know it.
                              J.H.

        The verses are a much better commentary on
the scandal surrounding the death of Sir Thomas
Overbury than on the treatment of John Hoskyns,
and it is likely that John was making a comment
on the death of the other prisoner in the Tower
who had met his end in 1613. In 1615, a verse
which could in any way link King James with the
treatment of Sir Thomas Overbury would only be interpreted in the very worst way. John had apparently not learned to stop being witty. But at
least he was free once again, even though limited
to his brother's house. His family was with him,
and he could now get to know his baby daughter and
renew his close relationship with his young son.
Within a month he would be back in Hereford, and
then be free of all travel limitations. It would
be two years before he was totally clear of the
results of his witty endeavors, but in spite of
that, he was ready now to renew his practice,
develop his landholdings in Hereford, and help his
brothers and their families when they needed his
assistance. It was a rather late start: he was
already fifty years old. At the same age his
friend John Donne would only have nine years of
life to go. But Hoskyns had twenty-three years
ahead of him, and he was going to keep his strength
and his wit the whole way, gaining honors and real
estate as he went.

                              491

Footnotes for Chapter XIV

1. MS. Malone 19, p. 148 (Osborn, p. 208) is headed "Mr Hoskins wrott in the windowe when he came out of the Tower" but Carreglwyd Papers, Ser. II, 218, in the National Library of Wales, has "Traditus in custodiam A°: Domino 1614 12° Jacobi: Re 8° die Junij." The tense of the verbs seem to favor the earlier date.
2. "Verses made by Sergeant Hoskins," Carreglwyd Papers, Series II, 218. Aubrey tells the unlikely story that "He, with much adoe, obtained at length the favour to have his little son Bennet to be with him; and he then made this distich...." (Clark, I, 422) The poem is found in the English version in Sloane 4130, f. 93v ("Ad Beniaminum filium") as well as the eleven manuscript versions listed by Osborn, p. 292.
3. Harewood MSS. In Osborn, pp. 41-42. The fourth letter is in a different hand with small and meticulous printing, but the signature is by Ben.
4. Lansdowne 702, f. 54. This is the manuscript described by Disraeli, in his Curiosities of Literature, Vol. III (1881), p. 133, which Osborn was unable to find (p. 219). It is made up from letters from Aubrey to Wood as well as other extracts from Wood's notes.
5. Ibid., f. 57v.
6. Dick. p. 257.
7. Dick, p. 258.
8. Bald, pp. 228-29.
9. Dick, p. 123.
10. Clark, p. 419. In Osborn, p. 212.
11. Dick. pp. 305, liii.
12. Lansdowne 702, f. 9v. "This acct Mr Wood had from Mr Tho: Henshaw at Kensington." Henshaw also had "an excellent Latin copie in rhythme in the prayse of ale" of Hoskyns that has been lost. See Clark, p. 418. Henshaw was the uncle of Benedict's wife Ann.
13. H.M.C., Cowper, Vol. I (1888), p. 87.
14. I have used as a base the poem found in Sloane 2023, f. 60v (eliminating an opening quatrain

on the previous page), but changed the spelling of names and inserted "carelessly" for "popishlie" from Chamberlain, I, p. 557. Another version is in the "Letter Book of Sir John Holles," H.M.C., Portland, IX, 165. Osborn, p. 38, quotes a version from Malone 19, p. 95, and refers to yet another in Rawlinson Poetry, 26, f. 2v.

15. Sloane 4130, f. 92v. In Osborn, pp. 202-3.
16. A.P.C. 1613-1614, pp. 548-49.
17. Chamberlain, I, p. 556.
18. Sizergh MSS. In Osborn, p. 70.
19. P.R.O., Bishops Certificates Hereford E 331/6, on a sheet of institutions dated 9 October 1615. Also in the book of Institutions in the Vicars Choral Library, Hereford, p. 27. The annual income from this post was the second largest in the diocese. See John Duncomb. Collections (1804), p. 502.
20. Bishops Cert. Here. E 331/6. On 7 June 1615, Oswald and another merchant tailor, Simon Price, acted as bond for £17 18s 10d (P.R.O. Composition Book 15, E. 334, f. 48).
21. Harley 6947, ff. 252-53. Osborn uses this version, pp. 206-8. Besides the twelve versions which she notes, p. 293, the poem appears in Rawlinson B. 151, as "Mr Hoskins his dreame in the Tower. 1614." It omits stanzas 4, 5, 7, 12, 13, and 14. The punctuation is much clearer, and it supplies the word "me" in stanza 15, which I have added without brackets. There is another version of the short form among the Hoskyns papers at Harewood.
22. If this age is correct, it would mean that Benedict was born either quite late in 1609 or before 25 March 1610, as other records indicate his birthdate as 1609.
23. Oswald, John, Thomas, Philip, Dr. John, Charles, and William. William must have died at or near birth as John nowhere else mentions him. He is listed as one of Margery's children in Charles Robinson, The Mansions of Hereford (1872), pp. 133-34.
24. Ben's children by Francis Bourne.
25. Thomas Taylor, William's younger brother.

26. Osborn substitutes "kisse" for the last word from other mss.

27. Miscellany of the Abbotsford Club, Vol. I (Edinburgh, 1837), pp. 131-32. It is introduced (p. 129) as "JOANNIS HOSKYNS/SUPPLICATIO AD REGEM." In Osborn, pp. 203-4. Also found in Harley 1221, f. 76v, as "John Hoskins New-yeares gift to the Kings Matie": Harley 6038, ff. 20v-21; Sloane 4130, ff. 92-92v.

28. Harley 1221, ff. 77-77v. In Osborn, pp. 205-6; also Harley 6038, ff. 21-21v.

29. A.P.C. 1615-1616, p. 46.

30. Chamberlain, I, pp. 581-82; S.P.D. James I, 1611-1618, LXXX, 38, p. 275.

31. English Reports, Vol. 80. King's Bench Division, pp. 1168-69; under "Edward Bulstrode Reports (1688)."

32. Sizergh MSS; also in Harley 1221, ff. 99v-100; in Osborn, pp. 70-72.

33. pp. 6,8.

34. A.P.C. James I, 1615-1616, Vol. II, pp. 193-94.

35. Ibid., pp. 191-92, 194.

36. Carreglwyd Papers, Ser. II, 218 (N.L.W.) This entry as well as the attached version of "Sic luo..." was made by Robert Branthwaite at Crease (or Cruse, at Goodrich in Herefordshire). There can be no doubt about the authenticity of these entries. Branthwaite witnessed a document for Hoskyns exactly one week after his release from the Tower. See the following chapter.

37. Wood, col. 614; also in "Bishop Kennett's Collections," Lansdowne 984, f. 92v.

38. Chamberlain, I, p. 602; S.P.D. 1611-1618, LXXX, 115, p. 289.

39. S.P.D. James I, vol. 86, #16.

40. Both Mss., Harley 1221 (f. 71v) and Harley 6038 (f. 12), contain other Hoskyns poems in close proximity. Harley 6038 credits it to the same "J:H:" as the "New Year's Gift to the King." Harley 1221 has it just before both the "New Year's Gift" and the Cornwallys letter. Osborn prints it as a doubtful verse, but acknowledges as "likely that the six lines are by Hoskyns." p. 302. She knew only the Harley 6038 version.

Chapter XV

Restoration

The next six years were a series of ups and
downs for John, both in his personal and public
life. The King apparently remained convinced for
at least three of those years that Hoskyns was his
enemy, and worry over the royal displeasure may
have been a factor in John's weakening physical
health. Certainly for the first time in his life
he was sick almost as often as he was well. He
and his wife began to fight with each other at the
same time, and his older brother, Oswald, died,
leaving a large family in John's care. But in
spite of his troubles, John continued to put all
his effort into building a solid financial base for
all of the branches of his family, and he grew in
grace at the Middle Temple, taking on positions of
greater and greater responsibility. At last, in
1621, he was appointed a Judge in Wales, and only
the further honor of becoming a Serjeant-at-law
still eluded his grasp. Perhaps most important for
his future, though, was the indication, in being
appointed a Judge, that James had finally forgiven
him.

As we have seen, upon being released from the
Tower, John was limited to his residence in London
until the end of Term. This meant that he had to
empower someone else to look after his interests in
Hereford. His brother Thomas could fulfill that
function in the estates around Llanwarne and Llan-
garren, but Titley was too far away to be included
in that task. Dr. John was busy with his own affairs. So, on 28 June 1615, John appointed another man to look after his property in Titley. His
autograph letter of commission is among the manuscripts in Winchester College.[1]

Be it known to all men by these presentes that
I John Hoskyns Lord of the mannor of Titley for
the terme to me granted by the warden ę scholers
clarkes of the college of S^t mary of Oxford in

Winchester haue made ҽ constituted ҽ doe make
ҽ constitute Richard Knight of Lyonhalls in
the com̄ of Heref gent my Steward of the said
mannor to take a surrend^r of one copyhold tene-
m^t from william Austin esq^r ҽ Anne his wyfe
daught^r ҽ heir of philip Gryme late of London
to be regranted to Thomas Gryme ҽ Margaret his
wyfe accordinge to the custom of the said man-
no^r 28 Jun 1615

J: Hoskyns

Robert Branthwaite was the witness. This gentleman is especially interesting as it was he who was
the source for the Carreglwyd copy of the two sets
of verses which Hoskyns cut into the Tower window.
Branthwaite was in London at the time of John's release and carried the commission back to Herefordshire. The commission was a formal statement of
what was already an acknowledged fact, for on the
following day back in Herefordshire William Austin
and his wife Anne surrendered one messuage, "lately
of Thomas Grymes deceased" to the Lord of the Manor,
and "Richard Knight Steward" was one of the signa-
tories.[2]

Usually James Dalley acted as steward for Titley, but Hoskyns wanted to have the matter of copyhold estates clearly established and under his own
control after his legal difficulties in the spring.
Dalley had earlier been reasonably efficient in the
handling of the manor court arrangements, but he
became increasingly lax through the years whenever
other business kept Hoskyns from personally visiting the manor to look after his affairs. The role
of the steward was an important one in the whole
matter of collection of fines, taxes, feudal dues,
etc. Individual items were often small; the heriot
on the Thomas Grymes property, for example, was only fourteen shillings.[3] One rent was a mere four-
pence a year.[4] Fines ranged from fourpence to five
shillings. In 1613 Hoskyns had set forth a number
of regulations the breaking of which would incur a
fine,[5] such as "vsurping the comon wth his Cattell."
There was a five shilling penalty for not filling

496

up a sawmill pit. Gathering acorns in the common woods would cost the miscreant 3/4. Anyone removing timber from the common woods would pay ten shillings for each offence. Lumped together these small items made up a respectable income for the Baron of the manor; indifferently collected, they amounted to very little.

One court meeting presided over by Dalley on 23 August 1616 is well recorded, probably because Hoskyns had been visiting the manor earlier that summer. Edward Greenly had cut down eleven young saplings in Hoskyns' woods and also cropped three oaks. John Knight cut down five saplings. Thomas Tristram, Edward Wellington, Walter Price and Roger Godwyn cut down firewood. John Stevens cut down a tree "neer the Churchyarde." Thomas Gryme made a poundbreach (the illegal removal of an object impounded) against the bailiff. Walter Lucas was fined for "making of a Sawpitt in Tytleys woodes and for not fillinge of the same againe." And so on; all the offenders were fined in due course.[6] There was also a list of various fines for transfers of land, recordings of rents paid, and the payment of the heriot on Edward Wellington's land, which was forty shillings.[7] There was a list of those who were missing at the meeting of the court session which was sent to Hoskyns for his attention, and there was also a notice of the death of Thomas Glover since the last court, and "his son Richard Glover is next of kine to be brought in as heire to the same howse."[8] In these court records a good view of life on a small manor is given, but it is evident that all of the details could be lost to an absentee lord of the manor if he could not completely trust the steward he had appointed to oversee his rights.

In July 1615 Hoskyns went back to Hereford with his family, and from his house in that city caught up with news of his relatives and the business of his various farms. But it was soon apparent that for John to move upward in his chosen field, the city of Hereford was not the proper base, and once again he petitioned the Privy Coun-

cil. On 21 July 1615 the Council granted him permission "to repair to London and Westminster Hall
for his practice in law."[9] Thus released from his
confinement in Hereford, Hoskyns finally was a totally free man, no longer having to report his movements to the court in London.

Back at the Middle Temple, he would have found
that Richard Martin and Francis Ashley, the latter
a friend both at the Temple and in Parliament,
were moving up towards being Readers, both of them
serving at the cupboard in the autumn term for
1615. On 27 October Martin was chosen as Reader
for the Lenten term and Ashley for the autumn term
in 1616.[10]

October was a busy month for Hoskyns as well
as the Court of James. It had been a long time
since Sir Thomas Overbury had succumbed to poison,
but the news had finally gotten around London, much
to the political and personal discomfort of King
James, who was immediately linked to the sordid
plot because of his closeness to Rochester and his
wife, both of whom were implicated in the murder.
We are able to follow Hoskyns' interest in the e-
vents through two letters written in the middle of
the month. On 14 October he wrote to his wife:[11]

Sweet hart I am alive & in health, desirous yf
it be gods will to take further paynes for the
supportation of a poore estate, wherein gods
favour to our prayers may effect more then the
strength of our labours. Your sonne John Boorne
is well, & hath a special affeccion to musique
& sayth he will goe to the dauncinge schoole,
but keepes his study & good order wherein I beseech the Lord that I may continue hym. I have
ben with my lord Chauncelour & found hym most
lovinge & honourable in his favours to me. My
lord Chyefe Justice came home yesternight from
the Kinge wth whom as the generall report is
(& I thincke it was so) he was to relate the
state of the cause of the poysoninge or attempting to poyson S[r] Thomas Overbery in the Tower,
what Mr. Page[12] shall relate to you therin is

that wch I receyved from them to whom the Lieuetenant hymselfe spake it. I pray God I may get
my money of the Lieuetenant before any danger
fall to hym, for concealing what he now hath revealed whatever it be. And let us draw home our
eys eares & senses from others cases to ourselves & gods greate mercy in our preservation.
I heare Mrs Kempe came on friday wth her sonnes
Smith & Jeffreys[13] & that yesterday her man
sayd to my man she would speake with me. I will
goe to her & doe whatever I can for y^r sake. but
to go abroad is not our order it is the office
of a sollicitor. I wish she had a skilful one
for her ease & mine....

The letter is interesting on several counts:
that Sir Thomas Egerton was continuing his friendship and kindness to Hoskyns was of the greatest
importance to John now and later. John Bourne's
interest in music followed that of his stepfather,
just as did his interest in dancing; but in spite
of that temporarily diverting interest he continued
in his practice of the law and acted as an assistant to his step-father in the years ahead. Ben's
sister, Mrs. Kempe, seems always to have depended
on John in her legal difficulties, and that confidence was well-founded. It must have been a
little trying for him, however, to have this added
family burden to shoulder as we have no evidence
that she ever paid him for his services. But most
interesting of all is his comment on the Overbury
case. He was clearly avoiding any danger of writing down rumors of the case. Any written document,
in the wrong hands, would be a danger to him. He
undoubtedly was sorry that he had written the short
poem which could be interpreted as a comment on the
case. His personal involvement was more in relation to the luckless Sir Gervase Helwys, who never
did manage to pay back the £50 that he owed Hoskyns. Such a large sum of money (equal to more
than half of his total salary for serving in the
long first Parliament under James) must have been
a crushing loss to John at this critical point.

Sir Thomas Overbury was the extremely handsome

and intelligent favorite and mentor of Sir Robert
Carr. Carr shared Overbury's good looks, but not
his intelligence; what he lacked in wisdom he made
up for in luck and a good eye for political advancement, however, and Sir Thomas hitched his
wagon to the rising star of James' court. All was
well until Sir Thomas tried his best to dissuade
Carr, the then Earl of Somerset, from helping with
the annulment proceedings of Frances Howard (daughter of the Earl of Suffolk and great niece of
Northampton) against her husband, the Earl of Essex, so that Somerset himself could marry her. The
lady never forgave Overbury and not only succeeded
in having him imprisoned in the Tower in 1613, but
supplied him servants who were to poison him. Overbury, one of the real literary lights of the
period and the man who brought the literary form
of the "Character" to full bloom, died on 15 September 1613, after five months of close imprisonment.

Sir Thomas had matriculated from Queen's College, Oxford, in 1596, at 14, and had his B.A. by
1598. At the same time, he had officially entered
the Middle Temple on 30 July 1597,[14] being bound
with his father, Nicholas Overbury. When Sir
Thomas was knighted in June 1608, his father, on
the same day, received his judgeship in Wales.[15]
Hoskyns was closely associated with the older Overbury for many years, both in the Middle Temple
and Parliament, and in later years they shared the
same circuit in Wales through nearly two decades
of service.

But at the moment Hoskyns was concerned about
the fate of the Lieutenant of the Tower, who had
sought to save himself by telling the King's Secretary, Sir Ralph Winwood, about all of the events
of the summer of 1613. Helwys was really quite a
decent fellow in his way, but he had become more
and more intangled in the web of Howard intrigue
during the slow poisoning of Sir Thomas Overbury.
He did his best to act as an honest guard, and it
is undoubtedly due to his restraint and basic honesty that Overbury lived as long as he did. But

500

Helwys was up against superior forces, and in the
end all of his care did not suffice.[16] The fact
that Hoskyns was still in close enough contact with
Helwys to have his information almost at first-hand
from the principal informant in the case is sufficient reason for us to trust him when he advises
Ben to keep quiet about the whole situation. Perhaps he had even had some intimation of Overbury's
fate from Helwys before he left the Tower, for the
Lieutenant was not the most circumspect man in the
world, and rumors of the murder were circulating
for some months before Winwood and Chief Justice
Coke broke the case open in October.

Two weeks later,[17] Hoskyns wrote to Ben once
again, now able to give many more details of the
events transpiring in the city. On 23 October,
Richard Weston, the principal agent of Frances
Howard and one of the two actual poisoners of Overbury, was tried and condemned. Two days later, as
Hoskyns indicates, he was executed at Tyburn. A
large group of sympathizers with the Howard party
rode over to Tyburn to try to get Weston, who admittedly had been given a very bad trial, to deny
his guilt. Of the men that Hoskyns mentions, Sir
John Lidcot is a special case, however, for he was
Sir Thomas Overbury's brother-in-law and had been
one of the few men who had been able to talk with
Sir Thomas in the Tower; he wanted Weston to make
a clear confession.[18] Mrs. Turner was indeed the
next to be tried and found guilty, but although
Helwys was examined many times during the week, he
was not put on trial until November. The unhappy
man, who thought he was clearing himself by letting
the secret of the murder out, never seems to have
realized that by doing so he made obvious his own
participation, although his was the sin of omission
rather than commission. He was condemned on 16
November and executed in the Tower on the 20th.
His successor was not Sir John Keyes, as Hoskyns
indicates, but John Donne's father-in-law, the sto-
lid and sure Sir George More. King James was not
about to take any chances on further difficulties
because of a weakness in the principal officer of
the Tower of London.

...On Wednesday last Weston was executed for poysoninge Sr Thomas Overbery, yesterday the Lieuetenant of the Tower, Sr Gervase Hellwisse was committed to Sr John Swynnerton & Sr John Keys was sworne Lieuetenant. Sr John Wentworth & Sr John Lidcot & Mr. Sackvile were committed for askinge questions of Weston at his execucion. Sr John Hollis & Sr Tho Vavasor were sent for for the same cause but appeered not. On thursday last the Earle of Som'sett was convented before the lords Commissioners but I heare of nothinge confest by hym. Mrs Turnor was examined on thursday she shalbe shortely tried, but the generall report is that the lievetenant shalbe tried on tuesday next. Soe it will goe hard with me for my 50^l yf it goe ill wth hym. I pray you therefore returne some money by Mr Philips^{19} to pay Winchester rent, for part of the 14^l is gone for a gown, & part for other things.

I have ben favourably heard but I had but few clientes. I dyned on Sunday wth the Countesse. Y^u must needs send her som Turneps seed...

For your steele I would gladly heare how much is delivered, and I would but heare that it is once delivered for Oswald lookes for it & every man else for every penny that I ow nay I tooke but two fees before my commitment for wch I moved not & I thancke my clients both, they came & made me move for the both wthout further fee or thancks. So I hope I shall grow perfectly out of debt & ow nothinge but a care of our children & myselfe, for as my Lord Chauncelour and my lord Cooke told me I hope I shall be the better whilst I live I am so well disciplined. I am much comforted wth the honorable words both of the Lord Chauncelour and the M^r of the Rolls both privately & publiquely but discomforted by the present state of the Chauncery the mill grynds slowly. It pleased the kinge in discourse of Sr Thomas Overbery to say that the Earl of sommerset dealt falsely with hym as he did wth me. for he promised to speake for his deliveraunce & spake not & promised to speake for me but spake agaynst me.

502

Sturgeon is at 23^s a kegge. Yf it please y^u to have any y^u shall, but the longer it stays the more I shall fynde when I come. I wonder I heare not from Thomas nor Harry Wathen.[20] Thomas promised to rayse the ponde head. I would have him cut the outlett straighter through the end of the stanke though the ditch fall to runne a furrow lower yet it will runne more easily & continually. I pray y^u in any case let Thomas presently bargayn with workmen to quicksett all my ringe hedge by the perch to make a ditch halfe a foot broader & deeper then the best is usually & to sett two rows of quick-sett, this wynter must not be lost. I would have som body bwy me som pere trees at Dymocke[21] & set them at Bernithen I told Thomas where. I troble y^u wth to much husbandry. I love y^u only & infinitly. god keepe you all & blesse our children.

I heare nothinge from yu by this carrier.

28 Octb. 1615.   J.H.[22]

Some of the references to his personal life and friends are clear, but others are not. Ben apparently sent the money he requested, for the records at Winchester indicate he paid his annual rent of £8 13s 4d on time. It is not possible to identify surely who "the Countesse" was, as John was friendly with several, but as the reference falls in a paragraph dealing with Ben's estates, it would seem to be Elizabeth, Countess of Winchelsea, a not-too-distant relative of Ben's through the Moyle family and the mother of John's good friend Sir Heneage Finch.

John was continuing his friendly relations with Egerton and Coke (who was in the process of over-stepping his power in the prosecution of the Over-bury trial and about to lose his position at Court to the more tactful Sir Francis Bacon) and Sir Julius Caesar, the new Master of the Rolls; but what the specific case in Chancery he refers to was, it is not possible to discover. It may have been that of his brother, Dr. John, who was involved with a

503

suit against tenants of St. Oswald's hospital the
following June. The item of greatest interest in
the letter is the note of King James' remark concerning the Earl of Somerset, who was before long
to join the long list of those convicted of the
murder of Overbury. The easiest explanation of
John's comment is that Somerset was the man who
stood in the way of John's release from the Tower
in November 1614, when he had expected to be set
free. It is perfectly possible that Somerset
thought that Hoskyns knew of the rumors of Overbury's poisoning because of his acquaintance with
Helwys, but the easier explanation is that he simply was furious at John for his statements about the
Scottish favorites, of whom Somerset was chief.

The comments on his brother Thomas are typical
of John's relations with his younger brother, which
were never terribly warm.

Meanwhile he continued to watch out for Ben's
son, John Bourne, and on 20 November the young lad
moved into his stepfather's rooms at the Temple
(replacing Christopher Jones)[23] where he would stay
until his death.

* * * * *

The following year was a busy one for John.
Although Thomas Coryat's volume of letters from Asmere was published, naming John among the circle
of wits at the Mermaid Tavern, there is no indication that he now had much time for writing poetry.
As a matter of fact, he would have reason once a-
gain to regret some of his previous wit before the
year was out. In the meantime, he was busy about
his younger brother's business. Dr. John's difficulties give us the first complete record and example of John's method of handling a case in Chancery. As we have seen, in February 1615, Dr. John
had obtained the Mastership of St. Oswald's Hospital
near Worcester. The position entailed the running
of houses for four poor hospitallers and the upkeep
of a chapel. The income was derived from the lands
connected with the Hospital and amounted to some

£300 a year. In other words, it was a considerable plum for the new minister. It was lucky for Dr. John that he had Bishop Benet as his patron at the time that his brother fell into such strong royal disfavor. But by June 1616, the Doctor discovered that he had more troubles in collecting his money at St. Oswald's than John did at Titley, and he pressed a suit in Chancery against the troublemakers among his tenants, especially Thomas and Mary Barnes, John Coucher, and Henry Thomas. John acted as his counsel.

The legal problem was a rather sticky one. Originally the Master's place belonged to the Dean and Chapter of Worcester Cathedral, but by "lapse of tyme it did acrew to Our Late Souerayne Lorde King James."[24] The question to be decided was whether leases from Worcester were binding or whether the new grant from the King took precedence.

As in so many cases in Chancery in the seventeenth century, the witnesses were nowhere near London and the Courts of Law in which the real estate cases were decided. As a result, the lawyers for the plaintiffs and defendants had to develop "Interrogatories for witnesses" which were then given to a commission which handled the depositions of those witnesses in the home territory. As one reads through the many cases stored up in the Public Record Office, the fine hand of John Hoskyns makes its appearance in these Interrogatories. There is a precision and neatness in the logical order which sets his cases apart from most of the other cases of the time. It is no wonder that, once he recovered from his political difficulties, he won preferment in the legal profession. But it makes even more strange Aubrey's statement that Hoskyns was worse at law than at his other pursuits.

On 22 June 1616, a commission was given two sets of interrogatories, one for the plaintiff, "John Hoskyns minister, and Doctor of Lawe, master of the Hospitall of Sayncte Oswalldes neere Worcester," and the other for "Thomas Barnes, Mary his wief, and others deffendanntes."[25] Hoskyns' re-

505

morseless questioning never lets up. As he cannot
be there to press home his point personally, he
makes his questions have the same effect. It is
not the redundant language, which is common to all
interrogatories, that is so effective, but the
movement of the questions. Still there is the
tolling of a bell present in the constant opening:
"Do you know or have your heard?" and the closing:
"Declare the trueth hereof at lardge" of each
question.

Dr. John's problems and accusations come
through quickly in the questions: 1. Do you know
the parties, the plaintiff and the defendants?   2.
Do you know the Hospital of St. Oswald's, "for the
maynetenannce of a master, and foure poore brethren"? (What looks like a simple question becomes
the basis for John's winning of the case.) 3. Do
you know of a "faire dwellinge" built there? Who
lives there? How many have lived there? 4. Was
there a chapel with bells and a churchyard filled
with trees? Did you or any other person pull down
the chapel? Under whose orders? Did Mary's late
husband, Thomas Barnes, take away the stones?
(Thomas formerly held the hospital by lease.) To
what use did he put them? Did he use them in his
own house? Who took away the Bells, etc.? "what
value do you think or have heard?" 6. Were there
any trees in the churchyard, especially "was there
one tree, called the preaching Elme"? Were any
sermons preached there? How often? Is it cut
down, by whom, for what use, by whom, what value?
Were any of your ancestors buried there? Has it
been plowed? By whom, how often? Was there any
corn growing in it? Who had it? 7. Were there
four houses belonging to the Hospital for the poor
brethren, and "are there in the said howses foure
poore men nowe dwellinge?" What are their names,
who put them there, how are they maintained, how
much is their yearly pension, and when is it paid?
"What parishe church do they now resorte vnto to
heere divine service?" Do they sit together? Are
their houses now being repaired? 8. Do you know
Thomas Hitchcock, "sometymes the baylief, servant,
or agent vnto Sir John Boorne, or vnto or for the

506

Deane and chapiter of Worcestor?" 9. "Did he intermeddle with or dispose of any possessions or
rents of the Hospital?" When did he do so and to
whom? What have you heard him say about who really owns the Hospital, who gets the rent, and so on?
10. Do you know the dwellings of Thomas and Mary
Barnes... (and eighteen others)? What are their
values? 11. Dr. Powell was the previous master of
the hospitall and lived in the house there. Are
the notes in this book his handwriting? Did he
give it to the Dean and Chapter of Worcester? 12.
What other lands belong to the hospital that have
been concealed? 13. What privileges has the hospital enjoyed? 14. Did you know that John Coucher
conveyed his lands to his son? When did he do it?
Has he gotten any rents? How much? 15. Has Henry
Thomas also gotten profits from the land even
though they were conveyed to his son? 16. "What
else do you know?"

The Depositions were taken by the commissioners on 23 September 1616. The answers to the
questions by the witnesses all seem to lead to a
clear case for Dr. John. Thomas Evet declared that
Thomas and Mary Barnes lived in the fair house by
the hospital. Thomas then took the stones away
and built a house for himself at Barbon. Thomas
Hitchcock was the one who cut down the trees, which
were worth four or five shillings each. Hitchcock
was also growing barley in the churchyard, and he
claimed that he had a lease to do so from Nicholas
Udall, who was Master of the Hospital eighteen
years before. Then Edward Price, a brickmaker of
St. Nicholas, Worcs., said that a Richard Nash of
Worcester had bought some of the stone and that
Hitchcock had ordered Price to dig up some of the
foundation. Price also used to collect rents for
the Hospital, and the yearly value of all of the
rents was about eighty pounds. Other witnesses
gave more details; basically their testimony was
the same.26

Then we get the case for the defense, and all
of Hoskyns' argument appears to fall apart. The
questioning runs this way: Did Nicholas Udall,

Clerk, a Master of the hospital, give a lease to
John Harford? Did Harford give it to Arthur Dedicot, and did Dedicot sign it over to Sir John
Bourne? Did his son, Anthony Bourne,[27] grant the
premisses to Richard Walker and lease the rents
to Sir Thomas Bromley, late Lord Chancellor of
England? Did Bromley transfer that lease to John
Coucher? (The defense had the lease in their possession.) Did Coucher grant the lease to certain
friends at the rate of £15 a year each? Were not
the tower, bells, etc. all pulled down before any
of the defendants had any claim to any of the property? Did not Edward Thomas have the rights to
the land from Thomas Evet (the father of the first
witness) and then give it to his daughter? All of
the witnesses immediately agreed to all of the
points in the case of the defense, including the
£15 yearly rent. It looked as though Dr. John had
lost all of the benefits of his new position.

But his lawyer brother did not give up the
fight. He had laid his case on the basis of the
foundation of the hospital, the grant of lands for
the purpose of the upkeep of a poor peoples' home
and the religious cure of their souls. For the
time being he merely made sure that Dr. John was
established as the legal Master of the Hospital and
that the court was made aware of the situation in
general: that Dr. John had paid the usual fees upon
his appointment, that the defendants were occupying
all of the lands and buildings connected with the
hospital, that they had pulled down the Chapel,
detained their required tithes, etc. Then he
waited until the case could be heard again.

On 25 October 1617, he brought the case back
to Chancery in London, arguing that Udall's lease
was illegal because it went against the nature of
the Hospital and the principles of the endowment.
The court agreed that Udall's lease was "odiens"
for that reason. They "did forbeare to make anie
decree at that tyme... but advised the Defftes to
yeld vnto the plaintiff some good advancmt towardes his & the said poore peoples maintenance," because the tenants should not have stuck to the

508

lease knowing that it was wrong. They also appointed two judges to arbitrate the case and set
the valuation. Dr. John would have half the true
value of the land until the lease was determined;
then he would receive the whole. Dr. John immediately showed real Christian spirit and agreed to
take only one third in order to help the defendants
out. On 19 April 1618 at the Guildhall in Worcester, the list of rents for the defendants was
decided on the basis of proof given by Dr. John.[28]
Thus the situation stood for over a decade until
1631.

But if John was having success in difficult
law cases, he was still not having any luck in politics. In the summer elections of 1616 in the city
of Hereford, he was finally elected mayor, after
many years of service in official positions in the
city. There are various indications in Parliament
records that at some point Hoskyns was a mayor, but
each of these leads has proven false under investigation. The fact is that we have a complete list
of the mayors of the city of Hereford throughout
John's lifetime, and he appears nowhere in them.
Many of the mayors were his close friends and associates in legal matters. For the year 1616, however, the name that appears in the mayoral list is
not one of the men that is usually encountered in
the records for the city, one James Rod. It is
really of no importance who Rod was; the important
fact is that he was the second choice of the citizens. Their first choice was John Hoskyns, M.P.,
deputy steward of the city and counsellor of law.
James I was not the type to forgive quite so quickly, however, in spite of what he might have said
concerning the Earl of Somerset's speaking against
Hoskyns. What he did in the case of the mayoral
elections in Hereford remains one of his major
legal inequities, and it remained buried in the
records of the British Museum until 1960.[29]

On 21 August 1616, James wrote to the Corporation of Hereford,

Trusty and welbeloved wee greete you well. We

509

are given to vnderstand that choice is made of
John Hoskins (who so notoriously hath fallen into our heavy displeasure, for wch cause he was
removed from being yor Recorder, and that
worthely.) to be the Mayo^r of yor Towne, this
next yeare. If he had bene chosen by the generall consent of the Corporacion, wee should
haue had reason, to haue charged yow, wth want
of duty and discretion, but being credibly informed, that he hath obtayned that place, by
faction and vnderhand practises, wch he caryed
by some few voices, we haue thought good to sig-
nifie vnto yow this our pleasure, that yow admit not the said Hoskins to that office or dignitie, but vpon the receipt of these our letters, yow proceede to a new election, and make
choice of such a one to represent our person,
qualified in all respects, both in point of Religion and in duty and Loyalty to the advancement of o^r service.

Given at o^r Court at Grafton the 21th of August
1616.^{30}

None of the charges which the King levels at Hoskyns, except the monarch's displeasure, make any
sense. Hoskyns was the most logical choice in the
city for the position. The fact that the King says
that Hoskyns had been the Recorder of Hereford before he removed him, which appears nowhere in the
somewhat spotty records of the city, only makes the
election more meaningful. It was obviously a personal act of James to which he did not even try to
give the appearance of legality by using the Privy
Council as his tool. The fact that the letter appears only among the collection of Scudamore papers
gives us a further hint of what may have happened.
Sir James Scudamore and Hoskyns were never friendly, and as Deputy Steward Hoskyns had accused the
Scudamores of misusing their power in the shire in
regard to fishing rights. In October 1617, John
would write to Ben, "Sr James scudamore is heere I
neyther know nor much care to what purpose." Scudamore apparently reported the election to the
King, made up a story of a forced election, and

510

urged the King to put pressure on the city. Under the circumstances, the Corporation felt that they had to acquiesce to the royal pleasure, and Hoskyns never was allowed to take office.

With this very clear indication that James had not forgiven him, John may have felt that he should take a greater role in the events in London which drew favorable attention from the King. This year's great social event was to be the celebrations connected with the creation of Prince Charles as Prince of Wales. As usual, the Inns of Court took a major role in the festivities. On 11 October 1616, "Messrs. Bastard and Martyn, Masters of the Bench, Hoskyns, T. Warre, and Malet, Masters of the Utter Bar, and Bevis and Bate, under the Bar, are intreated to take care concerning the barriers at the creation of the prince, and for provision concerning the furnishing of them with armour and other necessaries."[31] The first three were, of course, old school chums. The idea they hit upon seemed a good one at first: to put on a martial display for the active young Prince. It would be a lot less expensive than the great masque put on for the wedding of Prince Charles' sister, and the younger members of the House could be the participants. For the moment no one could see any difficulty arising from the idea.

Then, on the last day of October, the celebrations began, with Charles coming down the river by Royal Barge to Whitehall. He was greeted at Chelsea by the Lord Mayor and Aldermen of the City of London, and the river banks were packed with sightseers. John Howe says of the display, "there was ... at the Cities charge in honour of his highnesse creation, more particular, pleasant Trophies and ingenious deuices met him vpon the water then euer was at any former creation of any Prince of Wales."[32] Then, on 4 November, Charles was formally installed as Prince of Wales, Duke of Cornwall, and Earl of Chester. That night the four Inns of Court put on their display. "They included a martial display of mimic combats called 'the Barriers,' given at Whitehall on the evening of the Investiture, by

511

gentlemen from the four Inns of Court."[33] Ten men
were selected from each Inn, "who fought at Barriers viz. the one halfe against the other."[34] No
one of any note represented the Middle Temple, but
Ben Jonson wrote the speeches that were delivered
to the Prince and his father. The result was not
outstanding. "Our Ynnes of Court gentlemen caried
themselves but indifferently at the barriers the
night of the Prince's creation but specially in
theyr complements wherin they were not so gracefull
as was to be wished and expected, but in requitall,
they played the men at the banquet." A "barrier,"
of course, was the low wall that ran between the
lists in chivalric contests. The men in charge of
the event, including Hoskyns, had supervised the
erection of these "barriers" in the Banqueting
House at Whitehall, and after the forty participants had made their compliments to the King and
young Prince, they were supposed "in way of honourable combate to break three staves, three swords,
and exchange ten blowes apiece."[35] But there had
been too long a period of peace, and the young law
students were not terribly martial in their appearance nor courtly in their approach. The King noticed.

On 22 November Martin submitted an expense account from his committee for the Middle Temple's
part in the Barriers. Members of the Inner Temple
were assessed thirty shillings for each bencher,
fifteen for each barrister, and ten for all others.[36] The charge would probably have been less
at the Middle Temple. Under any circumstances, it
was a good deal less than the previous celebration,
and James may have noticed that as well. The following June he suggested to the Inns of Court that
they supply six hundred volunteers "to practise in
martiall discipline."[37] But James had very little
power over the Inns of Court, and no volunteers
stepped forward.

It may have been during 1616 that John acted
as counsel for the widow of Sir Horatio Townsend;
certainly it was before Lord Chancellor Egerton
died in 1617. The story found in MS. Sloane 1757[38]

512

gives us another view of John as a lawyer and of
his practice of carrying his wit into the court
room, at least when a close friend was sitting in
the chair:

Master Hoskins Serjeant at Law, being of Councell
in Chancery for the Lady Town send, (Relict of
Sr Horatio) that stood in Contempt vpon Proces
The S^{r}jant having pleaded long, and well for his
Clyent, The Lord Chancellor Elsmeere asking him
But M^r S^{r}jant What can you say in discharge or
excuse of the Contempt? I hope (said the S^r-
jant) your Lordsh^p will consider, how easy a
matter 'twas for a Lady that in her youth, had
been of great account, if in age she chancd to
fall into Contempt. The Lord Chancellor smyling
at the Seriants conceit, past by the Contempt.

John was not, of course, to become a Serjeant-at-
Law for a number of years, but the recorder of the
anecdote undoubtedly wrote it down or copied it a
number of years later, when Hoskyns had risen to
the heights of Serjeancy.

Hoskyns seems to have gone back to Hereford
after his annual trip to Winchester to pay his
rent, and his mind would have turned to his farms,
for as he rode, the dust swirled up around him.
Howe says of this year, "This Sommer and haruest
was so dry, that Passengers were anoid with dust in
the high wayes, the 20. of Nouember."[39] He must
have talked over the family property with his
brothers, and they decided to let him take over
control of the home farm. Dr. John was caught up
with his own affairs in Ledbury and Worcester (moreover, he was now obligated to his brother for his
law suit concerning St. Oswald's); Thomas was busy
at Bernithen acting as overseer for John and becoming more and more subordinate to him. On 14 January 1617, Thomas and Dr. John surrendered the lands
which they held in Monkton from their father's estate to their brother John.[40] Some idea of the
value of Monkton can be gained from the fact that
when Thomas Brown and William Breton purchased the
property in 1553, they paid £1596 7s 8d.[41] The

value would have increased considerably in the next sixty years. The father must have turned over in his grave, for he had done everything he could to keep just this transfer from taking place. He could not have foreseen what events would transpire in the years following his death, however. One does feel sorry for Thomas, though, as he comes more and more under the control of John. It is not only the legal records that give that feeling; Ben seems to have felt that her husband was treating his brother badly as well. It is true at the same time that this sibling struggle is the only indication of John's doing less than we might wish for one of his relations, and his mother continued to live comfortably in her own home in Monkton, apparently agreeing with John's activities.

On 16 January, two days later, John renewed the lease on the Monkton property with Edmund Browne of Harewood.[42] One of the reasons that Hoskyns seemed to be worried about his growing property was that in many cases the land was held on long-term leases which required a steady rental payment no matter what problems might arise with drought, tenants' problems, rebuilding of houses, etc.

* * * * *

Although he now held the Monkton property without any worry about his brothers' interests, John continued to live in the city of Hereford, and early in 1617 he had to pay a tax of 15d for keeping a horse in the city.[43] Then he went back to London, but he must have wished he had stayed in the relatively uncomplicated west. On 8 February 1617, Chamberlain wrote to Carleton,

> But now for matter of rimes Hoskins the lawier is in a laberinth beeing brought into question for a rime or libell (as yt is termed) made some yeare and halfe agon. Yf he find not the better frends yt is feared he shalbe brought into the Starchamber and then he is undon. Yt is saide they have him in a dilemna either to confesse or to denie yt upon his oath, and then they have

514

sufficient witnes to convince him. The best
hope they have is that my Lord Chauncellor is
his frend, but he hath greater adversaries.[44]

We do not know positively who the adversaries were
nor even which poem is involved. There are four
possibilities for the verse: it might be the poem
on the Parliament Fart, for in Add. MSS. 23,229
that poem is specifically referred to as the "Parliament Libell." But Chamberlain had already sent
that poem to Carleton, and it certainly was extremely well-known long before this. If Hoskyns
were to be in trouble about it, that trouble would
have come up at the same time as his imprisonment.
It could have been the final verse cut into the
Tower window, but that scarcely seems libelous.
Much more likely is the short verse on hearing a
Prince's secrecy. Although the poem is probably
about Sir Thomas Overbury, it could now, with the
downfall of the royal favorite, Somerset, be seen
as a comment on him. Under either circumstance, it
would be read as a criticism of the fickle-minded-
ness of King James. Its composition date would
also seem to fit Chamberlain's description best.
There is the further possibility, of course, that
it is a poem that no longer exists.

The adversary problem is linked to the poem
itself. Somerset was a very real opponent of Hoskyns, but he was in no position to bring pressure
to bear on anyone, as he was sitting in the Tower
of London, pardoned from the death penalty but not
from the conviction of complicity in the Overbury
murder. One possible "greater adversary" than
Chancellor Egerton was George Villiers, Duke of
Buckingham, but that new favorite of James helped
Hoskyns out of his troubles. The other clearly
greater person was the King himself, and there is
reason to believe that James was still attacking
Hoskyns at every chance. There are many examples
of the King's vindictiveness, but perhaps none
quite so petty as his continued attack on Hoskyns.

Whatever the actual circumstances, Hoskyns
was in big trouble once more and was forced to call

515

on his closest friend at court for help. According to Minna Prestwich, in her biography of Lionel
Cranfield, John was actually back in the Tower of
London.[45] This is a little hard to believe as the
letters we have do not indicate anything so extreme.
But he was at least under house arrest in his chambers at the Middle Temple.

Cranfield was now one of the Masters of Re-
quests to King James, and through him John received
Buckingham's help. It may be that John knew that
Buckingham had been against him, but his letter to
Cranfield does not indicate that in any way:

To the right worshipfull Sr Lionell Cranfield
one of the mastrs of the Requests to his Ma^{ty}
S^r
Examininge my hart this sunday morninge wth
the word of truth. I reade wth mine eys that
wch I feele wth my hart He loveth much to whom
much is forgeven. pardon me therefore yf I desire y^u again to remembr my eternall thancks to
that sweete Conduict of the kinges m^{r}cy my h^{ble}
Lord the truly noble Earle of Buckingham this
merit of his becommes as visible to the world
as yf it had ben conferd vpon a more eminent
man, nay more, & is of greater accoumpt lyke a
light in a darke lane more conspicuous & bene-
ficiall then a torch vpon the top of powles.
now men take notice that he p^{r}fers vertuous &
mercyfull acts before any oth^r p^{r}vaylings what-
soev^r, the same labour & intercession to his m^r
my gracious Saueraigne that pacified his displeasure towards me might haue procured a greate
advancement or obtayned a greate suict for an
other
So ev^r will I value it & so eu^r will I proportion my thanckefullnes. And as I stand pardoned
by his Maiesty so may it not be offensive that
I desire I might goe protected agaynst all others who not wthstandinge may question me som for
their malice, som for that in som construccon of
those v^{r}ses they might take themselues to be
parties grieved nothinge will acquitt me a-

516

gaynst all but his Maiesties pardon vnd^r the
greate seale wch yf it be fitt to be moued to
his M^{ty}, (for I beseech y^u thincke I dare not
craue any thinge that my Lord shall doubt to
doe.) then haue I sent yu heerin inclosed a note
for his M^{ties} signature wch beinge superscribed
the rest will passe of course And I shall live
& dye wth prayer in my hart & mouth for my Lord
of Buckingham and yf please god I could wish myselfe a greater man that I might doe yu greater
service by whose worthy & lovinge care & meanes
only I obtayned this favour from my Lord   So I
rememb^r my service yu & my Lady & pray for the
recouerry of her health

Mid Temple

Y^{r}s to commaund & Deservedly

Sunday   J: Hoskyns

  2 Martij[46]

The enclosed note was the usual document for such
an occasion:

   It is o^r pleasure that yo^u drawe vp a pardon
for John Hoskyns Esquire to passe vnder o^r
greate Seale in such forme as yo^u shall thinke
Convenient

To o^r Atturney generall[47]

The Friday nights at the Mermaid Tavern had paid
off. One reason that he may have gotten off so
lightly was that the King left London on March 14th
for a six month trip to Scotland.

   Life returned to normal very quickly, but
there is some indication that Ben was becoming dis-
enchanted with her husband's repeated difficulties
with the King. On 6 June John wrote to her of his
affairs and sent the letter off with William Taylor.[48]

   Sweet hart. I only write to the intent y^t y^u
should have it under my hand that I love y^u better then myselfe & all the world besides. how

517

we doe Taylor can tell y^u somtymes in the day.

I have sent y^u a small token of amber I pray y^u were it on y^r brest for my sake wthout alter-acion. be good to Besse & Dicke, & pray to god that my lord keeper[49] continue his honorable favours to me. I thancke god it begyns to be excellent well. Were it not for spendinge money I would be in Kent a little while for our work lasted till this day & on munday com sevennight begyns agayn. loose not the month & season to cutt down ridde & fell all the bushes in Breni-then wood. I hope the house is covered walled lymed & glazed. Meete me there when I comm down. I pray y^u be earnest with Thomas yf he mortgage the reversion of Trelewisdee to me I will acquitt hym for the 100^l he owes me wch he sayth is but 80. as yf he would the payinge use to be paym^t of the principall. yf so then I will intreat my sister Kempe who now hath money enough to discharge the 40^l to Gryffyn for hym, & pay as much more of his debts as that Rever-sion is worth & any time during his lyfe he shall redeeme it paying use. untill god send hym a sone of his own I know noe fitter heyr for hym then my sonne yf he marry let his wyfes por-tion redeem all & let hym & my mother live out of debt.

Good sweet hart survey y^r selfe & in this tyme let it not be to late to weede out all presumtu-ouse malicious and bitter branches of affeccon or send me word there wilbe no amendment nor rest for me in Herefordsheere, & I will keepe such a diet as by som gout or stone shall end me the sooner. God blesse my boy & your grand-child who wilbe a meanes that I may take away my boy the sooner. I have gotten a day for the Doctor's cause. I will doe anythinge for any of y^u all but I pray y^u skorne me [not?] for it. I end the happyest man in the world yf y^u love me otherwise most

miserable

6 June 1617   J. Hoskyns.

The letter is valuable for our understanding of

John's family relationships in many ways. Dr. John
had married his own brother's step-daughter, Frances Bourne, at some point within the past two
years, probably in the first half of 1616. And
now they had their first child, Charles, Ben's
first grandchild. Thomas is revealed as a person
who could not seem to clear himself of debts and
was more and more beholding to his brother. This
also explains why he was willing to sign over his
rights in Monkton. Now he was being nudged into
giving up his rights to still another piece of
land. It was part of the property that linked the
estate at Bernithen with the Monkton farm. Obviously Thomas gave up the land as it is not mentioned in his will. John's statement about Thomas
making Bennet his heir unless Thomas gets married
and has a son of his own sounds a little harsh, but
it must be remembered that Hoskyns looked after
the affairs of other people's children throughout
his life, as well as his own son's.

But the last paragraph of the letter indicates
the coming cleavage between John and Ben. As I
said before, there is evidence that part of the
problem lay in John's treatment of Thomas; part of
it may have been the result of such long periods of
separation from one another. Perhaps Ben felt that
John was beginning to use her a little like Thomas,
as an overseer for his estates. But perhaps even
more, she was tiring of his constant trouble with
the King, the danger of imprisonment, the worry
over his future. Whatever it was, John's letters
tend to indicate that Ben was the one who grew unhappy with the marriage relationship rather than
he. But then, we only have his side in the letters.

On 29 June he wrote to his wife again,[50] and
the bitterness of the split becomes ever more apparent. His attack on her for having someone else
help write a letter from his little son Bennet
seems a bit overdone, unless he is suspicious of
her fidelity. If his reasons for Ben's keeping his
letters are true, it is too bad, but it is still a
lucky break for us, as we would otherwise never
have learned so much about him.

Ben: I perceyve by the stile of y^r last letter
that little Ben my sone did not dictate all to
y^u wch y^u wrote but I discover som other phrase
therein then y^r own. and yf in things of such
privacy y^u are fortified wth counsayll and assistance it were best for me write no more. for
yf I write good letters, y^u keep them to silence
me yf displeasing letters y^u reserve them to
quarrel wth me & howsoever I shalbe sure to
heare of them agayn. Only yf I send y^u gold I
am suer never to heare of it agayn   therefore I
send y^u by my Cosen Jones^{51} two peeces. y^u that
are so well advised need no advise of myne,
therefore look to the mill & all y^r state yourselfe. god geve y^u wisdom & not to think y^u
have it. yf I should say I will love y^u as well
as y^u love me it were in other wives cases happy to them. But I love y^u and since y^u answer
it not, god helpe me, & god forgive y^u & blesse
y^r children & myne & geve us grace to place our
love on hym that never fayleth to love us though
we be his enemyes.

29 June 1617.   Your poore husband

whom once y^u loved J. Hoskyns.

The situation between them was enough in itself to draw him back to Hereford, but there were
the usual business affairs of the city as well. He
wanted to vote in the elections for Mayor early in
August and did so.^{52} He and Ben seem to have
worked out their differences temporarily. Perhaps
he got mad enough to frighten Ben, who appears to
have felt that she was relatively safe in his affection. Whatever it is, she must have written him
a much friendlier letter that autumn, which he answered from London on 16 October 1617:^{53}

Sweet hart

for gods sake be comforted in hart & assured
in mynd that I love y^u more then a thousand
lives of myne own yf I were to have them suc-
cessivelye and fram'd at my pleasure.

My brother Doctor is comme. My Lord Compton
is Lord president for any thinge else I have
yet but seene the Citie & Westminster hall...
let Ben learne to write & David to, for Ben it
will be of necessity for he must learne to make
a latyn vulgar or sentence shortely & that must
be written. I daylie pray for y^u & y^r little
sicke daughter & for all the family. Remember
my most loving commend^{ns} to my sister & her
daughters, & forget that I was cholericke it
was nature not malice for in reason & judgem^t I
am nothinge but love and kindnesse.

Dr. John not only had his room at the Hereford
house of his brother but also stayed at John's
chambers in the Temple on his visits there. Both
of them would have been interested in the appointment of William Lord Compton as Lord President of
the Marches of Wales on November 24th, which explains why he was able to report the King's decision before the actual investiture took place.
Compton became the first Earl of Northampton of the
new Compton line on 19 July 1618. The 1614 death
of Henry Howard had brought the earlier line to an
end. Hoskyns was to have good working relations
with the new Earl and even composed a piece of
music for his pleasure: Aubrey wrote a note to
himself to "Get the song or speech of serjant Hoskyns of the earl of Northampton, the Lord President
of Wales."[54] Unfortunately he did not get it, and
it has been lost.

Young Ben, or Bennet, or Benedict, was now
nearly eight years old, and his father was pushing
his education, perhaps faster than his mother
wanted it. Within three years he would be moving
to London, as John had intimated in his June 6th
letter, and his father wanted him prepared. Of
David we know nothing but the name. It is likely
that he was Ben's "page", temporarily replacing
the "Tom" of the poem "A Dreame." Just as the
young William Taylor had received his education at
the same time as John Bourne, so this David would
have received lessons at the same time as his
charge. Mrs. Kempe, Hoskyns' sister-in-law, con-

tinued to live with her sister throughout this period, bringing up her daughters, and a son Robert, who was still in his minority in 1630. What Robin Kempe, the husband, did until his death in 1628 is never mentioned.

Two weeks later John wrote again, on 30 October.[55] Sir Ralph Winwood, the King's Secretary, had his wish granted that he would never see another Parliament.

...Secretary Winwood is as dead as my lord byshop. Sr James scudamore is heere I neyther know nor much care to what purpose. My brothers cause is heard & the order is enclosed in the pap^r wrapt up in this lett^r I have not receved the mony of Mr Alford[56] as yet but shall upon the day. I supt the last week with Mr Alford & this night I sup with hym agayn... My brother cannot comm down till about the tenth of November, for about that tyme the tenants of the hospital are to be treated wth what they will receve yearely till the lease expire. I will send you mony & other things when I have them, in the meane tyme be merry & thancke god of a poore husband that is not the worst of husbands

The news of the death of Robert Benet, Bishop of Hereford, was bad for both Hoskyns brothers. He was John's close friend and Dr. John's patron. But neither could be back in Hereford to see their friend pass away on October 25th, for it was on that day that the St. Oswald's case was heard in Chancery and John won the decision for his brother. John knew of his wife's interest in Dr. John's affairs, which explains why he sent the court order along for her to read.

On November 11th he wrote again, sending the letter home with Dr. John.[57] His relations with his brother Thomas seem to have reached a new low.

Sweet hart. My brother Doctor is loath to carry money but when I see what is lefte me then I will seeke som returne and comme myselfe as soon

522

as I can. yf there be any thinge else besides
a gown for the wynter that y^u want I pray y^u
send me word. I heare that my brother Thomas is
so foolish as to come up in the worst tyme of
the yeare to no end that I know of except it be
to drincke wth Thomas Hynde. I had rather he
stayed at home & procure me elmes to be sett at
Brynithen and the quick sett hedge to be made
that he & I talked of level from the upper gate
poste at the end of the lane by the barne to the
upper corner of the meadow underneath Biddle-
stons meadow.58 and to sett wallnuts, chest-
nutts, beechmaste, ashenkeys & akornes, & for
any thinge heere I can better doe it for hym
then he can for hymselfe... I am sorry to heare
that y^u want wood, yf Thomas had ben honest of
his promise it could not had ben so. but doe
not y^u spare any money to keepe yourselfe & your
family in health farre better to spend money &
have health then have sicknesse & want money...
I have spoken wth your new lord president. I
have no ambition but to comme out of debt & enjoy myne own in quiet. And whereas y^u write to
me not to be cruell I shalbe glad to serve y^u,
so y^u will not be in perpetual quarrell wth me.
And I am now old & expecte to be more contemt-
ible, & therefore to passe unmedled wth. But
never looke to have any in this world love y^u
better....

He lived up to his promise and headed west as
soon as he could get away. This time he had a real
plum in his possession, and he had not forewarned
his wife. If she had been surprised at his sudden
willingness for her to spend as much as she wanted
or needed, she now found the reason. On 25 November
1617 he was made Commissioner of all the lands in
Hereford of the Neville family.59 Edward Neville,
Lord Abergavenny, at the urging of his son and
heir, Sir Henry, gave Hoskyns the power of attorney
in dealing with land leases and purchases. John's
commission would be a healthy fee in each case,
and the Neville lands were very large. Sir Henry
had been a close associate with Hoskyns in the Parliamentary cause in the first Parliament of James I,

although he had shifted sides in 1614, He also had been among the company of wits in London. His younger brother, Christopher, had been imprisoned along with John in 1614. Perhaps they felt that they owed Hoskyns something. More likely, though, they both appreciated his legal ability and his wit. Sir Henry had a good sense of humor himself. Several of the stories in that collection of very funny and often very rude jokes which Sir Nicholas L'Estrange made in the early seventeenth century deal with Sir Henry and his wife. The Earl of Dorset once asked Sir Henry "how he went to worke to gett such handsome children of such an ill fauoured woman as his wife; O my Lord sayes he, I am like Aesops Cocke, I can digg pearles you see, out of a Dunghill."[60] Knowing Neville, he probably recounted the conversation at his own dinner table in front of his wife. Another story may well concern a dinner party in which Hoskyns took part. The sense of humor matches rather closely with his:

> The Lady Neuill would needs carue a peece of cheese, with superlatiue commendations, to a good witty merry gentleman then at the Table, and when he had tasted, ask't his opinion; Madame sayes he, the cheese it seemes is your owne, and therefore you haue some reason to like it, but I professe, for my part, I would neuer desire to eate worse; she rashly apprehending the worse sense, grew very angry, till he explained his meaning.[61]

Dinner at Sir Henry's was never dull. One time he told of a woman on one of his estates who came to his court and made

> a pittifull complaint how such a man had rauisht her; he granted a warrant, and the fellow was brought: and vpon examination, the wench hauing made her strongest allegations, the fellow confes't he had carnally knowne her, but not without her consent; for if it please your worshippe, sayes he, she tooke vp her smocke very willingly; O Lord, S^r, sayes she, If I had not done so, he kept such a wimbling, as he had bor'd a

greate whole in my smocke presently.[62]

Hoskyns went right to work on his job as Commissioner, and on 9 January 1618 he completed five
land transactions for the Nevilles.[63] The total
yearly rents involved were £13 3s 9d, and the payments for the leases themselves were £10 9s 9d, of
which Hoskyns no doubt collected a healthy part as
the man who "for divers other good causes, and con-
sideracions, them especially mouinge" brought a-
bout the transactions. One of the interesting side
notes is that for the first time we find John involving still another brother in his legal activities. Phillip Hoskyns signed all of the leases as
a witness, along with John's regular clerk, William
Taylor. Phillip remains the least-known member of
John's immediate family, but that he was close to
John is indicated by the fact that he made his own
son John his eldest brother's godson. Phillip managed the farm at Didley for his brother for many
years.

* * * * *

Having fulfilled his duties to the Nevilles
for the moment, John left immediately for London.
It was to be an extremely busy year, but it started with an uncustomary sickness for a man of John's
strength. Like many a very strong and healthy man,
he reacted with fears of immediate death. On 6
February, he wrote a letter to his wife that reads
as much like a will as it does a letter.[64] There
is a kind of death-bed honesty about the whole letter which makes one feel as though he were telling
the whole truth about their marital problems. He
admits his own faults freely, but he also places a
good deal of blame on Ben's quickness of temper and
her forcefulness of temperament. There is no over-
statement in his prophecy that she will find no
other husband who will deal with his children as
well as he has dealt with hers. Even here, as
fearful of his future as he is, he shows as much
care for his stepdaughter Bess as he does for his
own two children. What rankles the most is his
brother Thomas, and he does not restrain himself
from charging Thomas with lewd vices and lack of

525

thrift; that this man, even though he is a brother, should have to get a pension out of John's estate worries him almost more than his own state of health.

   This is now the 8th day that I have kept my bedd. yesterday I tooke a purge by Doctor Giffords advise. he would had me this day ben let blood I would stay till this frost thaws: he would not have me stay. And I am willinge to doe as please hym for he doth all things discreetely & safely. There are but 3 ways eyth^r this suddayn obstruccon̄ wi̅ll bringe death wch is most welcom of all and to speake the truth I most earnestly desire it. first to enjoy my savious secondly I have seene enough & known enough & to much of this world: thirdly God hath led me by his hand past the difficulties of malice, misery & debt, there is but one enemy to conquer, death, whom my saviour hath conquerd for me, & I longe to step over his backe.
   And when I am gonne an old objection will be ended, whether I wanted65 others or others wanted me. I shall synne no more; I shalbe reprehended no more. the second way is yf this be but a cold it cannot be longe my strength or physicke will break it. The third is yf it grow to be consumption I shall have the longer tyme to repent but that will be the most miserable of all. I shall have them sawcy with me that ought not to be so. I shall be uprayded to be a waster of a poore estate. it grieves me of what is lost already. to save the rest & obtayn peace: it were best dye now, & best dye heere where no body dares interrupt my thoughts. To be a true Judge of myselfe I thincke the greatest part of this is Melancholy yet god graunt never worse melancholy possesse my mynde. b̄e y^u merry for I feele no payne but a deep longe cough somtymes labour for breath w^thout any payne & som daunger to be chockt when I sleepe. this ten days I have eaten once a day towards night well enough but w^thout any greate desire my stomach is so full of flagme. yet somtymes I am thirsty as I drincke seldom but physicke drincke & that

not 2ise a day. the losse of my pracktise makes
me sadde. I know you could be contented to endure me longer wth money. yf I scape this and
come home be not froward be not crosse, w^thdraw
not y^r hart nor counsayll from me pracktise not
upon me reprehend me no more. for then my next
sicknes I will certaynly dy yf I cann: & would
now yf I could. the reason may be guessed: doe
y^u thincke that I see not what I doe amisse.
doe y^u thincke I speak not more bitterly to my
own hart for every offence then you cann? doe
y^u thincke it can be pleasinge to me to see y^u
suffer such things und^r y^r eys & authority as
y^u doe in others & reserve y^r gale[66] for me?
This hath made me ask, I have been somtymes
stunge a fortenight to breake out in a rage.
but god & y^r soule knows who begyns. Selfe &
sudden will & presumtion above y^r sex in y^u: riot & misdiet in me must be amended. I by the
laws of god am y^r governor you are not mine.
Yf y^u desire a sole supremacy marry no more when
I am dead: thére be enough that can speake y^u
fair & undoe y^u, and y^u shall fynd none to
deale wth myne as I have dealth with y^rs
Chaunge that wicked axiom wch y^u repeat so often
that y^u desire to be kyndly used though it be
by a dissembler. for I dreamt I saw a dissembler pawninge y^r plate, sellinge y^r leases,
feastinge in y^r house & putting my boy to keepe
his hawks & dogges & y^u makinge much of hym. I
will leve y^u all & therefore give me leve to
leve y^u this, and I pray y^u make bett^r use of
it then to grieve. For god knows I desire y^r
health & contentment rather then my own lyfe.
When I am gonne never doe what y^u suddaynly desire or determin, follow no counsayll of them
that flatter y^u geve them good words or rather
money then the governm^t of y^rselfe. be not
tyed to the service of any one to much for y^u
will so endure anythinge rather then loose such
a one, that y^u & y^r children will become servaunts ere y^u be aware, & therefore harken for
exchaunge in tyme & use them all well. Stuff
not y^r house wth to many people. let my boy be
continually kept at his booke choose an honest

527

man for Besse, for little Dicke neyth^r y^u not
I but god must provide an husband. It grieves
me that the livinge wch I shall leve y^u is so
little & that he must have a pension out of it
in whom there never was courage, & now I descry
snekinge lewd vices & unthriftines. I have bitterly reproved hym. I hope he will amend therefore speake not of it. Will Harbin^{67} stays
heere to bringe me home yf it be gods will yf
I comm geve me no ill words yf I comme not y^u
are ridde of one that offended you much. I pray
you forgive hym for gods sake & he with all his
soule prays for y^r health & contentment in this
world & to see y^u in the kingdom of heaven longe
hence.

God blesse the poor children   J. Hoskyns.

Under John Gifford's friendly care, he not only recovered but also did not need to return to
Hereford. Gifford was a lifetime friend and now
treated his Wykhamist associate with all the attention he could ask. And on 30 March Hoskyns must
indeed have felt that he had turned the corner.
Either Buckingham or Cranfield seems to have persuaded the King to forgive Hoskyns completely, for
the monarch sent a writ to the Mayor of Hereford,
ordering the city to pay the money they owed John
for his service in Parliament:

It was ordered by Phillip Symonds Esqr Mayor
and w^t· major part of the Common Counsell of
the s^d Citty of Hereford that they of y^e Common
Counsell every of them within their Wards wth
some others shall assess their Wards with a
Double tax for the satisfyeing of John Hoskins
Esqr late one of the Burgesses of the Parliament for the S^d Cittye of 92$^{\pm}$. Allowed him by
the Kings Writt now in the Sheriffs hands for
his Parliam^t Expences for 9 hundred ℘ Odd Days
after the rate of 2^s per Diem.^{68}

With this long overdue payment John was able to
clear up outstanding debts and look forward to an
even more successful future.

But if the year had begun with false fears of his own death, the spring brought real news of his older brother's death. Oswald had led a successful life as a merchant tailor in London and had even managed to marry the daughter of the head of the Guild of Merchant Tailors, Randolph Wooley, the man to whom Dr. John dedicated part of his book of sermons. Oswald had eight children when he died, and one more was on the way. But only the first, William (named after his uncle who had died as an infant or young child), was a boy. In order followed Mary, Magdalen, Elizabeth, Elinor, Margery, Katherine, Thomasina, and then, posthumously, Frances. William was named executor in his father's will, but he was only slightly older than John's son Bennet and was, therefore, completely dependent on the care of his uncles.

By 10 April 1618, Oswald felt sick enough to draw up his will, a duty that a surprisingly large number of people of the time left until the very last minute. Somewhere within the next two weeks he died, and on the 27th the will went through Probate.[69] Responsibility for the large family was shared equally by John and Dr. John. Oswald apparently did not trust the business acumen of his wife. Except for her legal portion of the inheritance, she simply remains unmentioned. It was certainly not a sign of a lack of affection, but Oswald wanted his children safely taken care of.

The city of London had a quite remarkable system of guaranteeing a just division of an estate: one third went to the wife, one third to the children, and one third could go to specific bequests. The third due to the children was handled through the City of London Court in the Guildhall, and the records kept are extraordinarily precise. Executors of a will were made to present a complete record of all money, land, personal possessions, debts, outstanding income, etc., of the deceased and the City of London personally received the money due to the children. They then put this money out to trusted persons, usually personal acquaintances of the deceased recommended by the ex-

529

ecutors, taking a recognizance which bonded the
receiver for an amount that included the actual
money from the estate that he was to pay to the
children plus an amount that could reasonably be
expected as interest. If the person under bond
fulfilled the obligation to the children, however,
he was not charged for whatever money he himself
gained in the way of interest. Such a recognizance was a valuable situation for a person, as he
had a good deal of money to work with in order to
make more money for himself. The hitch was that on
the twenty-first birthday of each child, or on the
day of marriage of the girls if they married before they were twenty-one, the person under bond
had to appear in the Mayor's Court in London with
the exact amount of cash called for in the recognizance. In some cases the Court also required
that those receiving money look after the children,
providing food, clothing, and housing.

Oswald's will is quite straightforward. He is
the only member of his family that did not begin
his will with a long statement of religious beliefs and statements of hope in the divine will.
First, he divided his estate "accordinge to the
Custome of the Citty of London," between his wife
Elizabeth, his children "as well alreadie borne as
that his wife is nowe Conceaved withall equallie
betweene them," and a series of specific bequests.
First, he left his two smallest children, Thomazin
and the one not yet born, an added £300 apiece.
Among his specific bequests he gave Osias Churchman, who was another Merchant Tailor and former
servant of Randolph Wooley, £20 "in Consideracion
to doe his best indeavor for gettinge in of his
Debtes"; "To the Companye of the Marchantaylors
for a dinner on the day of his buriall Thirtie
poundes"; and to all of his servants the usual
black mourning gowns. He gave his lands to his
wife "duringe her life and after her death to William his sonne and his heires." What remained after his debts were paid was to be divided equally
among his children. Although he made William his
sole executor, "he beinge in his minoritie he
maketh and ordeyneth his lovinge brothers John

530

Hoskins Doctor of the Civill lawe and John Hoskins Esquier Administrators of his goods and Chattells duringe the mynoritie of his said sonne William." Actually, the main burden fell upon John. For the next three months he and his brother were busy clearing up his brother's accounts, and it would be four years before all of the recognizances were cleared through the Guildhall.

On 7 May John and his brother appeared before George Bolles, the Mayor of London, and placed themselves under an obligation of £1000 to bring into that Court within two months a "perfact Inventory in writing vpon their oaths theren conteyning all and singuler the goods Chattells rights and creditts plate Jewells and ready Money and Debtes wch were the said Testato^rs at the tyme of his death...."70

The next morning he wrote to Ben:71

Sweet hart. we are in health & pray for y^u. Concerning y^r resolution touching comminge hither I leve it to god & y^r mynde. things must be as god geves occasions. Y^r daughter72 wrote from Ledbury that you were gonne to Bath wth my sister Kempe, & Mrs. Harbyn wrote that her mother was gonne & left her wth you. Yf y^u want any thinge that is to be had hence let us know we will procure it by gods helpe. Above all things make much of y^rselfe for y^u are the only comfort that is lefte me. I pray y^u let Ben be encouraged to learne & to write. I looke for a letter from hym. God blesse hym & Besse & Dicke & francke & Tom & all that are alive, & are to come, for when Charles died Ben succeeded when I went to Tower Dicke was geven us: and if god send us another for Oswald It is his mercyfull supply....

If the David of the earlier letter had been a replacement for Tom Taylor, he had now returned to his own home, and Tom was once more part of the family. John and Ben seem to have become reconciled; at least their relations were better for the

531

time being.

On 19 May he wrote again.[73] Oswald's estate
was apparently more complicated than John had expected. It must have doubly angered him that
Thomas was causing trouble just at the moment that
he was working on their dead brother's estate. And
the fact that the citizens of Hereford were giving
him still further trouble in the collection of his
rightful pay for Parliament only angered him more.
It was a fortunate thing that Sir Francis Bacon
was now clearly on his side.

> Sweet hart I feare we shall not see y^u this
> Whitsontyde for we have not yet put of the shop
> & wares being a matt^r of 4000^l & above & we
> have great debts to pay & som to receave w^{ch}
> will aske continual attendaunce... Thomas would
> know whether he shall receve 60^l of Maynston.
> I would have hym tell hym that I respect not
> his title to BrynIthen but his intention to
> quarrell & his good will wch he shews yf he re-
> fuseth to release. It were best for hym to doe
> soe least I put on foote a title from oth^r Mayn-
> stons to Pykefield. Notwthstandinge yf y^u neede
> mony doe as y^u will. The cytizens have peti-
> cioned to barre me my fees. My Lord Chauncelour
> awnswerd he would geve them no helpe neyther in
> law nor equity. I thancke them for their good
> will. the und^r shieryf awnswers me it shalbe
> payd to whom I pleased--I say to y^u....

Within the next four days he received a letter from
Ben which indicated that she had misread his previous message of 8 May. This exchange is the best
evidence we have that Ben was able to manufacture
hurt feelings out of whole cloth. No wonder that
Frances preferred being on her own in Ledbury than
with her mother. John tried to smooth the troubled
waters, but it was growing more and more clear that
he should try to return to Hereford as soon as possible.

> ...I perceve by franck's letters to her husband
> she had rather be at Ledbury then wth y^u. I

pray y^u therefore love y^rselfe best & next love
them best that love to be wth y^u. I am glad yf
y^u are at Brynithen, though it seemes Francke is
unwillinge to goe wth y^u. Sweet hart I never
denied y^u leve to goe to Bath I rather much desired that y^u would goe, & when I heard y^u were
going was sory that y^u had not servants to attend y^u & was carefull to have sent to y^u. I
thincke myselfe borne to no bett^r purpose then
to procure y^r contentm^t in all things & rather
desire to dye then to fayll in it. I dare not
write all the love that I beare towards y^u for
feare least y^u keepe my letter as an Evidence
agaynst me when y^u turne curst yet I canot forbeare to professe my selfe

Y^r truest servant

23 May 1618.   J. Hoskyns.[74]

On 19 June Mr. Ford was named Reader at the
Middle Temple for the Autumn, and Hoskyns was appointed along with James Whitelocke and two others
to stand at the Cupboard.[75] Thus began the sequence of positions leading to his own election as
Reader. It must have been a mixed pleasure for
him to be given this duty at a time when he had so
many other tasks to attend to. On July 9th he was
back in the Lord Mayor's court with his brother to
report their activities in clearing up Oswald's estate. This time they bound themselves for an additional £2000 until such time as they brought in
a record of all "doubtfull and desparate debtes"
which Oswald had incurred and also brought to the
court "good and sufficient sureties to be bounde
for the true and sure payment of soe much thereof
as shalbe founde due and belonginge to the said
Children...."[76] Oswald's estate was not quite as
great as he had thought in his will, and John's
statement to Ben about the large debts was no over-
statement. As a matter of fact, Oswald's entire
estate turned out to be only slightly over £1000,
as the third which legally came to all the children
amounted to only £338 8d. The bulk of their inheritance (over £2000) came not from their father,
but from their grandfather, Randolph Wooley.

Late in July Hoskyns finally made it back to
his home in Hereford. His brother's affairs had
made him all the more aware of his own family, and
it seems likely that it was during this summer
that he drew a pen sketch of himself and family.[77]
His step-son, John Bourne, was his close companion
now at the Middle Temple and warranted an important
position in the family; his step-daughter Bess was
always a favorite and would take over the running
of his household on the death of her mother. His
wife almost disappears in her head-covering, but
that should not surprise us considering their
fluctuating relations. The two young children are
treated with delicacy and love. But the main interest is on Hoskyns himself, with his large nose
and somewhat receding hair. His strength and humor
are both apparent, more so than in the finished
portrait on the other side by the skillful minia-
turist of the time, also named John Hoskyns. This
professional portrait gives us a sense of strength
and vitality, but it flatters John in a way that
his own self-portrait does not.

While he was at home in Hereford, he received
a letter from Sir Thomas Coningsby, inviting him
and his wife for a weekend visit to his estate at
Hampton Court, eight miles north of Hereford, on a
bend of the Lugg River.

Well esteemed Mr. John Hoskins
In my afaires at the Assises you were one of
them in list of my direction to Tho. Eaton to
be entreated to employ the skill of your profession, untill we heard that you were not returned from London; and since he informes me
that you cominge home but soddenlie, would not
(I thancke you) of your own accord stand to
looke on where I had matter of interest & reputation; and nowe beinge by the good successe
of them at leisure to thinke of other things
amongst the rest there occurred a further consideration to perfect (if God will) my pious intentions in your neighborhood there. And for
that purpose doe desire conference with you,
and an houres examination of particulars. And

doe hereby invite you to kepe the second Saboath
of August here with me. And that you wilbe
pleased soe to direct your journey as that you
may be here on the Saturday night by fower of
the Clocke that we may have leisure to consult
& over-reade and afterwards to sett down & perfect that (yf yt please God) wch is yet imper-
fect, untill when I leave you to your other
good occasions, and ever rest

> your very loveng Freand

> Tho. Conyngesbye

If you will bringe
Mrs. Hoskins to take the
aire of our gardens   Hampton Courte
I will bid her welcome.   30 July 1618.[78]

Coningsby's "pious intention" was the hospital that
he founded in 1614 on Widemarsh St., just on the
city limits of Hereford. Evidently he had not completed that work by 1618 and wished to do so. His
friendship with Hoskyns is clear from his letter,
as is his trust in his friend's ability.

There was much to do in the intervening days,
and John was not able to vote in the mayoral elections on 3 August,[79] but as his close friend John
Clarke received all of the votes except for Clarke's
own (he diplomatically voted for an ex-Mayor, John
Warden), Hoskyns' presence was not really necessary. John was probably down at Bernithen, trying
to get Thomas to do the work around the estate that
had not been accomplished through his instructions
in letters to Ben. Moreover, a new idea had come
to him: it would be far easier for him to take
care of Oswald's large and helpless family if they
were on one of his own pieces of property than if
they remained in the city of London. The obvious
place for them was in one of the large houses and
spacious lands of Monkton or Bernithen. But moving the family into Bernithen would take some careful preparation, preparation which he was not likely to wish to entrust to Thomas. In the meantime,
he set his sister-in-law up in his own home in
Hereford to await the arrival of her child.

After his visit to Hampton Court on the weekend of August 8th, he journeyed south to Monmouth
to renew his commission from Lord Abergavenny as
Steward and Commissioner for the Neville lands.[80]
He then had to return to London immediately to take
his post at the Cupboard, arguing the fine points
of law for the instruction of the law students of
the Temple. But by 5 October he was back in Hereford for a by-election.[81] His main purpose for returning to Hereford, however, was to pursue his
plan for Bernithen. On 8 October he bought 5 acres
of fertile land which extended right into the town
of Langarren.[82]

By the 16th he was back in London again, and
the travelling had taken its toll, for he was sick
once again. On 16 October he managed to talk the
Benchers of the Middle Temple into letting him have
another chamber next to his own added to his present rooms.[83] Perhaps he was already planning for
a space for Bennet when he would be admitted during John's term as Reader. Then, on the 24th, he
wrote to Ben.[84] Sick as he was, he still could
plan for the best use of his lands in Bernithen
and take on the duties of a substitute father for
his brother's family. If his manner about the
naming of Oswald's child seems more than a little
brusque, it must be remembered that he took his
duties within the Hoskyns macro-family very seriously, especially now as the eldest living male.

...I am free from the cough but only in the
morninge a quarter of an howre. I am faynter
& weaker then ever but wth no payne. It hyn-
ders my gaigne for what wth hillary termes sicknes & the two last termes busynesse upon my
brothers death & the heavynesse of my spiritts
now that cannot endure to stirre abroad & meete
occasions of employment, my harvest falls short
of my other yeares.
...I would have so many bought of all fine
fruicts as shall sett the ground called the Coni-
gree at Brynithen all over. It is the ground
eastwards the house where Thomas sayd a fine
orchard would be made. Let them be sett a fair

536

distance asund^r that they may not shadow the
ground. Let the ground be well fenced in & let
no rother beasts comm into it nor shall comm
these 4 yeares. The profitt of it will be made
as gaignefull by corne, at first wth oates or
barly & plow it flatt & afterwards by hay for
it well easyly be made meadow.
        ...yf my sister hath a boy let hym be called
John or Randolph yf a girle let it be Francke[85]
& let Francke be godmother--Godfather Mr. Clarke
eyther of them Mr. Pember, Mr. Crumpe, Mr.
Warden, Mr. Doctor Benson Mr. Harbyn Mr. Jef-
feryes or any other of no lower degree then
these & I pray y^u let no sparinge be of expense
to lay her down as handsomly as she was wont in
this town, her own estate shall discharge it.
The maydes will speake of it heere & therefore
good Ben let it be well donn...
        ...God send my sister a safe delivery. looke
to her at that tyme, she may be a little out of
time y^u must hier an handsom keeper, that may
be Mrs. Atkyns besides her midwyfe & maydes....

        Another reason for his melancholy besides his
physical state was the impending death of his
friend Sir Walter Ralegh. Ralegh had been allowed
to try one more search for gold in the Americas,
but he had once again aroused the wrath of the
Spanish, whom James was trying to placate. It gave
James the excuse he wanted, and on 28 October Ralegh was tried for his former supposed act of
treason, convicted, and, on the following morning,
beheaded. There were very few who saw any real
justice in the act. It did not endear the chief
prosecutor, Sir Francis Bacon, to Hoskyns either,
even though Bacon had been helpful to John recently.

        Another of the Prince d'Amour associates was
also on his deathbed. Hoskyns' closest friend a-
mong the wits, Richard Martin, had risen quickly in
recent years and found his efforts crowned with the
position of Recorder of the City of London, one
which would have eventually "made" him financially.
James Whitelocke said that Martin was made Recorder
"by sollicitation of sir Lyonell Cranfeild, master

of the requestes, being tolde it shold be done for
him, but he must be thankful." Martin then gave
out some two or three hundred pounds, not realizing how much was expected; but he discovered that
he was expected to give Sir Edward Zouche £1500.
Zouche was paying Sir Thomas Vavasor £3000 for taking over his new position as Marshall of the House.
(Vavasor had survived his implication of complicity
in the Overbury case.) And so it went, up the
chain, with the final person getting the greatest
benefit from the musical chairs being the King himself. Martin did not have anything like £1500, so
"This money was layd downe by sir Lyonell Cranfeild
for mr. Martin, but it lay so heavye at mr. Martin's hart after he knewe of it, that he fell ill
and heavye upon it, and toke his chamber and never
came forthe untill he was caryed to buryall."86
The story is a nice one, but it is not very likely
that a man-about-town like Richard Martin was so
unschooled in the ways of the Jacobean court, especially with as close a friend as Lionel Cranfield; it was smallpox, not melancholy, that carried him off on 31 October.87 Even Aubrey's version has more of the ring of truth to it than
Whitelocke's: "I thinke he dyed of a merry Sym-
posiaque with his fellow-Witts."88

We have seen many indications that the Mermaid Tavern group kept together through the years
on an informal and individual basis, but none are
more pleasant than the series of events following
Martin's death. According to Aubrey, Hoskyns wrote
a short Latin poem that was placed on Martin's
Bible.89 Martin evidently left his Bible to his
friend Hoskyns, and John used it as a memento mori.
He addressed the Bible in close personal terms,
"thou who holdest the words of eternal health [or
salvation]." It is a love-pledge of friendship
and sadness; he asks that while he lives, it will
keep him mindful of Martin, of death, and of God.

Then the friends set up a monument to Martin
in the Temple Church. It is one of the very few
monuments that escaped the devastating bombing of
the Temple in the second World War. One of the

nice ironies of history follows from Anthony à
Wood's statement: "There was no Person in his time
more celebrated for ingenuity than R. Martin, none
more admired by Selden, Serjeant Hoskins, Ben.
Johnson, &c. than he."90 Martin's monument now
stands directly over the tomb of John Selden. On
Martin's monument is the Latin epitaph which Hoskyns wrote in memory of his dead friend. Just as
it should be, there is a wonderfully light touch
to the inscription, especially located as it is in
the church of the Inns of Court: "Hail, reader!
Martin lies here; if you don't know him, ask others. Meanwhile, think of your own tomb." Then he
addresses Martin as Jurisconsult (but the typical
passerby would also be a lawyer or at least training to be one) and tells him to put everything up
to prayer, and anything that is left to litigation,
and "time will be, for you, eternal." That, of
course, can also be read as "you will have eternal
life," which gives it a more acceptable meaning for
a church, but Martin would have appreciated the
double meaning. The intricacies of lawsuits could
often seem as long as eternity itself. At some
time after Martin's death, John, Chris Brooke, and
Hugh Holland gave Lionel Cranfield a portrait of
Martin with a dedication.91 They all recognized
what Cranfield had done for their mutual friend
and wanted to express their appreciation. It would
have been hard to forget their old friend as they
passed through the Temple church daily. Kneeling
in prayer, dressed in his red and black robes, Martin remains to this day an attention-getting figure.

     One irony of Hoskyns' inscription to Martin
was that John was now to be involved in one of
those interminable lawsuits that seemed to stretch
to eternity. Every lawyer must run up against
someone like Alice Williams some time in his life,
but it must have seemed just a bit too much at the
end of this year for John. On 23 November 1618,
she went before Sir Francis Bacon, now Lord Verulam, and argued, through her distinguished lawyer
Francis Williamson, that five years before she had
lent Hoskyns the sum of £27 on the condition that
in one year he would pay her back £29 14s. She

admitted that he had paid her small amounts at
several times, totalling some ten pounds. In her
charge she says that Hoskyns doth "most vnconsion-
ablie and vniustlie contrarie to all equitie and
good consience vtterlie" refuse as well as "intending vtterlie to defraude yor Oratrix." Williamson
toned all that down to "refuse to pay" and "these
being due unto yor Oratrix." Apparently he was already a little suspicious of her charge. She goes
on to say that this money is "all the meanes she
hath to preferr or mayntayne herself."[92] Hoskyns

> Answered the said Bill or a Bill to the same ef-
> fect in all things And the Bill and Answere was
> referred to Mr Williamson beinge her owne Coun-
> cell and if he found anie reason of her com-
> plaint to order what he though fitt for her, if
> he found her Complaint to be clamerous ꝙ false
> then to take order for her punnishm^t who seeing
> the said Bond menconed in the said Bill and the
> paym^{tes} indorsed vpon the same and a certificate
> of her disposicon ꝙ behavioure from the maior
> ꝙ Chief Cittysons of the Cittye of Heref where
> shee was borne and had lived disorderlye a longe
> tyme tould her that there was nothinge due to
> her ꝙ soe he must reporte, wherevpon shee
> rayled at him ragiously that shee forced him to
> send her to Bridwell by the Constable of Far-
> rington Extra after wch tyme shee sensed [sic]
> her clamoures against this defendant.[93]

For the time being, Hoskyns was free of the woman,
but it was not to be for very long.

* * * * *

In general, 1619 was the best year for John
since before the Addled Parliament. No major tragedies among his family or friends marred the passage of days, and although the marvelous banqueting
hall at Whitehall burned down on January 12th and
Queen Anne died on March 2nd, neither of these e-
vents were of the kind to bother Hoskyns. He may
not even have been in London for the first, and he
managed to help clear up some of Oswald's accounts
as a result of the second. On 20 January 1619 he

540

was in Winchester, signing another ten year lease
on Titley, and on the 29th the Parliament of the
Middle Temple, which Hoskyns was soon to join,
chose James Whitelocke for the Autumn Reading.
Whitelocke and Hoskyns were again two of the four
barristers appointed to stand at the Cupboard for
Lent.[94]

The death of Queen Anne led to the usual formal ceremonies connected with the death of royalty.
She died on March 2nd at Hampton Court, and a week
later her body was brought to Denmark House in the
Strand.[95] The burial, however, did not take place
until the Saturday before Whitsunday, May 13th.[96]
One of the reasons for the delay was that the King
fell very ill following his wife's death and remained on the danger list until April. Meanwhile,
on 15 March, Hoskyns wrote from Hereford to his
old friend Lionel Cranfield, who was Master of the
Wardrobe as well as Master of the Wards and Liveries. The letter is addressed on the outside: "To
my moste Honored frynde Sr Lionel Cranfild K^t m^r
of the wardes and Liueryes:"[97]

My humble service ℮ prayer for y^r happynesse.

our Seruants of my brothers shop in watling-
street writ to me that the provision of blacks
for the Queenes M^{ties} funerall is committed to
yr charge ℮ desier to be recommended to yr re-
membrannce that they may furnish part of it S^r
yf please yu so farre to favour them when they
receue the kings money we shall tell yu how
well it spends in better meate then the proclamation allows vs at this tyme, when the ayre
is so infected wth the smell of redde hearinge
that it is thought it will turne backe the Spanish fleete our liewetenantes are all fethers
our clownes all iron our beacons themselues are
ready to spitt fier whereby yu may see how ill
the Spainards comminge is taken. I desier only
that yu will thincke me a thanckefull man ℮
so vnd^{r}take for me to my Lord Marquesse for
whom and y^u I could dye brauely wth a good will
in a good cause ℮ till then I will live

541

Heref this xvth of   Y^r servant
Marche (1618) ⌈1619⌉   J: Hoskyns

John frankly catches the mood of the country
towards the growing power of Spain, with King James'
strange vacillation between trying to please Spain
with proposals for a Spanish match for Prince
Charles on one hand and his support of his strongly
Protestant son-in-law Frederick on the other. John
knew he had nothing to fear in being witty with his
old friend. He could even risk having Cranfield
tell Buckingham, who had been made Lord Admiral in
January, that he was ready to serve him in battle.
At 54 it was a safe offer, but it gives a good indication of how secure John now felt with the King's
favorite.

The reason that he was in Hereford seems to be
that he was sick once again. At least he took this
opportunity to write his first will. It may simply
be that with so many people dependent upon him, he
wanted to make sure that his affairs were in strict
order in case of any accident. After all, he was
now looking after his own mother, his wife's family, his own children, and the entire family of
Oswald. As a lawyer he was bound to realize the
difficulties which would arise if he were to die
intestate. Whatever the reason, we are given a
complete picture of his state of affairs just at
the point at which he began to become really successful in his chosen field of law.

My last will & testam^t

J. Hoskyns

Gracyous god I geeve thee humble thanckes for
all thy mercyes And I beseech thee for thy
sonne Jesus Christe his sake forgeeve mee my
sinnes And receaue my soule into thy kingdome
by this my last will I bequeathe my body to
Christyan buryall in full Assurance of the Re-
surrecion and Constant faith of my salvacon
All my landes of any freehold estate I geeve to
Benedicta my wife to take all the profits duringe the time that shee shall continue sole and

542

Vnmaryed payinge after her maryage to Bennet my
sonne yearely xvj^l a yeare after he shall ac-
complishe the age of xij^o yeares... [from 12 to
15 Bennet was to receive £16 a year; from 15 to
17, £20; from 17 to 21, £30; from 21 to 25, £40;
from 25 to 32, £50] ... And after xxxij^{en} 100
markes a yeare during her life in her Cover-
ture[98] The said paymts to be made at the
feastes of S^{ct} Michaell tharchaingle and than-
nunciacon of the blessed virgyn S^{ct} Mary yearely by even porcons. And if any of the said
somes be behinde and vnpaid at any of the dayes
aforesaid then I will that my said sonne Bennet
shall enter vpon all or any my said landes of
tenements and the sonne to keepe in his possession vntill he be fully satisfyed the said seu-
rall somes and the Arrerages and x^l over; I doe
will that all my debtes be paid not only out of
my personall estate but out of my landes and
tenements though my sonnes Annuitye be there by
diminished And I doe will that out of my personall estate there be payd 200^l to Elizabeth
Boorne and 200^l to Benedicta My Daughter, I doe
geeve to M^{ris} Fraunces Hoskynes my Daughter in
law one of my best kine, I doe geeve to my brother Mr Doctor Hoskynes the two ringes now vpon
my finger And fouer of my best bookes, I doe
geeve all the rest of my goodes to my sonne in
law Mr John Boorne I doe geeve to my mother a
peece of gould of xxij^s and one of my best
sheets to make her a shrowde, I doe geeve to
my two brothers Thomas and Phillip Hoskyns my
two swordes the eldest to choose, I doe geeve
John Hoskyns my god sonne sonne of my said
brother Phillip sixe sheepe I doe geeve to my
brother Mr Doctor Hoskyns my second best geldinge And to my sonne in law Mr John Boorne my
third geldinge; I doe geeve to William Taylor
iij^l a yeare for three yeares after my deathe to
be receaued out of the profits of a meadow mortgaged to me by John Dunne;[99] I doe geeve to every other of my servants xxx^s a peece, I doe
geeve to my sister M^{ris} Elizabeth Kempe two
peeces of gould of xxij^s a peece to make for a
ringe I doe geeve to my sone Bennet Hoskyns my

silver bason and Ewer my two best Coverlets and
Carpets to be delivred vnto him at the Day of
his maryage, And I doe geeve my said bed and
furniture in my mens Chamber to my daughter
Benedicta to be delivred vnto her like wise at
her day of maryage, I doe geeve to the poore
of All saints wthin the Citye of Heref xl[s] And
to the poore of Lenwarne xx[s] And to the poore
of Lengarren xx[s] I do geeve to my brother M[r]
Doctor Hoskyns the landes that I bought of M[r]
Thomas Morgan[100] to be sould to make restitucon
of the money to my brother Oswaldes Children by
wch it was bought And I doe pray him to geeve
my wife good allowance for keepinge my brother
Oswalds Children and widdow; And of this my last
will I doe make Benedicta my wife executrix And
I doe ordaine my brother M[r] Doctor Hoskyns and
John Bainham esqr assistants to her and to her
vse And I doe geeve to M[r] John Bainham a smale
guilte wyne boule And I desire my wife to take
care of the poore childe at Lyonhalls[101] In
witnes that this is my last will and testament
I haue here put my hand and seale the xxiij[th]
Day of March in the yeare of our Lord god (1618)
[1619]

                              J Hoskyns:[102]

Both from the letters and this will, it is clear
that Hoskyns expected Ben to remarry almost immediately after his death. Fate decreed otherwise, for
he was the one to outlive the other.

    On 11 April John took a further step. He had
apparently put his title to Monkton in his son's
name; now he turned that property over to Oswald's
wife. According to a fragmentary indenture among
the papers of The Mynde in the National Library of
Wales,[103] on that day Bennet demised "all his LoPP
in Mounton" to Elizabeth Hoskyns, including "one
sheepcott with divers other houses and edifices and
one garden and orchard... together with one close
of land called the Croft adioyning." The indenture
goes into great detail about all of the fields and
meadows, by name. Unfortunately the total sum of
money involved is lost. John signed the indenture,

and Elizabeth's son Will signed as a witness.

On 11 June 1619 Hoskyns was named first of those to stand at the Cupboard for Whitelocke's Reading that August,[104] and for the two weeks following August 2nd, he took part in his friend's Reading. Along with his legal duties, he supplied Whitelocke with a buck worth 13/6 and gave him a gift of £3 6s.[105] Whitelocke kept a full account of all of the money that he spent (over £41 for venison alone) and received, with all of the names of the givers. It was a costly position, as Hoskyns was to discover the following spring; in all, Whitelocke spent £239 9s 9d. The gifts from his fellow barristers were a necessity to keep the Reader from going into debt. The Reading ended on Friday the 13th, which may be why Whitelocke simply said, "I ended the Fryday senighte after I began." Ben Hoskyns was not the only superstitious person in Jacobean England.

> That nighte, half a skore of the gentlemen, of whiche my underlector was on, and two of my stewards that wear under the bar, mr. Ticheborn sun and heir to sir Walter Ticheborn and mr. Raynesford sun and heir to sir Henry Raynesford, mr. Hoskins, mr. Borlase, came withe me to Windsor, wheer I layd in a buck, and thear they bore my charges, and the next day I came home, and sume of them withe me, and stayd untill Munday, and then went back.[106]

It was a pleasant ending to their hard work. During the Reading Whitelocke admitted his son Bulstrode without any payment fee, as was the custom.[107]

On 29 October, Hoskyns was elected Reader for the following Lent. At the same time Mr. Tynte was fined for not standing at the Cupboard during Whitelocke's Reading, which meant that Hoskyns and his associates had more than their usual share of work in interpreting and arguing the law cases for the students of the Temple.[108] He was not worrying about the past this autumn, however, as he was deeply involved in one of the most important trials of the period.

With the fall of the Earl of Somerset the carefully nurtured power structure of the Howard family began to fall apart. Northampton had been the guiding mind of the family, and his death in 1614 had robbed the rest of a real source of advice in times of trouble. Not only had the entire group fallen into disrepute because of their active assistance in defense of Somerset; the disreputable handling of the nation's financial affairs by the Earl of Suffolk in his position as Lord Treasurer had endangered the entire country. In his attempt to build his own fortune, he had misused almost every power of his office. Finally, on "Sonday the 19. of July in the after-noone, the King tooke away the Staffe from the Lord Treasurer at White-hall."109 In the autumn the case was brought into the Star Chamber, and one of the persons accused was Sir John Bingley, the Remembrancer of the Exchequer. Hoskyns was called upon to plead his case, and John was up against the toughest opposition in the realm, for Sir Francis Bacon brought the charges against the Howards and Bingley and Sir Henry Yelverton was in charge of the prosecution. Hoskyns was joined with his friends Heneage Finch and Christopher Brooke and two others, Sir Thomas Richardson, a Serjeant-at-law, and Thomas Pyne, in the defense and did a masterful job, in spite of the poor pleading of Brooke. Sir John Bingley's case was important enough to be written up as a legal precedent in the Law Reports.110 As we know that Hoskyns was Bingley's main defense attorney, it is interesting to follow the events of 10 November 1619.

Yelverton, the King's Attorney, charged Sir John Bingley, Writer of Tallies, with abuses in office and for extortions. Bingley was supposed to have extorted and withheld diverse sums of money from several persons, who were named. There was then a general charge that the accused had also extorted from others. After the accused answered the charge, the Attorney set out to prove his point.

546

One example that he gave was the holding back of
money that was supposed to go to "Capt. Baugh, and
others, pyrats." Hoskyns rose from his seat in
court immediately and stopped the Attorney. It
was the kind of legal point at which he was very
sharp. He argued that the charge about Capt. Baugh
was "of another nature then the particulars were
of; the particulars being for extorting and taking
part of the Kings mony from such as were to receive
it out of the Exchequer," which did not hold for
the case in point. The question here was not of
extortion but of breach of trust. Also, this was
a new piece of evidence, and the defendants had not
had time to examine it for the defence. If Bingley had had time, "he could have made clear proof,
that he had not delt unjustly therein: and he
shewed forth many acquittances, purporting (as was
affirmed) the full payment of all the said mony
which now the Court could take notice of, being
not proved in the books: and thereupon the defendants councel prayed the judgment of the Court,
whether the matter of Baugh should be urged against
him, as an offence punishable upon the information,
as the case standeth?"

The Court weighed this matter gravely and gave
the opinion that if a bill charges certain particulars of one nature and concludes with a
general charge of others of the same nature,
not naming them, then the plaintiff has liberty
to prove any charge he can upon the general
charge and those shall be accepted as good
proofs against the dfdt by way of aggravation
only, and so as some of the particulars be
proved. This case tended to expound and give
power and limitations to the general rule rather
than cross it.

A plaintiff should not make his charge on the basis
of a few particulars and then examine a great many
more on the basis of a general charge: he should
"not make two or three particulars as a drag-net,
to draw all a mans life in examination, when he
shall not have convenient knowledg to make his defence, which all men ought to have." Secondly the

547

general accusation must be of the same kind as the
particular charges. Since the case of Baugh and
the pirates violated all three principles, and

> it was impossible for the defendant to make that
> defence unto it, as happily he might have done,
> wherein no man ought to be intercepted: and
> therefore the whole Court was of opinion, that
> the said Sir John Bingley ought to be proceeded
> against for the matter concerning the said Baugh
> and pyrats upon the proofs now made against him,
> but that he ought to be admitted to his just de-
> fence, if he shall be questioned for it.

It was a good motion of defense and was properly appreciated by everyone connected with the
case. Unfortunately for the lawyers involved, Suffolk's guilt was apparent to everyone, and all they
could hope to achieve was a lessening of sentence.
Three days later Chamberlain wrote to Carleton a-
bout the case as it stood in the late afternoon of
November 13th.

> The Lord of Suffolkes cause hath possessed the
> Star-chamber nine or ten dayes... There were
> five dayes of accusation, and fowre for defence,
> which was so well inforced by theyre counsaile
> Sergent Richardson, Henneage Finch, Pine, Hos-
> kins, Brooke and others (though the last named
> was sometimes ridiculous and did more harme then
> goode) that many auditors of goode judgement
> thought all devills not so blacke as they are
> painted, but upon Master Atturnies replie yes-
> terday matters are found so fowle, that the
> Lord of Suffolke is this day fined at an hun-
> dredth thowsand pound, to imprisonment in the
> Towre during the Kings pleasure, and what other
> penalties I know not, for yt is the first newes
> taken fresh from the Lord Cooke as he spake yt
> ... Sir John Bingly is censured at 5000li and
> this is all I can say of this matter on such a
> sodain as I am to finish this letter for yt is
> thought they will not end nor rise in the Star
> Chamber till five or sixe a clocke.[111]

548

On 23 November, Dr. John wrote to his sister-in-law cum mother-in-law and with proper pride told of his brother's success in the case. For it was a successful defense in spite of the ultimate verdict. Suffolk's fine was reduced, as was Bingley's, and the Earl and his wife spent only a week in the Tower. Sir John Bingley was understandably grateful and remained a very close friend for life; indeed the two families were later joined by the marriage of their children.

Good Mother
It is not amisse that W. Hoskyns is returned, he should have ben sent and delivered in another manner. I knowe noe newes but that the ould Lord Treasurer & Sir John Bingly this day com to be censured in the starre chamber, where my brother spake of late for Sir John Bingly with greate applause and to good purpose for himselfe for his client and for the common wealth
.... 112

The immediate cause of the letter was to confirm the return to London of young Will Hoskyns. Dr. John was right; the boy should not have been sent out to Hereford until the financial obligations were met in the Mayor's court in London. After all, he was the legal executor of the will. It was an incredibly busy time for John. While he was engaged in the Bingley case, he was also clearing the accounts of his brother Oswald, and that process had turned suddenly more complicated than they had expected. On 16 November he and Dr. John petitioned the court for a ruling concerning the children's estate from the will of their grandfather. 113 Meanwhile they went ahead with the clear part of the estate, and on 23 November they brought two former friends of Oswald with them to act as recognitors for the children's legacy. Ozias Churchman and Daniel Hollingworth, both merchant tailors, bonded themselves to pay £253 11s 8d into the Treasury of the City when called for on the maturity of William and either the maturity or marriage of the eight daughters, in equal parts to each. 114 The same day John and Dr. John signed two

549

recognizances on their own. The first was £80 guaranteeing that they would "deliver to the saide orphans such plate as was given them at their Christning."[115] The second was for £2400, guaranteeing the payment of £300 each to the first seven children from the estate of Randolph Wooley, who died before Thomasina and Frances were born.[116] Then on 25 November, the Mayor's Court agreed to John's recommendation on Oswald's estate. He had found that Wooley, in his will, gave Oswald and Elizabeth the "rest and residue of all his goods." That meant that at Oswald's death the two of them possessed the Lease of Wooley's house and of plate, etc., to the value of £926 2s 1d. John and his brother had mistakenly included this in the inventory of Oswald's estate. John suggested that the lease, plate, etc. should be allowed Elizabeth, and the Court agreed.[117] Elizabeth was now comfortably off, but the whole estate was still not settled. The business had to be disposed of and the debts paid. It would be another three years before John could fulfill all of the terms of the will and the Orphan's Accounts.

* * * * *

Early in 1620 John focused his attention on the upcoming Lenten Reading, when he would have to show his legal ability to all of his fellow lawyers in the Middle Temple. The position of Reader was a very difficult one. Besides working out the cases which were to be argued for the benefit of the young law students and preparing his assistants for the roles that he wished them to play, the Reader was on the spot to show his legal ability before the best lawyers and judges in the country. They had been through the same situation in their own careers, but that was not likely to make them any more understanding in their criticisms of the Reader's performance. And, of course, besides worrying about the Reading proper, the Reader had to oversee all of the meals, banquets, and ceremonies during his fortnight's term of office. Members of the Court as well as members of the Middle Temple had to be invited and treated with due magnificence. In the long run, all of this was worth-

550

while, as the Reader not only automatically became
one of the Masters of the Bench and member of the
Parliament of the Middle Temple, but also came in
line for available judgeships and appointment to
the prestigious position of Serjeant-at-law.

On 11 February 1620, "Mr. Jo. Hoskins is confirmed to be Reader for next Lent, and Mr. Whitlock
is chosen assistant. Messrs. Triste, Curle, Greene,
and Southe are appointed to stand at the Cupboard.
Messrs. Ri. Mansell, Fr. Keate, Jo. Wells, and Jo.
Page are appointed to provide the Reader's feast."
[118] It was the practice for the Reader to have
two assistants, Benchers who had already served as
Readers.[119] As it was, John and his close friend
James Whitelocke would have to work doubly hard
with the other Assistant missing, but they had been
working together on Readings for the previous two
years and knew well enough what to do to make up
for the missing Bencher. All of the other usual
positions were filled. The Reader had four Cupboardmen who were next in seniority in the House to
be apointed to the office. He also had four Stewards (two of whom were Barristers and two still
"under the Bar") to direct the preparation for the
Feast and to share in the expenses of that final
Feast. The Cupboardmen attended the Reading and
debated the points of law raised by the Reader.
They were stationed at the Cupboard, a square or
oblong table near the Bench table, which was the
center of all the Ceremonies. All announcements
were made there, for example. The Reader also had
a retinue of hired men who were dressed in his
livery. John put on a very great show, and if his
brother is right, his expenses far exceeded the
£240 spent the previous August by Whitelocke. The
Reading started on 6 March and, according to Dr.
John, ended on the morning of the 17th. Dr. John
wrote to Ben at the end of the first week:

Good mother wishinge y^u health and happines
from heaven

I can acquainte y^u wth nothinge amisse, y^e
readinge is halfe gon over in good fashion, all

(except myself) are very rich and brave for y^e
tyme, and nobly disposed for y^e honor of m^r
Reader a reasonable portion of Lords have ben
at his table allready and ȳ^{e} greate marquesses
meanes to be heere to morrowe beinge sunday;
others on tuesday and on thursday friday we
breake our fast$_t$and away, I heare not yeat of
any strangers y^t com downe. I beleeve it will
be tuesday followinge y^e next weeke ere y^u see
any of y^e company som escapes and slipps y^u
shall not knowe it hath gon well wth abundance
yea superfluity rather then want; beyond readers
of other howses and former tymes they say. my
brother Boorne hath donn his exercise well, and
m^r Reader goinge to ye hall at 7 of ye clocke
cannot conclude his matter vntill allmost 2
they say preachers are longe, but sure ye lawe
is very tedious ye thinges y^u sent vp were well
handled I sawe them taken out of ye hamper, and
they will serve on sunday to morrowe. I pray
y^u send noe more for m̄^{r} pyes[120] chamber is full
of his kindread. Mr Salmon py and m̄^{r} Lampre py
we have fewe of this last because ye ladyes have
learned your neighbours skill to longe for any
thinge God send vs a good end....121

The day before the end of his Reading, John
admitted "Mr. Benedict, only son of John Hoskines,
esq., Reader, specially; bound with Charles Cockes
and Walter Kyrle, esq.; no fine, his father being
Reader."[122] But the eleven year old boy was probably not present at this Reading and would not actually begin his studies for another few years. If
he was present, he undoubtedly returned home immediately, as his father, after all that talking,
would need a rest. He would also have to examine
his badly damaged treasury. The money for Oswald's
children had come into his possession at just the
right time.

From this point on he would be a Master of the
Bench of the Middle Temple and would be expected to
be present at each meeting of the Parliament, which
decided policy for this most important of all the
Inns of Law in London. The Parliaments met three

times in Michaelmas term, the first and last Friday and the Friday before Allhallows; twice in every other Term, the first and last Friday of the Term, in the evening. As the last Reader, John was excluded from the meeting on the evening of 5 May until the very end; then he entered and James Whitelocke, his "immediate predecessor welcomes him thither with an Oration."[123] Then Hoskyns gave a formal answer, and the Treasurer of the Parliament, in a third oration, welcomed him.

John attended his first full meeting of the Parliament of the Temple on 26 May, not only joining many of his close friends who had previously been Readers, but also Benjamin Rudyard, who was made a member of the Bench because of his new position as "Surveyor of the Court of Wards and Liveries." Cranfield was taking the whole group up with him![124] Before the next meeting of the Parliament, on 28 June, Whitelocke was given notice of his forthcoming appointment as Serjeant-at-law. It must have made John a trifle envious and a bit nervous as to whether, with his long record of monarchical displeasure, he would follow in due course. On 30 June Hoskyns and Ford were named as Assistants to Thomas Triste for the Autumn Reading. John's old friend Aegremont Thynne was one of those named to the Cupboard.[125]

But aside from that two weeks in August, John seems to have been busy back in Hereford. For one thing, the City of Hereford was reorganizing its constitution. On 12 July 1620 a new charter for the city was drawn up, establishing a "Common Council" of thirty-one members. Sir John Scudamore was named first and John Hoskyns second.[126] As the election list in 1618 contained just thirty-one names, it appears that the citizens who had worked together through the years, exchanging offices and positions, decided that they should incorporate in such a way that they would jointly run the city under a legal charter. There are many possible reasons, such as a growing feeling that the Mayors were not as efficient as they should be. It may also be that they felt that with the new organization, the

553

King could not interfere as easily in their internal affairs. For whatever reasons, John was now more intimately tied to the affairs of the city than ever.

And he continued to purchase more land, no doubt as the safest investment for the money he was holding in trust for Oswald's children. On an indenture of 5 August 1620 made before Thomas Jones, a Justice of the Peace for Hereford whose name directly followed Hoskyns' on the new Common Council, John Newton and his wife sold a 100 acre estate known as Newton and Greenway to John Hoskyns for "a competent somme of money... in hand paid." 127 The land is directly west of Monkton, on a long section of good farmland sloping towards the southeast, down to the Garren Brook. It was that brook, flowing through Langarren, which tied together most of Hoskyns' lands in central Hereford. Having sold his rights to Monkton to Elizabeth, he took advantage of the same good countryside for his own crops. Were he to die, the lands which were bought with the children's money would be right next to their mother's. In completing the purchase, he brought his young son and heir Bennet as one of the witnesses, as well as John Bourne's new wife, Margaret. Margaret was her husband's first cousin, the daughter of Elizabeth Kempe.

On 1 September, he bought land directly from Thomas Jones himself. He paid £200 for a 90 acre estate called the Heald in Little Wilton.128 This land, like some previous purchases, adjoined the Bernithen estate, but this time to the east. Bernithen now extended from below the town of Langarren to the "Brook called Luke," a distance of over two miles. At its broadest part, from the Langarren-Ross road to Biddlestone, it measured a mile. When he had purchased the original property in 1612, the Delehays had claimed it was worth £1500 although John only paid £700 for the property. By now the size of the estate had nearly doubled.

Back in London he was caught up in the events that were pushing James, much against his will, towards another Parliament. His son-in-law, Frederick, had accpeted the crown of Bohemia in August 1619, but he lost it at the Battle of the White Mountain in November 1620. Meanwhile, the King attempted to take advantage of the public enthusiasm for Fredrick by calling for contributions for Bohemia. On 3 October 1620, Hoskyns' name appears as one of the Justices of the Peace who were "contributories to the loan for Bohemia."[129] But voluntary contributions were not sufficient, and the King found it necessary to call another Parliament. Hoskyns was more concerned with his own business than he was with another session in the House of Commons however. In late November he went back to Hereford to make sure that his name was not submitted as one of the M.P.'s from Hereford. It is unlikely that the Common Council would have purposely antagonized the King on this point, although Parliament itself was ready to take up Hoskyns' case as a point of Privilege. There is no evidence that the King forced John into standing down from any elections, but the fact that he did not run for the office may have impressed James favorably.

* * * * *

Back in London in January, Hoskyns must have had mixed feelings as his old friends took their places in the Commons chamber. Parliament opened on 16 January 1621 but then adjourned until the 30th. The first Bill was not read until 3 February, and on that day John wrote to Ben:

Sweet hart[130]

I have been very heavy harted and trobled in sleepe & wakinge wth imaginations that y[u] are sicke or dead. but yf god be so merciful to me that y[u] are alive I have sent y[u] all the outward & inward comforts against this miserable weather that I could suddenly prepare. scarlet kersey in a boxe, white wth direccions on it to y[u] A capp, a wastecoate, a pair of draws for y[r] thighs, a pair of germashes for y[r] legges, & a pair of pantofles, a seller or cabinet of waters, six halfe pynt square glasses viz[t] aqua

555

caelestis, Doctor Monfords Cordial water, lymon water, cynnamon water, wormwood water, Rosa solis water.

Sir Walter Py is atturney of the Court of Wards. All my labour is to represse the lower house from questioninge my comittment the last parliament & to keepe them from revivinge the kings displeasure. I thincke whatever they doe they will not hurt me, as they promise me, but they will provide for ever agaynst the lyke as they say.

The kinge in his sollemne first speech layd all the falt of braking the last parliam^t upon the undertakers. I have my health I have no cold nor cough but seldom, but when I doe cough I spitt blood. I am somewhat full & short breathd but better then when I parted from y^u. for gods sake & for all those childrens sakes doe what y^u can to live, and be not curst when y^u are well. medle not wth me but to provide the best things y^u can for the house & me. forbeare your censure & speeches & bestow them on y^r sone Boorne, & that servaunt that is lyke to undooe us all.

I can & will love y^u better than they that flatt^r y^u & bett^r in earnest then any flatterer can devise to dissemble. Now doe I imagine y^u skorne this letter. I would not have y^u doe soe, but if y^u doe I will endure that & ten thousand tymes worse rather then lose y^u as curst as y^u are & I am the only old poore man on earth that truly loves y^u

J. Hoskyns

Two days later, on April 5th, his friend from the previous Parliament, Edward Alford, with whom he often had dinner in London, made the first motion for a petition to the King for freedom of speech in Parliament.[131] True to his word, however, he did not mention Hoskyns' name nor did he go into any details concerning cases from the previous Parliament. But Alford's motion was given immediately to the Committee on Privileges for action.

John's letter raises the very real possibility that he had contracted tuberculosis some few
years before when he was under the care of John
Gifford. Certainly the coughing up of blood was
not a good sign. If this is the case, his physical
condition otherwise must have been really remarkable to allow him to operate with as busy a schedule as he did for the rest of his life.

On 9 February he was at the evening session
of the Middle Temple Parliament when he and Triste
were confirmed as assistants to Edward Curle for
the Lent Reading. It must have been a difficult
time for all, as Curle died before April 17th, when
his chamber was vacated. It may even be that the
Reading had to be called off, or at least shortened, which would explain why John and Thomas
Triste were again named as Assistants to the August Reading of Thomas Greene.[132]

More important to Hoskyns--and certainly to
all of England--was the fall from grace in April
of Sir Francis Bacon, Viscount St. Albans, Lord
Verulam, Lord Chancellor of England and Keeper of
the Privy Seal. The Parliament, this time with
the Lords joining the Commons in the attack, was
out after the abuse of monopolies that had grown
steadily since the reign of Elizabeth and had increased enormously at the same time as Buckingham
rose in favor with James. The King tried to withdraw graciously from the trouble, but Parliament
was not ready to stop. After attacking some of
the smaller fry of the court, they went after their
former member. He was accused of accepting gifts
from suiters, and he unhesitatingly acknowledged
his guilt, pleading at the same time that he never
allowed those gifts to influence his judgement and
that he did not do anything that everyone else did
not also do. Although both statements were probably true, it did not save him, and he retired to
St. Albans to continue his writing on the new
scientific method of inductive reasoning which is
ultimately far more important than any of his actions in the political entanglements that made up
so much of his life. Hoskyns was moved immediate-

ly to verse. He really never had liked Bacon, and
it may be that the Bingley case had only reawakened the earlier dislike. There is a key pun in
the poem that he now wrote: he considered Bacon a
bore, just as he had intimated back in 1599 in the
Directions. The poem is a clever set of puns in
English, at least one of which was once again on
the borderline of danger. He really accused the
King of giving in to the pressures of Buckingham
in dropping Bacon. Perhaps the nastiest crack of
all is the remark about Bacon's relatives who
joined in the accusation in order to keep receiving gifts (the dative).

Sr Fra: Bacon. L: Verulam. Vicount St Albons.[133]

Lord verulam is very lame, the gout of go-out
                                        feeling;
  who (therfor,) beggs the crutch of state, with
                                falling sicknes wheeling.
Disease, displeasd greeves sore, that state by
                                hidden fate shold perish:
  vnhappy, whom no hope can cure, nor high pro-
                                tection cherish.
Yet can I not but marvel much at this, in common
                                        reason,
  that bacon shold neglected be, when it is most
                                in season.
Perhaps the game of Buck, (now come,) hath vili-
                                fied the Bore,
  or els his Crescents are in waine, that he can
                                hunt no more.
Be it what t'will, the relatiues, their antece-
                                dents moving,
  decline to case accusatiue, the dative too much
                                loving.
The red-rose-house lamenteth much that this so
                                fatal day
  shold bring the fall of leafe in March, before
                                the spring in May.
St Albans much condole the losse of thy great
                                vicounts charter,
  that suffering for his conscience sake, is
                                turn'd Franciscan Martyr.
His men look sad, and are sore grieu'd, so sud-

> denly to see
> the hogshead that so late was broach'd, to run
> so neare the lee.

Meanwhile the Parliament, after voting subsidies both for the King's expenses and also for the army in the Palatinate, proceeded to draw up a petition in justification of the subsidies which set forth the state of European affairs from their point of view. They suggested that the King declare war against Spain, the head of the Catholic League, and marry Prince Charles to a protestant. This angered the King, and he replied with force, among other things saying that he considered himself "very free and able to punish any man's misdemeanors in parliament, as well during their sitting as after. Which we mean not to spare hereafter upon any occasion of any man's insolent behaviour there."[134] It was a lucky thing for Hoskyns that he was not in the Commons, as his answer would undoubtedly have landed him right back in the Tower. As it was, the House drew up A Protestation, on 18 December 1621, proclaiming their Parliamentary privileges and denying the King's right to imprison members at his own will. The cases of Hoskyns and his fellows in 1614 had brought Parliament to a position of recognizing their need to stand together or to fall separately, and that action of the King in 1614 underlay much of the debate in this Parliament. Hoskyns was, therefore, a part of the Parliament without even being present.

Meanwhile he used his free time to prepare for changes in his home base. On 12 May, the morning after a meeting of the Middle Temple Parliament, he wrote to Ben, who was visiting her sister-in-law at Monkton. As usual he was moving about rapidly, this time looking after his wife's business affairs in Kent. He shared his wife's feeling that she came from a socially superior family. The Moyles were one of the leading families of Kent and first cousins of the Earl of Winchelsea.

To my Mrs Ben. Hoskyns at Mounton.[135]

559

Good sweet hart this is whitsonday. I had busynesse heere till friday last & must be heere a-
gayn on friday next. this morning I promised
to be at Rochester for busynesse there to-morrow.
I am now goinge to the Tilt boat & my man goes
about wth my horses... I will see y^r 2 sisters
& y^r broth^r & come up again presently. I meane
to be so fine as that they shall not laugh at
y^u for having a sloven to y^r husband....

Hoskyns was in good shape financially and
planning the last major purchase of his life. The
time had come to set up his own family on a large
estate now that he had taken care of the rest of
his extended family. On 5 June he wrote to Ben
from London.[136]

Deare hart

God send y^u health. y^r parliament men[137] will
tell y^u all the parliament news. For me first:
for my health I thancke god I am better then I
was wth you, the reason is early risinge & somtymes fastinge one meale increaseth breath &
diminisheth fatt. Next for Mr Parry he is des-
perately selfe willed. he denyeth somm duc
reconings, wanteth som evidences to make good
his title, & yet would compell me to sett furth
his title to be good, & will have me to proceed
& take what assurance pleaseth hym & pay what
he demaunde. he will never be in order unless
his brother or som reasonable man were heere to
over-rule hym. For my being a welsh judge it
is as constantly spoken by all great & small
even to my face as yf it were so. and every
judge in the welsh circuit & sergeants in West-
m^r would have me believe, & it is as true a report as the commission for pressing mayds to
Virginia.[138] Yet I will not say it is impossible because som of the greatest doe warrant
it, but I pray god it nev^r may be except it be
more gods will then myne. be merry & make y^r
selfe stronge to take in good part what ev^r fall.
yf it be better then we deserve y^u will rejoice
the more lively yf it be but as we deserve y^u

shalbe the more contented. yf worse then we do deserve y^u shall endure it the more courageously. be assured the greatest preferment I looke for is to be gods servaunt &....

John was in the process of exchanging his manor of Arkeston, which was next to his holdings in Didley, with Stephen Parry, who owned the manor of Morehampton, in the Golden Valley. He had bought Arkeston from Sir Charles Morgan at the same time as the Willock's Fields property, apparently as a possible location for his own major estate; but when Morehampton became available, he decided on a trade with Parry.[139] Stephen was related to the poet Rowland Vaughan, for whose book Hoskyns had earlier written a dedicatory poem. Vaughan owned Newcourt, which is directly across the river Dore from Morehampton. The Morehampton estate was a very large one, sloping southwards to the Dore, with a large house and moat. Today there is just a single farm building near the river and on the other side of the road from the original house, which is no longer standing. Tradition has it that the large timbers of the Morehampton house were used to support the church in Vowchurch, where Ben was buried. If this is so, then the house at Morehampton was indeed a large and substantially built manorhouse. The Dore river valley is a beautiful one, perhaps the most beautiful in all of Hereford, which accounts for its local title as the Golden Valley. William Camden says it was named "for the golden, wealthy and pleasant fertility thereof. For, the hils that compasse it... are clad with woods; under the woods lie corne fields on either hand, and under those fields most gay and gallant medowes."[140] John had been long in choosing his own manor, and when he did, he picked the most beautiful of all the properties which he was to own. Once he had made his choice, he wasted no time in moving his family there and making his home a place of special interest. For the moment, though, he was concerned with all of the last-minute details of the exchange, which included the shifting of title of many different pieces of land, for Morehampton was a very expensive piece of real

561

estate--approximately £3000. The Arkeston property was worth £1600. Will Harbyn was lending or
repaying John £1000, and Mrs. Jeffrey was doing the
same for another £100. We do not know exactly how
much more John had to put down.

The other news of the letter was also significant. Although John obviously did not want to
raise any false hopes in Ben, the appointment to
the circuit in Wales was clearly on the way. His
old friend Nicholas Overbury was the senior judge
of the circuit and would be a great help in gaining
Hoskyns the position. More importantly, Lord Compton favored him and so did Lionel Cranfield, both
favorites at Court; they gained the support of
Buckingham, and that trio guaranteed the monarch's
agreement. It was certainly not as lucrative a
position as the one to which James Whitelocke had
been appointed in Chester two years earlier, but
it was a good one all the same. On 14 June his
clerk William Taylor wrote more of the details to
Ben:[141]

...my M[r] I praise god is in health and in the
kinges favoure and by his gracious guifte by
the meanes of the Marquesse Buckingham, my lord
President & the M[r] of the wardes (with whom my
M[r] dyned a Sunday last at Greenwiche) is made
fellow Justice with M[r] Oxenbury within the
Counties of Carmarthen Pembrooke and Cardigan
with the towne of Haverford West, and the bur-
rough of Carmarthen. although the place be not
soe benefyciall as other english Circuits yet
it is a stepp to preferment And I doubt not but
it will grow greater; The gray geldinge must be
well kept for he must be the sumpter horse: M[r]
Parry and my M[r] are fully agreed for morehampton
for M[r] Parry upon Agreement betweene himself and
M[r] Morgan is contented to take Arkeston and the
Mills at sixteene hundred pounds. Meares courte
and Hungerston my M[r] keepes for his securitye
for his other monyes due, and M[r] Harbyns one
thousand pound being paid and M[ris] Jeffreys one
hundred pounds there will not be much due to M[r]
Parry; M[r]. Boorne is to be called to the barre

tomorrow being fryday; M^r. Clarke is in health
and intendeth to ride my M^r's circuite with him
as his favourite wch will beginne the third of
September....

The friendships of the Mermaid Tavern had finally
led to a real case of preferment.

Cranfield had understandably felt that he was
to be the next Lord Chancellor, on the fall of
Bacon, but he was mistaken. He lost that position
to the Dean of Westminster, John Williams. But
the King, in attempting to make up for Cranfield's
disappointment, at the beginning of July created
him Lord Cranfield of Cranfield and then made him
Lord Treasurer. This success was short-lived, for
on 29 May 1624 Cranfield, now Earl of Middlesex,[142]
was deposed and fined £50,000 for misuse of his
office. The temptations of success had been too
much for him. It may well have been his fall from
office that ended the successful rise of Hoskyns
and kept him from appointment to the more lucrative
judgeship which Taylor predicted in his letter to
Ben. For the moment, however, John had the best of
friends in a position to help him out.

Meanwhile, John had to prepare for the move to
Morehampton by mail. On 26 June he wrote to Ben
again, with a quick survey of news.[143]

Sweet hart god graunt we may live together and
all turne to our good. god graunt we may answer
every one their own every penny wilbe payd for
morehamton by the end of the next moneth. proceede to goe thither. I thincke I shall troble
y^r patience wth a welsh judge, & therefore let
Ben proceede to be a barrister for John Boorne
loyters.
Y^r prebendary Williams is a privie counsaylor
& not assuredly lord-keeper. We are sealinge
of writings I shalbe ridde of Arkston only the
little mannor of Meres Court stays in pawn with
me for about 300^l.
Evry man calls for money nobody pays. god
help us....

563

John was mistaken in doubting the advancement of
Williams, who was made Lord Keeper on 10 July, but
he was right about John Bourne's failure to pass
his examinations for the bar as Taylor had too san-
guinely predicted. He was apparently disappointed
in having to give up so much of his previous landholdings to get Morehampton, but in spite of his
complaints about his financial dealings, he was obviously pleased with the way things were going.

One of those who was not calling for his money
was Dr. John Gifford. But now that Hoskyns had recovered from his bout with what may have been tuberculosis, he was not only happy to pay his old
friend £5 but prepared to write a latin poem to go
along with it. The poem was probably written soon
after the actual appointment to the judgeship was
made, but John was now sure enough of the grant to
word his poem as he did even in late June. He was
also sharpening his wit for writing latin verse a-
bout his new property at Morehampton. John begins
even in the title to condense his language in a
double use of the title "Doctor," for Gifford is
both a Doctor of Medicine and his Doctor: "Hoskins
conualescens ad Giffordum medicinae Doctorem et
suum. 144 Hoskyns says he is giving a tithe of his
salary as Judge, his "Jameses, money received by a
fiscal hand" (the fiscus was the state treasury).
If Gifford refuses, "the wage perishes with the
perishing judge," for we are not as men allowed to
be ungrateful, although we are allowed to die.
Then John makes a nice twist: Gifford should not
look upon the money as a gift, but purely as pay,
since "he who is yours has nothing of his own which
he could give." Then comes a line whose internal
repetition of sounds of "me" and "fec" are impossible to reproduce in translation: "Me fecit Deus,
infectum medicina refecit." "God made me; Medicine
[the art of healing] remade me when I was sick.
I am God's because I live; I am the doctor's because I am well." John then ties up his poem with
a legal image that does not live up to the balance
of the previous lines by saying that the person who
is not solvent is put in chains, since the debtor
is equivalent or equal to his money. The poem is a

warm gesture on the part of a busy and somewhat
harried lawyer to an old friend who had treated
him over a considerable period of time and restored
him to health without asking for any money.

On 3 July 1621, John finally received his appointment as Judge: "3 July A Grant to John Hoskyns Esq of the Office of one of the Justices in
the Countye of Carmarthen Pembrocke and Cardigan--
dureing pleasure."[145] Hoskyns replaced one William
Reeves[146] as second Justice; Overbury remained the
Chief Justice. Hoskyns was to tour the circuit
twice a year until his death in 1638. The duties
of the two justices was that they "shall in likewise hold and keep Sessions twice in every year, in
every of the same Shires, and shall also have yearly of the King's Majesty fifty Pounds for his fee."
[147] They each received £30 a year besides for
their meals and expenses, but from that they had to
pay the expenses of any clerks or assistants whom
they took along. From William Taylor's letter it
appears that John Clarke went along the first year.
Later, when he was old enough, Bennet joined his
father in the annual trips. The sessions were to
last six days in each shire during each of the two
circuits, so a good two months of the year were
spent on this work, in all kinds of weather, and on
horseback for much of the time. Through it all
Hoskyns managed to maintain his sense of humor, although even now he was approaching sixty years of
age. An added benefit or duty was that as one of
the Justices, he became a member of the Council of
the Marches of Wales, joining his friend James
Whitelocke there as well as his patron for the present position, Lord Compton, the Lord President.[148]

It had taken seven years, but now John was
free of all taint from his activities in Parliament. He had very close friends in Court to look
after his interests, he had managed to buy an estate which pleased him both in its size and location, and he was the pater familias of an extended
family that included cousins as well as nieces and
nephews. Financially, he was beyond any greater
worries and had a solid income beyond the transient

565

fortunes of law cases in individual terms in London and the assizes in Herefordshire. He was, in every regard, a successful man. There was but one further post that he obviously wanted, loaded with honor and income, and that was to be but two years away.

Footnotes for Chapter XV

1. WCM <u>18957</u>. Osborn was not aware of any of the documents relating to Titley at Winchester College.
2. WCM <u>18955</u>. Knight is also named as "Senescall" on an undated note of surrender, WCM <u>18956</u>.
3. WCM <u>19023</u>. Records of Court Baron proceedings at Titley from 1613 through 1625 are found in WCM <u>19022</u>, <u>19023</u>, <u>19038</u>, <u>19089-91</u>, <u>19093</u>, <u>19094</u>, <u>18953-56</u>.
4. WCM <u>18953</u>.
5. WCM <u>19089</u>.
6. WCM <u>19038</u>. Only the last fine had the sum of money involved recorded.
7. WCM <u>18953</u>. Again, most of the figures are missing.
8. WCM <u>18954</u>.
9. <u>A.P.C.</u> James I, <u>1615-1616</u>, p. 274.
10. Hopwood, II, 592, 596, 598.
11. <u>Sizergh MSS</u>; in Osborn, pp. 72-73.
12. William Page was the Hoskyns' next-door neighbor in Widemarsh St.
13. Elizabeth Kempe had three daughters, one who married William Jeffreys and another Edmund Smith.
14. Hopwood, I, 376.
15. William McElwee, <u>The Murder of Sir Thomas Overbury</u> (1952), p. 27.
16. McElwee covers in detail the months of Overbury's imprisonment and his death. pp. 75-128.
17. Osborn prints the date of the letter as 17 October, but it was actually written on the 27th and 28th of the month.
18. For a description of the events concerning the Overbury case mentioned in this letter, see McElwee, pp. 190-196.
19. Fabian Phillips, a Herefordshire lawyer whose friendship with Hoskyns had been noted by the Privy Council a decade earlier. See Chap. 3.
20. Harry Waythen was a descendant of the David Waythen who sold John's father property in Trevase in 1567.
21. Dymock was four miles south of Ledbury and nearly fifteen miles northeast of Bernithen.

22. Sizergh MSS. Osborn follows Henry Hornyold-
    Strickland's transcription of "Mr. Sarcevile"
    rather than "Mr. Sackvile", who was one of
    those called into the Star Chamber for his ac-
    tions. Letter in Osborn, pp. 73-75.
23. Hopwood, II, 599. As John Bourne paid a fine
    of twenty shillings for the move, it appears
    that Hoskyns had done a good deal of renovat-
    ing of the chambers since he had moved in.
24. Details of the whole suit are given in the
    Chancery Depositions C.2. H 45/19; 6 May 1631.
25. C.21/H 57/3. Sheet 1 is Hoskyns' interroga-
    tories; Sheet 2 contains the answers. The re-
    maining sheets contain the interrogatories and
    depositions for the defendants.
26. One of the witnesses was Richard Best, the yeo-
    man brother of Charles Best, Hoskyns' close
    friend at the Middle Temple and the "Orator" of
    Le Prince d'Amour. The Bests were from Cother-
    idge, Worcs.
27. Anthony Bourne was apparently capable of any
    indecent or illegal act. In 1582 his wife
    Elizabeth wrote to Dr. Julius Caesar, asking
    him to act as her lawyer to divorce Anthony,
    who had left her five years before for another
    man's wife, after spending all her dowry. Now
    he was trying to get the court to make her take
    him back so that he could spend the rest of her
    money for his mistress and their children. He
    had apparently threatened her with death and
    then moved an Italian cut-throat in next door
    to her in order to spy on her. Her daughter
    was to marry Edward Conway. Articles filed a-
    gainst Anthony indicated that he had threatened
    his own mother's life, beat one of the servants
    so badly that the man died, caused a riot at
    Oxford with his gang and was thrown out of the
    University, nearly drowned an old man, and
    written a letter to Queen Elizabeth's Solicitor
    General, Sir Thomas Bromley, threatening Brom-
    ley's life. Add. MSS. 23,507 (Caesar Papers),
    ff. 204-05; Add. MSS. 23,212 (Conway Papers),
    ff. 7ff.
28. C21/ H38/ 12.
29. First reported in Whitlock, "John Hoskyns, Al-

most Mayor of Hereford," <u>Transactions of the Woolhope Club</u>, Vol. XXXVI, Part III, 1960.

30. <u>Add. MSS. 11,053</u>, f. 77.
31. Hopwood, II, 610.
32. Stow, <u>Annals</u>, p. 1025.
33. Williamson, <u>The History of the Temple</u>, <u>London</u>, pp. 275-76.
34. Stow, p. 1026.
35. Williamson, p. 276.
36. Edward Foss, <u>The Judges of England</u>, Vol. VI, 1603-1660 (1857), p. 43.
37. Hopwood, II, 618.
38. F. lv. The story is headed "Of Serjant Hoskins."
39. Stow, p. 1026.
40. N.L.W., <u>Papers from The Mynde</u>, <u>Mynde 1520</u>.
41. The original deed is among the MSS. at Harewood.
42. <u>Mynde 278</u>.
43. <u>Sheepskin Bags 1616-1619</u>.
44. Chamberlain, II, 52.
45. Prestwich refers to an uncatalogued letter in the Cranfield collection among the <u>Sackville MSS</u>. from Hoskyns to Cranfield. <u>Sackville MSS 4710</u> (her numbering) in P.R.O.
46. <u>Sackville MSS</u>. (Cranfield) <u>M990</u>. Cranfield's wife did not recover. She died on 6 July 1617.
47. Sackville MSS 7824.
48. <u>Sizergh MSS</u>; in Osborn pp. 75-6.
49. Sir Francis Bacon succeeded Egerton as Lord Keeper on 7 March 1617. He did not become Lord Chancellor until 4 January 1618. Apparently he had treated John with respect in spite of their previous disagreements.
50. <u>Sizergh MSS</u>; in Osborn, pp. 76-7.
51. Probably Christopher Jones, his former chamber-mate at the Temple.
52. <u>Sheepskin Bags 1616-1619</u>. His friend Philip Symonds was elected.
53. <u>Sizergh MSS</u>; in Osborn, p. 77.
54. Aubrey (Clark), I, 328, under "Herifordshire."
55. <u>Sizergh MSS</u>; in Osborn, p. 78.
56. Edward Alford, M.P. from Colchester in both the 1603 and 1614 Parliament, was a brother-in-law of Ben and Elizabeth Kempe, as Elizabeth's daughter Margaret refers to him in her will as "my uncle."

57. Sizergh MSS; in Osborn, pp. 78-9.
58. John was ordering a mile-long hedge along the northern boundary of Bernithen. Three years later he bought more property at the far end of the estate, beyond Biddlestone.
59. The Commission is mentioned in an indenture on 9 January 1618 among the Abergavenny MSS. in the National Library of Wales, #742.
60. Harley 6395, "Jests and Stories," #52.
61. #123.
62. #103.
63. Abergavenny MSS. 742, 743, 750, 760, 1465.
64. Sizergh MSS; in Osborn 79-81.
65. "needed."
66. "gall."
67. William Harbyn and his wife were close friends of both John and Ben from Hereford.
68. Collections of Herefordshire, Mss. Hill, Vol. 4, p. 205. Also quoted in W. R. Williams, The History of the Great Sessions in Wales, 1542-1830 (1898), p. 168.
69. The Will is 30 Meade in the Probate Registry in Somerset House.
70. Repertory Book 33, 1616-1618, f. 289, in Guildhall Library.
71. Sizergh MSS.; in Osborn, p. 82.
72. Frances, now living in the rectory at Ledbury.
73. Sizergh MSS.; in Osborn, pp. 82-83.
74. Sizergh MSS; in Osborn, p. 83.
75. Hopwood, II, 629.
76. Repertory Book 33, f. 360v.
77. For a discussion of the portrait of Hoskyns and the sketch on the back, see Osborn, pp. 303-5. I have placed the sketch two years earlier than Osborn because of the ages of the children. If the two small children are Ben and Dick, they are much more likely four and eight than six and ten.
78. Sizergh MSS.; in Osborn, p. 256.
79. Sheepskin Bags 1616-1619.
80. Abergavenny MSS. 646.
81. Sheepskin Bags 1616-1619.
82. Indentures in the Sizergh muniment room. There were two parcels, called Langstons Meadow and the Home. The owners were John and Alex Donne

and John Jones.
83. Hopwood, II, 632.
84. Sizergh MSS.; in Osborn, pp. 83-84.
85. As the child was a girl, it was duly named Francis.
86. Liber Famelicus, p. 63.
87. Prestwich, p. 100.
88. Aubrey, p. cii.
89. Aubrey (Clark), II, 48; in Osborn p. 209.
90. Athenae Oxoniensis, Col. 441.
91. Aubrey (Clark), II, 53.
92. Chancery Cases C2, James, I, W15/25.
93. C2, Charles I, W28/23, Sheet I.
94. Hopwood, II, 634. The DNB incorrectly says that Hoskyns was the Lenten Reader in 1619.
95. Somerset House had been renamed Denmark House on the fall of the royal favorite.
96. Stow, p. 1031.
97. Saville MSS 9331; reported in HMC, Fourth Report, Part I (1874), p. 315.
98. "Protection of her husband." O.E.D.
99. Langstons meadows near Langarren.
100. These included the Manor of Arkeston and part of the manor of Didley which was part of a lawsuit we will consider later.
101. Just south of the estate at Titley. No other clue to this child can be found.
102. Sizergh MSS. Osborn incorrectly dates the will 24 March. She also states that he wore 6 rings rather than 2 (pp. 85-86).
103. #274.
104. Hopwood, II, 638.
105. Liber Famelicus, pp. 71, 73.
106. Ibid., p. 74.
107. Hopwood, II, 640. Bulstrode became famous in his own right, writing a history of England that William Penn, Governor of Pennsylvania, edited for publication. Henry Fielding noted it in Joseph Andrews as one of the more boring histories of the nation. Bulstrode also became Keeper of the Great Seal.
108. Hopwood, II, 641.
109. Stow, p. 1029.
110. English Reports, Vol. 80; under Sir James Ley's Reports (1659), pp. 67-8.

111. Chamberlain, II, 272-73.
112. Sizergh MSS; in Osborn, p. 257.
113. Repertory Book 34, 1618-1620, f. 251v.
114. Letter Book GG, 1617-1620, f. 20; also in Orphans Recognizances 2, 1590 to 1633, f. 200; Rep. Book 34, f. 262v.
115. Orphans Recog. 2, f. 359; Rep. Book 34, f. 263v.
116. Orph. Rec. 2, f. 359; Rep. Book 34, ff. 262v-263.
117. Rep. Book 34, f. 264.
118. Hopwood II, 646.
119. Middle Temple Bench Book (2nd ed.; 1937), p. xv. The duties of the Reader are described pp. xviii-xx.
120. Sir Walter Pye, the neighbor at the Mynde who, as a former Reader, would have had no reason to be present at the Reading.
121. Sizergh MSS, quoted in part by Osborn, p. 50.
122. Hopwood, II, 646.
123. William Dugdale, Origines Juridicales (1666), p. 201.
124. Hopwood, II, 640. Rudyard had been among the Benchers since 15 October of the previous year.
125. Hopwood, II, 653.
126. Williams, History of the Great Sessions in Wales, p. 168; John Duncomb, Collections towards the History and Antiquities of the County of Hereford (1804), p. 356.
127. NLW, Lease Book of The Mynde, Mynde 608. Final concord on a question of a fine connected with the property was reached 7 September 1620, Papers from The Mynde, #153, 368.
128. Indenture in Sizergh Muniment Room.
129. HMC Portland, Vol. III (1894), p. 13.
130. Sizergh MSS; in Osborn, p. 87.
131. C. J. I, 510.
132. Hopwood, II, 660, 662, 664 (under 15 June 1621).
133. MS Rawlinson B. 151, f. 102v. It is also in Harley 6038, ff. 27-8, with the rest of Hoskyns' political verse. Osborn cites MS Rawlinson Poet. 117, f. 22.b. as well. In the B. 151 version, the poem, on the page facing

two of Hoskyns' other poems, ends with the statement: "Thought to be done by Mr Hoskins of Hereford." It is dated "April 1621."

134. Davies, The Early Stuarts, p. 26.
135. Sizergh MSS; in Osborn, p. 88.
136. Sizergh MSS; in Osborn, pp. 88-89.
137. James Rod (who replaced John as mayor) and James Weaver represented Hereford City.
138. There were several "con men" at this period of history who travelled about England pretending to have such a Commission and taking money from unsuspecting families and towns to "exempt" them from such a danger. Osborn notes examples from SPD 1611-1618, p. 586, and Chamberlain's letters.
139. C. J. Robinson, The Mansions of Herefordshire (1872), pp. 2, 161.
140. William Camden, Britannia, London, 1637, p. 617.
141. Sizergh MSS; in Osborn, p. 51.
142. Created Earl in September 1622.
143. Sizergh MSS; in Osborn, pp. 89-90.
144. Harley 3910, f. 54v; in Osborn, p. 213.
145. PRO, SPD James I, 141, f. 344. Listed in S.P.D. James I, 1619-23, CXXIII, p. 272.
146. Another one of the ironies of fate is that the man who had served with Overbury bore the same name as the young man who had poisoned Overbury's son in the Tower of London.
147. Williams, Great Sessions, p. 13.
148. Ibid., p. 167.

Chapter XVI

Serjeant-at-Law

It took John and his family the better part of
a year to complete the move from Hereford to their
new home at Morehampton. In August he completed
his last term of duty at Middle Temple Readings,
serving as Assistant to the Reader, Thomas Greene.[1]
By 3 September he was on the road in Wales in his
new position as judge, and the next month he was
back in London for two meetings of the Middle Temple Parliament. It was not until the first of
March 1622 that he actually began to designate himself as "John Hoskyns of Morehampton" instead of
the more familiar "of Hereford."

Part of the reason for the slow pace at which
he accomplished the move to Morehampton was the
weather in the late fall and winter:

The last weeke of Nouember, began a great
Frost, which continued the first weeke of December, so as the Thames was frozen all ouer, so as
the people went ouer the Riuer in diuers places,
and then it thawed, and the weather continued
very milde and gentle, vntill the 20. of January, and then it began to Freeze more extreame-
ly then it did before, and continued vntill the
12. day of February, so as all sorts of people
went ouer all places ouer the Thames... also
there was diuers Boothes that sold drinke and
other things vpon the Ice....[2]

Besides, there was a great deal to do in moving from his large house in Hereford to the even
larger estate in the Golden Valley. Morehampton
was an impressive place. The entire farm area of
over five hundred acres was on the usual south-
facing slope down to the river Dore. The main
building was very large and included a chapel and
a hall that measured 42' by 60'.[3] It was surrounded by a moat that is still visible. Aubrey
went into considerable detail in his description

of the estate:

    I will now describe his Seate at Morhampton
(Hereff.). At the Gate-house is the Picture of
the old fellowe that made the fires, with a
Block on his back, boytle and wedges and hat-
chet. By him, this distich:--

    Gratus ades quisquis descendis, amicus et
                                  hospes;
      Non decet hos humiles mensa superba Lares.[4]

By the porch of the howse, on the wall, is the
picture in the margent:--[5]

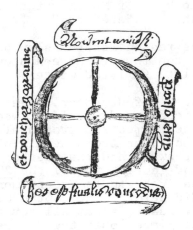

Above it are these verses:--
    Stat coelum, fateor. Copernice; terra movetur;
      Et mutant dominos tecta rotata suos.[6]

In the Chapelle, over the altar, are these two
Hebrewe words

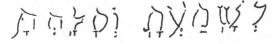

and underneath this distich

Hac quicunque orat supplex exoret in aede,
  Nec pereant servis irrita vota tuis.[8]

Here is an Organ that was Queen Elizabeth's. In
the gallery, the picture of his Brother Doctor
in the Pulpit, Serjeant in his Robes, the Howse,
Parke, etc.; and underneath are these verses:--

Est casa, sunt colles, lateres, vivaria, lym-
                                         phae,
  Pascua, sylva, Ceres: si placet, adde pre-
                                         ces.[9]

In the first leafe of his Fee-booke he drew the
picture of a purse... in the margent,

and wrote Χιδωμεν δσΧίνδω underneath, out
of Theocritus.[10]
   On his picture in the low gallery are writt
on his deske these verses... [Then follows the
eight line stanza "Undecies senos."] [11] These
verses with a little alteration are sett on his
monument.
   In the Garden, the picture of the Gardiner,
on the Wall of the Howse, with his Rake, Spade,
and water-pott in his left hand.
   By it, this distich:--

Pascitur et pascit locus hic, ornatur et or-
                                         nat:
  Istud opus nondum lapsus amaret Adam.[12]

Under severall venerable and shady Oakes in the

577

Parke, he had seates made; and where was a fine purling Spring, he did curbe it with stone.[13]

Naturally, John did not accomplish all of the decorating and landscaping described by Aubrey in the early months of his tenure at Morehampton. It was to be a gradual process over the remaining years of his life. We know, for example, that the poem he wrote for his desk was written in 1631 or 1632. Several of the drawings mentioned are similar enough to the work of his Winchester days to make it probable that he did the drawing himself. The most important inscription is his poem on Copernicus; that such an outright acceptance of the new astronomical view should appear on the walls of a country estate on the borders of Wales is remarkable.

In the summer of 1621, however, most of the activity at Morehampton would have been the moving of furniture and household goods from Hereford and making sure that the harvest of the various fields was brought in for market. On September 3rd, the new owner was on his way to Wales on his new job, accompanied on his first circuit by his friend and city neighbor John Clarke.

Cardigan, Carmarthen, and Pembroke are the three most southwest counties in Wales, with coastlines on the Bristol Channel, St. George's Channel and Cardigan Bay. John and Sir Nicholas Overbury held sessions not only in the three principal towns of the counties, but also in Haverfordwest, which actually went by the title of Town and County of Haverford West. The Mayor of that town was an Admiral and under the charter given to the city by King James could hold an Admiralty Court. One of the first tasks the two judges had was to compile a list of the Sheriffs and Escheators in the three Counties for the court in London.[14] Escheators were officials who took notice within the County of any lands that were legally reverting to the Crown due to the death of an owner who died without heirs. One of the major problems of the officials in London was their inability to keep up with

events in the counties. As Ivan Roots has pointed
out,[15] the judges were almost the only sure way
the court had of keeping in two-way communication
with local governments. The farther away a county
was from London, the less able the King and his
agents were to know the true state of affairs in
the towns of the kingdom. There was no way even
of knowing the actual population at any given time,
and thus there was no way of being absolutely sure
that taxes were being properly levied. The activities of John and Overbury as they are shown in
various manuscript records indicate that they took
their job of being a communication channel seriously.

Even though John's home was already in the
west of England, it was still a considerable trip
to reach his circuit. From Morehampton to the
nearest of the towns in which he held assizes, it
was slightly over 80 miles of hard riding through
the Black Mountains. From Hereford it was ten
miles farther. The circuit itself was not much
easier a journey. Cardigan was 30 miles over the
moors from Carmarthen and 38 from Pembroke. Haverfordwest was only ten miles from Pembroke, but that
included a ferry boat ride across Milford Haven,
which could be very rough indeed in the winter
months. If the two judges wanted to take the
"short" way (26 miles) from Cardigan to Haverfordwest, they had to climb well over 1000 feet in
crossing Mynydd Preseli.

All four towns were port towns, and John's
experience on committees in Parliament stood him
in good stead in understanding the local problems.
One case on their first trip showed the attempt of
Hoskyns and Overbury to fulfill their duties completely. On 16 September 1621, they wrote to the
Privy Council:

...It maie please yor Lo^{ps} to be advertized
That whereas by his Maties proclamation declare-
inge his Maties grace, to his Subiects touching
matters complayned of as publique greevances
his Matie hath revived and required the straight

execution of a former proclamacion... in the
xijth yeere of his Maties Raigne wherebie for
the better preservinge of the manufacture of
Cloth wthin this Kingdome... the transportacion
of Sheepes woolls (amonge other thinges) out of
anie his Maties Kingdomes Isles or Dominions
either into forreine partes or from out of one
to the other is prohibited. And all Customers
and Officers at the Portes are required not to
permitt anie woolls to passe out of anie his
Maties Kingdomes Isles or Dominions, either vnder Colo^r of Carriadge from Porte to Porte or
otherwise oapenlie or privilie. And whereas
wee vnderstand that the woolls of the greatest
parte of the Counties of Pembrok and Carmarthen,
wherein wee serve as his Maties Judges, are vttered... to Clothiers of the Cittie of Bristoll
and of the partes of the Counties of Somersett
and Devon, lyennge vppon the River of Severne,
and there convirted into Cloth, wch woolls the
buyers, for more conveyniencie of carriadge,
doe passe vpp the said River to the English
Portes: vppon wch former proclamacion the Customer of the Porte of Mylford makeinge stay of
such woolls as were then bought in theise partes
by the said Englishe Clotheirs vnder pretence
that the passeinge of them from Porte to Porte
was forbidden, Wee doe likewise vnderstand that
Complainte thereof was made to yor Lo^{ps}: about
Easter terme 1615, And that yor Lo^{ps}: were
pleased therevppon to declare that the said for-
mer proclamacion was not to be expounded to pro-
hibite the carriadge of Woolls from Porte to
Porte, soe as the same were shipped for conveyniencie of carriadge onlie to be converted into
Clothe wthin the Kingdome, And that yor ho: letters were directed to the... then Lo: Treasurer,
to giue order to the said Customer of Mylford
for dischardge and settinge at libertie the
woolls soe restrayned. Nowe it maie please yor
Lo^{ps}:... wee are given to vnderstand, that the
Customer of Mylford hath againe latelie restrained the carrieng awaie of the said woolls
of theise Counties from out of that haven or the
Portes thereto belonginge, to the said Englishe

580

Portes, vppon the former pretence that the same
is prohibited by this late proclmacion (Notwth-
standinge the Clothiers doe offer bondes to retorne certificate from the Englishe Portes of
theire landing the said woolls there) by meanes
whereof the woolls in theise partes are fallne
in price to the greate greevance of the Inhabit-
auntes... (whoe affirme that they have noe other meanes to vtter theire woolls): wherevppon
at theire earnest suite wee haue presumed to
make knowne the same to yor Lo^{ps}: humblie leav-
inge the redresse and releife to yor ho: consideracons and wisdomes. And soe wee humblie
take leave and rest at yor ho: further service
and to be commaunded[16]

John had been involved in the discussion of
the grievance that led to the King's initial proclamation. Now he discovered that any simple solution to a given problem is likely to raise more
problems. But with Lionel Cranfield sitting in
the Privy Council as Lord Treasurer, John could be
sure that his plea would receive a sympathetic
hearing.

By the 12th of October John was back in London for a meeting of the Middle Temple Parliament.
On the 26th, when they met again, they noted that
all of the gentlemen "except Masters of the Bench
have repaired their chambers and the stairs leading thereto at their own cost"; but new repairs
were needed.[17] And at the meeting on 23 November
John Bourne finally was called to the degree of the
Utter Bar.[18] His step-father must have felt re-
lieved that he had shepherded his wife's son
through his education successfully. Benedicta
would receive them happily back in Hereford, and
John would now have a full barrister helping him
with his duties both in London and in his affairs
at home.

But William Taylor was still accompanying his
master on most of his journeys and acting as witness to legal documents. John's position as Commissioner of lands for the Nevilles was coming to

an end. He had sufficient work to make up for the
loss of this source of revenue, and trips to Abergavenny to handle the details of these dealing were
more than he needed. On 15 January 1622 he signed
two leases as "of the Citie of Heref," indicating
that the move to Morehampton had not yet been completed.[19] On 1 March, however, he signed another
lease, this time as "John Hoskins of Morehampton."[20]

There were just two further pieces of business
for John to complete for his old friend, Sir Edward Neville;[21] then, on 26 May, a William Baker
of Abergavenny became the new Commissioner.[22] Baker was a tenant of the Nevilles, having rented a
Fulling Mill in Abergavenny two years before.
John was free to concentrate his attention on his
own land and on the positions he now held.

While changing his residence from the city of
Hereford to Morehampton, John apparently felt that
it would be a good idea to indicate his continuing
interest in the activities of his friends in the
city. He still remained one of the principal landholders of Hereford and would continue to be involved in the political life of the city. But at
this point he gave a present of three volumes to
the Vicars Choral Library of the Cathedral. They
are beautifully bound with his name, "Iohn: Hoskins: Esq:," tooled into the leather at the top
and his initials, "I H," an inch high on either
side of a 4½" abstract design in the middle. The
first was The Annales of Cornelivs Tacitvs/ The
Description of Germania/ MDCXXII, "Ex dono Mᵣⁱ
Johanis Hoskins Armigeri." The volume was printed
by John Bill, London. The second was The Historie
of Gvicciardin Containing the Warres of Italie and
other parts, printed by Richard Field, a native of
Stratford who printed Shakespeare's Venus and A-
donis. The volume was published in 1618. John
also presented the library with a copy of Observations upon Caesars Commentaries, by Clement Ed-
munds, but it is currently missing from the library.

Francis Godwin had followed Robert Benet as
Bishop of Hereford, and his background insured not

only that he and John would enjoy each other's
company but that he would appreciate the gift of
these three volumes. He was a good astronomer,
and it is claimed for him that he was the first to
know the true movement of the moon (he would have
liked John's latin poem on Copernicus when he visited Morehampton). He was "a good man, a grave
divine, a skilful mathematician, an excellent
Latinist, a great historian, and an incomparable
antiquary; a fine preacher, strict liver, diligent
in his studies, and applying himself much to matters of religion."[23] Godwin worked closely with
Hoskyns on Cathedral matters until his death in
1633.

In 1622 John lost one of his oldest friends,
the epigrammatist John Owen. Not surprisingly,
he immediately wrote a Latin epitaph for Owen that
would have been appreciated fully by its subject.[24]
Anyone who walks by Owen's Tomb who is not destitute of wit is called upon to note that Owen lies
near this column and warned not to tread upon the
Poet of epigrams (Hoskyns is using the word Poet
in the Greek sense of "maker"), "for the Avenging
epigram treads upon the world." It had been some
time since John had written an epitaph, but he had
not lost his skill.

By the end of May, Hoskyns was busily involved
in Hereford business and caught in a legal conflict
between friends. When the new Charter was sought
and obtained from King James three years before,
there was some conflict between the jurisdictions
of the city and the Cathedral. The Common Council
created by the Charter had gathered political,
legal, and financial control of the city under itself. It was to meet the first Monday in August
yearly, and it both elected and could remove the
Mayor.[25] But the Charter expressly stipulated that
"these our letters patent shall not extend themselves in any thing to the prejudice, damage, or
detriment of the bishop and chapter."[26]

On 27 May James Wilcox petitioned the Privy
Council for redress concerning the action of Hos-

kyns' old friend John Clarke, who had been Mayor at the time of the institution of the new Charter. Wilcox claimed that Clarke taxed the city £300 for the expense of the Charter, which he (Wilcox) did not intend to pay since it did not prove beneficial to the city, "but was got up for the benefit of Clark, who wanted to be Town Clerk for life."[27] An appeal had been made to the Privy Council, and the whole subject was referred first to the inhabitants of the city, then to the President of Wales, and finally to Sir Walter Pye and John Hoskyns. Wilcox requested dismissal, with the payment of expenses, for being summoned on the cause, "though living under the Bishop's fee, and therefore exempt from all taxations." The Council referred the case to Pye and Hoskyns.

Four days before that same day, the Bishop, Dean, and Canons of Hereford got into the act.[28] They claimed that the Mayors and Aldermen of the city had invaded the rights and liberties of the Dean and Chapter, and even though the matter had been referred to Pye and Hoskyns, Wilcox, who was the Bishop's tenant, "has been summoned for non-payment towards the city charter." They asked that if the case were to be heard before council, both the Charters of the city and of the Cathedral should be used, and that in the meantime any suits against individual persons should be suspended.

Pye and Hoskyns went to work immediately and reported back to the Privy Council on 1 June. That same day Henry Herring and Evan Price, describing themselves as two poor men of Hereford, asked the Council to dismiss them of any Charter charges, again charging that Clarke was acting for his own profit. Herring claimed that since he lived in the Canons See at Hereford, he was exempt.[29]

Pye and Hoskyns came up with different evidence, but they left the final judgement up to the Privy Council. They carefully left the basic claims of the Bishop unquestioned.[30]

...wee find Walter Jones Jeuan Price and Henry
Heringe to bee free men of the Cittie of Herefford and doe conceave them subiecte to the
paymente of the sommes vpon them assessed. And
that James Wilcox inhabiteth w^thin the precincts
of the said Cittie, but alleageth that he is
w^thin the Lo: Bushopps of Herefford Libertie,
the truth of wch allegacon doth not yet appeare
vnto vs, but wee knowinge the said Wilcox to
have receaved benefitt from the said Cittie en-
deavored to perswade him to paymente, wch he
refuseth And the Lord Bushopp beinge present
prayed a time in the Cuntry to make proofe that
the said Wilcox was w^thin his ffee and so ex-
empted. All wch wee leave to yor. Ho^ble consideration.

The records for the rest of 1622 and early
1623 are remarkably sparse concerning John's activities. Hoskyns does not even seem to have made
the circuit in Wales this autumn, for his name is
missing from the court record at Haverfordwest. A
man named Easton shared the judicial duties with
Overbury.31 The only activities that we are sure
he was engaged in were those connected with his
brother Oswald's estate, and they prove that he
was well enough to be attending to his affairs. On
9 July 1622 John and Dr. John had completed working out the debts and assets of Oswald's estate
and were ready to be bound for the outstanding
money due to their nephews and nieces. Once again,
however, they decided to share the responsibility
of obligations with fellow merchant tailors of Oswald. The two Johns bound themselves to pay £123
4s 10d for the use of Thomasina and Francis Hoskyns "at such tyme as they shall seuerally & re-
spectiuely attaine vnto their seuerall ages of one
& twenty yeares or bee married." If either John
or Dr. John died or grew "into pouerty or decay,"
the other agreed to bring another person or persons into court as surety for the money.32 The
same day Thomas Morse and Richard Cockes bound
themselves to pay the sum of £80 9s33 to all seven
children when they attained the usual age of twenty-one or were married. John and Dr. John were

responsible for finding new sureties if either
Morse or Cockes died or grew into poverty.[34] They
were also responsible if Morse or Cockes failed to
perform their obligations.

* * * * *

The silence surrounding John's actions at this
period extends from early July through the fall and
winter. Then, in Easter term 1623, he reappears in
an unlikely lawsuit. A man called King had brought
a charge against Hoskyns that he had illegally tak-
en four parcels of cloth, and the jury had found
in the plaintiff's favor. Hoskyns appealed his
case to the King's Bench. There he won on the
basis of an error being made in the judgement. The
case is reported in Henry Rolle's Reports of The
English Reports, King's Bench Division.[35]

The plaintiff had charged that Hoskyns had
taken "un parcell containant 18 yards, & auter 20
yards, & duaram aliarum parcellarum." The jury had
found the defendant guilty in regard to 5 parcels
of cloth. The judge reversed the judgement made
in Common Pleas because it was not set forth that
the first parcel containing several yards of cloth
actually contained "divers parcells." The jury
had found the defendant guilty of 5 parcels while
the plaintiff had only declared him guilty of 4.
John's legal wit had won another verdict for him,
whatever we may think of the merits of the case.

Later in the Spring, at the Middle Temple Parliament on 2 May, "On the motion of Mr. Hoskines,
a Master of the Bench, his son, Benedict, shall be
admitted in expectancy to his chamber in Essex
Court, a great part of which Chamber was built by
himself." The fourteen-year-boy was to be admitted
"gratis, and free from all duties of the House
(pensions excepted) till he come into commons."[36]
He had actually been admitted during his father's
Reading three years before. This entry merely
acted as a reminder to the Treasurer that no fine
was to be levied when the boy joined his father in
their Essex Court chambers.

Meanwhile on 23 May John Bourne was once a-
gain fined for missing the Lenten Reading.[37] The
Reader for Lent was John Bramston, and he, Hoskyns,
and Aegremont Thynne were about to enjoy an appointment coveted by every Barrister in England.

On 26 June 1623 John Hoskyns was raised "to
the state and degree" of Serjeant-at-Law by King
James.[38] The list included 11 names, three from
the Middle Temple (Thynne, Hoskyns, and Bramston),
but four others were to be added before the official ceremonies took place in late October. On 27
June, the Middle Temple Parliament met to congratulate their fellows and to make sure that the next
Reading would go forward with no complication:
"As Messrs. John Hoskins, Aegremont Thynne, and
John Bramston are appointed by the King's writ Serjeants-at-Law, it is ordered that Mr. Bramston
shall read for the first week of next Autumn reading for his second reading, being the junior of
the said serjeants."[39]

The Serjeant-at-Law ranked immediately below
a Knight, and equally with Justices of either
Bench.[40] The Serjeants were chosen by the Lord
Chief Justice of the Common Bench and the Privy
Council, with the assent of all the Justices. Usually seven or eight men of "the discreetest persons, that in the forsaid general study have most
profited in the Laws" were chosen at a time from
among those who had spent at least sixteen years
in the general study of the law. Their names were
presented to the Lord Chancellor, who charged them
to be present before the king on a certain day "to
take upon him the state and degree of a Serjeant
at Law."[41]

The call of 15 Serjeants in 1623 was much
larger than usual. For example, when Whitelocke
was made a Serjeant in 1620, there were just two
men called. The very size of the call raised
doubts in the minds of some about their quality as
a group. Chamberlain seems to reflect that attitude in his letter to Carleton on 12 July 1623:

The new sergeants have their writts and prepare
alredy for their great feast in Michaelmas
terme... I do not well know their number nor
their names, but they say that in all (old and
new) they are five and twentie, more then they
have ben seen or can stand at that barre.
Master Hoskins is one of this call and George
Crooke was much graced by the King at Greenwich
on Sonday was sevenight beeing knighted and made
one of his sergeants: Master Noye, Thomas Crew
and fowre or five more wold not accept the fav-
or and so are left out.42

On 25 July Chamberlain went further in his questioning of the call:

I have not knowne so great a call for number,
though for other abilities they are thought to
come short of many or most that went before
them. Sir George Crooke, Sir Henneage Finch
the recorder, Thomas Crew, Damport, and Hoskins
are the prime men, the rest of the fifteen being of litle note or name.43

There was a good reason for anyone to want to
be left out. This year it was more costly than
usual to be appointed. Normally the expenses were
great enough, as described by William Dugdale. The
new Serjeants had to keep a great dinner "like to
the Feast of a King's Coronation; which shall continue and last for the space of seven dayes." Each
of the Serjeants had to pay at least 400 marks for
those celebrations. Then the new Serjeant had to
give gold rings to "every Prince, Duke, and Archbishop being present at that Solemnity; and to the
Lord Chancellor and Lord Treasurer of ENGLAND, a
Ring of the value of XXVI s. 8d." Every Earl,
Bishop, Lord of the Privy Seal, Chief Justices,
Baron of the King's Exchequer, was to get a ring
costing £1. A ring of 1 mark went to every Lord
of Parliament, Abbot and notable Prelate, Knight,
Master of the Rolls, and Justice. Less expensive
rings went to the Chamberlains, officers and notable men in the King's Court. Even the court
clerks were to get some sort of ring. And finally,

the new Serjeant was to give rings to his friends.
He also gave liveries to his household and friends
who were to wait upon him at the time of the official ceremonies. Dugdale sums up the reason for
all the expense: "Neither is there any man of Law,
throughout the Universal World, which by reason of
his Office or profession gaineth so much as one of
these Serjeants."44

The King saw an opportunity to make money for
himself out of a large call of men who could look
forward to profiting handsomely from the appointment. He does not seem to have been the least bit
subtle about his aim. Each person accepting the
call was to pay £500 for the privilege directly to
the King. Edward Foss, in his volume The Judges of
England, says, "scarcely any office was granted in
this reign without a fee to King James: not even
the serjeants escaped. Sir John Bramston, speaking of the great call of fifteen serjeants in 1623,
says that his father 'gave 500 l. for a present to
his Majestie (as did all the rest of that call) as
I find by an acquittance for the monie.'"45

Finding the ready cash for the expenses connected with his new position must have taken much
of John's time during this summer and fall, but we
have no record of any desperate measures that he
might have taken. No property had to be sold, for
example, nor are there any letters that would indicate any panic within the household over financial matters. Apparently he had his finances well
in hand and could look forward to the greatly increased income that the position of Serjeant would
bring.

But as October passed, John would have had to
supervise the purchase of rings and liveries, and
prepare for housing his family, friends, and servants in London for the great occasion. The £500
had been given to the King on the day he was presented to His Majesty and agreed to receive the
state and degree of Serjeant. It was at that time
he had also sworn on the Holy Bible to fulfill his
role as Serjeant and been told how to act on the

589

day of the actual investiture.46

At some time previous to the actual call, the
newly-elected Serjeants "assembled each in the Hall
of his Inn, learned addresses were delivered and
a purse of gold de regardo or by way of retaining
fee were given each, who were then rung out of the
Society by the chapel bell."47   But the Society
did not collect any money for their honored trio
until four days after the investiture. On 27 October the Middle Temple Parliament ordered "For the
roll of Messrs. John Hoskins, Aegremont Thynne,
and John Bramston, serjeants, each fellow is assessed at 3s 4d. according to the ancient order."48

23 October dawned dark and damp, as the weather had been dismal for some time. Chamberlain had
described the entire Michaelmas term as "a sad season by reason of the continuall wet."49   Early in
the morning wines and cakes were sent to one of the
Serjeants' Inns for the Judges and Serjeants and
to each of the Inns of Court that had members to be
created Serjeant that day.50 All the Benchers and
members of the Society joined in the refreshment.
Then the Benchers and Barristers from each Inn went
to the Serjeant's Inn, two by two, led by the Warden of the Fleet and his Tipstaves, with the Marshall of the Common Pleas going ahead, bareheaded.
There they were joined by the Serjeants, and all
together they went in the same manner to Westminster, arriving about 9 a.m. Chamberlain described
them as going "dabling on foote and bareheaded
save their beguins to Westminster in all the raine."
The new Serjeants then put on their new robes--a
long Priestlike robe colored "Murrey and Mouse-
color" with a Cape about the shoulders with lamb-
skin fur, and a hood with two linen bands--entered
Westminster Hall and moved to a spot directly opposite the Court of Common Pleas,

Where the Court being set, and all business
ceasing, two of the old Serjeants recede from
the Barr with a solemn Conge, and go towards
the new Serjeant; and when they come to the mid-
way betwixt him and the Court, they turn their

590

faces towards the Court, and make a second Conge; and when they are come to the said new Serjeant, they make their third Conge towards the Court. And then, after a little pawse, they proceed to the Court again, with the new Serjeant betwixt them; making their three Conges.

What happened next on the day in question is not totally clear. What should have happened is that the Chief Justice of the King's Bench would give a formal exhortation and declare a Writ of his own making in law French. The most ancient Serjeant present then would answer in defense and ask the Writ to be read. "And so being read and pleaded, and entry made thereof by the Prothonotary; the second antient Serjeant offereth emparlance thereto."

According to John Hacket, in his Scrinia Reserata (London, 1693), what actually happened was that Lord Keeper John Williams gave a long oration on the history and condition of the role of Serjeant:

> you are the Principal of all that practise in the Courts of Law... you are the chief Servants at the Bar... You are next in the Train of my Lords the Judges... You are, by reason of your Degrees, our Letters of Recommendation unto the Kings Majesty, for his Choice and Election for the Judges of the Kingdom... That Gold which you give away... implies that by your Labour and Gods Providence, you have attein'd to the Wealth of a fair Estate... Then your great and sumptuous Feast is like that at a Kings Coronation.[51]

However, Hacket is so wrong in the rest of the details surrounding the speech that it is perfectly possible he has put it in the wrong context. The speech itself sounds very much as though it were given on the day the new Serjeants were called before the King and agreed to receive the position of Serjeant.

591

At any rate, after the Writ had been pleaded
before the new Serjeants, or the Lord Keeper had
delivered his speech, they passed by the Bar into
the Court and knelt before the Chief Justice to
take the Oath of Supremacy. The Clerk of the
Crown then read the Serjeant's oath:

> Ye shall swear well and truly to serve the Kings
> people as one of the Serjeants at the Law; and
> ye shall truly counsail them that ye be retained
> with, after your cunning: And ye shall not de-
> ferr or delay their causes willingly, for covet-
> ise of money, or other thing, that may turn ye
> to profit: and ye shall give due attendance, ac-
> cordingly, so help ye God.

Each Serjeant then swore accordingly and the Chief
Justice placed on his head, with the solemnity of a
knight's helmet,[52] the white quoif of silk, which
is "the principal and chief insignement of habit,
wherewith Serjeants at Law in their creation are
decked; and neither the Justice, nor yet the Serjeant, shall ever put off the Quoif, no not in the
King's presence, though he be in talk with his
Majesties Highness,"[53] and the hood on his shoulders. When all were invested properly, the Court
arose, "and all depart."

The next appointment for the day was back in
the City at the Middle Temple. Richard Howe, in
his continuation of Stow's _Annales_, says that "the
Duke of _Richmond_, the Lord Keeper, the Lord Treasurer, with others of the Priuy Councell, and also
Alderman, Lumley, Lord Maior elect, and 17. Aldermen of London"[54] were present. Chamberlain adds
to this list "the French, Venetian, and States ambassadors, with all the counsaile and great men
about this towne." But all did not go well, as
Chamberlain notes, "and after dinner to Powles,
where the Dean preacht, though yt were sixe a
clocke before they came; and that all might be
sutable, their (though otherwise plentifull and
magnificent) was so disorderly performed, that yt
was rather a confusion then a feast."[55]

592

One of those who had been caught in the rain
along the way that day was the preacher at St.
Paul's when the group assembled at 6 p.m. John
Donne, Hoskyns' long-time friend and fellow poet,
was now Dean of St. Paul's and addressed the illustrious assemblage on a text from I Timothy 1:8,
"We know that the law is good, if a man use it lawfully." It used to be thought that the famous
sickness that put Donne to bed later this same autumn was caused by his catching cold during the
day's activities. That no longer matches what we
know about his sickness, which was a form of epi-
demic fever then sweeping London.[56] But it may
well have been a cold contacted on October 23rd
that weakened his constitution enough to make him
a prey to the "spotted fever" that followed. From
that sickness, of course, came one of Donne's major
prose works, his Devotions Upon Emergent Occasions.

John's family was undoubtedly present in London to share in his triumph. His stepson, John
Bourne, was working with him on his cases. Dr.
John would be there, squiring his sister-wife and
mother-sister. This would be another good chance
to meet friends of the new Serjeant and lay plans
for his own advancement at Court. Later this winter John wrote to John Coke, who owned Hall Court
in Much Marcle, Herefordshire, and was currently
working in the Navy Department, on his way up to
becoming Secretary of State. He asked Coke to in-
tercede with the King for a position for Dr. John.
On 8 March 1624, Dr. John himself wrote to Coke,

My brother serjeant sent unto you to move His
Majesty that the members of our Hereford Church
might have a free election of a Lecturer, because I had good reason to think their voices
would fall on me. The means which have been
used for another betray might and violence. I
had much rather amend my means in another pas-
toral charge, and so end my days, than hang upon any Cathedral. I am willing to make a journey and wish I were the prince his chaplain.[57]

Coke arranged to have a Commission set up to study

the situation, and eventually Dr. John received
the Lectureship.[58] He did not, however, receive
the appointment as Prince Charles' chaplain.

* * * * *

Meanwhile John went about his business. Howe's
entry of 1623 identifying him as Recorder of Hereford once more raises questions about the exact
role John played in the city, as did King James'
previous letter. That he was still concerned a-
bout the governance of the city and its welfare is
not to be questioned, even though he now signed
himself as being from Morehampton. He was certainly a member of the town council, and he may well
have sat in on some of the cases we have records
for during 1624.[59] Elinor Andrews, a widow, complained that James Frank swears, is drunk, calls
his neighbor "whore," his mother "bitch," beats
his mother and wife, and so on. The Council committed him until he could find some people who
would act as sureties for his good behavior. The
Council was notified that the "Pumpe next vnto the
Kings Ditch is out of repaire, and hath been dry
this haulf yeare." John Butler ended grace at dinner with the comment "And the Divell take m^r maior," so the Council bound him over to the next
Sessions. Thomas James and his wife were accused
of gaming in their house, but no action was taken.
And on 19 June the Council collected the assessment for the first subsidy voted by the Parliament
currently sitting in London. John does not appear
among the list of taxpayers in Widemarsh St., as
he used to, but he is first on the list of Commissioners, paying a land rent of £5 20s, the largest in the city of Hereford. The next largest payment was only £3 12s. He did appear among the
Widemarsh St. taxpayers of the First Fifteenth
(Parliament had voted the King three Subsidies and
three Fifteens) that same day, paying 6s 8d, by
far the largest payment in the entire group. And
John kept the best interest of the city government
in mind wherever he was. It is almost certainly
his influence, for example, that led the Earl of
Northampton to write from Ludlow on 21 November
1624 to Sir John Scudamore, telling him to treat

the Mayor and City Council with more respect.⁶⁰

Meanwhile, he found he had overextended himself on landholdings. Although much of the property he had bought would be used to cover monies
he held in bond for his nieces and nephews, at the
moment they were more than he could supervise with
his duties as a circuit judge and Serjeant-at-Law.
He was also undoubtedly cash poor after the drain
on his reserves caused by the gifts he had had to
spread around during the call to the Serjeancy.
So, on 10 April 1624, John leased to one John Howe
the main house and much of the surrounding land at
Bernithen. The annual rent was £65, a considerable
amount, especially as he added a proviso that Howe
was not to do any plowing unless he was given permission by Thomas Hoskyns. And we already know
how close track John kept of Thomas' work. Howe
was obviously a friend. John and Benedicta kept
the right to use one room at Bernithen when they
visited there together. And for the privilege of
renting the corn crop on the lands at Trecelley,
Howe had to pay one fat hog and a couple of capons
each year.⁶¹

Five days after signing that lease, John got
involved in the first of two major lawsuits for the
year; in this one he was the complainant. He had
owned more than eighty acres of land just north of
the town of Didley on the Pontrilas-Hereford road
for over a decade and had had trouble with tenants
the whole time. On 15 April 1624 he submitted his
case to the Lord Keeper. He claimed that about
forty years earlier Richard Pierce "was seysed in
his demesne as of ffee of the mannor of Didley...
wch mannor Consistes of desmesnes and services
vizt service of free & Customary tenants theiore
rents and other Duties all the ffree tenants howld-
inge theire tenants of the said mannor by knights
service rent herriott and suite of Coorte...."
Pierce mortgaged the property to James Garnons of
Trelough, and Garnons conveyed the same to one
Warren of Didley, who "by his last will and testa-
m^t appoynted the same to be sould for 600^{li} by one
Morse and one Atkins his executo^rs...," who "payed

sevenscore poundes more to the said Richard Pierce
and had from hym as absolute conveyance and then
sould the same to Richard Hoskins gent and his
heyres." Richard, John's cousin, being unable to
pay the £600, plus the £130 more which had become
due "by bargin and sale feoffm^t fyne and other
good conveyances conveyed the same to yor orator
and his heires aboutes twellve yeares past." Then
William Parry of Grafton (a town just north of
Hereford), who claimed to have some title to the
rents and services of the manor of Didley, "for a
Competent somme of money" released his title to
John, so that for the past ten years John had
owned the manor "wthout iust clayme and tytle of
any other person to be owner of the said mannor or
any parte therof."

     But Charles Rogers, his son Thomas, John Mor-
gan, and John Quarrell, "beeinge men of greater estate and power then the rest of the tenants... and
beeinge freehoulders and owinge to yor orator
theire seuerall rentes and services and duties for
the landes they hould of the said mannor... havinge
gotten into theire handes diuerse evidences writ-
inges surveyes Recognitions and Coort Rolles belonginge to yor orrator concerninge the said mannor
haue of late deteyned their rentes and denied ...
theire ancestors willingely payed." Furthermore
he says that they have mixed up the lands which
they hold from the manor with lands that they hold
from other landlords by "defacinge the meeres and
boundes therof that yor Orrator cannot knowe where
to distrayne for his rentes and services and soe
is Remediles at the Comon lawe." John then says
that the two Rogers and John Morgan divided the
lands at Willockes bridge between them, part of
which were of the manor of Didley, bringing a yearly rent of 17d and other services, "by postinge of
it of, from one to an other ȝ and from one parcell
of land to an other." And they have refused to
pay and have tried to "wthdrawe conceale and de-
tayne" the rents for the past ten years. Quarrell
had lands worth 5s per year rent, with services
and herriotts which he, his uncle, and his grandfather paid to Garnons and Parry, "yet only out of

596

some private mallice to yo[r] orrator denieth to pay
the same" or show which of his lands are liable
for rent. John asks for a writ of subpoena for
the three of them to appear in Chancery to answer
his charges and show what lands they hold in Didley, what services are due, and what rolls they
have kept.[62]

The Court, on 3 May, assigned four men to take
testimony from the defendants. We have the depositions for both sides in the case, and it gives
us once again an opportunity to see how much more
skilled in questioning John was than most lawyers
of the time. He left nothing to chance as he pur-
sued the legal point he was trying to establish.

1. Did you know that John Quarrell, the grandfather of the defendant, was a tenant of Didley,
and did he hold certain lands under the manor?
"was he ever amearced for not appeering at the
Courte of the said mannor. did he sometimes appear & was sworne of his homage" Have you ever seen
any of the Court Rolls of the manor?... "and doe
y[u] knowe the same Rolls, and are the same nowe
showed vnto yo[w] the same Rolls."

Then he moves into his usual litany: "Do you
know or have you heard--" 2. that it descended to
4 coheirs and then to 6, and that Edith Parry, wife
of James Garnons, was a coheir and that James Garnons received rents of all the tenants as they
were allotted to the 6? And that Lewis her son received the rents as her heir, and after his death
William Parry, and so on. 3. that William Parry
granted to the Complainant, John Hoskyns, all his
right "and that all the other tenaunts but the nowe
defend[te] haue and doe paie their severall rentes
to the p[lt] since the said Release?" 4. that John
Quarrell, the grandfather, was owner of the lands
now occupied by the defendant and paid rent to
James Garnons, then Lewis Parry and William Parry?
"If yea what rent did hee paie declare the trueth."
5. that when John Quarrell died, "after his death
there was an herriott paied... on the land defdt
holds." 6. "that the Defend[t] John Quarrell hath

shewed a p^rtended free deede & haue yo^u seene the
same... doth the same beare date before the death
of John Quarrell the Graundfather... and did he
[the grandfather] notwthstandinge continue the
paiem^t of his rente and other service afterwardes."
Did the uncle John Quarrell pay herriots and rents
set for the same land? If so, where, when, and to
whom?

    Hoskyns was out to prove a record of payments
that was more important than any deed, but he was
also intent on showing that the deed that Quarrell
possessed was a forgery or at least one with no
legal force. 7. Do you know or have you heard that
"at the tyme of the date of the said p^rtended free
deede, Jenkyne Peerse was not receauor or owner of
the rentes of the said mannor yf yea whoe then receaued the same did Edith Parry or her husband...
and doe yo^u knowe that Jenkyne Peerce neaver had
the interest of the said Edith" 8. Did you see the
present deed sealed and delivered? What was the
sale price and was it ever paid? Why wasn't it
ever produced or why weren't the rents claimed to
be released until the present owner purchased the
land or until the witnesses to the deed were dead?
9. Has John Quarrell ever "moved yo^w or any other
to procure any release... of ye rente of fiue shillings per annum to himself since the p^{lt} purchased
the said mannor..." if so, what "did he or they offer to give yo^u & what conference was between you"?

    Then he moved to the Rogers. Did the witness
know or had he heard 10. that Charles Rogers "hath
byn heeretofore accompted tenaunte to the mannor of
Didley or the other dfdt Thomas Rogers... hold any
lands in the mannor of the p^{lt} or Bishop of Heref."
If so, what lands or services? 11. that Charles
Rogers has been paid a yearly rent of 17d for lands
in the manor of Didley, or any other rent to the
Lord of the manor? If so, when and to whom? "and
did hee procure seuerall rentes, Besides the rent
due for the Tenem^t wch George Smithe houldeth and
the landes wch the Widdow Greene nowe houldeth &
did they pay their rents besides the defdts rent"
12. that Rogers confessed that he had turned the

lands for which he owed rent to Hoskyns over to John Morgan of Kilpeck, deceased, or his father; did you hear him say that these lands should be charged the same rent? "did yo^u see him take his corporall oathe voluntaryly vpon a bible or any other booke... that the said rentes ought to be paied" 13. that Rogers lands were part of the property of John Carwardine and part of a larger parcel of lands containing your and his "and the rente accordingly devided and apporcioned vizt xvij^d on his parte and xvj^d vpon yo^{rs}" 14. "Itm what oth^r matter or thinge doe y^u knowe matteriall or effectuall for the Complainante, Declare the trueth of y^r Knowledge therin at lardge."63

The set of interrogatories for the defense is in very bad condition, with much of the writing illegible or totally rubbed out. Each question begins with "Does nott yo^u knowe" or "Doe y^u knowe" and is much simpler in approach generally: 1 & 2. that Jenkin Pierce, father of Richard, once owned the manor in question and had fields there called Willocks fields, consisting of 80 acres, and of a pasture called the Home and another pasture called Higgins Meadow, which Thomas Rogers, father of Charles Rogers purchased for himself and his heirs. Afterwards he built a dwelling house and other buildings. (This is an exact description of the land that John purchased twelve years before.) 3. that Charles Rogers purchased for himself and his heirs other parcels of the said meadow and pasture from Jenkin Pierce and/or his son Richard? "Declare what are those parcells." 4. who holds the said manor now and by what rent? "Declare the troth And doe nott yo^u knowe... that the pasturage & meadow called the Home were part of the manor and have been held by the Lord Bushopp of Hereff." 5. that Charles Rogers for years paid no rent and that John Carwardine had not demanded any rent of him? 6. that Charles sold all his lands in Didley "before such time as the said Compt p^{r}chased the said ‹manor› of Didley or the Chieffe Rentes thereof or anie parcell of the same" and that he "had noe landes Tentes or hereditamentes there for the space of these Tenne yeares" 7. that all the lands

of Charles and Thomas Rogers were part of the manor
of Didley and that Jenkin Pierce released John
Quarrell's grandfather from all tithe interest for
the land? 8. Do you know what Rents are or always
have been due to the Complainant and when and how
much one ought to pay?64

The rest of the sheet is too illegible to follow. But in a way the case had been lost in the
interrogatories. The defendants were trying too
many lines of defense at the same time, and John
had anticipated all of them in his questions.

The answers to the interrogatories already
show the effect of the questions themselves and the
necessary conclusion of the case. The defendants
had chosen witnesses poorly. Of the six who answered, only one gave testimony that raised any
serious questions.

On 21 May the Commissioners took testimony in
Hereford from both the defendants and the witnesses. First the four Commissioners listened to the
defendents, who naturally took exception to the
whole charge. They agreed that there was originally a manor known as Didley, but that "the same
mannor was longe sithence dismembred and sundrie
parcells thereof haue binne conveyed aliened and
sould away to sundrie persons." They own such
lands which they have purchased with "greate sommes
of money." They do not know whether any rents were
ever due on the land. Charles Rogers said that
there was a meadow in St. Devereux named the Home
which passed between him and William Morgan, and
that there was some pretense about a 17d annual
rent that James Garnons claimed and that Rogers
paid for some years to Garnons and others, "butt
whether the same were due or nott this Deffendent
doeth nott knowe." After that weak answer, John
Quarrell took up his defense along much the same
lines. He said that there was a rent of 5s claimed
on his land, "buth whether anie such Rent were due
or nott" was of no importance since "the same was
lawefullie extinguished by a sufficient deede in
writinge dated aboutes 19 March 13 Eliz. One Jen-

600

kin Pearce, father of Richard Pearce, then lord of
the mannor conveyed to his grandfather John Quarrell all rents, suits, herriotts," etc. Quarrell
apparently did not realize that Hoskyns had successfully cut off that path of retreat. Thomas
Rogers simply claimed that he did not own any land
that was chargeable to pay rent to Hoskyns. They
then all testified that there is "a Custome and
vsage allowed and putt in practize wthin the said
... parish that if anie man bee seized of anie
messwage... and doeth alien... anie parte thereof
... then the Rent soe to bee aportianed should
yssue... out of the messwage parcell thereof onelie." It is an interesting theory but not one
liable to hold up in a court of law, especially
one based in London. The defendants denied owing
any free and customary services, knowing any pattern of sales shown in the Complainants bill, being aware that during the past ten years the Complainant had "binne seized of the said Mannor and
of the Rentes, and services thereof." They justified keeping any bills or rolls they possessed because it was their land. They denied having refused to pay or perform services to the Complainant that their ancestors performed to former lords
of the manor or having "Confounded anie their
landes." They did confess that they had refused
to pay any rents demanded of them by Hoskyns, for
they did not recognize his title. They also denied any combination to defraud. Quarrell denied
that he paid any 5s rent and denied he held any
malice towards Hoskyns. All then asked to be dismissed with their costs "in this behalfe wrongefullie and wthout Just Cause sustained."65

The witnesses for the defense were not very
helpful. John Carwardine, aged 71, said he knew
all the persons involved in the case and the various pieces of land, but he did not know "of anie
Chieffe Rent paiable to anie Chieffe lord out of
the same p^{r}misses." Robert Smith, 60, had the same
knowledge of people and places, but he added that
when Thomas Rogers, father of the defendant
Charles, purchased his land, he built a dwelling
house on it and afterward furnished it. William

601

Overton, 56, said his father built the house for
Rogers and that before that house was built, there
were no buildings on the property.

Two Thomas Quarrells answered the interrogatories of the defendants. The first sat squarely
on the fence when dealing with the principal issues involved. Thomas Quarrell the elder of Didley, aged 46, "hath beene Blayliffe of the said
mannor" for twenty years. "Whether there bee anie
such Custome that the rent Essueinge out of the
said mannor is to bee paid out of the messwages
onelie he knoweth not butt duringe all the time
that hee was Baylieff he did vsuallie gather the
Rent att the said messwages." He was also present
when Lewis Parry "seized a Cowe for a herriott vppon the decease of John Quarrells grandfather of
the nowe Deffendant at wch time the said Defft John
Quarrell said yo^{w} may take her as a guieft butt if
itt did bee my ⟨ ⟩ yo^{u} shall neuer haue anie, sithence wch time there was nott anie herriott paid;
but William Parry claimed a herriott after the
death of John Quarrell vncle to the nowe the Defft
butt there was not anie paid." It would seem that
although Quarrell did not want to get into trouble
with his cousin, he also was interested in being
bailiff to Hoskyns if the Serjeant won the case.

Thomas Quarrell of Hereford, aged 40, gave
the principal support for the defense. He said
that on 7 April (a week before John presented his
case in London), he had gone with the defendant
John Quarrell to visit Richard Pierce, son and heir
of Jenkin Pierce, "sometime Lord of the said mannor
of Didley," to find out if "there were not a deede
of a generall release made by his said ffather Jenkin Pearce" to John Quarrell, grandfather to the
defendant. Richard had told them that his father
had sealed such a deed and that Richard himself
"had entred into bond of 100^{li} for performance of
the Contentes of the said Deede," which bore the
date of 13 March 13 Eliz. Since that deed, neither
Jenkin nor Richard Pierce "receaued anie Rent out
of the landes in the Tenure of the said Deffte
John Quarrell." The evidence was the best the de-

602

fendants had to go on, but Hoskyns had already established that Pierce could not dispose of land
that he did not own.

The last of the defense witnesses was Richard
Rogers, aged 34, son of Charles. He testified
that his father had no "estate or interrest in anie
Land<u>es</u> or Tent<u>es</u>" in Didley for the past 12 years
according to h<u>is</u> certain knowledge, for he had conveyed them all away.[66]

Hoskyns called just two witnesses, as that was
all he needed to prove his case. The identity of
the first raises some questions. It is another
Thomas Quarrell of Didley who had been bailiff of
the manor of Didley. But instead of being "about
46" he is 44, and he has no comparative age desig-
nation such as the other Thomas's "the elder." It
may well be that he is the same person as the previous witness, now having decided to place himself
squarely on John's side in order to secure the position of bailiff once again. He testified that he
knew everyone involved and that the defendants were
tenants of the manor of Didley and that John Quarrell presently held lands under the said manor. He
had yearly collected the rent of the defendant's
grandfather and uncle, as he was the bailiff of the
manor (but now is the bailiff of the defendant--al-
though not likely for long after this testimony!).
He said that the grandfather and uncle held the
same lands held by the defendant and had paid the
same rent of 5s yearly to Lewis Parry. He confirmed that when the grandfather died about twenty
years before, "one Cowe was paid to Lewis Parry...
in the name of an herriott...." Charles Rogers,
who used to be one of the tenants of the manor,
promised to pay the sum of 17d annually for the
two meadows called the Home and Higgins Meadow
which he held under the manor. He did pay that
rent upon his taking over the property from the
widow Greene and the tenements in the possession
of George Smith. The deponent was present when an
argument occurred between the Morgans and Charles
Rogers about the payment of 17d rent on the Home
and Higgins Meadows property, "att wch time the

said Charles Rogers tooke vpp a prayer booke and tooke his oath therevppon that the said Rent of xvij^d ought and was paiable out of that parte wch was by him sould to the said William Morgan" and that William Morgan then sent his son John to Hoskyns to agree to pay the same rent annually. Quarrell also testified that Charles Rogers said that he had usually paid the rent before his sale of the meadow "butt knewe nott whether the same were due now."

All of Hoskyns' points had now been verified. He did call one other witness, however: George Smith, aged 70, said that he held a parcel of land for which an annual rent of 16d is due and Charles Rogers held the other, on which Rogers had sometimes paid the yearly rent of 17d. They both came to their land by inheritance from a common great-grandfather.[67]

Although we do not have the final court decision, it is easy to discover what it was, since we know of Hoskyns' dealing with the Didley property. He had won his case easily and clearly. I have gone into the case as fully as the documents allow since it reveals both John's technique as a lawyer, his care in preserving his own rights, and the detail with which he handled even the smallest sums. The amount of money which he had insured from the rents involved would not, during the course of his lifetime, ever pay for the expenses of the suit itself. But he had established the clear title of the manor with all its privileges for his own family when they inherited it.

The day before the Interrogatories were taken, John saw his best hope for advancement struck down. On 20 May 1624, Lionel Cranfield was imprisoned in the Tower on charges of corruption. Prince Charles and Buckingham, who had been his patrons, now had turned on him and ordered impeachment proceedings. On 29 May Cranfield was deposed, fined £50,000, and released three days later. He had remained in power long enough to be of great help to John at crucial periods of his life, and they would remain close friends, but he was no longer in a position to gain the ear of the principal courtiers of the realm for his friends of the Mermaid Tavern.

In late August, John was off to the west, but when he returned from his Welsh circuit in the autumn, he became deeply involved in a law suit between the Canons of the Cathedral and Edward Broughton of Canon Pyon, a manor seven miles northwest of the city of Hereford. The case was to occupy much of John's time for the next two years. It is interesting not only because we see how well he worked within the court system to win a case for his client, but also because we get a sense of just how much it cost a client to carry on a case at law--we have a record of all expenses except one: what John himself was paid.

The Broughtons had been the holders of Canon Pyon since the 1560s under a series of 40 year leases from the Dean and Chapter of Hereford Cathedral. The present holder of the land, Edward Broughton, was described by Aubrey as a descendant of an ancient family, a puritan, and a Committee man of Herefordshire, "who learned to use composted Soape-ashes to improve land near Bristol, where they polluted the harbor water by throwing them away." Aubrey was more interested in Broughton's famous daughter Elizabeth, however. He did not know whether she was born at Canon Pyon or not,

but there she lost her Mayden-head to a poor young fellow, then I beleeve handsome, but, in 1660, a pittifull poor old weaver, Clarke of the Parish. He had fine curled haire, but gray. Her father at length discovered her inclinations and locked her up in the Turret of the house, but she getts down by a rope; and away she gott to London, and did sett upp for her selfe. She was a most exquisite beautie, as finely shaped as Nature could frame; had a delicate Witt. She was soon taken notice of at London, and her price was very deare--a second Thais. Richard, Earle of Dorset, kept her (whether before or after Venetia I know not, but I guess

before). At last she grew common and infamous
and gott the Pox, of which she died.
   I remember thus much of an old song of those
dayes, which I have seen in a Collection: 'twas
by way of litanie, viz:
        From the Watch at Twelve a Clock,
        And from Bess Broughton's buttond smock,
        Libera nos Domine.[68]

She was famous enough to warrant a poem by Ben Jonson on Broughton's pox.

   But in 1624 her father was more concerned a-
bout his land than his daughter. The manor of
Canon Pyon was a very large one.[69] The original
lease of 30 January 1561 included the manor and all
its lands, water stangles (areas covered by water),
and fish pools, tithes, work silver (a place where
silver is smelted), and so on; wards of marriages,
hawkinge, etc. The annual rent for this large estate was to be 43 quarters of wheat and 200 heaps
of oats (a quarter contained 8 bushels and there
were 3 heaps in a bushel). The monetary equivalent
for that amount of grain, based on a yearly average
was £74.

   The original lease was for forty years, and
it was renewed on 18 June 1569. On August 1580,
Eleanor Broughton became administrator of the manor
for her husband, and nine years later, as a widow,
she was given a lease for another forty years. On
10 July 1600 Edward Broughton came to the lease as
the assignee of his mother Eleanor. He apparently
met his obligations to the Cathedral until 1619,
when he started withholding his rent. The rent was
paid under a series of covenants to the various
members of the Chapter, and Broughton faulted on
seven of those covenants for the period 1619
through 1623. In 1624 the Dean and Chapter decided they had waited long enough and brought suit
against Broughton in the King's Bench. They decided to concentrate on just one covenant rather
than trying at that late date to collect on all
seven, and the one they chose was one that in 1619
and 1620 was assigned to Robert Burghill but in

1621 was transferred to Dr. John Best, vicar of Lugwardine and one of the Canons of the Cathedral.[70]

Some time during 1624, a King's Bench decision had awarded Dr. Best £40 for outstanding debts and £17 in court costs. Best had chosen John Hoskyns to represent him and the Cathedral.[71] John would naturally have wanted to do his best in this case, and the record shows that he gave it a great deal of attention during the next two years. He may also have wanted to further his brother's application for the Lectureship by putting the Chapter in a position of obligation for his valuable services.

The records of the case as they exist in the Cathedral library begin on 17 November 1624. Broughton, with John's old Parliament friend Sir Henry Yelverton as his counsel, was the plaintiff. John argued that the case had already been decided in this court (King's Bench), but that the plaintiff had brought a writ of error in order to reverse the judgement in Common Laws. Yelverton replied that the plaintiff had already paid £40 penalty and only owed twenty shillings. He wanted any further action on the part of the defendant injoined. The court ordered that the plaintiff should forbear proceeding on the writ of error, and the defendant was injoined against any further action until the case was heard by this court. Robert Rich noted that all counsel were to meet at the Judge's house in Chancery Lane on 1 December, "by consent of all parties."

On 27 January 1625, Dr. William Prichard wrote to Dr. Best from Morehampton, sending along an order from the court that had been granted upon a motion submitted by Serjeant Hoskyns. "If y^u belieue Mr Broughton will performe the ord^r and Reporte, wthout a decree, it will saue a greate chardge." If not, Best was to let Prichard know.

Dr. William Prichard was a solicitor that John used regularly to handle the details of cases when he could not be present. For example, on 16 March

Justice Whitelocke ordered both parties and their counsel to be present in his lodgings in Hereford on Monday the 21st, at 2 p.m. John would have been on his own circuit in south Wales at the time and would not be able to attend, so Prichard attended instead. Prichard was a university man with a Doctor's degree, but he apparently found working for John very congenial since he is shown as a close family friend as late as 1629. He certainly did not suffer financially from the association; the Best case alone brought him at least £9 7s 4d.

The reason for the March session in White-locke's lodgings was an "order in Chauncery for reference to Sr James Whitelocke." On 12 February, John had told the court that Dr. Best had an order from the King's Bench that ordered all parties to submit to Justice Whitelocke. Justice Washington, who was presiding at the court session, told White-locke to find "how far forth ye Deane and Chapter have been dampnified." He also was to decide whether to continue or dissolve the injunction. Whitelocke "took paynes therein but Broughton would obey no order of him & therevpon ex^{ted} his bill in Chancerie to wch answ^r is made & ye bond being 40^{li} wherevpon recouerie was had ye performance of Broughtons Indenture of lease being broken in seaven seuerall covenantes & yssue taken vpon one of ye covenants wilfullie broken, yet prayeth releife of ye Court & had an Iniunction although iudgm^t was given in ye Kings Bench."

The night before the meeting at Whitelocke's lodgings, Dr. Best gave John a present of an 18/5 sugar loaf. He then listed the item under his expenses for the lawsuit. It is probably the only payment that John received during the entire two year period.

A week later England was suddenly thrown into mourning for the death of the King. James died in the morning of 27 March 1625, at his favorite retreat at Theobald's, the comfortable manor house built by Lord Burghley just west of Waltham Cross in Hertfordshire. On 4 April the late King's body was brought to London from Theobald's and laid in state in Denmark House in the Strand until the morning of 7 May, when it was taken to the funeral at Westminster Abbey. The funeral service was all that James could have asked for. His hearse "was more Royally adorned, than hath beene knowne for former Princes," and the procession included King Charles and "all the Nobility, and chiefe Clergie of the Land, with diuers Ambassadours, and all his Seruants and Officers, and a great number besides, all in mourning habites."[72] Undoubtedly John was there with the rest of the Serjeants-at-Law, anxious to be seen by the present King for doing his duty and paying his respects to his father. But John's feelings must have been very mixed as he looked at the corpse of the man who had treated him so harshly ten years earlier. He took no part in writing latin verses on the death of James nor on the accession of Charles to the throne.

The country returned to normal quickly. King Charles went off to the coast almost immediately to welcome his new bride from France, and White-locke went back to work on the Best-Broughton case. He had a list of the debts involved drawn up and submitted to him. During this process, Dr. Best had heard a request from Broughton's counsel for a Mr. Seaborne to do the calculations and, against the advice of Dr. Prichard, had agreed to the arrangement. Seaborne not only came up with practically the same amounts that had formerly been claimed by Dr. Best but was honest enough to add a note for £9 14s 4d because "I forgate to reckon for the heapes of all these 5 yeares after ij heapes to euery quarter of wheate in toto 10 heapes."

The price of a bushel of wheat fluctuated considerably during the period: from 3s 4d, to 6s 8d. Oats, on the other hand, remained constant at 20d a year. All told, including the additional reckoning by Seaborne, Broughton had accumulated a debt of £22 17s 8d. "Expenses in the suite at common lawe, allowed by Sr James Whitelocke" were £17 11s. Later additional expenses amounting to £4 18d were

609

added by the time Justice Whitelocke's Report was
confirmed in Chancery. So by May 1625, the original debt plus allowable expenses amounted to £45 2d.

Before Justice Whitelocke submitted his report, John wrote to the Dean of the Cathedral:

S^r by god_es_ loue I will see y_u_ as soone as eu^r
I com pas_t_ S^{r}ieant_es_ Inne. yestrday broughton was wth me to outface me. Doctor Best
dealt vnwisely to submitte hymself by bond to
m^r Sebornes arbitrem^t to be made by a day vp-
o_n_ a commissio_n_ fro_m_ the marcches ⟨ wittnesses to be examined but the day was past ere I
came vp ⟨ nothinge donne but he Broughton
commes vp to make affi_d_avit that the death of
the kinge detrmind the autority of the Councell ⟨ so he was hindred, their autority was
p^{r}sently renewed. ⟨ howsoev^r Doctor Best a-
lone could not submitt the cause of the Church
to arbitrem^t it is now res integra
Justice Whitlock will pepper hym wth a report
when y_u_ are well y_u_ shall com to hym all had
ben donne ere this had Doctor best not referd
it but as soone as I haue the Report y_u_ shall
heare more I take it it is ready but not
brought into the Registr quan_tum_ vales me ama
et quan_tum_ amas vale. vxorem ⟨ filiam ⟨ fra-
trem mes noua saluta quibque salutem a deo opt
maximo indulgend_um_ stremus apud eu p^{r}cibus
concendo
          tibi serviens
           J: Hoskyns[73]

Whitelocke was indeed ready with his report,
dated 20 May 1625. He says that he had heard both
sides. The plaintiff, Broughton, alleges that the
Dean and Chapter received the verdict for £40 in
King's Bench, so only a 20s loss remains from the
breach of covenant, and he desires relief. The defendant answers that it is true that

the bond was condiconed for performance of Covenants of a lease of a mannor wth tithes wch the
def. holds wch Covenant_es_ are for reparacon of

houses for not counttinge waste in woods for
giueing entertainement to theire officers at
theire Courtes there to be held and for paye-
inge severall measures of Corne or petty Comons
to severall prebendaries in the Church And that
theis severall Covenantes being broken to their
damage aboue the value of the forfeiture of the
bond they comenced suite thervpon and tooke issue as by lawe they ought onely vpon the breach
of one Covenante wch the now plt then def ought
to prove performed,

notwithstanding the other damages. Whitelocke
finds that at the King's Bench, the Dean and Chapter got £40 debt and £17 odd money costs from the
suit. It was then "referred to me for mittigacon
of the Judgment by consent of parties if I could."
In these investigations he found cause for Broughton to pay the defendants £30, but Broughton de-
clined that reference and preferred his own Bill in
this court. On again looking the whole case over,
Whitelocke says,

I thinke it reasonable that the plt in this
suite doe pay vnto the Defendant the somme of
thirtie poundes And for that the defendantes in
this suite are by this order debarred of about
thirtie poundes more recovered at the Comon Lawe
I held it fitt that the nowe Complainant enter
into a new bond of Fortie poundes condiconed as
the former was wch if he refuze to doe it is
reasonable the nowe defendantes should take
their advantage against the complt at the Comon
Lawe.

Whitelocke's report was accepted in a decree in
Chancery on 28 May, upon a motion by Serjeant Hoskyns. A week later, on 4 June, Prichard wrote to
Dr. Best, warning him that Broughton intended to
move "at the seale," even though Prichard had
warned him not to. Broughton's counsel "prtended
that during the referrence to Sr James, yu consented Mr Seaborne should mittigate the Judgmt."
As noted in John's letter, this tactic did not
work, however, and Whitelocke's report stood. And

611

indeed there is a decree ratifying the former order present among the Best-Broughton papers. And that is where the case stood for nearly six months.

Meanwhile the usual sorts of activities continued. Thomas, John's brother, on 2 June 1625, bought twenty-two acres of land in four different parcels around Bernithen for £40.[74] The land was actually purchased for John as part of the Bernithen estate.

By June the plague that had started in the late winter in London had grown markedly. The King's death was only one of scores of thousands that year in England. On 1 July the situation had become so bad that the Middle Temple Parliament decreed that "There shall be no Summer reading this year, by reason of the great increase and danger of the sickness."[75] By 18 November the sickness was still so great that the Middle Temple Parliament had to meet at Reading. It must have been a welcome duty to John to have to go far west on his circuit in September. We know he was there as, on 19 September, he and Nicholas Overbury signed a final concord on a case at the Great Sessions at Haverfordwest.[76]

The plague was the worst that England had suffered since the Black Death during the reign of Edward III in the middle of the fourteenth century. Between 22 December 1624 and 23 December 1625, within London and in the suburbs of the city, 63,000 people died, 40,313 of the plague. A glance at any of the church records of the time reveals the effect of the sickness. In an ordinary year a given church would have a folio page given over to the recording of births, marriages, and deaths, with the first and last more or less taking about the same amount of space. For the year 1625, there are usually a few births recorded, fewer marriages than usual, and then folio page after folio page of deaths, showing whole families wiped out, almost entire parishes decimated.

The death that happened at Morehampton probably had nothing to do with the plague since there was only one at the time; but by whatever cause, on 6 October 1625, Benedicta died, leaving John a widower. That there had been times of strain between these two we have already seen, but that there was also a real love and affection between them that outlasted the times of difficulty seems equally true. John had loved his adopted family as his own and had always treated the offspring equally.

Benedicta was buried up the river from Morehampton in the quiet church of Vowchurch, and John had a tablet mounted on the wall, with an inscription in Latin he had written himself. It began with the usual identification of the deceased: Benedicta, the oldest daughter of Robert Moyle of Burkwell, in the county of Kent, gentleman, wife first to Francis Bourne of Sutton St. Cleares in the county of Somerset, gentleman; then to John Hoskyns of Morehampton in the county of Hereford, Serjeant at Law. She was "Pia, formosa, prudens, pudica": pious, beautiful, prudent, chaste. Having reached the age of 50, she died 6 October 1625. Here Jesus awaits his servant. Then follows a quatrain, also in Latin:[77]

Here lies Benedicta, of whom no one of family,
Virtue or pious tongue can speak evil
She was wife of Bourne and Hoskyns and mother of
offspring
To each, daughter of Moyle, servant of God.

At about the same time that Benedicta died, another death appears to have spurred John into writing another epitaph, although he is not usually credited with its composition. The nephew and very close friend of Sir Henry Wotton, Sir Albertus Morton, had married Elizabeth Apsley, one of the Ladies in Waiting to the Queen of Bohemia, in 1624. A year later he was dead, and soon after, she followed him to the grave. Three years later, Sir Henry Wotton wrote a letter to his friend John Dynely, who was in attendance on Queen Elizabeth, and included the following postscript:

613

If the Queen have not heard the epitaph of Albertus Morton and his lady, it is worth her hearing for the passionate plainness:
    He first deceas'd. She for a little tried
    To live without him: lik'd it not and died.

Authoris Incerti[78]

The epitaph was published in Reliquiae Wottonianae as being by Wotton, and that attribution has remained unchallenged in spite of the wording of the letter, which has been taken as a self-effacing remark by Wotton.

    The couplet immediately became popular and appeared in both manuscript and published form quickly. In all but one case that I have seen, it appears anonymously, although editors have, in several cases, added a note about its appearance in the Reliquiae. The one specific attribution is in Harley 6038,[79] where it forms but two lines of a longer epitaph which is assigned to "J:H:" In the other cases in which those initials are used in this manuscript, the poems so identified are those by John Hoskyns. There is no reason to believe other than that the complete poem is by John; and there is certainly no reason to credit the two stanza poem to Wotton:

    Here Lye two Bodyes happy in their kinds
    the rich Apparel of two noble minds
    All blessings they familiarly did know
    wch either earth or Heaven could bestowe.
    She first deceased, He for a little try'd
    to liue wthout her, likt it not, & dy'de.

    They had noe Children, whence we truly say
    the good of all their Offspringe in them Laye.
    For they ingross'd their Heyres right, & did
                                            prove
    their owne Inherito^rs in Grace, in Love,
    Neither to others nor themselves a trouble
    Whose Soules are one, & yet reward is double.

                        J:H:

There are, of course, several possibilities about the origin of the poem. In the full version, found also in <u>Harley 1221</u>, the order of death of the married pair is incorrect, as it is in all but one version besides the <u>Reliquiae</u>. John may have gotten the facts wrong when he wrote the poem and sent it off to his friend Sir Henry. It was certainly his version rather than Sir Henry's which formed the model for other copyists. Another possibility is that John, following the early poetic play that he and Wotton indulged in, saw a copy of Wotton's couplet and built a longer poem around it as a gesture of friendship, again, making an error in the order of death. I believe that Hoskyns wrote the entire poem. By 1628, when Wotton transcribed the poem, John was back in Parliament and taking a strong stand on the Petition of Right. Wotton would have been politic in not identifying the writer to the sister of the present king, Charles, who was having no better luck with Parliament than his father had had. The epitaph style is very much like that of Hoskyns, and there is no example of Wotton's poetic style that would identify the couplet as his. He did indeed, in 1625, write a longer poem in praise of Morton, "Tears at the Grave of Sir Albertus Morton (who was buried at Southampton) Wept by Sir. H. Wotton," but the couplet bears little resemblance to Wotton's longer poem. Even if he did write the couplet, there is no reason to doubt that the other ten lines are by Hoskyns.

* * * * *

On 16 February 1626, John was in London to continue his pleading of the Best-Broughton case, but he was also trying to clear up a family problem. Will Hoskyns, eldest son of Oswald, had run off and married against the advice of the family, and it had proven disastrous. John brought a bill of annulment and won the case. At the time of his first letter to his step-daughter Bess, the final decision had not been handed down, although the case itself had ended.

To his very lovinge daughter Mrs Elizabeth

Boorne at Morehampton
                    give these.
   My cosen Wills cause is this day ended. M^rs
Morgan is to pay 200 marke fyne to the king for
her selfe, & a 100 marke a peece for Sr Jasper
Carpenter & Taylor & if they be not able to pay
themselfs then she is to pay and all fower are
committed prison, and the pris^r and her mayd &
Taylor never to be vsed as wittnes in the spiritual Coorte to proue the marriadge. And yf it
proue a marriadge then Mrs Morgan is to pay a
1000 marks porcion, and Mr Danncer & Mr Blayrich
Barrys bonds are to stand for performaunce of
this decree and besides shee is to pay all the
costs of suite wch shalbe allowed by the Coorte.
Bid Wills sisters give thankes to god & pray
for hym and for themselfs, and by this example
learne to be wise, to feare god & be advised by
theire best frends. Let my daughter Megg:
Boorne haue any money that she shall want, for
I have receaued money of hers, desire Parrot to
be diligent in all husbandry. Comend mee to my
Cosen Richard Hoskins and yf he want any little
somme of money let him haue it let the keep[er]
be remembred to looke to the parke & to the Con-
yes. I am not licke to come home till the Sys-
ses be past in Glouc, wch will be about the 16
of March.
   My man hath written for my horses to be heere
about the 3 of March, At wch tyme send word
what fysh or other things yo^w will haue, And
good Besse be carefull & serue god... Will &
Ben & Lewis are in health & mery wth mee. Lewis
shall come downe shortly, But Will & Benn may
stay heere yf the sickness Increase not. pray
for vs all, wee will pray for yo^w. forgett not
to put forward the gardinge. god blesse yo^w &
Dick and all the rest.

                    yr Lovinge father
                    J: Hoskyns.[80]

   The letter is of interest for a number of reasons. Will was considerably under the age of
twenty-one, as he did not sign the Orphanage Ac-

616

counts in London for his share of his father's estate for another four years, and then, not until
he was married. Which Morgan family he had married
into is not at all clear; at any rate, he seems to
have been happy to escape from the marriage. Perhaps Elizabeth was already interested in her young
cousin; by 1630, even though she was at least seven
years older, she would become his wife in another
move by John to consolidate the Bourne and Hoskyns
families. That may be the reason her step-father
gives her so many of the details concerning the
case. John was certainly now in the position to
ease up on the cash flow out of his chest in Morehampton.

John was also remaining quite close with his
cousin Richard. The problems with the property he
had bought from Richard had not impaired that
friendship. John handled many of Richard's land
difficulties over the years, and Richard's wife
Ann moved to Monkton as a widow. "Lewis" is Lewis
Powell, who was to act as a clerk for John later,
as had his father, Thomas Powell. At this point
he was probably a companion for Ben. William Taylor had once again violated John's trust, and his
name never again appears in the letters or as a
clerk in John's various legal transactions. Both
he and his brother Tom did, however, die about this
time.

The day after he wrote to Bess, John was in
Westminster again, pleading Dr. Best's case, this
time before the new Lord Keeper, Thomas Coventry.
There had been a note in the court records for 24
November 1625 that Edward Broughton had still done
nothing about obeying the order of the King's
Bench. Now, on 17 February 1626, John reviewed
the record of various court decisions and said,
"the plt will neyther paie the sd xxx^{li} nor enter
into any new bond, but doth now proceede vppon his
Writt of error which he had formerlie waved as a-
foresaid." The Lord Keeper immediately ordered
that Dr. Best proceed "wth proces vppon the decree,
to inforce the plt to the performance thereof." He
also awarded Dr. Best costs for the whole suit in

617

this court.

The results were the same as before. Broughton took advantage of a momentary delay to forward
his own cause. On 20 May 1626, Sir John Mitchell
ruled that he saw no reason for any charge of contempt against Broughton, and that if Dr. Best did
not prove such a charge, he would have to pay all
costs. Mitchell also said he saw no reason why
Broughton should not have his old bond if the new
one was taken.

That brought John back into court on 17 June.
He stated to Lord Coventry that all of Broughton's
excuses were lies as far as the real events were
concerned. He reiterated that the important point
was that Broughton had not obeyed the Court. The
resulting Court order takes on a new tone. It orders that the plaintiff shall, on 1 August next,
"peremptorily paie vnto Do^r Best the said £30 &
costs" and Dr. Best is to return the old bond on
making a new one. On his side Broughton is to release the writ of error on their charge of contempt, but they shall have to prove the charge or
pay costs. So each side had won its immediate
point, and John was obviously not worried about
proving the charge of contempt with all of the evidence of Broughton's lack of action. Broughton was
not through with his delaying action, however, and
in September the Dean and Chapter notified the Lord
Keeper officially that Broughton had done nothing.

Meanwhile John had been busy at other matters.
As he had told Bess in his last letter, he had been
to the Assizes at Gloucester, and it is possible
that at that time he met a charming widow who was
to occupy his attentions during the next few months.
On 12 March he had undoubtedly attended a meeting
of the Council of the Marches of Wales in Ludlow,
for they were hearing a case from his circuit.[81]
On 4 April John and Nicholas Overbury were on their
circuit and hearing a case in Carmarthen.[82] On 18
April John probably helped his cousin Richard and
Ann his wife, in preparing a petition to the House
of Lords that asked that their cause against "the

618

Custos and Viccars of the Quire in the Cathedral
Church of Hereford" might be heard by their Lordships or referred by them to the Lord President
and Council of Wales.[83] And on the last day of
August John took the opportunity to add another
four acres to the Bernithen property by buying a
close of land for £17. He was only one purchase
away from completing the land transactions on the
property that would fulfill his obligations to his
brother Oswald's children.

Then, after riding his circuit for the fall
term, he returned to London determined to finish
off the Broughton case for the Dean and Chapter of
the Cathedral. It had been hanging on long enough.
On 23 October 1626, he opened a hearing before Sir
Richard Moore and Sir John Heyward at the Court of
Rolls by restating the claims and declaring that
Broughton had still not paid. The Court acted
quickly: "It is therefore ordered that the said
plaintiff bee solempnly Committed to the prison of
the Fleete there to remayne vntill he shalle submitt himself." The judges especially ordered him
to submit to Mr. Justice Whitelocke. On 5 November Broughton's counsel claimed in court that
Broughton had paid the £30 and felt that incorrect
costs had been charged. The Court disagreed and
ruled that they stood. The next day Sir Richard
Moore appointed a 2 p.m. meeting for Broughton in
his chamber in the Elm Court of the Middle Temple,
following which, on 13 November, he issued a report that on examination of the evidence, he agreed
that Broughton was in contempt. Back in Court on
16 November, John opened the hearing by showing
Sir Richard's Report. The Court ruled that Broughton's counsel had one week to disprove the contempt
charge or Broughton would go to the Fleet. (His
counsel had been successful in delaying the order
of 23 October.)

On the day that Broughton's counsel was to
have disproved the contempt charge (23 November),
he appeared before the Lord Keeper and said that
Broughton had always been willing to pay. John was
suspicious, however, and attended Chancery on Nov-

ember 24th and 25th to see what Broughton might argue in his defense. On 27 November, Broughton's counsel made a motion that claimed that Broughton had never prosecuted a writ of error. At the same time an affadavit was submitted by Walter Wheeler that he had served a subpoena on Broughton for all the costs. So, on 1 December, Broughton was ordered to pay all the costs for the contempt charge as well. By this time John apparently had other things to do, as he had his friend Serjeant Athowe plead Best's case. But it was undoubtedly John who decided that an act of leniency on the part of Dr. Best would bring the whole matter to a conclusion. On 7 December 1626, Dr. Best and the Dean and Chapter notified the Court that they were willing to relinquish the £40 costs charged by Sir Richard More. They thought it "reasonable that the plt pay vnto the Def^{tes} the some of xxli in discharge of all cost̲es." Broughton assented, and obviously he finally paid, as the case was closed.

The case is an excellent example of the use and misuse of the law in 17th Century England. Everyone lost by it in the end except the lawyers, and, in the case of John, even he apparently lost, although by his own choice. In the final analysis the one who lost the most was Edward Broughton, who sought to circumvent the law in every way possible. Had the Dean and Chapter not retained as dogged a legal representative as John, however, Broughton might have gotten away with his scheme. Even if he had, though, he would have spent more on legal fees than he owed on his lease to the Cathedral.

The lists of expenses that are joined to the various court orders give us a good idea of just how expensive it was to pursue a case in court at the time. A large amount of the cost to the Dean and Chapter was the work of William Prichard. There are such entries as "To Mr Prichard Serieant Hoskins his man per billa̲m & for soliciting 2^{li} 17s 0"; all told he was paid nearly £10 for his work. There are entries such as "To Mr Serieant Hoskins his men to cary ye Lawe book̲es to London̲, & to take care of them̲ 2^s." There were costs for the writ of error and copies of rulings as well as payments to the Judge's men for their activities ("To Mr Justice Whitlockes man at Serj.'s Inn at the hearing vpon the reference out of Kings Bench 2^s 6^d").

The most important entries, of course, are those for the lawyers pleading the case in court. "To Counsell for a motion in the Kinges bench for execution after Mr Broughtons refusing to stand to Sr James Whitelockes order xx^s," "S^{r}iant Bramston to defend the mocon" £1. Serjeant Athowe received £2 for his work on 1 December 1626. Finally we think we will have a clear picture of the money that John made as a Serjeant. For example, "To Mr Serieant Hoskins himself for a motion at ye Rooles Octob. 23. 1626. for Mr Br^s Committem^t for abusing S^r Ja: Whitelocke, & for a reference to Sr Rich: Moore com. ye Attachm^t"--and then appears a blank space. Entry after entry indicating John's activities for Dr. Best, such as "To attend in Chancery & ye Rolles on Thursday Novem. 23 to see if any good cause should be alledged for Mr Broughton to avoyd his comittem^t," appears in the expense sheets, and always there is a blank space in the margin where the sum should appear.

It is easy enough to judge what the entries should have been from the payments to the other Serjeants in the expense accounts. A Serjeant could expect to be paid either £1 or £2 for an appearance in court depending on the duties expected of him there. Why are John's entries left blank, therefore? I think the answer is quite clear and is indicated by the final decision on the case. As long as there was any question as to who was going to pay the costs of the long litigation, John refused to accept payment from the Dean and Chapter because of his long friendship and association with that group. In the last action, he offered to have his costs removed from the expenses in order to get a final settlement which would draw Broughton's legitimate debts into the hands of Dr. Best, who had not received his payment for all those years. John had known what it was like to have his rightful income held back when the city of Hereford re-

621

fused to pay him for his days in the first Parliament of James. He could sympathize with Dr. Best, and he could visualize further delaying actions by Broughton unless some sort of compromise was reached. The difference of £20 between what the Court judged as legitimate costs and what the Dean and Chapter and Dr. Best settled for in the final statement of costs is almost exactly what the expense sheets indicate John would have received for his work on the case. This generous act is yet another sign of the friendship that John showed in very practical ways to those in Hereford who were close to him. I suspect that it was a rare act in the history of 17th century legal practice.

All this time John had continued to live in his chambers at the Middle Temple, partly because John Bourne and Benedict were living there and also because he had invested a good deal of money in refurbishing them and keeping them in good condition. He was not the only Serjeant who was breaking the rules of the Temple in this way. The rules were very clear: once a Serjeant had been rung out of the Temple on the day of his Call, he was supposed to move all of his belongings over to one of the two Serjeants' Inns. It was, admittedly, rather difficult to force a Serjeant out if he did not have the good grace to move on his own. After all, these people worked in the law courts together, and Judges that the Middle Temple barristers had to argue before were chosen from the ranks of the Serjeants. At the same time, something clearly had to be done to make room for new students coming in. John was to be at the center of the controversy as it built up during 1627, and his old antagonist Sir Walter Pye was to be the moving force in the Temple for change.

Sir Walter, Attorney of the Court of Wards and Liveries, was chosen Treasurer of the Middle Temple on 13 October 1626,[84] and part of his duties was the assignment of new students to chambers in the Inn. On 24 January 1627 John Cockes of Castleditch, Herefordshire, entered and was bound with Thomas Cockes and Benedict Hoskyns.[85] It seems to have been his plight as far as assignment of chambers is concerned that triggered the following action by the Parliament of the Inn. On 26 January, they ruled that "No Serjeant-at-Law after he has taken his oath and been solemnly invested in his robes, had any right to retain or dispose of his chamber, which then accrues to the House to be disposed of."[86] The next month the Inn had to go through the process of collecting money for a new Serjeant, and they became rebellious. On 1 February 1627, Sir Nicholas Hyde of the Middle Temple was made a Serjeant-at-Law and one week later was sworn in as Lord Chief Justice of the King's Bench. Then on 4 May 1627 the Middle Temple Parliament moved that they would no longer give a Serjeant the gift of £10. No Serjeant was to be allowed the use of a chamber, nor was he to move to the upper end of the hall any more. "...neither shall the company here or of New Inn be summoned to attend his going to Serjeants' Inn or to Westminster Hall."[87] They were fed up.

Their next action came as a result of another death close to John. Sometime early in May, John Bourne died at Morehampton and was buried next to his mother in Vowchurch. His step-father wrote a Latin epitaph on the young man as he had for his mother:[88]

Noble Bourne spent harmless years
    Reading much, understanding much, saying
                                        little.
A lawyer, he did not enrich himself by pleading
                                        cases,
    Laying store not in having riches but in
                                        dying.

The Serjeant had treated his step-son well all his life, even though letters to Benedicta had indicated that he thought young John was lazy. The epitaph gave the very best reading possible for the young man's life. Certainly the necessity to write epitaphs had reawakened John's skill in the form. The epitaph for Benedicta had been very straightforward, giving little evidence that it was written

623

by a skillful Latinist and wit. This later one
was much cleverer. First there is the nice pun
that the son of Benedicta and Francis is indeed
"noble born." The full meaning of one phrase "cal-
lens plurima" would run something like "gaining
knowledge of a great many things through experience," and it reminds the reader of John's remark
to Benedicta to "forbeare your censure & speeches
& bestow them on y^r sone Boorne." The third line
is both a compliment and, for those who knew of
John Bourne's lack of activity, an accurate description of his behavior as a lawyer. The last
line is a skillful use of a very few words to relate Bourne's life to Christ's advice not to lay
up treasures (locans lucrum) on earth but in heaven.

John wrote another epitaph, one of his most
admired pieces, before the year was out. On 11
August 1627 Anne Prideaux, the six-year-old daughter of John Prideaux, who was Regius Professor of
Systematic Theology at Oxford and rector of Exeter
College, and who later became Bishop of Worcester,
died and was buried along with her sister and her
mother in St. Michael's Church, Oxford. Their
monument still hangs on the wall of the church.
John wrote an epitaph for the young girl either at
the request of her father or of her grandfather,
William Goodwin, who was Dean of Christ Church:

On Mrs Anne Prideaux daughter of Mr Doctor Pri-
deaux Regius Professor.
        She dyde at the age of 6 yeares.
            [On a young Gentlewoman]
Nature in this small volume was about
To perfect what in woman was left out.
Yet fearefull least a piece so well begun,
might want preseruatives when she had done,
Ere she could finish what she vndertooke,
Threw dust upon yt, & shut vp the Booke.[89]

As soon as the Middle Temple Parliament heard
that John Bourne had died, they ruled that John
Cockes should move into the chamber of Benedict
Hoskyns in place of Bourne. The record indicates

that he paid a fine of £13 6s 8d;[90] it must mean that John had done such a good job of fixing up the rooms that they now called for a much higher fee than the rest of the chambers around them. John, however, refused to let Cockes move in.

One reason may be that he was thinking about something else. During Easter term he had had to answer a remarkably strange charge. It is contained in a record of "Serjeant Hoskin's Case" before the King's Bench.[91]

He was indicted for not paving of the Kings high-way in the county of Middlesex in S. Johns street, _ante tenementa sua_: and in the indictment it was not shewed, how he came chargeable to pay the same; nor was it shewed that he was seised of any house there, nor that he dwelt there, nor was it averred that he had any tenement there. The opinion of the Court was, that the indictment was incertain; for it might be that his lessee dwelt in the house, and so the lessee ought to have repaired it, and also mended the high-way. And for these incertainties the indictment was quashed.

John was not as fortunate in his continuing battle with the Middle Temple Parliament. On 8 June appears the record:

Mr. John Cockes, lately admitted by Mr. Treasurer to the part of a chamber late of Mr. John Bourne, deceased, with Mr. Benedick Hoskines, now in the possession of Mr. Serjeant Hoskines, father of the said Benedick, shall have (while Mr. Serjeant has use of the chamber) a place in the said chamber to set a bed in, and a convenient study. After Mr. Serjeant's departure a competent partition of the chamber shall be made between Benedick Hoskines and Cockes.[92]

The Parliament was increasingly angered by the failure of the Serjeants to leave when they should. The next item they dealt with was strongly worded: "Serjeants-at-Law now lodging in any

chambers of this House, shall have warning to depart before Hilary Term next." There must have
been some reason for John to be so recalcitrant.
There is evidence that he was in failing health
and did not want to move from his familiar quarters. At the same time, he was legally one of the
holders of Serjeants' Inn in Fleet St., a property
owned by the Dean of York Cathedral. On 16 July
he signed an indenture for that property along
with twenty-three other Justices and Serjeants-at-
Law, including Chief Justice Nicholas Hyde, Whitelocke, Henry Yelverton, Thomas Athowe, Aegremont
Thynne, Bramston, and Henneage Finch. The indenture grants them the Tenement in Fleet St. known
as Serjeants' Inn in Fleet Street, to have and to
hold for 40 years at an annual rent of 53s 4d.[93]
The rent was remarkably low, just over 2s apiece,
for the distinguished and wealthy group involved.
Of course there were other expenses which the men
of law shared, and they were responsible for the
upkeep of their own chambers; but basic costs were
still very slight. During the time of struggle between John and the Middle Temple, he was using his
rooms at Serjeants' Inn as guest chambers for his
friends and clients, as indicated by his remarks
to the Dean of Hereford Cathedral in his letter
during the prosecution of the Broughton case.

But John was still not about to move, nor to
let Cockes into the family rooms. On 23 November
1627 the Parliament had to move that "Mr. Treasurer
and Mr. Wotton shall view Mr. Hoskines' chamber
where Serjeant Hoskines now lieth, to a part whereof Mr. John Cockes is admitted, and do right therein in accordance with a former order."[94] Whatever
the results of that investigation, neither John nor
his fellow Serjeants left their chambers; so, on
8 February 1628, the Parliament put a specific
deadline on their move. All Serjeants were to "remove before the feast of the Annunciation next."[95]
That worked; there are no more entries on the subject.

Meanwhile the summer of 1627 was busy with
legal affairs in Wales. On 30 June John met with

626

the Council of the Marches of Wales at Bewdley, a-
bout twenty miles due east of their usual meeting
place in Ludlow. The next day William Murray
wrote to Edward Conway, who had just been raised
to the title of Viscount,

My most Honored Lord

The offenders name I haue begd of his M^{tie} is
W. Marten his offence a rape committed upon
the body of Margaret Sandford in the Countie of
Hereford { the Judges of that circuit are S^r
Jhon Dodderidge { Sr William Jones. my humble
desire is they may ase from the King be commaunded to appoint councell in his M^{ties} name
to prosecute the offence Sergeant Hoskins being particularely named for one { suche others
ase the Judges themselues will thinke fitt.
this is all the request an this particulare of

Your Lordships humble
seruaunt[96]

Conway moved fast, as did the king. The next
day Charles sent a message to the Justices involved, but he did not name John specifically:

Trustie and welbeloued wee greet yo^u well wee
are informed of a foule Rape committed by one
William Martin vpon ye Body of Margaret Sandford in o^r Countie of Hereford We thanke god
that these offences are not frequent, And wee
doe hold it requisite for deterring of others,
when such offenses are committed that exemplary
punishment should be inflicted vpon ye offendors. And therefore being informed that the
said Martin is of such Condition as he may in
likely hood finde meanes to stopp or deferre y^e
prosecution of Justice, wee haue thought good
to recommend it vnto yo^u to take into your
spetiall Care the examination of his Cause, and
by ye vsuall and legall waies and appointing of
such Counsell as yo^u shall thinke good, to see
a faire { iust prosecution of the facte mentioned according to o^r lawes and as to Justice
shall be agreable[97]

There is no reason to doubt that the Justices
appointed John as counsel according to the request
from the friends of the plaintiff. But it is also
true that John was not feeling too well. The
deaths of his wife and step-son, both apparently
dying intestate, had reminded him of the necessity
of bringing his own will up to date. On 23 June
1627, he drew up an addition to his previous will,
making sure that all of his estate would be cared
for. The handwriting is rather shaky throughout
and nearly breaks down towards the end. On the
outside of the document is the description: "a
scedule to Seriant Hoskyns will."

23 Jun: 1627 O god for Christ Jesus sake forgiue me preserve me The four closes that I pay
for to my broth^r Thomas bought of Donne neere
BrynIthen I will that my brother Thomas shall
convey & dispose of as my brother Doctor Hoskyns shall require hym and I devise my lease &
landes at Lookeham Barkshes to be disposed of
by my executors to the same vse that I haue
geven my oth^r landes I meane both the lease
& the fee farme yf m^r Treswell hath gotten for
me of the kings he hath the writings. my lease
of Tytley is almost expired and must be renewed
I hope the College will not aske above x^{li} fine
of me. I doe besides the fine geue to the warden & the ten fellows my eleven Sergeant_es_
ringes the best to the warden the next to the
subwarden & the choyse accordinge to their
antig'ty. I doe make my sonne Bennet Hoskyns
ioynt executor wth my broth^r Doctor and at his
age of one & twenty yeres I geue hym equall interest power and autory^{ty} in all my estate wth
my brother god blesse hym & my daughter and
all my broth^r Oswald_es_ children & my broth^r
philip & the Doctors all my brothren & my wives
children & grandchildren
Mid Temp vt ante[98]   J: Hoskyns

But John was not about to die; indeed in some
ways he was to take a new lease on life and add
to his already large family.

Footnotes for Chapter XVI

1. Hopwood, II, 664.
2. Stow, p. 1034.
3. See Osborn, p. 237.
4. Welcome you arrive, you who come down here, a
   friend and guest:
   This distinguished table does not suit these
   lowly Lares (or household gods).
5. An adequate translation of the words of this
   symbol has escaped every language professor I
   have consulted.
6. See Chapter 14, p. 475 for translation.
7. "And when thou hearest, forgive." I Kings 8:30.
8. Whatever anyone prays or raises in supplication
   in this house,
   Let not the prayers of your servants be spent
   in vain.
   Aubrey mistakenly gives a reference to I Reg.
   8:30. John has actually taken the idea from
   Solomon's great prayer at the opening of the
   Temple and adapted it to his own small chapel.
9. Here is the house, here the hills, quarries,
   Park and clear springs,
   Pastures, woods, and harvests: if it pleases,
   add your prayers.
10. "We hold the fruits of Hoskyns." There are
    several puns in the Greek, including an ob-
    vious reference to testicles held in a purse.
11. The translation of this poem, perhaps written
    by John himself, is to be found under 1631.
12. This place nourishes and is nourished, adorns
    and is adorned:
    Adam, not yet having fallen, would love this
    work.
13. Aubrey (Clark), I, 419-20. I have used the
    order of the description by Oliver Dick in his
    edition.
14. HMC, 13th Report, Rye and Hereford Corpora-
    tions, Dovaston MS., f. 109b, p. 264.
15. Ivan Roots, "The Central Government and the
    Local Community," in The English Revolution
    1600-1660, ed. E. W. Ives (1968).
16. SPD James I, Vol. 122/130.

17. Hopwood, II, 666.
18. Hopwood, II, 669.
19. N.L.W., Abergavenny MSS, 646, 675.
20. Abergavenny 787. The scribe incorrectly dated this indenture as "20 James I" instead of "19 James I."
21. Abergavenny 714, 348.
22. Abergavenny 643. Baker's Commission is dated 20 Feb. 1623, but it indicates his assumption of the office the previous May.
23. John Duncomb, Collections towards the History and Antiquities of the County of Hereford (1804), I, 488-89.
24. Harley 3910, f. 57; in Osborn, p. 210.
25. Duncomb, I, 357.
26. Ibid., p. 307. The Charter is given at length on pp. 355-59.
27. S.P.D. James I, 1619-1623 (1858), CXXX, 116, pp. 397-98.
28. Ibid., CXXX, 117, p. 398.
29. PRO, S.P.D. James I, Vol. 131, #2
30. Ibid., #3.
31. N.L.W., Poyston 74.
32. Orphans Recognizances 3, 1619 to 1627, #94, ff. 48v-49v; also Orphans Recognizances 2, 1590 to 1633, f. 241.
33. Recognizance Book 2 indicates a sum of £84 9s, and since this is the entry later signed by the inheritors, it would seem to be the correct one.
34. Orphans Recognizances 3, #95, f. 49v.
35. Vol. 81, Henry Rolle's Reports, part II (1676), p. 888.
36. Hopwood, II, 681.
37. Hopwood, II, 682.
38. P.R.O. Patent Roll James 21, Item 12, C66/2306. Osborn said that the call was for 13, using Hacket as a source. The records and comments at the time indicate the number was 15.
39. Hopwood, II, 684.
40. Alexander Pulling, The Order of the Coif (London, 1884), p. 36.
41. Dugdale, Origines, p. 111.
42. Chamberlain, II, 506.
43. Ibid., p. 518.
44. Dugdale, pp. 112-3.

45. Edward Foss, The Judges of England, Vol. VI, 1603-1660 (London, 1857), p. 31. Pulling quotes Foss in The Order of the Coif, p. 257, footnote 1.
46. Dugdale, pp. 111-2.
47. Pulling, pp. 229-30.
48. Hopwood, II, 686.
49. Chamberlain, II, 518.
50. The description of the activities of the day is taken basically from Dugdale's Origines Juridicales, pp. 136-8.
51. The oration runs from p. 110 to p. 113. Pulling also states that the Lord Keeper could be the speaker for the occasion.
52. Pulling, p. 230.
53. Dugdale, p. 113.
54. Stow, p. 1035. Sir Richard Baker, A Chronicle of the Kings of England (1645), p. 442, also notes the feast for the Call of 15 Serjeants at the Middle Temple Hall.
55. Chamberlain, II, 518.
56. I.A. Shapiro, "Walton and the Occasion of Donne's Devotions," R.E.S., N.S. IX (1958), p. 18.
57. H.M.C., Earl Cowper, K.G. at Melbourne Hall, Derbyshire, Vol. I (1888), p. 160.
58. Other letters on the lectureship controversy are on Ibid, p. 168 (24 August 1624); S.P.D. James I, 1623-1625 (1859), CLXXIV, 70, p. 379 (16 November); Ibid., p. 387 (22 November).
59. Hereford City MSS., Vol. 4, 1600-1644, ff. 34, 36, 39, 54, 40, 46.
60. Add. MSS. 11,053, Scudamore papers, f. 91.
61. Sizergh Muniment Room, Lease dated 10 April James 22.
62. P.R.O., Chancery Proceedings--Mitford, C8/30/56, Sheet I. The order for the Commissioners is on Sheet 2. John Bourne signed the document.
63. P.R.O., Chancery Case C.21, H22/10, Sheet 3.
64. Ibid., Sheet 1.
65. C8/30/56, Sheet 4.
66. H22/10, Sheet 4.
67. Ibid., Sheet 2.
68. Aubrey, p. 40.
69. All of the information on the Best-Broughton

case is contained in the Vicar's Choral Library of Hereford Cathedral, Index 3406, 3047.

70. He seems to have been either a brother or cousin of John's friend Charles Best, the Orator of the Prince d'Amour. Best died in 1637 and was buried at Lugwardine, where there is a waist-length painted bust in full ecclesiastical garb. H.M.C., Herefordshire, Vol. II, East (1932), p. 154.

71. Besides John's other relationships with the Cathedral which we have noted, his name is listed as "serjeant-at-law" among those who had contributed to the building of the College quadrangle of the Cathedral. Woolhope Club Transactions, 1868, p. 273.

72. Stow, p. 1041.

73. Index 3407.

74. Sizergh Muniment Room Indentures.

75. Hopwood, II, 701.

76. N.L.W., Poyston 79.

77. Among the family papers at Harewood. Aubrey also has the final four lines (Clark ed., I, 424).

78. Smith, Wotton, II, 311.

79. F. 11v; it is followed directly by the poem on the "Prince's Secrecy" and a few folios later by John's "New Years Gift to the King," both ending with the same "J:H:" The twelve line version is also in Harley 1221, f. 71 but without attribution. It is followed by the "Prince's Secrecy" and later by the "New Year's Gift." Just the couplet beginning "She" appears in Add. MSS. 15,227, f. 94; Add. MSS. 11,811, f. 2, has the couplet beginning "He" and the index of first lines refers to the Reliquiae; Add. MSS. 30,982, f. 31, has the couplet headed "on a gentleman dying presently after his wife"; Add. MSS. 25,707, f. 100, entitles the couplet "A epitaph of two louers"; Lansdowne 542, f. 56, entitles it "On a Gent: soone dying after his wife." Camden added the couplet along with John's "Upon a young Gentlewoman" among the epitaphs "nearer to our times" and introduced it "Upon two Lovers who, being espoused, dyed both before they were married."

(p. 438) There is always the chance that the manuscript tradition is accurate and that Wotton lifted two lines from Hoskyns' poem on a totally different pair, altered the death order to fit the occasion, and sent it off as a poem that the wife of Frederick would have liked about two of her former favorites. In Reliquiae Wottonianae (1685), the couplet is headed "Upon the death of Sir Albert. Morton's Wife" (p. 389) and follows a seven stanza poem on Morton himself (pp. 388-89).

80. Sizergh MSS.; in Osborn, pp. 90-91.
81. N.L.W., Derwydd 686.
82. N.L.W., Derwydd 252.
83. Fourth Report of the Royal Commission on Historical Manuscripts, Part I (1874), p. 9.
84. Hopwood, II, 711.
85. Hopwood, II, 715.
86. Hopwood, II, 715.
87. Hopwood, II, 720.
88. Aubrey (Clark, ed.), p. 424. Osborn did not know when Bourne died, locating the date as "sometime between 1624 and 1627." (p. 294)
89. Lansdowne 777A, f. 60v. The poem is among a collection of poetry by William Browne of the Inner Temple, but it is not designated as by Browne, as most are. The collection includes many elegies and poems about Middle Templars. William Camden also includes the poem in his collection of epitaphs, although not among those directly attributable to Hoskyns (p. 438). Also in Harley 3910, f. 4; Sloane 1446, f. 65; Add. MSS. 15,227, f. 89; Egerton 2421, f. 2v, where it is with other Hoskyns epitaphs; Egerton 923, f. 65; Add. MSS. 25,303, f. 163, among a group of Hoskyns' poems; and Facetiae: Musarum Deliciae (1817), II, 238. Osborn incorrectly lists entries for this poem in Sloane 1827 and Harley 6917. One of the nice coincidences of history made William Prideaux Courtney the author of John's biography in the D.N.B.
90. Hopwood, II, 721.
91. The English Reports, Vol. 78, King's Bench Division, Godbolt's Reports (1653), No. 481,

p. 400. Dr. Prideaux was a witness in a case at the King's Bench that same term, and John and the Doctor may have reawakened an old friendship at that time, leading to the request for the epitaph written in August.

92. Hopwood, II, 723.
93. H. C. King, ed., Records and Documents concerning Serjeants' Inn Fleet Street (1922), pp. 118-20.
94. Hopwood, II, 727.
95. Hopwood, II, 729.
96. S.P.D. Charles I, Vol. 70, #2, dated 1 July 1627. Summary is in S.P.D. Charles I, 1627-1628 (1858), p. 239.
97. S.P.D. Charles I, Vol. 70, #7, dated 2 July 1627; summary in S.P.D. as above.
98. Harewood MSS.

Chapter XVII

A New Life

On Sunday, 9 December 1627, John wrote a letter to someone he trusted well and who knew of all his affairs at Morehampton, preparing for the activities of the following week:

...I thinck the matter to morrow wilbe so farre settled as that we shall need no other help but gods blessinge wch is drawn down by the prayers of them that feare hym. Provide all things as well as y^u can yf it please god we will be at Rosse on friday night. Thither must be brought som good coach with fower horses for I know not how we shalbe provided further. We are in hope of my Lady Comfields coach for part of the way. I had brought one downe from London had not a foolish report caused a doubtful letter to be written to me but now I will cut off all possibilities of rumours, & therefore I must make suddein provision. Sir Samuell Awbrey Mrs Candish Sir Giles Brugges & every frend must be tried. my sister Kempe hath a good coach so hath my Lady Bodenham. but who hath horses. yf any knows any noble gentleman that now would furnish me I would truly requitt hym, & in such a case never troble frend more yf it please god, & be ever hereafter able to doe the like to another... Commend me to Mr Howarth tell hym how yf he can help us it shalbe a worthy frendship. There must be horses sent to Oxford to be there on St Thomas eve to bring down Will Hoskyns & Ben Hoskyns they meane to keepe Christmas wth us. there must be an hogshead of sacke from Monmouth (I thincke best) or else from Hereford to walke with our Claret. take care for the coach horses to be had at this tyme and goe presently about it day & night... Study the coach way where to breake hedges & how to avoyd deepe & dangerous ways. So god speede us and y^r

J. Hoskyns.

> Mistake me not, no man now resisteth me, we
> want nothing but coach & horses.[1]

The letter was probably not addressed to his step-
daughter Bess, who was to receive a similar note
two days later, for John expected the recipient to
bring the coach and four to Ross and be familiar
enough with the way to act as a guide for the return trip. The friends and neighbors mentioned as
possible aids in an hour of need are those one
might expect under the circumstances. "My Lady
Comfield" is not identifiable, but John may have,
in his haste, miswritten the name and meant "Lady
Cornwall"; Lady Cornwall was Katherine Harley of
Brampton Bryan Castle who was now the widow of
Thomas Cornewall, Baron of Burford. Sir Samuel
Aubrey was High Sheriff of Herefordshire in 1622
and a fellow contributor to the Cathedral College
quadrangle with John. He lived in Grendon, near
Ross. Sir Giles Bridges was High Sheriff in 1625
and lived at Wilton Castle at Ross. Lady Bodenham
was the widow of Sir Roger Bodenham of Hereford,
who had been one of the major participants in the
1609 races. And Mr. Howarth was a neighbor at
Whitehouse near Turnastone, just across the river
from Vowchurch.[2]

The cause of all this preparation was the marriage on the following day of John Hoskyns and Isabel Riseley Barrett in the Parish Church of Great
Rissington, Goucestershire, just up the hill from
Bourton-on-Water and five miles northwest of Burford. The church register for that period is missing from the church safe and can no longer be used
to check out the strange, indeed unexplainable, entry in W.P.W. Phillimore's Gloucestershire Parish
Registers. Marriages (1914): "John Hoskins, Servant at Law and Mrs. Habett Barrett Harding." The
marriage had been licensed on 7 December. The of-
ficiating priest was certainly the rector of Rissington from 1604 to 1650, the Rev. Thomas Whittington, Isabel's brother-in-law.

Isabel was the oldest daughter of William
Riseley of Chitwood, Bucks., and had three sisters

and three brothers. She had already been married twice when she became Mrs. Hoskyns, the first time to one Thomas Heath, the second to Devereux Barrett.[3] Barrett, of Hanham House in the Parish of Bitton, Gloucestershire, had died in March 1622. In his will,[4] he left Isabel the sum of £500, the "lease of Hannum Howse" and "the Mano^r of Shelswell in the Country$\bar{e}$ of Oxford, leased to Sr William Cope of Hardwicke, Oxon." He also left her most of his personal possessions. The description of the rest of his property gives us one indication of where John may have met his new bride. Barrett had considerable interest in the Registership of St. David's in Pembroke as well as a house in Tenby. He left his sisters houses in Llampeter Velfry and Tenby, Pembroke. One of these sisters, Jenett Barrett, was married to Rice James of Haverfordwest. It is not at all unlikely that John heard of Isabel from her in-laws during his riding of the circuit in Pembroke, perhaps even meeting her at the Assizes. Since Hanham House and Bitton are just outside the city of Bath, however, he may have met her there.

His new wife was financially well off, if not rich, and had no children. She was not a young thing or inexperienced in marriage, and she was probably looking for the same kind of companionship that John sought. The day after the marriage, December 11th, John wrote to his stepdaughter from Rissington, reassuring her about her new stepmother. Benedict had apparently given his approval of the new member of the household, and there is no doubt that Isabel fit quickly into Morehampton, not as head of the house, but as a quiet member. Bess remained John's agent at home, even after his marriage.

Daughter Besse[5]
y^u shall have a godly worthy mother-in-law kynde & quiet. let as much be provided for her content as y^u cann, & I thancke y^u for what y^u have donne allready. Ben wonne her for me as he came up; y^u & Dicke are her daughters she longes to see my neeces. at this tyme she brings a

637

neece of her own & one mayde & two men with her.
I thincke y^u are every one of y^u as happy as I
in the match. Comend me to my sister Kempe--
tell her she wilbe a lovinge compannion for her,
& is somewhat lyke her for stature & makinge.
Commend me to my daughter Margarett Boorne &
tell her I hope she will thancke me for her.
Let us all pray to god with thanksgevinge for
the least of his benefitts & humble supplication
for his pardon for our synes. Mr Edwards[6] this
bearer hath woundrously bound me to hym so hath
Mr. Griffith lloyd who will come with us wth one
man only. I pray god we may be so happy as to
have a coach & good horses meet us at Rosse upon fryday night. Mr Edwards will tell you the
rest....

The fact that John should write on the morning after his marriage indicates both the quiet contentment he must have felt with his new wife and his
sincere admiration and affection for his step-
daughter.

Christmas would have been a particularly joy-
ous period for the Hoskyns tribe at Morehampton
that winter, with everyone welcome from the various
properties that made up the family holdings. Will
and Benedict would have brought the latest news
from London to their sisters and cousins, and all
would have been trying to make the new "mother"
feel at home.

But the quiet of the country was soon to
change to the unaccustomed activity of Parliament,
for John was about to re-enter that form of public
life. On 12 February 1628, William Reed, the High
Sheriff of Hereford, called for "a free and an indifferent Choise according to the Statute in that
behalfe provided of twoe Burgisses of the most fytt
and discreete menn of yor said Cytty to be of the
Parliam^t."[7]

Two weeks later 38 citizens of Hereford signed
their names as having chosen Sir John Scudamore and
John Hoskyns as their representatives.[8] As there

638

was no love lost between these two, we can suppose that John made his plans on his own, both for his traveling back and forth between Hereford and London and for his stay in the city, where he was now comfortably established in his new chambers in Serjeant's Inn Fleet Street. He was not far enough away from the Middle Temple to make it inconvenient to attend any early morning committee meetings there.

One of the nice elements of his move to Serjeant's Inn was that he was now in the parish of St. Dunstan's-in-the-West, whose parish priest was John Donne. The Middle Temple was also within the parish, but it maintained its own church. There were close relations with St. Dunstan's, however, and the banquets during the Summer Reading were always held in the church hall.[9] But now Donne was literally John's parish priest, and since we know of John's sincere religious attitudes and practices, we can presume that he saw Donne as often as the latter appeared at his church, which was reasonably often in the year 1628.

The 1628 Parliament turned out to be one of the most important sessions in British history. Charles had called it for the express purpose of raising money to support his government, but the Commons turned it into a meeting for drafting the famous Petition of Right, one of the corner stones of the British "Constitution" (and the American Bill of Rights). The entire session lasted less than a year, and it was in recess seven months of that time: from 26 June 1628 until 20 January 1629.

John's role in the Parliament was perhaps even more important than it had been in previous sessions, but he was a great deal more circumspect in what he said. He did not change any of his earlier positions, however, and he was obviously respected by his fellow parliamentarians for the role he had played. At the age of 62 he was not quite as eager to volunteer for the same number of Committees as he had earlier, but Parliament had learned that separate Committees were not the best way to accomplish major business anyhow.

Monday, 17 March 1628, began auspiciously e-
nough, with all the due forms being followed for
the opening of Parliament. Then

> About Two of the Clock in the Afternoon, his
> Majesty, having rid in State to Westmynster Ab-
> by, and there heard the Sermon, preached by the
> Bishop of Bathe and Welles, and being set in the
> Upper House, sent for the Commons, to come up
> unto him; where his Majesty made a short Speech
> unto the Lords and Commons... And, in the End,
> his Majesty directed the Commons to go down into
> their House, and chuse them a Speaker, and to
> present him unto his Highness upon Wednesday af-
> ter, at Two of the Clock.
> The Commons being come into their House, and
> settled, Mr. Treasurer brake the Silence, put-
> ting them in mind of the Work of that Day, viz.
> the Election of a Speaker; nominating and com-
> mending unto them, as very fit Man for that Pur-
> pose, Sir John Finch Knight, the Queen's Attor-
> ney General: Who being thereupon called upon,
> excused himself, [by] his Insufficiency for so
> great an Employment; [but, by] his Speech, in-
> creased the Desires of the House [towards] him;
> so as, with a greater Acclamation than [before,
> he was] called to the Chair....10

Sir John, cousin of John's close friend Sir Heneage Finch, had good reason not to want to sit in
that particular chair, and by the end of the Parliament he would have to be held in it forcibly by
Members of the House. The lines were already drawn
in what was foreseen to be a difficult session.
The King had attempted to influence the elections
as his father had in 1614, but had similarly failed
The Bishop of Bath and Wales, William Laud, would
be under strong attack by the end of the year, and
the current favorite of the King, the Duke of Buckingham, would be dead. Moreover, the two houses of
Parliament would, for the first time, be working
together in confronting the King. That alliance
would be, however, short-lived as Commons tried to

640

push too hard on religious issues that the Lords, with their high proportion of Bishops, simply could not agree to.

Meanwhile, two days later, on Wednesday the 19th, the King made a small mistake that raised the first opposition from the House, as they felt they had been slighted. The incident reveals just how much on edge everyone was as Parliament opened. When Charles came to Parliament that afternoon, "Word was brought by Mr. Crane, unto the Serjeant at Arms attending the Commons House, that his Majesty was ready, and expected the Speaker, and the House." The Commons were offended "that Mr. Maxwell, Knight of the Black Rod, did not come himself to bring this Message, as had formerly been used." Some M.P.'s said that "Mr. Speaker elect should not stir, till they had received the Message by Mr. Maxwell himself"; others "(howsoever they acknowledged this to have been a great neglect in Mr. Maxwell, and wrong to the House) because his Majesty stayed for them, advised, that they should not now further insist upon it, but go up: And so they did."[11]

When Commons returned to their own chamber later in the afternoon, they had one bill read which had been introduced during the previous session but not acted on: "An Act to restrain the Passing or sending of any to be Popishly bred beyond the Seas." It could not have been more appropriate a Bill in foretelling the end of the Parliament a year later. There was scarcely anyone who questioned what the ultimate conclusion of the session would be. The country was angry over Charles' action in levying forced loans from unwilling citizens and imprisoning those who refused to pay. As one observer of the new Parliament remarked, "It is feared... because such patriots are chosen every where, the parliament will not last above eight days."[12] There would be days in which Charles probably wished he had only allowed it to last that long.

The next day, Thursday the 20th, the Committee

641

on Privileges was set up, and it was huge; but John tactfully chose not to serve on it for all the obvious reasons. He still did not want his 1614 experience used as an example in any formal grievance.

Then the House showed that they had learned from the experience of the past three sessions. There was no longer any doubt that the Committee of the Whole was the best way to avoid individual pressure on members by agents of the king, the best way to bring about unanimity on protests against actions by the king, and the surest way of making the House of Lords listen to points under contest between the two houses. As was to be said a number of times this session, "the Strength of this House is in the Number of our Members." First they decided that "A Committee for Religion, of the whole House" would meet every Monday at 2 p.m. in the House throughout the session "and have Power to send for any Parties, Witnesses, or Records; and to hear Counsel."[13] The Commons was on the attack against Arminianism and the increasing power of the high church party led by Bishop Laud.

Next, there was to be "A Committee of the whole House, for Courts of Justice... upon every Tuesday, during this Session" and it was to have the same powers. The role of the Justices in upholding the King's arbitrary imprisonment of those who had refused to agree to forced loans had raised substantial doubts among many Englishmen as to the separate jurisdiction of the courts. A Committee for Trade of the whole House was to meet every Thursday. They would consider the continued use of royal impositions on materials entering and leaving the country. But the real thrust of the session was made clear in the decision to establish "A Committee of the whole House, for Grievances... at Two of the Clock... every Wednesday, and Friday." It was from these meetings that the Petition of Right was to emanate. Then, having decided on their course of action, the House decided to take Communion at St. Margaret's church on Sunday, April 6.[14] It had been a long day's work and had revealed a remarkable unity among the members.

Almost immediately the Commons began to move
on the issues of the King's right to tax without
Parliament's approval and his right to imprison
without cause. John was slow in getting involved.
He did not volunteer for the first Committee to
meet with the Lords on 21 March and accepted no
committee assignments until 3 April, over two weeks
after the session started. Of course, he did
serve on Committees such as that for the "Bill a-
gainst the Passing over of Recusants Children"
which involved all the lawyers of the House.[15] On
the afternoon of Thursday April 3rd, the Committee
of the Whole decided "To have a select Committee,
to frame a Bill concerning pressing Soldiers, employing Men as Ambassadors, fit for the Service of
the King and Subject." Serjeant Hoskyns was named,
along with his friends Henry Martin, John Selden,
and William Hackwell, to the Committee which also
included the Lord Treasurer, the Secretary, and two
of the leading figures of the House who were to
grow in importance during this and succeeding years,
Sir Edward Coke and Sir Thomas Wentworth, the latter who had been a victim of an enforced loan of
King Charles and who had not yet switched sides to
be a leader of the monarchist forces. The instructions to the Committee give little hint of the important issues involved: "to take into Consideration the Framing of a Bill concerning the Pressing
of Soldiers, foreign Employments, and such like;
so as the same may be regulated for the Service of
the King, and Good of the People."[16] The Bill was
aimed directly at the King's misuse of power in regard to forced loans and illegal imprisonment.
Some of those persons who had refused to pay the
loans had, rather than being sent to prison, been
forced to serve on board ships. Fifty men had been
forced to accept press money for serving the King
of Denmark. The fact that the Danish King had been
driven out of Germany and that this defeat had been
followed by Buckingham's decisive defeat at the
hands of the French on the Isle of Re in 1627 had
not made the King's actions any easier to accept.

Regular business of Parliament went on as usual, and on 8 April, John was made a member of a

Committee to consider "An Act for the Establishing and Confirming of the Foundation of the Hospital of King James, founded in Charter-house, in the County of Middlesex...."[17]

The House was deadly serious about thwarting those actions of the King which they considered to be illegal and aimed against the rights and privileges of the House and all Englishmen. On 9 April they ordered that "The House shall be called upon Thursday next Week; and every Member of the House then to attend, upon Pain of 10 1."[18] £10 was a remarkably high fine, amounting to more than any M.P. would receive as pay for the entire session of this Parliament. And the business of 17 April turned out to be important enough to warrant the call: "A Committee, of all the Lawyers of the House, to meet, and prepare a Bill for the Repeal and Continuance of Statutes."[19] Up until this point, they had been dealing with grievances piecemeal by passing resolutions against unparliamentary taxation, against a denial of a writ of habeas corpus, refusal of bail, etc. Such an approach had led to conflict with the House of Lords, who were worried about what seemed individual attacks on the King's prerogative. With the more inclusive Bill on Statutes, they sought to "reaffirm the validity of old statutes safeguarding the liberty of the subject and interpret them in the sense the commons thought right."[20]

On 28 April,[21] a second reading was given to "An Act concerning Liberties of Parliament" and Mr. Serjeant Hoskyns was named along with Coke, Selden, Benjamin Rudyard, and others. The Committee was to meet on Wednesday afternoon (the 30th) in the Exchequer Chamber, and "all that will come to have voice." The liberties of Parliament were considered part and parcel of the liberties of all Englishmen, so the House reaffirmed the Committee on Statutes and placed that Committee in the mainstream of English constitutional actions:

Upon Question, a select Committee to be named, of some Lawyers, and others of the House, for

the present Framing of a Bill, therein expressing the Substance of the Statutes of <u>Magna</u>
<u>Charta</u>, and other Statutes, and of the Resolu-
tions made in this House, concerning the Liberty of the Subjects, in their Persons and Estates,
without One Negative.

The Committee had all lawyers named to it, and it
was to meet this same afternoon at 3 p.m., in the
Inner Temple Hall.[22] John was back in the heat of
the battle with the King.

Charles sought to head off the potential danger by telling the House that he was willing to
promise to follow the old Statutes as long as they
were willing to follow the laws of their forefath-
ers without trying to change them by adding new explanations. But he remained adamant that his prerogatives should not be curtailed. It was at this
point that Sir Edward Coke suggested that the two
Houses join together in submitting a Petition of
Right to the King that would set forth their grievances. Such a petition would in fact have the
force of law. The King was caught; obviously the
best way to halt the movement of the opposition was
to dismiss Parliament, but he needed the money that
only they could vote.

By May 21st general agreement had been gained
between the two houses, but the matter of wording
had become a stumbling block. The Lords were, of
necessity, seeking wording that the King could live
with, yet they shared many of the feelings of their
friends and associates in the lower House. After
all, there was little difference in outlook between
a man like John in the Commons and his friend James
Whitelocke in the Lords. On the 21st, the Lords
sent two messengers to request "a free and present
Conference, in the Painted Chamber, about the great
Business."[23] The House agreed to the meeting, but
decided to listen, not to speak, then to report
back to the House as a whole. Sir Edward Coke did
the reporting of the speech of Lord Keeper Coventry. The Keeper raised four objects: 1. the Petition was a reservation (or "Saving") upon the Stat-

utes; 2. it would bring ill effects, as in the reservation mentioning "in Articuli super chartas";
3. the Petition uses new words, "Sovereign Power",
rather than Prerogative; 4. this not fit for the
Petition, since it is a Petition of Right. It is
the desire of the Lords "to correspond with us in
all our just Proceedings;" therefore, it ought to
be granted by everyone "that the Intention of both
Houses" is "to maintain the just Liberty of the
Subject, and not diminish the just Prerogative of
the King." They feel, therefore, that the additional words they suggest to the Commons statement
would be helpful in that the Commons Petition is
"not in the words of the Laws" and their addition
is "necessary for the King's Satisfaction." The
men chosen to report from the Lords, with their
assistants, then met in Sir Edward Coke's chamber
late in the afternoon "to agree about the Reasons
concerning the Addition propounded." Commons was
to meet again the following morning at 7 a.m.[24]

The meeting on the morning of Thursday the
22nd of May was to be a crucial one. The decision
of how to handle the request from the Lords in such
a way as to retain the agreement to submit the Petition to the King as a statement of both Houses
was critical to the success of the entire project.
Therefore they put a man into the chair that would
be able to handle the meeting in the best possible
way--and that was Serjeant Hoskyns. At 7 a.m. the
House met and "Upon Question... resolved into a
grand Committee, to consider of the Addition propounded by the Lords, together with the Reasons delivered by the Lords for it; and to strengthen our
Reasons against the Addition; and to consider, what
is fittest thereupon to be done further." Hoskyns
took the Chair and the meeting started.

First he ordered "That no Man shall, during
the Debate by this Committee, go out, without Leave
of the Committee; and, that the Serjeant shall
stand without, and suffer no man, to go out, that
hath not Leave of the Committee; and, that no Member of the House stand in the Entry." The lesson
of 1614 had been learned well. No one was to be

646

allowed to report out individual speeches or to represent the House as anything but a united group. Sir William Herbert did leave at one point and was immediately sent to and asked to return. During the morning the Lords asked if the Commons were ready for a meeting, but the House replied that they would be meeting all day and would send a message when they were ready. As a matter of fact, the Committee not only continued that afternoon but met the next morning at 7 a.m. once again.

Late in the morning of the 23rd, Hoskyns was able to report officially to the House from the Committee of the Whole "that they have agreed upon the Arguments, both for refuting the Lords Arguments for the Addition, and of our, against the admitting it; and that they have distributed all into a rational Part, to be delivered by Sir H. Martyn, assisted by Sir N. Rich, and Mr. Pymme; and the legal, by Mr. Glanvyle, assisted by Mr. Selden, and Mr. Mason." The House then told the Lords they were ready, and the representatives went up to the upper chamber. When they returned, the House heard a report "that both the Gentlemen, that spake, have deserved especial Thanks from this House, for performing the Service enjoined them by the House, to the great Honour thereof. Whereupon a general Expression of Thanks to them, with Acclamation and putting off Hats."

For the next few days[25] there was continued discussion between the Houses, but Commons had already decided on the form of the Petition. They had it read twice, ordered it to be ingrossed, and agreed to have it read once more before it was presented to the King. Then, in a conciliatory move, they gave a second reading to "An Act for the Grant of Five intire Subsidies, granted by the Temporality:--Upon Question, committed to a Committee of the whole House.--Wednesday Morning, Nine Clock."[26] At some point in the debates on Subsidy, John took his usual position on the subject. Indeed, his statement could have been made in either of his first two Parliaments: "That knowing our own rights, we shall be better enabled to give.

Two legs go best together, our just grievances and our supply; which he desires may not be seperated, for by presenting them together, they shall be both taken, or both refused."27

The next day was another busy one. The Petition of Right had been ingrossed and was read again, followed by a debate on how to present it. The decision was to send the Petition to the Lords, have both Houses present it to the King, and ask the King to give his Answer to the Petition to the full Parliament. Sir Edward Coke was to deliver the Petition, "with Thanks for their Signification of their Purpose of joining in this Petition with us." There was a temporary delay from the Lords, and then,

A Message from the Lords, by Justice Jones and Justice Whitlocke; That the Lords having received the Petition, have read it thrice, and, with one unanimous Consent, voted it, though they had voted it before. For moving the King, for the Manner of giving his Answer; for that the same concerneth both Houses, the Lords desire a present Conference, in the Painted Chamber, if it may stand with the Conveniency of this House.28

On the 28th, the King agreed to meet with both houses in the Banqueting House at Whitehall to receive the Petition. He then began ten days of delaying actions, offering ambiguous and evasive answers. There is no wonder that he did so.

The Petition, "concerning divers rights and liberties of the subjects", begins with a recital of the statutes alleged to have been broken and of the grievances for which redress was now provided. It then proceeds to ask: (1) that no man hereafter should be compelled to make any gift, loan, benevolence, tax, or such like charge, without common consent by act of parliament; (2) that no free man should be imprisoned or detained without cause shown; (3) that soldiers and mariners should not be billeted upon

648

private individuals against their will; and (4) that commissions for proceeding by martial law should not be issued in the future.[29]

On Thursday the 29th the King asked Parliament not to recess for the holidays but to finish the session. The Subsidies had not yet been voted, and he did not want them to leave until they had acted on his needs. At the same time he avoided a direct answer to the Petition. On 3 June he sent an answer to the Petition that was so unsatisfactory that the House deferred its consideration for three days.[30] On the 5th the King sent another message and the House immediately resolved itself into a Committee of the Whole to "consider, what now fit to be done, upon this Message, and Command, now delivered from his Majesty; and for the Safety of King and Kingdom." They were obviously afraid that Charles was about to respond as his father had in 1614; thus, "Upon Question, every Member of this House free from having spoken any thing un-dutifully, from the Beginning of this Parliament, to this Time. All business called off."[31] Another message from the King on the 6th stirred them to another Committee of the Whole, and they met all day with the doors shut. Finally, on Saturday the 7th, they joined with the Lords once more in re-questing of the King a clear and satisfactory an-swer to the Petition. As no further avoidance of the issue was possible, especially if Charles wanted the Subsidies voted, at 4 p.m., he came to Parliament, met with both Houses, and said, "Soit droit fait come est desyre."[32] Parliament had its way, if perhaps in a less hearty manner than it could have wished.[33]

As soon as the King had assented to the Peti-tion, the mood of Commons changed, mainly as a re-sult of the speeches of Sir John Eliot, M.P. from Cornwall, one of the leaders of the 1624 Parliament. He was "the greatest orator of his generation,"[34] a hothead, and a strong believer in the supremacy of Commons. He had been angry at the conciliation that had taken place to assure the joint efforts of the Commons and Lords and now pressed for a

series of Remonstrances to the King, the first a-
gainst Bishops Laud and Neile and the royal favorite Buckingham, and the second against the collection of Tonnage and Poundage "as a breach of the
fundamental liberties of the kingdom, because these
duties had never been granted to Charles I by parliament."35

These actions by Commons were done without
support from the Lords and were more than Charles
could bear. On 26 June he prorogued Parliament,
following a powerful speech in which he attacked
the Petition of Right: "The profession of both
houses, in time of hammering this Petition, was no
ways to intrench upon my prerogative, saying, they
had neither intention nor power to hurt it. Therefore it must needs be conceived that I have granted
no new, but only confirmed the ancient liberties of
my subjects."36 Speaking directly to the Judges
that were present, he said, "for to you only, under
me, belongs the Interpretation of Laws: For none of
the Houses of Parliament, joint or seperate (what
new Doctrine soever hath been raised) have any
Power, either to make, or declare, a Law, without
my Consent."37 The judges, by their actions following the dissolution of Parliament the next winter, showed that they agreed with his statement.
Meanwhile, the only immediate result of the Petition was that Charles no longer tried to exact any
forced loans But in the long run, the Petition
represented a real defeat for the monarchy at the
hands of a united Parliament.

And on another point Parliament needed to
have no further worries.

This Summer there was a great Army prepared for
forraigne seruice, whereof the Duke of Buckingham was Generall, who went to Portsmouth, to
set all things in readinesse for present dispatch: And vpon Saturday the 23. of August, as
hee was going thorow his Hall, which was filled
with Commaunders, and Strangers, suddainly and
vnexpectedly Iohn Felton a Lieutenant, stabd the
Duke into the breast with a knife, and slily

650

withdrew himselfe, vndiscerned of any to doe
the fact, the Duke stepping to lay hold on him,
drew out the knife and began to stagger, the
bloud gushing out at his mouth, at which dreadfull sight, certaine Commanders with their
strength held him vp, the Duke being depriued
of speech and life.[38]

When the bystanders tried to find the murderer,
Felton stood forth and admitted that he had done
the deed. He felt that he had done a service to
his country, and many agreed.

When the news of Buckingham's assassination
reached John, however, he was undoubtedly on his
way to his fall circuit in Wales. On the prorogation of Parliament, he had returned to his own affairs in Hereford. He had hardly had any time to
spend with his new wife before he went off to London, and his usual affairs needed attending to.
The family that surrounded him was now growing into
maturity. His "manager" of Morehampton, Bess, had
a suitor from outside the family, a young man named
John Bowen who wrote tediously flowery letters in
the current courtierly fashion.[39] We have no way
of knowing whether Bess returned the young man's
affection or whether she was already emotionally
attached to her cousin Will.

John continued to prepare the Bernithen estate for the settling of Will and his sisters' inheritance from their father. On 29 July 1628 he
bought 18½ acres of land in Trecelly, all of which
were surrounded by other lands that John already
owned.[40] The deeds mark a new stage in John's
life. He had completed all of his land purchases
and could now concentrate on developing his present holdings and decide which lands were to be
left to which of the children. From now on Bennet
was to be at his side most of the time. The young
man was still a year and a half from his call to
the Bar, but he was sufficiently trained to be of
immense help to his father. And there was a bond
of affection that shows up not only in John's desire to have his son with him in his work, but in

651

the letters of Bennet over the remaining years of his father's life.

When John returned from his Welsh circuit, he turned his attention to the Manor of Titley, which he had mentioned in his previous will as being close to renewal time. James Dalley was once again Steward of the Manor for John and had been doing a poor job of it. John's instructions are precise:

Mr Dalley

I thanke yo^w that yo^w write vnto me that there wilbe cause of houlding of a corte wch I am willing shalbe done but I will knowe first what estates are to passe from whome to whome and of what land_es_ and what shalbe my heriott. ffor fines and amerciament_es_ I never receaved any whereof I gave not an acquittannce of the receipte vnder my hand and that because they shall establishe a custome of fines certayne by p^rsident from me. I pray yo^w therefore pro_v_ide all the corte Rowles ready that yo^w haue hadd in yor tyme and warne the baylief to haue ready all estreat_es_[41] of heriott_es_ ffynes issues and amertiament_es_ and trespass_es_ and sales in the wood and lat_e_ spoiles and kutting of Saplin_cs_ This being sent vnto me at this Sessions vpon a dayes warning yo^w shall haue a co^rte kepte and I or my Sonne wilbe there p^rsent for nowe yo^w knowe there is but Saterday and there canne be noe travelling vpon Sunday and then but Mundaie then the Sessions. Soe yo^w see there is noe tyme convenient for my travell and warning of a co^rte, and the Craft nor will of the tenant_es_ shall snatch or Surprize me vpp, and I will haue every one of them knowe that the passing of an estate shall deser_u_e a iourney hither and a composic_i_on and I will gladdlie know whoe dares make a_n_ alterac_i_on of an estate aboue one yeare and I not know of it or a corte not kepte. Soe wth thankes to yo^w for yor care I pray god keepe yo^w and I take my Leave

Morehapton   ℞ rest
26 Sept   yr frend
1628   J: HOSKYNS:[42]

652

Notations on the back of this letter indicate how profitable the Manor of Titley was to John. It is no wonder that he demanded care on the part of Dalley to protect his interests. Sample entries include five oxen--£15; five kine--£10; eleven Store Cattle--£15; three calves--30s; one mare--20s; twenty-six sheep of all kind--£5; swine--6s 8d; one brass pan, one pott--50s; other items, including "On leas of a howse xx^s, barley and otes in the barne vij^{li}; "debtes by specialty Mr Sayer vj^{li} xij^s Mr Carpenter vj^{li}," etc.; and notes such as "Jo: Boyle alien to his Daught^{tr}."

* * * * *

John had expected to return to Parliament on 20 October, which was the time set by the first prorogation, but King Charles put off the session until 20 January 1629, allowing another quiet Christmas at Morehampton for the Hoskyns family. In the first session Parliament had gotten their Petition of Right, and Charles had gotten his five Subsidies. The second session was to produce nothing but increased anger on both sides and an eleven year period of the King ruling England without benefit of Parliament.

As Edmund Howe summarized it in his continuation of Stow's Annals, Parliament began again on 20 January, "but concluded nothing."[43] Commons, making no attempt to secure the agreement of the Lords, immediately attacked the impositions or duties levied by Charles since the previous session, especially those levied against one of their own members, the merchant John Rolles, who had had his goods confiscated for refusing to pay the impositions. More importantly they moved to the attack on Arminianism and on the whole issue of who was responsible for the state religion of England, the clergy in Convocation or the Parliament. The attack was clearly directed against Laud.

Arminianism took its name from the Dutch theologian James Arminius or Harmensen, who opposed Calvin on the doctrine of predestination. But the Arminian "party" had more to say about the nature

653

of the church than it did about theological issues.
To the Arminians, with Laud as their leader, the
English Church was but one branch of the universal
catholic church. As Laud said, the church, in Rome
or London, is "one in substance but not one in condition of state and purity." His position on the
Bible was that "the key that lets men into the
Scriptures, even to this knowledge of them that
are the Word of God, is the tradition of the
church." And Protestants have "not left the church
of Rome in her essence but in her errors."44   In
order to support the break of the English church
from Rome, the Arminians sided with the monarchy
in saying that the King and his Bishops were the
legitimate leaders of the Christian Church in England, responsible for the purifying of Roman errors. To Puritans, the threat of Arminianism was
the danger of a return to Roman Catholicism. To
the supporters of Parliament against the royal prerogative, the Arminians were a political threat
against any further growth in the power of Parliament. The debates of 1629 heralded the eventual
action of the Parliament in destroying the power
of the Bishops and disestablishing the Church of
England during the period of the Civil Wars. The
future was inherent in the person of the man who
sat in the chair during the meetings of the Committee of the Whole on the discussions on religion,
John Pym, M.P. from Tavistock, who became the
leader of the anti-monarchy forces in 1640. Pym
already saw Parliament as the only power that had
the strength or the competence to confront the
growing power of the Arminian faction under Laud.

Hoskyns spoke three times for the record during the Committee of Religion debates. He did not
disagree with the Arminians on doctrine, but he
was very strong in his judgment that Parliament
should be a major force in the deciding of the
stance of the Church of England on any issue. On
31 January 1629, the Committee resolved first that
they would debate the issue of Arminianism. The
issue actually discussed was what power the King
and Convocation (hence the Bishops) had. "Nothing,
said Selden, could be called a public act of the

654

Church which had not received the assent of Convocation."45 Hoskyns went much further:

> Serjeant Hoskins. That by the Church is to be
> understood all the beleevers of the Church, and
> the Convocacion house is not to be termed the
> church nor hath power to doe a publique act;
> for that only is said to be a publique act which
> is considered of, debated, disputed and resolved
> on by the King and all the State.
> The papists and we agree all in the Scripture
> and differ only in the interpretacion, and for
> that wee offer to be tryed by the 3 generall
> Creedes, the 4 first generall Councells, and
> all the antient fathers that wrote in the first
> 400 yeares.46

John's speech was effective enough to bring the debate to a close for that day.

On 14 February the Committee launched into a
discussion of the way Roman priests had been let
loose, reprieved, allowed to escape, and so on.

> By question resolved to send to Mr. Atturney to
> know whether he received from the Counsell a
> direction to procede according to the Instruc-
> tion in those papers: whether he did proceede:
> what instructions he gave Mr. Longe: and then
> concerning the Bayle: by what authority. And
> why he bound them to appeare before the Counsell
> table: and why he had not acquainted his Ma-
> jestie that these men were not bayled by law,
> if he received directions to bayle them.

John saw the deeper question involved and put the
Attorney in a most difficult position. There were
ten Jesuits who had been sent to Newgate. Their
indictment had charged them with being priests although there was no hard evidence that was true.
"Serjeant Hoskins. To ask the Atturney why he gave
direction to indicte these as priests: the only way
to have them escape." Then John trapped him in a
way that might block Charles' support for his Attorney General: "Another question: seeing the

priests had purchased lands: why he took not care to search out this land for the King."47

Three days later the Committee was on the same general subject, especially trying to find out about Mr. Long and his work as a representative for the Attorney. There was also discussion about registering of recusants in London, the great increase in their numbers, and so on. John returned to the previous issue, however, the act of the Attorney in setting bail for known Catholic priests. His old sense of humor returned, and no doubt the Commons appreciated the analogy he drew: "Serjeant Hoskins: never the like to lett a whole Colledge of Jesuits to Bayle. There have bene wolves in Wales, and foxes in the Isle of Wight: if they were now; the people wold not lett them to Bayle."48

There was precious little humor in this session of Parliament, however, and on 21 February 1629, John made a request he had never made before: to be excused from Parliament. Although it was granted, the Recorder was a bit mixed up: "Mr. Serjeant Hoskyns, being a Judge of a Circuit, and ... Mayor of ... have Liberty to go down; and to return with all convenient Speed." Having forgotten the name of the second person who was excused that day,, he left a record that has misled many scholars to insist that John was a Mayor.49

He had no need to return. Parliament was adjourned from 23 February to the 25th, and then to 2 March. It would have been adjourned that day as well, at the order of the King, but members of Commons physically held the Speaker in his chair while Selden gave an impassioned speech and the House passed three resolutions:

that whoever should introduce any innovation in religion to bring in either popery or Arminianism should be accounted a capital enemy of the king and kingdom; that whoever should advise the levying of tonnage and poundage without parliamentary sanction should incur like denuncia-

656

tion; and that whoever should pay tonnage and poundage, under those conditions, should be held a betrayer of the liberty of the subject and a capital enemy of the king and kingdom.[50]

Two days later, on 4 March, Charles issued a Proclamation dissolving Parliament, and on the 5th, he went in person to Westminster and dissolved the Parliament, denouncing the Commons and praising the Lords. John was undoubtedly very glad to be on horseback in the depths of Wales.

Most of the records for the year dealing with John have to do with his family. On 25 April 1629, "Mr. William, son and heir of Oswald Hoskines of London, esq., deceased, specially bound with Benne Hoskines and John Cockes, gents."[51] moved into his step-father's old chambers, but he never finished his studies of the law, if indeed he even started. As a matter of fact, he never learned to spell or write very well. It may be that John simply wanted to provide lodgings for him in London so that he could travel with John and Bennet.

Before Will joined John and Bennet in London, John had written a letter to Elizabeth Bourne at Morehampton. Bess was finding her duties as head of the household more than she felt she could bear. She had written to her brother-in-law, Dr. John, telling of her unhappiness. John's letter is a combination of hard-headed business and inherent affection. He was certainly nurturing a close relationship between Bess and her cousin:

Bes[52]
It was to much for you at my partinge to weepe & to write to y^r broth^er that you could not write for weepinge. the cause wch you wept for was that all was spent, nothinge layd vp. that may be a causelesse weepinge when I am dead. spare y^r teares the meanewhile. spend y^r care & labour rise early take an accoumpt of every bodyes worke cramme not vp the fellowes of the basest companie wth hott beef & mutton every meale, that they keepe no place cleane. I will

657

not bwy their dunge so deare. Let the buttery
be regulated... Geue Will. Hoskyns good counsell, & when I come home I will propose more
vnto you. fare well good Besse, remember now I
leve you none to be hiered to chargeable worke.
Let my own servaunts doe the things that are
downe in a note & call vpon them to doe it daylie....

The interesting omission in all of the letters
of this period is his wife. Perhaps he simply
felt it was wrong to mention his wife in letters to
his step-daughter, but the fact that he never even
asks Bess to convey any message to her is baffling.
The easiest explanation is that he always sent a
letter to her at the same time that he wrote to
Bess and that Isabel disposed of his letters. But
the inevitable conclusion is that he did not feel
that she played any role in the running of his estate. His earlier statement that she was to play
the part of mother to the children does not appear
to have come true. She apparently lived a life
quite separate from the daily affairs of the manor.

On 6 June 1629, he wrote to Bess again, this
time a very long letter. It is filled with details
of planting, planning, stock management and all
the other daily activities of life on a large estate. But one can understand why Bess was dis-
couraged by the load.

Besse[53] I pray y^u remember there are now four of
Morehampton house at London besides myselfe &
three servaunts & that the use of their portions
wch is after the rate of 500^l a person must be
spent heere upon them at least, wch is after
the rate of eyght score pound a yeare at eyght
in the hundred. & all that must be saved &
spared out of the expense of Morehampton house,
& y^u need not be ashamed to alleage this excuse
eyther to the family or straungers. I doubt
Rowland Jones is a weake bayliff or steward &
can forcast nothinge for the provision in the
house for people or abroad for cattle. let it be
therefore remembered how many load of hay were

provided the last yeare, & yet y^u wanted & now
y^u have five coach-horses perpetually in the
house. See how many cattle y^u had the last
yeare what fother y^u spent how many you are lyke
to wynter this yeare & let proportionable provision be made for them. Tell Rowland Jones...
to divide the kyne & the younge beasts the stone
colts & geldings from the mares, & those that I
must use to be best kept. that he very foolish-
ly hath not donne so but eaten up altogether...
Consider what corne y^u bought this last yeare
above what grew at home & forecast to bring
corne or teythe upon the ground. there be portions of the Prebends to be sold upon St Peter's
day as Allensmore Kingston Webton & the Holds-
by...

Tell Mr Ward[54] that his sister & I have
thought upon helpe for hym heere at London & so
wish hym to take his tyme to comme up. Tell
Zachary Wilson that I myslyke his running to
the Alehouse as soone as I gave hym money except he amende his falt in that & labour hard
upon myne arras he shall never fynde me in that
falt to geve hym a penny... let old dick french
provide & make a lyme kyll betwixt the parke &
John Mericks ground, let stubbs be digd & lyme
burnt & let Rowland Jones with the advise of
John Sheldon & Robin Hughs choose ground for
fallow & terne the next yere in New street
ground & the furre wood... consider whether so
much be gotten in the stocke of cattle as is
spent in hyringe of grounde & bringinge hay, yf
there be not, sell som of the stocke to save
bringinge hay & hiering ground, keepinge only a
plow of exen and necessary kine. Let Rowland
Jones lykewise consider whether there be need
to put two bullocks more to the teeme for the
manuringe of John Mincks ground & the further
wood and whether there be any ready for the yoke
... for all matters of husbandry I thincke John
Hughs can geve best counsayll for he is an excellent good husband.

Daughter there are many & serious thinges to
consider of, & I pray y^u keepe this letter and
reade it dayly, for y^u neglect & forget many

659

things & disappoynt me...

Well to conclude great payments of porcions
grow on, y^{r}self are one. I have no ready money
it must be made out of rents & saved from expense in house keepinge or out of sales of land
& if we cannot live wth our land how shall we
live without it. Where the money is there our
porcions. Doe y^r best serve god all of y^u & let
y^r Girles hear the youngest children words &
let them teach them or read to them the principles of relligion....

yor poore sorrofull father in law
J. Hoskyns.

Apparently three of Will's sisters were in
London along with Will. John was well aware that
his responsibilities under the terms of the Orphanage Accounts were coming near. He had invested all
of the money he received in land so that he was
cash poor, as he advised Bess to tell others. For
a man who lived as close to the land as he had done
all his life, it would have been criminal to consider selling property in order to meet his commit-
ments. The only way out was to make the land pay
the money that was coming due. His reminder to
Bess that her own dowry had to be raised in the
same way certainly helped to keep her mind on her
duties. His remarks about the "portions of the
Prebends to be sold upon St. Peter's day" refer to
the rent due on leases from Hereford Cathedral for
the property in Didley. And his complaint that
Bess had visited Dr. John without telling him has
a slight touch of jealousy about it. He undoubtedly knew that his role of taskmaster meant that he
was robbed of some of the affection that Bess felt
for his and her brother.

The details of life at Morehampton revealed
in these letters and the financial obligations
that had to be met on a daily basis can be fleshed
out by other records of the time. Among the papers
of the Duke of Portland at Welbeck Abbey is a list
of wage rates for servants and laborers in Hereford in 1632.[55] A bailiff of husbandry like Rowland Jones received an annual salary of 53s 4d; a

husbandman's annual salary was 40s. Day laborers were paid according to the season. During the winter a laborer received 6d a day if food was not provided, 3d if it was. From Candlemas day through harvest, he received 8d a day without food or 4d with. A mower or reaper received either 12d a day or 6d; a woman reaper received 8d or 4d. Thatchers, carpenters, and masons were paid either 12d or 6d a day. Their helpers received either 8d or 4d. A maid servant received an annual salary of 20s. And the highest paid servants were dairymaids, who received 96s 8d.

On 6 September John sent a brief note to Bess, this time from Bernithen, where two of Oswald's daughters, Mary and Magdalen, now lived. Whatever the differences had been between John and Bess, they now seem to have been cleared up, and he was his usual affectionate self.

Daughter Besse. This gentleman was my brothers workeman and is still for that house. He knowes my cozens in London and I sent him by my house that he might see howe my cozens are and noetifie my cozen Mary and Magdulen of it. I pray you bidd him heartiful welcome for indeed he is a very honest man and one that did my brother much good service. He will convey anie letter that you will to them....
yo[r] loving father[56]

And John was sharing other responsibilities as well. When he journeyed to Winchester in December this year, he took Bennet with him and turned over the lease of Titley to his son. He continued to take responsibility for the estate, but he was making sure that as he drew near the age of 65, his son would be well taken care of. On 20 December 1629 Nicholas Love, Warden of Winchester, leased the manor of Titley to "Bennett otherwise Benedicte Hoskins of the Middle Temple London Esq[r]" for ten years. He was to pay Winchester "all such summes and summes of money as shall fortune to bee made for woods vpon any woodsale of selling of trees over ρ aboue fortie shillings yearlie." The fine

for any default was to be £5.[57] John had duly
paid the annual rent and fine of £38.13.4. at the
time of this new lease. But then begins the very
strange set of gaps in the record for which there
is no explanation. Bennet paid the annual rent the
following December and again in December 1632, but
nothing for the other years during the rest of his
father's lifetime.[58] There is no comparable act
of generosity on the part of the Warden of Winchester in allowing a leaseholder to maintain his
lease without payment of rent for such a long period time. All of the amounts due were made up by
1644, but they were paid by the next leaseholder,
or "farmer" of Titley, Richard Frampton. Neither
John nor Benedict was ever charged for any default.
There is simply no explanation for this situation
except that Winchester held its old alumnus in
such respect that it allowed him (and his son) to
fall behind in payments with the expectation that
some day the debts would be repaid.

Two months later, on 11 February 1630, Bennet
completed his legal training at the Middle Temple
and was called to the Bar.[59] Following in the
family tradition, he missed the following three
Readings and was fined. He was too busy working
for his father to fulfill the usual obligations.
But his activities with the Middle Temple continued, and long after his father had died, he was
elected Treasurer of the Middle Temple in 1664,
three years after he had served as Lenten Reader.
Bennet continued many of his father's activities,
as we have already seen. He was one of the Justices on the Carmarthen circuit from 1654 until
his death in 1677, represented Hereford in Parliament from 1646 till 1659, and was an ardent supporter of Parliament, being commissioned to raise
trained bands and volunteers in Hereford in 1642.[60]
There is little doubt that in the war against the
King, he took delight in avenging his father's imprisonment.

* * * * *

Some time in January or February 1630, John
wrote an undated letter to Bess, the last we have

662

of his family letters, telling of both his financial worries connected with Will's annulment and
John Bourne's wardship. On her death, Margaret
Bourne gave her two executors the wardship of the
young boy, which offended Hoskyns' sense of the
Hoskyns-Bourne family. He apparently immediately
paid the executors for the wardship rights and got
the child back. But it cost a good deal of money.
His attitude towards his nieces was that of treating them as members of his family.

Bes.61 I ow fiue pound ten shillings to Mr Phil-
ips62 for light gold wch he returned. the doctor calls for it now as I take horse. I pray
you send it hym & let Pereth make hast to gett
in the rents. I thancke god I am out of payne
& I hope aft^r a little ridinge to be stronge a-
gain. I had not leasure at home to thincke vpon any thinge of myne own. now I fynde that I
shall haue occasion to lay out much money the
suiet in the Arches to reu^erse Will Hoskyns
mariage & the fynding of the office & payinge
the fine & charges for Jony Boornes wardship.
You see howe the neyghbours are mynded they
thincke I must serue their turnes & neglect &
overthrow all my own busynesse. take you heed
of them & suffer them not to incroch vpon you...
you will loose much by mislaying when any thinge
hath not lately ben seen it wilbe easy for any
to say I neu^er knew what is becomme of it a
longe tyme, & so steale it. & so I must still
pay for new. Oth^er things are spoyld by beinge
cast in holes & corners. Let the gentlewomen
rise early & learne to know god that made not
the day for sleepe & let them be sure idlenes
is moth^er of all evill & the tyme of temptacion
to lewdnes, & pride. God blesse them... Let
none be absent at prayers. & let the gentlewomen know that I will take notice wch of them
is most early riser, diligent, humble & geven
to thrive & they shall fare the bett^er for it
though my sone & daughters haue the lesse, &
they that are contrarywise geven (wch god forbidd) I shall the lesse pytie them when their
own rodd beats them. Let them looke vpon Robin

663

Kempe & see what it is to be proude of false
hopes. God blesse & defend & guyde & preserve
you & them & Dicke.

Robin Kempe's false hopes apparently lay in
the fact that his mother, Elizabeth Kempe, had died
soon after she wrote her will on 9 February 1628,
although it was not proved until 31 December 1630.[63]
In the will Robin's sister Margaret was left a
great deal of the family holdings and Robin was
made the ward of Mrs. Kempe's son-in-law William
Jeffers.

Meanwhile Margaret also died, having written
her will on 27 October 1629.[64] A Margaret Bourne,
widow, was buried in Bath on 26 December 1629,[65]
and this is almost certainly John Bourne's widow
even though Margaret's will was not brought to probate for another six months. Margaret had apparently returned to Bath on the death of her husband,
and she identified herself as being of that City.
To her son John she bequeathed a number of specific
silver objects, like spoons and jugs, as well as
some bedding; to her daughter Elizabeth Bourne (who,
like her brother, must still have been in her minority), she left her own clothes and all the silver plate not given to John. She bequeathed "vnto my brother m^r Dco Hoskins fortie shillinges to
buie him a seale gold ringe wherein shalbe ingrav-
en my owne fathers armes, and my name sett vnder
the armes... vnto my sister Hoskins [Dr. John's
wife Frances] a mourninge gowne."

The next entry undoubtedly caused some problems. She bequeathed to her daughter all the
rights and possessions held in the parish of Middleton in Hereford "which was given or bequeathed
vnto mee by my naturall mother deceased." But the
will of Elizabeth Kempe was not proved until December 1630. In that will Margaret was given the
leases which her mother held from the Bishop of
Hereford.

Margaret's will goes on to bequeath "vnto the
executors of this my last will the wardshipp of my

664

said sonne John Bourne duringe his minoritie...."
All of her other possessions were bequeathed to
her daughter. The executors were to be her cousins
John Alford and Richard Godfrey, and "my loving
vncle Edward Alford Esqr and my lovinge brother
John Hoskins doctor of the Ciuill lawe" were named
overseers of the will "to see the same duly performed accordinge to my true intent and meaninge."

Margaret, for all her possessions and legally-
trained husband, could not write her own name, but
signed the will with her mark. It is ironic that
John is not mentioned in either Margaret's or her
mother's wills since he had taken care of all of
their legal affairs without payment ever since he
married a member of the Bourne family. Dr. John
was the one whom the family loved. He, of course,
never had to put any pressure on them to get their
affairs in shape, nor did they feel indebted to him
for past favors as they would with the Serjeant.
Benedicta may also have prejudiced them against
John during the period of their disagreements. Her
relatives were more than willing to use his ability
and knowledge, but they did not apparently feel
close to him.

But John was not happy about the will; it violated his sense of family. Dr. John and Edward
Alford, as overseers of the will, would certainly
have supported John's appeal for paying off the
executors for the wardship, but it cost a great
deal of money at a time John could ill afford it.

Also during the winter of 1629-1630, Will and
Bess decided to get married, once the annulment
proceedings had been satisfactorily completed.
John had been advising Bess quietly on the side,
as his letters indicate. Now everyone in the family got involved. Will's sister Mary, one of those
living at Bernithen, was in charge of the wedding
dress and trousseau. On 6 March 1630 she wrote to
"her good coussin Mis Elizabeth Bourn at Sargant
Hoskins house at morehampton in the gilde vally."

moste intyerly beloued sister

I ame glad you are in health I haue receued
your letter with the pattourns and am sory that
amounge them you could not fitt your selfe with
better coullers for your gowne and peticoat be-
leue me my coussin mary is deceued in sayeing
that noe yonge gentillwomen are married in blake
for I asuer you the time is strangly altred now
and tharefor I hope you will pardon me if your
gowne be black and your petticoat carnydine dam-
mask you saie you will bestowe one gowne vpon
your self sweet let me heare by the next carryor
what you will willingly bestowe vpon one or
whether you will haue a coat it is amost nete
ware I maid me on of baies and it stoud me in
three pound ten sheilling and it was drest but
with a smal siluer laice and I thinke for v or
vi pound you maye haue a veri nete one maid as
for Bennidactas and nels stoufe you shal haue
it the next carryor thous with my sencear loue
to your selfe and my brother with the rest of
my sisters I commite you and them to the protection of him that is the gidder of vs all
Your truly loueing sister
Mary Hoskins[66]

Sometime in the middle of April Will and Bess
were married, almost certainly by Dr. John. By the
24th Will was back at the Middle Temple, writing
"To his Beutious Wife M[rs] Elizabeth Hoskyns att
Morhampton... With hast."

Sweet Harte
    The Continuall thought of yor most intire Loue
douth Cause mee in all my Praiers and all my
other actions Chifely to desier yo[r] good and
Content for that is the only thinge, that I can
Joy in I pray lett mee Heare how my Granmother
doth and all my sisters, for I my silfe doth
long to imbrace thy sweet Corps, my sisters
Heare are in good health and longe to see yo[u].
and so I whom will euer Continue
Yo[r] most Lovinge Husband tell Death
Will[m] Hoskyns[67]

Will must have left for London almost immediately after the wedding, for on the same day he wrote his letter, Mary wrote to her new sister:

Sweet Sister
My entier loue sallutes thee and this is but to till thee that my hart bids god giue you ioy and grant you as many good daies as Isaac and Rebecca had and I besheech the lord to power his blessings vpon you... and that you may haue as much content in this life as euer anny had or as much as I desier my selfe... my hartes delight I am sorrye that it was my misefortune to be abcent at that time I so much desiered and longed to see but it doth suffiesse me to hear that it was vnited with much ioy and content to you... In the mene time remember my duty to my mother and my saruies to my ante with my loue to all my sisters and my cousin Mary and Benedicta and till her my coussin Be hath bought the House[68] for her gowen and nells of what I know not and they are amakeing and 4 vest[69]

Mary was her father's daughter and carried on the merchant tailor traditions. Why she was unable to get to the wedding is not clear. Certainly she was able to travel, as she was to be in London within a week. Her letter is particularly interesting because it contains one of the possible references to the Serjeant's wife, Isabel, her "ante."

On 1 May Will wrote to Elizabeth from the Middle Temple again. It would seem from the ending that he and Bess were taking a good deal of teasing from his bevy of sisters and cousins:

Deare harte
...beseach the lord to giue me that observuation to follow yo[r] good instructions and admonitions, which louing soule I will striue aganst nature to performe my last promis, for thous admirable nots that you noted in your louing leater, I will produce my labore to perform them by gods louue sweet Creatuor my selfe douth long to behould thy beautious Continance of thy sweet face, and besieds to cease thy imbrasing hands,

667

which I trust in allmiti god I shall shortly
and so I rest, youers to be commanded, youer
sisters ar in good health, I pray remember my
duty to my mother pray leat not this be seane[70]

The relationship between these two was a fascinating one. Will had made a bad error in choice
of a first marriage partner. Bess, who was considerably older, was continuing to follow her step-
father's advice in counseling Will, so that she
seems at times to have been as much his mother as
his wife. Yet Will's letters are passionate as
well as affectionate in such a way that they seem
to indicate that Bess shared that passion.

A week later, on 7 May 1630, Will, Mary, and
Magdalen went to the Alderman's Court in London
with one of John's assistants to receive the money
due them from their father's will: "John Edwardes
servant to John Hoskins S^{r}ieant at lawe here present doth depose vpon his Corporall oath that Mary
Magdalen and William... ar of the full ages of xxj
yeares and upwardes." Mary then acknowledged herself fully satisfied of the Recognizances held by
Messrs Churchman and Hollingworth for £253 11s 8d
in money and £30 18s 5d of plate; and of the bonds
held by John and Dr. John for £80 and £2,450. Then
Magdalen and Will did the same.[71]

Actually they did not receive most of the
money they had signed for. The day before, Hoskyns had accompanied Will and his two sisters at a
special hearing in the Probate Court. Will was
now of age and thus the sole executor of the will,
although it is difficult to believe that he did
anything without consulting his uncle. At that
hearing Mary and Magdalene testified that they
were of age but were renouncing their bequest.[72]
Yet the next day they signed as having received
their inheritance, and the Orphanage Court was established to insure against any tricks being played
of the kind that were obviously going on. When
Mary died, she had not yet received all of the
money that was coming to her from her father's and
grandfather's estates, but she had received some.

There is no way of knowing what the sums involved were at any one time.

There is no reason to believe that any of the children were being forced against their wills to agree to some underhanded plan by John. We know that Bess was aware of the financial condition of the family and where the money had gone that John held in bond for his brother's children. Will, both as Bess' husband and executor of the will, knew as well. There was the choice of selling off parts of Bernithen, which was going to end up in Will's hands anyway, for the immediate cash, or to wait for the money to be raised off the land. Mary and Magdalene were already living at Bernithen and doing so in comfort. It would be only natural for them to agree to renounce the terms of the will on a temporary basis since they had no reason to doubt that eventually they would receive all that was coming to them. When the rest of the children had their portions come due, there was less problem in receiving the money, so Oswald's children not only received what they inherited, but the family continued to have at least one major estate in Hereford as a result of John's careful investments.

In spite of family complications in 1630, John got back to doing a good deal of writing once more. Perhaps it was triggered by the publication in London that year of All the Workes of Iohn Taylor The Water Poet. A long section of that book was called "Laugh, and be Fat: or, A Commentary vpon the Odcombyan Banket." In it Taylor wrote, "All these Noblemen and Gentlemen that are named in this following book, did write merry commendatory verses, which were called the Odcombian banquet, and were inserted in Mr Coriats booke, intituled, Coriats Crudities: Vpon which verses, I haue seuerally and particularly paraphrased." All the old friends were there in parody: Henry Neville, John Harrington, Henry Goodyer, John Donne, Richard Martin, Hugh Holland, Christopher Brooke, Lionel Cranfield, Inigo Jones, John Gifford, John Owen, Thomas Bastard, Michael Drayton, and John Davies. John would, of course, be most interested

in the one on page 74: "Iohannes Hoskins, Cabal-
isticall, or Horse verse." Taylor went at his 34
line paraphrase with a verve:

    Hold, holla, holla, weehee, stand, I say,
    Here's one with horse-verse doth thy praise dis-
                                              play:
    Without all sence, or reason, forme, or hue,
    He kicks and flings, and winces thee thy due.
    He maketh shift in speeches mysticall,
    To write strange verses Cabalisticall;
    Much like thy booke and thee, in wit, and shape,
    Whilst I in imitation as his Ape.

But he certainly adds nothing to the original poem.

      The occasion for John's own poem for the year
was a good deal more serious, however.

    Saturday the 29. of May 1630. betweene the
    houres of 10. and 11. in the forenoone, was
    borne the most High & Mighty Prince Charles, at
    Saint Iames neere Charing crosse. The next day
    beeing Sunday, the King with the great Lords of
    his Councell, and others came to Pauls Church
    by Coach, about 8. of the clocke, in the fore-
    noone, and was by the Bishop, Prebends, and
    Quier of Paules, met and receiued at the great
    West doore with solemne singing of Te Deum
    Laudamus, assisted with Sagbot and Cornets, and
    being ascended neere the Quier, the Organs gaue
    like Assistance: The King sate in the Bishopps
    seate, during the celebration of Gods diuine
    seruice, the Creed beeing sung, the King went
    vp to the Altar, and made his offering, all bee-
    ing finished, hee went into a roome and heard
    the Sermon at Paules Crosse....[73]

John was present on the occasion; he witnessed the
strange appearance of a star during the daytime
(an eclipse occurred the following day), and he
later sat down to write a Latin poem on the occasion as well as an English translation.[74] In one
manuscript there is additional information about
the poem: "Certaine verses sent from Serjeant

670

Hotchkins, to one Mr Hryne of Bramford, who then preached at Pauls crosse, on that day the King came thither to offer up his oblation, at the altar for the birth of his sonne."75

Vpon the birth of the Prince

While at the Altar of St Pauls ye King
  Approached with a gratefull offering;
At noone a starre appeard. Tell me Deuine,
That preached'st riddles, why it did then shine?
  To the Western world a Prince was newly borne,
And th'East to morrow in Ecclipse will mourne,

On 7 July 1630 Hugh Davis became the organist of Hereford Cathedral. He was a graduate of New College in 1623, and it is very likely that he was the person with whom John worked in composing "an antheme in English to be sung at Hereford Minster at the assizes; but Sir Robert Harley (a great Puritan) was much offended at it."76 This would seem to be period at which John did a great deal of other writing. Aubrey describes his literary activities:

He wrote his owne Life, (which his grandsonne Sir John Hoskyns, knight and baronet, haz) which was to shew that wheras Plutarch had wrote the Lives of many Generalles, etc., Grandees, that he, or an active man might, from a private fortune by his witt and industrie attain to the Dignity of a Serjeant at Lawe--but he should have said that they must have parts like his too. This life I cannot borrowe.
He wrote severall treatises. Amongst others:--
    a booke of style;
    a method of the lawe (imperfect)
His familiar letters were admirable.77

As we are fully aware of the accuracy of Aubrey's remarks on the book of style and John's familiar letters, it is all the more tragic that the autobiography has been lost from among the family papers.

There seems to have been little to disturb

671

the even tenure of his days during 1630. Many old
friends were now beginning to depart. Kit Brooke
had died early in February 1628. Dr. Sharp died
late in 1630. John Donne became very ill during
the summer of 1630 and would die on the last day
of March 1631, a year that brought death to those
even closer than his poetic friends. And in 1633
Hugh Holland, who had been a close friend of Buckingham, died and was buried in the Abbey.

* * * * *

We next pick up records of his activities on
6 May 1631, when John once again acted as counselor
for his brother Dr. John in an argument before Lord
Coventry. He recounted all of the activities connected with the suit of St. Oswald's that we have
previously studied in 1617 and 1618. Since then,
he claimed, the defendants "suffer to be comitted
div^{rs} greuious wast__es__ and delapidac__i__ons in div^{rs}
of the houses ₽ wast in the meadow__es__ pastures ₽
Wood__es__" for which Dr. John will be liable. Dr.
John wants the court to order things so that the
condition of the property, possession of leases,
location of who does repaires, etc., will all be
made clear. The defendants in their reply say that
their houses arc in better shape than ever, that
they haven't hidden any leases, and so on. Nothing
had really changed apparently from the bitterness
of the earlier dispute in spite of Dr. John's generous treatment of the offenders.[78]

But Dr. John was soon to be beyond caring a-
bout the problems of St. Oswald's hospital. He
died in August; the exact date is unclear. The
Ledbury Register records his burial as 13 August.[79]
Aubrey says he was buried on the 9th, which is
simply inaccurate.[80] And the D.N.B. says he died
on 8 August. That, however, is probably only a
guess based on the date in Aubrey. It may be that
Aubrey substituted the day of death for the burial.
At any rate, John lost more than a brother; he lost
a close friend and associate through the years.
The rest of the family lost the best-liked member
of that extended family. We do not know who wrote
the Latin poem for Dr. John's monument in Ledbury;[81]

672

but it would be very surprising if it were not his brother John. There are two reasons for questioning the authorship: it is never ascribed to John, whereas the other family epitaphs are, and, ironically, the wit is too obvious. The word order of the first line is also remarkably awkward: "Under foot Doctor here lies of Laws Hoskins," a man who taught the pious and who revealed in his life the piety he taught. Here the people of Hereford mourn their Lecturer in his tomb, and the church in Ledbury is wet with tears. His double duties increased his honor but tired him out in his watchful care. His congregation was fortunate to have one who devoted his time in Christ to them and died in the middle of his diligent work.

John had little time to mourn his brother. He had to be off on his usual circuit in the west. On his own he sent a list of "such as are fitt to be Shierifes" in the three counties to the Earl of Bridgewater, now Lord President of Wales, which was received at Ludlow on 22 September.[82] Overbury seems to have caught up with John, however, and felt a more formal document should be sent by both of them. So he and John then sent another report of the lists of both potential Sheriffs and Escheators from the three shires. This report was received by the Earl on 28 September.[83] John's signature is very shaky, indicating that the death of his brother had struck him hard. He was feeling his age more than ever before.

But death had not finished gleaning his friends. In December 1631 Sir Heneage Finch, John's fellow Serjeant at Law and Recorder of London, died. He was the fourth son of Sir Moyle Finch. Aubrey said of John, "He made the best Latin epitaphs of his time; amongst many others an excellent one on < > Finch, this earl of Winchelsey's grandfather, who haz a noble monument in Eastwell in Kent." Andrew Clark filled in the missing identification as "Sir Moyle."[84] That gentleman could indeed have been "this earl of Winchelsea's grandfather" depending on when Aubrey wrote the observation, but the Latin epitaph was

not on Sir Moyle but his son Sir Heneage, who was
the grandfather of the first Earl of Aylesford and
the sixth Earl of Winchelsea (who was also the
second Earl of Nottingham). The seat of this family was the great estate of Eastwell in Kent, built
by Sir Thomas Moyle, Heneage's great-grandfather.
Sir Thomas was the brother of John Moyle, Benedicta's great-great-grandfather, so John's wife and
his co-Serjeant at Law were third cousins once removed.

During World War II tanks were stationed a-
mong the trees of this great manor near Ashford in
Kent and became a target for German bombers. A
single bomb hit the lovely church nestled directly
on the Pilgrim's Way to Canterbury and destroyed
all but the tower and the south chancel. Luckily
that chancel is where the tombs of the Moyles and
Finches of this period were located, and they were
undamaged. There is a sarcophagus containing the
bodies of Sir Thomas Moyle and his wife Catheryn
Jurdayn and listing the names of their two daughters and spouses: Katheryn Moyle and Sir Thomas
Finch, and Ann (or Amy) Moyle and Sir Thomas Kempe.
Nearby is a large marble monument with the reclin-
ing figures of Sir Moyle Finch and his wife, beautifully executed in life size. Around the monument
are the names of their children: Theophilvs, Heneage, Thomas, John, Heneage, Francis, William, Robert, Elizabeth, Elizabeth, Katherine, and Ann.

There is no epitaph on either of these two
monuments, but next to that of Sir Thomas, there
is a white marble slab, framed by gray marble, and
on it is the Latin epitaph written by John, un-
touched by time or war. All the necessary information is there in a remarkably short space. Francis,
Heneage's brother "least in age but not in affection" and heir raised this modest monument along
with his cousin Thomas Twisden to Heneage Finch,
Knight, Serjeant at Law, Recorder of London, and
Speaker of the House of Commons in the second Parliament of King Charles, who, besides being the
best of patrons, husbands, and friends, was the son
of Moyle Finch and his wife Elizabeth, who survived

674

her husband and was honored with the titles of Viscountess of Maidstone and Countess of Winchelsea; by his second wife Elizabeth Cradock[85] he had two daughters, and after two years, seven months, and twenty days of lawful marriage, he yielded up his spirit most calmly (he was struck by a dropsy) into the hands of his Saviour, whom he had served most constantly, 5 December 1631, at the age of 50 years, 11 months, and five days.

You have here (O may you never die), alas too
                                              quickly,
The Tomb you asked for while alive.
          Surely renowned virtue
Undefiled faith, unconquered constancy,
Gracious Justice refuse to die.
Among the leaders educated in sacred letters
You ranked second to none in goodness.
Why do we envy a person rapt into heaven by God
His posterity will hardly see his equal on earth.

     The poem is one of classical ease and clarity, with none of the wit and cleverness that marked John's earlier works. It is a simple statement of praise for a person whom John obviously liked and respected, one who had attained considerable position at an early age, not only because of his family connections, but as a result of his own ability.

     Also during this winter, John's niece Mary died. Due to her illness, she had moved over to Morehampton to be cared for by her sisters and perhaps her mother, who also died some time during this period. As we could predict from the wording of her letters, she began her will, written on 1 November 1631, with a strong statement of faith. Most of her bequests if not all were dependent on the state of her inheritance:

     ...Item for my worldly meanes which are fallen or shall fall in right vnto mee by Grandfathers Will or my fathers Will or otherwise I thus dispose of The first I give to the Church where I shall be buried two pound<u>es</u> Item to the poor five pound<u>es</u> Item I give and bequeath my broth-

675

ers eldest Child my bason and Eure Item I give
to my sister Magdalen one hundred pound... Item
the rest of my porcion I give to all my sisters
to bee equally devyded, onely to my Vncle Pig-
coate whom I make and appoynt myne Executo^r
twenty three poundes that he may see this my
will truely and faithfully fulfilled....86

Will and his sisters Elizabeth Hoskyns and Magdal-
en Hoskyns were witnesses. Once again we are faced
by the almost unintelligible fact that the will
was not probated for an extremely long time, in
this case until 17 June 1635.

* * * * *

The rest of the winter and spring wore on un-
eventfully. John went off on his usual circuit
and took his place on the Council of the Marches
of Wales. Meanwhile Will's wife no longer had the
worries of Morehampton to bother her. John's
daughter Benedicta was now old enough to take over
those responsibilities so that Bess could concentrate on caring for Will and looking after her
young sisters-in-law. In March another member of
John's extended family died, this time his sister-
in-law Anne, the wife of his brother Phillip and
mother of his godson John. On 22 June John's long-
time friend James Whitelocke died at his house at
Fawly, Bucks.87 It was but another reminder of the
possibility of death.

John had been thinking of his age, recounting
his blessings (as indicated in Aubrey's account of
his autobiography), and facing what seemed to be
his own approaching death. Sometime in 1631 or
1632, either on his birthday or soon after, he
wrote the Latin poem that was on his desk under 88
his portrait in the low gallery at Morehampton.
Later on it would be carved on his tomb in Abbey
Dore. He may also have written the English version that is among the family papers at Sizergh
Castle:

Years sixty six, I have with vigour Past,
But Death, my daily Thought, is come at last;

676

My sayings, writings, Deeds, of trifeling Play,
Lett endless Silence, in her Bosom lay:
Be my wrong Dealings, by my Heir redres't,
That no complaint, my Ashes may molest:
And what's to God, from a vile spendthrift, due,
To Christ, for Payment with his Blood, I sue.
                           in my name,

The ending of the poem is much more powerful in
the Latin, as he addresses Christ directly: "I
entreat you, O Christ, to release me [from my debt]
through thy blood."

     With his mind on his own death, John went a-
bout straightening out his affairs. Dr. John had
been one of the executors of Oswald's will and had
been a co-bondsman with John for the legacies of
the children. It was necessary to insure that the
commitment to those children was carried out without danger in case of his own death. On 3 July
1632, therefore, John took his son Benedict into
the Orphans Court in London before Robert Bateman
and had him sign on to the bonds in the place of
Dr. John.[89] As Bennet was to inherit John's estate, the remaining cousins were taken care of.
At the same time John realized that it had been
some time since his last will and two important
events had occurred: Bennet had reached the age
of maturity, and his brother Dr. John had died.
On 31 July 1632, therefore, he sat down to write
another will undoubtedly believing it would be his
last:

My Last Will the Last of July 1632 J: Hoskyns:

The same p^{r}face y^t was to my former will, in-
serting in a fitt place, that to my great grief,
and most sensible touch of my owne mortality,
my brother Dr Hoskyns is dead, and my brother
Oswalds eldest daughter, and his widdow, and
(out of Gods mercifull abridgm^t of my care I am
married againe to a religious honest Gentlewoman; my Daughter in law Elizabeth Boorne is
married to my brother Oswalds eldest sonne, and
my sonn is called to ye barr and as well experienced in my own estate as my selfe

677

recite what prouision I had made for my Daugh-
ter--
and because (I thanck God) shee is now of the
age of 18, and vndergoeth ye whole gouernm^t of
my house; and desire him out of his gratious
prouidence to send her a good husband, wherin
it may not bee so convenient for her to expect
the Distribucion of my whole estate, and ye satisfaction of my brothers childrens porcions and
my Debts, I doe giue her (if my sonn and shee
shall soe thinck fitt) for a p^{r}sent porcion 700
the best trees growing vppon all my grounds and
what y^t shall not make vpp of 1000^l I desire my
sonn to make vpp shee conveying all lands that
shee hath vnto him and this to bee her porcion
(if her brother and shee doe not otherwise agree)
and that they may agree is my last praier vppon
my last blessing
my debts are: 150^l. to M^r· Badbye 90
200^l to Mr Gibsonn
450^l for which Mr Churchman is bound with mee.
The porcions that shall arise to 5 of my brothers children which are of full age and whereas
I acknowledged a Judgm^t of 1000^l to the 2 eldest Daughters that was onely for securitye of
their porcions due in ye court of Orphans whereof they acknowledged satisfaction before they
had receaued it my Cosin William hath likewise
a bond of 1000^l from me for paiem^t of his porcion abating the charges of suites for him and
the suinge out of his liuerye.
There lyes in m^r Churchmans hands 500^l (if my
Cosin Magdalen will giue a generall release of
all demands due to her as well of her porcion
that shall grow due by augmentacion of our next
account as of the 100^l y^t is giuen to her by her
Sister. I am contented shee shall haue that
whole 500^l though her part will not arise to it
and God grant shee bee not seduced in choise of
a husband, but that shee maye bee blessed therin If my Cosin William will be contented to exchange his lands in London and Middlessex with
my sonn and giue him a generall release of all
his owne porcion & his wyfes I doe will that in
exchange of those somes and for his full satis-

faction hee shall haue all my lands at Bernythen
and the Held to him and the heires males of his
body by his now wyfe, the remainder to the
heires of his males body generally the remainder to my sonn and his heires paying to y^e
heires females of William Hoskins body 1000^l
and if hee accept of this then I giue him 6 ox-
en. 6 kine. 100 sheepe. 4 sowes and 200^l in
money to beginn the world with all. for the
paiem^t of the porcions of the rest of my brother Oswalds children I desire (as in my former
will) all possible speed maye bee made but I
forbeare to p^{r}scribe any speciall waye thereof.
besides the inheritance of my recognizance my
sonn is particularly bound in the co^{r}te of Orphans for the performance thereof. I desire my
sonn after all debts and legacyes paid to lett
John Hoskins my good nephew & faithfull seruant
hold the manno^r of Dydley for ten yeares at 20^l
per annum at some tyme in their 2 liues
I giue my 2 brethren as in my former will I haue
giuen them.
John Boornes land is fallen vnto him by his
fathers death yet I giue him within 3 yeares after hee is 21 yeares old and married the summ
of 50^l and at the birth of his 3^d child 50^l more.
for my brother D^{rs} children. I leaue it to my
sonnes godly discretion to help them by annui-
tyes or the reuercion of Mounton after my Brothers Dayes
I giue the rest of my clerks and seruants as in
my former will and to Sara Powell as in my former will, and I revoke and disanull all former
willes otherwise then they are heerin related
vnto
My wyfe is sufficiently prouided for but for a
particuler seale of my true loue I doe will
there bee p^{r}sented vnto her a purse and 20^l in it
All my Lands in the realm of England I giue to
my sonn and his heires for euer. all my leases,
chattles, plate, householdstuff, cattles and
goodes whatsoeuer I likewise giue him with my
praier to God and his blessing vppon it and I
beseech the Lord to bless my daughter my brother
Oswald and my brother D^{rs} children my brother

679

Thomas and my brother Phillipp and his children.
and for Jesus Christ his sake to remitt our
sinns and revnite vs with them that are departed
in his euerlasting Kingdome of this my Last
will I make my only sonne ɍ heir Ben Hoskyns my
only executor[91]

Only the last few lines were written by John, in a
very shaky hand. The rest was written from dicta-
tion, read to him, and signed before three witnesses.

There is no doubt that John had overextended
himself in land purchases, making payment of legal
debts next to impossible. But he refused to let go
of land to raise cash. Mary had died without getting her legacy; Magdalen was still waiting for
hers. Will was being forced into "retirement" from
the city of London to a life of farming, albeit on
a fine estate. The livestock given him to begin
his farming amounted to well over £50. But John
was giving his son Bennet plenty of time to build
up his fortune in order to pay the legacy to Will's
children. All in all the next generation of Hoskyns would do well by the Serjeant's death and estate, but they would have to wait and would have
to agree to his terms in order to get the benefits.

The remarks about Isabel are very pleasant,
but they do not give us much to work with in trying to establish their relationship. But Isabel
was not to receive her new purse and £20, for she
was to die before John. He still had six years of
active life ahead.

Footnotes for Chapter XVII

1. Sizergh MSS; in Osborn, pp. 91-2.
2. Identifications are from Appendix II of the Woolhope Club Transactions, 1868, pp. 272-76. Mrs. Candish remains unidentified.
3. Harley 1151, "Visitation to Buckinghamshire 1634," f. 83v.
4. Somerset House, 28 Savile. Written 16 October 1612; proved 18 March 1622.
5. Sizergh MSS.; in Osborn, p. 92.
6. John Edwards became one of Hoskyns' servants.
7. Hereford City MSS., Vol. 4, 1600-1644, f. 55.
8. Ibid. ff. 56-7.
9. Whitlock, "Donne at St. Dunstans," Times Literary Supplement, 16, 23 Sept., 1955.
10. C.J. I, 872.
11. Ibid.
12. Davies, The Early Stuarts (1952), p. 38.
13. C.J. I, 873.
14. Ibid.
15. C.J. I, 877; 29 March.
16. C.J. I, 879; 7 April; on 8 April this Committee was ordered to meet again 10 April.
17. Ibid.; to meet 9 April in Court of Wards.
18. C.J. I, 881.
19. C.J. I, 885.
20. Davies, The Early Stuarts, p. 38.
21. That same day Hoskyns was added to the Committee on "An Act for the better Ordering of the Office of the Clerk of the Market, and Reformation of false Weights and Measures." C.J. I, 889; "this Afternoon, in the Court of Wards." The Committee met again 27 May. (p. 905).
22. Ibid. The Committee on Statutes also met on 3 and 8 May. (p. 891).
23. C.J. I, 902.
24. Ibid.
25. The events of May 22 and 23 are recorded C.J. I, 903.
26. C.J. I, 905.
27. Ephemeris Parliamentaria (1654), p. 140.
28. C.J. I, 905-6.
29. Davies, p. 39.
30. C.J. I, 908.

31. C.J. I, 909.
32. C.J. I, 910.
33. Although the Petition was certainly the main
    order of business, other Bills were considered
    during the political maneuvering of Parliament
    and King. On 10 May John had been put on a
    Committee handling Herbert's Decree. (C.J. I,
    895. 13 May, in the Exchequer Chamber.) On 19
    May all Knights and Burgesses of the Four
    Shires were placed on a Committee for "An act
    for exempting the Counties of Gloucester, Wor-
    cester, Hereford, and Salopp, and of the Cities
    of Gloucester and Worcester, and of the Coun-
    ties thereof, from the Jurisdiction of the Lord
    President" of Wales. (C.J. I, 900. 24 May.) On
    23 May he was on the Committee for "Confirma-
    tion of Letters Patents, made by the late
    King's Majesty, unto John Earl of Bristoll, by
    the Name of John Digby, Knight." (C.J. I, 903.
    26 May; Bill passed 31 May.) And on 16 June,
    as the session headed for a rocky ending, John
    was named to the Committee on Hamond's Estate.
    (C.J. I, 913. 17 June.)
34. Davies, p. 40.
35. Ibid.
36. Quoted in Davies, p. 40.
37. C.J. I, 920.
38. Stow, p. 1044.
39. Sizergh MSS.; in Osborn, p. 257.
40. Sizergh deeds.
41. True extracts or copies of fines, amercements,
    etc. entered on the rolls of a court to be
    levied by the bailiff. O.E.D.
42. Winchester Archives 19024.
43. Stow, p. 1043.
44. Cambridge History of English Literature (1932),
    VII, 157.
45. Samuel R. Gardiner, The Personal Government of
    Charles I, 1628-1637, Vol. I (1877), p. 59.
46. Commons Debates for 1629, Notestein & Relf,
    edd. (1921), p. 120; from "Nicholas's Notes."
47. Ibid., p. 211; from "Grosvenor's Diary."
48. Ibid., p. 220.
49. C.J. I, 932. Osborn repeated this error in her
    biography.

50. Davies, p. 43,
51. Hopwood, II, 747-48.
52. Sizergh MSS.; in Osborn, p. 93.
53. Sizergh MSS.; in Osborn, pp. 94-97; she followed the order of Henry Hornyold-Strickland's arrangement, although she knew of Margaret Bourne's will.
54. Apparently Nick Ward, who was wasting his time at Morehampton. Probably the son of John Ward, a Hereford City friend of John. See Chap. 4.
55. H.M.C., Duke of Portland, Vol. 3 (1894), p. 31.
56. Sizergh MSS.; in Osborn, p. 97.
57. Lease Book A, WCM 22999.
58. Bursar's Accounts 1624-1644.
59. Hopwood, II, 773.
60. Middle Temple Bench Book (2nd ed., 1937), p. 119.
61. Sizergh MSS.; in Osborn, pp. 93-4.
62. Fabian Phillips.
63. 135 St. John.
64. 53 Scroope.
65. Bath Register, II, 353.
66. Sizergh MSS.
67. Sizergh MSS.
68. The O.E.D. gives one reading of "howse" as a covering of textile material.
69. Sizergh MSS.
70. Sizergh MSS.
71. Repertory Book 44, 1629-1630, ff. 230-230v. Signatures are in Letter Book GG 1617-1620, f. 201. "Paid" entries were made in Orphans Recognizances 2, 1590 to 1633, ff. 200, 359.
72. 30 Meade.
73. Stow, p. 1045.
74. MS. Rawlinson, Poet, 26, ff. 11v; in Osborn, p. 214. The English stanza is in Egerton 923, f. 57; Add. MSS. 30,982. f. 28v. Osborn's reference to Harley 6071 is incorrect.
75. Add. MSS. 15,227, f. 37v. The ms. entry not only has both versions of the poem, but the date of the poem, that of the Prince's birth, and that of the solar eclipse. Mrs. Hyrne is said to have responded to John:
    Ein Misael de Israeli
    stella non est Israeli

683

Astra regunt homines sed regit   astra Deus.
Secreta Dei, revelata nobis, et
filiis nostris.
There is a note on the third line which explains Mrs. Hyrne's poem: "The Text was, out of
ye history of Sampson in ye booke of Judges:
Si non arasses cum vitula mea, non solvisses
aenigma meum." [Judges 14:18]
In N.L.W., Carreglwyd, Ser. II, 217, along with
other Latin verses by Hoskyns, the Latin version of this poem is found with another Latin
poem on the same subject: "6 Junij 1630. A cop-
pie of verses made by D^r. Sharpe & Sergeant
Hosgins vpon ye appearance of a starr that day
in ye sermon tyme at Powles crosse ye Kinges
ma^{tie} beinge present of the byrth of ye prince."
It is pleasant to find that John and Lionel
Sharpe, now Archdeacon of Berkshire, had remained friends over the years following the
Addled Parliament. Latin version also found
in Hengwit MS. 275, #267 Peniarth, p. 52, with
a full description of the event.
76. Aubrey (Clark ed.), I, 419. Aubrey made a note
to "gett it," but unfortunately he failed to do
so.
77. Aubrey, Dick ed., with additions from Clark,
I, 421.
78. P.R.O., C.2 H45/19.
79. In Hereford City Library.
80. Aubrey (Clark, ed.), I, 424.
81. Thomas Blount's Collection, II, f. 11.
82. Among the Ellesmere Papers in the Henry E.
Huntingdon Library, EL 7374.
83. EL 7373.
84. I, 419; Aubrey as usual had trouble with his
generations.
85. They were married in the parish church of St.
Dunstan's-in-the-West, almost certainly by
John Donne, the parish priest.
86. 71 Sadler.
87. English Reports, 79, p. 833.
88. See Chapter 16. The poem appears in Aubrey as
noted; among the Sizergh MSS. here quoted; in
N.L.W. Carreglwyd Papers, Ser. II, 218, dated
1634 (listed in H.M.C., 5th Report, Part I,

p. 409); and <u>Lansdowne 702</u>, f. 54v; Osborn used
the version in <u>MS</u>. <u>Rawlinson</u> <u>D.727</u>, f. 94. The
Sizergh MS. has a headnote that the verse was
written in 1632 or 1633. It may well be that
the Serjeant wrote the poem at the same time
that he wrote his next will, but there is more
reason to place it at a time closer to his 66th
birthday, when we know he was doing a good
deal of writing.

89. <u>Orphans Recog</u>. <u>5</u>, ff. 75, 75v, 76, 76v, 91-91v;
   <u>Rep</u>. <u>Book 46</u>, ff. 280v-281v; <u>Orphans</u> <u>Recog</u>. <u>2</u>,
   ff. 200, 241, 359.
90. In earlier letters John had dealt with Badby
   on affairs for Elizabeth Kempe.
91. Harewood MSS.

Chapter XVIII

The Allotted Span

The final six years of John's life began un-
eventfully enough with the usual circuit in Wales.[1]
When he returned to London a few weeks later, he
was drawn back into a case that lasted for four
years. It really had been going on for fourteen
years already.

On 25 October, Alice Williams, whom we first
met in November 1618, came before Lord Keeper
Coventry in Chancery and filed a new complaint a-
gainst John. She said that about fifteen or sixteen years before she had lent him £17 on the condition that he pay her back £19 14s within a year
(she had reduced the original figures by £10).
When "yor Oratrix came to demaund her money...
[Hoskyns] willed yor Oratrix to leave the bond
with him till the morninge... and to repaire to
him... and he would either pay her the Interest
and renue the bond for a twelue monthe more, or
else pay her all her Money." Williams went on to
claim that when she went back the next morning,
John "p^{r}tended to haue such busines that he could
not haue then leasure to make a newe bond, but intreated yor Oratrix to take 40^s parte of the interest," and she endorsed the bond for that and
was told to come back for the rest. Once John had
the bond, he "slipt into the Country, and since
then she hadn't been able to get either her bond
or her money. She admitted that he had "vpon her
often importunity paid her att severall tymes the
some of Six poundes... wch yor Oratrix perceivinge
did doe her no pleasure by reason it was paid her
by such small driblettes," demanded the rest in a
single payment, but he refused and would pay her
no more. Now she wanted it all and wanted a subpoena to bring him into court.[2]

Young Bennet was in court, ready to respond to
the charge, no doubt using an argument already
drawn up by his father. He simply retold the his-

687

tory of the case:

> the said plaintiff beinge a person disordered
> in her life and distracted in her wittes and
> soe still continuinge did heretofore not only
> deliver or cause to be delivered divers iddle
> and clamourous peticions against this Def^te to
> the lorde Chancellor... but alsoe did aboute
> thirteene or fowerteene yeares since... procure
> her self to be admitted in forma pauperis and
> did exhibitt a bill agaynst this defd^te in this
> court pretendinge the same debte vpon the same
> bond... wth all other vntrue surmises.

John had answered the charges then, and Mr. Williamson of Lincolns Inn, who had since died, was
assigned as her counsel. John had "agreed in open
Courte... that the same shoulde be referred to her
owne Councell to heare and to determayne... if he
found the said suict causelesse and vniust would
take order for her punishment wch was accordingely
referred." When Mr. Williamson informed his client that

> noethinge was due vnto her she fell into an
> outragious exclamacion and raginge... Mr Wil-
> liamson... sent her to Bridewell there to be
> punished, ffor wch course of wandringe and lewd
> lyfe in this towne vnder pretence of suict a-
> gainst some others... she hath bin seuerall
> tymes committed to the same prison... laste
> terme she in a madde manner as this Defd^te was
> standinge at the Common Pleas barre came be-
> hinde him lept on his backe and thrust into his
> necke a subpoena... to wch this Defd^te appeared
> and by his Attorney demaunded what he should
> answeare and nothinge was shewed against him
> and nowe this terme she served him wth an other
> subpoena....[3]

The image of the old prostitute leaping on to
the back of the aging Serjeant in the middle of
Westminster Hall while he was arguing a case would
have struck his friends and perhaps even himself
in his younger years as very funny indeed, but no

doubt he was tired of the continuation of such a senseless case after all these years. Alice Williams was not about to disappear, however. She may have been slightly mad, but she was even more tenacious. Unfortunately there is no safeguard in the common law against a person bringing suit against another, no matter how worthless the complaint.

Young Bennet was becoming completely conversant with all of his father's affairs, as John's will had stated. Late in November he and his father were ready to take care of the next round of payments to his nieces under his brother's will. On 29 November Thomas Price, who identified himself both as a gentleman and from Morehampton, swore before the Orphans Court that Elizabeth and Eleanor Hoskyns were both over twenty-one and still unmarried. The two girls were present and each received the sum of £22 14s 11d as the share of the estate that was in the hands of John Hoskyns.[4] They also signed as being satisfied of their portion of the Ozias Churchman bond.[5] Elizabeth, like her sister Magdalen, appears not to have learned how to sign her name and put down only her initials. There are notes on all of the recognizances that the two were paid their full inheritances in spite of the clear statement that each had received only slightly over £22 from their uncle.[6] As the sum of money that they did acknowledge receiving bears no resemblance to any amount that they should have received (over £300), we are again faced by the mystery of how John was able to prove to the court's satisfaction that the terms of the will had been carried out with the payment the girls received that day. The easiest explanation would be that he presented the girls deeds to small landholdings in lieu of cash, probably property bordering the main Bernithen estate.

John now felt that some bonds should be rewritten since five of the children had supposedly received their legacies. So, on 4 December 1632, before they all rode back together to Morehampton, he and Bennet signed a new recognizance for money

689

due to Margery, Katherine, Thomasin, and Frances, in conjunction with Ozias Churchman and James Fawcett[7] and one by themselves for money due to Thomazin and Frances.[8]

After John had turned over the official lease of Titley to Bennet, he continued to make sure that the estate was run properly by his steward, James Dalley. In June 1630, for example, he held a baronial court there, and the care with which the records were kept indicate that Dalley had learned his lesson from John's strongly worded letter.[9] For the next two years, Bennet took over his father's duties and held courts on 21 March, 14 November and 12 December 1631 and 14 August 1632.[10] No courts were held for the next two years, and then Bennet allowed Dalley to run the court.[11] The record immediately reveals a return to the same sloppiness that had bothered John before. Neither John nor Bennet seems to have bothered to attend a court at Titley from that point on.[12]

While John and Bennet were visiting Titley, however, they also looked in on their cousins and kept up to date on their affairs. On 16 March 1633 Thomas Hoskyns of Shobdon, a town not far from Titley, was involved in a number of cross suits with a William Perry. Their case was examined before the Lord President and Council of the Marches of Wales. John was undoubtedly present but not taking much part because of the close family connection. The cause of all the difficulty was the fact that on the last day of December 1632 Thomas had cut down a small tree on his own ground, not worth more than six pence. Perry and his family filed a suit against Thomas, his wife, and some other members of his family for "severall supposed assaultes" on Perry at the same time and in the same place. Thomas agreed at this point to refer the case to a third party, Thomas Abberley, Clerk.[13] There the case rested for the time being. When it reopened, John would be representing his cousin as counsel.

Meanwhile, Bennet had fallen in love. On 14

March 1633, he wrote from Morehampton,

> Sweet Valentine
> I thancke you for enrichinge my mynde with the
> contemplacion of those many vertues I haue al-
> ready discouered in you. I beseeche you vouch-
> safe mee soe much Loue as maye make mee acc-
> quainted with the rest, (since none can bee ab-
> sent from you,) for I vowe if there bee true
> Loue of infinit extent; (as my conscience and
> harte tell mee there is) with it I honor and
> affect you, and you alone....14

The girl he was addressing came from a distinguished and wealthy family. She was the daughter of Sir John Bingley, the person whom John had
defended so well in the great extortion case of
1619. Bingley had, of course, been convicted, but
everyone knew how well John had performed his duties as Counsel. A friendship had developed and
lasted through the years which allowed for the
children to meet each other in London. The love
the young people felt for each other is obvious in
the letters written by Ben. That correspondence
also gives us a view into the waning days of John's
life. Ben's depiction of his father is warm and
understanding. Their mutual affection was real and
lasting. And we also gain a good idea of young
Ann Bingley--well-educated, witty, and beautiful,
characteristics she shared with Ben's mother.

The marriage took place in early summer, as
the first letter Ben wrote to his new wife is
dated 10 July 1633. Ann was staying at Temple
Combe, on the edge of Blackmoor Vale in eastern
Somerset, while Ben had reached New Sarum on his
way back to London. The letter begins, "Now that
you haue made mee yor Husband" and ends "excuse mee
to yorselfe for forgetting to buss you 100000000
tymes more then I did thus hoping to bee better
accquainted with & praying for you I am...." In a
p.s. he adds, "I hadd a desire to superscribe the
name of Hoskins first vnto you because I am to
blame (yf any body) for it."15 By August she had
moved temporarily to Morehampton, where, on the

sixth, he addressed a letter saying that he hoped
to be with her "this tyme to morrow."16 This ide-
ally-matched young pair were to have two sons. The
first, who was named after his grandfather, inherited his father's baronetcy and became the second
president of the Royal Society; the second, who was
named after his cousin William, appropriately e-
nough became a draper in London, following in his
great-uncle's footsteps. Ann, who was to die before her husband, was buried next to her father-in-
law in Abbey Dore.

One of the reasons we have so many letters
from Ben to his wife is that business kept him on
the road with his father. For example in September
1633 they were in Carmarthen where, on the 18th,
the Common Council there "were called to an ac-
countt by Sr Nicholas Ouerbury, knight and John
Hoskyns, seriant att Law... for the Monies receaved
towards the buildinge of the ffree Schoole...."17
Later that month John wrote a letter to the Earl
of Bridgewater that sounded more like Hotspur than
John Hoskyns:

My honorable goo [sic] Lorde,
    It was not out of any vndutyfullnes or any ar-
regation of any power to myself that I denyed to
send by this gentleman any supplies of more
shreryffes names for I shalbe ready to discov^r
to y^r Lordshep not only what others are next
ability, but a Roll of the abilities, alliances
ꝗ inclinations of ev^{r}y particular man of quality in evry sheere of our circuict to my best
knowledge. And I haue it ready it wantes but
fayr writinge. but vpon a messuge ore terms by
a gentleman whom I nev^r saw before, to send more
shreryffs names then the statute required ꝗ
wthout my broth^r Overburyes privity was a thinge
that I made som doubt of. because I haue found
it of ill consequence. by the pracktise of som
labouers to free to chaunge sheryffes in one
yeare fell out three shreryffes to be prickt in
those three sheeres that were not so good men
as three chief constables in my country And
one of them worth but 40^l a yeare was serve [?]

692

to Enterbery [?] the then Lord President at
Harford West 3 tymes wth the helpe of his
frendés I haue herein sent y^r lordshep the
true state of them that are named. to morrow
I will attend y^o wth the names ę abilityes of
more w^thin our sheere will hardly fall out^18

John thought the issue was important enough to warrant writing to Bridgewater in his own handwriting
so that the Lord President would know that no one
was miscarrying a message.

Sometime during the late fall or early winter,
Isabel fell sick, and John, who probably had married again with some idea of having an help meet
for his old age, found himself caring for and worrying over his slowly weakening wife. It appears
that he spent almost the entire winter in the west,
attending only to those legal duties that could be
fulfilled in Wales or in the city of Hereford.
Ben was, therefore, forced to spend his first
Christmas away from his new wife, who had returned
to London and was living quite contentedly in her
aunt's house in Old Street, Kensington. It was at
this home of the Henshaw's that some of John's
lost poetry was last seen, according to Aubrey in
later years. We do not know why Ann remained in
London for over a year, but there is some evidence
in the letters that Ann may not have wished to
leave the social and literary life of London for
the farmlands of Hereford.

On his way to Morehampton for Christmas Ben
wrote to Ann, when he was "within 7 miles of Morehampton safely and soe is my noble frend Mr Price."
He reports that "my mother in law is vppon recou-
ery" and that he has "done my father Bingley the
seruice of obteyning a Cooke." Bennet was not a
poet like his father, but this year he tried his
hand at light verse to make up for his absence
from Ann:

Twere well enough if I this Yeare
gaue thee a Hogshead of Stale beere
or if I thought 'twould make thee merry

693

The like proportion of good Perry
or such like things, but what is spent
in Common gives thee nor Content
Therefore I Chose a Drugg to send
which on none other thou shalt spend
But if it doe thee good Beware
for then the whole house hath a share.
Thy health a Common Banck would bee
But most of all would enrich mee[19]

It should be remembered that about this time Bennet asked Ben Jonson if he could become one of the
"Sons of Ben," the poetic hangers-on of the great
poet. Jonson's reply was "No... I dare not; 'tis
honour enough for me to be your Brother: I was
your Father's sonne, and 'twas he that polished
me."

By Christmas Isabel had recovered even more,
as in an undated letter a few days later, Ben
wrote to Ann that on St. Stevens day, December 26,
several people "came to welcome my Motherinlaw into the parlor and to congratulate her recouerye
which wee all ioye for." Then he gives us a picture of the assembled family and John's obvious
happiness over his son's choice for a wife: "My
father drinckes to you all each meale nor doe any
of vs forgett our seruices to any, nor yor commands (hitherto very strictly kept) to lye alone.[20]

On 7 January 1634 Ben was with his father at
the Quarter Sessions in Hereford when he again
wrote to Ann. The weather had been miserable: "I
hope this yeare will gett erely better then hee
begann for on New yeares Eue our very land and
houses were moued but are come to their wonted
stations againe, And that wind that then was bois-
terous vnder the earth doth now dominere aboue it."
The letter ends with greetings from Benedicta, who
"hath sent you some cloth of her owne directing to
bee made."[21] It is clear from all of the correspondence from this time on that Benedicta and Ann
became very close friends. John had gathered a-
round him a loving community of relatives, lacking
any of the coolness if not plain bitterness that

694

had at times characterized his own and his father's generations. His activity in developing an extended family had worked.

Isabel's recovery from her illness did not last long. On 13 January, Ben sent another letter off to Ann in London: "It is now tyme to talke of a Returne my desire was to speed it but my fathers commaund lyes vppon mee to attend him vpp to bee a staff to his age and a comfort to him now grieued with my Mothers relapse into sickness."22 There is no doubt that John took the decline in his wife's health and her death very hard. It made him depend on his son more than the latter would have wished, of course, but that dependency was also a sign of love, and Ben knew it.

They did get back to London, however, for the Williams case was still alive in the courts there. On 13 February John submitted his formal answer to another bill of complaint from Alice Williams. There is a certain querulousness in the tone of the answer which is easy to understand: "he conceaveth that he suffers extraordinarilye In beinge ordered to Answere the said Bill, Former proceedings of this Corte the quality of the Complainant & this Defent beinge well considered." He then repeated all of the activities that had taken place since 1618, including the eventful day in Chancery. When he appeared in court in answer to the subpoena, nothing was alleged against him. Now Williams has found some old copies of her original Bill which she is using to start the case up once more. John (through his son Ben, who signed the statement as his father's attorney) then tells the full story of how the case started:

> it is true that her ffather and her mother be-
> inge poore people in the Cyttye of Hereford
> caused this Deftes wief to entreate this Defente
> to be of Councell... in an accion of Debte vp-
> on Bond... for paymt of twenty pounds to be trid
> in Guyldhall London wch bond was entred into by
> a yonge man her fellowe servant in Mr Hopwoods
> house in newgate Markett for a satisfaccion of

695

too much familiarity that had bin betwixt them,
the said yonge man pleaded non age at the tryall before my Lord Coocke at Guyldhall and produced the church booke, but because the same
was written all wth one hand and because the
acte... seemed not to be the Acte of an Infant
My Lord directed the Jury and they found a ver-
dicte for the plaintiff and after Judgm^t the
said yonge man... brought a Writt of Error and
therevpon this Defend^t and one Mr Morse her attorney drewe the Matter to composicion and shee
received aboute thirty pounds Mr Morse complayned that w^thin two or three dayes shee had
spent about fower pounds of it, and willed that
the residue shouldbe brought vnto this Defen^t
wch was brought accordingly in winter in the
eight yeare of our late... James and this Def^t
would not receaue it w^thout puttinge of it forth
for her benefitt and givinge of her a bond for
the same, wch he gaue her of fifty pounds for
paym^t of twenty nine pounds fourteene shillings
wch was principall and Interest for one yeare
But w^thin fewe dayes after shee brought the bond
ꝑ said shee would not haue it put to interest
but would haue it for her selfe and her friends
as shee had neede of it and so p^rsently receaved
some parte and soe came from tyme to tyme soe
often ꝑ for soe small parcells for herselfe her
ffather her mother ꝑ kindred to whome shee gaue
it in vaine-glorious fassion that this Defend^t
was wery of her ꝑ haueinge written the seuerall
parcells that shee receaved on the backe of the
bond ꝑ wittnesses therevnto offred her all that
remayned beinge aboute three pounds, w^ch, shee
beinge distempred in her witts threwe aboute
the Chamber ꝑ gathered vp only a eleaven shillings of it and deliuered vp the bond to this
Def^t willinge him to cancell it ꝑ shee would
come for the rest as shee had neede of it w^ch
shee receaved at seuerall tymes ꝑ more to the
some of aboue thirtye pounds and wherupon this
def^t by her good will cancelled the said Bond
And afterwards aboute fifteene yeares since being a vagrant in this Towne ꝑ being app^rhended
by officers counterfitted that shee had a suite

696

in lawe ρ soe procured herselfe to be admitted
in forma pauperis to sue this Def[t] in this Co[r]te
w[ch] suite was ended by M[r] Williamson as aforesaid the money apperinge to be paid by the seuerall Indorsm[tes] of the said Bond aboue twenty
yeares since ρ the said first suite beinge ended aboue fifteene yeares since soe that this
Deft conceaveth it shee ought not to beene a-
gayne in forma pauperis w[ch] admittance shee
sheweth to eu[r]ye constable to prviledge her
selfe from beinge comitted to Brydwell wyther
for her vagrancye and lewde lief shee hath beene
there thrice comitted ρ she is there well knowen,
ρ should be againe comitted were it not for the
priveledge... for shee is well knowen to be disordered in her lief distracted in her witts, ρ
soe shameles ρ vnwoemanlieke that shee hath not
only abused this defen[t] but divers knightes ρ
gentlemen of like sorte wth impudent slanders
ρ exclamacions.[23]

Bess Broughton was not the only woman from Hereford
to garner a wide reputation in London as a prostitute. John's lengthy answer should have finished
the case, but it didn't.

John and Ben headed back to Hereford and Wales
soon afterward, once again leaving Ann behind. On
7 March 1634 Ben wrote from Hereford, giving Ann
the news from Morehampton: "I thanck Godd my Motherinlaw liues though shee keepes her Chamber and
the rest of our frendes heere are in health, the
Springe (notwistanding the Ecclipse) proues forward wee are at our Salladdes and Nosegayes already neither is your Cloth for a Bedd very back-
ward for with the 5 yardes and a half you haue wee
shallbee able to make vpp 20 yardes by Easter."[24]
Ben was getting ready for Ann's joining him at
Morehampton.

If the Hoskyns household had the continuing
cloud of Isabel's impending death hanging over it,
it also had the good news of impending birth. Ann
wrote Ben the good news on 7 April, and he dashed
off a quick note to tell her that he would join

697

her in London on the 21st or 22nd. "I shall bee
double dilligent and grieued that I can nott cure
euery quame that your great belly costs you Godd
bless you and it."25 Six days later he wrote her
again, obviously trying to relieve any doubts she
might have as to where she would lie in. "if the
housewifry heere make not sufficient speed to yor
liking wee will find some meanes at London to accomodate you with a Bedd."26

   It is difficult to discover whether or not
Ben and his father got to London in April, but
probably not. By the first of May he wrote a very
melancholy letter to Ann: "the ground of my Sadness is partly because my Mother is fallen very
sick againe." The letter is written while Ben is
on his way to join Ann the following day. He sends
her word of John's affection for his daughter-in-
law: "you shall now receaue a Ring which Serieant
Weston the new Baron of the Excheq^r bestowed on my
father and hee made mee the Conveyance of it and
his Loue to you."27 John had remained in Morehampton with his dying wife.

   During the week of 9 May, while Ben was in
London asking for a delay of the Court's action in
the Williams case so that further depositions could
be taken,28 Isabel died. Her death left John in a
very depressed state of mind that lasted for several months and affected Ben and the rest of the family as well.

   But the family business pressed upon John,
and he had to travel to London once again in order
to help out his cousin Thomas Hoskyns of Shobdon,
on the 14th. The case of the six penny tree had
gotten out of hand. It seems that the Thomas Abberley whom Thomas had agreed to use as a Referee
in his case against William, because he had professed "much scincerity and that he would deale indifferently," had turned out to be a great friend
of Perry before he made the judgment and was "in
that respect noe indifferent Arbitrator." Thomas,
therefore, had "discharged him from medlinge with
the said matters," but Abberley had meanwhile or-

dered Thomas to pay the original 6d and legal costs of 50s or forfeit the enormous sum of £100. The main point that John made in defense was that there is no reason for Thomas to "forfeit one hundred poundes for not paying fiftee shillings six pence and not doinge some other lesse trifles in the same awarde menconed." Thomas, "being a poore man and much impoverished with suites & vexacions and willing to purchase his peace" offered to pay Perry the 50s 6d for the bond to be cancelled, but Perry refused and put the bond in suit in the Court of Common Pleas. Hoskyns says that Thomas' attorney in that suit, mistaking Thomas' instructions, appeared and agreed to the bond, "to the vtter overthrow of your Orator and of his poore wife and Children" unless the suit is "prevented by your LoPP in this his Maties most Hoble Court of Chauncery." John asked that a subpoena be issued to bring Perry into the Chancery to answer these charges.29 It would appear that the best John could do for his cousin was to get him off with costs and the price of the tree. As there is no record of a decree or order for this case, the contestants obviously settled their disagreement out of Court.30

Meanwhile Ann had left London and moved to Morehampton. On 26 June Ben was on the road "I know not where I am what I doe or how the tyme passeth" when he wrote her a short letter. The reason for his mental state is shown more fully in a note that he probably wrote from Hereford:

This is that Mercury that I promised to send that I might know your commandes. And how you all doe; whom I hadd prvented by coming my self last night but that I hadd infused melancholy by discorse with my Father in the Afternoone and knew not how to carry soe great a burthen soe farr by night.

John was taking Isabel's death badly.

By the time Ben and John headed west for the Welsh circuit, however, the melancholy had turned to joy. John was now a grandfather, and the succession for which his estate had been built up was secure. He must have shared the happiness that bubbles over in Ben's letter from Carmarthen on 1 August 1634 to his wife in Morehampton:

Little thoughtest thou (O Wooman in the strawe) to heare the Tautologie of my true Loue till I returned in person a Captive to thy Sweetness or if you were in hope to heare how strange maye it seeme that I (if there bee any Egoity) should without mixture of the language of my profession, speake in the Dialect of Loue, but what I doe now is not my Invention nor determined phrase but a meere dischardge of the abundant vrgent thoughtes of my heart; I am Covetous of the newes of yor healthy & yor eldest Sonnes & ought to reioyce that I haue not kingdomes at my dispose. for I should turne them all to foostooles for if there bee any ommission of my duty respects Loue and service to ye rest you are to blame whilest I was mine owne I p^{r}sented it but now I am

yor Ben: Hoskyns[32]

Ben had been studying his father's book on style! The new member of the Hoskyns family, born on 13 July, was once again named John, but to avoid misunderstanding, he was immediately referred to as Jack by his parents, especially to avoid any mix-up with John's godson John, the child of Phillip.

On 29 September 1634, John, Earl of Bridgewater, was officially inaugurated as Lord President of Wales. Serjeant Hoskyns, as a member of the Council of the Marches, was in attendance and therefore was present in the evening to watch one of the major events in English literary history, the first performance, under the direction of the musician Henry Lawes, of A Mask, later to be called Comus by eighteenth-century editors, by the young poet John Milton. The younger members of the Egerton family, John, Thomas, and Alice, took the leading roles, and Lawes himself played the role of the Attendant Spirit. John had retained his close

700

association with the Egerton family ever since he had persuaded the original Lord Ellesmere, Sir Thomas Egerton, to write a letter to Winchester and New College in support of Dr. John's election to Oxford in 1598. John would have been as conscious that evening as his friend Henry Wotton was three years later when he read <u>Comus</u> that a new master had appeared on the <u>English literary</u> scene, a man whose religious and political principles closely paralleled his own. It is unfortunate that the documents of the Bridgewater collection in the Huntington Library do not detail the events of that evening performance, but we can be sure of the magnificence of the occasion from other records which indicate the Earl's standard of hospitality.

On 28 November 1634, John drew up a new list of Interrogations to be given to the witnesses on his behalf in the case of Alice Williams. Once again, the interrogations show the careful building of the case, covering all the points at issue and tending to an inevitable conclusion for the Court to draw. They begin by asking the witnesses if they know the plaintiff and the defendant "and of what accompte eyther of them are and of what truth in theire Dealings declare yor knowledge."

Itm Do you know the bond now shewed vnto yo^w and the indorsm<u>^{tes}</u> of the said bond is yor name eyther written or menconed on the backe of the said bond Are the names of William Taylo^r William Prichard, Thomas Morse Epiphan Haworth, Christopher Jones, Henry Bayley, Thomas Taylo^r... there written to testifie paym<u>^{tes}</u> of c^rteyne summes for discharge of the said bond are those persons of Credditt And is yor name written wth yor owne hand and is the rest of the wittnesses names subscribed wth their owne hands... and wch of them be dead ρ wch liueinge Itm did yo^u knowe the plainante to haue bene disordered in her lief ρ distempered in her wittes and a wandrar or runnagate haue you knowen her punished in heref or in London ρ And doe yo^u thinke that she hath gotten a priveledge to sue in forma paup^ris to keep her selfe

701

from being Comitted to Bridwell..,
Item Doe yo^u know anie Certificate made from
the Maior Aldermen and others of the best sorte
of the inhabitantes of the Cittye of Heref heretofore conc^{r}ninge the plainante behauiour ɛ her
suite doth the paper now shewed vnto yo^u Con-
teyne the said Certificate...
Item are yo^u a Wittnes to the bond in question
haue yo^u seene the same since in the hands of
the Defte cancelled or other wise Did yo^u know
the plte to resorte often to the Defendentes
Chamber for seu^{r}all somes of money ɛ to haue receaued the same Did yo^u then knowe her at anie
tyme Complayne that the Deft kept the said bond
from her Did yo^u know Christofer Jones Esqr
was he then Chamberfellowe to the Deft.
Item Did yo^u know the Deft Complayne of the
plainantes often Comminge for the said Money by
parcells ɛ her wasteinge thereof ɛ that in the
end when she had spent all she would trouble
the Deft Did yo^u see the Deft offer her a whole
heape of money ɛ will her to take all that was
due to her ɛ vnpaid Did yo^u see her throw the
said money abrode folishly refusinge to take it,
ɛ yet lawghinge ɛ grininge snatcht vp some few
shillings sayinge that should serue her torne
then ɛ departed Did the Defte writte downe vpon the said bond what she then did, did she
then desire to haue the said bond or noe
Item were the seu^{r}all papers of the said bond
nowe shewed vnto yor vntorren ɛ vnrent when yo^u
sawe it at anie tyme heretofore but one sheete
or halfe sheete of papere vndevided did yo^u then
cast vp all the paym^{tes} indorsed vpon the backe
of the said bond to what some doe they arise
ɛ how much more is that then is due by the said
bond ɛ how longe was the same in payinge... what
other matter or thing doe yo^w knowe that maketh
for or concerneth the Defte[33]

On 15 January 1635 the depositions of five
witnesses were taken at the new Market House in
Hereford. The first was William Morgan of Howton,
the original owner of some of John's holdings in
Didley. He testified that he had served John "for

702

fiue or six yeares as one of his Clerkes duringe
wch tyme and euer sithence this Deponte neuer knewe
but yt the Defendente was and is accompted for a
right worpll honest Gentleman in his Dealinges."
Alice Williams, on the other hand, "is a turbulent
peeuishe woman of behauior by the reporte of her
Countrie men and partly to this Depontes knowe-
ledge." He says that he knows the bond, signed it,
and believes that William Taylor also signed his
name to two notes of receipt. He believes that
Taylor's witnessing was true "because he found ye
said Taylor honest and iust in all his dealinges
dueringe the tyme this Deponte and the said William
Taylor serued the Defendte...."

    Epiphan Howorth of Whitehouse [Whitehouse was
across the river from Morehampton], Herefordshire,
aged 67, said that he has known John for forty
years and has often seen the Complainant. Howorth
acknowledged his own signature for a receipt of
40s paid to Williams and believes the rest of the
sums were paid also. He was present when

    the Complte came to the Defte demaundinge money
    of him at wch tyme the said Defte began to ex-
    postulate wth her and alleadged before this de-
    ponte to this purpose yt he had ouerpayd her of
    the some of money by her demaunded, wherevpon
    in regard of her clamour this deponte wished the
    said Defte to lett her haue somewt more; where-
    vpon ye said Defte at this Depontes request
    gaue her som moneyes and shee departed well con-
    tented as this deponte then conceaued....

    Henry Bayley of Hereford, aged 57, was next.
He acknowledged his signature on a receipt of 20s
which he saw paid Williams. He said that he

    was prsent in London in the Middle Temple in
    the Deftes chamber when ye said Defte had told
    a crtaine somme of money and layd it downe vpon
    the table to the Complte, wch moneys shee re-
    ceaued and went out of the chamber wth the same,
    and came againe into the chamber whilest this
    deponte was there, and threw the same or some

parte thereof downe vpon the table againe, and
yet in a malepert and furious manner did snatch
vp some parte of the same money againe and went
her way wth it. . . .

John Clarke of Hereford, aged 48, repeated
the former testimony about John and Alice William's
character and said that when he was Mayor of Hereford he and the Aldermen and Justices of the Peace
made out a certificate about the behavior of Williams which the Commissioners now have. All of the
signatures on the certificate were of Justices of
the Peace except for Epiphan Howorth.

Thomas Morse of Pencoyd was the last witness.
He had served John for about four years. He repeated the same information on the reputations of
the two persons involved and acknowledged that the
signature on a receipt of £3 by Williams was his.
He also said that he believed that the signatures
of all the others were in their handwriting.[34]

Another year and a half were still to pass before any final action was to be taken in the case.

By the end of January, John and Ben were back
in London from the Welsh circuit, and they made
sure that the depositions were delivered properly
on the 28th of that month. A letter from Ben that
spring is especially interesting because of the
insight it gives us about Ann's literary taste: "I
haue sent Downe the Spiritt of Amber if my Cosin
John Hoskyns can gett it I haue spoken to Mrs
Susan and shee sayes yor Shakespeare is at Temple-
combe."[35] Unfortunately, this copy of the First
Folio of Shakespeare is missing from the family
treasures along with the complete copy of John's
poems. Ann was well read. Besides her taste for
Shakespeare, she had interesting opinions on other
poets of the day. Perhaps Ben had told her of his
exchange with Ben Jonson. Aubrey remarks that
"'Twas an ingeniose remarque of my Lady Hoskins,
that Ben Jonson never writes of Love, or if he
does, does it not naturally,"[36] One wonders what
she thought of the poetry of John Donne.

704

It may be that it was during May 1635 that
Oswald's daughter Margery married Edmund Bagshaw,
of Basmey in Bedfordshire, for in June Ben and
John were busy trying to get that family's accounts
straightened out a bit. On 17 June 1635, Margery
went into Probate Court with them as witnesses concerning her sister Mary's will, which had not been
acted on for four years.[37] Margery was anxious
that her portion of her father's and grandfather's
estate, as well as her legal portion of Mary's
will, should be obtained for her dowry. Whatever
may have been the earlier arrangement with her
sisters, Margery was given her full share of her
father and grandfather's estate, as there are no
indications of any discrepancies in the records of
the Orphanage Court of London on the next day, 18
June 1635, when Margery and Bagshaw signed as satisfied with their payments of the legacies due
Margery.[38] John never was able during his lifetime to meet all of the obligations to his nieces
and nephews, but each time a payment became due,
he managed to get closer to his goal.

In September he was riding the Welsh circuit
again, on 14 September holding a court with Overbury at Haverfordwest[39] and on 25 September sending
the annual lists of Sheriffs and Escheators to the
Earl of Bridgewater from Cardigan. This time Overbury wrote the covering letter to the Lord President. John's shaky signature indicates that age
was definitely beginning to take its toll.[40]

But it was not affecting his wit. Aubrey recounts an event at Morehampton that Christmas, unfortunately getting the name of the person wrong:
"Sir Robert Pye, Attorney of the Court of Wardes,
was his neighbour, but there was no great goodwill
between them--Sir Robert was haughty. He happened
to dye on Christmas day: the newes being brought
to the Serjeant, said he, The devill has a Christ-
mas-pye."[41] The neighbor was, of course, Sir Walter Pye, owner of The Mynde, the great estate just
to the north of Monkton. John and his brother Dr.
John had been punning on the name of their neighbor, whom neither of them liked, for years. John

now felt that a return to his old habit of writing
epitaphs was called for, and soon the following
sestet was circulating around London:

Epitaph[42]

On Sr Walter Pye, Attorney of the Wardes,
    dying on Christmas Day, in the morning.

If Any aske, who here doth lye,
Say, tis the Deuills Christmas Pye.
Death was the Cooke, the Ouen, the Vrne,
No Ward for this, The Pye doth burne,
Yett serue it in, Diuers did wishe,
The Deuill, long since, had had this Dishe.

Perhaps the death of Sir Walter stirred John
to think once more about his own death and his
will; more likely the fact that he was now approaching the end of the allotted span of life
prescribed by Moses in Psalm 90 led him to write
still another will, this to be his last one. He
now trusted his son completely in all his affairs.
He had seen how close Ben was to all the members
of the extended family: better to trust to Ben's
good judgment than to load him with duties of following out specific bequests. As his financial
affairs were still not what he had hoped they would
be, he resigned the task of straightening them out
to his son. On the last day of January 1636, probably just after returning from the Welsh circuit,
he sat down in the presence of his godson and two
friends, John Prince and Francis Ellis, and dictated his will:

I doe giue to my sonne All my Landes rents & re-
vercions whatsoeuer and wheresoeuer to him and
his heires forever. I give him alsoe all my
leases plate housholstuffe and goodes and Chattles whatsoever and I praie God blesse him and
I thanke God for him, I give my daughter nothinge but what it shall please him to bestowe vpon her when hee is able nor anie thing then
vnles her husband & shee sufficiently release
and convey vnto him all their estate and title
in all the landes that I purchased in her name,

706

when itt shall please god that my sonne shall
haue discharged all my debtes which I hope in
god hee will doe, and I praie Godes speciall
assistance in itt then I intreate him to remember my purpose in my last will before this
towardes my Cosen John Hoskins, my Cosen Richard Hoskins children John Borne and my ser-
vantes and to doe somwhat therein In what
measure hee thinkes fitt and shalbe able for
the burthen that lyes vpon vs nowe is greate,
I doe revoke all former Willes and of this I
make my sonne Bennett my sole executo^r In witnes whereof I subscribe my name and putt my
seale the last day of January 1635[6] 43

That he put his trust in the right place is
shown by the marvelous indenture of 11 March 1642
in which Benedicta's husband, John Markey of Ross,
sells various pieces of property owned by his wife
to Ben, his cousin William, the Serjeant's godson
John, and Dr. John's son Oswald (who was then
studying at Cliffords Inn) for five shillings and
"the yearelye rent of one Red rose att the feast
of St John the Baptist if the same be lawfullye
demanded." In return for this sale, they guarantee
to pay Benedicta and her husband £40 yearly and
above that all the rest of the rents and income
from the property as long as they live.44

And by mid-year John was finally free of the
burden of the Alice Williams case. On 15 June
1636 a final hearing took place in Chancery, during which the judges reviewed all of the evidence
from 1610 to the present, including all of the depositions. Williams had tried one final trick,
but John's godson appeared as a witness to halt
that:

it also appeared that the plt depending this
suite and since publicacion in this Cause hath
given the Defs^r a Release vnder her hand and
seale wch was now read, the plt neuertheles pretending that the same was gayned from her vpon
the defs^res promise of paym^t of the residue of
the money due vpon the said bond, wch the Def

707

failed to performe as was alleaged but inasmuch
as it appeared by the testamonye of one John
Hoskins gent now deposed in Court viua voce
that the said Releas was read vnto to the plt
before the sealing and Deliuie thereof who did
seale and Deliver the same as her Act and deed,
and that noe money was then given or promised
to the plt in respect thereof....

(The court also noted that "the plt never made any
proofe att all of any of her allegacions nor examined any one witnesse in the Cause but put the
Defs^r to much Caustes expence.") The final sentence must have brought a great sigh of relief
from the aging Serjeant: "This Court therefore
sawe noe Cause att all to giue the plt any Releife
but doth ord^r that the matter of the pltes bill be
from henceforth clearelie ₹ absolutelie Dymissed
out of this Court."[45]

* * * * *

For the next year John went about his business
as usual, riding the circuit, attending the Council
of the Marches in Ludlow, the quarter sessions in
Hereford, and the courts in London. During the
summer of 1637 John was dangerously ill at home.
In a letter dated 17 September, Ben wrote to Ann
from the Middle Temple and added a postscript that
asked her to "tell my Sister my Father thanketh
her for her great care of him in his sicknes." Benedicta was obviously still in charge of the household at Morehampton. In that same note, Ben indicated that there were still problems with his
cousins' estate: "I wish my Cosins were payd, but
wishers etc." In spite of his sickness, John had
still managed to ride the circuit before returning
to London. He had not lost his sense of humor:
"My father remembers his Loue to you and is reasonable well (I thanck Godd) considering his long
iourney but exclaimes against the hardness of his
sadle whose Difficulty (as hee sayes) is beyond
the dyscription of Orator or Poet but you know
where the fault laye." The plague was abroad in
the city and seventeen had died of it that week.
Ben was not about to worry his wife too much, how-

708

ever, and limited his information to that statistic: "that is permitted to you to know and that Taverner my Lo: Chamberlaines Secretary is dead... Serieant Heath is Kings Serieant." Ben and his father were not planning to return to Herefordshire for at least six weeks.[46]

Ann's brother was visiting her at Morehampton during this period, possibly because she had been sick with whatever had struck down John. Ben had opened his letter of the 17th with the remark, "You are welcome abroad," which would indicate that she had just recovered from an illness. At about the same time he seems to have written another letter from the Middle Temple including a postscript "Tell my brother I haue receaued both his letres & remember my seruice to him & my sister & Cosins." In this letter he was more open about the plague situation in London: "Mr Serieant spoke of buying a beaver for Jack, and certainly (though I need one myself) yor boye shall not bee vnprouided... praye for mee too, for though the plague killed but 107 last weeke yet other diseases heere are from which Godd keepe vs if it bee his will...."[47]

If they did return at the end of October, it was only briefly, for on 26 November, Ben wrote to Anne from the Middle Temple again with news of friends, and on 4 December he wrote from his father's lodgings at Serjeant's Inn. He and his father had planned to leave for the west that day, "but now The tedious [?] spitefull business of my Cosins seekes to keepe our bodyes assunder whose mynds haue nearely reioyned."[48]

John seemed to sense his own impending death, no doubt partially because of the death this year of one of his oldest and closest friends, Ben Jonson. He became more and more obsessed with attempting to clear up his brother's legacy. At times the situation obviously frayed everyone's temper. In one undated letter from the period, Ben lets his feelings show through clearly: "Excuse my vncivill departure from my sister & Cosins without a kiss you know I was not in ye humo^r."[49] Unfortunately,

709

John never saw the resolution of the problem. But
Ben acted as quickly as he could after his father's
death. In 1639, the three remaining legatees were
all paid their shares of their father's will,[50]
and all the recognizances were ordered to be cancelled and delivered up to Ben.

But John and Ben made it back to Morehampton
for the Christmas holidays of 1637, the last the
family was to spend together. In spite of the
tensions over the legacies, made all the more tense
by the fact that two of the cousins had reached
the age of 21 and may have delayed their marriages
because of the lack of ready money for their dowries, the holidays were happy ones, with giving of
gifts all around. Although John and Ben had to
get back to London immediately, they did not forget the happy times together at Morehampton; and
on 27 January 1638 Ben sent back thanks to his
brother, sister and Cosins for the "new yeares
guifts they gave mee."[51] But legal business was
uppermost in his mind. John had a final case to
take care of. During Hilary Term, that began on
22 January, that case was heard in the King's Bench.

A man named Ceely had said to Hoskyns, "Thou
art forsworn in a Court of Record, and that I will
prove." When Hoskyns brought a charge of slander
against Ceely in Common Pleas, the judge had said
it was not actionable. The attorney for Hoskyns
(probably Ben), however, claimed it was the same
as if Ceely had said, "He was a perjured person."
The argument on Ceely's side was that he did not
say which Court of Record nor that it was while
giving evidence to any Jury. The Judges, Jones,
Berkeley, and Croke (and later Bramston, who was
absent at the hearing), decided for Hoskyns "that
the action well lay... and it shall be taken that
he spake these words maliciously, accusing him of
perjury."[52] John was not about to let his hard-
won legal reputation be besmirched.

Part of his duties in the winter and spring
of 1638 was to report to the Privy Council on the
sale of wood by a Mr. George Mynne in Carmarthen.

710

John now had a new associate on the Welsh circuit.
Sir Nicholas Overbury decided that he had had e-
nough at the age of 88 and retired, although he
lived to the ripe age of 94. Timothy Tourneur, who
had been a Solicitor for the Council of the Marches from June 1627, became Chief Justice of the
Carmarthen circuit, replacing Overbury on 25 July
1637.53 On 24 May, the two Justices wrote to the
Council:

According to yor Lo^{pps} lettres of the 25th of
February last wee haue inquired of the particulars therein mencioned to be complayned on concerning destruccion of woods by George Mynne
Esquier And we find that by his Ma^{tes} lettres
patente dated the 26th of July in the 12th yeare
of his Ma^{tes} raigne he hath power to fall and
convert into charcoale such woods as he then had
or should buy wthin 12 miles of Whitland Abbey
in the County of Carmarthen wth non obstante
the Statute of 7:E:6: of the Assise of fuell
and i Eliz: against converting tymber into Charcoale wth some cautions of view to be first
taken by his Ma^{tes} surveyor and certified to
the Exchequar that there is none of the tymber
fitt for shipping, and that he must first offer
by proclamacion to sell the tymber to the Countrey and to leaue standells etc. We find that
before this patent he had obtayned a bargaine
of woods in Whitsland Forrest or Whittland wood
this did consist all of tymber sufficient for
building and husbandrie after this he obtayned
a bargaine of wood in Pembrokeshire wthin 12
miles of Whitland Abbey and 12 miles of Hauer-
fordwest of one Mr Barlow in wch there is noe
considerable porcion of tymber And that Mr Barlow hath growing vnsould neere twice as many
acres of wood (as he sould to Mr Mynne) wch is
for the most parte Tymber and sufficient to
supply the wants of the countrey for many ages
as we conceaue and wch he hath vndertaken to vs
shalbe kept for that end and we find that the
countrey hath not in fower yeares last past
bought of him 8 acres of wood he haueing 200
acres reserved of wch he deliued vs a bundary.

711

Now for Whitland wood it is the stocke of tymber in those partes and the greater halfe is
cutt downe and many of the trees stocked vp by
the rootes and the rest is in falling and here
we conceaue a restraint is necessary. as also
that M[r] Barlow be restrayned to make any other
woodsale for Iron workes. And soe we humbly
take our leaue and rest

> At yo[r] lops further Commaund most readie[54]

John was supposed to deliver the letter to the
Council in May or June, but he did not do so.
Tourneur made a note at the bottom of the document
that "this certificat was in London wth M[r] Sergeant hoskins at the tyme of the date[24 May] and
all Trinity terme after and because neither partie
demanded it he brought it back into the countrey
where he dyed." One of John's servants then gave
it to Tourneur when the judge went west for the
circuit in September. Tourneur rode the circuit
alone that month, for John was not replaced by his
successor, John Platt, until the following January.[55]

Following Trinity term in London, John returned to Morehampton and went across to Hereford
in August for the Assizes as usual. Aubrey tells
a tale of what happened that is so perfect for the
end of Hoskyns' life that many have doubted its
truth. According to Aubrey, John was witty on his
own deathbed:

> Not many moneths before his death (being at
> the Assises or Sessions at Hereford) a massive
> countrey fellowe trod on his toe, which caused
> a Gangrene which was the cause of his death.
> One Mr. Dighton of Glocester, an experienced
> Chirurgian who had formerly been chirurgian in
> the Warres in Ireland, was sent for to cure him;
> but his Skill and care could not save him. His
> Toes were first cutt-off. The Minister of his
> Parish had a clubbe-foote or feete (I think his
> name was Sir Hugh). Said he, Sir Hugh (after
> his toes were cutt off) I must be acquainted
> with your shoemaker.[56]

But Aubrey was not making up the story. His
friendship with John's son and grandson had provided him with intimate details of the Serjeant's
life as we have noted before. We have external
and contemporary verification of the truth of
John's witty end.

On 18 August 1638, Sir Marmaduke Lloyd, who
had been bound with John when he entered the Middle Temple in 1604 and had risen to the position
of Judge on the Glamorgan, Brecon, and Radnor circuit in Wales, wrote to the Earl of Bridgewater
with the usual list of Sheriffs required each year,
and then sent the latest news:

> This place at this tyme affoords nothing woorthy
> of yor LoP^s intelligence: only I hearde this
> day, that m^r Serieant Hoskins lyes very sicke
> (in extremis) & I doubt yor next newes wilbe,
> that (diem clausit extremum) he had a sore in
> his legge, wch fell into his foote, & by the
> ignorance of an vnskillfull Chirurgian, his
> toes haue gangrened, & 4 of them haue beene
> cleane cutt off; & it seemes all the deade part,
> not quite cutt off: so that his foote gangrenes
> further, & his foote, or legge must be cutt off:
> yet in this extremity, he is merry, & will dye
> iestinge, as Sr Tho: Moore did: but not withe
> the losse of a heade, but withe the losse of a
> legge: There came one to see him, who had a
> stumpe foote, & had it cutt off: & the Serieant
> askt him who was his shooemaker, the man de-
> maunded of him, why he askt that question. Be-
> cause saithe he, I feare I shall haue occasion
> to vse yor Last, to make a payre of bootes by,
> for my use: when I haue lost my foote: (mors
> illi ludus, mors illi lucrum)[57]

John would have been delighted with the comparison with the author of Utopia. His sense of
humor had carried him and his family through the
dark days of his imprisonment in the Tower, and
now it lightened the atmosphere in Morehampton,
as his family gathered around to be with him at
his death. The story is all the more poignant be-

713

cause of the nature of his death. Gangrene in itself is a very painful cause of death; an operation on his foot in the mid-seventeenth century
would have been excruciating. But, as Lloyd observes in Latin, "to the person for whom death is
a game, it is also a gain"--in St. Paul's meaning,
"For me to live is Christ and to die is gain."

On 27 August, the game ended at the age of 73.
John had played it well, both for himself and his
family. His position as a leader of the wits of
his day had been maintained to the end; his reputation as a latinist and prose stylist had remained
unchallenged; he had risen to the height of his
profession in spite of political setbacks; he had
kept the admiration of his friends in Parliament
for his bravery; and he had brought together a
large family of brothers, sisters, and cousins who
obviously loved and respected each other. They
were all financially safeguarded for the future although it would take his son to bring the family's
affairs together finally. He was buried immediately in Dore Abbey, just two miles down the road from
Morehampton in the Golden Valley, and it was only
fitting that his own poem Vndecies senos should be
the epitaph on his tomb in the chancel of the
great Cistercian abbey nestled among the hills.
Later the tomb was moved to the first chapel on
the right when his daughter-in-law joined him.
There is a long latin poem also carved on the tomb,
raised by the "two Bens, Bene and Dicta." It cele-
brates his three lives of service, to the courts,
to poetry, and to the state, but the unknown poet
could not equal John's own quiet prayer: "To Christ,
for Payment with his Blood, in my name, I sue."
Aubrey quotes another epitaph on the Serjeant by
Thomas Bonham of Essex, in which John's classical
background is praised with references to Solomon,
David, Amphion, Plato, Solon, Astraea, and Thalia.[58]
But John's own quiet wish that his son take care
of his debts rings more true for the old man.

John Hoskyns has not survived the centuries
as his friend John Donne has, nor is it likely
that the full collection of his poems that has

been lost would alter the situation radically.
But, to paraphrase Robert Frost about his own future reputation, John lodged some pebbles that
would be hard to get rid of. If a widespread appreciation of Latin poetry should ever return,
Hoskyns will receive his proper appreciation. And
no study of the development of English prose style
is possible without reference to his work. But
perhaps even more important than either of those
accomplishments, he stands as one of the best representatives of his age, involved in all aspects
of Elizabethan, Jacobean, and Caroline society. To
follow his life is to follow the main drift of
English history as it moved from the glories of
Elizabeth's reign to the onset of the revolution.
Unfortunately his country shared little of his wit
and tolerance as it headed inexorably into civil
strife. But his son and grandson carried on their
predecessor's activities, points of view, and intellectual vigor. He would have been proud of
Ben when, in 1676, he was created a Baronet, but
he would have been even more proud when, in 1682,
Sir John Hoskyns, young "Jack" to his admiring
grandfather, was elected the second president of
the Royal Society, following Sir Christopher Wren
to that position. His praise of Copernicus, painted on the walls of Morehampton, had become em-
bodied in his own descendant. Had he lived to see
that day, he would have written an appropriate
witty latin epigraph to celebrate the occasion.

Footnotes for Chapter XVIII

1. N.L.W. Curt Maur 731; 580.
2. Chancery Cases, C2 Charles I, W28/23, Sheet 2.
3. Ibid., Sheet 3.
4. Repertory Book 47, 1632-1633, ff. 46v-47v.
5. Letter Book GG, 1617-1620, f. 201.
6. Orphans Recognizances 2, 1590 to 1633, ff. 200, 241, 359.
7. Orphans Recognizances 5, 1630-1636, ff. 91-91v; Rep. Book 47, f. 55; Orph. Recog. 2, f. 411.
8. Orph. Recog. 5, ff. 91v-92v; Rep. Book 47, ff. 55v; Orph. Recog. 2, f. 411.
9. Winchester Archives 19095 d, e.
10. 19095 c; 19095 a, b; 19096 a, b; 19097, 19098 a.
11. 19098 b, c.
12. Dalley held courts 17 Dec. 1635, 5 Jan, 26 Jan, 8 Apr., 17 June, 18 July, 15 Dec. 1636, and 16 Feb. 1637; 19098 d, 19099 a-k, 19100 a-e, 19101 a-b.
13. Chancery H 30/37.
14. Harewood MSS. Burke's Peerage says that Benedict (whom it calls Bennet) married the daughter of Sir Henry Bingley in 1634. The entry is wrong on both the year (as evidenced from the following letter) and the father's name, as indicated by the inscription on Benedict's tomb (John H. Matthews, Collections...., Hereford, 1912, p. 144; see also Robinson, Mansions, p. 133.)
15. Harewood MSS.
16. Harewood MSS.
17. N.L.W., 12,358D, The Records of the Corporate Borough of Carmarthen... Elizabeth... George II, pp. 55-56.
18. Ellesmere 9538.
19. Harewood MSS.
20. Harewood MSS.
21. Harewood MSS.
22. Harewood MSS.
23. C2 Charles I, W28/23, Sheet 1.
24. Harewood MSS.
25. Harewood MSS.
26. Harewood MSS. 13 April 1634.
27. Harewood MSS. "ye Kalends of Maye."

28. Chancery Decrees & Orders 1634 B, f. 504v.
29. Chancery H30/37.
30. There were three reasons for judgment not appearing in Chancery Court Orders: 1. the Plaintiff decided to take it no further; 2. the case was settled out of court; 3. a Plea was entered for the purpose of getting depositions on the record.
31. Harewood MSS.
32. Harewood MSS.
33. C21/W18/18, Sheet 1.
34. Ibid., Sheet 2.
35. Harewood MSS.; 25 April 1635.
36. Aubrey, p. 178.
37. 71 Sadler.
38. Letter Book GG, f. 201. Payment entries are marked in Orph. Recog. 2, ff. 200, 241, 359; Rep. Book 49 notes that Margery also received her portion of the plate due her, ff. 241-42.
39. N.L.W., Poyston 91.
40. Ellesmere Papers, EL 7198. It was received in Ludlow 28 September.
41. Aubrey, p. 171.
42. Add. MSS. 23,229, f. 50. As Osborn indicates, both this version and that in Add. MSS. 25,303, f. 151, are anonymous. But their location in the mss. and Aubrey's anecdote leave no reason to question the attribution; in Osborn, p. 214.
43. 127 Lee; in Osborn, pp. 241-42.
44. Harewood MSS.
45. Chancery Decrees & Orders 1636 B, C.33/172, f. 473v.
46. Harewood MSS.
47. Harewood MSS.
48. Harewood MSS.
49. Harewood MSS.
50. On 14 February Katherine signed the Orphanage accounts with her husband Albyn Roe of London (Letter Book GG, 1617-1620, f. 201; Repertory Book 53, 1638-1639, ff. 108-9); on 17 October Thomasina signed with her husband Edward Thomas of Cardiff (Letter Book GG, f. 201; Rep Book 53, ff. 320v-321); and on 3 December Frances signed, having reached the age of 21 (Letter Book GG, f. 201; Rep. Book 54, 1639-

1640, ff. 29v-30v.)
51. Harewood MSS.
52. English Reports, 79, Sir George Croke, p. 1039.
53. W. R. Williams, The History of the Great Sessions in Wales 1542-1830 (Brecknock, 1899), pp. 12, 168.
54. S.P.D. Charles I, Vol. 390, #166, f. 235.
55. Williams, p. 168.
56. Aubrey, p. 171.
57. MS letter in the Bridgewater collection in the County Record Office, Shirehall, Shrewsbury, sent to me by Mary C. Hill, County Archivist.
58. Aubrey (Clark ed.), p. 423.

A

Abberley, Thomas, 690,698–99
Abraham (and Lot), 259
Achilles, 50, 60
Acland, Sir John, 288, 292, 325
Aesop, 159
Aleppo, 387
Alford, Edward, 246, 450, 556, 569, 665
Alford, John, 665
Allen, Cardinal, 71
Alleyn, Edward, 70
Amphion, 121
Anna Perenna, 65–6
Andrewes, Lancelot, 46
Anne, Queen, 540–41
Apollo, 35, 183
Apology, The (House of Commons) 200, 355, 358
Appeltree, Thomas, 27
Apsley, Elizabeth, 613–615
Areopagus (Club), 56
Aristarchus, 2, 472
Aristotle, 50, 57–8, 98, 147, 161
Arkeston, Manor of 561–63, 571
Arminianism (James Arminius or Harmensen), 642, 653–54
Arthur, King, 40
Arundel, Count, 302, 475
Ascham, Roger, 144
Ashley, Francis, 104, 428, 498
Asmere, 386–87, 389
Aston, Sir Roger, 239–40, 290 380
Athena (Minerva), 58, 62, 183
Athowe, Serjeant, 620–21, 626
Atkins, Mr. 595
Aubrey, John, 1, 4–6, 11–13, 17–20. 23–5, 32–3, 37, 41–43, 49–50, 77, 81, 83, 87, 105, 119, 171, 173–74, 215–

Aubrey, cont., 216, 220, 284, 293, 300–1, 313, 328, 393, 405, 453, 462, 472, 492, 505 521, 538, 575–78, 605–6, 629 632–33, 671, 673, 676, 684, 704, 712–14, 717–18
Aubrey, Sir Samuel, 635–36
Austin, William & Anne, 496
Ayliffe, John, 85

B

Bacon, Edmund, 458–60, 462
Bacon, Francis, 3, 13, 27, 70–71, 138, 142–43, 164, 166, 190, 193, 196, 199, 207, 226 227, 238–40, 245–46, 253, 292, 311, 324, 348–49, 351, 362–63, 423, 427–28, 430, 434–37, 439, 443, 503, 532, 537, 539, 546, 557–59, 562, 569
Bacon, Nathaniel, 198, 209,354
Bacon, Nicholas, 13, 27
Bacon, Roger, 88
Badby, Mr., 678, 685
Bagshaw, Edmund 705
Bailey, Henry, 701, 703
Bainham, John 544
Baker, Richard, 8
Baker, Sir Richard, 46, 106, 382, 631
Baker, William, 582
Balch, Elizabeth, 387
Bald, R.C., 189, 212, 390, 393 422, 474, 492
Bancroft, Richard (Canterbury) 232, 244, 354, 390
Banwell, 169, 405, 424
Barlow, Mr., 711
Barnes, Thomas & Mary, 505–7
Baroque, 117, 138–40, 337

Barrett, Devereux, 637
Barrow, Isaac, 17
Bartesham, 479
Baskervilles, 302
Baskerville, James, 303
Baskerville, Thomas, 303
Bastard, Thomas, 31, 46, 58,
   109, 112, 311, 382, 511, 669
Bate, John, 379, 440
Bath, 87, 531, 533
Baucis & Philemon, 299
Baugh, Capt., 547-58
Beaumont, Francis, 18, 115,
   392, 420
Beaumont, Henry, 209
Beeston, Hugh, 209, 290, 320
Benet, Robert, 179, 218, 376,
   406, 409, 424, 479, 505, 522,
   582
Bennett, John, 209, 291, 321
Bentley, G. E., 375, 421
Berkeley, Maurice, 196, 268,
   326, 367, 427, 437, 710
Bernithen Court, 127, 401, 406,
   407, 423, 503, 513, 518-19,
   523, 532-33, 535-37, 554, 570,
   595, 612, 619, 651, 661, 665,
   679
Berry, Richard 326
Best, Charles, 122-23, 136,
   568, 632
Best, John, 123
Best, Dr. John, 411, 607-12,
   617-22
Best, Richard, 568
Bevan, Mr., 406
Bilson, Thomas, 159, 166
Bing, Robert, 391
Bingley, Sir John, 546-49, 558,
   691, 716
Blount, Thomas, 19, 138, 189,
   684
Bodenham, Roger & wife, 302,
   635-36
Bodin, Jean, 191

Bolles, George, 531
Bond, John, 390-91
Bond, Thomas, 292, 326
Boorne, Richard, 183
Botticelli, 63
Boughton Allow, 104
Bourne, Sir Anthony, 508, 568,
Bourne, Elizabeth (Hoskyns),
   169-70, 296, 406, 424, 486,
   518, 525, 528, 531, 534, 543,
   615-18, 636-38, 651, 657-68,
   676-78
Bourne, Frances (Hoskyns), 170,
   296, 406, 424, 486, 519,
   531-33, 543, 664
Bourne, Francis, 87, 96, 98,
   104-5, 167-70, 187, 418,
   424, 493, 613, 624
Bourne, John Robert, 169-70,
   296, 406, 408, 417-18, 424,
   486, 498-99, 504, 521, 534,
   543, 552, 554, 556, 562-64,
   568, 581, 587, 593, 622-25,
   631, 633
Bourne, Johnny, 663, 665, 679,
   707
Bourne, Margaret (Kempe), 554,
   616, 638, 663-65
Bourne, Walter, 169-70
Bowes, Jerome, 289, 316
Bowyer, Robert, 133, 136, 209,
   224, 234, 246, 253-54, 256,
   276-80, 285, 336
Bradshaw, Dr., 334, 376
Bramston, Sir John, 587, 589-
   90, 621, 626, 710
Branthwaite, Robert, 494, 496
Breinton, 404, 407, 423
Brereton, Mr., 255
Breton, William, 20, 513
Briareus, 143
Bridges, Sir Giles, 635-36
Bridwell Prison, 540, 697, 702
Bristol, 88, 101, 169, 187
Bromley, Sir Thomas, 508, 568

720

Bromwich, Richard, 177
Brooke, Christopher, 95, 180–
81, 198, 236, 262, 255, 271,
284–85, 289, 315, 318, 354,
382, 386–87, 390–91, 395,
436–38, 441, 445, 451, 465,
539, 546, 548, 669, 672
Brooke, Giles, 291, 322, 427,
464
Broughton, Edward, 605–12,
617–22
Broughton, Eleanor, 606
Broughton, Elizabeth, 605–6,
697
Brown, Alexander, 380
Brown, Frederick, 187
Brown, William, 633
Browne, Edmund, 19, 514
Browne, George, 19
Browne, Thomas, 14–5, 19–20,
513
Bruce, John, 425, 464
Brugge, Thomas, 407
Buckingham, Duke of, 48, 209,
515–17, 528, 541–42, 557–58,
562, 604, 640, 650–51
Buckley, Richard, 291, 322
Buckwell, 169
Budge, John 298
Bulstrode, Henry, 432
Burdett, William, 105
Burrell, Robert, 472
Byton, 127

C

Cadiz, 107
Caesar, 476, 481, 582
Caesar, Sir Julius, 502–3, 568
Calvert, Samuel, 394, 399
Calvin, Jean, 653
Cambridge Univ., 207, 210, 253–
54, 366–67
Camden, William, 3, 23–5, 48,
50–3, 56–7, 77–9, 84–5, 107–8

Camden, William, cont., 133,
217, 253,345, 561, 573
Camerata, 56
Campion, Thomas, 382
Candish, Mrs. 635, 681
Canon Pyon, 605–6
Cardigan, 562. 565, 578, 581,
705
Carew, Sir George, 202, 209,
322, 345, 353, 490
Carey, Sir Robert, 302
Carleton, 322, 326, 399, 458,
460, 462, 467, 484, 490,
514–15. 548. 587
Carmarthen, 562, 565, 578–81,
618, 710–12
Carr, Robert (Rochester and
Somerset), 373–74, 399, 498,
500, 502–4, 509, 515, 546
Carwardine, John, 599, 601
Catesby, Robert, 221, 223
Cato, 372
Cecil, Sir Edward, 368
Cecil, Sir Robert, 34, 190
Cecil, William (Burghley), 53–
54, 64–71, 91, 319
Ceely, Mr., 710
Chaloner, Thomas, 290, 320
Chamberlain, John, 322, 393,
399, 423, 458, 462, 467, 477,
484, 490, 493–94, 514–15,
548, 569, 587, 590, 630–31
Chambers, E.K., 425
Chapman, John, 55, 101, 105,
117, 130, 167–68, 413, 425
Character, The, 500
Charles I, King, 137, 277, 301,
302, 396, 398, 461, 511–12,
542, 559, 593–94, 604, 609,
627, 639ff., 653ff., 670
Charles II, King, 670
Charles of Anjou, 453
Chaucer, Geoffrey, 288, 319
Chauncey, Henry, 92
Chepstow, 88

Chitty, Herbert, 42
Churchill (Somerset), 169,187, 267, 405, 424
Churchman, Osias, 530, 549,668, 678, 689-90
Chute, George, 302
Chute, Walter, 452, 454, 456-58, 476-78
Cicero, 50, 140, 143, 147-48, 307
Clark, Andrew, 17-20, 81, 83, 86, 189, 220, 327, 393, 395, 492, 629, 673, 718
Clarke, James, 175, 405, 478, 537
Clarke, John, 175, 368, 402-5, 535, 537, 563, 565, 578, 584, 704
Clarke, 177, 368
Clement, Dr., 406, 410, 425
Clement IV (Pope), 453
Clink, Liberty of, 187
Cockes, John, 622, 624-26,657
Cockes, Richard, 585-86
Cockes, Thomas, 101, 552, 622
Coke, Sir Edward, 432, 485, 489, 498, 501-3, 548, 643-6, 648, 696
Coke, John, 593-94
Colepepper, Dr., 125, 405
Colphabius, Radulpho, 393-94
Columbus, Christopher, 145
Comfield, Lady, 635-36
Committee of the Whole, 224, 257, 263-64, 338, 435, 450, 642
Composition, 195-97, 228-29, 233, 243-45, 344, 351-53, 355-56, 365, 369-70, 431
Compton, William, Lord (Northampton), 521, 523, 562, 565, 594-95
Coningsby, Thomas, 302-3, 311, 534-35
Connock, Richard, 395, 398,421

Constantinople, 389
Conway, Edward, 568, 627
Cope, Anthony, 243, 291, 323
Cope, Walter, 289, 317, 323, 326, 442-43
Copley, William, 105, 132, 179, 257, 424
Copernicus, 88, 474-75, 576, 578, 583, 715
Corbet, Richard, 3, 132
Coriolanus, 155
Cornwall, Thomas & wife, 303, 636
Cornwallis, Sir Charles, 202, 209, 429, 432, 456, 459-63, 468, 475-77, 489-90, 494
Coryat, Thomas, 381ff., 395-7, 420-22, 487, 504, 669
Cotton, George, 331
Cotton, Robert, 217-18, 285, 290, 320, 353, 377, 390-91, 447, 465
Coucher, John, 505, 507-8
Counter-Renaissance, 140
Court Terms, 93
Coventry, Sir Thomas, 617-19, 645-46, 672, 687
Cowell, Dr. John, 344-50, 356, 378
Cox, J. Stevens, 131
Cradock, Elizabeth, 675
Craford, Mr. 339
Cranfield, Lionel, 3, 382,395, 397-98, 421, 422, 465, 516-7, 528, 537-39, 541-42, 553, 562-63, 569, 581, 604-5, 669
Crewe, Randolph, 427, 430, 436 450, 452
Crewe, Thomas, 438, 441, 444, 458, 588
Croft, Herbert, 219, 248-50, 272, 341, 351, 368
Croke, Sir George, 710, 718
Croll, Morris, 138-40, 164-65
Crompton, Dr. Thomas, 291,321

Comwell, Sir Oliver, 262, 280, 431
Crook, Sir John, 283, 288, 315, 323
Crooke, Sir George, 588
Culpepper, Thomas and John, 424
Cupid, 135
Curle, Thomas, 179

D

Dalley, James 496-97, 652-53, 690, 716
Daniel, Samuel, 158
Dannett, Thomas, 291, 322
Dashfield, John, 106
Davenport, Sjt., 588
Davies, Godfrey, 190, 212, 379-80, 681-83
Davies, John, 18, 31, 47, 90, 94, 96-100, 105, 112, 132, 156, 311, 332, 573, 669
Davies, John, of Hereford, 47-48, 123, 311, 382
Davies, Roger, 176-77
Davis, Hugh, 671
Day, Angel, 165
Dedicot, Arthur, 508
Delehay, John, 401, 405-7, 423, 554
Delehay, Morgan, 406
Delehay, Walter, 407, 423
Denman, Mr., 170
Denton, Thomas, 339
Devereux, Penelope, 322
Dick, Oliver, 174, 188, 328, 492, 629
Didley, 217, 269, 405-7, 423-424, 525, 571, 595-604, 660, 679
Digges, Dudley, 382, 428, 431, 438-39, 444
Dighton, Mr., 712
Dingley, Thomas, 20

Disraeli, Benjamin, 492
Divine Right, 191, 199, 337, 349
Dodderidge, John, 484-85, 627
Donne, John, 3, 5, 7, 30-32, 46, 48-50, 55, 58-51, 70-72, 86, 92, 95, 100, 102-3, 107, 112-2, 115, 117-19, 125,132, 137, 144, 165-66, 180-81, 187, 196, 287, 311-12, 317-318, 322, 324, 326-28, 368, 370, 381-82, 387, 390-93, 395, 398, 399, 413, 427-28, 441, 452, 474-75, 491, 501, 592-93, 639, 669, 672, 681, 704, 714
Donne, John (Hereff.), 543, 570, 628
Donne, Henry, 46
Dore Abbey, 676, 714
Dore, River, 561, 575
Dorset, Richard, Earl of, 605
Dover Court, 169, 187, 405, 407, 423-24
Drake, Sir Francis, 72, 135, 144-45
Drayton, Michael, 382, 669
Drummond, William, 23-24
Drury, Sir Robert, 292, 324, 368
Drury, Elizabeth, 59, 324
Dudley, Robert (Leicester), 73-4
Dugdale, William, 92, 131,136, 572, 588-89, 630-31
Duncomb, John, 20, 290, 319, 572, 630
Dunne, Dr. Daniel, 253, 290, 319
Dyer, Edward, 234, 276-77
Dynely, John, 613
Dyott, Anthony 326

E

Eaton, Thomas, 534

Egerton, John (Bridgewater), 3, 285, 673, 692, 700-1, 705, 713; children, 700

Egerton, Thomas, Lord Chanc., 4, 124-25, 177-78, 180, 256, 311, 326, 342, 350, 357,365, 367, 390, 397, 399, 407,435, 489, 498-99, 502-3, 512-13, 515, 518, 569

Egerton, Sir Thomas, 317, 487

Eliot, John, 649-50

Elizabeth, Queen, 27, 64,67-73 78-9, 112, 132, 144, 155, 181-85, 190-91, 210, 234, 284, 317, 352, 472, 577, 715

Elizabeth, Princess, 182,412-4 434-35, 437, 453, 613-15,633

Essex, Earl of, 3, 71-2, 98, 107, 137, 144, 176, 182, 219 419, 429

Eton, 208

Eure, Lord, 400-1, 423

Evet, Thomas, 507-8

F

Fates, 62-3, 117, 184

Fawcet, James, 690

Fawkes, Guy (John Johnson), 221-23

Fawley Court, 97, 676

Felton, John, 650-51

Fettiplace, Thomas, 132, 179, 257, 424

Fielding, Henry, 571

Finch, Francis, 674

Finch, Heneage, 285, 438, 503, 546, 548, 588, 626, 640, 673-75

Finch, John, 640, 656, 674

Finch, Moyle, 673-74

Fiore, P.A., 189

Fleissner, Kenneth, 36, 85

Fleming, Baron, 351

Fleminge, Mr., 70

Fletcher, Giles, 106

Fletcher, John, 106, 420

Fletcher, Phineas, 106

Fletcher, Richard, 18, 47, 106-7, 132

Fogassa, Reniger, 121, 123

Ford, Mr., 484-85

Ford, William, 389, 533, 553

Fortescue, John, 326

Foss, Edward, 569, 589, 631

France, 215, 221, 242, 360, 454

Freeman, John, 328

Freere, James, 405

Freke, Thomas, 326

Frobisher, Martin, 27, 72

Frost, Robert, 199, 715

Fuller, Nicholas, 196, 209, 225-26, 231, 233-37, 244, 249, 252-53, 259, 263, 265, 271, 288, 316, 340-41, 361, 372, 375, 431-34, 436-38, 441

Fuller, Thomas, 299-300, 307, 313, 328, 392

G

Gager, William, 89, 131

da Gama, Vasco, 144-45

Gardiner, Samuel, 369, 378-80, 682

Gargrave, Richard, 292, 324

Garnet, Henry, 224

Garnons, James, 595-98, 600

Garrard, George, 390-91

Garrick, David, 175

Gawdy, Phillip, 292, 324

Gethyn, Thomas, 8

Gifford, John, Dr., 30, 46,58, 98, 382, 526, 528, 557,564-65, 669

Giles, Edward, 458

Glanvile, Mr., 647

Glastonbury, 87-88

724

Glenham, Charles, 475
Globe Theater, 414–15
Godwin, Francis, 582–85
Golden Valley, 101, 561, 575, 714
Good, John, 291, 323
Goodrich, 401, 423, 494
Goodwin, Sir Francis, 200–2, 438
Goodyer, Henry, 95, 166, 202, 285, 289, 317–18, 382, 395, 421–22, 427, 669
Gosse, Edmund, 464
Graces, 68
Grant, Mr., 360
Gray's Inn, 190
Great Rissington, 636–37
Greene, Thomas, 551, 557,575
Greene, Widow, 598, 603
Greenwich, 68
Gresham, Thomas, 53–4
Greville, Edward, 209, 288, 316
Greville, Fulke, 56, 95
Grey, Catherine, 473, 489
Grierson, Herbert, 118, 132, 134
Griffith, John, 288
Griffith, Dr., 416
Grosart, Alexander, 54, 57, 83
Grymes, Thomas & Margaret, 496–97
Guicciardini, 582
Guilpin, Edward, 102–3
Gunpowder Plot, 221ff., 245, 439, 471
Gwillim, Thomas, 334, 376, 470

H

Hacket, John, 423, 591, 630
Hackwell, William, 7, 20,207

Hackwell, cont.,285, 386,390–91, 430–31, 437–38, 441,446–47, 449, 465, 643
Hall, Joseph, 47
Hamlet, 170, 182
Hampton Court, Hereff., 534–36
Hancock, Henry, 74
Harbyn, Will, 528, 537, 562, 570
Hardy, Harry, 289, 319
Hare, Mr., 195, 241
Hare, John, 292, 324
Harford, John, 508
Hariot, Thomas, 315, 474
Harley, Sir Robert, 37, 101, 137–38, 303, 372, 671
Harley, Thomas, 101, 137
Harmer, John, 39, 125, 127,412
Harrington, John, 3, 117, 285, 382, 669
Hart Hall, 46
Hastings, Francis, 263, 358
Hatton, Christopher, 73–4, 77–82, 156, 164
Haughton, Richard, 289, 317
Haverford West, 562, 578, 585, 612, 693, 705
Hayman, Robert, 294
Heald, The, 554, 679
Heath, John, 216, 307, 312–14, 328
Heliogabalus, 121
Helwys, Gervase, 458, 477, 484, 489–90, 499–502, 504
Henry, Prince,307, 350, 359, 382, 389, 394, 396, 398, 413, 429
Henshaw, Thomas, 492, 693
Heraclitus, 122
Herbert, Edward (Cherbury), 58, 368, 377, 413
Herbert, George, 58, 65, 209, 213
Herbert, Henry (Pembroke), 58,

Herbert, Henry, cont., 109,301
Herbert, William (Pembroke),
   301, 310, 489
Herbert, Sir William, 445
Hercules, 143, 384
Hereford Cathedral, 4, 37,
   57, 179, 189, 407, 409, 411–
   12, 415, 493, 582, 584, 593–
   94, 605–11, 618–22, 632
Hereford, City of, 99, 174–79,
   188, 208, 218–19, 272, 298ff.
   528, 532, 541, 553–55, 582–
   83, 594, 704
Herford, C.H. & Simpson, P.,
   23=4, 41, 420
Herring, Henry, 584–585
Heyward, Sir John, 619
Heywood, John, 46, 312
Hicks, Michael, 326
Hill, Mary C., 718
Hill, Nicholas, 3, 475
Hitcham, Robert, 285–86, 289,
   317–18
Hitchcock, Mr., 461
Hitchcock, Thomas, 506–7
Hobart, Sir Henry, 349, 355,
   431
Hobbes, Thomas, 192
Hoby, Edward, 209, 211, 235,
   253, 290, 319, 321, 377,446,
   450–51
Hoby, Thomas, 209
Holcroft, Thomas, 289, 317
Holland, Hugh, 48, 382, 387,
   390–91, 395, 421, 539, 669,
   672
Hollingworth, Daniel, 549, 669
Hollis, John, 292, 325, 428,
   493, 502
Homer, 2, 307
Hopwood, Charles, 131–36, 190,
   220, 280, 424–25, 567–72,
   629–34
Hornyold-Strickland, Henry,
   188, 328, 568, 683

Hornyold-Strickland, Thomas,
   188, 296
Horseman, Thomas, 326
Horsey, Jerome, 289, 316
Hoskyns, Alice, 8–11
Hoskyns, Ann (Bingley), 492,
   691ff., 716
Hoskyns, Anne (Baker), 8–11
Hoskyns, Benedict (Bennet),1,
   2, 5, 24, 137, 174, 179,295–
   97, 376, 406, 469, 480–81,
   486, 492–93, 518–21, 529,
   531, 534, 537, 543–44, 552,
   554, 563, 565, 570, 586,616,
   622, 624–25, 628, 635, 637–
   38, 651–52, 657, 661–62,
   677–80, 687ff.
Hoskyns, Sir Benedict, 20, 489
Hoskyns, Benedict (Moyle), 96,
   105, 131, 169–75, 187, 296,
   333–34, 400–411, 423–24,469–
   71, 477–88, 498–99, 501–4,
   517–28, 531–37, 542–44, 549,
   555–56, 559–63, 581, 593,595,
   613, 623–24, 674, 691, 706–7
Hoskyns, Benedicta, 469, 479–
   80, 486, 518, 528, 531, 534,
   543–44, 570, 637, 667, 676,
   678, 694, 708, 714
Hoskyns, Charles, 12, 69, 124,
   216–17, 269–70, 313, 370,
   493, 531
Hoskyns, Elizabeth, 8–11, 18
Hoskyns, Isabel (Riseley),636–
   38, 651, 658, 667–68, 679–80,
   694–95, 697–99
Hoskyns, Johane, 8–11, 18
Hoskyns, John (1510), 6
Hoskyns, John (1522), 6
Hoskyns, John (grandfather),
   7–11, 18
Hoskyns, John (uncle), 7–11,
   18–20, 99
Hoskyns, John (father), 7–11,
   13–16, 74–5, 257, 266, 269–

726

Hoskyns, John (father) cont., 271, 275

Hoskyns, John, birth, 5; crest 13, 20; Westminster 23-8; Winchester 28-40; New College 45ff.; duel 49; Terrae filius 81-2; Middle Temple 87ff.; Deputy Steward 176-79, 215, 249, 257, 296, 309; Mayor 509-11; imprisonment 469ff.; Commissioner of Neville 523-25; Serjeant 587ff.; Judge 560-62, 565; portrait 534; wills 542, 629, 677,706; poems 32,34, 51-7, 58, 64, 77, 79, 89, 106-10, 113-17, 182, 185, 283, 294, 298, 382, 393, 399, 469, 475-76, 479, 482, 490, 538-39, 558, 564, 576-77, 613-14, 623-24, 670-676, 706; Fustian speech 119; Directions 1, 34, 41, 49-50, 56-7, 77, 80, 90-2, 99-101, 119-20, 137ff., 171, 173,180, 191-92, 207-8, 254, 303, 307, 417, 558; other writings 87, 164, 463, 521, 671

Hoskyns, Dr. John, 8-12, 45, 124-27, 170, 182, 217, 269, 296, 313, 333, 408-12, 419, 425, 469, 477, 479, 486-88, 493, 495, 503-9, 513, 519, 521-22, 529-33, 543-44, 549, 551-52, 577, 585, 593, 628, 657, 660, 664-65, 668, 672-73, 677; children: Oswald, 707, Charles, 519

Hoskyns, John (painter) 534

Hoskyns, Sir John, 301, 671, 692, 700, 709, 715

Hoskyns, Margaret, 8-11

Hoskyns, Oswald, 12, 24, 75,99, 103, 167, 170, 269-70, 278, 370, 397, 477, 484, 493,495, 502, 529-33, 536, 540, 542, 544, 549-50, 552, 554, 585, 615, 619, 628, 657, 669,677; wife Elizabeth 529-30, 535, 544, 550, 675, 677; children, Elinor, 529, 689; Elizabeth, 529, 676, 689; Frances, 529-30, 550, 571, 585, 690, 717; Katherine, 529, 690, 717; Magdalen, 529,661, 668-69, 676, 678, 680, 689; Margaret, 529, 690, 705; Mary, 529, 661, 665-69, 675-77, 680, 705; Thomasina,529-30, 550, 585, 690, 717; William, 529-31, 545, 549, 615-17, 635, 638, 657-58, 660, 663, 665-69, 676-80, 707

Hoskyns, Phillip, 12, 217,269-70, 376, 401, 423, 493, 525, 543, 676, 680, 700; son John, 543, 676, 679, 700, 704, 706, 707-8; wife Anne, 676

Hoskyns, Richard, 407, 423-24, 596, 616-18, 707; wife Ann, 617-18

Hoskyns, Thomas (1522), 6, 20

Hoskyns, Thomas, 12, 217, 269-70, 401, 493, 495, 503-4, 513-14, 518-19, 522-23, 525-26, 528, 532, 535, 543, 628, 680

Hoskyns, Thomas (of Shobden), 8, 11, 407, 690, 698-99

Hoskyns, William, 12, 493

Hoskyns, William (uncle), 8-11

Howard, Frances, 399, 498, 500-1

Howard, Sir George, 339

Howard, Lord Thomas, 72, 107, 125-26

Howarth, Epiphan, 635, 701, 703-4

Howe, John, 595

Howes, Edmund, 511, 592, 594,

Howes, Edmund, cont., 653
Hudson, Hoyt, 1, 135, 137,164-
  66
Hughes, Mr. 474
Hughes, John, 659
Hungerford, Edward, 288, 316
Hurdman, George, 175
Hurdman, Walter, 177, 192, 218
Hyde, Lawrence, 193-94, 289,
  318-19, 444
Hyde, Nicholas, 427, 623
Hynde, Thomas, 523
Hyrne, Mrs., 683-84

I

Ilchester, 87ff., 96
Iliad, 62
Ingraham, Arthur, 285, 395,398
Irving, Washington, 25-6, 41
Isocrates, 50, 160

J

Jacob, Lady, 110-11, 134
James I, King, 41, 57, 69,176-
  77, 182, 184-86, 189-90,
  191ff., 215, 218-19, 221ff.,
  287, 291-2, 297ff., 314,325,
  331ff., 386, 396, 409, 412-
  14, 419, 421-22, 427ff.,
  469-74, 477-84, 488-91, 495,
  498-504, 509-12, 515-17,521,
  523-24, 528, 537-38, 542,
  546-48, 554-59, 563, 565,
  583, 589, 594, 608-9
James, John, 410
James, Richard, 290, 321, 341
James, Thomas, 415
Jeffreys, William, 499, 537,
  567
Jegon, Bishop, 70-71
Jenkins, Henry, 193-94, 288,
  316
Jerusalem, 381

Jesuits, 224, 242, 332, 655-
  656
Jewers, Arthur, 187
Johnson, Robert, 247, 252,
  290-91, 321
Johnson, Samuel, 51, 144
Johnson, William, 392
Jones, Christopher, 101, 257,
  504, 520, 569, 701-2
Jones, Inigo, 284, 311, 315,
  382, 387-88, 390-91, 395,
  414, 421, 669
Jones, Margaret, 6
Jones, Margery, 6, 270-71,
  480-82, 493, 519, 542-43
Jones, Rowland, 658-660
Jones, Thomas, 6-7, 74-6
Jones, Thomas, J.P., 407, 554
Jones, William, 627, 648, 710
Jones, William (Much Birch)14
Jonson, Ben, 2, 3, 18, 23-5,
  34, 41, 56, 92, 138, 165-6,
  277, 284, 287, 311, 315,
  381-82, 387-88, 390-92,413,
  420, 472, 512, 539, 606,694,
  704, 709
Juvenal, 467

K

Keate, Francis, 551
Keats, John, 40, 392
Kemp, Will, 307, 381
Kempe, Elizabeth, 169, 499,
  518, 521-22, 531, 543, 554,
  567, 569, 635, 638, 664,685;
  son Robert, 522, 663-64
Kepler, Johannes, 474
Kerry, Dr., 411, 415
Kettel, Ralph, 37
Keyes, John, 501-2
Keynes, Sir Geoffrey, 286,394
King, Mr., 586
King James Bible, 39
Kirby, T.F., 18, 136

Kirton, James, 90, 94-6, 285
Kirton, Robert, 95
Knevet, Thomas, 223, 288, 290, 320
Knight, G.B., 41
Knight, Richard, 496, 567
Knollys, William, 126
Kyrle, Edward, 551, 557
Kyrle, Henry, 99
Kyrle, Walter, 552

L

Lacon, Francis, 302, 339
de Lacy, Hugh, 6
Lake, Arthur, Dr., 333, 376
Lake, Sir Arthur, 322
Lake, Thomas, 253, 291, 322
Lancaster, Duke of, 240
Langland, 272
Laud, William, 640, 642, 654
Lawes, Henry, 700
Leander, 117
Le Comte, Edward, 189
Ledbury, 57, 409-10, 531-32, 672-73
Leigh, Sir John, 291, 323
L'Estrange, Nicholas, 28, 286, 298, 524-25
Lewes, Sir Edward, 302
Lewknor family, 106, 323
Lewknor, Edward, 209, 253, 291, 323, 372
Lewknor, Lewis, 253, 285, 291- 92, 324, 339, 372, 382
Libitina, 183
Lidcot, John, 501-2
Lincoln's Inn, 97, 413
Lipsius, Justus, 34-4, 147
Llanthony Abbey, 5-6, 19
Llanwarne, 5-6, 13, 19, 99, 544
Lloyd, Lodowick, 166
Lloyd, Marmaduke, 101, 713-14
Long Sutton, 87, 169

Love, Nicholas, 661
Lovelace, Richard, 209, 292, 324
Lower, William, 289, 317
Lucina, 183
Lucretius, 30
Ludlow, Henry, 283, 315
Lyly, John, 141-42, 154, 159

M

Macassay, Sir Lynden, 131
Machiavelli, 147
Mackreth, William, 105
Madan, Falconer, 79, 393
Magellan, 145
Magna Carta, 344, 357, 378
Malet, Mr., 511
Mallory, Andrew, 255
Mallory, John, 342
Manfred, 453
Manne, Thomas, 368
Manners, Edward (Rutland), 70
Manners, John (Rutland), 70-1
Manners, Roger (Rutland), 70-1
Manningham, John, 101, 179, 189
Mansell, Richard 551
Manwood, Peter, 326-27
Manwood, Roger, 327
Marino, Giovanni, 143
Markey, John, 707
Mars, 62, 183
Marston, John, 47
Martin, Henry, 30, 46, 58, 185, 196, 285, 336, 643, 647
Martin, Richard, 47-9, 96, 98- 100, 105, 121, 156, 184, 193- 94, 207-10, 253, 271, 284- 85, 291, 311, 315, 322-23, 361, 366-67, 381-82, 386-88, 390-91, 395, 398, 421, 427- 29, 446, 464, 498, 511-12, 537-39, 669
Martin, William, 627
Mary, Queen, 72, 78, 412

729

Mason, Mr., 647
Matthews, John H., 19, 716
Matthews, Toby, 166, 196,209, 285
Matthews, Dr. Toby, 154, 166, 196
Maxwell, Mr. 641
McClure, Norman, 423
McElwee, William, 567
Medea, 116–17
Meg Goodwin, 305, 328
Merchant Tailor's School, 97
Meredith, Richard, 168
Meres Court, 562–63
Mermaid Tavern, 2, 17, 36, 95, 381, 389–92, 422, 436, 504, 538, 563, 605
Mennis, Sir John, 315
Michelchurch, 15–16, 270
Middle Temple, 87ff., 413, 418, 552–53, 559, 575, 581, 586, 590, 612, 622–26
Middleton, Hugh, 415
Mildmay, Thomas, 302
Milton, John, 98, 232, 448, 700–1
Mitcham, 382
Mitchell, John, 618
Mitchell, Williams, 227, 276, 331, 374, 428, 464, 467
Mitre Tavern, 393, 395, 398
Mocket, Docket, 390
Monkton, 5–6, 13, 16, 18–20, 45, 96, 127, 175, 269–70, 513–14, 519, 535, 544, 679
Moon of London, 305
Moore, Francis, 209, 289, 318, 442
Moore, John, 289, 317
Moore, Richard, 619–21
Moore Smith, G.C., 136
Moorton, George, 98
Moorton, Robert, 98, 131
More, Anne, 180–81
More, George, 180–81, 195–96,

More, George, cont., 198, 202, 209, 212, 228, 242, 253,271, 284, 292, 317, 325–26, 358, 361, 367, 431, 438, 441,452, 501
More, Sir Thomas, 46, 713
Morehampton, 50, 127, 561–64, 575–78, 582, 594, 612–13, 623, 635, 638, 653, 658, 660–61, 675–76, 693–94, 697, 699, 705, 708–10, 715
Morgan, John, 596, 603
Morgan, William, 600, 603–4, 702
Morgan, Thomas, 334, 376, 544
Morris dance, 298ff., 313–14, 328–29, 339
Morris, William, 231, 276,288, 316, 350
Morse, Thomas, 405, 423, 585–86, 595, 696, 701, 704
Morton, Sir Albertus, 613–15
Mounson, Thomas, 210, 291,321
Mountague, Edward, 235, 332, 447
Mountague, Henry, 194, 275, 443, 455
Mountague, Dr., 390
Mounteagle, Lord, 222
Moyle, John, 674
Moyle, Robert, 169, 187, 613
Moyle, Thomas, 674
Moyle, Walter, 104
Muses, 59ff., 116
Mynne, George, 710–11

N

Nash, Richard, 507
Neale, Bp. of Lincoln, 205–7, 448–452
Nelson, John, 26
Nestor, 299, 307
Neville, Christopher, 454,456–58, 463, 524

Neville, Edward (Abergavenny), 523, 582

Neville, Henry, 88, 209, 236, 247, 253, 285, 367, 382,395, 427, 429, 431, 438, 445,454, 523-25, 536, 581, 669

New College, 40, 45ff., 58, 124-26, 182, 216, 411

Newcourt, 310, 561

Newgate prison, 26

New Inn, 48, 96-7

New Philosophy, 475

New River, 415

Newton, John & wife, 554

Nonnington, 409-10

Howard, Henry (Northampton), 397, 399, 428-29, 439-40, 449, 456, 459-63, 500, 521, 546

Percy, Henry (Northumberland), 223-34, 257, 474-75, 489

Norton, 410-11

Norwich, 381

Norwood, Henry, 132

Noy, William, 289, 318, 588

O

Odcombe, 382, 396, 421

Offa's Dike, 127

Oking, 242

Orcop, 19, 217

Orpheus, 63, 121

Osborn, Louise, 1, 17-18, 42, 83-4, 117, 132-37, 164-66, 220, 284, 287, 315, 323, 327-29, 380, 421, 423,425, 468, 492-94, 567-73, 629- 30, 633, 682-83, 685, 717

Overbury, Nicholas, 167,252, 285, 500, 562, 565, 573, 578-81, 585, 612, 618, 692, 711

Overbury, Thomas, 321, 387,491, 498-504, 515, 567, 573

Ovid, 30, 36, 65

Owen, John, 3, 30, 46, 49,58, 293-95, 311, 382, 583, 669

Owen, Roger, 288, 290, 319, 339, 436, 439, 441, 444-45, 447, 458

Oxenbridge, Robert, 291, 323, 367

Oxford, Univ., 46, 72-4, 207, 253-54, 415-17

P

Pady, William, 291, 321

Page, William, 175, 567

Page, Mr., 498, 551

Palatine, Count, 29, 412-14, 431, 434, 436, 439, 453, 542, 555, 559

Pandora, 183

Panofsky, Erwin, 135

Parker, John, 290, 320

Parliamentary Party, 226-27, 331, 372, 428, 437

Parma, Duke of, 60, 71-2

Parrot, Henry, 85

Parrott, James, 291, 322, 432

Parry, Blanche, 310

Parry, Eustace, 339

Parry, Stephen, 560, 562

Parry, Thomas, 442-32

Parry, William, 176-77, 596- 97, 602

Parrye, Lewis & wife, 177,597, 602-3

Peake, Edward, 288-89, 318

Pembridge, Anthony, 219, 247, 271-73, 333, 368, 375

Pembroke, 562, 565, 578-81, 618, 710-12

Pembroke, Countess of, 58

Pembroke, Simon, 26

Penecoyd, 14-16

Penn, William, 571

Percival, Mr., 34

731

Percy, Thomas, 221-23
Perry, William, 690, 698-99
Perryne, Henry, 176-77
Petition of Right, 615, 639,
   644-50
Phelips, Edward, 192, 242,261-
   64, 268, 271, 273, 285, 292,
   326, 341, 349, 359, 377,386-
   388, 413, 418, 420, 430, 447
   463, 477
Phelips, Robert, 382, 386-88,
   395, 439, 447, 463
Phellpotts, Roger, 175, 310
Phillimore, W.P.W., 636
Phillip II, 454
Phillips, Edward, 83
Phillips, Fabian, 76, 502,567,
   683
Phillips, Richard, 101
Phillpott, H.W., 19
Philpot, John, 302-3
Pierce, Jenkin, 598-603
Pierce, Richard, 595-96, 599,
   601-2
Piggott, Kit, 259, 280, 287,
   290, 319
Plague, 185, 190, 256, 274,
   297, 309-10, 365, 612, 708-9
Playfer, Mr., 119, 135
Polden, Mr., 133
Polybius, 159
Poole, Henry, 288, 316, 382
Pory, John, 290, 317, 320-21
Powell, Dr., 507
Powell, Richard, 178
Powell, Thomas, 178; son,
   Lewis, 616
Prestwich, Minna, 422, 516, 569
Price, Edward, 368, 507
Price, Thomas, 689, 693
Prichard, William, 607-11,620,
   701
Prideaux, Anne, 624
Prideaux, John, 624, 634
Prideaux, William, 633

Prince d'Amour, 49, 119ff.,
   135-36, 315, 537, 568
Prittfoote, Henry, 74
Privy Council, 75-6, 206,218,
   222-23, 247, 268, 284, 309,
   322, 343, 351, 367, 430-32,
   441, 455-63, 473, 477, 484,
   488-89, 497-98, 510, 567,
   579-81, 583-85, 710-12
Proctor, Stephen, 342-43, 367,
   378
Prufrock, J. Alfred, 115
Pulling, Alexander, 131,630-31
Purchas, Samuel, 390-91
Purveyance, 193ff., 224, 228-
   30, 241, 244, 431
Puttston Minor, 409-11
Pye, Walter, 96, 99, 101, 552,
   556, 572, 584-85, 622, 625-
   26, 705-6
Pym, John, 647, 654
Pyne, Thomas, 546, 548

Q

Quarrell, John, 596-602
Quarrell, Thomas, 602-4
Quintilian, 150

R

Rainsford, Henry, 286-87, 545
Ralegh, Walter, 2, 13, 49, 78,
   92, 95, 107, 120-21, 123-24,
   135, 185, 294, 472-74, 489,
   537
Ratcliffe, Sir Edward, 396,421
Rawlings, Mr., 405, 424
Reade, William, 176, 638
Readings, Inns of Court, 93ff.
   104, 168, 179, 190, 408, 533,
   536, 541, 545, 550-52, 587
Recusants, 227, 332
Reeves, William, 565, 573
Reynolds, John, 395, 421-22

732

Reynolds, Mr., 84
Rich, Nicholas, 647
Rich, Robert, 607
Richard, Mrs., 400-1, 403
Richardson, Thomas, 546, 548
Ridgeway, Thomas, 325
Riseley, William, 636
Robinson, Charles, 18, 20,
  187, 493, 573, 716
Rod, James, 573
Roe, Albyn, 717
Roe, Thomas, 420, 452
Rogers, Charles, and son
  Thomas, 596, 598-604
Rogers, Richard, 603
Rogers, Peter, 389
Rolles, John, 653
Romulus, 327
Roots, Ivan, 579, 629
Rosenbach, D.A.S.W., 85, 133
Ross, 300, 635-38
Royal Society, 692, 715
Rudyard, Benjamin, 48-9, 96,
  98-9, 104, 120, 167-68,301,
  553, 572, 644
Russell, Thomas, 302

S

Sackville, Mr., 502, 568
St. Augustine, 159
St. Bartholomew's, 102, 170
St. Cross Hospital, 179
St. David's, 101
St. Devereux, 269, 600
St. Dunstan's-in-the-East, 97
St. Dunstan's-in-the-West,
  328, 393, 639, 681, 684
St. George's Field, 102
St. Giles, 394-95
St. John's College, Oxon, 97
St. Oswald's Hospital, 419,
  486-87, 504-9, 522, 672
St. Paul's, 592-93, 670
SS. Peter and Paul, 170, 187

St. Saviour, 26
Salisbury, Earl of, 218, 222-
  24, 349, 357, 360-61, 372,
  394, 397, 399, 489
Sandford, Margaret, 627
Sandys, Edwin, 196, 226-28,
  236, 246, 251, 253, 314,318-
  19, 341-42, 351-52, 355-56,
  361, 365-66, 377, 427-28,
  431, 433, 436, 438, 441,443,
  445-56, 458, 462, 467
Sanford, 169, 187, 267
Sargent, Ralph, 276
Savile, John, 456-58, 467
The Scots, 196-97, 215, 242,
  254, 259-60, 319, 322, 372-
  74, 428-29, 447, 453-54,
  461-63, 473, 475, 482, 504
Scudamore, James, 178, 201,
  302-2, 339, 510, 522
Scudamore, John, 175, 219,408,
  553, 594, 638
Seaborn, Mr., 411, 609, 611
Searle, Gilbert, 98, 132
Selby, George, 448
Selden, John, 3, 539, 643-44,
  647, 654, 656-57
Seneca, 55-6, 150, 165
Serjeant-at-Law, 587-93, 622-
  23, 625-26
Serjeants' Inn, 97, 590, 621,
  622-23, 626, 639, 709
Seymour, William, 473
Shakespeare, William, 13, 18,
  47, 51, 179, 286, 297, 311,
  333, 375, 392, 415, 428,
  582, 704
Shapiro, I.A., 18, 392-93,
  421, 631
Sharp, Lionel, 429-30, 459-63,
  476-77, 489-90, 672, 684
Sheffield, John, 326
Shirley, Thomas, 201, 326
Shobden, 99, 127
Shuttleworth, Richard, 75-6

733

Sicilian Vespers, 430, 453-54, 456, 459-60
Sidney, Sir Philip, 56-64, 71, 95, 98, 141, 146, 151, 159, 161, 322, 417
Simpson, Evelyn, 317, 327
Singleton, Thomas, 415-17
Sirenaicks, 381, 385, 387ff., 422
Sizergh Castle, 187, 296, 570, 676
Smith, Logan P., 41, 467
Smith, Edmund, 499, 567
Smith, George, 598, 603-4
Skipworth, William, 242
Socrates, 89
Somerset, Henry (Worcester), 301-2; brothers Charles & Thomas, 302
Sophocles, 56, 304
Spain, 69, 71-2, 215, 221, 242, 342, 399, 412, 454, 459, 537, 541-42, 559
Speake, George, 390-91
Spenser, Edmund, 57, 166, 302
Stafford, Edward, 209
Stansby, William, 391, 487
Star Chamber, 224, 477, 514, 546-48
Stationers' Register, 99
Staunton, Mr., 70
Stempe, Thomas, 39
Sterne, Laurence, 42, 305
Stow, John, 41, 80, 85, 106, 181, 190, 266-67, 275, 307, 380, 425, 569, 592, 653
Strowde, William, 326
Stuart, Arabella, 185, 294, 473, 489
Sturgess, H.A.C., 131
Suffolk, Earl of, 397, 399, 500, 546-49
Summers, Joseph, 213
Sutton St. Cleares, 87, 169, 613

Swift, Edward, 302
Swift, Jonathan, 283
Swindler, William F., 378
Swinnerton, John, 502
Symonds, Phillip, 528

T

Tacitus, 159, 372, 582
Tantalus, 483
Tarleton, 84
Taylor, John, 669-70
Taylor, Thomas, 481, 493, 521, 531, 617, 701
Taylor, William, 296, 328, 493, 517-18, 521, 525, 543, 562-65, 581, 616-17, 701, 703
Tey, Mr., 206, 361
Thalia, 59ff.
Thavies Inn, 95
Themistocles, 155
Theobald's, 608-9
Theocritus, 577
Thomas, Edward, 508, 717
Thomas, Henry, 505, 507
Thoms, W.J., 188
Thornton, Thomas, 57
Throckmorton, John, 318, 459
Thynne, Aegremont, 112, 209, 553, 587, 590, 626
Thynne, John 209
Tiberius, 372
Ticheborn, Walter & son, 545
Tintern Abbey, 88
Tipper, William, 233-38, 276-77
Titley, 99, 127-30, 216, 257, 270, 295, 405, 408, 412, 495-97, 505, 541, 567, 571, 628, 652-53, 661-62, 690
Tolderrey, Christopher, 291, 322
Tourneur, Timothy, 711-12
Townshend, Heywood, 20
Townshend, Sir Horatio's wife, 512-13
Townshend, Sir John, 292, 324

Trehearne, Phillip, 175
Tretire, 270
Trevase, 13–16, 567
Trevor, John, 289, 317
Triste, Thomas, 551, 553, 557
Trojan horse, 432, 439
Trumbull, William, 394, 399, 459–60
Turner, Mrs., 501–2
Turner, John, 179
Tuve, Rosamund, 17
Tyburn, 26, 501
Tynte, Edward, 105
Tynte, John, 104–5, 545

U

Udall, Nicholas, 507–8
Ulysses, 89
Undertakers, 419, 427, 436, 439, 441, 445
Union, The, 192ff., 244, 247, 254, 257–64, 274, 314, 350, 369
Urrey, David, 99

V

Vane, Francis, 253
Varney, The Ladies, 389
Vaughan, John, 100–1
Vaughan, Rowland, 101, 310–11, 328, 561
Vaughan, William, 99
Vavasor, Thomas, 502, 538
Venice, 381, 383–84, 396, 421
Venus, 183
Vere, Anne (Oxford), 64–9, 284
Vere, Edward (Oxford), 64–7, 284
Villiers, George, see Bucking-ham
Virginia Company, 210, 216, 370–71, 446, 560
Vowchurch, 561, 613, 623, 636

W

Wade, William, 326
Wake, Isaac, 477
Marches of Wales and four counties, 248–50, 351, 356, 371, 433, 438, 565, 618–19, 627, 682, 690
Wallop, Henry, 443
Wallwyn, James, 334, 376
Walter, Edmund, 76
Walton, Izaak, 31, 39, 41, 48, 180, 631
Walwyn, James, 99, 100
Ward, Nick, 659, 683
Ward, William G., 300
Warde, John, 368
Warden, John, 175, 369, 430, 537
Warner, Mr., 474
Warre, T., 511
Warren, Mr., 407
Washington, Justice, 608
Wayte, Thomas, 98–9, 105
Waythan, David, 13–4
Waythan, Harry, 503, 567
Weaver, James, 573
Webb, Thomas, 406
Wells, John, 551
Wentworth, John, 340–41, 352, 372, 374, 502
Wentworth, Thomas, 444, 446, 454, 456–58, 463, 643
West, John, 395, 398, 421
Westminster Abbey, 25, 48, 412, 432, 590, 609
Westminster School, 3, 23ff., 37
Weston, Richard, 501–2, 698
Whitaker, Lawrence, 382, 386–91, 420
White, Helen, 41
Whitehall, 297, 413–14, 512, 540, 648

735

Whitelocke, James, 97, 167, 286, 358, 408, 431-34, 436, 438, 441, 444, 446, 457-58, 464-65, 467, 533, 537-38, 541, 545, 551, 553, 562, 565, 587, 608, 611, 619, 621, 645, 648, 676
Whitelocke, Bulstrode, 545, 571
White Mt., Battle of, 555
Whitland Abbey, 711-12
Whitlock, Baird, 83-5, 164, 568, 681
Whitson, Mr., 405
Whittington, Thomas, 636
Widemarsh St., 171, 175-76, 295, 535, 567
Wight, Isle of, 99
Wilcox, Anne, 176-77
Wilcox, James, 176-77, 583-85
William of Wykeham, 12, 29, 50
William I, King, 40
William Rufus, King, 40
Williams, Alice, 418, 539-40, 687-89, 695-98, 701-4, 707-8
Williams, Henry, 334
Williams, John, Lord Keeper, 563-64, 591, 595
Williams, Mr., 387, 390
Williams, Thomas, 408
Williams, W.R., 20, 570, 572-73, 718
Williamson, Francis, 539-40, 688, 697
Williamson, J. Bruce, 131, 425, 569
Willson, David, 276
Wilson, John, 105
Wilson, Thomas, 138
Winch, Mr., 201, 237
Winchelsea, Countess of, 502-3
Winchester College, 12, 18, 23, 28ff., 41-2, 45, 99, 124ff., 208, 215-16, 257, 293, 412, 487, 495-96, 513, 567, 661-62

Wingfield, Robert, 276, 290, 319-20
Winter, Robert, 22
Winter, Thomas, 221-23
Winwood, Ralph, 435, 460, 500-501, 522
Witherspoon & Warnke, 41, 86, 164
Wood, Mr., 70
Wood, Anthony á, 2, 17-8, 20, 31, 72, 81, 83, 105, 131, 187, 409, 454, 472, 490, 492, 494, 539
Wood, Roger, 289, 317
Woodgate, Peter, 30-1, 77
Woodstock, 97
Wooley, Randolph, 529-30, 533, 550
Wotton, Mr., 334
Wotton, Edward, 57
Wotton, Henry, 3, 31-2, 41, 46, 49-50, 57, 71-2, 92, 98, 107, 132, 287, 381, 399-400, 412, 438, 455-56, 458-60, 462-63, 613-15, 633, 701
Wraxall, 101, 105
Wren, Christopher, 715
Wright, Christopher, 222
Wright, John, 221
Writhlington, 87, 96
Wroth, Robert, 193-94, 209
Wye River, 177, 208, 267
Wymarke, Edward, 291, 322-23

Y

Yaxley, Robert, 302
Yelverton, Henry, 196, 209, 232, 326, 404, 423, 427, 546, 607, 626
Yeovil, 87
Young, John, 292, 325

Z

Zouche, Richard, 417